Gold Medal Policing

This straightforward, easy-to-understand textbook inspires tools for improving job performance, productivity, and morale in law enforcement. The groundbreaking first edition of *Gold Medal Policing*, inspired by work with Olympic athletes, confirmed the importance of mental readiness in frontline policing excellence. Partnerships with policing and related fields positioned *Gold Medal Policing* principles across recruitment, multilevel training, web-based learning, and field assessment.

The second edition consolidates two decades of peer-reviewed research and training, reflecting new trends, lessons, contemporary issues, and proven tools. Drawing on insights from frontline officers recognized for their excellence, including coach officers, it introduces an Operational Readiness Framework rooted in scientific principles. This framework systematically assesses physical, technical, and mental readiness, creating a detailed police-specific profile. A comprehensive literature review informs current police preparedness practices. Mental readiness is upheld to strict, measurable standards, akin to traditional physical and technical readiness. Best practices from exceptional officers are isolated, and operational benchmarks and strategies are established. The ultimate result is to empower officers to excel in the practice of their profession.

Gold Medal Policing is indispensable for law enforcement leaders, scholars, students, and aspiring officers.

About the author

Credit: Elizabeth Siwicki

Judy McDonald is an Adjunct Professor in the School of Epidemiology and Public Health with the Faculty of Medicine at the University of Ottawa and former Associate Director at the McLaughlin Centre for Population Health Risk Assessment. She earned her PhD from the University of Westminster, UK, specializing in operational readiness for high-risk professions. Her applied research over the past three decades has focused on understanding readiness strategies in diverse population groups working in high-risk and demanding professions where excellence carries serious life-or-death consequences. Study populations have ranged from Olympic athletes to surgeons and air traffic controllers. Her initial study with Ottawa Hospital surgeons revealed parallels between surgical and Olympic athlete mental-readiness practices, acclaimed as a landmark in the medical community. Subsequent research illustrated the need for systematic mental training in the high-stress world of air traffic control, leading to mandatory trainee courses and an "Advanced Situational Awareness Program" for seasoned controllers, flight service specialists, and trainers in Navigation (NAV) Canada. This pioneering perspective underpins her work in operational risk assessment, now successfully applied in policing, as well as other high-performance occupations such as dentistry, financial auditing, and Sherpa high-altitude guiding. McDonald extends her expertise globally, supervising, lecturing, and conducting workshops. Her efforts advance operational readiness for high-risk professions, safeguarding lives.

ROUTLEDGE SERIES ON PRACTICAL AND EVIDENCE-BASED POLICING

Books in the Routledge Series on Practical and Evidence-Based Policing disseminate knowledge and provide practical tools for law enforcement leaders and personnel to protect and serve the public and reduce crime. With an aim to bridge the "translation gap" between frontline policing and academic research, books in this series apply sound scientific methods as well as practical experience to make everyday police work safer and smarter. These books are an invaluable resource for police practitioners, academic researchers, public policymakers, and students in law enforcement and criminology programs to guide best practices in all aspects of policing.

Police Misconduct Complaint Investigations Manual, 2nd Edition
Barbara Attard & Kathryn Olson

Police and YOUth
Everette B. Penn & Shannon A. Davenport

Twenty-One Mental Models for Policing
A Framework for Using Data and Research for Overcoming Cognitive Bias
Renée J. Mitchell

Public Corruption in the United States
Analysis of a Destructive Phenomenon
Jeff Cortese

The Wicked Problems of Police Reform in Canada
Laura Huey, Lorna Ferguson & Jennifer L. Schulenberg

Human Rights Policing
Reimagining Law Enforcement in the 21st Century
Peter Marina & Pedro Marina

Interviewing Vulnerable Suspects
Safeguarding the Process
Edited by Dr Jane Tudor-Owen, Dr Celine van Golde, Dr Ray Bull & David Gee MBE

Reframing Police Education and Freedom in America
Martin Alan Greenberg & Beth Allen Easterling

Gold Medal Policing
Operational Readiness and Performance Excellence, 2nd Edition
Judy M. McDonald

Gold Medal Policing

Operational Readiness and Performance Excellence

Second Edition

Judy M. McDonald
Université d'Ottawa | University of Ottawa

uOttawa
www.uOttawa.ca
L'Université canadienne
Canada's university

NEW YORK AND LONDON

Designed cover image: Accurate Design and Communication Inc. and Sloan Associate Press

This edition published 2025
by Routledge
605 Third Avenue, New York, NY 10158

and by Routledge
4 Park Square, Milton Park, Abingdon, Oxon, OX14 4RN

Routledge is an imprint of the Taylor & Francis Group, an informa business

© 2025 Judy M. McDonald

The right of Judy M. McDonald to be identified as author of this work has been asserted in accordance with sections 77 and 78 of the Copyright, Designs and Patents Act 1988.

All rights reserved. No part of this book may be reprinted or reproduced or utilised in any form or by any electronic, mechanical, or other means, now known or hereafter invented, including photocopying and recording, or in any information storage or retrieval system, without permission in writing from the publishers.

Trademark notice: Product or corporate names may be trademarks or registered trademarks and are used only for identification and explanation without intent to infringe.

First edition published by Sloan Associate Press 2006

ISBN: 9780367702878 (hbk)
ISBN: 9780367700232 (pbk)
ISBN: 9781003145493 (ebk)

DOI: 10.4324/9781003145493

Typeset in Palatino
by Deanta Global Publishing Services, Chennai, India

Contents

Abstract xviii
Academic and police endorsements. xix
My sincere thanks. xxi
Forewords xxii
Tables and Figures xxv
Mission. xxx
Roadmap for readers: Who and where to look. xxxi
What's new and improved in the second edition?. xxxiii
How I got here xxxvii

1 **Redefining readiness: A blueprint for peak performance in policing.** 1
   Abstract 1
   A. Excellence redefined 2
   B. Gold Medal Policing research approach 4
       Bridging risk and performance. 5
       Expansion to operational readiness 6
       Operational Readiness Framework:
           A standardized tool 7
       Research that stands up in court. 8
   C. Insights from the field: Coach officers' solutions 9
       The vital role of coach officers 9
       What coach officers look for in trainees. 11
       Strategies to enhance training 12
   D. 20 Key strategies for navigating the science
       of peak performance 13
   Notes. 15

2 **Insights from current research on policing excellence** . . 18
   Abstract 18
   A. Predictors of police performance 20
   B. Police performance stressors. 21
   C. Critical analysis of "Road to Mental Readiness"
       (R2MR) Program 24
   D. Physical competencies in policing. 25
   E. Technical competencies in policing 27

F. Mental competencies in policing. 29
G. 20 Key strategies from current research for
    enhancing police performance 32
Notes. 33

3 Police under pressure 35
Abstract 35
A. Reimagining coaching and frontline dynamics 36
B. Frontline police challenges: A closer look. 38
    Standardized assessment. 38
    Categorizing police challenges. 39
        Heightened-risk situations. 40
        Complex situations 41
        Emotionally-charged situations. 43
        Coaching/Leading 44
        Unfamiliar situations. 46
        High-risk individuals 47
        Unprecedented circumstances 48
C. Performance blocks: *"Barbs and jabs"* 49
    Categorizing police performance blocks 49
    Operational performance blocks. 52
        Operational general blocks 52
        "Crises"... "Pucker factor" 54
        Shift-work fatigue 56
        Public disrespect. 58
        Downtime (lulls) and routine tasks 60
        Car collisions 61
        Court appearances 62
        Personal fears and skepticism 63
        Team dynamics. 65
        Resource shortcomings 66
        Operational rookie errors (Aggressiveness,
        General patrol issues, Lack of safety, Poor
        reports, Unrealistic expectations, Poor
        containment, Other officers' anxiety,
        No action plan, Discipline problems,
        Negativity, No basic law, and Lack
        community contacts) 68
    Organizational blocks. 73
        Workload 75
        Public complaints. 76

       Female-policing coping issues 77
       "Not being promoted" 80
       Other organizational blocks. 82
    External performance blocks. 85
    Changes in performance blocks over time 87
       Impact of performance blocks. 87
          Immediate Needs 88
          Serious Blocks 91
          Individual Blocks. 92
       Summary of police performance block measures . . 92
       Trends in performance blocks. 94
  D. 20 Key challenges and performance blocks in policing . . 96
  Notes 98

4 The readiness equation 102
  Abstract 102
  A. Measuring what matters: Inside the minds of
     excellent officers. 103
     Striking the right balance 103
     Trends in preparedness 105
     Mental readiness dominance across occupations . 105
  B. Exceptional officers speak out on readiness 107
  C. Influential factors 109
  D. Successful and disappointing performances. 111
     Readiness during successful performances. 111
     Readiness during disappointing performances . . 113
     Readiness in successful versus disappointing
       performances 114
  E. Performance indicators for preparedness. 115
     Benchmarks for technical and physical readiness . 116
     Benchmarks for mental readiness 117
  F. 20 Key strategies for measuring readiness and
    success in policing 120
  Notes 122

5 Physical readiness in policing 125
  Abstract 125
  A. Officer Safety 127
     Proper handcuffing 129
     Body search 130
     Fitness and wellness. 132

    Physical discipline 132
    Shift-work strategies 134
    Fatigue strategies 136
    Long-term rest strategies. 138
    Injury management strategies. 140
    Containment in environmental conditions 141
    Strong safety sense 143
  B. Use of Force 144
    Firearms and gunpoint arrest 146
    Equipment readiness: Checks and electronic aids . 148
    Defensive tactics 149
    Physical control with appropriate use of force . . . 150
    "Reasonableness" 153
  C. Vehicle Operations 154
    Vehicle safety. 155
      Collision-avoidance strategies. 156
      Lights and sirens 157
    Multitasking 159
    Vehicle reversing. 162
    Patrolling the environment 162
    Strategic traffic stops 163
  D. 20 Key strategies for physical readiness in policing . . 165
  Notes 167

6 Technical readiness in policing 170
  Abstract 170
  A. Proficiency in law 172
    Knowledge and application of laws 173
    Court procedures 175
      Court appearance strategies. 175
    Arrest authorities 179
    Use of force principles. 181
    Effective apprehensions 183
  B. Verbal communication 185
    Prevention of conflicts and de-escalation (Tac com) 186
    Good articulation and appropriate tone. 188
    Active listening 189
    Community rapport and humor 191
      External communication. 192
    Effective interviewing. 194
  C. Written communication 196

           Systematic note-taking 196
           Timely reports 199
           Suitable reports 201
      D. Knowledge of police service and community 203
           Police service 204
           Policies and procedures 207
              Review and interpret internal resources 208
           Internal communication 210
           Community composition and resources 213
      E. 20 Key strategies for technical readiness in policing . 216
      Notes 218

7 **Mental readiness in policing** **224**
   Abstract 224
   A. Assessment of mental success elements 225
   B. Commitment 227
      Empathy 230
      Professional Discipline 231
      Job Satisfaction 235
      Responsible Leadership 236
      Understand "the Job" 238
      Loyalty: Dedication and Pride of Uniform 240
      Motivated to succeed: Competitive and Job
         Security 242
   C. Confidence 244
      Quality Training 245
      Control Environment 247
      Police Mentors 249
      Seek support: Family and Camaraderie 249
      Grounded: Recognition, Thanks, Education,
         Faith, and Luck 251
   D. Positive Imagery 253
      Techniques: Vivid Imagery and Visual Triggers . . 255
      Opportunities to Visualize 258
   E. Mental Preparation 261
      Strategic Resource Plan 263
      Positive Thinking 266
      Clear Objectives and Plan 268
      Minimize Interruptions 269
      Recognize Risks 270
      Psyching: Rituals and Preparation Locations 271

   Psyching Rituals 271
   Preparation Locations 273
 F. Full Focus. 274
   Present and Mindful 276
   Anticipation 277
   Equipment Confidence 279
   Teamwork and Trust. 281
   Emotional Intelligence: Enjoyment, Rhythm,
    and Relaxation 282
 G. Distraction Control 284
   General Control Practices. 287
    De-Escalation 287
    Involvement of Others 289
    Task Orientation 291
   Specialized Control Practices. 293
    "Crises" Refocusing 294
     Brief pause 294
     Preferred alternative actions 296
    Public Disrespect Refocusing 296
    Public Complaint Refocusing 298
    Downtime (Lulls) and Routine Tasks Refocusing . . 299
    Workload Strategies 301
    "Not Being Promoted" Refocusing 303
    Female-Policing Coping Strategies 305
 H. Constructive Evaluation 306
   Self-Evaluation. 307
   Feedback from others: Team, Formal, Informal,
    Public, and Suspects 309
   Coping: Take Ownership and Draw Lessons. . . . 312
 I. Influential factors and trends for success practices. . . 314
   Overall influence by factor groups. 314
   Most influential factors 316
    "Elite" officer distinct practices 317
    "Patrol-only experience" distinct practices . . . 318
    Gender factor profiles 319
    Language and ethnicity 320
   Least influential factors 320
   Trends in mental-readiness practices 321
 J. 20 Key strategies for mental readiness in policing . . . 324
Notes 326

8 Police leadership at all levels 332
Abstract 332
A. "Gold-medal" senior leadership 333
B. Management under pressure 336
    Senior police management challenges 336
    "Crises" 337
C. Effective leadership tactics 339
    Endurance 340
    Team building and partnerships 340
    Engagement 342
D. Leadership in the field 343
    Sergeants' perspectives 344
    Leadership beyond ranks 345
    Supervisors' dilemma 346
    Attitude and actions 347
E. 20 Key strategies for police leadership 348
Notes 350

9 Knowledge transfer: Conclusions 352
Abstract 352
A. Police Operational Readiness Index 353
B. Confirmation of mental success elements 354
    Assessment of mental readiness 354
    Range and consistency of practices 359
C. Confirmation of technical and physical success
    elements 361
    Benchmarks for technical readiness 361
    Benchmarks for physical readiness 363
D. Performance blocks in policing 363
    Identification of performance blocks 363
    Impact of performance blocks 365
E. "Watch items" (emerging problems and initiatives) .. 368
    Potential impact of teamwork on individual
      accountability 368
    Potential downside to generalized strategies ... 368
    Shift in workload dynamics 369
    Artificial intelligence integration with mental
      training 369
    Promotional realities 369
    Recruit selection and training 370

Proven initiatives for women, public protocol,
and offense-defense mastery 370
F. Influential factors on success skills 370
Most influential factor profiles 371
Less influential factors 374
Factors profile development 375
G. 20 Key summary conclusions 376
Notes 378

10 **What's next? Recommendations and leadership directives** 379
Abstract 379
A. Customize recruitment, selection, and retention
guidelines 380
B. Create multilevel self-assessment tools 385
C. Target career and succession planning 387
Specialty-unit skill profiles 387
Supervisor's Guide. 388
D. Develop e-learning programs 388
E. Promote a frontline-recognition plan 389
Formal recognition 390
Frontline organizational problem-solving 391
Frontline "buy-in". 392
F. Establish a corporate curriculum 392
G. Create a high-performance mental training program. 394
Overview of police mental readiness 394
Full Focus with Use of Force training 395
Distraction Control training 396
Career and succession planning 398
Progressive success-skills training. 398
H. Enrich the internal role-model function: Coach
officers, trainers, and mentors 399
Enhancement of the Coach Officer Program 400
Identification of ideal trainers 402
Support mentor-officer skill-set matching 403
I. Pursue publication opportunities 404
J. Promote further related research 405
K. 20 Key summary recommendations 406
Notes 408

11 Executive summary: Gold medal policing: Operational readiness and performance excellence . . 411
Introduction 411
The mission: Enhancing law enforcement excellence . . . 412
Approach 412
Knowledge transfer: Results and conclusions 413
    Police Operational Readiness Index (ORI) 413
    Confirmation of mental success elements 413
    Confirmation of technical and physical success elements 414
    Performance blocks in policing. 414
    "Watch items" (emerging problems and initiatives) . 414
    Influential factors on success skills 415
Recommendations 416
Summary 417

Bibliography 419

Acknowledgments 453

Appendix A: Evidence-based rigor: study design 456
Abstract 456
A. Collaborative partnerships. 457
    Collaborative necessity 457
    Mutual benefits and equitable contributions 458
    Founding champions 459
    Other important project contributors 460
B. Study background. 461
C. Study overview 463
    1. Academic aim and rationale. 463
    2. Overall changes to the second edition 464
D. Descriptive analysis. 465
    1. Subjects 465
    2. Instruments. 466
    3. Sampling procedure 466
    4. Data collection and statistical analysis. 467
    5. Limitations and attempts at controlling investigator bias 468
E. Operational definitions. 469

xvi ■ Contents

    F. Influential factors 474
        Background factors 474
        Developmental factors. 476
        Police distinction factors 477
    G. Investigative framework 478
    Notes 482

Appendix B: Predictors of police performance 486

Appendix C: Police performance stressors 496

Appendix D: Critical analysis of the "Road to Mental Readiness" (R2MR) program. 505

Appendix E: Physical competencies in policing 515

Appendix F: Technical competencies in policing. 526

Appendix G: Mental competencies in policing. 537

Appendix H: Challenging situations in frontline policing. ... 551

Appendix I: Temporal changes in performance blocks 2003-2019 553

Appendix J: Calculations for the differences in the importance of readiness in policing over 17 years. 556

Appendix K: Overall importance of operational readiness by factor. 557

Appendix L: Successful performance readiness by factor. ... 558

Appendix M: Disappointing performance readiness by factor 561

Appendix N: Orlick's Wheel of Excellence: Mental readiness success elements 562

Appendix O: Temporal changes in mental readiness practices 2003–2019. 564

Appendix P: Police field training assessment and progress report 565

Appendix Q: Officer X's top 10 Gold Medal Policing quotes and lessons 569

Appendix R: Police simulation training focus assessment 574

Appendix S: Officer X's Top 10 Commitment and Confidence quotes in Gold Medal Policing. 576

Appendix T: Coach Officers' 25 teaching tips 578

Index 581

Abstract

This straightforward, easy-to-understand textbook inspires tools for improving job performance, productivity, and morale in law enforcement. The groundbreaking first edition of *Gold Medal Policing*, inspired by work with Olympic athletes, confirmed the importance of mental readiness in frontline policing excellence. Partnerships with policing and related fields positioned *Gold Medal Policing* principles across recruitment, multilevel training, web-based learning, and field assessment.

The second edition consolidates two decades of peer-reviewed research and training, reflecting new trends, lessons, contemporary issues, and proven tools. Drawing on insights from frontline officers recognized for their excellence, including coach officers, it introduces an Operational Readiness Framework rooted in scientific principles. This framework systematically assesses physical, technical, and mental readiness, creating a detailed police-specific Operational Readiness Index that profiles police preparedness. A comprehensive research review informs current police preparedness practices. Mental readiness is upheld to strict, measurable standards, akin to traditional physical and technical readiness. Best practices from exceptional officers are isolated, and operational benchmarks and strategies are established. The ultimate result is to empower officers to excel in the practice of their profession. *Gold Medal Policing* is indispensable for law enforcement leaders, scholars, students, and aspiring officers.

Academic and police endorsements

The book is organized with a logical, appropriate structure. Finding out all the changes that have taken place in policing, police training and society in the last 20 years was valuable.
—**Police Training Instructor**, anonymous peer reviewer

This is a unique resource. I cannot think of any book that competes. The closest competition would be various articles about leadership and performance motivation.
—**Sergeant and Chief Instructor**, anonymous peer reviewer

Even with my military tactical experience, I said to myself reading the book, 'That's a good idea. I could use that.' It feels authoritative and credible. The strategies would actually benefit other frontliners in the broader LE community like CBP, Homeland Security, ATF, DEA, Secret Service, as well as applying to EMT, SpecOps, firefighters, SAR, etc.
—**Cemil Alyanak**, Special Operations Recon Unit Commander

We can personally relate to this. It's not just another f---ing manual… You know what? There'll be an immediate buy-in.
—**Constable >10 years on**, anonymous frontline feedback

I'd make it a mandatory read at all levels. If you do that, you'd actually have leadership by example. Leading and teaching young officers is the ideal for our profession.
—**Constable <5 years on**, anonymous frontline feedback

The academic underpinnings allow evidence-based improvements in police response, individual performance, and training for new officers. Integrating technical and physical readiness broadens the scope to examine excellence, often overlooked by sports psychology books that concentrate mainly on mental techniques.

—Michael G. Tyshenko, PhD, Senior Analyst,
Risk Sciences International

The author's personal credibility, the imagery from frontline quotes, and lived experience of identified high-performing officers enhances the practical scenarios—such as compliance versus hypervigilance; hurry-up and wait; court time overlooked.

—Andy Rhodes, Retired Chief,
United Kingdom, OBE, QPM Service

The mental readiness section is absolutely crucial in helping officers learn and become proficient at policing. Recommendations to improve performance are very thorough to benefit academy staff or field training officers in law enforcement.

—Morgan J. Steele, Assistant Professor,
School of Criminal Justice, Leadership, and Sociology,
Fort Hays State University, United States

My sincere thanks

I extend my heartfelt gratitude to the 81 outstanding frontline police officers, including coach officers, who generously shared personal and professional details not typically disclosed to civilians. Their openness and candor have laid the groundwork for invaluable mentoring, benefiting not only guidance provided by this work but also the training of future officers. For many officers, the interviews provided a much-needed catharsis, allowing emotions to surface in those whose professions demanded emotional restraint. I am deeply privileged that these officers opened up and allowed me to delve into the human side of policing.

I am grateful to the management and instructors at police colleges and services for implementing new strategies informed by frontline officers' insights, fostering innovation. Your commitment to excellence is inspiring.

Forewords

As a police chief, I highly recommend *Gold Medal Policing, 2nd Edition*. It offers diverse officer perspectives and genuine communication that is very relevant in today's challenging policing environment. With a retirement bubble upon us and the need to increase recruiting, this edition's insights are invaluable. The identified officer traits provide vital guidance for candidates dedicated to a career in policing and can guide training curriculums to enhance skill sets. Emphasizing mental preparedness recognizes its crucial role in managing critical situations. Officers at all ranks will benefit from reading the book.

Eric Stubbs, Chief / Chef
Ottawa Police Service / Service de police d'Ottawa
ottawapolice.ca
Ottawa, Canada

Policing is a protean term; it means different things to different people. I served 35 years as a police officer, working in three policing organizations that were variously called Constabulary, Police, and Service. I also worked with police organizations in Europe, North and South America, and Africa. Despite the differences in policing styles across the globe, one constant remains: the professional care that officers reserve for each other.

This is important because police organizations worldwide are facing testing times. Recruitment is more challenging, and experience is being rapidly lost as officers either retire early or join for much shorter duration than previous generations of officers. Rates of mental health issues are rising, and navigating the system to find the right leaders lacks clarity.

Gold Medal Policing, 2nd Edition, is a welcome resource that can help confront these challenges. It is based on social scientific principles and research. The perspective is broad, drawing on information from different public sector services. It provides solid study tools and practical advice for implementing change.

While the system cannot suit everyone, *Gold Medal Policing* goes a long way to getting there.

Victor Olisa, QPM, PhD
Strategic Advisor to Police Scotland
United Kingdom

McDonald's Operational Readiness Framework is rooted in sound scientific principles, and cuts across different professions servicing public health and safety. Its transdisciplinary approach facilitates a profound understanding of risks confronted in diverse high-performance environments. Being invited inside these professional circles demonstrates McDonald's ability to earn trust within multiple constituencies and to access candid insights from highly respected individuals. With the author's decades of experience in preparedness, high-performance and human behavior, the framework can be tailored to any profession or challenging life-events.

This work is based on highly innovative research with purposive sampling of excellent officers and coaches, ensuring confidence in identified best practices. Systematically evaluating qualitative and quantitative evidence across physical, technical, and mental readiness domains, this work yields detailed, profession-specific profiles of high performers.

The value of this framework extends beyond policing, with applications as diverse as specialized surgery and air traffic control, to even the broader readership of *TIME* magazine. This scientific body of work can incentivize leaders to integrate readiness competencies into corporate values, enhancing decision-making and organizational initiatives. *Gold Medal Policing* synthesizes evidence that is generalizable and transferable to other high-risk professions demanding high performance to ensure efficient, equitable, and cost-effective risk reduction in a variety of emergency-response situations.

Daniel Krewski, PhD
Chief Risk Scientist
Risk Science International

Tables and Figures

2.1 Summary of Evaluation Standards and Measures to Predict Police Performance 20
2.2 Summary of Police Performance Stressors 23
2.3 Summary of Police Physical Competencies 26
2.4 Summary of Police Technical Competencies 28
2.5 Summary of Police Mental Competencies 30
3.1 Police Performance Block Measures 51
3.2 Operational Rookie Errors 71
3.3 Workload Block Details 76
3.4 Public Complaint Details 77
3.5 Female-Policing Coping Issues 78
3.6 Impact of Police Performance Blocks by Weighted Average 89
3.7 Summary of Police Performance Block Measures 93
4.1 Police Overall Importance of Readiness 104
4.2 Overall Importance of Readiness across Different Professions 106
5.1 Shift-Work Strategies 135
5.2 Fatigue Strategies 136
5.3 Car Collision-Avoidance Strategies 157
6.1 Court Appearance Strategies 176
6.2 Internal Communication Strategies 211
7.1 Professional Discipline Practices 232
7.2 Understanding "the Job" Practices 238
7.3 Vivid Imagery Practices 256
7.4 Strategic Resource Plan Practices 264
7.5 Positive Thinking Practices 267
7.6 Preparation Location Practices 273
7.7 Anticipation Practices 277
7.8 De-escalation Practices 287
7.9 Involvement of Others Practices 289

7.10 Task Orientation Practices 291
7.11 Performance Blocks and Specialized Related
       Control Practices.. 293
7.12 "Crises" Refocusing...294
7.13 Public Disrespect Refocusing 296
7.14 Public Complaint Refocusing 298
7.15 Downtime and Routine Task Refocusing 299
7.16 Workload Strategies 302
7.17 "Not Being Promoted" Refocusing....................................303
7.18 Female-Policing Coping Strategies 305
7.19 Practice Tendencies by Factor.. 315
7.20 Elite Officers' Distinct Practices... 317
7.21 Patrol-Only Experience Distinct Practices 319
9.1   Detailed Summary of Mental-Readiness Success
       Element in Policing 357
9.2   Mental Success-Element Practices Tally 360
9.3   Detailed Summary of Technical and Physical
       Readiness Success Elements in Policing 362
9.4   Performance Block Tally 364
9.5   Summary of Performance Block in Policing 366

Figures

1.1 High-Performance Professions: Common Traits 3
1.2 Operational Readiness Framework for High-Risk
      Professions... 8
1.3 Try this... 11
2.1 Extended Mental-Health Continuum 24
3.1 Challenging Operational Situations 40
3.2 Operational General Blocks 53
3.3 Operational Rookie Errors 70
3.4 Organizational Blocks 74
3.5 Differences in Performance Blocks in Policing over
      17 Years 95
4.1 Police Overall Importance of Readiness 104
4.2 Differences in the Importance of Readiness
      in Policing over 17 years... 105
4.3 Influential Factors in Policing... 110
4.4 Comparison of Overall Importance of
      Operational Readiness by Tactical Experience 111

4.5 Comparison of Successful Performance Readiness for Officers by Military Experience 112
4.6 Comparison of Disappointing Performance Readiness for Officers by Elite Officers 113
4.7 Comparison of Successful and Disappointing Performances Readiness for Officers by Elite Officers 114
7.1 Orlick's Wheel of Excellence 226
7.2 Commitment Practices 228
7.3 Confidence Practices 245
7.4 Positive Imagery Practices 254
7.5 Mental Preparation Practices 262
7.6 Full Focus Practices 275
7.7 Distraction Control Practices 285
7.8 Constructive Evaluation Practices 307
7.9 Differences in Mental-Readiness Practices in Policing over 17 Years 322

Photos

0.1 Now adapted as an interaction training aid xl
0.2 Identity, compassion and commitment xl
0.3 Equipment comfort xli
0.4 Utilizing a spike belt xli
0.5 Advanced mentoring xlii
0.6 Tactical Trainer xlii
0.7 Improvising with creamers xliii
0.8 Equipment precision and confidence xliii
0.9 School Resource Officers xliv
0.10 Being tased xliv
0.11 After only 15 minutes xlv
0.12 By example xlv
0.13 Catching the bad guy… xlvi
0.14 … always gets played out in training… xlvi
0.15 How I got here xlvi
0.16 Canine Officer xlvi
0.17 … Iko xlvi
0.18 "Delivering the package" xlvii
0.19 Mock disasters xlvii
0.20 University researchers xlviii

0.21 My detailed instruction xlviii
   5.1 Safety starts with proper handcuffing, and mastery ensures confident apprehensions. Credit: Ottawa Police Service, 2024 129
   5.2a At the frontlines of dissonance, navigating the tempest means balancing rights and safety. Credit: Libby Nelson, Vox, Bing, 2016 151
   5.2b Taming chaos. When situations heat up, training kicks in to navigate the ethical maze. Credit: Zou Fa, PXHere, Bing, 2024 151
   5.3 Mastering safe driving in all conditions: prioritize space, exercise caution, and anticipate hazards. A Traffic Escort method for traffic and intersections: Scan, study, select. Credit: Columbus Indiana Police, Bing, 2024 155
5.4a and b 24-7, maintaining visibility and situational awareness is crucial, even during seemingly routine stops. Credit: Ottawa Police Service, 2024 164
   6.1 Tech-savvy policing: From body cameras to crime mapping, the digital transformations of modern law enforcement. Credit: Ottawa Police Service, 2024 173
   6.2 Facing the bench: Officers undergo rigorous preparation for court appearances. Credit: Nick Youngson, Picdedia, Bing, 2024 178
   6.3 Every police arrest requires intelligence, professionalism, adaptability, and confident authority. Credit: Ottawa Police Service, 2024 180
   6.4a-c Strategic conversations infused with credibility, persistence, and empathy lay the groundwork for trust in policing from the first seconds of an interview. Credit: Anna Collins, Femanin, Bing, 2023; Pexels, Bing, 2024; Ed Vulliamy, The Guardian, Bing, 2015 195
   6.5 Mastering the balance between detailing incidents with evidence and ensuring thorough documentation without overwhelming is essential. Credit: Ottawa Police Service, 2024 ... 201

6.6 Walking the fine line between protocol and practice is crucial for staying current and upholding what's right while navigating evolving policies. Credit: Ottawa Police Service, 2024 209

7.1 Missing moments and making sacrifices to serve others in the name of community protection. Credit: Cape Charles Wave, Bing, 2012 241

7.2 Evolving one's frame of mind from "society sucks" to empathy and understanding is a journey supported by home and uniform. Credit: AI NOW Institute, Bing, 2019 250

7.3 The mindset: Safety first, scene managed, support each other. Need to plan resources well ahead, run equipment checks, review procedures, liaise with external resources—always ready to adapt as required. Credit: Unison, Bing, 2017 265

7.4 Confidence with equipment is non-negotiable—it's typically just you and your gear sometimes. A "packing ritual" ensures you know where everything is—no thinking, just action. Credit: Chris Yarzab, Action Alliance, Bing, 2015 279

7.5 Leading others requires a firm commitment to the team and the mission. Internal support and quick problem resolution are key to maintaining order and focus. Credit: Russ and Tiña De Maris, RVTravel, Bing, 2022 290

Mission

1. **Mission statement**
To provide law enforcement personnel with guidance in identifying, preparing for, and operationalizing high-performance strategies and tactics for the frontline, ultimately enhancing results and saving lives.

> *Law enforcement officers on the frontline encounter increasingly complex and unpredictable situations.*

2. **Guiding principles**
   a) Ensuring high standards in a demanding high-risk profession will promote a healthy, prepared police workforce—and, by extension, a safer community.
   b) Employing a systematic approach will give leaders confidence to replicate and adapt evidence-based tactics for recruitment, training, and evaluation.
   c) Examining the strategies of top frontline officers will reveal current best practices.
   d) Sharing authentic and authoritative insights from exceptional frontline officers, including coach officers, will inspire and empower others.
   e) Predicting future trends by contrasting current data alongside information from 20 years ago.

3. **Academic aim and rationale**
   a) *The primary purpose* was to complete analyses on operational readiness in policing in three competencies—physical, technical, and mental readiness—by obtaining physical and technical competencies from a Provincial Coach Officer Advisory Group.
   b) *The secondary purpose* was to update the mental-readiness data from excellent coach officers.
   c) *The final purpose* was to develop resources for practical implementations in policing and other law enforcement professions.
   d) *Rationale*: To improve the operational readiness (performance) of frontline police officers by developing a model based on "excellent frontline" officers that will help frontline police officers achieve performance excellence by:

- enhancing curriculum design and training
- increasing consistency (rather than relying solely on best practices)
- reducing mistakes
- decreasing inefficiencies

Roadmap for readers: Who and where to look

Three-tiered readership—This easy-to-understand analysis offers practical tips for improving performance in law enforcement, based on evidence. It is a must-read for frontline officers, supervisors, senior managers, and academics focusing on excellence in policing.

1. **All readers are invited to…**
    a. dive into this *court-defensible research* that reveals how exceptional frontline police officers and coach officers, akin to many emergency responders ensuring public safety, excel in challenging situations
    b. explore strategies for *maintaining consistency* beyond just best practices, being prepared at a moment's notice, managing distractions, staying focused, and developing high-stress coping skills
    c. evaluate how mental readiness aligns with physical and technical readiness to enhance one's own *overall operational performance*
    d. gain insights into the *human aspect of policing* through candid accounts shared by exceptional frontline officers
    e. scan the *20 key strategies at the end of each chapter* to apply evidence-based practices into daily decision-making, training, and career planning

2. **Frontline law-enforcement officers**
Think of verbatim quotes from exceptional officers as evidence-based research and education with a soul. How you see, judge, and act affects your safety. Your commitment, confidence, and mental-readiness practices can be both separated and integrated into your physical and technical practices. It is essential throughout your career to broaden and improve different strategies and tactics for situations that unfold quickly. See Chapters 3 to 7 related to police challenges, and details for overall operational competencies aligned with physical, technical, and mental readiness.

3. **Police leadership: From police executives to instructors, coaches, and supervisors**
Are you ready to read a publication that captures almost everything that keeps you awake at night? Decisions taken based on opinion alone, in the absence of evidence, tend to yield greater unpredictability, where organizational initiatives can fall short. Adopting a scientific perspective, leveraged from uncensored insights provided by exceptional officers on everyday challenges, leads to setting and delivering sound standards, vital for organizational safety and defense. See Chapters 8 to 10 related to leadership at all levels, knowledge transfer and what's next. Chapter 11 has the Executive Summary.

4. **Academics: Those interested in evidence-based research in the policing domain**
Preparedness in frontline policing significantly influences public health and safety. A comprehensive review of literature spanning 20 years informs this investigation. Purposive sampling of top frontline officers ensures confidence in a scientifically grounded approach. The Operational Readiness Framework offers a replicable, measurable model for addressing risk assessment. This framework systematically integrates qualitative and quantitative evidence into a detailed, police-specific readiness profile. See Chapters 1 and 2 for the conceptual framework and extensive research review, then find detailed versions and references of six themed research reviews in Appendices B to G. The study design is in Appendix A.

What's new and improved in the second edition?

The first edition of *Gold Medal Policing* garnered worldwide attention in plenary sessions; supplied a straightforward, easy-to-understand textbook for training institutions; and inspired tools for improving job performance. Since then, partnerships have developed between extraordinarily skilled professionals in policing and, quite unexpectedly, individuals in related fields. Increasingly, the insights of high achievers were respected and followed. With this came much opportunity to position *Gold Medal Policing* principles where those high achievers deemed necessary, from recruitment, multilevel training and curriculum design, to field assessment.

This second edition summarizes the last 20 years of related studies, measures any significant departures from the original findings, identifies lessons learned, and shares tested tools. Readers can expect the following new, updated, and reorganized content:

1. **Expansion to operational readiness** The methodology has evolved. What originated as a mental-readiness assessment, based on work with Olympic athletes, has grown to a fully integrated "Operational Readiness Framework." The framework provides a very transferable, empirical approach to preparedness with a new risk-assessment perspective. Its replication across vastly different occupations goes beyond policing to neurosurgeons, air traffic controllers, and Sherpa guides. The framework provides insight into performance excellence, especially with regard to mental readiness—which, while critical, is typically neither defined, recognized, nor emphasized in high-risk professions. Operational readiness is now deconstructed into its three main competency areas—physical, technical, and mental readiness. Performance indicators measure these competencies. The performance indicators are illustrated through the practices of

excellent frontline leaders. These practices are job-specific and detailed through the testimonies of these recognized officers.

2. **Extensive research review**: A comprehensive literature review of 343 articles for the period 2000 to 2022 was undertaken, compiling the six emerging policing themes—performance predictors; physical, technical, and mental competencies; performance stressors; and critiques on "Road to Mental Readiness." Each theme was condensed, with expanded versions provided in the Appendices. Graduate students, research assistants, and experts contributed in this process. As a result, this second edition updates issues related to operational readiness and mental readiness, while integrating physical and technical readiness.

3. **Updated data**: Data were collected again using purposive sampling to investigate the preparedness of recognized frontline leaders. While the first edition was based on data from 48 "exceptional" frontline officers (identified by both peers and supervisors), the second edition added new data from 31 excellent active coach officers. The newly collected data were compared with the original data for similarities and differences between the two datasets. Both data were combined for further analysis through various statistical analyses such as qualitative measures of overall operational readiness and quantitative measures of consistency, correlation, and weighted averages.

4. **Changes in practice**: The study design enabled temporal changes to be identified in policing practices over 17 years from 2003 to 2019. This approach provided insight into new focus, trends, changes from the original findings, and effectiveness of the framework in frontline policing. By tapping into what coach officers think, it was possible to assess which best practices in 2003 for mental readiness were still useful in 2019.

5. **Quotes throughout the book** were scanned by multiple reviewers. They agreed that effective practices and inner thoughts of some of the best officers were captured and made available to others through these testimonials. Most quotes were

viewed as timeless and retained. Any text seen as dated or less impactful was removed, and new quotes were added as needed. A peer reviewer's request for additional female officer quotes was accommodated. Over the years, several officers offered their "Top 10" which was subsequently included. Officers and instructors have consistently commented that the testimonial format is valuable for promoting classroom discussion and personal reflection by officers.

6. **Tool development** is a new chapter that captures lessons learned in implementing many of the evidence-based recommendations from the original *Gold Medal Policing*. Tools have been included for recruitment strategies, curriculum revisions, blended learning, and field/scenario assessment. One peer reviewer commented that "this update evaluates the practicality and operationalized use of the framework and its tools, something many other psychology performance books often lack." Sharing these knowledge-transfer tools is intended to encourage further use and refinement in policing and other related law-enforcement professions. Online resources are also referenced that include ready-to-use templates. These training tools can improve police response, individual officer performance, and provide training to new officers, especially in the area of mental fatigue and stress.

7. **Contemporary policing issues** are infused into the book to expose varied applications for the Operational Readiness Framework, particularly with respect to preparing for challenging situations. The framework can guide officer responses to current issues such as: counter-terrorism, hate crimes, mass protests, relationship building within racialized communities, and body-cam evidence. The book also provides a performance context for frontline officers and management to discuss optimal mental wellness for operational readiness.

8. **Layout and terminology** were modified for improved flow. For instance, the opening text is streamlined by excluding the Executive Summary and partnership detail. The new framework

incorporates consistent terminology and labeling of competencies, performance indicators, and practices. The methodology flow is more concise, presenting the empirical blueprint in Chapters 1 and 3 and delving into detailed academic rigor in Appendix A.

9. **Who can benefit**: Each chapter is summarized to accommodate different readers, for instance those on the frontline, in management, or in academia. Impact statements and critical evaluations of the book have been collected to offer a precise range of worth. The primary audience is police officers, coach officers, instructors, supervisors, trainees, recruit applicants, and management. However, it has also benefited related law-enforcement workforces such as military personnel, customs border patrol and security providers, as well as university and college students in disciplines spanning sports psychology, criminal behavioral profiling, criminology, and criminal law. Recently, it has been suggested that the book can also be advantageous to government officials interested in risk management and communications, performance excellence, and operational readiness.

10. **Amended scope**: *Gold Medal Policing: Operational Readiness and Performance Excellence, 2nd Edition* retains the "Gold Medal Policing" branding from the first edition while replacing "Mental Readiness" with "Operational Readiness" due to the broader context and application. Producing quality research goes far beyond academic or scientific spheres, especially when conducting field research with high-risk professions. This field research has enabled a direct link to be drawn between police preparedness and high performance, and to offer foundational practices that influence safety, productivity, and morale, while aligning perfectly with key law-enforcement principles. Peer reviewers from both North America and Europe have ensured methodological rigor of academic research. As a result, it is expected that this book will not only inspire and challenge officers, but also empower them with a broad, evidence-based toolkit to be good at their jobs.

How I got here

I've been tased, bitten by dogs, and now find solace in a little extra coffee. Gaining an invitation into an inner circle to conduct research by senior management of Ottawa Police Service was a nod to my past work, but the real measure of success lay in the views of the frontline. Building rapport and earning trust among highly respected individuals demands a genuine connection with their colleagues on the frontline—*news travels fast in either direction.*

The adaptation of the "Athletic Interview Guide" into a "Police Interview Guide" was more than just reviewing external research and internal police documents. Three intense months of ride-alongs and training days were about getting to know official (and unofficial) police jargon, understanding frontline procedures, deciphering both spoken and unspoken issues, finalizing the study methodology through open dialogue, and establishing a rapport at all levels within the Service.

From an academic standpoint, I approached frontline officers (Constables or Sergeants) confidentially one-on-one, asking two fundamental questions: What defines an "excellent" officer, and could they give me with some names?

As the Principal Investigator, prior to conducting interviews, I engaged in 5 presentations, 25 briefings, 27 full-shift ride alongs, 13 group training days, and 15 breakfasts and lunches by invitation. Additionally, I prepared 43 sets of confidential, anonymous summaries for officers involved to approve my note-taking of the day's experiences.

My participation in frontline police activities was extensive, covering everything from city-wide patrol calls and a first-hand Taser experience to being a tail-gunner in a Level 5 Escort, participating in a 5-hour John School, and engaging in mock hostage negotiations. Each experience was a privilege and a crucial step in establishing openness and trust within the Service before commencing the selection and interview process.[1]

Photo disclaimer: The following photos capture the cultural immersion that was central to the success of the initial study. Please note that these photos, taken during the research pilot phase, are highly selective and in no way representative of the participating interviewees in this study.

Notes

1 Participation and observation of frontline police activities included: City-wide patrol calls, a first-hand Taser experience, cellblock tour, breaking and entering investigation, Basic Officer Driving Test, high-pursuit training (classroom and practical), handcuffing drills, tail-gunner in Level 5 Escort, funeral escort, prostitute sweep, outdoor canine track, mock bomb call, 5-hour John School, school drug search, Mobile Command Post tour, school visits, use-of-force refresher training, parade briefings, drug bust, indoor shooting range practice, outdoor sniper training, breathalyzer testing, radar traffic stops, mock hostage negotiation, a rare 10-78 response ("officer needs assistance"), political demonstration with Public Order Team, rural ride along, airport surveillance, close combat training, bite-suit training, and… *it was a privilege and a vital part of establishing candidness and trust within the Service prior to beginning the selection and interview process.*

PHOTOS 0.1–0.21 How I got here

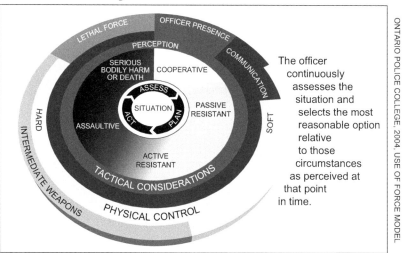

Now adapted as an interaction training aid, *to think, when I began I didn't know what "Use of Force" meant—the gold standard for an officer's legal response options. I was quickly steered to the Professional Development Centre for the mandatory annual full-day refresher course for all sworn officers.*

Identity, compassion and commitment *play a strong role in performance excellence as seen at this memorial service for a senior patrol officer.*

Equipment comfort *must be learned. Proper fitting, regular duty belt tests and simple hand taps are rituals that reinforce an officer's technical readiness. Equipment skills are second only to an officer's ability to communicate effectively— "your mouth is your first defense tool."*

Utilizing a spike belt *demands timing, accuracy and team trust in de-escalating a high-pursuit situation.*

Advanced mentoring *from a seasoned patrol officer is a much sought-after opportunity. Cst. Cheryl Arnott benefits from the advice of respected colleague Sr. Cst. Eric Jones. This process begins as a rookie, where a coach officer role models basic best practices such as a drive-by at traffic stops and informal debriefs.*

Tactical Trainer *Cst. Larry McNally's (center) leadership and expertise are maximized at a special internal workshop series for patrol officers. Quick response, situational awareness, and volume-driven solutions are the trademarks for patrol.*

Improvising with creamers, *Csts. Steve Carroll (left) and Craig Bowman (top right) explain to me the essential role of patrol officers in their rigor to maintain proper containment. Visualizing and role-playing multiple scenarios creates automatic responses.*

Equipment precision and confidence *takes on many forms, including bicycle training for community policing. Community Resource Officers have a knack for external networking and even developing a strong rapport with suspects.*

School Resource Officers *are masters at listening, simplifying messages, managing their time and using diplomacy with parents, school Boards, and politicians (children's handcuffing demonstration by Cst. Susan Wright).*

Being tased *is a lesson you need only learn once. Restraint by Cst. Leo Benvenuti (left) and Sgt. Mark Hayes (right).*

After only 15 minutes *of a slow-moving stealth exercise, I asked Tactical Officer Cst. Steve Boucher, "Excuse me, but why are you taking a break?" He handed me his 75 pounds of uniform to try on. Civilians beware... reality is not always what it seems!*

By example, *my instructor Cst. Nick Mitilineos (left) reinforced that the skillfulness of being an accurate sniper comes from 60% preparing, 10% shooting, and 30% debriefing and cleaning up. I was proud when told, "You did not blink."*

Catching the bad guy...

... always gets played out in training...

... with the same rituals and effort as the real thing. Team of Cst. Jamie Soltondyke (right) and dog Barney.

Canine Officer *Cst. Dan Berrea prepared me well. However, getting into a "bite-suit" can mean only one thing...*

*... **Iko**—with his training, agility and powerful jaws—has the advantage.*

"Delivering the package" *means the Escort Team must constantly adjust to changes in waiting times and variable driving speeds. Performance demands that the rhythm and preparation for all conditions are anticipated. Traffic Escort excels in meticulous appearance, public negotiation, and driving safety. This Mock Level 5 Escort with Cst. Amerjit Sahota (left) and Sgt. Brian Mieske (right) illustrated how traffic flow is always treated with cautious respect—like a veteran sailor shows for the sea.*

Mock disasters *allow municipal emergency measures teams to coordinate complex multi-service responses. Left to right: Judy McDonald, A/Insp. Alain Bernard, Emergency Management Mgr. John Ash, Supt. Pat Hayes, and Cst. Denis Hull.*

University researchers *involved with transcribing and coding the anonymous inter- view data underwent high-level security clearance and police briefings. Left to right: Shawn Amyot, Jennifer Allen, Tim Murphy, James Galipeau, and Insp. Michael Rice.*

My detailed instruction *on the art, science, and discipline for a pristine military- style spit polish was provided by Former "Gren" (Grenadier Guard) and Deputy Chief Larry Hill (left).*

Photo disclaimer: The following photos capture the cultural immersion that was central to the success of the initial study. Please note that these photos, taken during the research pilot phase, are highly selective and in no way representative of the participating interviewees in this study.

Gold Medal Policing, 1st Edition, garnered the attention of police applicants, police services, police colleges, and related fields in protective services. My connection with the Ontario Police College, where I consulted and taught for over 10 years, allowed me to actively shape the curriculum, design tools, establish evaluation criteria, contribute to e-learning, and script scenarios. I facilitated training courses such as Coach Officer, Leadership, Train-the-Trainer, and Recruit Orientations. Regular feedback on the book highlighted its versatility in classrooms, as reflective reading, and as a valuable resource. Requests for training extended to municipal services and educational conferences. This hands-on application of evidence-based research provided valuable insights into the immediate needs within policing.

In 2020, Routledge, the book publishers, were gearing up for a special emphasis on evidence-based policing books in the upcoming years and were actively pursuing more well-researched and practically useful additions to their portfolio. The prospect of a *Gold Medal Policing, 2nd Edition*, had piqued their interest, with specific affirmation that "It looks ideal." So, I started working on the second edition of *Gold Medal Policing*, researching, writing, and consolidating lessons learned.

1

Redefining readiness

A blueprint for peak performance in policing

> **SPOILER ALERT**
>
> Coach officers provide insights on essential competencies needed for excellence and operational readiness in policing.

Abstract

This chapter delves into performance excellence in policing. First, by drawing parallels between elite athletes and peak performance, focusing on identifying specific, measurable skills that redefine excellence and distinguish exceptional performers. Secondly, it showcases the robustness of the Gold Medal Policing research approach across diverse high-risk fields, highlighting its adaptability, court-defensibility, and evidence-based nature. Coach officers contribute insights into fostering fully proficient frontline officers with the capacity for independence. The chapter advocates for a practical, evidence-based approach tailored to police culture, involving frontline peers in defining excellent officer qualities, establishing performance indicators, and teachable practices. Additionally, it emphasizes the need for risk assessment and management to elevate preparedness and performance in managing emergencies. Finally, it concludes by summarizing 20 key takeaways for those interested in investigating performance excellence within policing.

DOI: 10.4324/9781003145493-1

This chapter discusses peak performance in policing in four sections:

A. Excellence redefined
B. Gold Medal Policing research approach
C. Insights from the field: Coach officers' solutions
D. 20 Key strategies for navigating the science of peak performance

A. Excellence redefined

At the heart of this book is the pursuit of performance excellence across three critical areas: physical, technical, and mental readiness. Guided by insights from a Coach Officer Advisory Group, performance indicators were meticulously reviewed. Building upon the first edition[1], mental-readiness practices were updated and integrated with physical and technical practices to ensure overall operational readiness. The ultimate aim was to develop resources with broader applications in policing and other law enforcement professions.

To produce peak performers, skills that we *know* separate the *best* from the *rest* need to be developed. The Olympics showcase many forms of excellence, evident in the 2024 Paris Olympics, from first-time gold medalists like Chinese tennis player Zheng Qinwen, remarkable precision by British shooter Nathan Hales, proud efforts from IOC Refugee Team athletes Muna Dahouk and Dorsa Yavarivafa to enduring forces like American gymnast Simone Biles[2].

Excellence is critical in high-performance professions, such as surgery, air traffic control, and policing, where failure can have serious consequences, including illness, death, financial loss, embarrassment, and public safety issues[3]. While these professions differ from world-class sports, they share similar performance qualities, demanding dedication, discipline, and commitment to achieving exceptional outcomes[4,5,6]. See Figure 1.1.

High Performance Professions: Common Traits

FIGURE 1.1 High-Performance Professions: Common Traits

Individuals in these roles:
- must perform at their peak during specific periods, often facing high-pressure situations
- are directly responsible for their performance
- have finite time frames for execution
- possess highly specialized skills
- require steady nerves
- have accumulated thousands of hours of practice and training

These professions significantly impact community well-being, with research suggesting that evidence-based practices, similar to those in medicine, could greatly enhance effectiveness in policing[7]. Understanding human factors in emergencies is crucial for skill development[8].

> **Lives at risk**—*In policing, you have to fine tune your skills and lives are in the balance because if it. In some ways policing is very much like a lot of the high skill jobs, like being a surgeon. We do it with a gun or with words as opposed to a scalpel. A life is just as much in the balance with me—not as close at-hand and not all the time with every movement—but it can be.*
> —Female officer

What qualities make the "best of the best" in various professions? The criteria for superior performance vary depending on the situation. For instance, while some strive for "perfection," others prioritize getting the job "done."

> *Perfection is not attainable, but if we chase perfection we can catch excellence.*
> —Vince Lombardi, Super-Bowl-winning coach[9]

> *Done is better than perfect.*
> —Sheryl Sandberg, Chief Operating Officer at Facebook, former VP at Google, and World Bank economist[10]

In a world where top athletes must perform under intense pressure, frontline police officers face the ongoing challenge of dealing with high-stress situations, often involving life-threatening consequences. Textbook solutions frequently fall short, and support is often limited. Policing demands heightened public awareness, such as identifying hate crimes, mental-health issues, and potential complaints. Given this ever-changing environment, officers need adaptive skills on the frontline.

Training for peak performance has long been used to equip top achievers to consistently excel and achieve greatness. Military research on high-risk operational personnel found job-specific teamwork, adaptability, sound judgment, and physical endurance to be key factors in making informed decisions[3].

Frontline uniformed officers must demonstrate *individual* readiness through a blend of technical expertise, physical abilities, and mental sharpness throughout their shifts. Efficiency and resilience are paramount in delivering dependable performance at critical moments.

B. Gold Medal Policing research approach

Identifying the practices exhibited by informal leaders on the frontline can spark positive cultural shifts within a workplace. *Gold Medal Policing, 1stEdition*, focused on 48 exceptional frontline officers (anonymously identified by both peers and supervisors), presenting a comprehensive understanding of police-specific mental-readiness practices for advanced performance excellence. Mental-readiness skills, proven contributors to peak performance among Olympic athletes[6,11] and high-risk professions[12,13,14], were central. The book was peer-reviewed and used as a textbook in municipal and provincial police training courses for recruits, coach officers, trainers, and supervisors.

This second edition, now including input from a Coach Officer Advisory Group and 33 currently active coach officers, delves deeper. Through in-depth interviews and investigator-led questionnaires, this research uncovers the physical, technical, and mental competencies enabling the "best-of-the-best" to excel. It reveals:

- ♦ How they consistently perform, remain ready-on-demand, effectively manage distractions, maintain sustained focus, and develop coping strategies to navigate challenges.
- ♦ How their mental readiness aligns with their physical and technical prowess, contributing to overall operational excellence.
- ♦ What practices have changed over the past 20 years.

Bridging risk and performance

To fully prepare, a shift is necessary—one that recognizes the importance of mental preparedness and integrates it with physical and technical practices, especially in high-risk environments.

Risk-science research highlights assessing threats and employing multiple innovative methods for preventing and managing risks[15].

Frontline officers are expected to handle emergencies and community issues, whether as part of a corporate initiative or independently. The real risk lies not in substances or products, but in how officers perceive, understand, and respond to dangers. Their readiness and performance represent an organization's liability, serving as the first line of defense and ultimately impacting the health and safety of the population. Enhancing their skills to stay ahead matters for first responders, especially in rapidly evolving situations.

Defining risk is crucial. It's not just what we tell children to avoid, but also a concept addressed through scientific disciplines like law, medicine, and engineering. Risk is what good leaders factor into all their decisions. It encompasses anything leading to harm—such as loss of life, money, livelihood, or peace. Some might say, "If you do something stupid, something might go wrong." But can something be done about risk? Can experts using data, models, theories, or expert opinions truly influence, even save, lives and livelihoods?[16]

Predicting performance excellence and preparedness is possible. By defining challenges from a frontline perspective, outlining optimal performance under these conditions, and determining how "the best" prepare, respected risk-science practices are followed. Models play a crucial role in understanding complex situations, distilling real-life processes into formats that can be examined to understand how they work. Though models simplify reality, useful ones pinpoint critical elements to manage complex situations.

Essentially, all models are wrong, but some are useful.
—George Box, British statistician[17]

Today, quality assessment combines science and experience. With advanced tools and technologies, experts can better understand, communicate, and manage risk. Using statistics within a bona fide assessment model can reliably quantify data to inform decision-making, safety, fiscal responsibility, and performance. A standardized tool would address risk assessment and management in unexpected contexts.

Expansion to operational readiness

What began as a mental-readiness assessment for Olympic athletes has evolved into a robust and integrated "Operational Readiness Framework." Operational readiness hinges on striking an appropriate balance between physical abilities, technical know-how, and mental sharpness without overreaching or underestimating each competency.

The present framework offers a pragmatic, evidence-based approach to readiness, modernized with a risk-assessment perspective. Expanding beyond policing, it now serves vastly different high-performance environments like neurosurgery and air traffic control[18,19,20]. By isolating and quantifying key readiness competencies, it proves beneficial across these fields. Notably, it has advanced surgical excellence by assessing mental preparedness among surgeons, enhancing focus during procedures[12]. Air traffic control has implemented situational awareness training for both trainees and experienced controllers[19,21,22]. This adaptable methodology extends to other diverse fields like dentistry, social work, global health, and even high-altitude Sherpa guiding[13,14,23,24].

In vital, high-risk professions, thriving professionally and personally is not coincidental. Performance markers and teachable practices are imperative. The Operational Readiness Framework establishes rigorous yet flexible standards, validated by real-world expertise, tailored to each profession. It stands as a versatile, comprehensive tool, offering access to performance potential and mastery of preparedness.

Operational Readiness Framework: A standardized tool

The Operational Readiness Framework (ORF) assesses operational preparedness using both quantitative and qualitative measures. It is a scientific framework that considers:
- the real challenges faced by frontline professions that significantly impact society
- the resolve to uphold high standards when excellence is expected
- the hardwired competencies within these high-performance professions
- the need to extract both spoken and "unspoken" issues among exceptional, confident individuals
- the sharing of best practices through an empirical approach

This framework, depicted in Figure 1.2, is based on individual in-depth interviews and guided questionnaires conducted with outstanding individuals, anonymously identified by their peers and supervisors. They articulate challenging operational situations, the relative importance of readiness (physical, technical, and mental) for optimal performance, and personal preparedness practices. Final calculations yield "performance indicators," exemplified by the practices of exceptional frontline leaders. Job-specific weighting for the three competencies—physical, technical, and mental readiness—creates an Operational Readiness Index (ORI) for the profession, serving as benchmarks for curriculum design, training, and evaluation. Candid quotes are retained to illustrate various applications and promote future critical thinking, self-reflection, and self-assessment. For a detailed methodology see Appendix A: Evidence-Based Rigor—Study Design.

FIGURE 1.2 Operational Readiness Framework for High-Risk Professions

Research that stands up in court

The framework leverages different viewpoints and policing approaches of "excellent" officers to determine the qualities that distinguish exceptional performance. After the first book release, a defense lawyer hailed *Gold Medal Policing* as a court-defensible, evidence-based document defining an "excellent" officer. This endorsement shows the robustness of both the framework and the investigative process in discerning the hallmark qualities of superior policing.

Understanding the importance of physical, technical, and mental readiness, alongside tailored police strategies, can empower frontline officers to navigate challenges better.

> *This framework serves as a great preparedness tool for current military security and defense training exercises. It has extraordinarily broad knowledge from respected sources (police, surgeons, etc.) with academic validation.*
> —Former Commissioned Officer and pilot with the Canadian Air Forces

While performance psychology typically addresses stress management across various domains such as sports, arts, high-risk professions, and business leadership, it often overlooks overall readiness for top performance[25]. This framework is different. It is tailored specifically for professions like policing, providing a comprehensive approach to profession-specific readiness, particularly in achieving policing excellence. The frontline perspective resonates with authenticity and authority, providing credible guidance on what may or may not be a risky situation or decision.

C. Insights from the field: Coach officers' solutions

The vital role of coach officers

Coach officers set examples and foster positive attitudes to help trainees improve. Selected by their supervisor based on their ability and completion of Coach Officer Training, they serve as role models for honorable job performance. These experienced officers bridge the gap between Basic Constable Training and operational policing for new recruits[26]. Their responsibilities include exposing recruits to diverse learning experiences, assessing their performance with timely feedback, and addressing problems during field training. They also ensure trainees are aware of training requirements, document trainee performance, and provide comprehensive progress reports and evaluations throughout the training period. In turn, trainees are expected to sign and understand field-training documents, maintain a daily activity log, record attended Ten Code calls, actively participate in training, demonstrate mastery of taught material, show initiative and integrity, maintain a good fitness level, and comply with regulations and procedures[27].

> **Clear standards**—*A lot get on and think, "Hey, I'm on the police force now. I want to be Chief. Yeah." I was a Coach Officer for four and a half years... I let it be known, "If you're going to screw around or have problems, I'll really push the Police Department to fire you. If they don't, I'll go push them."*
> —Canine

Ultimately, the coach officer's job is to enable trainees to become competent frontline police officers who can independently provide safe, courteous, and effective patrol services. Measurable performance indicators are invaluable tools for coaches to improve consistency, reduce errors, and increase efficiency on the frontline. To understand the training needs of frontline officers, it is logical to seek insights from experienced coach officers.

Competencies for coach officers. Coaches believed that the following practices are crucial to excel at coaching:
- strong communication skills
- ability to set clear objectives
- effective feedback techniques
- capacity to identify and assess potential problems
- skills to assist individuals in improving their performance

Coaches noted that trainees often struggle not due to lack of knowledge or physical ability, but rather due to issues like overconfidence or lack of confidence, lack of initiative, and difficulty staying focused.

> **Coaching sports**—*I also coach basketball and hockey teams about stress preparation. There is value in preparedness like goal setting, getting the reps and simulation scenario to develop competency in whatever—in athletics before going on the court/ice or police giving testimony.*
> —>15 years on

Stay in touch—*I have done a lot of coaching, supervising, mentoring and instructing. I always try to stay aware that the field changes the second you step away. I strive to stay in touch with what it is like out there.*

—>15 years on

Lasting coach impressions—*I brought a lot to the table—thanks to some coaches over the years. One, in particular, was always preaching, "You've got to visualize! Keep your head up! Be ready to go!" In the professional sporting world, if YOU don't do it, they get someone else. You're only as good as your next play. Like thinking you're invincible. Yeah, yeah, yeah… it doesn't matter that you were 100% last week—I don't care—it's what you're going to do for me THIS week.*

—School Resource, >10 years on

What coach officers look for in trainees

> **Try this**: I would challenge any officer reading this to think of an "excellent" officer and list the traits that make you believe that person is exceptional. You may also want to think of someone you feel should not have gone into policing, and list the traits that make you believe that person is not suited for the job.
>
> ♦ Now, mark beside each trait whether it is predominantly a physical (P), technical (T), or mental (M) trait (see definitions in Chapter 4).
>
> ♦ Do you have a clear dominance or pattern in the traits you judge "excellent" and "poor" performers?
>
> ♦ If you find the list that follows of *"Qualities coaches look for in trainees"* seems reasonable, these numbered traits are sorted as: Physical (#s 2, 8, 13); Technical (#s 5, 6, 12, 14); Mental (#s 1, 3, 4, 7, 9, 10, 11).
>
> ♦ Do you see the clear dominance of mental traits coach officers gave to judge "excellence" in policing?
>
> This exercise illustrates why *mental readiness* is generally an influential factor in performing with excellence. It further reinforces a checklist of competencies respected as skills rather than inherent talents.

FIGURE 1.3 Try this

Coach officers collectively shared the following related to desired trainee qualities, crucial competencies needed to excel as a coach, and common coach-officer issues, along with suggested solutions to improve training outcomes for frontline coach officers.

Qualities for policing excellence:
1. ethical behavior both on and off duty (M)
2. prioritization of officer safety (P)
3. leadership skills (M)
4. the ability to follow directions (M)
5. effective communication skills (T)
6. proficiency in applying the law (T)
7. consistent work habits (M)
8. multitasking abilities (P)
9. maturity (M)
10. personal initiative (M)
11. sensitivity toward victims and diverse communities (M)
12. knowledge of the law (T)
13. maintaining a professional personal appearance (P)
14. familiarity with police service and community they serve (T)

Strategies to enhance training

In striving to enhance new officer training, coach officers have identified several persistent challenges:

1. insufficient time to expose recruits to a variety of meaningful calls
2. inconsistency in field training manuals
3. absence of a valid assessment instrument
4. generally poor documentation practices

Practical solutions to address these issues and improve training outcomes were shared by coaches.

1. *Improve time efficiencies* by assigning daily log entries to trainees, fostering equal responsibility and accountability. Incorporate adult learning principles and develop a flexible delivery format that caters to the diverse needs of trainees.

2. *Establish a single field-training manual* with a comprehensive and cost-effective framework.
3. *Develop valid assessment instruments* based on evidence-based research, incorporating concrete and measurable indicators to nurture the growth of "peak performers" rather than settling for "satisfactory" outcomes.
4. *Utilize court-defendable research* that highlights the significance of mental skills. Coaches could relate to evidence that mental-readiness skills[28], which can now be measured and taught, significantly contribute to improved performance.
5. *Streamline documentation practices* by generating progress reports that accurately reflect trainees' learning processes and competence progression. It is crucial to obtain approval from trainees, coaches, and supervisors to ensure accountability.

By prioritizing this input from experienced coach officers, their expertise shaped the development of streamlined training tools (see Chapter 10). This approach ensures that the current data collected aligns with the practical insights and knowledge of those who have extensive experience in coaching frontline officers.

D. 20 Key strategies for navigating the science of peak performance

As a summary, below are the key steps taken in researching peak performance for policing.

1. **Collaborate to analyze:** Collaborate with police training institutions and services to conduct a comprehensive training needs analysis, emphasizing ethics, leadership, and communication.
2. **Assess competencies:** Engage coach officers to assess real challenges and hardwired competencies vital for police excellence.
3. **Improve manuals:** Respond to coach officers' needs for a single, comprehensive field-training manual and valid assessment tools to ensure consistent and effective officer training.

4. **Isolate key skills:** Aim to uncover and develop skills that we *know* distinguish outstanding police officers.
5. **Build in knowledge transfer:** Engage "excellent" officers to share their diverse perspectives to build a valuable database for knowledge transfer and continuous improvement in policing performance.
6. **Emphasize proven performance:** Recognize the importance of mental readiness in achieving peak performance—such as focusing and managing distractions—both in policing and in high-risk professions.
7. **Be cross-disciplinary:** Understand the parallels between elite athletics and frontline policing, emphasizing readiness-on-demand, consistent performance, and steady nerves.
8. **Use science:** Review and incorporate current scientific evidence on performance excellence and operational readiness in policing.
9. **Find a balanced approach:** Analyze the balance of physical, technical, and mental readiness needed for successful policing through a systematic, research-based approach.
10. **Measure "excellence:"** Use a standardized tool to measure how "excellent" officers use mental readiness in achieving excellence.
11. **Tailor police readiness:** Follow a practical, evidence-based approach to define operational readiness in policing, tailoring investigations to police culture and adapting language and scenarios.
12. **Use evidence-based tools:** Expect that a reliable framework for readiness has adaptability to various high-performance settings beyond policing.
13. **Identify the risks:** Apply risk assessment and risk management, and consider human factors to elevate preparedness and performance in managing emergencies.
14. **Gain frontline buy-in:** Involve frontline peers in defining the qualities of excellent police officers, and select top-performing officers anonymously identified by both their peers and supervisors.
15. **Conduct quality sampling:** Utilize anonymous sampling and in-depth interviews to identify the physical, technical, and mental competencies of "the best" officers.

16. **Separate individual from core practices:** Determine the individual and common practices that make these officers excellent performers.
17. **Create a police profile:** Systematically weigh quantitative and qualitative evidence to establish profession-specific profiles.
18. **Set markers:** Establish performance indicators and teachable practices to be a fully functioning officer.
19. **Promote readiness:** Enhance the understanding and adoption of readiness competencies through presentations, workshops, publications and tools.
20. **Reduce risks:** Encourage risk reduction in emergency response situations with scientific advice, informed by evidence-based, real-world practices.

Notes

1 J. McDonald, *Gold medal policing: Mental readiness and performance excellence.* New York: Sloan Associate Press, 2006.
2 J. Mendoza, "Olympic medals today: What is the medal count at 2024 Paris Games on Monday?", *USA Today*, August 5, https://www.usatoday.com/story/sports/olympics/2024/08/05/olympic-medals-today-medal-count-paris-games-aug-5/74668390007/, 2024.
3 J. J. Picano, Roland, R. R., and Williams, T. J., "Assessment and selection of high-risk operational personnel," *Military psychology: Clinical and operational applications,* pp. 326–343. https://books.google.ca/books?hl=en&lr=&id=3LtzEAAAQBAJ&oi=fnd&pg=PA326&ots=8wCTxIy4Tu&sig=nXzekuuaIHIrDGWTbP0V6fONc50&redir_esc=y#v=onepage&q&f=false, 2022.
4 J. Roach, "Managing "key events" can be the fastest route to success," *Management Review,* vol. 71, no. 4, p. 56, 1982.
5 J. McDonald and Orlick, T., "Excellence in surgery: Psychological considerations," *Performance Enhancement,* vol. 2, pp. 13–32. http://www.zoneofexcellence.ca/free/surgery.html, 1994.
6 M. Sarkar and Fletcher, D., "Psychological resilience in sport performers: A review of stressors and protective factors," *Journal of Sports Sciences,* vol. 32, no. 15, pp. 1419–1434. https://doi.org/10.1080/02640414.2014.901551, September 2014.

7. L. W. Sherman, "The rise of evidence-based policing: Targeting, testing and tracking," *Crime and Justice*, vol. 42, pp. 377–431, 2013.
8. C. Owen, *Human-factors challenges in emergency management: Enhancing individual and team performance in fire and emergency services*. Ashgate Publishing, 2014.
9. M. D. Estes, *Do better! Be better!*, eBooks2go. https://indiereader.com/book_review/do-better-be-better/, 2023.
10. S. Sandberg, "Lean in-women, work and the will to lead," *NHRD Network Journal*, vol. 8, no. 2, pp. 137–139. https://doi.org/10.1177/0974173920150225, 2015.
11. T. Orlick and Partington, J., "Mental links to excellence," *The Sport Psychologist*, vol. 2, pp. 105–130, 1988.
12. J. McDonald, Orlick, T. and Letts, M., "Mental readiness in surgeons and its links to performance excellence in surgery," *Journal of Pediatric Orthopedics*, vol. 15, no. 5, pp. 691–697. https://doi.org/10.1097/01241398-199509000-00027, 1995.
13. J. McDonald, Dahal, G. P., Tyshenko, M. G., Sloan, D. A. and Sharma, S. K., "Operational readiness: Links to Sherpas' peak performance in tourist mountain-guiding," In A. P. Adhikari, G. P. Dahal, I. Mahat, B. Regmi, K. Subedi, & S. Shrestha (Eds.), *Sustainable livelihood systems in Nepal: Principles, practices and prospects*. Kathmandu: International Union for Conservation of Nature, Nepal Country Office (IUCN Nepal), pp. 281–308, 2016.
14. J. McDonald and Hale, K., "Mental readiness for frontline workers in homelessness services in Ottawa, Canada," *International Journal on Homelessness*, vol. 2, no. 1, pp. 80–104, 2022.
15. D. Krewski, Westphal, M., Andersen, M.E., Paoli, G.M., Chiu, W.A. and Al-Zoughool, M., "A framework for the next generation of risk science," *Environmental Health Perspectives*, vol. 122, pp. 796–805. http://dx.doi.org/10.1289/ehp.1307260, 2014.
16. Risk Science International, "RSI," 25 January 2022. https://risksciences.com/.
17. G. E. Box and N. R. Draper, "Essentially, all models are wrong, but some are useful," *Statistician*, vol. 3, no. 28, p.1919, 2013.
18. J. McDonald, Orlick, T. and Letts, M., "Mental readiness in surgeons and its links to performance excellence in surgery," *Journal of Pediatric Orthopedics*, vol. 15, no. 5, pp. 691–697. https://doi.org/10.1097/01241398-199509000-00027, 1995.
19. J. McDonald, *Mental readiness training for air traffic control trainees: Course manual*. Transport Canada, 1–16, 1993.

20 J. McDonald, "Mental readiness: Focusing on the cutting edge," *Archives of Pediatric Neurosurgery,* vol. 3, no. 2. https://doi.org/10.46900/apn.v3i2(May-August).95, May–August, 2021.
21 NAV Canada, *Situational awareness module: Train the trainers manual.* Ottawa: NAV (Navigation) Canada, pp. 1–124, 1997.
22 NAV Canada, *Situational awareness module: Participants manual.* Ottawa: NAV (Navigation) Canada, pp. 1-82, 1998.
23 McDonald, J., and Paganelli, C., "Exploration of mental readiness for enhancing dentistry in an inter-professional climate," *International Journal of Environmental Research and Public Health,* vol. 18, no. 13, pp. 7038–7055. https://doi.org/10.3390/ijerph18137038, 2021.
24 J. McDonald and Gyorkos, T., "Operational readiness for conducting global health research abroad," *Canadian Journal of Public Health,* vol. 107, no. 4–5, pp. 387–389. https://doi.org/10.17269/cjph.107.5555, 2016.
25 K. F. Hays, *Performance psychology in action: A casebook for working with athletes, performing artists, business leaders, and professionals in high-risk occupations.* American Psychological Association, 2009.
26 E. Knights and Barath, I., "These experienced officers are the gateway between the OPC Basic Constable Training (BCT) program and operational policing," *Blueline: Canada's Law Enforcement Magazine.* https://www.blueline.ca/problem-based-learning-and-coaching-police-professionals-4950/, November 16, 2017.
27 Ontario Police College, "Police trainee field training manual," Queen's Printer, pp. 1–77, 2009.
28 T. Orlick, "Wheel of excellence." http://www.zoneofexcellence.ca, October 25, 2003.

2

Insights from current research on policing excellence

> **SPOILER ALERT**
>
> Current evidence and existing know-how fuel informed decision-making and outstanding performance.

Abstract

This chapter explores the latest research on police performance, covering six dominant areas: what makes a good police officer, what stresses them out, and how well programs like the "Road to Mental Readiness" (R2MR) work. Also included are the physical, technical, and mental skills officers need. Evidence-based uses of research for making well-informed decisions in law enforcement are also emphasized. Some key findings include new ways to support officers' well-being, such as self-diagnostic tools, fitness programs, and updated policies. The implementation of training that helps officers become more risk-ready, communicate effectively, and build good relationships with communities is also discussed. The importance of cultivating positive leadership and emotional resilience is highlighted. The chapter concludes with 20 top strategies, backed by current research, to help officers improve their performance, enhance community relations, and prioritize their safety, health and wellness.

DOI: 10.4324/9781003145493-2

This chapter discusses current research in police performance in six dominant themes:

A. Predictors of police performance
B. Performance stressors in policing
C. Critical analysis of "Road to Mental Readiness" (R2MR) Program
D. Physical competencies in policing
E. Technical competencies in policing
F. Mental competencies in policing
G. 20 Key strategies from current research for enhancing police performance

Forming opinions without considering evidence can render them superficial. Backing up our beliefs with current evidence and integrating it into our thinking cultivates well-informed perspectives. Police officers and partnerships often rely on traditional law enforcement responses, neglecting evidence in strategy development[1]. However, an expanding evidence-based police movement seeks to understand research and its effective implementation[2,3].

A police instructor's feedback prior to writing this second edition was:

Learning from current literature review stands out for me as key in developing superior performance when teaching mental readiness.

—Police College Instructor,
anonymous peer reviewer

Building on the first edition of *Gold Medal Policing* (GMP1), extensive research examined operational readiness and high performance in policing. A total of 343 articles from 2000 to 2022 were reviewed, providing evidence for six dominant themes in this chapter. The outcomes of this extensive research serve to introduce the background review for this study. Detailed versions and references for each theme are presented in Appendices B–G. Here are the findings:

A. Predictors of police performance[4]

Accountability within law enforcement necessitates adherence to quality, cost efficiency, productivity, performance, and citizen satisfaction standards. Achieving public safety and ethical policing requires defined officer performance criteria. Frontline perspectives lack sufficient performance research. Current research highlights four key performance standards across 39 articles: Selection Criteria (39%), Organizational Directives (29%), Training Principles (16%), and Leadership Development (16%), with 16 unique measures identified (Table 2.1).

TABLE 2.1 Summary of Evaluation Standards and Measures to Predict Police Performance

STANDARDS	*Selection Criteria*	*Organizational Directives*	*Training Principles*	*Leadership Development*
MEASURES	Psychological profiles	Community relations	Core competencies	Informal leaders
	Physical performance	Public confidence	Scenario-based training	Supervisor engagement
	Problem solving	Appropriate use of force	Applied ethics	Females in authority
	Ethnic diversity	Wellness and performance	Critical thinking	Leadership styles

Five recommendations to advance performance excellence in law enforcement:

1. **Update core competencies** with newer predictive performance measures. Prioritize attributes such as composure, maturity, responsible conduct, and controlled self-assuredness, while avoiding counterproductive traits like aggressive, impulsive, or anti-social tendencies.
2. **Enhance public trust and confidence** by employing both traditional and innovative community-policing metrics. Leverage data on citations, response times, and creative

problem-solving tactics to boost community safety perceptions. Account for the impact of local crime rates and victimization to ensure a comprehensive perspective.
3. **Integrate problem-solving scenarios** into officer screening, training, and leadership development. Foster sound judgment through real-world and simulated frontline situations, focusing on ethical decision-making, appropriate use of force, and performance under pressure.
4. **Expand wellness initiatives** to enhance the physical and mental health of officers. Address concerns like anxiety, sleep disorders, and other issues impacting performance, particularly in areas such as driving, safety management, and injury prevention.
5. **Foster leadership** at all organizational levels through both formal and informal channels. Recognize attributes like courage, community engagement, mentoring, and advocacy for diversity and inclusion.

Please refer to Appendix B for a more detailed, referenced, and peer-reviewed version of the *Predictors of Police Performance*.

B. Police performance stressors[5,6]

Over the past two decades, have perceptions of stress within policing changed significantly? Chronic workplace stressors impact key aspects such as job satisfaction, motivation, and performance. These stressors include time pressures, staff shortages, ambiguous workload, excessive training demands, limited job control, equipment deficiencies, and work-family conflict. Notably, increased attention has been directed toward addressing post-traumatic stress disorder (PTSD) and law enforcement suicide. The adaptation of the military-based R2MR program to policing seeks to counter stigma, yet confidentiality remains an obstacle. An extensive review identified 35 articles dedicated to police performance stressors.

Identifying stressors and blockers can advance refined stress management tools. Operational and Organizational Police Stress

Questionnaires (PSQ-Ops and PSQ-Org) provide stress thresholds categorized as low, moderate, and high. These stressors align with three classifications: Operational (inherent to the job), Organizational (from workplace dynamics), and External (outside job factors linked to workplace stressors) (Table 2.2). By understanding and addressing these stressors, officers' well-being and overall effectiveness can be significantly improved.

Five recommendations to address police stressors:
1. **Develop confidential self-diagnostic technologies** to track stressors impacting officers' well-being and performance. Understanding the interaction of stressors is crucial for effective tool design.
2. **Implement support initiatives**, including coaching, mentoring, and positive officer-management relationships, to foster a compassionate work environment. Address hindrances that impede activities like time off, exercising, socializing, and training.
3. **Address sensitive issues** often overlooked in police research through open dialogue with informal leaders. Tackle topics like promotional complacency, job satisfaction disparities among patrol and non-patrol officers, inclusion of minority officers, and fundamental rookie errors.
4. **Establish workplace health and fitness programs** for all officers to improve physical health, mental well-being, energy levels, job satisfaction, and performance.
5. **Promote work-life balance strategies** to minimize conflicts. Encourage creative solutions through inter-professional collaborations beyond law enforcement.

Please refer to Appendix C for a more detailed, referenced, and peer-reviewed version of the *Police Performance Stressors*.

TABLE 2.2 Summary of Police Performance Stressors

CLASSIFICATIONS	PERFORMANCE STRESSORS			
	Operational		Organizational	External
	General	Rookie Errors*		
Primary stressors >75% officers reported in GMP1 Frequently noted in current research	*Crisis* *Jaded/sceptical* *Lulls/routine* *Shift work* Female-policing issues* Personal fears* Public disrespect* Pain and injury**	Aggressiveness*		*Fatigue*
Secondary stressors <75% officers reported in GMP1 Less frequently noted in current research	*Court appearances* *Others' complacency* *Team/Peer mistrust* *Work conflicts*	Basic patrolling issues* Discipline problems* Lack community contacts* Lack of safety* More positivity*	*Equipment limitations* *Ethnicity issues* *Leadership* *Mistrust administration* *Poor support* *Preferential treatment*	*Day-to-day pressures* *Family-work conflicts*
	Car collisions* Climate conditions* External specialists* Getting lost* Lack of information* Previous calls*	No action plan* No basic law* Other officers' anxiety* Poor containment* Poor reports* Unrealistic expectations*	*Training issues* *Workload* Changes* Coaching issues* Lack of feedback* Politics* Promotional complacency* Public complaints* Other e.g., Laws*	

Source: *Gold Medal Policing* (McDonald, 2006) (GMP1).

Notes: Italic font in the main body of the table indicates stressors found in both GMP1 and GMP2 reviews. *Found only in GMP1. **NOT found in GMP1.

C. Critical analysis of "Road to Mental Readiness" (R2MR) Program[7]

Employee wellness is vital for productivity, with mental health and job-specific stressors becoming increasingly significant. Military research underscores the importance of seeking assistance to mitigate Operational Stress Injury (OSI) and PTSD. Canadian data revealed that many military members with disorders refrained from using available services due to stigma. In response, the Canadian Armed Forces (CAF) launched initiatives in 2007, resulting in the "Road to Mental Readiness" (R2MR) program, adapted for first responders and law enforcement in Canada.

An extensive review of R2MR research yielded 53 articles, including 16 that were editorial-style and not scientifically peer-reviewed, used solely for descriptive purposes. The analysis focused on five categories:
- R2MR program description
- Evidence supporting R2MR
- Evidence criticizing R2MR
- R2MR program advancements and adaptations
- R2MR fit with research on high performers

To achieve high performance, excellence is paramount, transcending basic skill levels. An Extended Mental-Health Continuum was created to recognize the range of wellness necessary for peak performance, extending beyond mere basic health and skill levels (Figure 2.1).

FIGURE 2.1 Extended Mental-Health Continuum

[1] McDonald (2006)
[2] Adapted from Road to Mental Readiness: Mental Health Continuum Model (Barath, 2017)

Five recommendations from the R2MR literature analysis:

1. **Enhance programming** for greater engagement, addressing diverse mental-health needs and predicting PTSD through enhanced training and policy development.
2. **Conduct research regularly to validate training delivery** for maximum impact, improving measurements and exploring applications beyond the military.
3. **Address feelings of inadequacy** among supervisors and instructors by incorporating professional mental-health and counseling support.
4. **Invest in e-tools** for personal assessments, addressing privacy concerns and sensitively observing signs of mental illness.
5. **Develop performance-readiness strategies** covering all risks, adapting proficiency based on job and environment specifics.

Please refer to Appendix D for a more detailed, referenced, and peer-reviewed version of the *Critical Analysis of "Road to Mental Readiness" (R2MR) Program.*

D. Physical competencies in policing[8]

Regular fitness, self-defense, and use of force training remain crucial for officers to meet physical requirements. Different regions expect varied tasks and skills from police officers. "Perishable Skills Programs" allocate 14 annual training hours for firearms, suspect arrest and control, driver training, and tactical communication. As frontline roles carry high risks, robust methods for assessing physical readiness are vital.

A rapid review of 29 articles on physical police competencies revealed four main high-performance standards. Most researched was Use of Force (39%), followed by Officer Safety (24%), Physical Demands (21%), and Vehicle Operations (15%). Eleven specific measurement approaches were identified within these standards (Table 2.3).

TABLE 2.3 Summary of Police Physical Competencies

STANDARDS	Use of Force	Officer Safety	Physical Demands	Vehicle Operations
MEASURES	Defensive tactics	Safety training	Fitness testing	Motor-vehicle events
	Force at mental-illness calls	Protective equipment	Environmental stamina	Officer compliance
	Equipment proficiency	Injury status		
	Cultural and gender challenges			

Five recommendations to advance physical competencies in law enforcement:

1. **Increase training time and frequency** to enhance equipment proficiencies like marksmanship and tactics, forming critical muscle memory for violent encounters. Combine physical training with critical thinking and mental adaptability, situational awareness, and decision-making for improved practice quality.
2. **Prioritize competence in handling mental-illness calls** with empathy and reduced force, guided by evidence-based use of force policies, such as using Tasers instead of guns.
3. **Implement tailored scenario training** covering survival, threats, mental-ill encounters, active-shooter response, and complex driving maneuvers, fostering safety awareness for various situations.

4. **Analyze risk versus protection**, considering factors from public threats to hours behind the wheel. Officer acceptance and use of protective actions and equipment are highly dependent on risk perception. Address environmental, cultural, and gender factors affecting protective gear usage and injury risks.
5. **Emphasize protective driving measures** to address common threats of vehicle fatalities and roadside incidents, encouraging officers to reduce driving incidents and researchers to focus less on use of force.

Please refer to Appendix E for a more detailed, referenced, and peer-reviewed version of the *Physical Competencies in Policing*.

E. Technical competencies in policing[9]

Police officers rely on technical skills for daily tasks, including tactical, analytical, communicative, and legal abilities. Agencies must train and measure these skills for officers' technical excellence. Communication and interpersonal skills are crucial for enhancing safety during dangerous situations, such as giving clear instructions and collaborating with other professionals. Active listening, problem-solving, persuasion, and conflict management are key.

A rapid review of 51 articles on technical police competencies identified four main high-performance standards. Most researched was Knowledge of Police Organization (40%), followed by Understand Community (27%), Knowledge and Application of Law (25%), and Verbal and Written Communication (8%). Thirteen specific measurement approaches were identified within these standards (Table 2.4).

Five recommendations to advance technical competencies in law enforcement:

1. **Deploy mobile technology effectively**, integrating body cams, video surveillance, social media, and dataflow

TABLE 2.4 Summary of Police Technical Competencies

STANDARDS	Knowledge of Police Organization	Understand Community	Knowledge and Application of Law	Verbal and Written Communication
MEASURES	Policing philosophy	Special-interest groups	Local, provincial, federal laws	Articulation
	Policies, procedures, protocols	Street-drug use	Situational tactics	Note taking and reporting
	Organizational culture	The media	Technology resources	
	Counter-terrorism impacts	Community partners		

platforms with traditional policing in high-risk areas to reduce street-level crime.

2. **Strengthen articulation training for rookies** through on-scene debriefs and simulation exercises to communicate effectively during challenges like hate crimes, mental-health incidents, suicide attempts, and overdoses, fostering de-escalation and peaceful resolutions.
3. **Facilitate collaborative information-sharing** through interactive platforms, improving community relations and public-image branding. Encourage frontline officers to exchange information with other service providers for increased efficiency and preventive efforts.
4. **Invest in specialized counter-terrorism training** and enhance mental-health literacy and accessibility to services within police departments to address terrorism threats and reduce risks of depression and PTSD.
5. **Embrace community-policing strategies**, engaging local communities in crime prevention and adapting to evolving laws. Enhance citizen satisfaction, perceptions of order, and

police legitimacy while effectively managing public complaints, negative media reports, and social media interactions.

Please refer to Appendix F for a more detailed, referenced, and peer-reviewed version of the *Technical Competencies in Policing*.

F. Mental competencies in policing[10]

Mental readiness is vital for police success, akin to world-class athletes performing under pressure. Orlick's Wheel of Excellence, a model for athletic success, is applicable to policing. The model comprises seven success elements: Commitment, Self-Belief, Positive Images, Mental Readiness (or Preparation), Full Focus, Distraction Control, and Constructive Evaluation (adapted to include Coping).

Reviewing mental police skills identified 69 crucial training skills for frontline work, grouped into 23 measures predicting high police performance based on the Wheel of Excellence. Comprehensive research across 64 articles revealed all seven high-performance standards present. Commitment was most studied (30%), followed by Constructive Evaluation and Coping (22%), Self-Belief (17%), Distraction Control (12%), Full Focus (10%), Positive Images (5%), and Mental Preparation (4%)

The organization of these standards is supported by four other existing models for assessing mental readiness: Mental Toughness Questionnaire-48 (MTQ48), Emotional Intelligence Model (EQ), Train (your brain) like an Olympian, and "Psychological Resilience in Sport Performers" (Table 2.5).

Five recommendations to advance mental competencies in law enforcement:

1. **Identify and refine less-dominant success elements**, combining Positive Images with Mental Preparation and Full Focus with Distraction Control for more effective training and evaluation.
2. **Emphasize ethics** to address moral dilemmas, misconduct, profession discipline, and biases impacting decision-making

TABLE 2.5 Summary of Police Mental Competencies

STANDARDS	Commitment	Constructive Evaluation and Coping	Self-Belief	Distraction Control	Full Focus	Positive Images	Mental Preparation
MEASURES	Ethics	Formal evaluation	Quality training and practice	Emotional control	Situational awareness	Motor-imagery training	Rituals
	Ethics training	Public feedback	Support systems	Car collision avoidance	Anticipation	Stress reduction	Goal setting
	Leadership connection	Debriefs	Recognition and thanks	Refocusing			
	Job engagement	Coping	Maturity and culturally grounded				
	Competitive	Leadership directives					

(e.g., victimization, racism, and priorities). Research on commitment to laws, regulations, and the organization is critical for officer development.
3. **Inspire officer commitment** through successful police leaders who role-model openness, meaningful exchanges, and job engagement. Address concerns of seasoned patrol ranks related to being undervalued to ensure positive coaching and training.
4. **Focus on emotional control** for managing distractions, leadership, stress reduction, and interpersonal skills. Implement practices like visualization and controlled breathing to enhance coping and performance.
5. **Cultivate resiliency** through individual and organizational responsibility, supporting coping with trauma, preventing stress injuries, and enhancing performance. Utilize preventive mental skills, drills, peer debriefing, and wellness support to reduce PTSD risks.

Please refer to Appendix G for a more detailed, referenced, and peer-reviewed version of the *Mental Competencies in Policing*.

In conclusion, this extensive research review establishes a robust foundation for evidence-based approaches to address operational readiness and high performance in policing. The identified key themes, encompassing performance predictors, stressors, mental health, and competencies, underscore the significance of blending up-to-date evidence with existing knowledge to formulate superior strategies for police officers. The recommended strategies from this review, along with an empirical framework and insights from exceptional frontline officers and coach officers, will inform and ground future directives in this book.

Gold Medal Policing aims to offer continuous enhancement and effectiveness in law enforcement practices to cultivate a more resilient, highly proficient, and skilled workforce. Integration of these evidence-based insights by policymakers, leaders, trainers, and those on the frontline can result in a safer and more effective policing environment for both officers and the communities they serve.

G. 20 Key strategies from current research for enhancing police performance

As a summary, 20 key strategies supported by current research to enhance performance in law enforcement are listed below.

1. **Foster compassion:** Develop confidential self-diagnostic technologies for officer well-being, supporting initiatives to foster compassion at work.
2. **Use more dialogue:** Engage in open dialogue with informal leaders to address sensitive issues.
3. **Target work-life balance:** Implement workplace health and fitness programs, and promote work-life balance strategies.
4. **Research current training methods:** Conduct ongoing research to develop effective and risk-ready training programs.
5. **Support performance wellness:** Enhance performance-specific mental-health training and policy development, and incorporate mental-health teaching support for instructors.
6. **Post online resources:** Utilize downloadable e-tools to enable anonymous and confidential personal assessment of performance and well-being.
7. **Improve readiness training:** Implement risk-readiness strategies, and provide extensive and frequent training for equipment proficiency.
8. **Practice empathy:** Practice less force, greater empathy, and accessing resources when handling mental-illness calls.
9. **Train with scenarios:** Create tailor-made scenario training for varied situations emphasizing tactical and protective driving measures.
10. **Anticipate risks:** Conduct risk analysis and implement protection measures on the frontline.
11. **Be tech savvy:** Utilize mobile technology and AI for effective policing and improved resources and decision-making.
12. **Choose words:** Train in word precision and varied tone for effective communication and community rapport.

13. **Share information:** Foster collaborative information-sharing for community relations.
14. **Update specialized training:** Deliver specialized hate crime and counter-terrorism training to inform frontline risks.
15. **Address public needs:** Embrace community-policing strategies to build trust and gain citizen satisfaction.
16. **Train for success:** Modify training and evaluation to include open dialogue on successful and less successful practices.
17. **Know biases:** Place emphasis on ethics to address decision-making biases on complex issues.
18. **Lead by example:** Inspire commitment through positive formal and informal leadership at all levels.
19. **Steady nerves:** Focus on emotional intelligence and control to reduce stress.
20. **Practice personal wellness:** Cultivate resiliency through preventive personal mental skills and organizational wellness supports.

Notes

1 K. Bullock and Tilley, N., "Evidence-based policing and crime reduction," *Policing: A Journal of Policy and Practice,* vol. 3, no. 4, pp. 381–387. https://doi.org/10.1093/police/pap032, 2009.

2 K. Lumsden and Goode, J., "Policing research and the rise of the 'evidence-base': Police officer and staff understandings of research, its implementation and 'what works'," *Sociology,* vol. 52, no. 4, pp. 813–829. https://doi.org/10.1177/0038038516664684, 2018.

3 L. W. Sherman and Murray, A., "Evidence-based policing: from academics to professionals," *International Criminal Justice Review,* vol. 25, no. 1, pp. 7–10. https://doi.org/10.1177/1057567715576174, 2015.

4 N. Vyas, McDonald, J., Kirkwood T. and Tyshenko, M. G., "Predictors of police performance," In J. McDonald, *Gold medal policing: Operational readiness and performance excellence,* 2nd ed. London: Routledge, pp. 497–504, 2025.

5 N. Vyas, McDonald, J., Kirkwood, T., Cheng, C. and Tyshenko, M. G., "Police performance stressors," In J. McDonald, *Gold medal policing:*

Operational readiness and performance excellence, 2nd ed. London: Routledge, pp. 497–504, 2025.
6 J. McDonald, 2006. *Gold medal policing: Mental readiness and performance excellence* New York: Sloan Associate Press, 2006.
7 M. Abu-Alhassin, McDonald, J., Kirkwood T. and Williams, M., "Critical analysis of Road to Mental Readiness (R2MR) Program," In J. McDonald, *Gold medal policing: Operational readiness and performance excellence*, 2nd ed. London: Routledge, pp. 505–514, 2025.
8 M. G. Tyshenko, McDonald, J., Niyati Vyas, N. and Kirkwood, T., "Physical competencies in policing," In J. McDonald, *Gold medal policing: Operational readiness and performance excellence*, 2nd ed. London: Routledge, pp. 515–525, 2025.
9 M. G. Tyshenko, McDonald, J., Kirkwood T. and Ali-Ndi Ringnyu, C., "Technical competencies in policing," In J. McDonald, *Gold medal policing: Operational readiness and performance excellence*, 2nd ed. London: Routledge, pp. 526–536, 2025.
10 M. Abu-Alhassin, McDonald, J., Kirkwood, T., Williams, M. and Cheng, C., "Police mental competencies," In J. McDonald, *Gold medal policing: Operational readiness and performance excellence*, 2nd ed. London: Routledge, pp. 537–550, 2025.

3
Police under pressure

> **SPOILER ALERT**
>
> Any call can turn violent—physical strength doesn't guarantee safety or prevent being thrown down a flight of stairs.

Abstract

This chapter explores the challenges and stressors faced by frontline police officers, emphasizing the impact of limited resources, stress, and feeling undervalued on safety and morale. Officers encounter diverse, unfamiliar and emotionally-charged situations that involve high-risk scenarios and complex procedures. Operational, organizational, and external stressors shape their on-duty experiences, with operational stressors and rookie errors being significant. Managing public complaints, street disrespect, and routine tasks amid shift changes and personal anxieties adds to their burden. Addressing these challenges requires robust support mechanisms, including recruiting the right people, providing training, and offering realistic guidance. The chapter concludes by outlining 20 key challenges and performance blocks in policing.

This will establish the first phase of the Operational Readiness Framework in categorizing challenging situations and performance blocks in policing. The views of excellent frontline officers and coach officers are reported in four parts:

A. Reimagining coaching and frontline dynamics
B. Frontline police challenges: A closer look
C. Performance blocks: *"Barbs and jabs"*
D. 20 Key challenges and performance blocks in policing

A. Reimagining coaching and frontline dynamics

Current research highlights common stressors among individuals in high-risk occupations, affecting personal safety, productivity, and well-being. These stressors include limited resources, heightened stress and fatigue, feeling misunderstood or undervalued, strain on human resources, inconsistent performance, and knowledge transfer gaps[1]. Such stressors can lead to diminished overall well-being, and even a desire to quit.

> **Misunderstood**—*Too often we get feedback, whether from a superior officer, the public or the Communications Centre, wanting us to do more with what we have. We don't have enough manpower. These guys work very, very hard. It bothers me when we're not understood.*
> —Patrol Sergeant

Compounding stressors intertwine, potentially leading to other stress-related conditions like post-traumatic stress disorder (PTSD). For instance, fatigue can trigger family disputes, worsening worry and sleep issues, perpetuating fatigue, hindering recovery, and reducing performance[2,3,4,5]. Law enforcement now recognizes everyday stressors, such as inadequate support, low organizational commitment, and family-related stress[3].

Coaches and informal leaders play a crucial role in shaping attitudes. Retired Chief Andy Rhodes emphasizes the urgency of addressing these challenges. By revamping coaching dynamics, a healthier and more productive environment can benefit recruits, seasoned frontline officers, and coaches alike.

> **Toll on coaches**—*Policing research[1] has shown that our tutors form 50 percent of our attitudes. What are the belief systems of coaches for new recruits? I have seen mid-service coach officers, although "excellent," with higher fatigue, higher stress, lower well-being and who feel less valued than any other group. Is it helpful for them to influence new recruits in this state? We have to do better.*
> —Retired Chief Andy Rhodes,
> United Kingdom, OBE, QPM Service

The military's Road to Mental Readiness (R2MR) program aims to raise mental-health awareness and reduce stigma among police[4]. While stress assessments and personality tests can be valuable tools[2,6], frontline officers may perceive them differently. Maintaining confidentiality and anonymity is crucial, considering the unique stressors encountered on duty.

Assessment tools have their limitations. While stress tests may help, frontline officers may find them burdensome. They often provide numerical values for various stressors but offer limited solutions. The key lies in seeking professional help immediately or attempting to reduce stress levels[5].

> **Assessment drainage**—*I feel stressed from juggling multiple priorities, and exhausted from having to be "resilient." Stress tests are "suckage in my life" with numerical values for deaths, injuries, surgeries, doctor's appointments, moods, financial troubles or whatever the obstacles or challenges. But the recommended solutions boil down to either seek professional help immediately or stress less, do more and be happier.*
> —Patrol

Informal opportunities for discussion and support from coach officers, peers, and the organization may be the most effective way forward in mitigating negative stress[6]. Real-world frontline issues from fellow officers and coaches follow in this chapter. Best practices for handling these issues, including distraction control strategies, are detailed in the subsequent Chapters 5 to 7, providing valuable insights to support officers in managing stress and maintaining optimal performance.

B. Frontline police challenges: A closer look

Standardized assessment

Officers were asked, "What frontline situations are challenging (… *and make you sit up a little straighter*)?"—just as athletes would relate to an Olympic competition. They discussed calls they had been active in attending within the past few months.

Challenges: "If you screw up, people die." Officers are often asked to perform under complicated, stressful, or high-risk circumstances, as well as to attend what they consider to be "routine calls." However, all scenarios must be viewed with caution as illustrated in these sample quotes.

> **Not looking foolish**—*Barricaded suspects are a huge challenge. If you screw up, people die. The biggest thing that keeps you going is not looking foolish in front of your peers. You don't want to be the guy that everybody discusses at lunch. We are highly critical people.*
>
> —Tactical
>
> **"Routine" calls**—*Always remember, even though you've been to 20 break and enters that month, the person who just got broken into has never been broken into before. To walk in and say "Aw, it's nothing"… You have to realize that this person has just been violated—this is their home. That's the other side of complacency. It falls into the public eye and public perception. Why are you doing the job you're doing? Why are you here in the first place?*
>
> —Patrol

Perceived challenges in policing often stem from officers' familiarity with risk, their recognition of potential danger, and their skill level. Calls are classified into seven categories based on previous research, ranging from life-threatening to coaching responsibilities.

Whether or not situations are perceived as being "challenging" may stem from an officer's:
- familiarity with risk versus others who rarely face it
- ability to recognize potential danger versus others who may not
- lack of the necessary skills and thus uncomfortable versus others with the related skills

Categorizing police challenges

Calls are classified into seven circumstances based on previous research[7,8,9], ranging from life-threatening to coaching responsibility. These challenges significantly affect personal safety, productivity, and well-being.

On average, each officer identified three of the seven types of challenges (refer to Figure 3.1). There is little consistency in their selections as a group. While most officers (77%) recognized heightened risk situations, over half regarded complex (56%) and emotionally-charged (50%) situations as primary operational challenges. Fewer identified challenges related to coaching or leadership (47%), managing high-risk subjects (13%), or handling unprecedented events (6%) as challenging (see handout in Appendix H: Challenging Situations in Frontline Policing). Officers with prior experience in another police service reported fewer challenging situations overall ($p = 0.081$).

> **Hate crimes and terrorism**—*As a member of the Provincial Hate Crime and Extremism Team, instructor for the Provincial Hate Crimes Course, and former chair of the Federal Hate Crime Task Force on Training, the focus on hate crimes and terrorism in this book is a welcome addition.*
> —Sgt. Ali Toghrol,
> Hate & Bias Crime Unit, Ottawa Police Service

> **Tunnel-vision**—*I've lived tunnel vision in combat. As a leader, one often experiences the loss of "tactical periphery," necessitating a 360-degree awareness from left to right, and*

from down to up, despite having a lookout on your six... Stress can come at law enforcement even without a weapon being fired your way.

—Special Ops Commander

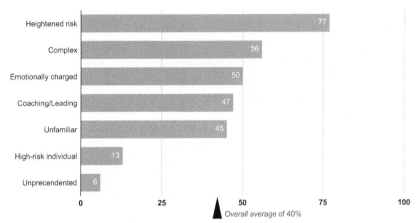

All officers on average reported 40% of the challenging situations (3 out of 7 challenging situations per officers).

FIGURE 3.1 Challenging Operational Situations

Heightened-risk situations

Heightened-risk situations typically involve life-threatening conditions or significant injury. Officers with previous rural experience (65%) or those from other police services (42%) mention these challenges less frequently. Heightened-risk situations are defined as follows:

> "confirmed" weapon call • suicide attempted with weapon • "legitimate" hostage taking • domestics • stolen cars pursuits • B & E in progress • barricaded person call • dynamic entry • lock down (for bomb threat) • bar or drug blitz • high-risk tracks • explosive detection scenario • high speed escort • high-risk vehicle takedowns • bank robberies • live fire in the mix • 6.5-hour day in an intersection • delay in/access to back-up • nothing is "routine" • not recognizing the potential risks • when

it's the "real deal" • feeling nervous with "tunnel-vision warp"

The real deal—*This is the "real deal." You talk about preparedness—that's when the wheels start turning. What are we going to get into? How are we going to deal with it? We just keep going through it and through it, asking ourselves the questions and reflecting on all those potentials. Our training is driven by the operations we do and the high-risk calls. The ones that are challenging are probably that 20%, because you know they are the "real deal." This is not somebody who "thought" they saw somebody with a knife.*

—Tactical

Tunnel-vision warp—*To this day, certain calls make me nervous. You're on the way to a scene and you're in this tunnel-vision warp. The radio is blaring, the computer is going and calls are still coming in. Information is being added to updates on the call that you're racing to. You're just thinking, "What am I gonna do?" and trying to drive [laughs].*

—Traffic Escort

Breach the door—*When you are called, you really have to be at the top of your game… With search warrants, drug warrants, you never really know what you're getting into until you actually breach the door… They may say there are guns in the house, but you never know.*

—Tactical

Complex situations

Complex situations, characterized by their intricate and multi-phased nature rather than being life-threatening, are mentioned more often by males (65%) than females (27%), all Canine officers, and those with prior Traffic Escort experience (88%). Conversely, officers with Patrol-only experience or previous Neighborhood Resource Team (NRT) roles mention complex situations much less frequently (30%). Complex situations are defined as follows:

complex entry (double entry, distraction devices) • demonstration (prostitute) "sweep" • call volume for service • school drug search • long canine tracks • intersections on Level 5 Escort • sexual assaults at school • involvement of external agencies, parents, officers • mass traffic accident chaos • multi-injuries • handling a lot all at once • bound by protocol/guidelines • racing to call while radio is blaring, computer is going, calls coming in, still getting updates • hate crimes • suspected terrorism • being quick and observant • circumstances bound by protocol, guidelines and changes • school fight-at-large with reoffenders • getting a good witness statement • limited resources

Re-offenders—*The call came in as "a fight-at-large in a high school." I get there, see the look on the V-P's face, he gives me the name of the subject… and I said, "Okay, now this is going to be something. Do we have some witnesses?" "Yeah, they're over there in my office." I went and spoke to the witnesses, and knew these guys were re-offenders. I said, "Okay, we've got some good evidence here. Let's go after them."*
—School Resource

Complex situation: *"For two seconds, you're just literally dumbfounded."*

Multi-vehicle injuries—*Arriving first on the scene of a mass traffic accident—multi-vehicle injuries everywhere—just chaos. Everybody's screaming at you, traffic is backing up. For two seconds you're just literally dumbfounded. Then, you have to report everything back: Assess injuries, make sure the fire and ambulance is coming, react to life-threatening stuff, get barricades, call the City, get street cleaning going, reroute traffic, call for other units. You have to do all of this at the same time, so you kind of go, "Oh my God, what am I doing?"*
—Neighborhood Resource

Quick *and* observant—*One of the biggest challenges is being quick while at the same time being very observant.*
—Patrol

All at once—*You can get screwed up when a whole bunch of stuff is occurring all at once. It becomes very confusing. You've got two radios going talking to Patrol and to Tac, and you're trying to talk to the Duty Inspector face to face.*
—Tactical

Emotionally-charged situations

Emotionally-charged situations trigger personal and emotional responses, particularly for female officers (73%) compared to males (43%). Emotionally-charged situations are defined as follows:

> accident or incident with an officer ("… a whole different dynamic—especially if you know them") • policy versus "what's right" • special relationship pressures with subjects (e.g., relative, friend) • emotional relationship • graphically violent situations • injury or violence against a child • personal physical or mental fatigue • low team morale • parental involvement • feeling like a politician • handler-canine issues • complacency at repetitive calls • not looking foolish with peers • promotional process with A-types • personal fear • "I wish this wasn't my call" feeling • feeling misunderstood or undervalued • team pressure, like being the last guy on the truck

Another officer—*There may be an officer that's not going home tonight. This really sucked… from the start. I was lying in bed (my wife is used to phone calls in the middle of the night). "What's that?" When I described it to her, I knew from my voice that this was different. This is going to take a lot of fortitude. Driving in it's like, "I wish this wasn't my call. I wish they hadn't phoned me. Yeah, this is what I'm supposed to do, but man… this is going to be a tough one."*
—Tactical

I can sleep knowing—*I had a case where a biker affiliate was recruiting 17-year-old girls into prostitution. I spent two hours trying everything to get through to one of these girls not*

to go back. We take the oath and we're not allowed to talk about anything on the job, but could I sleep at night if I didn't tell her what she is getting herself involved in? She went back to the bikers and told them everything—they might sue us. I could be hung out to dry but I will continue to do the right thing, as opposed to what policy states. At least I can sleep knowing this girl had the chance.
—School Resource

Special relationship: "This was different. This is going to take a lot of fortitude."

Team pressure—*There's nothing worse than being last guy in the truck. When I put my stuff away, I know where everything is—I don't have to hunt around. If you were lazy the night before and didn't do that, then you're taking extra time.*
—Tactical

All A-types—*The promotional process, it's very competitive with A-type personalities—everyone wants a leg up on the other guy.*
—Patrol

Coaching/Leading
Coaching others on duty increases complexity and responsibility while decreasing the sense of control. Almost half of all officers (47%) find coaching situations challenging as defined below:

> official Coach Officer role • liabilities with young officers • simulations • range training • team projects • recruit not performing but father is the Supt/Chief • first day with a new recruit • coaching someone more skilled requires more preparation • feeling the added responsibility as leader • when you miss a step • keeping it current to avoid boredom from repetition • dealing with a "tv cop" outlook • pressures when mentoring • assessing a poor trainee • trainee not willing to accept feedback • balancing coaching with other duties • managing time

and priorities to address key skills • building rapport while assessing • managing expectations

Missed a step—*We might have been too quick to clear the call and get going on the report—we knew we were done soon. I skimmed over her report when I needed to go line-for-line. I don't want to train somebody to miss those obvious steps. I didn't show her that one step that we should have done that night. That hit home.*

—Patrol Coach, >10 years on

Coaching others: "I didn't show her that one step that we should have done that night. That hit home."

Beat boredom—*The challenges in training is keeping it loose, keeping it current, and keeping it interesting because a lot of the training we do is repetitive. When you keep repeating things, you get bored. If you start losing interest, your skill level will start to drop.*

—Tactical

More responsibility—*When you have a rookie with you, you've got an added responsibility.*

—Patrol Coach

TV cops—*Some of them coming on have a funny outlook on policing—some think it's like cops on TV. This job isn't all action—it's a lot of mundane stuff too.*

—Patrol Coach

Know them—*My platoon is an extension of my family. I've become a mentor to them and I take this responsibility very, very seriously. Their wellbeing is paramount because if they are in a good frame of mind and reasonably happy, they'll do good work. That makes my job easier. So… treat them with respect. Trust them. Educate them. Know them. Why is their behavior or work performance changing? What's going on in their lives? Help them deal with it.*

—Sergeant

Unfamiliar situations

Unfamiliar situations, uncommon to a specific officer but familiar to others, are often mentioned by more experienced officers with more years on the job than those with fewer years (45% versus 8%), higher-ranking officers (Sergeants 60% versus Constables 29%), and "Old School" males (48% versus "New School" 13%). The frequency increases with high-risk specialty units, from lower-risk (NRT, School Resource Officer [SRO] 8%) to Patrol (33%) to high-risk (Tactical, Canine, Traffic Escort Units 56%).

Unfamiliar situations: "Just resist the urge to light your hair on fire and run around."

However, NRT officers reported unfamiliar situations as challenging less frequently than other officers (10% versus 42%), as did those who speak multiple languages (23% versus 46%). Unfamiliar situations are defined as follows:

> common rookie pressure situations • "every day is different" • threat that this could be the "big one" • traumatic situations—afterwards "nobody gave a shit" • working with dogs • unfamiliar building or neighborhoods • first time drawing gun or shooting • anywhere I haven't been tested yet • a search without warrant for weapons • the unknown • lacking necessary skills • inexperienced area and not recognizing the potential risks

Search without a warrant—*Let's say there's a possibility of doing a search without a warrant for weapons and particular charges. I'm not all that experienced in that area. I've never been an Investigator. I rely on five years on Patrol, six years on Tactical, and then my two years as a Supervisor.*
—Elite officer

New location—*If I've never been before, I'll just try to listen to the radio and go to the area. If I have been, then I'll try and identify who the actors are involved, "Oh yeah, this guy, I've dealt with him before. He's got weapons" or "this guy isn't so*

bad" or "the wife is this and that" or "there's a lot of drugs" or "there's kids involved"—a lot of factors.
—Neighborhood Resource

Can't assume—*Assess calls as you go along. Be prepared for different scenarios, but don't play scenarios over in your head, because every call is different and you can't assume anything. [For example], at a domestic call you have to be prepared for anything. It could be non-violent or a full-blown violent call. You've got to mentally prepare yourself. Keep your cool, stay calm and deal with it as it happens.*
—Patrol, >10 years on

Not tested yet—*There are scenarios I haven't been tested in yet. I've been through them a thousand times in training but the question is, when it's time for the real deal, what's going to happen?*
—Tactical

First-time "crisis"—*If I have to do it for the first time, it's a crisis. Just try to resist the urge to light your hair on fire and run around. Try to be cool.*
—Elite officer

High-risk individuals

High-risk individuals, either victims or offenders, create stressful conditions for officers. These challenges are infrequently mentioned by officers in general (13%), less so by those with only a high school education (8%), never by college graduates (0%), and most often by those with a university background (33%). Those with tactical training (33%) or prior police-related experience (27%) are also more likely to identify high-risk individuals such as the following:

MHA/EDP (Mental Health Act/Emotionally Disturbed Person) • drunk call • large group fights between persons who know each other • evidence of criminal record • known HIV positive • groups with a violent reputation (known to carry gun, fight police, be full patch HA [Hells Angel])

Pain thresholds—*Any call has the potential to be violent. If someone is mentally disturbed, you have to be fully conscious of it all the time. Know the pain threshold you're dealing with. You think you're bigger and stronger, but that doesn't always work. Some person who's 90 lbs. but mentally disturbed can friggin' throw you down a flight of stairs.*

—>15 years on

Charged-up—*We used to have a saying when faced with a charged-up individual… "How much adrenalin is he packing?" We had even come up with a scale of 1 to 3.*

—Military combat experience

Reaction to police—*For a mental-health call and a warrant of apprehension, you have no idea what you're dealing with. You don't necessarily know the ins and outs of the person's mental instability, let alone their reaction to police. Nobody likes to see us coming because generally something bad has happened or is about to happen.*

—Female officer

Unprecedented circumstances

First-time procedures and unprecedented terrain involving "the unknown" or exceptional circumstances are rarely mentioned (8%) as a challenge, except for those with prior tactical training (22%) or female officers (16%). These unprecedented circumstances are defined as follows:

> first-of-its-kind procedure • using new equipment • implementing new procedures or policies • striving for exceptional results • world-class sniper training • being someone driven to "find the stolen car" • training for extreme circumstances • constantly setting new traps to challenge dogs • having a request for your personal expertise • needing perfect timing • trying something not typical

> **Not typical**—*We did an impaired driving project that meant a lot to me. Usually, Ride Programs are on highway off-ramps but, since we were getting complaints from the local community*

about drunk drivers, we set up in a residential neighborhood. That is definitely not typical but we got a lot of people and the feedback was phenomenal. People were really thankful. They'd never seen that.
—Neighborhood Resource

In frontline policing, navigating these challenges while dealing with scarcity of resources and high stress is crucial for improving overall performance and well-being. Subsequent chapters examine how top officers achieve physical, technical, and mental readiness in difficult situations.

Recognizing your strengths and limitations boosts confidence. A consolidated handout of challenges in Appendix H: Challenging Situations in Frontline Policing can help refine existing strategies, identify areas needing specialized attention, and explore mentoring opportunities and career development.

C. Performance blocks: *"Barbs and jabs"*

Categorizing police performance blocks

Officers often find it uncomfortable to recall disappointing performances. Officers expect to do well, want to do well, but sometimes fall short. Unexpected results, unmet objectives, a less than perfect job, dissatisfaction from citizens, or poor teamwork can lead to this discomfort. Distractions before and during calls can undermine confidence, compromising performance and leading to discouragement.

> **Complaints**—*There are a lot of lows, a lot of negatives but you have to turn it positive because nobody else is going to do it. Nobody calls the police to say, "Just wanted to say you're doing a good job!" (Laughs). They call to complain and we fix their problem. You try the best you can, and sometimes it backfires and they complain about your work. You know what, we're not all perfect.*
> —>10 years on

> **"Resiliency" fatigue**—*I feel stressed from juggling multiple priorities, and exhausted from having to be "resilient."*
> —Police Instructor

Officers face numerous obstacles that disrupt their performance, which are often referred to as "barbs and jabs." Stressors can be viewed as positive challenges like workloads and complex tasks, or hindrances like hassles and bureaucratic red tape[10,11,12]. They identified 45 stressors that affect their behavior, health, and reasoning, impacting blood pressure, impulse control, anxiety, focus, motor skills, and decision-making. These stressors can result in wrongful arrests, excessive use of force, memory issues, burnout, and coping difficulties[13].

Various tools exist to measure police stress[14,15] and its effects, including alertness, aggression[15], trauma, and coping methods, particularly regarding post-traumatic stress disorder (PTSD)[17]. These include the California Psychological Inventory (CPI-434), Critical Incident History Questionnaire (CIHQ), PTSD Checklist Civilian (PCL-C), Police Stress Questionnaire-Organizational (PSQ-org), and Police Stress Questionnaire-Operational (PSQ-op). They reveal significant stressors and gender differences[6,16]. However, some officers argue that these stress tests are not truly useful.

> **Stress-test *"suckages in your life"***—*There are numerical values for deaths, injuries, surgeries, doctor's appointments, moods, and financial troubles. If you score over 330 then "Seek professional help immediately." Whatever the obstacles, adversities or challenges, the problem solution is to stress less, do more and be happier.*
> —>15 years on

Identified by "excellent" officers as performance blocks, the stressors that follow warrant concern, particularly for those less experienced. Quantifying and understanding them can foster open dialogue and insight to resolve or avoid stress-related issues.

Performance blocks can be grouped into three distinct sources of pressure: Operational, Organizational[7], and External Performance Blocks.

Operational Blocks arise from the nature of the job, including crises, arrests, shift work, court, and public disrespect. Rookie operational errors, such as "aggressiveness" and "poor containment," are significant on the frontline and have been isolated.

Organizational Blocks stem from the structure, personnel, workload, supervisory action/inaction, and limited resources within the organization.

External Blocks are experienced beyond the workplace, such as daily pressures, family conflicts, spousal worries, and work-life imbalance.

Quantifying performance blocks: Exceptional officers identify 45 performance blocks that hinder their optimal performance. Operational Blocks are most dominant, making up 63% (28 out of 45) of the total blocks, with General Operational comprising 36% and Rookie Errors the remaining 27%. Organizational Blocks account for about one-third (15 or 33%), while External Blocks only make up 4% (2 out of 45)—refer to Table 3.1. Remarkably, rookie errors, previously not mentioned in existing research[7,15,17], are highlighted as significant impediments to top officers' performance. For the complete research review, see Appendix C: Police Performance Stressors.

TABLE 3.1 Police Performance Block Measures

PERFORMANCE BLOCK TYPE	NUMBER (#)	PERCENTAGE (%)	AVERAGE # AND % PER OFFICER
Total Performance Blocks	45	100	22 (49%)**
Operational Blocks*	28	63	14 (50%)
General Blocks	16	36	9 (53%)
Rookie Errors	12	27	5 (44%)
Organizational Blocks	15	33	7 (46%)
External Blocks	2	4	1 (40%)

Notes: *Operational Blocks combine General (36%) plus Rookie Errors (27%).

**On average, each officer reported 49% of the Performance Blocks (22 out of 45 stressors per officer).

On average, officers listed 22 out of 45 total blocks (49%), with each block type consistently represented at just under half (Operational 50%, Organizational 46%, and External 40%).

Operational performance blocks

Operational stressors are inherent in police work, encompassing physical duties, community interaction, and inherent risks in "doing the job." These stressors can lead to various psychological, physiological, and cognitive issues[18], including sleep disturbances, feelings of hopelessness, powerlessness, hostility[6], and family-related challenges[19]. Reactions to stressors are influenced by individual qualities, organizational culture, and the environment[20]. For instance, by their fourth year, all new recruits acknowledged a rise in cynicism, adopting an *"everybody lies"* outlook, which fosters group bonds and internal humor[1].

Shift work and fatigue, especially in extended schedules, lead to poor sleep quality, affecting performance, safety, and productivity, and can escalate sick leave, injuries, conflicts[21,22], and even suicidal thoughts[2]. Police officers often face health issues like pain, injuries, heart diseases, and musculoskeletal disorders, exacerbated by job-related stress and the physical demands of prolonged vehicle use[23]. Workplace health programs are typically underutilized[24], relying heavily on officer motivation and adherence to recommendations[4,25]. Additional stressors like personal fears, routine work, unwanted waiting, and non-essential calls can lead to distraction and negative work attitudes[9,26,27].

Overall, there are 28 Operational Blocks categorized into General Blocks (16) and Rookie Errors (12).

Operational general blocks

Frontline officers identified 16 Operational General Blocks, covering crises, shift-work fatigue, peer mistrust, and others' complacency, as detailed in Figure 3.2. Additionally, stressors like personal fear, public disrespect, and climate conditions were revealed in interviews. Six of these blocks were directly addressed with officers, who shared personal refocusing strategies, surpassing current research findings (see Chapter 7: Mental

Police under pressure ▪ 53

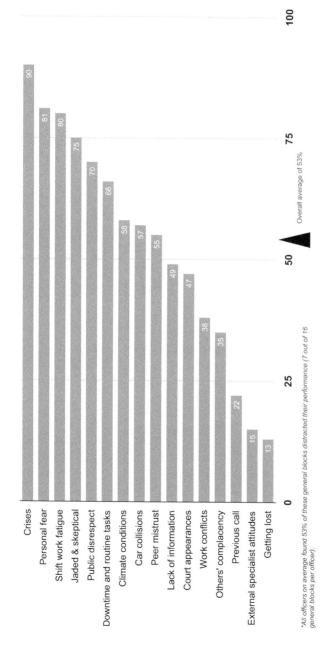

All officers on average found 53% of these general blocks distracted their performance (7 out of 16 general blocks per officer).

FIGURE 3.2 Operational General Blocks

Competencies—Distraction Control). Notably, these interviews provided a greater level of detail than current research, including stressors such as personal fear, public disrespect, climate conditions, external specialists' attitudes, previous calls, and getting lost.

Based on research trends and pilot discussions, officers were directly questioned about 6 of the 16 General Blocks and provided personal refocusing strategies. These blocks include crises, shift-work fatigue, public disrespect, downtime and routine tasks, car collisions, and court appearances. The remaining General Block areas were also discussed, covering personal fears and skepticism, team dynamics, and resource shortcomings. Specialized strategies for addressing these blocks are detailed in Chapter 7: Mental Competencies—Distraction Control.

"Crises"… "Pucker factor"

A critical situation can improve or worsen in seconds depending on the officer's response. Officers are hesitant to label a situation "a crisis" (more commonly known as a "pucker factor"). A "crisis" was reported as the highest (90%) of the 45 blocks, yet only 79% identified clear strategies.

> **Crisis**—*[A crisis is] anything that's out of my control—which is a lot of things. There are times I think, "I shouldn't be on patrol," because it consumes me. I want to make sure my officers do the call RIGHT and a lot of times they take shortcuts, or that's how they were trained.*
>
> —Patrol Sergeant

Crises in research include things like a colleague needing immediate assistance, multiple injuries or deaths, shootings, child trauma, and serious vehicle crashes[17,28]. Frontline officers defined "a crisis" using the following examples:

- 10-78 (Officer needs immediate assistance) … *full pause, as nothing else quite compares*
- child in trouble
- getting surprised, plan goes south
- weapon appears, missed the shot

- anything that's out of my control (which is a lot of things)
- my own panic reaction
- "I'm in trouble" (ironic and tragic)
- something I haven't yet been tested in
- others taking shortcuts and not doing it RIGHT—all the ramifications

Officers admitted feeling shocked, sick, or emotional, with a "gut reaction" either aloud or internally, when first facing a "crisis." These immediate reactions are as follows:
- shock wave, gut-wrenching
- stomach just turns, sick feeling
- instant panic, terror, "I'm shaking"
- "Sh--!," "God, where is he?"
- tunnel vision, dumbfounded, freeze
- the "Holy f---s" when you pull up
- body feels hot, sweaty palms
- breathing and heart rate changes
- unnerving feeling, heart in your throat
- emotions just go rampant
- can almost FEEL the adrenaline flow
- could make a mistake

Facing personal fear can paralyze an officer, making it hard to act during a call or in any given high-stress situation. Maintaining composure during and immediately after a crisis is vital.

> **Fear, personal crisis**—*Paralyzing fear is where you get in there and you're so scared fighting that you can't do anything but think of your flight. There's nothing else. You can't do anything. You can't think straight.*
> —>15 years on

> **Unexpected risks**—*Almost getting hit by a car. I stopped a car on a major road and was talking to the driver. A car got cut-off and didn't see me because he was behind a bus. He came onto the shoulder where I was. I had to literally jump onto the hood of the car I had stopped or I would have been...*
> —Traffic Escort

Fear: "Anybody who says they don't get scared in this job is bullshi--ing you."

Time slows down—*For 90% of our calls, I don't have time even to pause. There's no time to think, so I don't feel nervous—I don't feel anything. Time slows down, everything seems to focus and I'm not panicked. If I have time to think about what will happen when we get there, then I'll get a little bit of a rush.*

—Canine

10-78 chill—*You get to know people's voices and you can hear it in their voice when they need help—it's not their regular way of talking. When I hear an officer screaming for help on the radio... that gives me a chill.*

—>10 years on

Child involved—*A call saying a child's been hurt bothers me. It sends a chill down my back when children are involved. I usually go to those right away.*

—Canine

Fear, unknown factors—*It affects us. I've gotten scared. Anybody who says they don't get scared in this job is bullshi--ing you. It's the unknown factor. You hear things going on—yelling, screaming, or shots fired. Then I hear there's an officer down and I just wanna go in and kill. You have to sit back and count to 10—but it's tough.*

—>15 years on

Shift-work fatigue

The majority of officers (80%) cite shift work and the demands of rotating schedules as hindering their performance. They outline its effects:

- can't eat, have a poor diet and irregular meals
- can't sleep, never feel rested with irregular sleeping times
- only getting three or four hours of sleep during those shifts
- affects my body's balance, have general fatigue
- disrupts family life in general and during holidays, limits time with spouse and kids

- affects my mood and appetite
- struggle with sleep deprivation and exhaustion from toll of long-term night shifts
- further changes to schedule are made by management
- getting older makes it harder
- requesting a change

Long workdays and interrupted sleep are frequently standard, even an expected way of doing business in policing[2]. When fatigue becomes overwhelming, officers note a decline in performance, compounded by low solution rates. While most officers (79%) have general fatigue strategies, only 69% provide strategies specifically for coping with shift work, indicating a lack of consensus on effective solutions.

Fatigue: "For anybody working shift work… You are rarely, if ever, physically at your peak."

Family—*I first became an SRO for convenience. I was a good street cop—a go-getter, hard worker, putting a lot of time in, doing lots of charges. But I had some young kids. One day my son said he would wait for me. I was working an afternoon shift. At 10:00 p.m. he was still waiting for me. He didn't want to go to bed, fell asleep on the couch. I thought, I've been on the road for 12 years, maybe it's time I get away from shift.*
—School Resource

Shift changes—*There has been stress here—the shift is constantly changing. They can't seem to make up their minds.*
—>10 years on

Meals—*Eating at all hours. It's 4:00 in the morning and you're working night shift—dinner or breakfast? Your brain tells you something, your body tells you another. You want to eat eggs, but you'd rather eat a burger and fries. What time is it?*
—>15 years on

Motorcycle fatigue—*The long days are tiring, especially riding the motorcycle—you're a lot more mentally and physically fatigued than in a car. You're constantly looking for hazards,*

shifting gears, looking around—and trying to do a job on top of that.
—Traffic Escort

Exhausted—*Nights kill me. I get three or four hours of sleep on my nights and it's just not enough. I'm totally exhausted. Once 4:00 a.m. hits, I'm done. I didn't mind night shifts at the beginning but 10 years is too long for night shift.*
—Patrol,>10 years on

Aging—*As you get older, shift work gets a little bit harder.*
—School Resource

> *Shift work*: "Night shift killed me. I couldn't sleep. It's shift work that's going to be the end of me... I'll do them every now and then."

Hate it—*Can't stand it. Night shift killed me. I couldn't sleep. It's shift work that's going to be the end of me. I had to get off the nights. I'll do them every now and then but it's just not healthy for me.*
—School Resource

Rarely at physical peak—*For anybody working shift work, I don't think you ever physically feel good because you're always tired. You get through it, but are you at your peak? No. You are rarely, if ever, physically at your peak.*
—Patrol Sergeant

Public disrespect

The barrage of disrespect encountered on the street is often the most shocking realization as a new police officer. While they expect disobedience and profanity from those abusing drugs and alcohol, rebellious youth, and detainees, they are surprised by the frequency and casualness of sarcasm, smugness, threats, and criticism directed at them. It is the

- sarcasm towards the policing profession
- monotonous donut jokes directed at the uniform
- smugness from kids
- rudeness from individuals using their "taxpayers" status
- threats to use political influence
- criticism from former police officers

Recent studies look at how public disrespect is connected to police legitimacy, legal cynicism, and procedural justice. Factors like perceived violence[29], fairness during traffic stops[30], racial/gender disparities[31], and neighborhood variations in misconduct complaints[32] are influential. Legal cynicism involves distrusting policing but still valuing it for community safety[33]. Views on the law, fairness in procedural justice, and unwritten street rules are interconnected and shape individual opinion[34].

Strategies for dealing with public disrespect were reported by 73% of officers, balancing the 70% reporting it as a serious block, as illustrated below:

> **Donut jokes**—*The donut jokes hurt because I work out but it's the public's perception. It goes with the job. I usually say, "I'm a New-Age Officer, I drink apple juice and eat muffins." [Laughs].*
>
> —Female Patrol

> **Uncooperative public**—*If somebody called me saying they have this issue but they're going off at the mouth and not being cooperative, I just walk away. As long as I've covered all the areas, I say, "Call the police back when you've calmed down. Right now, I'm wasting time here." If they say, "I pay taxes!" I say, "Right now there's probably somebody out there who needs our help, and who's going to be more cooperative than you are."*
>
> —Patrol, 5 to 10 years on

Preconceived notions: "Police are a visible minority—that was a big shock for me."

> **Preconceived notions**—*Police are a visible minority—that was a big shock for me. It's not near what blacks or gays go through but, going to the door, I am already hated. People have preconceived notions of who I am and what I'm like. I went to a wedding—a person at the table found out we were police and attacked us. I get into the trap of thinking average people like the police and I keep kicking myself for it.*
>
> —School Resource

Cultural factors—*Because a lot of people come from countries where police officers are not good people, they look at us in the same light.*

—Patrol, <5 years on

Downtime (lulls) and routine tasks

High-risk professions, often action-oriented, face challenges during downtime or routine situations. Contrary to common beliefs, air traffic control incidents are more prevalent in low-traffic periods and sunny weather, showing anomalies and loss of separation increase when workload is moderate or low, and complexity is normal[35,36,37]. Similarly, in high-altitude guiding, 80% of accidents among climbers occur during the descent due to fatigue and complacency. Tourists capturing photos often unhook themselves from harnesses, casually step back for a shot, and slip into hazardous situations[11].

Lulls are significant distractions for 66% of officers, with 71% reporting the ability to regain focus after downtime. However, there is no consistent pattern in their responses, suggesting a need for better skills in dealing with passive distractions. Officers are mentally and physically eager to make quick decisions, and efficiency is crucial in minimizing public aggravation during calls. Unexpected or prolonged delays waiting and watching can be painstakingly long, leading to impatience and frustration. Slow, routine phases or observer roles are often perceived as boring, causing momentary inattention to the details.

Examples of downtime include slow shifts, passive activities like watching or supervising others, repetitive calls, false alarms or "stupid" calls, and waiting for information or equipment replacement.

Complacency versus hyper-vigilance: Officers swiftly switch from complacency to hyper-vigilance upon a call, but perceptions of danger vary. For instance, repeated fire alarm sounds may trigger complacency for most but hyper-vigilance for some. Nine officers denied ever feeling complacent in routine situations, highlighting the sobering reality of their experiences—they or their partners had been shot.

Uneventful calls—*Close to 50% of 911 calls are the same thing and you're wasting your time. That's certainly a frustration, especially when your time can be better spent.*
—Patrol, >10 years on

4:00 a.m. lulls—*Between 4:00 a.m. and 5:30 a.m.—THAT'S hard. I get out, drive away, find a lot and just relax. I don't fall asleep because I'd wake up at 11:00 a.m. with a 10-78!!*
—>15 years on

Hurry up and wait—*I like to get calls—I like the excitement. Most of them end up as, "Hurry up and wait." (We should have that in Latin for our motto.) It's always, "Hurry up! Go, go, go, go!" and then "Wait, wait, wait, wait," and then they finally give up. Not that you wanna shoot somebody—but you get pumped for it.*
—Tactical

False-alarm complacency—*We answer hundreds of house alarms. I always park about three or four residences down and walk in but a lot of these young guys STILL pull up right to where they're going because they assume it's going to be a false alarm. That's terrible, terrible complacency. They aren't always false alarms. At best, you'll risk losing the bad guy. At worst, you could get yourself hurt. In police circles, complacency is one of the worst things that we face right now.*
—Patrol Sergeant

Car collisions

Performance stress related to vehicle collisions was reported by 57% of officers, while strategies to mitigate this stress were reported by 73% of officers, indicating effective management by excellent officers. A criticism of other officers is:
- ♦ over-reacting, driving too fast, or being poor operators
- ♦ an ongoing risk of driving a big vehicle in traffic
- ♦ erratic public reactions to a cruiser (e.g., swing over like a beacon, freezing, changing normal driving patterns)

Running red lights—*Running through red lights with lights and sirens on will get you into an accident more than anything else. People don't know how to react to it.*
—5 to 10 years on

Whoosh—*I saw my life flash before my eyes not long ago. My light turned green and I proceeded. A guy ran the red light at about 90 km/hr. Whoosh. He just missed the front of my car. I pulled him over, gave him a ticket and then, after, I sat there and cried. I couldn't believe it.*
—Patrol Sergeant

Collisions—*I backed into a fire hydrant and poked out the red light on the cruiser. Fire hydrants normally have the flag up in the wintertime, this one didn't. Another one, I was actually responding to an emergency call and looking at my laptop at the same time. I bumped into somebody in front of me.*
—Patrol

Cruiser winter-driving—*A police car is rear-wheel drive and it's a powerful engine. It's terrible in the snow. If you have somebody in that vehicle who doesn't have much driving experience, it's going to add stress.*
—Patrol, <5 years

Why are you rushing?—*Going to calls lights and sirens is fun, but you've got to use your head. You see guys and girls going lights and sirens to alarms. It's an alarm! By the time we get notified, it's a six- to seven-minute time delay and chances are the guy has cleaned out whatever he wanted and he's gone. You're going to this call lights and sirens? You could cause an accident and hurt somebody. I'm not badmouthing people for doing it—their intentions are usually are good. You've got to take a step back. Why are you rushing?*
—Canine

Court appearances

After completing a call, officers' coping mechanisms are further tested. The justice system can be mentally fatiguing in its demand for accountability and can hinder future responses to a similar call. Nearly half (47%) find court appearances challenging, with divergent views. Some find them nerve-wracking and discrediting, as they try to exploit errors and show incompetence. Others see them as a waste of time, a joke, and not about justice. Nevertheless, 73% of officers have strategies to cope with court appearances.

> **Court, wasted resources**—*Almost every time I go to court, I see stupid things happen which are just a waste of money. Legal loopholes and the way the criminal aspect is handled—it's just bullsh--. Officers on the road are getting very, very fed up with it.*
> —Traffic Escort

> **Court, accountability**—*As a police officer, you're expected to make split-second—life and death—decisions based on the tools you have. Whereas down the road you have these lawyers who are paid much more to sit back and look at everything for weeks or months. They dissect it and then criticize you based on what you decided in a couple of seconds.*
> —5 to 10 years on

> **Court, fatigue**—*Court's a pain in the a-- as far as I'm concerned. I realize it's something we have to go through, and it's part of the job, but if you've been up for 36 hours, you hope you don't have to get up there on the stand. It's extra time off and a little extra pay, but for what? My health? You can keep it. I'd rather be healthy.*
> —Female Patrol

Personal fears and skepticism

The majority of excellent officers (81%) grapple with personal fears, ranging from panic and injury to death. Considering their expertise, less experienced officers likely face even greater stress. Additionally, 75% express caution and concern about the inherent cynicism resulting from working the "bad side of society" day in and day out.

> **Injury worries**—*Just coming off a bad one. It affects everybody personally when you have an injured officer. The worry of how seriously injured the officer is, motions of going through*

to tell the family about it—those would probably be the worries for me.

—Patrol

Expectations—*In Canine, if you catch anybody in the first year, good for you. If not, don't worry about it. It takes a good year to gel as a team. Putting too much pressure on yourself and the dog is a mistake. You're on stage every call—your peers are watching and if you don't succeed, they're judging you. You have to deal with that pressure, especially when you're new. Keep calm. Don't push too hard, because when you push too hard, you get anxious and make mistakes.*

—Canine

Self: "She screamed and I yelled... I was disappointed with myself."

Personal "danger zone"—*When I get annoyed, THAT seems to be the danger zone. Because it goes from annoyed to irritated—zero to 60. I just get this foul, foul mood. It's not somebody else so much as it's me.*

—5 to 10 years on

More compassion—*She screamed and I yelled, "RELAX!" I probably swore at her. It was more or less just a gut reaction but she was hysterical and I should've had more compassion. I was trying to shock her out of the emotion she was showing. I was disappointed with myself.*

—>15 years on

Public disobedience—*People will crumple a ticket you just served them and throw it on the ground. It's very hard to stay focused but... I try to be very professional. "Sir, please pick that up or I'll have to give you another ticket for littering." You're kind of pissing them off even more but I'm just being professional about it.*

—Traffic Escort

Use of force—*I get most upset having to be physical with somebody. I get frustrated. "Why did you make me have to do that?"*

—<5 years on

Ungrateful public—*The girl was a prostitute but she had hope and she needed help. We did so much for her—we went above and beyond. And then there was this robbery and she was the ringleader. Her attitude towards us completely shifted. She went from this nice person who needed help—and who we gave all we knew how to—to calling us names because she had been caught. It was like a slap across the face. We were pretty disappointed because we gave everything we could to this person, only to be called these horrendous things in the end. I did help her one more time and she's in rehab now, so it ended up good. But you're talking about years of work on this one person who pretended to want our help.*
—Neighborhood Resource

Death glares—*Sometimes it makes me sick what you have to do to get cooperation when you walk into their home. You bear the brunt of every mistake, attitude and rudeness of every police officer a person has met or even heard about—and you know that going in. That's the same feeling you get when you walk into a High School for the first time—the death glares.*
—School Resource

Team dynamics

Officers are uneasy about relying on complex teamwork in policing, where success hinges on the competence of various roles from patrol officers, specialty teams, and a dispatcher. This dependency can lead to interpersonal tensions. Fifty-five percent of officers highlight team mistrust, coupled with concerns about others' complacency and subpar effort (35%).

Chickens—*You've got a fight call and you call for back-up... "Chickens" take their time getting there.*
—Patrol, >15 years on

Trusted officers—*WHO you're going to the call with is a HUUUUGE factor. Some officers—if they tell you to do something, you do it without thinking. No problem. There's obviously a reason why. Officer X—nobody trusts. We're not even*

going to this call until we have more people coming and someone tells me what the hell is going on.
—5 to 10 years on

Non-risk takers—*You get guys who just won't do a thing. They don't care or they're scared to get in trouble.*
—Canine

Sick leave—*People come into work when they're sick. They don't like taking sick days because it costs money. But if you're sick, you're sick. Take it when you need it—that's what it's there for.*
—Patrol, >10 years on

"Individuals"—*The whole team concept is lacking. There are too many individuals out there and it's hurting our service. You want things for yourself, but in the end, you have to play as a team. Do your part, then it's easier for everyone else and you have a lot more success.*
—Sergeant

Confrontation—*I remember a guy walking in to the parade room and screaming at another guy, "You f---er, I'm never taking any more of your f---ing calls or covering your f---ing a--." That's the way it used to be: "You better f---ing pull your pants up, or else."*
—>10 years on

Work conflicts—*There are some officers that I won't talk to or make eye contact with. It comes down to respect—I'm just so thoroughly embarrassed that some of these officers wear a uniform. Just for opening their mouths, I'll turn and I'll walk away.*
—Female Patrol

Resource shortcomings

Remaining General Blocks include a lack of information, equipment limitations, getting lost driving in unfamiliar areas, and concerns with external specialists. Over half of officers (58%) are negatively affected by environmental conditions, from weather and insects to the filth and germs they are regularly exposed to.

Noise—*It was very loud inside the building. You couldn't talk to the guy next to you. We relied on hand signals and were almost yelling at each other, just to get information back and forth. But the noise wasn't a nuisance—it was just there for us to deal with.*

—Tactical

−30C, long term—*Because we're 24 hours a day, 365 days a year, climate does come into it. We took a call in February, where it was −30C. We started rotating guys, but one of the guys was very tenacious and kept saying "No, I'm fine." IT WAS −30C. He came back in two hours later and said, "I can't go back out, I'm done. I've stayed out too long."*

—Tactical

Winter-gear planning—*If I don't have proper clothing, I'm a liability instead of an asset—because of discomfort. My hands and feet get cold and I can't concentrate. You think ahead and make sure you have proper winter gear, but sometimes you get caught. You suck it up as much as you can.*

—>15 years on

Where are you?—*You have to know where you are at all times. That is HUMUNGOUS. Glance up at every corner and if you can't see the street signs, then you'd better know a landmark. That night, we were looking for someone who had taken off from another officer. I found him and they said, "Where are you?" I didn't know because I had never worked that area before and I wasn't paying attention. I should've known better because my Training Officer used to drive down the street, stop the car and say, "Where are you?" If I didn't know, I'd suffer some serious embarrassment.*

—Neighborhood Resource

(Unexpected) equipment readiness—*We had our sniper gear, but midway through the incident, we got re-tasked. We didn't have our full complement of equipment—it was embarrassing. My partner and I said, "That will never happen to us again. We will have everything."*

—Tactical

Fire halls—*When I hear stuff like, "Oh, the Fire Department guys are so busy!" Gimme a f---in' break. I see the calls in the [Patrol] cue. Guys are clearing 'em and bang, another call. How often do you go by a Fire Hall and they're actually out on a call? Not too often. The job is dangerous and I respect them, but it's apples and oranges.*

—>15 years on

Operational rookie errors

Working with rookies or inexperienced officers is a significant challenge in emergency response. While there are moments of pride, concerns about their impact on team performance loom large. Research often overlooks the effects of rookie errors, yet interviews reveal their significant impact.

On-scene rookie instruction alters the response dynamics. Officers reported feelings of:
- losing control but still being held responsible
- settling for less than perfection
- trying to teach those with low skill levels
- being stressed by the increased complexity
- combating the boredom and frustration of having to watch
- longing to have "fun" again by doing it all

According to excellent officers, 12 Rookie Errors were identified, with aggressiveness (80%) standing out (see Figure 3.3). This excessive attitude elevates anxiety, poses needless risks, disrupts public communication, and aggravates team cohesion. Other less frequently reported errors involved training deficiencies in basics, safety lapses, containment issues, reporting inaccuracies, disciplinary problems, and maturity. See Table 3.2 for more details.

"Dirty Harry sh--"—*The biggest complaint about a lot of kids on now is they're too gung ho—they're into this Dirty Harry sh-- and they wanna take on the world. They walk into a place putting on the gloves—pulling out their sticks, pulling out their spray. But if you're a bad guy, that's gonna make you more aggressive. I've walked every beat in the city and I've never had* to do that sh--. There's a time and a place to bring the hammer down.

—>15 years on

Aggressive driving—*We see how some of the young patrol officers drive to calls. The big joke is, if we're going to a call and come to an intersection, we watch for cruisers more than we watch for people [laughs]. It's true!*

—Tactical

More rapport—*Rookies don't allow people to talk. They haven't learned that there's "passive control" and "active control." You can control a situation by allowing a person to vent and then dealing with the situation with some compassion or sense of duty. You can say, "You've done this. I'm going to have to bring you to the station. There's some paperwork. You can get yourself a lawyer and we can discuss what's going on." Even though you're still watching what they're doing, talking to someone like that when you're making an arrest results in less aggression and need for physical contact. Should the need for physical control come up, (snaps fingers) deal with it fast, and then deescalate back to a normal tone of voice.*

—5 to 10 years on

Note-taking safety—*They have this thing where they have to write everything in a notebook. Instead of observing what's going on and getting it up here in your head, they flip open a notebook. They're writing while the situation is still going on. It's a safety concern.*

—Patrol, <5 years on

Rookies driving: "The big joke is, if we're going to a call and come to an intersection, we watch for cruisers more than we watch for people!"

Poor containment—*I go to gun calls and they're milling around in front of the residence—no cover, no concealment, talking to people with their hands in their pockets—absolute, HUGE mistake. If I'm talking to you on the street and my hands are in my pockets, how am I going to defend myself if you decide to take a swing at me? I can't.*

—Tactical

70 ▪ Police under pressure

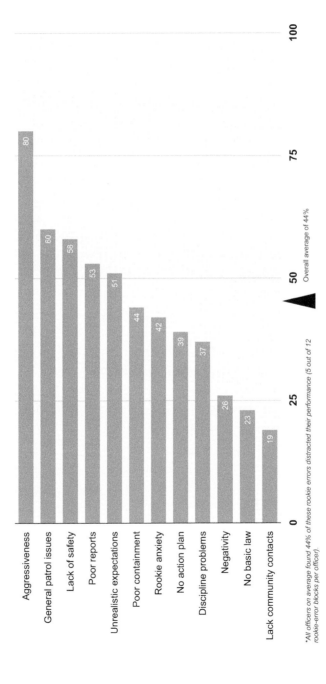

*All officers on average found 44% of these rookie errors distracted their performance (5 out of 12 rookie-error blocks per officer).

FIGURE 3.3 Operational Rookie Errors

TABLE 3.2 Operational Rookie Errors

Operational Rookie Errors	Weighted Average %
Aggressiveness: rush, no backup, over-react, know-it-alls, poor verbals, everything #1	80
General patrol issues	60
Lack of safety: no safety or absurd, no decisions, play it too safe, no initiative	58
Poor reports: poor writing, tracking, and admin skills; not timely, incomplete, or too thorough	53
Unrealistic expectations: be a Detective, not want to patrol, no life experience, whine with 3 years on	51
Poor containment: leave, not done properly, importance of "how" to do it	44
Other officers' anxiety: annoying behavior of fellow officers	42
No action plan: no tactical approach, options, technical knowledge, or procedure	39
Discipline problems: uniform, shoes, too many questions, hair, disrespectful	37
Negativity, more positiveness: change attitude to be more creative, improvising, fun, and enthusiastic	26
No basic law: interpretation, rights, practical; e.g., Young Offenders Act, traffic searches	20
Lack community contacts	19
Overall average	44

Note: All respondents on average found 44% of these rookie errors to block their performance (5 out of 12 rookie-error blocks per officer).

Proper notes—*Generally, you remember what people say to you. Don't quote people in your notebook—it's not going to stand up in court. When you're on the stand, you're going to say, "This is a paraphrase of what was said." If you start reading word-for-word on the stand, the defense lawyer will jump all over you, "How do you know if you've missed a word? It could be a key important word." I tell my rookies to put important things and times in their notebooks, but after you make an arrest. Make sure the situation is calm, and then you can do your notes.*

—Patrol, <5 years on

Unrealistic expectations—*"The brand new guy wants summer holidays. Well, he's not getting summer holidays and neither am I, because there's a guy with 18 years on platoon. He's going to get summer holidays because that's what WE owe HIM—HE does not owe us." A lot of people feel like they're owed. When they're recruited they're told they'll be on a NRT [Neighborhood Resource Team] in three years. It's a reality with the young group but it absolutely sends the wrong message.*
—5 to 10 years on

Negativity—*Sometimes all it takes is one person to get really, really, really negative about something and you can see a snowball effect. Whereas, if one person's really positive about something, I don't see that the snowball rolls quite as fast. It can certainly affect the platoon or the workgroup.*
—Patrol, >10 years on

Lack of respect—*One thing I despise is when we don't respect each other on the job. I don't care if you don't like each other—we're not all going to be best buddies and go drinking after work. When you're working, you do your share, and you respect your partner—him or her.*
—Neighborhood Resource

Disciplinary—*Nobody wanted to go to the call. Nobody wanted to do the paperwork. They all want is to drive around. There's times where I've gotten on the radio, "Go to the scene now! Don't mess around." I'm not an NCO but "Go to the scene now." Somebody has to go. And I've heard this, "Oh, I'll check the area." "No. You were dispatched a call. Go to the call." I even send the Dispatcher a message sometimes, "Send them to the call now. You let me know when they get there because they have to go there."*
—Neighborhood Resource, 5 to 10 years on

No contingency—*Sometimes there's no way around deviation from the plan but what we don't do well here are contingency plans. If something happens, it's up to the guys on the ground to do whatever.*
—>15 years on

Community contacts—*When I was on platoon, I focused on knowing who my bad guys were. That's fantastic, but take the time to go into that store to get to know that shop owner. Get out there and get to know people. That's valuable— a lot of times they know who's doing the robberies up the street. I never took the time to do that and it's the biggest thing I learned. On Patrol, you don't really have the time but you can make time. If you're on your lunch and you've got 5 minutes left, take that 5 minutes, walk into that store and just say, "Hello, this is who I am." That way, they'll know your name and face and the next time there's an issue, maybe they'll come to you.*

—Neighborhood Resource

Community versus hard-core—*In my younger years, I was a Patrol Officer at heart. I didn't see the benefit of Community Policing. As I get older, I do. It has its place. Just like hard-core patrolling has its place.*

—School Resource

Organizational blocks

The organization itself can stress officers and impact their performance. Factors include overbearing bosses, ineffective policies, resource shortages, organizational culture, excessive bureaucratic red tape, equipment problems, unfair workloads, incompatible partnerships, and lack of support or feedback. Officers also struggle with role ambiguity, feeling unappreciated, and dealing with hoax calls or difficult people[38,39].

In-depth interviews yielded richer insights than currently available research. Among the 15 Organizational Blocks (see Figure 3.4), the top four reported by over half the officers directly relate to organizational effectiveness—Workload (75%), Lack of Leadership (63%), Bureaucracy (61%), and Fewer Resources (60%). Heavy workload remains prominent, compounded by insufficient communication and control[2,9]. Limited resources further impede effective policing[2,40]. Poor supervisory support and a negative work environment, marked by discrimination, harassment, lack of confidentiality, and lack of compassion, contribute to

74 ■ Police under pressure

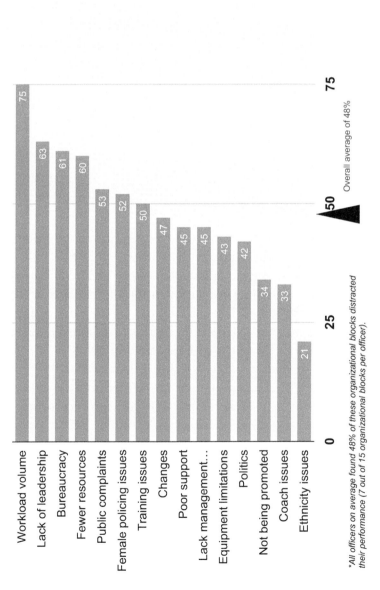

*All officers on average found 48% of these organizational blocks distracted their performance (7 out of 15 organizational blocks per officer).

FIGURE 3.4 Organizational Blocks

feelings of isolation and can worsen symptoms of PTSD, especially among female officers[9,18].

Officers were directly questioned about four Organizational Blocks—workload, public complaints, female-policing coping issues, and lack of promotion. They shared whether these blocks hinder performance and offered personal refocusing strategies.

Officers from ethnic minorities may face challenges in sustaining a policing career, including concerns about exclusion, racism, perceived inequality in promotions, and hostile reactions from friends and family[41]. Exceptional officers openly admit stress due to ethnicity issues, politics, coaching issues, and unspoken cultural clashes, discussed under "Other organizational blocks."

Organizational Blocks are discussed as follows:
- Workload*
- Public complaints*
- Female-policing issues*
- Not being promoted*
- Other organizational blocks

*See Chapter 7: Mental Competencies—Distraction Control for corresponding strategies.

Workload

Workload is rated as the top performance blocker by 75% of officers. They feel that excessive work volume limits preparation time, encourages too much multitasking, necessitates longer hours, and requires better call screening. Only 64% of officers reported strategies, amplifying the issue. Strategies for managing volume include improved time management, finding enjoyment in the job, accepting the pace, and developing better scheduling (see Table 3.3).

> **Confusion**—*You can get screwed up when a whole bunch of things start to happen. It becomes very confusing where a whole lot of stuff is occurring all at once. You've got two radios going talking to Patrol and to Tac, and you're trying to talk to the Duty Inspector face-to-face.*
> —Tactical Sergeant

TABLE 3.3 Workload Block Details

	TOTAL RESPONSES Ranked by %
Workload strategies	64
Workload block	75
Less quality: time limited to prepare, too much multitasking, other things happening	
Redirect resources: need more patrols, waiting for backup, short for containment	
Volume: hard long hours, reports backed up, interruptions	
Less control: too many calls, no control for ridiculous	
Screen calls: false alarms: stupid calls, hard to avoid complacency	

Team workload—*Working out on my lunch was my way of renewing myself. But when it's really, really, really busy and you're part of a group, it's hard to leave those people for an hour, knowing that they've gotta pick up the slack.*
—Patrol, >10 years

Quantity-not-quality policing—*Front line policing has changed 100%. Before, we were allowed to do police work: To hunt down, harass and arrest the bad guy. Now patrol is just a band-aid on the situation—they're just going from call to call to call. They're over-tasked. It has changed from quality work to quantity work. They're not chasing bad guys, they're just answering calls for service.*
—Sergeant

Public complaints

More than half (53%) of the officers identify Public Complaints as problematic. Leading concerns include unfair depictions of their work and the volume of unscreened complaints reaching the frontline. However, a higher number of officers (68%) report having effective strategies, ranging from prevention to acceptance, defense, and confidence in the system (see Table 3.4).

TABLE 3.4 Public Complaint Details

	TOTAL RESPONSES Ranked by %
Public complaint strategies	68
Public complaint block	53
Unfair: not reflective of work, dig gets complaint vs demo get thanks	
Volume: too many, control, ridiculous	
On your record, not just, accessory only	
Hesitate next time to go after crime	

Innocence first—*It's horribly unfair sometimes. The Department looks at it as if you've done something wrong. You're not innocent until proven guilty—you're always guilty. It's really stressful on officers when they get complaints.*
—Patrol Sergeant

Fear of investigation—*What I fear most is not the complaint but being falsely put under investigation. That trickles in to how you deal with people on the street. In the back of my mind, I'm thinking, "If there's a complaint against me, how is this going to be perceived?" In some situations, you don't want to have anything to do with it because it might bounce back on you—it's fear of investigation. That's a general feeling within all police officers and it's not right.*
—Neighborhood Resource

Female-policing coping issues

In 2003, 82% of female officers identified gender-related performance blocks, such as the "macho" environment, rejection, stereotyping, and perceived preferential treatment, while only 19% of male officers expressed concern about better opportunities, status-quo interests, and physical limitations. Currently, only 6% of coach officers acknowledge this issue, bringing the overall average to 52%.

Although officers believe that female-policing issues have improved, current research indicates that female officers may still

TABLE 3.5 Female-Policing Coping Issues

	TOTAL RESPONSES Ranked by %
Female-policing coping strategies	45
Female-policing block	52
Females with concerns relating to female policing	
Macho environment: alpha male-dominant, not helpful	
Rejection: don't want you, harsh judgment	
Perceived physical limitations: backup, need extra support	
Over-achievement: demands to over-compensate, must constantly prove yourself	
Stereotyping: "given" job, no skills, minimal duty	
Perceived opportunities: easy access to good jobs during pregnancy, lateral training, exposure	
Males with concerns regarding female policing	
Better opportunities: easy access to good jobs during pregnancy, lateral training, exposure	
Rejection: don't want females, harsh judgment	
Macho environment: alpha male-dominant, not helpful	
Physical limitations: backup, need extra support	

experience higher stress levels due to bias, shift work, and various environmental factors[2,9]. Furthermore, change may be slower in some police services and countries. Details on female-policing issues are well defined specific to both genders in Table 3.5. Female officers have developed specific coping strategies such as recognizing improvements, offering alternative approaches, seeking peer support, making personal adaptations, and confronting issues as they arise (see Chapter 7: Mental Readiness—Distraction Control: Refocusing).

> **Fair share**—*The ole, "Would you mind printing that guy? I don't want to ruin my nails." There are women who aren't rolling up their sleeves and doing their fair share. THAT pisses me off. But it also pisses me off for a guy too. One recruit I had was*

scared of his shadow—he would lock himself in the cruiser. My hat goes off to him, he knew to get out.

—Female Patrol

Willing to try—*I don't really have a lot of use for women police officers. If they get a big guy who wants to walk away, they can't stop him. But it doesn't matter what physical stature you have, it's how much fight is in you. There are more good male cops than there are female cops but there are lots of good female officers because they're willing to try.*

—>Male, 15 years on

Male attitude—*Some of the things that have happened to women they don't play up now. It's kind of scary… Those [men] changed their behavior, but I'll bet you they haven't changed their attitude.*

—Female, >15 years on

Awful things—*It's not as easy as it's portrayed to be. I've been through absolutely terrible things that had everything to do with the fact that I am female. I could tell you some pretty awful things about officers.*

—Female Patrol

Brotherhood?—*"Call to brotherhood"… not so much anymore. It's lost that, as far as I'm concerned. I'm guilty of this: I remember when they first got women on the job… I was not a "woman-basher," but I was influenced by a few guys. They'd say, "Oh, look at this. A couple of girls trying to arrest a ruby and they're, 'Oh sir, come here.'" They weren't that good. They weren't as intimidating as a guy would be.*

—Male, >15 years on

Female: "I've been through absolutely terrible things that had everything to do with the fact that I am female."

"Small-Man Syndrome"—*In the platoon I was on, the guys talked down to people and got into fights. They treated people like crap. And there was a time when I tried to be like that. A Staff Sergeant pulled me aside one day to talk to me about my "Small-Man Syndrome" attitude. He*

said, "Who do you think you are? You're treating people like crap." I was in tears. I thought that's how I was supposed to behave. If he had not said that, I probably would have continued down that ignorant path. That's how the guys behaved and that's how I thought I had to be.
—Female School Resource

"Not being promoted"

"Not Being Promoted" as a block ranks low at 34%, with 59% of officers reporting refocusing strategies for lack of advancement. However, the fact that 66% of high-achievers do not see this as an issue may signal serious concerns for future succession planning, possibly indicating a lack of motivation for advancement. Most officers interviewed cope with disappointment by avoiding the promotional process, trivializing advancement, or seeking lateral transfers. Only a small percentage believe that with effort, persistence, and confidence, they can succeed in promotions. This is surprising considering these officers were selected for excellence. While *promotional complacency* is acknowledged, research on the topic remains limited, aside from exploring female officers' reluctance to seek promotions[27,42].

Hoops, shift work—*Yeah, I guess eventually someday, but right now, I've got no desire to do it because of the hoops that you've got to jump through and the shift work that they're on.*
—School Resource

Content, uninterested—*No. I haven't been seeking that at all. I'm very content where I am right now. That may change in a few years, or sometime down the road, but for now I haven't been pursuing a promotion.*
—Traffic Escort

Detective, same money—*As far as not being promoted, I could honestly care less. There're ways to get around the monetary end of it anyway. Detectives are making the exact same money as Sergeants.*
—Female Patrol

Unfair opportunities—*What happens is someone on Patrol, who's not worth a damn, will get pregnant, and get the opportunity to go roll with Indent or CISB, because they need somebody to help out. They get the experience all because of a physical thing, and before you know it, they never come back to Patrol. Whereas someone who's pounding the street for a few years will get refused opportunities. If you don't have the merit then you're getting it for the wrong reasons. Yes, you can help out there, but then back to Patrol to be a good officer or a good representation of police smarts. You need to be sound in your bottom level, ideally 4 to 5 years to see all different variety of calls, maybe be in leadership roles at times, and get well-rounded. I see people with two years go.*

—Patrol, >10 years on

Not done it yet—*I haven't written yet but I'm going to soon. I probably won't go through the promotional process anyway. I think it's a hoop-jumping exercise that's incredibly flawed. I want to write to be qualified and able to get my Senior Constable pay.*

—>10 years on

BBQs to supervisor—*That almost sent me to the water tower, watching people rocketing by you… Two people put in their portfolios. One having barely any time spent doing police work but was involved in organizing a BBQ, and they will get more points than I did. Well, I organized a drug raid… Some who have just been promoted haven't had their a--es in police cars for years, and even when they did, they spent a lot of time hiding in it… Suddenly they're a frontline Sgt back in a uniform and going to these dangerous calls and organize things… How can you organize a fire scene? You've got to block traffic as a supervisor when you've never done it as a Constable?*

—Patrol Sergeant

Buzzwords—*The next portfolio I put in basically wasn't changed except I shoved all the words in there that they told us they didn't want to hear, and I got promoted.*

—Patrol

Other organizational blocks

The remaining organizational blocks cover coaching issues, ethnicity issues, the promotional process, politics, and unspoken, stigmatized issues where there is a clash of cultures.

Coach issues

Although Coach Issues were generally ranked at 33%, the majority (77%) of the 31 coach officers in 2019 identified it as a stressor. They reported four major coach officer concerns that include:
- low standards: lower expectations, settle for less, coaches too young
- low pay
- career issues: held back to coach, overworked, burnout
- no recognition: importance, interest versus good teacher, rookie abuse—"Generation Me"

Coaching or mentoring was perceived as the most successful skill for confidence after training. However, the Coach Officer position is categorized as an unattractive role while being a highly valued service to officers. This highlights the impact of coaching on staff and how extremely important it is to select quality coaches.

> **Coach's final say**—*If you don't give the coaches the respect or trust to actually have the final say, then what's the use? If you're going to say, "Thank you very much for your input," and then let that recruit out anyway. What's the use? That's why people aren't interested. Their opinions are that we're babysitters.*
> —Female Patrol

> **Lost pay**—*You can always get people to do something by offering them a little bit more money. We make two extra dollars an hour when we were coaching. Quite frankly, that's nothing. If you coach someone, you're doing the reports and they're doing the files. When those files go to court, they're going to go to court, you're not. As a result, you're losing the money that you would have made going to court. That one or two dollars an hour is burnt up by one or two court appearances that you miss. So, the financial incentive doesn't even exist.*
> —Patrol, >15 years on

Ethnicity issues

Internal stereotyping concerning ethnicity (22%) is deemed to be the most serious issue for Visible Minority-Aboriginal officers when they feel that their peers believe they were just "given the job" and have "no skills." On the other hand, racial slurs from the public are more uncomfortable for the colleagues of visible minority officers. Thus, ethnic-minority officers may face unique challenges, including reduced overall job satisfaction and feelings of disadvantage[27].

Other organizational issues

Like many professions, other organizational issues are captured by too much paperwork, not enough resources, inadequate training, political interference, and leadership problems. Many officers (61%) shared frustration with paperwork demands amid resource shortages (60%). They are divided (50%) on training effectiveness for crucial skills, compounded with equipment limitations (43%), and civilian-led decisions by those unfamiliar with the realities of frontline policing. Political influences (42%) are acknowledged as a constant disruptor, fueling frustration. Some lament changes imposed without consultation (43%), lack of management feedback (45%), and generally feeling unsupported (45%).

> **Paperwork versus quality**—*Two minutes of excitement, and two hours of paperwork… it's brutal. The duplication and triplication have made this job almost unbearable. I understand that we have to collect this information but what the powers that be don't understand is that there's got to be a better way. They're deterring officers from doing quality work—there's too much. If it was easier, their officers would work harder.*
>
> —Patrol, >10 years on

Paperwork: "Two minutes of excitement, and two hours of paperwork…"

> **Staff shortage**—*You know by all the calls stacked in the queue, you don't have enough staff on the road. You're not going to get your supper and you're not going to get to go pee. The more the little things pile up, the more stressed I get. One big thing, I*

can handle. But I have a hard time keeping all those little things in perspective.

—School Resource

Leadership, individual mentality—*Our team watches each other's back. On some platoons there are "individuals," and no team. That's not effective. Leadership causes that. Team members, if demoralized, break away thinking, "I'm going to do things on my own. I'm not being recognized—so who cares?"*

—Patrol, >10 years on

Training, bullsh-- days—*I'm a firm believer in training, but one of the first things they cut in the budget is training. Patrol Training Days are only 6.5 hours long now. They call them "Bullsh-- Days." Give them the meat and potatoes. Teach them how to do high-risk vehicle stops, how to interview people, how to stand properly. They get that in basic training, but it's all thrown in the garbage and they develop bad habits.*

—Tactical

Hiring: "It all starts at the ground level... people who are truly interested in serving the public."

Policy changes—*They keep adopting every new policy and bad idea that comes around and it continuously changes the order. [I once worked in a place that] was very streamlined and efficient. It was patrol-oriented and ran very smooth. You were out there to do your job and you had a lot of support. Here, it's constantly changing.*

—Patrol, >10 years on

Unsupported—*What also affects us at the end of the day is, if you screw up—even though you're trying something in good faith—there's a lack of support. At times, admin doesn't stand behind you.*

—Patrol

Politics: "Be prepared for change. It doesn't stop changing and it's all political."

Politics, changes—*The guys and girls at the bottom say, "This doesn't make sense, why are you doing this without our input?" Be prepared for change. It doesn't stop changing and it's all political.*

—Patrol, 5 to 10 years on

> **Equipment decisions**—*What frustrates me, and other people I've spoken to, is that it's a civilian who makes the decision on the expenses for our clothing. All officers were supposed to get these pants. They're Gore-Tex. They're over $200 a pair but they're invaluable. My regular patrol pants have frozen to me. Well, it was a civilian who decided we didn't need these pants—somebody who's never done the job, never taken an accident report in the freezing rain. They don't understand.*
> —5 to 10 years on

External performance blocks

An officer's frame of mind at the onset of a call sets the tone for the emergency response, though emotional upsets are forgotten once on-scene—but not all. Anxiety is physically painful, mentally preoccupying, and ultimately taxing on performance.

Research using stress surveys reveals how life events and work-family conflicts impact officers' health and work performance differently based on personality, especially affecting shift workers as well as younger and female officers[2], potentially leading to post-traumatic stress disorder[6,9]. Existing research lacks detailed insights, but interviews with exceptional officers who openly admitted experiencing performance blocks due to family conflict, failing marriage, and spousal fear of dangers provide valuable perspectives.

Family Conflicts (48%) and *Day-to-Day Pressures* (31%) significantly influence officers' performance habits, with officers speaking out about their families' sacrifices—typically evoking a deep sentiment of gratitude. The limited but compelling research available on police family stress suggests the need for more attention to this sensitive and understated issue in family police studies.

> **Mental fatigue**—*I have a lot of outside stuff with the Association. Mentally, it's hard to keep it up 18 hours a day. It wears on you.*
> —>15 years on

> **Motorcycle tiredness**—*The long days are tiring. Especially riding the motorcycle—you're a lot more mentally and physically fatigued than in a car... You're constantly looking for*

hazards, shifting gears, looking around—and trying to do a job on top of that.
—Traffic Escort, >10 years on

Post-shift—*I'm not tired there, at every shift, it's when I leave and I come down. Because there are a lot of times I drive home, and all of a sudden, I'm home. "How'd I get here?"*
—Female Sergeant

Physical confidence—*Physical condition is all relative. It can happen where you go to stop a car, for an innocent "no left turn" or a stop sign, and the guy just sprints and he's gone. It's obviously gonna be a stolen car or something's going on there. You have to have some sort of physical fitness to go after the guy—either for a foot-chase or to act on it. You look at some guys, Holy geez. I know I'm not in good shape, and that bothers me. I'm trying to get back into it. I should be better. I would feel more competent and confident.*
—Traffic Escort, >15 years on

Monotony—*It's big picture monotony that I don't like. I was in Patrol for four years and I took every course possible. I loved being a breath tech. I took the radar course, the mobile workstation, and the teacher's course. I always had my hands in some pot, just because I'm a high-energy guy—I like to do things. But after a while… it's not that I didn't feel I couldn't learn anymore, because there's always something to learn, but the job in itself started to become monotonous. I wanted to try something different.*
—Traffic Escort

> "Ahhhh, frig… and the stress builds. Not because of the job but how it impacts my life at home."

Spouse conflict—*It's funny, once you get a family, they start to take a higher priority. You like to think they're number one, so when the job creeps up it starts eating at you. You go, "Ahhhh, frig," and you have got to make some phone calls and the stress builds. Not because of the job but how*

it impacts my life at home. It's going to put some stress on my wife, which is going to show in how she reacts to me.
—Traffic Escort

Family priorities—*If you're having problems at home and you can't give 100%, sometimes it's better not to be [at work]. If all you're thinking about is how your little boy or little girl is sick, it's better that you're there with them.*
—Patrol, >10 years on

Day-to-day pressure—*Having served in the Canadian military and as a police officer, I would hypothesize that Canadian police officers have more key stress than any Canadian soldier since the Korean conflict. Canadian urban police officers in the major cities are day in, day out, picking up dead bodies in houses. When they send out a death call it's, "Oh ya. A dead body. Ha ha." We try to shrug it off, but we are still picking up a dead human being and it's not pleasant. The insults, the high-adrenaline calls…*
—Neighborhood Resource

Changes in performance blocks over time

The study looked at changes from 2003 to 2019 to see what police officers found stressful enough to block their performance. By asking current coaches about current blocks, which ones stayed important, changed, or were new could be identified. Data was compared from "excellent" officers in 2003 (48) to "excellent" coaches in 2019 (31) to see how things changed over time. The 45 blocks were ranked from highest to lowest impact, including how much they changed, and if they affected how their impact was ranked (see Appendix I: Temporal Changes in Performance Blocks 2003–2019 for detailed calculations).

Impact of performance blocks

Blocks are ranked as Immediate Needs (>75%), Serious Blocks (50–75%), or Individual Blocks (<50%) based on how often they were reported by the combined sample group. Some blocks shifted in impact level from 2003 to 2019, either increasing (+) or decreasing (–) in classification (indicated with (+) and (–) in Table 3.6). Seven blocks increased levels from Individual to Serious Block: Lack of leadership, Lack of safety, Climate conditions, Poor reports, Public complaints, Unrealistic expectations, and Training issues. Alternatively, four decreased from Immediate Need to Serious (Public disrespect, Downtime and routine tasks, Car collisions, Female-policing coping issues), and Court appearance moved from Serious to Individual Block.

Other blocks demonstrate an imbalance, showing a greater value than their associated strategies: Crisis, Shift-work fatigue, Workload volume, and Female-policing coping issues (indicated by * in Table 3.6 with further information in Appendix I: Temporal Changes in Performance Blocks 2003–2019). Conversely, four blocks showed a much lower value than their associated strategies: Car collisions, Public complaints, Court Appearances, and Not being promoted. Weight for the associated strategies for Public disrespect, and Downtime and routine tasks were comparable to the block weight.

Additional discussion follows on:
- Immediate Needs
- Serious Blocks
- Individual Blocks

Immediate Needs

This classification is identified when over 75% of the group reported the block. Only 4 of the 45 blocks reached this level of impact, all within Operational Blocks.

It is important to note that for both Crisis and Shift-work fatigue, more officers see them as blocks than there are associated strategies. Specifically, 90% see a crisis as a block, while only 79% have crisis refocusing strategies. Similarly, 80% see shift-work fatigue as a block, while only 69% have Shift-work fatigue Strategies in place. See Chapter 7: Mental Readiness—Distraction Control for strategies.

This Immediate Need level is of particular concern, which contains:
- Crisis 90% with 79% Crisis refocusing strategies
- Personal fears 81%

TABLE 3.6 Impact of Police Performance Blocks by Weighted Average

Block Impact (Immediate Need, Serious, Individual)	Performance Block	Block Type	Block Weighted Average (%)	Specialized Strategies
Immediate Need	Crises	General-Ops	90	79*
	Personal fear	General-Ops	81	
	Shift work fatigue	General-Ops	80	69*
	Aggressiveness	Rookie Error-Ops	80	
Serious Block	Workload volume	Organizational	75	64*
	Jaded & skeptical	General-Ops	75	
	Public disrespect (−)	General-Ops	70	73
	Downtime and routine tasks (−)	General-Ops	66	71
	Lack of leadership (+)	Organizational	63	
	Bureaucracy	Organizational	61	
	Fewer resources	Organizational	60	
	General patrol issues (+)	Rookie Error-Ops	60	
	Lack of safety (+)	Rookie Error-Ops	58	
	Climate conditions (+)	General-Ops	58	
	Car collisions (−)	General-Ops	57	73
	Peer mistrust	General-Ops	55	
	Poor reports (+)	Rookie Error-Ops	53	
	Public complaints (+)	Organizational	53	68
	Female-policing coping issues (−)	Organizational	52	45*
	Unrealistic expectations (+)	Rookie Error-Ops	51	
	Training issues (+)	Organizational	50	

90 ■ Police under pressure

Block Impact (Immediate Need, Serious, Individual)	Performance Block	Block Type	Block Weighted Average (%)	Specialized Strategies
Individual Block	Lack of information	General-Ops	49	
	Family conflicts	External	48	
	Court appearances (−)	General-Ops	47	72
	Changes	Organizational	47	
	Poor support	Organizational	45	
	Lack management feedback	Organizational	45	
	Poor containment	Rookie Error-Ops	44	
	Equipment limitations	Organizational	43	
	Politics	Organizational	42	
	Rookie anxiety	Rookie Error-Ops	42	
	No action plan	Rookie Error-Ops	39	
	Work conflicts	General-Ops	38	
	Discipline problems	Rookie Error-Ops	37	
	Others' complacency	General-Ops	35	59
	Not being promoted	Organizational	34	
	Coach issues	Organizational	33	
	Day-to-day pressures	External	31	
	Negativity	Rookie Error-Ops	26	
	No basic law	Rookie Error-Ops	23	
	Previous call	General-Ops	22	
	Ethnicity issues	Organizational	21	
	Lack community contacts	Rookie Error-Ops	19	
	External specialist attitudes	General-Ops	15	
	Getting lost	General-Ops	13	

Notes: *These blocks are significantly greater than their associated specialized strategies.

(+) Blocks that shifted up in impact level, e.g., from Individual to Serious.

♦ (Rookie) Aggressiveness 80%
♦ Shift-work fatigue 80% with 69% Shift-work fatigue strategies

Serious Blocks

Blocks are deemed "serious" when they are identified by 50–75% of the group. There are 17 of the 45 blocks within this category, 10 Operational and seven Organizational, ranging from Workload volume (75%) and Jaded and skeptical (75%) to Unrealistic expectations (51%) and Training issues (50%). Eight blocks, previously categorized as Individual Blocks, have elevated (+) to Serious Blocks, primarily linked to Rookie Errors and Organizational Blocks. Notably, Workload volume (75%) narrowly missed Immediate Need criteria but showed a marked increase of 25%.

Three Operational General Blocks, previously Immediate Need, namely Jaded and skeptical, Public disrespect, and Downtime and routine task, were downgraded (–). Female-policing issues also decreased within the Organizational Blocks category.

It is significant that more officers see Workload and Female-policing coping issues as blocks (75%; 52%) compared to the lower number of associated strategies (64%; 45%). In contrast, specific strategies related to Public disrespect, Downtime and routine tasks, Car collisions, and Public complaints were comparable or higher. See Chapter 7: Mental Competencies—Distraction Control for strategies.

This Serious Block level with associated strategies includes:
♦ Workload 75% with 64% Workload Strategies
♦ Public disrespect (–) 70% with 73% Public disrespect strategies
♦ Downtime and routine task (–) 66% with 71% Downtime and routine task refocusing
♦ Car collisions (–) 57% with 73% Car collision avoidance strategies
♦ Public complaints (+) 53% with 68% Public complaint refocusing
♦ Female-policing coping issues (–) 52% with 45% Female-policing coping strategies

Individual Blocks

These individualized blocks, noted by less than 50% of the group, total 24 of the 45 blocks ranging from Lack of information (49%) and Family conflict (48%) to External specialist attitudes (15%) and Getting lost (13%). They span all three block types: 14 Operational, 8 Organizational, and 2 External. Half (7 out of 14) of the Operational blocks were due to Rookie Errors. Court appearance was downgraded (–) from Serious to Individual Blocks. Three blocks showed significant shifts without changing classification: No action plan (+74%), Work conflict (+53%), and Others' complacency (+50%). Additionally, there is an implied complacency with the promotional process, ranking as a low block among "excellent" individuals, with 59% having specific refocusing strategies. Strategies for Court appearances (72%) were much higher than the reported block (47%). See Chapter 7: Mental Competencies—Distraction Control for strategies.

This Individual Block level with associated strategies includes:

- Court appearances 47% with 72% Court appearance strategies
- Not being promoted 33% with 59% Not being promoted refocusing

Summary of police performance block measures

Impact can also be quantified by block types, average blocks per officer, and block classifications. Operational blocks dominate overall (28 out of 45 blocks) and Immediate Needs (4 out of 4), with about half (24) classified as Individual Blocks. A third (15) are organization-based, split almost evenly between Serious (7) and Individual (8) Blocks. Only 4% are sourced as External Individual Blocks (see Table 3.7 for details).

TABLE 3.7 Summary of Police Performance Block Measures

| | | AVERAGE BLOCKS | BLOCK CLASSIFICATION | | |
| | | | IMMEDIATE NEED | SERIOUS | INDIVIDUAL |
PERFORMANCE BLOCK TYPE	RANGE of BLOCKS	Average # of blocks per officer (%)	# blocks (%) by >75% of officers	# blocks (%) by 50-75% of officers	# blocks (%) by <50% of officers
Overall total blocks	45 (100%)	22 (49%)	4 (9%)	17 (38%)	24 (53%)
Operational blocks	28 (63%)	14 (49%)	4 (9%)	10 (22%)	14 (31%)
General blocks	16 (36%)	9 (53%)	3	6	7
Rookie errors	12 (27%)	5 (44%)	1	4	7
Organizational blocks	15 (33%)	7 (46%)	0 (0%)	7 (16%)	8 (18%)
External blocks	2 (4%)	1 (40%)	0 (0%)	0 (0%)	2 (4%)

Trends in performance blocks

Changes in police blocks reporting over time provide insights into potential emerging trends. Blocks related to rookie officers, such as No action plan, Discipline problems, and Negativity, have seen significant increases (ranging from 56% to 74%), possibly reflecting new recruitment procedures or training gaps.

Additionally, General Operational Blocks, like Day-to-day pressures and Work conflict, have also risen substantially (each at 53%), perhaps due to reported growth in workload demands (25%), organizational changes (17%), and family conflict (15%).

Many performance blocks showed minimal change (<10%), such as Rookie aggressiveness, Jaded/skeptical, Court appearance, Ethnicity issues, Not being promoted, Getting lost, and Shift-work fatigue. This may indicate ongoing challenges within police culture.

Female-policing coping issues (–76%) and Public disrespect (–51%) suggest a decrease in their prevalence, possibly due to the development of associated strategies (45% and 68%, respectively) and organizational initiatives. However, coping strategies for Female-policing issues were lower (45%) than blocking performance (52%). Personal fear (–43%) is also lower, possibly linked to new offensive-defensive training initiatives.

Figure 3.5 illustrates temporal changes in performance blocks over 17 years. Significant decreases over time are depicted at the top with Female-policing issues, transitioning to no change in Getting lost, and ending with the greatest increase from No action plan (from rookies) at the bottom.

Police under pressure ■ 95

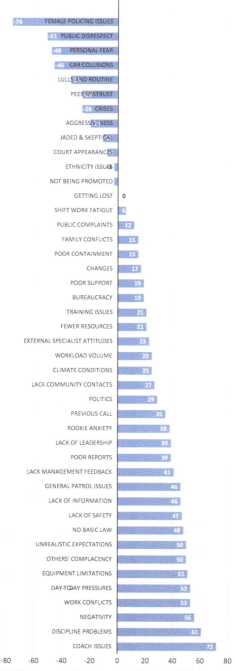

FIGURE 3.5 Differences in Performance Blocks in Policing over 17 Years

D. 20 Key challenges and performance blocks in policing

The following 20 key strategies summarize challenges and performance blocks in policing.

1. **Assess the "unknown:"** Dealing with the unknown in frontline policing can range from dangerous, complex, emotionally charged to unprecedented changes imposed by the service.
2. **Recognize common frontine challenges:** In high-risk jobs like policing, common challenges include limited resources, higher stress and fatigue, feeling undervalued, and inconsistent performance, which affect frontline safety, productivity, and morale.
3. **Prioritize personal stressors:** Police officers face operational, organizational, and external stressors, each with varying levels of importance and impact, and these can affect genders differently.
4. **Combat stress early:** Sudden or cumulative stress can lead to sleep problems, more sick days, family conflicts, and even thoughts of self-harm, influenced by individual traits and the work culture.
5. **Follow health orders:** The physical demands can lead to health problems like pain, injuries, heart diseases, and muscle disorders, but prevention relies on officers' motivation and following recommended steps.
6. **Handle daily stressors:** Dominant stressors include crises, public disrespect, routine tasks, shift work, car collisions, and court appearances, which can be distracting and frustrating in day-to-day operations.
7. **Ignore or counter public disrespect:** Police officers often face a shocking level of disrespect from the public, including disobedience, profanity, and rudeness from people under the influence, rebellious youth, suspects, or those from countries where law enforcement is negatively perceived.
8. **Ignore or correct public sarcasm:** Surprisingly, frequent and casual sarcasm, donut jokes, smugness from kids, rudeness from "taxpayers," threats to use political influence, and criticism from former police officers are common.

9. **Prepare for slow:** High-risk professions, like policing, can experience impatience and frustration during downtime, slow phases, or routine situations, particularly when delays happen unexpectedly.
10. **Assess personal alertness:** Some officers become complacent, while others stay hyper-alert due to past experiences when facing routine situations.
11. **Make shift-work adjustments:** Shift work poses a major challenge, affecting eating habits, sleep quality, family life, mood, and overall well-being, with aging making it even more difficult.
12. **Face personal demons:** Personal fears, concerns about making errors, feeling jaded, and dealing with pressure can weigh heavily on officers.
13. **Function with dysfunctional teams:** Team dynamics can be stressful due to mistrust among team members, ethnic issues, and the challenges of relying on others in high-pressure situations.
14. **Recognize struggle:** Despite improvements, female officers still face challenges in male-dominated environments, dealing with rejection, stereotypes, and perceived favoritism.
15. **Persist with rookies:** Working with inexperienced rookies can bring pride as a mentor, but it can also involve challenges such as excessive aggressiveness, lack of safety awareness, poor containment, inferior reports, unrealistic expectations, and discipline issues.
16. **Mentor the errors:** Proper recruitment, training, and mentorship are crucial to address rookie errors, improve safety, elevate team rapport, and build positive community connections.
17. **Tolerate bureaucracy:** The top organizational stressors are unfair workloads, coaching issues, excessive bureaucracy, limited resources, public complaints, and leadership challenges.
18. **Recognize gaps:** Ethnic minority officers may encounter extra obstacles in their careers, such as exclusion, racism, education gaps, and negative reactions from friends and family.
19. **Set persoal goals:** Many "excellent" officers lack motivation for the promotional process, raising concerns about succession planning, job satisfaction, and coaching issues related to low standards, lack of recognition, and low pay.

20. **Notice external conflicts:** Family conflicts often go unnoticed as a source of police stress, including domestic conflict, failing marriages, and spousal fears about officers' safety, leaving them torn between their job and personal life.

Notes

1 S. Charman, *Police socialisation, identity and culture becoming Blue*. Cham: Palgrave Macmillan, 2017.
2 J. M. Violanti, Charles, L. E., McCanlies, E., Hartley, T. A., Baughman, P., Andrew, M. E., Fekedulegn, D. and Ma, C., "Police stressors and health: A state-of-the-art review," *Policing*, vol. 40, no. 4, pp. 642–656. https://doi.org/10.1108/PIJPSM-06-2016-0097, 2017.
3 F. H. Zimmerman, "Cardiovascular disease and risk factors in law enforcement personnel: A comprehensive review," *Cardiology in Review*, vol. 20, no. 4, pp. 159–166. https://doi.org/10.1097/CRD.0b013e318248d631, 2012.
4 D. Fekedulegn, Burchfiel, C. M., Ma, C. C., Andrew, M. E., Hartley, T. A., Charles, L. E., Gu, J. K. and Violanti, J. M., "Fatigue and on-duty injury among police officers: The BCOPS study," *Journal of Safety Research*, vol. 60, pp. 43–51. https://doi.org/10.1016/j.jsr.2016.11.006, 2017.
5 J. Lepine, Podsakoff, N. and Lepine, M., "A meta-analytic test of the challenge stressor-hindrance stressor framework: An explanation for inconsistent relationships among stressors and performance," *Academy of Management Journal*, vol. 48, no. 5, pp. 764–775, https://doi.org/10.5465/AMJ.2005.18803921, 2005.
6 J. Wills and Schuldberg, D., "Chronic trauma effects on personality traits in police officers," *Journal of Traumatic Stress*, vol. 29, no. 2, pp. 185–189, https://doi.org/10.1002/jts.22089, April 2016.
7 D. McCreary, Fong, I. and Groll, D. L., "Measuring policing stress meaningfully: establishing norms and cut-off values for the Operational and Organizational Police Stress Questionnaires," *Police Practice and Research*, vol. 18, no. 6, pp. 612–623, https://doi.org/10.1080/15614263.2017.1363965, 2017.
8 S. Bailey*, Smith, S. and Williams, K., "Strive to thrive: Resiliency training for all levels of healthcare," in 6th Canadian Conference of Physician Health (CCPH), St. John's Newfoundland, October, 2019
9 S. Maguen, Metzler, T. J., McCaslin, S. E. and Inslicht, S. S., "Routine work environment stress and PTSD symptoms in police officers," *The Journal*

of Nervous and Mental Disease, vol. 197, no. 10, pp. 754–760, https://doi.org/10.1097/NMD.0b013e3181b975f8, 2009.
10 J. McDonald, Orlick, T. and Letts, M., "Mental readiness in surgeons and its links to performance excellence in surgery," *Journal of Pediatric Orthopaedics,* vol. 15, no. 5, pp. 691–697. https://doi.org/10.1097/01241398-199509000-00027, 1995.
11 J. McDonald, Dahal, G. P., Tyshenko, M. G., Sloan, D. A. and Sharma, S. K., "Operational readiness: Links to Sherpas' peak performance in tourist mountain-guiding," In A. P. Adhikari, G. P. Dahal, I. Mahat, B. Regmi, K. Subedi, & S. Shrestha (Eds.), *Sustainable Livelihood Systems in Nepal: Principles, Practices and Prospects.* Kathmandu: International Union for Conservation of Nature, Nepal Country Office (IUCN Nepal), pp. 281–308, 2015.
12 McDonald, J. and Hale, K., "Mental readiness for frontline workers in homelessness services in Ottawa, Canada," *International Journal on Homelessness,* vol. 2, no. 1, pp. 80–104, 2022.
13 N. P. Podsakoff, LePine, Jeffery A and LePine, Marcie A., "Differential challenge stressor-hindrance stressor relationships with job attitudes, turnover intentions, turnover, and withdrawal behavior: A meta-analysis," *Journal of Applied Psychology,* vol. 92, no. 2, pp. 438–454, https://doi.org/10.1037/0021-9010.92.2.438, 2007.
14 Lockey, S., Graham, L., Zheng, Y., Hesketh, I., Plater, M. and Gracey, S., "The impact of workplace stressors on exhaustion and work engagement in policing," *The Police Journal: Theory, Practice and Principles,* vol. 32258, pp. 1–17. https://doi.org/10.1177/0032258X211016532, 2021.
15 Gutshall, C., Hampton, D. P., Sebetan, I. M., Stein, P. C. and Broxtermann, T. J., "The effects of occupational stress on cognitive performance in police officers," *Police Practice & Research,* vol. 18, no. 5, pp. 463–477. https://doi.org/10.1080/15614263.2017.1288120, 2017.
16 A. R. Blais, Thompson, M. and McCreary, D. R., "The development and validation of the army post-deployment reintegration scale," *Military Psychology,* vol. 21, no. 3, p. 365–386. https://doi.org/10.1080/08995600902914727, 2009.
17 M. Martin, Marchand, A., Boyer, R. and Martin, N., "Predictors of the development of posttraumatic stress disorder among police officers," *Journal of Trauma Dissociation,* vol. 10, no. 4, pp. 451–468. https://doi.org/10.1080/15299730903143626, 2009.
18 R. N. Haarr, "Factors affecting the decision of police recruits to "drop out" of police work," *Police Quarterly,* vol. 8, no. 4, pp. 431–453. https://doi.org/10.1177/1098611103261821, 2005.

19 M. &. F. D. Sarkar, "Psychological resilience in sport performers: A review of stressors and protective factors," *Journal of sports sciences,* vol. 32, no. 15, pp. 1419–1434. https://doi.org/10.1080/02640414.2014.901551, September 2014.
20 J. P. Andersen and Gustafsberg, H., "A training method to improve police use of force decision making: A randomized controlled trial," *SAGE Open,* vol. 6, no. 2, p. 2158244016638708. https://doi.org/10.1177/2158244016638708, 2016.
21 B. Green, "Post-traumatic stress disorder in UK police officers," *Current Medical Research and Opinion,* vol. 20, no. 1, pp. 101–105. doi:10.1185/030079903125002748, 2004.
22 P. Dick, "The social construction of the meaning of acute stressors: A qualitative study of the personal accounts of police officers using a stress counselling service," *Work & Stress,* vol. 14, no. 3, pp. 226–244, https://doi.org/10.1080/02678370010026422, 2000.
23 S. Garbarino, Guglielmi, O., Puntoni, M., Bragazzi, N. L. and Magnavita, N., "Sleep quality among police officers: Implications and insights from a systematic review and meta-analysis of the literature," *International Journal of Environmental Research,* vol. 16, p. 885. https://doi.org/10.3390/ijerph16050885., 2019.
24 L. B. Larsen, Andersson, E. E., Tranberg, R. and Ramstrand, N., "Multisite musculoskeletal pain in Swedish police: Associations with discomfort from wearing mandatory equipment and prolonged sitting," *International Archives of Occupational and Environmental Health,* vol. 91, no. 4, pp. 425–433. https://doi.org/10.1007/s00420-018-1292-9, 2018.
25 D. Chan, Webb, D., Ryan, R. M., Tang, T., Yang, S. X., Ntoumanis, N. and Hagger, M. S., "Preventing occupational injury among police officers: Does motivation matter?," *Occupational Medicine,* vol. 67, no. 6, pp. 435–441. https://doi.org/10.1093/occmed/kqx076, 2017.
26 I. V. Carlier, Lamberts, R. D. and Gersons, B. P., "Risk factors for post-traumatic stress symptomatology in police officers: A prospective analysis," *The Journal of Nervous and Mental Disease,* vol. 185, no. 8, pp. 498–506. https://doi.org/10.1097/00005053-1997080, 1997.
27 J. McDonald, *Gold medal policing: Mental readiness and performance excellence.* New York: Sloan Associate Press, 2006.
28 C. Moad, "Critical incidents: Responding to police officer trauma," Fayetteville, AR: School of Law Enforcement Supervision. Criminal Justice Institute, 2011.
29 J. Jackson, A. Z. Huq, B. Bradford and T. Tyler, "Monopolizing force? Police legitimacy and public attitudes toward the acceptability of violence," *Psychology, Public Policy, and Law,* vol. 19, no. 4, pp. 479–497. https://doi.org/10.1037/a0033852, 2013.

30 L. Mazerolle, E. Antrobus, S. Bennett and T. R. Tyler, "Shaping citizen perceptions of police legitimacy: A randomized field trial of procedural justice," *Criminology*, vol. 51, no. 1, pp. 33–63. https://doi.org/10.1111/j.1745-9125.2012.00289.x, 2013.
31 R. S. Engel, "Explaining suspects' resistance and disrespect toward police," *Journal of Criminal Justice*, vol. 31, no. 5, pp. 475–492. https://doi.org/10.1016/S0047-2352(03)00052-7, 2003.
32 B. McCarthy, J. Hagan and D. Herda, "Neighborhood climates of legal cynicism and complaints about abuse of police power," *Criminology*, vol. 58, no. 3, pp. 510–536. https://doi.org/10.1111/1745-9125.12246, 2020.
33 H. Campeau, R. Levi and T. Foglesong, "Policing, recognition, and the bind of legal cynicism," *Social Problems*, vol. 68, no. 3, pp. 658–674, 2021.
34 R. K. Moule Jr, G. W. Burruss, F. E. Gifford, M. M. Parry and B. Fox, "Legal socialization and subcultural norms: Examining linkages between perceptions of procedural justice, legal cynicism, and the code of the street," *Journal of Criminal*, vol. 61, pp. 26–39.https://doi.org/10.1016/j.jcrimjus.2019.03.001, 2019.
35 P. Stager, Hameluck D, Jubis R. Underlying factors in air traffic control incidents. In *Proceedings of the Human Factors Society Annual Meeting*, vol. 33, No. 2, pp. 43-46. Los Angeles, CA: SAGE Publications. https://doi.org/10.1177/154193128903300209, Oct 1989.
36 NAV Canada, *Situational awareness module: Train the trainers manual*. Ottawa: NAV (Navigation) Canada, p. 124, 1997.
37 J. McDonald, *Mental readiness training for air traffic control trainees: Course manual*, Transport Canada, p. 61, 1993.
38 P. Brough, "Comparing the influence of traumatic and organizational stressors on the psychological health of police, fire, and ambulance officers," *International Journal of Stress Management*, vol. 11, no. 3, pp. 227–244. https://doi.org/10.1037/1072-5245.11.3.22, 2004.
39 C. Nelson, McDonald, J., Kyle, N. and Galipeau, J., "Evaluation of police excellence," In J. McDonald (Ed.), *Gold medal policing*. Sloan Associate Press, pp. 201–209, 2006.
40 W. Tengpongsthorn, "Factors affecting the effectiveness of police performance in Metropolitan Police Bureau," *Kasetsart Journal of Social Sciences*, vol. 38, no. 1, pp. 39–44. https://doi.org/10.1016/j.kjss.2016.07.001, 2017.
41 I. Waters, Hardy, N., Delgado, D. and Dahlmann, S., "Ethnic minorities and the challenge of police recruitment," *Police Journal*, vol. 80, no. 3, pp. 191–216. https://doi.org/10.1350/pojo.2007.80.3.191, 2007.
42 S. A. Guajardo, "Measuring diversity in police agencies," *Justice*, vol. 13, no. 1, pp. 1–15. https://doi.org/10.1080/15377938.2014.893220, 2015.

4

The readiness equation

> **SPOILER ALERT**
>
> Achieving excellence in challenging situations requires the right blend of physical, technical, and mental preparedness.

Abstract

This chapter assesses the significance of physical, technical, and mental readiness in policing, underlining the pivotal role of mental readiness for success. Using a standardized tool, officers' preparedness is systematically measured. Police readiness across two studies, 17 years apart, is compared. Similar testing reveals unexpected parallels with professions like surgeons, social workers, and Sherpa guides. The importance of mental focus alongside physical and technical expertise in perilous situations is highlighted. Disappointing performances are found to be linked to lower mental readiness. Performance indicators are refined to enhance officer training. Insights from coach officers center on ethics, leadership, and communication for better outcomes. The chapter concludes with 20 insights for gauging readiness and success in policing.

DOI: 10.4324/9781003145493-4

This chapter presents decisive insights into the relationship between operational readiness and performance outcomes in six sections:

A. Measuring what matters: Inside the minds of excellent officers
B. Exceptional officers speak out on readiness
C. Influential factors
D. Successful and disappointing performances
E. Performance indicators for preparedness
F. 20 Key strategies for measuring readiness and success in policing

A. Measuring what matters: Inside the minds of excellent officers

Decisively quantitative results demonstrate strong connections between mental readiness and frontline performance. Each set of (dependent) variables was analyzed separately, starting with the importance of mental readiness relative to technical and physical readiness. Differences between successful and disappointing performance consider (independent variable) factors like background and developmental distinction.

Striking the right balance

Performance Excellence: A critical assessment of physical, technical, and mental readiness.

Officers weighed the importance of physical, technical, and mental readiness for frontline excellence. Balanced definitions based on established occupational functionality[1,2,3,4,5] were utilized to define each competency as follows:

> *Physical readiness*: Physical health and fitness, personal safety techniques, coordination of tasks, environmental stamina, fatigue, food and hydration management.

Technical readiness: Knowledge and application of the field, verbal and written communication, knowledge of the service and community, operational logistics and resources.

Mental readiness: Commitment, confidence, positive imagery, mental preparation, full focus, distraction control, constructive evaluation and coping.

Officers determined that mental readiness contributes 44%, while technical readiness accounts for 30%, and physical readiness for 26% (see Table 4.1). Generally, a balance was reported between physical and technical readiness, with an emphasis on mental readiness (Figure 4.1).

TABLE 4.1 Police Overall Importance of Readiness

COMPETENCIES	Mean (%)	Standard Error	Standard Deviation
Physical Readiness	26	1.70	10.63
Technical Readiness	30	1.50	9.53
Mental Readiness	44	1.54	9.30
TOTAL	100		

Note: On a scale where readiness competencies total 100%.

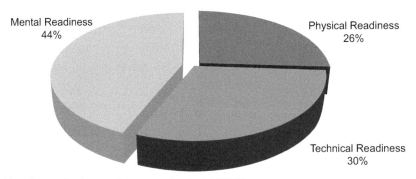

FIGURE 4.1 Police Overall Importance of Readiness

From the perception of highly proficient officers and coach officers, mental readiness clearly plays a major role in successfully dealing with challenging situations. This finding aligns with Orlick and Partington's study[6] on elite sports. Even with a conservative interpretation, given the standard deviation sizes, mental readiness must be deemed as at least equal to technical and physical readiness, if not more important.

Trends in preparedness

Comparing results from the 48 officers in the 2003 study and the 33 officers in the 2017 study, conducted 17 years apart, revealed differences. While physical and technical readiness decreased by 4% and 6%, respectively, mental readiness increased by 10%. This indicates that despite technological advancements and changes in the use of force, the overall impact was greater on officers' mental preparedness compared to their technical and physical preparedness. See Figure 4.2 and Appendix J: Calculations for the differences in the importance of readiness in policing over 17 years for comparison calculations.

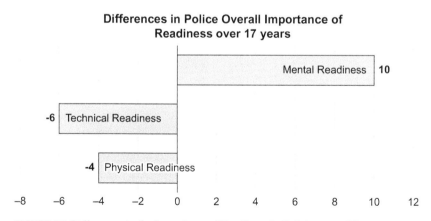

FIGURE 4.2 Differences in the Importance of Readiness in Policing over 17 years

Mental readiness dominance across occupations

Similar testing was conducted with high performers in various professions, from surgeons to Sherpa guides[7,8,9,10]. The results showed that:

- *mental readiness* was prioritized across all groups
- *technical readiness* was ranked second by police, emergency responders, and social workers
- *physical readiness* was ranked second only by athletes and Sherpa guides
- *distribution* was most even with Sherpa guides and widest with surgeons and social workers in homelessness services

Occupational differences are evident (Table 4.2). Mental readiness is a major contributor to peak performance, ranging from 37% for Sherpa guides to 48% for surgeons, while technical readiness varies more, ranging from 20% for athletes to 41% for surgeons.

TABLE 4.2 Overall Importance of Readiness across Different Professions

COMPETENCY	Olympic Athletes	Surgeons	Dentists	Social Workers	Sherpa Guides	Police
Physical Readiness	38	10	23	24	33	26
Technical Readiness	20	41	28	29	30	30
Mental Readiness	42	49	49	47	37	44
TOTAL	100%	100%	100%	100%	100%	100%

Despite unique aspects in each profession, unexpected similarities often emerge. Dentists' profiles[8] were more similar to social workers than to surgeons[7]. Unlike surgeons, dentists deal with conscious patients, often in pain or fearful. Similarly, social workers in homelessness services[9] frequently de-escalate tense situations, also akin to police profiles. For the same reasons, the police profile was found to be closest to that of social workers. Additionally, police profiles showed resemblance to high-altitude Sherpa guides[10], highlighting the importance of mental focus and composure in perilous situations alongside physical and technical expertise.

B. Exceptional officers speak out on readiness

Direct quotes from exceptional officers provide real-life, evidence-based, peer-to-peer insights shared throughout the book. These officers reflect on the essential balance and interdependence demanded by their physical, technical, and mental abilities. They highlight how each competency is essential for effective policing.

> **It varies**—*It's according to the situation. If you're going into a fight or have to go in with another officer, forget the technical and the mental, your physical is probably going to be your best tool at that point. If you're going into a domestic and bothered by the children crying, but no injuries, and a lot of lawyers involved and custody, well, your mental is going to help you a lot. And if it's a bank fraud, where they make a lot of statements, well, it's your technical for seizure of the envelopes, fingerprinting on the stamps, check writing where you forward it to Fraud for what evidence is needed to collect.*
> —Neighborhood Resource

> **Hand-in-hand**—*You have to be mentally ready, or else that could be your last day. You have to look at it that way. If you're not really physically fit, or ready, it could affect your mental state. If you're not mentally ready, it could affect your technical state. They all go hand-in-hand.*
> —Patrol

> **Mutually reinforced**—*The physical, the mental, the technical—you can't do just one—they're all related. Without one of them, you've got nothing. You can have the technical and the mental preparedness, but what if you're a big, fat slob that can't get up three flights of stairs without sitting down? You could be physically fit, but a friggin' wingnut who goes in blasting everything that moves.*
> —Tactical, >15 years

Officers often speak of the seriousness, challenges, and the possible consequences of error in their day-to-day dealings. The demands they face are unique. Physical readiness is crucial, especially in extreme conditions like cold weather, where necessary equipment is vital. Stress can quickly deplete physical and mental readiness. Technical readiness ensures officers have knowledge of the law, the organization, and the community, while mental readiness is essential for staying sharp and focused. These quotes help to emphasize the value placed on physical, technical, and mental readiness.

Physical readiness, the cold—*Physical fitness was no problem. It was the cold. It turned into a l-o-n-g drawn out call with this guy and it was BLISTERING COLD. You know, when the snow cracks when you walk on it… And it was as cold the next day too. Physically, I dropped down a peg.*
—School Resource

Mental readiness: "Maybe I'll get too old for the action someday, but I'll never get too old for the mental gymnastics."

Physical readiness, stress shield—*Without physical readiness, the other ones [mental and technical readiness] will crash, burn and fizzle. The stress will take its toll quicker.*
—Sergeant

Technical readiness, back-ups—*Technically, I have the resources. I have all my equipment: Two flashlights, one on my belt and one in my pocket, in case one runs out. I have two sets of handcuffs [laughs].*
—Canine

Technical readiness, know it—*Knowledge of the law is so incredibly important. If I had to, I could probably arrest you for something right now. If you don't know it, what's the use? And it is so much fun out there when you know.*
—Female Patrol

Mental readiness, never too old—*I'm still in uniform because I like the frontline—I like the action. Maybe I'll get too old for the action someday, but I'll never get too old for the mental gymnastics.*
—Patrol, >15 years on

Mental readiness, reminders—*Readiness starts when I put on my uniform. I never get dressed at home. I always make sure I do it at work. You understand the seriousness of what you're about to go and do.*

—Sergeant

For these officers, mental readiness is paramount, as it ensures confidence and control. It means having the ability to access knowledge, make the best use of experience, concentrate fully, and make constructive, accurate decisions at all times.

Stay focused—*Mental readiness has to be the top—you've got to stay focused. Physically, you've got to take care of your health—you have no choice. You can't let yourself go. Technically, you have to focus, but mental is the most important.*

—Sergeant

Balance—*You can be the most physically fit officer in the world—you can be Adonis and have people go, "Ooh! He's a big bastard!"… but no interactive skills or can't figure his way through a call. There needs to be a balance. I could just intimidate people, but I don't need to if I can get through this call with finesse.*

—Patrol, >10 years on

Attitude—*I go out and actively pursue bad guys. That's what I do. That's what I love doing. I always tell people when they ask, "You're not in the Detective's Office?" I say, "Why would I? I'm having a great time out there." I get to chase people into the ground. Chase them until they can't go anywhere. That's part of the job. That's the fun. That's the mental preparedness that I go through every day.*

—Neighborhood Resource

C. Influential factors

The excellent officers from the six frontline specialty units were analyzed based on three demographic factor areas for potential influence on performance—background, developmental, and police distinction.

Background factors include eight factors which officers are predisposed to upon entering a police service.

Developmental factors include nine factors which officers attain through former or current training and experience.

Police Distinction factors include five factors which officers earn while serving in policing.

Together with their respective descriptors, there are a total of 22 different individual factors (see Figure 4.3).

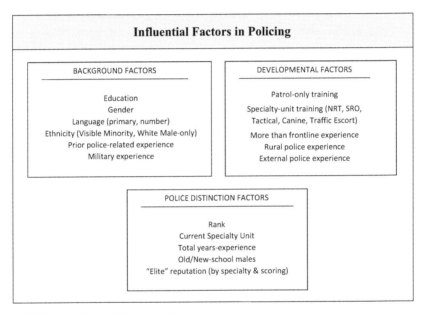

FIGURE 4.3 Influential Factors in Policing

Differences in the point distribution of these readiness components are noted among certain groups. A lower percentage of weight would be expected where:
- the actual job description requires a lower standard
- a higher than average baseline is assumed
- skill levels and confidence are higher than most

For example, officers with tactical or military experience gave less weight to physical readiness (25% and 24%, respectively),

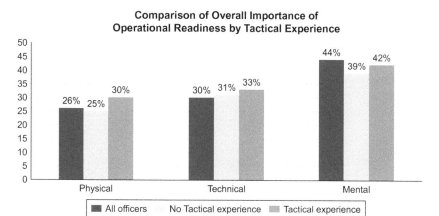

FIGURE 4.4 Comparison of Overall Importance of Operational Readiness by Tactical Experience

possibly because they assume a higher physical baseline (see Figures 4.3 and 4.4). Similarly, officers with prior police-related experience gave a lesser value to technical readiness (28%), possibly indicating more comfort in performing technical skills. Discussing such basic differences, regarding performance readiness between groups, lends itself to improved team building. See Appendix L: Successful Performance Readiness by Factors for additional factors.

D. Successful and disappointing performances

Readiness during successful performances

Officers were surveyed about their readiness just before a successful performance in a challenging situation they actively attended within the past few months. They rated their physical, technical, and mental readiness on a scale of 0 to 10, with 0 representing 0% ready and 10 representing 100% ready (Figure 4.4).

On average, readiness scores were consistently high, with all three aspects rated at 9 out of 10 during successful performances.

Officers with military experience, for example, scored themselves 5–6% higher in all three areas in terms of successful

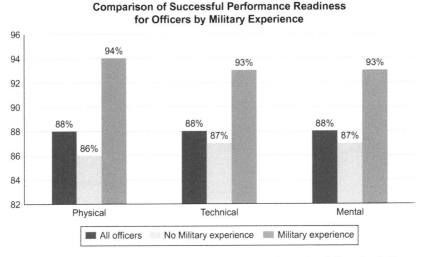

FIGURE 4.5 Comparison of Successful Performance Readiness for Officers by Military Experience

outcomes (see Figure 4.5 and Appendix L: Successful performance readiness by factors). This may indicate that best performance outcomes are attributed to oneself versus others or luck. Similarly, female officers scored themselves higher than male officers in physical readiness during best performances (p = 0.094).

In contrast, "elite" officers have as much as 10% lower scores, perhaps due to having higher standards (e.g., technical at 81% versus 91%, p = 0.067). The same tendency in technical readiness is seen among officers with previous Tactical Training (p = 0.096) or who are Caucasian (p = 0.064). Similarly, mental readiness is scored lower by officers with prior police-related experience and School Resource Officer (SRO) experience (p = 0.015 and 0.077, respectively).

Differences in the point distribution of these readiness components are noted among certain groups. This lower scoring would be expected where there is:
- a higher standard compared to others
- more attribution of success to others or luck than to self
- lower effort in preparation compared to others

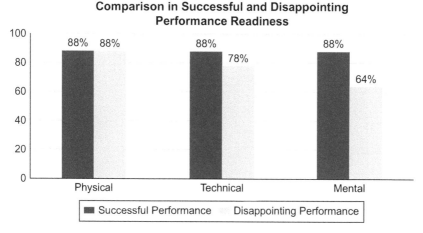

FIGURE 4.6 Comparison of Disappointing Performance Readiness for Officers by Elite Officers

Readiness during disappointing performances

Officers were asked to think back as to how they felt just before a disappointing performance in an equally challenging frontline situation, as compared to their best performance example. They were asked to rate their degree of technical, physical, and mental readiness at that moment on a scale from 0 to 10, with 0 representing 0% ready and 10 representing 100% ready.

On group scores for disappointing performances, physical readiness scored highest at 8.8/10, with a 10% decrease for technical readiness (7.8/10) and 24% drop for mental readiness (6.4/10).

Once again, elite officers scored themselves 7–9% lower than others in all three areas, suggesting that they may take more of the blame for errors than most (see Figure 4.6 and Appendix M: Disappointing performance readiness by factors). The same decreasing pattern was evident in

- mental readiness for Sergeants (p = 0.051)
- physical readiness for males and officers with prior police-related experience (p = 0.062 and 0.088, respectively)
- technical for officers with rural experience (p = 0.084)

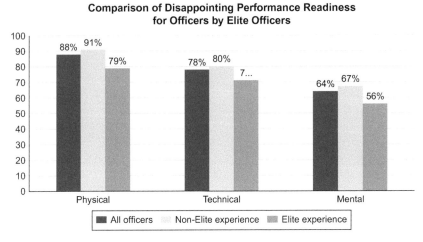

FIGURE 4.7 Comparison of Successful and Disappointing Performances Readiness for Officers by Elite Officers

Readiness in successful versus disappointing performances

In comparing successful and disappointing performances, mental readiness is the factor that shows the most significant change. Group scores show no difference between physical readiness scores, 10% decrease in technical readiness, and, the most significant drop, 24% in mental readiness. In turn, physical readiness scores high regardless of the outcome (see Figure 4.7).

Physical readiness: The Caucasian male groups (p = 0.079) are the only ones who find that their performance is impacted by physical readiness between best and disappointing performances.

Technical readiness: Variations and trends in technical readiness appear based on training experiences, years on, and background factors. Surprisingly, technical scores are not influenced by any of the three educational levels within officers (i.e., high school only, college only, university). This suggests that education is not a relevant factor in distinguishing technical readiness between officers. Officers speaking more than one language (p = 0.017**) as well as those with rural experience (p = 0.006**) reported technical differences between performances.

Without exception, officers with some form of frontline specialty training outside of patrol show more consistent technical readiness (i.e., Tactical, p = 0.002**; Canine, p = 0.008**; Traffic Escort, p = 0.014**; SRO, p = 0.014**; Neighborhood Resource Team [NRT], p = 0.016**). Sergeant rank (p = 0.008**) and officers with previous related experience (p = 0.014**) also minimize the technical difference. Technical preparedness also shows less change for elite officers versus the non-elite (p = 0.009).

Mental readiness: Regardless of their background, developmental, or police distinction factors, all of the officers interviewed show a significant difference in mental readiness between successful and disappointing performances. This is another indication that mental preparation has more weight or importance then physical and technical readiness.

E. Performance indicators for preparedness

Success skills: Redefining police best practices based on high performers.

Field training aims to create competent police officers who ensure safe, effective patrol services, minimizing liability and risk, and safeguarding the organization's interests. While traditional police training and evaluating have emphasized technical and physical skills, there is now a growing recognition of the importance of mental-readiness skills alongside these competencies[11]. To address this, performance indicators needed to be developed to acknowledge and enhance *all* the practices we *know* distinguish the *best* from the *rest*[12].

With the valuable input from a Coach Officer Advisory Group, comprised of respected coach-officer leaders from across the province, performance indicators were constructed as benchmarks for physical, technical, and mental readiness. To ensure practicality for frontline training and evaluation, they recommended approximately 12 performance indicators (PIs) for overall operational readiness. The Advisory Group envisioned a final Field Training Assessment tool of performance indicators and practices that would effectively integrate evidence-based findings.

Ultimately, physical, technical, and mental readiness PIs were detailed with matching practices to complete a Field Training Assessment tool. This two-page tool helps trainees understand what is expected of them for frontline policing readiness. It allows them to record their daily practices to show their skills. Once trainees comprehend these practices, they must exhibit full competence in *all* these expert and evidence-based performance indicators to ensure they are operationally ready—technically, physically, and mentally—for frontline duty. In this edition, the tool has been revised to reflect the current study (see Appendix P: Police Trainee Field Training Assessment and Progress Report). How these benchmarks were arrived at now follows.

Benchmarks for technical and physical readiness

The overall importance of readiness for challenging situations was used as the framework for the tool. To ensure practicality for frontline training and evaluation, 12 performance indicators were settled on, with 4/12 (33%) for technical readiness, 3/12 (25%) for physical readiness, and 5/12 (42%) for mental readiness, closely corresponding then and now to the actual weighted percentages for technical (32%, 30%), physical (28%, 26%), and mental readiness (40%, 44%) (see Appendix J: Calculations for differences in the importance of readiness in policing over 17 years).

The group worked on matching and refining the generic, occupational functionality definitions[1,2,3,4,5] of physical and technical readiness with current police training practices to create comprehensive and effective performance indicators for readiness.

Technical Readiness Performance Indicators, accounting for approximately 32% of police readiness, include:
1. Proficiency in Law
2. Verbal Communication
3. Written Communication
4. Knowledge of Police Service and Community

Physical Readiness Performance Indicators, accounting for approximately 28% of police readiness, include:
5. Officer Safety
6. Use of Force
7. Police Vehicle Operations

In Chapters 5, 6, and 7, each performance indicator is thoroughly described backed by current research and quotes from the interviews with top frontline officers. These testimonies of respected officers highlight important points and provide valuable insights from one peer to another, making learning easier.

Benchmarks for mental readiness

In *Gold Medal Policing, 1st Edition*[13], mental readiness was isolated and assessed using Orlick's "Wheel of Excellence"[14,15]. Orlick's model, based heavily on research with Olympic athletes[6], has proven applicability to other high-performance domains[8,16,17,18]. The "Wheel of Excellence" outlines seven important mental success elements for achieving excellence at critical moments in demanding high-performance domains. See also Appendix N: Orlick's Wheel of Excellence for a description of each success element.

From a theoretical perspective, *Gold Medal Policing* (2006) confirmed the transferability of these mental success elements to policing based on studying 48 excellent frontline police officers (anonymously identified by their peers and supervisors)—akin to the Olympic medal winners.

These mental success elements, renamed as performance indicators, were re-evaluated by "excellent" coach officers in this study.

Mental Readiness Performance Indicators, accounting for approximately 44% of police readiness, include:
1. Commitment
2. Confidence
3. Positive Imagery
4. Mental Preparation
5. Full Focus
6. Distraction Control
7. Constructive Evaluation

In Chapter 7, Mental Readiness in Policing, each success element is thoroughly presented and analyzed in multiple ways. In later chapters, they will be tailored to police terms and condensed into five performance indicators in proportion to the 44%.

♦ Firstly, the *success element is explained*, with its defining features broken down to align practices in the interview transcripts.

♦ Secondly, *percentage frequency counts* are calculated from the officer interviews, offering evidence for each of the success elements from Orlick's "Wheel of Excellence." These percentages are grouped into categories: over 75% of officers (highest usage), 50–75% of officer use, and less common but equally important practices used by fewer than 50%.

Interview quotes are included to emphasize intriguing character traits.

♦ Thirdly, *unconventional practices* are examined. Analyzing practices used by less than 50% of excellent officers helps uncover groups more likely to effectively employ these specialized practices. Furthermore, less common skills often have connections, meaning that using one skill can impact another. Officers who frequently use one skill also tend to utilize related skills when facing challenges.

Skill profiling: Directing career development for potential deficiencies or sought-after skills.

♦ Next, *notable quotes* from interviews are included to emphasize intriguing character traits. These respected officers' firsthand stories from their front-line experiences provide valuable peer-to-peer insights for learning.

♦ Then, *significant correlation relationships* are discovered, contributing to a deeper understanding of the success elements within policing. Chi-square tests, as an adjunct to the qualitative transcript analysis, were conducted on different mental-readiness practices and influential factors to reveal connections between certain variables.

♦ Lastly, *influential factors* on officers were compared based on 22 different Background, Developmental, and Police Distinction factors; see Appendix A: Evidence-Based Rigor: Study Design. For instance, specific specialty-unit experience (NRT, Tactical, etc.) led to significantly more use of less common practices.

These insights will help reshape police best practices based on high performers and offer guidance for *selecting trainers* for particular skills, *prioritizing training* for specialized groups, and *directing career development* for potential deficiencies or sought-after skills.

Range and consistency of practices. Officers' mental-readiness practices were assessed to further rank within and between success elements based on:

♦ the number or *range of practices* identified within each element, with consideration of their relative weight between elements

♦ the *consistency of practices* used by officers or the potential for individual differences among them

For instance, Positive Imagery, one of the seven success elements, was confirmed if all officers reported using visualizing practices. The total number of unique Positive Imagery practices determined its practice range. Officers differed in listing their full range of practices. To understand its importance, Positive Imagery practices were compared to those of the other six elements (its relative weight).

The material presented in the next three chapters is based on the qualitative and quantitative analysis of physical, technical, and mental readiness, and influential factors. It is comprised of exceptional frontline officers' perspectives from officer interview-transcripts, coach-officer consultations, and coach-officer questionnaires.

F. 20 Key strategies for measuring readiness and success in policing

The following 20 key strategies summarize the importance of physical, technical, and mental readiness in successful and disappointing performances.

1. **Consult coaches:** Access coach officers' insights on producing competent frontline police officers, emphasizing qualities like ethics, leadership, and communication, while addressing coaching issues and proposing solutions for improved outcomes.
2. **Approach readiness systematically:** Analyze physical, technical, and mental readiness needed for successful policing through a systematic, research approach.
3. **Explore preparedness tools:** Use a standardized tool to measure how prepared officers are, emphasizing the role of mental readiness in achieving excellence.
4. **Balance training:** Require a specific balance of physical, technical, and mental preparedness for effective policing, measured using a standardized tool.
5. **Share diverse perspectives for success:** Engage "excellent" officers to share their diverse perspectives on what is

important for success, forming a valuable database for learning and continuous improvement in policing performance.
6. **Be mentally ready:** Recognize mental preparedness in conjunction with physical and technical competencies as essential for optimal readiness, especially in demanding professions.
7. **Standardize training assessments:** Emphasize the need for a unified field-training manual and valid assessment tools to ensure consistent and effective officer training.
8. **Acknowledge and support frontline challenges:** Confirm that common challenges encountered by high-risk professions, such as limited resources, higher stress and fatigue, and inconsistent performance, also impact the personal safety, productivity, and morale of frontline police officers.
9. **View challenges by category:** Identify and categorize seven challenging frontline situations in policing, ranging from dangerous and complex scenarios to emotionally-charged cases using a standardized template.
10. **Seek reliable insight:** Define and understand difficult situations by seeking insight from exceptional frontline officers and coaches.
11. **Assess limitations and potential:** Consider officers' familiarity, risk awareness, and/or lack of necessary skills when assessing their perspectives on a given challenging situation.
12. **Plan for the unknown:** Anticipate unfamiliar terrain in frontline policing from: unprecedented changes imposed by the service, unfamiliar situations for the officer, involvement with high-risk individuals, coaching others, and aiming to achieve something exceptional.
13. **Measure mental preparedness:** Demonstrate strong links between mental readiness and frontline performance outcomes through quantitative results, equally important as technical and physical readiness.
14. **Understand consistency in performance:** Provide evidence that mental readiness matters in challenging situations, as supported by studies with elite sports and high-risk professions.
15. **Compare disciplines:** Link occupational readiness profiles by job requirements, baseline skills, and confidence levels,

such as high-altitude (Sherpa) guides and police officers who share a need for balancing physical and technical expertise with heightened mental focus and composure in dangerous situations.

16. **Benefit from structured mental preparedness:** Value mental readiness for its ability to provide confidence, control, and the capacity for constructive, accurate decision-making in challenging situations, observed in high-performing officers.
17. **Critique your performance outcomes:** Affect technical readiness through training and experience in different specialty units, while observing consistent fluctuations in mental readiness between successful and disappointing performances.
18. **Score your readiness:** Confirm if successful performances are associated with high readiness scores across physical, technical, and mental readiness, and these best outcomes are attributed to oneself versus luck.
19. **Track performance drops:** Check if disappointing performances show a drop in mental readiness scores, suggesting officers take more responsibility for errors.
20. **Work on all skills:** Develop performance indicators for physical, technical, and mental readiness to enhance crucial skills and improve training for frontline officers.

Notes

1 U.S. Bureau of Labor Statistics, "Occupational requirements survey: Visual overview for physical demands." https://www.bls.gov/ors/factsheet/visual-overview-of-physical-demands.htm, November 1, 2020.
2 D. Lechner, "Job Demands Analysis: Defining the physical demands of the work for post-offer and return-to-work functional testing." https://aeasseincludes.assp.org/proceedings/2007/docs/750.pdf, November 1, 2020.
3 I. General Healthcare Resources, "PTA physical demand summary." https://www.ghresources.com/wp-content/uploads/2014/06/Physical-Demands-Summary-PTA.doc, November 1, 2020.

4 Occupational Health Clinics for Ontario Workers Inc., "Physical Demands Analysis (PDA)." https://www.ohcow.on.ca/edit/files/general_handouts/PhysicalDemandsAnalysis.pdf, November 1, 2020.
5 D. Vatin, "79 core competencies for your resume, resumegenius." https://resumegenius.com/blog/resume-help/core-competencies-resume, November 4, 2020.
6 T. Orlick and Partington, J., "Mental links to excellence," *The Sport Psychologist,* vol. 2, pp. 105–130, 1988.
7 J. McDonald, Orlick, T. and Letts, M., "Mental readiness in surgeons and its links to performance excellence in surgery," *Journal of Pediatric Orthopaedics,* vol. 15, no. 5, pp. 691–697. https://doi.org/10.1097/01241398-199509000-00027, 1995.
8 J. McDonald and Paganelli, C., "Exploration of mental readiness for enhancing dentistry in an inter-professional climate," *International Journal of Environmental Research and Public Health,* vol. 18, no. 13, pp. 7038–7055. https://doi.org/10.3390/ijerph18137038, 2021.
9 J. McDonald and Hale, M., "Mental readiness for frontline workers in homelessness services in Ottawa, Canada," *International Journal on Homelessness,* vol. 2, no. 1, pp. 80–104, 2022.
10 J. McDonald, Dahal, G. P., Tyshenko, M. G., Sloan, D. A. and Sharma, S. K., "Operational readiness: Links to Sherpas' peak performance in tourist mountain-guiding," In A. P. Adhikari, G. P. Dahal, I. Mahat, B. Regmi, K. Subedi, & S. Shrestha (Eds.), *Sustainable livelihood systems in Nepal: Principles, practices and prospects.* Kathmandu: International Union for Conservation of Nature, Nepal Country Office (IUCN Nepal), pp. 281–308, 2016.
11 J. McDonald, *Gold medal policing: Mental readiness and performance excellence.* New York: Sloan Associate Press, 2006.
12 J. McDonald and Hoffman, R., "Gold Medal Policing overview to coach officers (ppt)," Regularly presented at the Ontario Police College, 2008-2016.
13 J. McDonald, *Gold medal policing: Mental readiness and performance excellence.* New York: Sloan Associate Press, 2006.
14 T. Orlick, "Wheel of excellence." http://www.zoneofexcellence.ca, October 25, 2003.
15 T. Orlick, "The psychology of personal excellence," *Contemporary Thought on Performance Enhancement,* vol. 1, pp. 110–122, 1992.

16 J. McDonald, Hale, K. & Kirkwood, T. Excellence in Homelessness Service: Evidence-Based Frontline Practices, *International Journal on Homelessness, 4(3),* pp. 1–19, 2024.
17 J. McDonald and Gyorkos, T., "Operational Readiness for conducting global health research abroad," *Canadian Journal of Public Health,* vol. 107, no. 4–5, pp. 387–389. https://doi.org/10.17269/cjph.107.5555, 2016.
18 J. McDonald, Orlick, T. and Letts, M., "Mental readiness in surgeons and its links to performance excellence in surgery," *Journal of Pediatric Orthopaedics,* vol. 15, no. 5, pp. 691–697. https://doi.org/10.1097/01241398-199509000-00027, 1995.

5
Physical readiness in policing

> **SPOILER ALERT**
>
> Keeping officers safe requires real-world scenario training, daily equipment checks, and vigilance.

Abstract

This chapter examines physical readiness in policing, focusing on officer safety, use of force, and vehicle operations. Officer safety practices, such as proper handcuffing and wellness, require legal authority, tactical strategies, and teamwork. Use of force involves firearms proficiency and defensive tactics, highlighting vigilance, threat assessment, problem-solving, and quick decision-making in emergencies. Tailored training is crucial, considering environmental factors and personal protective gear. Vehicle operations include collision avoidance and strategic traffic stops, demanding keen observation and rapid decision-making. Proficiency mandates acute driving skills, attention to detail, coordination, composure under pressure, and precise maneuvers. The chapter concludes with 20 strategies for physical readiness, providing valuable insights into the demanding yet essential aspects of law enforcement preparedness.

This chapter discusses physical readiness in policing in four sections:

A. Officer Safety
B. Use of Force
C. Vehicle Operations
D. 20 Key strategies for physical readiness in policing

Coach officers have defined three key performance indicators for assessing physical competencies. To efficiently evaluate overall physical competency in real-world scenarios, they identified specific practices for each indicator. These coach-officer performance indicators and informed practices were combined with current research findings as follows:

> **Officer Safety**: Performs proper handcuffing; completes thorough body searches (including sensitive areas); has good health and wellness (amid shift work and fatigue); maintains good physical fitness and injury management; can endure containment in environmental conditions; has a strong safety sense.
>
> **Use of Force**: Uses firearms effectively; can perform gunpoint arrest; maintains equipment ready; demonstrates evidence of defensive tactics; exercises physical control with appropriate use of force response option; understands "reasonableness."
>
> **Vehicle Operations**: Operates vehicle safely; multitasks while driving (e.g,. talks on radio, gathers information, checks plates); uses lights and sirens during emergency response; reverses cruiser using back window, not solely relying on mirrors; conducts effective patrolling of the environment; positions the vehicle appropriately during traffic stops.

Collectively these physical competency markers underscore the importance of safety protocols and well-being practices, proficiency in equipment usage and defensive tactics, and skilled driving techniques for policing. The Perishable Skills Program (PSP) in California, USA, is required to be completed annually by all law enforcement personnel: tactical firearms, arrest and control, driver training and awareness, and tactical interpersonal communication[1].

Police Use of Force research accounted for 39% of current physical publications, with a focus on defensive tactics, force at mental illness calls, equipment proficiency, and cultural and gender challenges. This was followed by research related to officer safety (24%), physical demands (22%), and vehicle operations (15%). See Appendix E: Physical competencies in policing.

> **Physical stamina**—*Physical readiness is huge. Without it, mental and technical readiness will crash, burn and fizzle. The stress will take its toll quicker.*
> —Patrol Sergeant

A. Officer Safety

Coach officers identified key practices that minimize risks and enhance officer safety. These practices relate to:

1. Proper handcuffing
2. Body search (including sensitive areas)
3. Fitness and wellness (amid shift work, fatigue, and injury)
4. Containment in environmental conditions
5. Strong safety sense

Prior to taking a call, most officers (75%) prioritize officer safety. During arrests and transportation, these practices require legal authority, tactical strategies, observation, memory, and camaraderie. Vigilance remains crucial, especially during night shifts and extreme weather, with fatigue management vital for safety. Managing shift work and fatigue, especially during continuous work and overtime, may necessitate additional recovery time. Physical fitness aids in stress relief, confidence, injury prevention, and overall well-being.

Officer safety—*There is no situation that can be considered a crisis unless it involves the officer… That's my main concern is to take care of their welfare and their safety first, and then deal with the call. That is the only kind of situation that causes me a bit of anxiety.*

—Neighborhood Resource

Police safety training involves officer survival, threat management, lethal and non-lethal situations, interactions with individuals with mental illness, response to active-shooter incidents, and safe driving practices. Notably, vehicle collisions cause more severe injuries and fatalities among officers than gunshots, emphasizing the need for improved risk assessment in training[2].

Policing is physically demanding, with a high risk of injuries, particularly upper extremity soft-tissue sprains and strains from confrontations with non-compliant offenders[3]. Cultural and gender challenges arise as high physical fitness requirements can be perceived as barriers to diversity[4]. Many officers have physical fitness levels exceeding the general population, but ongoing training and recovery are essential for maintaining health and performance[5].

Protective body armor reduces the likelihood of a fatal assault by 57%, while disarmed officers face over twice the risk of fatal assault[6]. However, body armor introduces biomechanical and performance impacts, such as increased exertion, longer task completion times, reduced work capability, balance and stability issues, and potential injury risks. Tactical gear can decrease power and agility, potentially increasing the risk of injury or fatality during duty[7]. Thus, body-armor selection should consider officers' fitness and ergonomic needs[8].

Environmental factors impact officers' physical, sensory, cardiovascular, and psychological well-being. Safeguard measures include enhancing trauma resilience, healthy lifestyle, vaccination protocols, and training to improve respiratory endurance, muscle resistance, and overall physical fitness. Adequate sleep and stress resilience improve memory recall during incident debriefings[9,10].

Proper handcuffing

Proper handcuffing ensures safety and effective law enforcement, protecting all parties involved. Incorrect handcuffing poses significant risks, especially from aggressive suspects or potential weapons. It provides control during searches and transportation in police vehicles, preventing unforeseen dangers. New officers need additional training for swift, appropriate, and confident handcuffing, rather than hesitating or engaging in unnecessary negotiations. Mental rehearsal enhances an officer's ability to handcuff effectively, improving timing and adaptability in various situations.

PHOTO 5.1 Safety starts with proper handcuffing, and mastery ensures confident apprehensions. Credit: Ottawa Police Service, 2024

> **Ridiculous**—*Some of the new Officers that I've watched on the street, they're handcuffing in the front, searching them without handcuffs, just dumb, silly things that shouldn't be done. Absolutely ridiculous, one day somebody is going to get it... If you decide you're going to let them go, take the handcuffs off, "Sorry sir," dust him off and be on your way.*
>
> —Tactical Sergeant

Two options—*I sat him down, explained why he had to be charged... "You have two options—we can walk down to my cruiser, nobody has to know, put the handcuffs on when we get there." And that's exactly what we did. Another kid, same scenario, he freaked out, so he got drawn to the ground, handcuffed and dragged out of the front of the school.*
—Female School Resource

Faking or not—*You get guys like that who will fake a seizure and then crack you in the head... I err on the side of caution. I'm still going to put the handcuffs on him.*
—Patrol

Rehearse—*Sometimes, if I'm just lounging around at home, I'll close my eyes and deal with scenarios in my mind. I "see" it, I'm there, outside my body, trying to deal with the situation. How would I handcuff the person?*
—Tactical

Cuff then search—*Once you know somebody's identity, you have power over them. I don't search anyone until after he's handcuffed and under arrest. Once you have them in the handcuffs, they're under your control.*
—Neighborhood Resource

Afraid to cuff—*New officers who are dealing with the scumbums on the street, their supervisor should turn them into hard-nosed cops—teach them to do their job and not get pushed around. You watch them on calls and they dance around with guys when they're perfectly arrestable. What are you waiting for? Arrest him. Handcuff him. Take him and put him in your car. But they say, "Well sir, you have got to do this, you have got to do that..." No! Grab hold of him! Let's go! But they don't do that. They sing and dance and afraid for whatever reason.*
—Tactical Sergeant

Body search

A Body search is multifaceted implying officer safety, legal authority, reasonable grounds, deception detection, and tactical strategies across different scenarios. Officers are reminded of the significance of continuously honing their safety skills, conducting consistent comprehensive searches (including sensitive areas), and having a firm grasp of the legal framework that governs their actions. Effective searches rely on experience, keen observation, and proper documentation. Furthermore, searching needs to use protective gear judiciously, consider potential presence of weapons, and adapt quickly during high-stress situations.

> **No complaint fears**—*I've never had difficulty searching vehicles or people. I never think, "What if this person complains?" If I have reasonable grounds that apply to an actual Section of the Criminal Code, that gives me the authority to apply the legislation. I encourage that kind of education. It builds confidence.*
> —Neighborhood Resource

> **Boots off**—*With this individual there was no physical gestures or threat or anything like that. You tend to let your guard down, and that's what I did there and started to take shortcuts. That's when I made mistakes. Now, I do every search the same—even if it's my father. The boots come off, everything comes off, without exception. That one event was enough to elicit the change.*
> —Canine

> **Backseat safety**—*Sometimes you need to perceive a person worse than they are. If I'm searching somebody and putting them into the back of your car, I want to be confident that they're not gonna hurt you when you're driving away with them (which is extremely important to me).*
> —Patrol

> **Time and place**—*A lot of guys are either wearing the gloves all the time, or as they're walking up to the address or inside the place as they think, "Oh geez, he's looking for trouble"—and they start putting on their defenses… If you're searching someone that you suspect may have this, then yes, by all means put on your protective clothing, either your gloves or whatever, and watch yourself. There's a way to do it. There's a time and a place when to bring the hammer down.*
> —Traffic Escort

Back pocket—*I searched his back pocket and he had three tickets on him from another traffic officer that he was able to suck in two days earlier. So now he had the double lie—but he didn't fool me… He was giving false names, getting experience and he knows he can lie and get away with it. I caught him. I felt good about that.*
—Neighborhood Resource

Consistency—*The guy in the back asked me if I would cuff him in front… the cuffs were too tight. I said, "No. Hang on, we'll be there in a minute." (We later found a gun in his boot.) That told me—no matter who they are or what the offense is— treat them all the same. They all get searched. If you're consistent, then you can't get criticized for searching somebody.*
—Canine

Fitness and wellness

Consistent physical conditioning is essential for minimizing risks in confrontations and serves as an effective stress reliever, promoting confidence and readiness when challenged. Maintaining Fiitness is a personal endeavor, with individual considerations and variations in the physical demands of different roles in law enforcement. Striking a balance between physical and mental health is important for excelling in the field. This includes physical discipline, strategies for shift work, fatigue and long-term rest, and injury management.

Physical discipline

More than half of the officers (63%) highlighted the importance of Physical discipline in a policing career. The regimen described includes regular exercise before or after a shift, together with proper and regular meals. Workouts were often mentioned as an opportunity for informally debriefing or enabling an officer to think through a problem. This trait is highly valued by elite officers and "New School" (<10 years) officers and all officers with prior police-related experience (77%, $p = 0.038$; 88%, $p = 0.034$; 100%, $p = 0.000$, respectively).

Workout debrief—*After a shift I like to work out. I'll work out while my brain is still processing everything, and it puts everything together.*
—Neighborhood Resource

Mornings only—*I have to work out in the morning, right at the start when I come into work or I'm not going to do it. I'm just not motivated. I'm motivated when I get here. By one o'clock in the morning, good luck.*
—Tactical

Energy—*When I work out before my midnight shift and get a good day's sleep, I am ready to go. I am pumped… I think you'd get less guys sleeping and less guys getting injured… You'd be able to handle situations a lot more and build up team camaraderie. I have young kids, and a lot of guys getting hired now are young with kids. I think it's very important.*
—Canine

Time management, coping—*Time-management skills are very important. However, coping skills have to work for you. Make sure you eat properly. Working out is a major de-stressor.*
—>10 years on

Stress reliever—*Physical fitness is a good stress reliever. Rough day? Go to the gym instead of slamming back a pint. It's huge—there's nothing like it. Get out some frustration from dealing with drunks and all that…. Physical fitness is key. You feel more confident and ready for situations.*
—3 to 5 years on

Physical goals—*They're getting away from the physical work of policing, and you see it, going towards the problem solving and crisis intervention… When I came in, I didn't stop 'til I hit 100 push-ups, and they'd go, "Only had to do 65." That's the way I've always been. If I want something, I'm going to blow the test out of the water. But they're getting away from all that stuff.*
—Neighborhood Resource

Presence—*Things turn ugly so fast, and if you can't defend yourself, get off the road!… Physical fitness is also the way you* *present yourself. I don't get many hassles. No one really challenges me too much.*

—Patrol

Defense—*I tie all those things into my job—my ability in the gym and my ability to defend myself and my partner. I have the same focus and I'm going to push myself as hard as I can.*

—Patrol

Injury prevention—*Physically, it all depends on the call... You have to be physically prepared or you're going to get hurt... We've had very few of our officers hurt. They're all physically prepared.*

—Canine

Shift-work strategies

Police shift work presents both challenges and benefits. Night shifts often cause sleep deprivation and exhaustion, while some officers appreciate the flexibility and better work-life balance. Day shifts can be draining due to administrative tasks, meetings, and reports. During quiet night shifts, officers seek ways to stay alert, often relying on caffeine and engaging with colleagues. Maintaining fitness is crucial, and integrating exercise into the schedule can improve readiness and build camaraderie.

Continuous work and overtime exacerbate fatigue, leading officers to desire more time off to prevent burnout. Fatigue varies among officers, influenced by individual fitness, coping mechanisms, and job demands. Some adapt well, while others find it more challenging with age, altering shift preferences. For many, determination to excel outweighs fatigue.

Most officers (80%) view shift work as a barrier to optimal performance. While 69% have strategies to manage shift work, 38% do not, indicating a need for expert advice to develop comprehensive plans. New recruits could benefit from the insights of experienced officers who have successfully adapted to the lifestyle impact of policing and demands of shift work (Table 5.1).

Interestingly, officers with only patrol experience and those with prior police-related experience report fewer strategies for managing shift work (61%, $p = 0.05$; 45%, $p = 0.06$, respectively). This highlights the importance of sharing effective coping

TABLE 5.1 Shift-Work Strategies

	TOTAL RESPONSES Ranked by %
Shift work block	80
Shift work strategies (… "not just fatigue")	69
Enjoy: flexibility, no crowds, always done it	
Sleep: disciplined sleep, regulate patterns/schedules/eating time	
Accept: part of job: knew it going in, just do it, job responsibility	
Effort and family support: call if late, balance with partner, coordinate logistics	

mechanisms within the force to enhance overall performance and well-being.

Accept—*Policing IS shift work. If you don't want to work shift work, then why are you doing this? Go find something else to do—work at a bank. It's becoming more common that people get hired on and then realize shift work is not for them. Then they turn around and expect to be accommodated. That's bullsh--.*

—Canine

Flexibility, benefits—*People who don't work shift work don't see some of the benefits. I like shift work because it gives me more time off, I get more stuff done and I still make the time for the family.*

—>15 years on

Avoid the routine—*I like the non-routine—I have more energy that way.*

—School Resource

Spousal support—*With families, it's harder. You rely on your spouse if you're not there on the weekends and you're gone during the week, too.*

—Traffic Escort

Alertness—*Night shifts are particularly hard. I like getting together with the people on my shift and talking, even if it's for a short amount of time. We'll park side-by-side and chat. That keeps me awake—you don't get stagnant.*

—Patrol

Fatigue strategies

Fatigue is a major stressor for 79% of officers, with 75% employing various strategies such as slowing down the pace, drinking more coffee, and maintaining disciplined sleeping habits. General fatigue and Fhift work complications deserve further consideration (see Table 5.2).

TABLE 5.2 Fatigue Strategies

	TOTAL RESPONSES Ranked by %
Fatigue block	79
Fatigue strategies (physical, mental, emotional)	75
Go easy: during high fatigue use slower pace, rest on the job, go easy, be realistic	
Ask for a change	
Stimulants: Coffee, coke, tea	
Get active: up from desk/car, interact, walk, talk	
Regulate sleep patterns: develop pattern, disciplined sleeping	

Officers with Patrol-only experience have the highest number of fatigue strategies (100%, $p = 0.071$), elite officers (46%, $p = 0.001$), and those with prior police-related experience (55%, $p = 0.023$) have the fewest. Elite officers, in particular, identify significantly less frequently the need for rest strategies (46% versus 91%, $p = 0.001$), and for rest in preparation (54% versus 67%, $p = 0.093$) compared with non-elite officers, indicating they may not see fatigue as problematic. In contrast, all Patrol-only experience officers report using one or more fatigue strategies. Effective strategies for sleep, fatigue, and recovery are crucial to performance and warrant further research.

Balanced life—*I'm pretty sensible: I balance my workouts and my diet. I'm not a drinker. My priorities are work and family. In between I take care of my own stuff. Hours of sleep go up and down with a big set of kids but when I really need a rest, my wife and I will compensate. Sometimes you have to take a* break. Do something unrelated that will clear your mental and physical state—just to get recharged?

—Patrol Sergeant

Fatigue rituals—*If I felt really tired, then coffee, a power nap, or washing my face in cold water—ice water. I'd go out for a quick, brisk walk around the area or just get out of the car and stand outside.*

—>15 years on

No more midnights—*I worked shift work for the first four or five years and… You're always tired. I didn't have trouble sleeping during the days. I just made sure my room was black and I could sleep. But I found I was almost sleeping too much. It certainly had an effect on the body so that's another reason I like Traffic. No midnights to worry about.*

—Traffic Escort

Adrenaline—*As far as being fatigued, day shift I'm often tired, but when a call like this comes in, your adrenaline takes over and you're rarely affected by physical fatigue… If you're so tired that you are, don't come to work.*

—Patrol

Socialize—*Don't isolate yourself—everybody else is in the same boat. Try to get talking, get laughing and then that will bring you out of it, for a bit.*

—Traffic Escort

Automatic—*I was tired and it was the end of shift… once I got there and decided to do it, the fatigue factor was irrelevant. Basically, it's just, "OK, I'm starting this, let's go do this." I stay in very good shape, so I was not worried about the fatigue factor—that will come at the end, when we're done, not at the beginning. It's irrelevant. You don't even think about it.*

—Canine

Music, coffee—*You've got to get yourself in tune. I usually make myself a cup of coffee and start listening to some tunes on the way to work to get me going.*

—Patrol, >10 years on

> **Naps, coffee**—*Fatigued, oh yeah, I'm ready for my two o'clock nap now, if it weren't for the coffee… [laughs]. Day-shifts for me are just killers. Up at 4:30, to be at work for 5:30 and I'm just drained. And it's administrative: meetings, all the reports, all that kind of stuff. I'm back in bed at 8:30 at night—literally. You just get through.*
>
> —Patrol

Long-term rest strategies

Getting proper rest also serves as a long-term coping strategy for 74% of officers. A sample of their ideas to ensure adequate rest include:

- get over what's keeping you awake
- guard against burnout
- install a hot tub
- separate work from home
- be disciplined in your scheduled sleeping and eating times
- develop a regular sleep pattern with rituals
- seek alternatives to policing through outside interests
- set personal time limits
- visualize to relax and relieve anxiety, gastric and general pain, and sleeplessness

All officers with English as a primary language and "New School" males (100%, $p = 0.08$ and 0.028, respectively), as well as Neighborhood Resource Team [NRT] and School Resource [SRO] officers (92%, $p = 0.064$) noted the importance of rest. In contrast, officers with Tactical experience (33%, $p = 0.02$) have significantly less strategies for rest.

> **Sleep discipline**—*Get your sleep! The odd time I skip a beat in my sleep and can't regain it for the rest of my shift. There's no easy way to regain that sleep. It has to be uninterrupted, and personal lives don't always allow that to happen. It's a domino effect. It's shift work. You have to take a hit. You may not get to sleep. Unfortunately, life goes on.*
>
> —Patrol, >15 years on

Days off—*I eventually manage to catch up on my days off. Other people have difficulty with ambient noise, and it has to be very dark. I'm not like that. I can shove earplugs in, and I'm gone for eight hours. I'm sleep-deprived, but luckily, I manage because I can sleep anywhere at any time.*

—Patrol, <5 years on

Burnout: "I know my body, and I know that if I keep pushing-pushing-pushing, I'll break down."

Five to eight hours—*You have to get your sleep. You have to. It's key. Talk to doctors, talk to anybody. You come in to a night shift and you've only had three hours sleep that day, it's dangerous, and you just don't feel like going. I try to get about seven hours. On a very good day I'll have eight. If I have less than five I'm a zombie. I feel it in my whole body.*

—Patrol

Time-off vs overtime—*There're times in the summer when there's always events going on. Sometimes we went a whole month with no days off, working 29 days straight, just because of shift changes. It's all overtime too, but after a while you'd rather have the time off.*

—Traffic Escort

Avoid burnout—*You shouldn't burn yourself out. Taking time off helps [laughs]. You have to refresh yourself. There are times we work weeks straight, no days off. I don't work crazy anymore. I know my body, and I know that if I keep pushing-pushing-pushing, I'll break down. I take the time that comes to me, and that's how I cope.*

—Tactical

External interests, support—*You certainly have to keep in touch with family or whoever's close to you. Whether its family ties or friends outside the Police Department, they keep you grounded. That's very important.*

—Neighborhood Resource

Injury management strategies

Alongside physical fitness is factoring in potential injury. Self-awareness is key in physical readiness, including knowing how to adjust one's pace to work effectively within a team. A holistic strategy is required for officers dealing with injuries, including physical preparedness, emotional well-being, and protocol adherence.

> **Your actions**—*Coming in sick—I used to drag myself in really sick. And then I thought, "If you're sick or distracted in any way, then you probably are better off not coming to work"—because of your decisions… your actions can affect a lot of people. Physical is important.*
> —Neighborhood Resource

> **Self-reliance**—*You have to be ready to take control, for example going to a fight. "I'm going to be in for a handful here. I have got to get myself ready to fight" because there's no one else available except one other person… Not that they're afraid or have the biggest intentions, but they're not going to win [laughs]. It wouldn't be fair to say but you know that. "Okay, I've have got to get myself ready to go here, because this could be ugly."*
> —Patrol

> **Capabilities**—*Even if my physical only needs to be 10%, it is an important factor. Sure, you can do the job hurt or with a sniffle. But if you're feeling shi--y, if you're physically tired or physically sick, where you can't do your job, you shouldn't be on.*
> —Tactical

> **Unpredictable**—*Physically, there's one situation that you're not going to recognize. You're going to end up meeting a guy who's 5'1, 160 lbs, but he's 9th degree black belt and he's going to just destroy you—charge you like a Raggedy Ann doll. And you're ready to go pick it up, because you finish what you started.*
> —Neighborhood Resource

Containment in environmental conditions

Successful containment operations rely on officers' commitment, collaboration, safety awareness, adaptability, and adherence to standard procedures. Officers must remain vigilant, alert, and engaged to their containment duties, even in adverse conditions or in seemingly routine situations. Effective containment is reinforced by officers' knowledge of geographic areas. Safety should always take precedence over bravado, and officers should readily acknowledge their limitations to ensure team safety.

Police rigor extends to extreme cold or hot conditions, where physical fitness alone may not suffice, and situations demanding endurance and adaptability, such as handling demanding tracks in harsh weather. Officers often endure discomfort and adapt without complaint, showcasing the mental fortitude and physical preparedness required to cope with rapidly changing external conditions and maintain operational effectiveness.

> **Fundamentals**—*Containment doesn't just apply to canine tracking. When you're the first officer on scene, no matter what the call is, there are a lot of general rules that are the same and apply to everything: containment, protecting the scene, and protecting evidence.*
>
> —Canine

> **Responsibility**—*Containment positions… a lot of them are happy to do it. Some aren't so happy. I've had people whine, "Well, I'm cold, I need replacement." "Well, you know what, the Tac guy standing beside you has been there as long as you have, and yes his equipment may be a little bit better but you know what, he's going to be there for another six hours, you're not. You're going to be there for another 20 minutes. You can bite the bullet and wait." Some are keener on doing their job than others. Some are here to just get a paycheck and go home.*
>
> —Tactical

> **Humility**—*Don't be so macho that you put somebody's safety in jeopardy. You're having a shi--y day, you may bring it to work—your thought processes won't be up to par. Twist your knee running—you may have to make some quick movements*

for the safety of the team. If there is something wrong, say, "I don't know if I can do it. Put me on containment." You want to be in the heat but somebody has to do containment.

—Tactical

Avoid boredom—*If I'm just doing containment on the building, on the perimeter, I think, "If he comes out the patio door, I'll put the shot here. If he comes out in the window, he's up a little higher."… It keeps you thinking all the time. I hate to get complacent and settled into the position where you go, "I'm starting to get really bored sitting out here." Oh, it's very easy to do… I am anal-retentive [laughs]. I like things here, here and my equipment lined up here. I like my kit bag organized a certain way [laughs].*

—Tactical

Reliance—*Especially for containment, as a CRO, I don't know the zones as well as my officers do, because that's THEIR zone. They know if there should be a light on in the school, where the doors are, which ones are usually ajar. I don't. I rely on them.*

—Patrol

Adjust—*Fitness was no problem, it was the cold. It turned into a l-o-n-g drawn out call with this guy and it was BLISTERING COLD. Physically, you have to drop it down a peg.*

—Tactical

Persevere—*When you first start, your heart is pounding. Just stand there, just stand there. The dog wants to go hard because he's not tired at all. But your body, what are you doing? There's snow, it's 30 below, you have lots of clothes on but then five minutes into it your heart adjusts, you're settled into it. Here's the pace and let's keep going.*

—Canine

Interdependence—*Being a team leader, I tell the guys, "OK, this is the way we're going to set up and we need to do containment at the back and at the front. We're going to need an immediate action and a plan." I give it to them, I let them go. I'll probably be part of the immediate action team. I'll be depending heavily on the guys that are there because of their experience.*

All that's going through my mind as we're going to the call so that I know we're going to be prepared.
—>Tactical, 15 years on

Strong safety sense

Fellow officers advise avoiding machismo and staying mindful of physical and mental conditions when making decisions. Cultivate strong safety skills, adopt cautious situational awareness, and have a pre-duty routine to gear-up. Avoid complacency, especially during solo assignments, and prioritize observation and memory over note-taking. Be ready with weapons in high-risk scenarios for swift, effective responses. Recognize and mitigate risks, adhere to procedures, and maintain constant vigilance for safety.

On the frontline, officer safety requires a cautious, common-sense approach, with criticism often directed at inexperienced officers for either unexpected aggressiveness or excessive caution. Elite officers, those with Canine experience, male officers, and those with English as their first language highly value safety (85%, $p = 0.08$; 100%, $p = 0.000$; 73%, $p = 0.027$; 91%, $p = 0.04$, respectively).

> **Near misses**—*I arrested a person for impaired driving. The dispatcher made a mistake when they ran the name. Nothing came up but he was a big-time drug guy. When I took the handcuffs off him he pulled out a gun out of his boot and put it to me. The Sergeant grabbed it out of his hand. I felt pretty stupid because I hadn't searched him properly.*
> —Patrol Sergeant

> **Males and females**—*Rookies, they're either overly aggressive or not aggressive enough— because they're not comfortable in their own skin. Hand-in-hand with that is indecisiveness. They know what to do but don't know if they should do it. Those are huge mistakes—but not with women. We don't have a problem with women becoming overly enamored with their new-found sense of power—males, always.*
> —Patrol Sergeant, >15 years on

Wait—*If you suspect there is something there and you go in by yourself, then you're asking for trouble. You just have to wait. Always by two don't make someone else risk their life to save your stupid a-- because you did something wrong. It's hard with the routine stuff, but you have to train yourself—Wait! This could be the day someone else is in there.*

—>15 years on

Shots-fired calls—*There are little officer safety things that we tend to notice more than anything else. Going to a "shots-fired call" without their gun out, and you're pretty sure we heard three hits. They'll say, "If you take it out, you have to put it in the Use of Force Report." Big deal. You're told when you can shoot it, but not when you can take it out. Get it out! That's why they gave it to you. On any gun call, it doesn't matter—get it out of your holster. It's no good to you there.*

—Tactical

Rituals—*I try to have a ritual… You've got to prepare for the scene. Are you going to be inside or back several hundred meters?*

—Tactical

B. Use of Force

The use of force in policing necessitates a blend of physical skills and judgment. Coach officers pinpointed specific practices for evaluating an officer's competency in employing use of force options. As markers, these practices encompass:

1. Firearms and gunpoint arrest
2. Equipment readiness: Checks and electronic aids
3. Defensive tactics
4. Physical control with appropriate use of force
5. "Reasonableness"

Police work demands a cautious approach involving rapid decision-making, threat assessment, problem-solving skills, and unwavering vigilance in urgent gun-related incidents, high-speed pursuits, and first aid/CPR situations. Preparedness involves meticulous equipment maintenance, proficiency in firearms and non-lethal tools, and the ability to safely subdue suspects. Ethical behavior, emotional control, and adherence to "reasonableness" principles shape measured use of force.

Moral dilemmas arise due to diverse community views and social status[11]. Continuous training is needed to keep pace with scientific and technological advancements[12].

Use of force instructors identified the need for more defensive tactics training, citing challenges like limited resources, training frequency, repetition, motivation, and liability concerns. Key skills include situational awareness, problem-solving, adaptability, decision-making confidence, and critical thinking for violent encounters[13].

Evaluating the use of force means measuring suspect resistance levels (from cooperative to deadly resistance) and officer force levels (from police presence to deadly force). Officers' perceptual biases make real-life case-study training imperative. De-escalation techniques, considering individual, cultural, and organizational factors, and accountability frameworks are essential in addressing aggression and violence[14]. The Problem Oriented Policing (POP) approach, which focuses on diagnostic research, tailored interventions, and impact evaluation, is effective[15].

Mental-illness calls are significant; in 2018, 25% of the approximately 1,000 people fatally shot by police were mentally ill. Crisis Intervention Team (CIT) programs offer specialized training, leading to increased officer satisfaction, diversions to psychiatric facilities, and perceived reduced use of force[16]. A review from 2007 to 2017[17] found that police responses to suicidal individuals often involve males who are between 35 and 40 years of age; single and/or having relationship issues; and have psychiatric disorders, substance-use issues, a lower socioeconomic class, unemployment, a history of suicide attempts, and recent police contact—either as a victim or a perpetrator. Stress-induced suicides are common, with triggers including adverse life events, domestic conflicts, terminal illness, job loss, lawsuit, and financial stress[18]. Many display violent behavior and are often armed, complicating responses to suicide-by-cop incidents, estimated between 10% and 36% of police shootings[18,19].

Proficiency in equipment use, such as marksmanship, is crucial to minimize collateral damage[20]. While caffeine is commonly used to mitigate fatigue among law enforcement and military personnel, it improves reaction times but not marksmanship accuracy[21]. Taser use varies, with policy concerns about training quantity and content, trainer qualifications, and Taser placement within the Use of Force Continuum. Further research is needed for evidence-based Taser policies and the safe substitution of force[22].

Firearms and gunpoint arrest

The officers' unwavering dedication to readiness highlights the gravity of firearm-related situations, where they must make life-altering decisions instantly. These high-risk calls come with inherent risks, including violence, knives, and firearms. Emphasizing a deliberate and cautious approach, even in urgent gun-related incidents, is crucial. Constant vigilance, continuous training in threat assessment and rapid decision-making, as well as adept problem-solving skills, are essential to ensure officer safety and effective responses to firearm-related incidents. This extends to scenarios involving high-speed pursuits and first aid/CPR situations.

> **Fear**—*Anything involving weapons—the ultimate for me being a firearm of any kind. Having to do with more of a fear challenge is if there's weapons involved because people around me could get hurt, my partners could get hurt, I could get hurt—I want to go home at the end of my shift.*
>
> —Patrol

> **Skill-sharing**—*I do know that since coming back from the Tac squad, I share my ability for training session—that was recognized by the brass. Everybody saw that I was doing that—more training sessions and they loved it.*
>
> —Patrol

Different coaches—*I spent many, many hours shooting firearms in the past. I'd say my skills with a firearm are fairly good. I'm a Range Safety Officer, and I'm really passionate about teaching… So, if your Coach Officer is a Range Safety Officer, yes maybe you're on the range three or four times during your 500 hours. If he's not, you have to rely on somebody else… Recruits exposed to different coaches have a more overall exposure to different skills and different knowledge.*

—Patrol

Safety habits—*As soon as you knock on that door, you find yourself going into your stance, putting your firearm away from the door, and being prepared. Yeah, it's going to be buddy again, but I'm still going to be prepared. As soon as I stand up straight (it's breathing now), I will automatically turn so that my firearm is away from where I am going.*

—Coach Officer

7-year-old dilemma—*Are you ready to handle a situation? Are you ready to pull a trigger if a seven-year-old points what you think is potentially a firearm or a toy at you, but you don't know if it's real? Could you pull? Could you fire your gun? Could you fire a gun at that seven-year-old?*

—Traffic Escort

Threat assessment—*Most of the calls we get sent on are high risk. There's usually a high level of violence—not just physical violence, it's knives and guns. The potential for serious bodily harm or death is there. In 80% of cases the violence is not there… Patrol guys are trying to validate the information while we're still surrounding the house or looking for a vehicle. The other 20%, when that call comes in, we know from the get-go that this was the real deal.*

—Tactical

Information gathering—*Just because a call comes to you as a priority one, it doesn't mean lights and sirens. My experience tells me that I'm going to get a lot more information if I have officers on the scene, approaching the situation cautiously, and listening to the airwaves.*

—Patrol

> **Oversights**—*Lots of people don't have any flashlights on their belt, because it's day shift. What happens if you go into a house that's dark? They did a drug raid, they didn't have any flashlights, they get inside, it's dark.*
>
> —Canine

Equipment readiness: Checks and electronic aids

Equipment maintenance necessitates meticulous checks and vigilance, ensuring officers are cautious and well prepared for duty. Understanding and readiness to handle firearms and non-lethal options are crucial. The Tactical Unit's sniper team exemplifies this dedication, spending hours on equipment adjustments and planning before practicing shooting, followed by thorough cleaning and inspection.

> *I'm prepared. I pride myself on doing things right.*

Like athletes, many officers (55%) take pride in their equipment, engaging in rituals like stocking their duty belt or tapping their gun for readiness. These physical rituals correlate with better recall using visual triggers (correlation = 0.375, p = 0.009). Equipment checking rituals are most common among Canine, Tactical, and Traffic Escort officers (72%, p = 0.08) and Visible Minority-Aboriginal officers (83%, p = 0.048). It is least likely among officers with Neighborhood Resource Team experience (20%, p = 0.092).

For 41% of officers, using electronic aids such as mobile data terminal (MDT)/mobile digital computer (MDC) or cell phone are essential for top performance. This electronic savvy also correlates with visual trigger for memory (correlation = 0.296, p = 0.041). These habits and technology enhance external communication (correlation = 0.338, p = 0.019), highlighting the critical role of equipment in police work.

> **Reaffirm**—*If I'm approaching a high-risk scene, I reaffirm where my equipment is. Sometimes it's just an informal touch—the gun's here. I go through informal touches of everything, knowing it's there, knowing it's available. You go through the normal checks at the beginning of shift with your weapon*

and your equipment. It's just a touch, almost a reassurance that it's there beside you.

—Patrol, >15 years on

Equipment backups—Technically, I have the resources. I have all my equipment: Two flashlights, one on my belt and one in my pocket, in case one runs out. I have two sets of handcuffs [laughs].

—Canine

Equipment updates—*I keep an eye on the equipment and make sure it's always up-to-date. Every now and again I test my pepper spray, to make sure it's working. Make sure that my gun and everything is clean. Things get frayed and every so often I'll go in and replace them.*

—Patrol

Quality equipment, quality work—*We do have a good police force. Good equipment. Good vehicles. Good technology. Good colleagues. It all makes for good police work.*

—Neighborhood Resource

Meticulous—*I always do things right. I pride myself on doing things right. I'm very meticulous… I have all my equipment. So, I'm prepared.*

—Canine

Checks—*Everybody makes sure their bike's OK—oil, full tank of gas, everything running OK. I make sure I've plugged in the radios—the helmet and the portable radio.*

—Traffic Escort

Awareness—*You have to be aware of the tools that you have: your sidearm, your hasp, and your pepper spray, whatever… Every call we go to, even if it's a kid stealing a gum ball out of a gum-ball machine, it's a gun call regardless, because we're bringing the ammunition.*

—Patrol

Defensive tactics

Defensive tactics training equips officers with the ability to safely and effectively control and, when required, subdue suspects, minimizing the risk of injury to all parties involved. The emphasis is on maintaining situational awareness, using appropriate force, and being well prepared in the line of duty. Officers recognize that sharing of knowledge and skills through continuous training sessions contributes to recognition and respect within the law enforcement community. Additionally, physical fitness is highlighted as a determinant of an officer's performance and their ability to engage professionally with the public.

> **Shared skills**—*I do know that since coming back from the Tac squad, I share my ability for training session—that was recognized by the brass. Everybody saw that I was doing that—more training sessions and they loved it… Really, I am very, very fortunate that I stepped back on the road. I was not put on a pedestal, but I was respected just based on what I had done on Tac.*
> —Patrol

> **Reliance**—*I was physically working out all the time, preparing myself, going to the range on our off days as a group, as a platoon. We were trained as best we could for any given situation.*
> —Patrol

> **Following policies**—*We don't stand back and let people get hurt but we have policies and procedures to follow… If you don't follow policy, you'll end up getting hurt and causing a bigger situation that won't help anyone.*
> —Patrol

Physical control with appropriate use of force

Officers must navigate ethical considerations and maintain control over their actions and emotions when employing force or dealing with the public or individuals in crisis. The shared experiences reveal how situations can escalate quickly, necessitating preparedness and adherence to training protocols. They also emphasize the potential impact of public complaints and the need for accountability in their actions, reflecting a commitment to responsible and measured use of force in their duties.

Physical readiness in policing ■ 151

PHOTO 5.2A At the frontlines of dissonance, navigating the tempest means balancing rights and safety. Credit: Libby Nelson, Vox, Bing, 2016

PHOTO 5.2B Taming chaos. When situations heat up, training kicks in to navigate the ethical maze. Credit: Zou Fa, PXHere, Bing, 2024

Justifiable—*Once it gets to the point where you have to use lethal force on someone, it's a matter of understanding what you can do and what you can't do.*
—Tactical

Burden—*I think back at the time, that responsibility I would've "possibly" been forced to take a person's life. Every cop, every day of his life has got that possibility taking place.*
—Tactical

Tactics while driving—*As soon as you get the call, you should be prepared how you are going to handle the call. You're always being updated by the dispatchers, so you should be prepared. "Ok, how is it? Is it escalating? What use of force options should I consider? If the guy bolts, should I get the dog out? What do I do if I show up first on the scene and there's no back up?" You're constantly getting information, but you still have to be able to drive to get there. You have to watch out.*
—Canine

Civility—*"GET OFF THE F---ING SIDEWALK!! YOU SHOULD BE ASHAMED OF YOURSELF!!" This kid turns around and goes, "F--- you."… One "f---," and I just wrecked an entire year's work. I can't believe I just did that… "You know what? I apologize. I shouldn't have done that. I can't believe I just did that. You're probably surprised to have a police officer apologizing to you, aren't you?"*
—School Resource

Frustration—*When I get the most upset is when I've had to be physical with somebody. Not that they've been hurt but that I had to exert physical force over them. I get frustrated, "Why did you make me have to do that?" That's my biggest frustration.*
—School Resource

Witnesses—*"POLICE. DON'T MOVE." As soon as my gun is out, that's what I'm saying, because I'm making him a witness. I'm making everyone else in the school a witness… If I'm talking, I'm breathing. This was part of my mental preparation.*
—School Resource

"Reasonableness"

Understanding and applying the concept of reasonableness in the context of police use of force is essential for ensuring safety and justifiable actions. Officers rely on their training and situational assessments to gauge the necessary level of force while carrying out their duties. This process involves carefully evaluating the behavior and circumstances they confront, weighing the necessity for force against the potential consequences. They must adhere to the principle of reasonableness to avoid unwarranted use of force in all encounters, even when dealing with threats, public scrutiny, or possible complaints, as this responsibility carries substantial liability.

> **Training**—*I just reverted back to the "Use of Force" training. The most important thing is my safety and the safety of others. I said, "If this guy's got a sword and he's swinging it, I'm at this level. If this guy doesn't, I'm not."*
> —School Resource

> **Liabilities**—*Young officers, they think it's just a bunch of gang members killing each other, so who cares, that doesn't make any difference—well, we still have a job to do. I think like that too sometimes, but once they call us, then we have to do what we're supposed to do. At the inquest, they're going to point at us for not doing this, not doing that… So, it always falls back on us. We're the people with the liability.*
> —Neighborhood Resource

> **Integrity**—*I'm going to keep doing my job. I've never been one to use unnecessary force, I don't tell little old ladies on traffic stops to f--- off or anything like that. I've had my public complaints and I've never lost a day's pay over anything.*
> —Patrol

C. Vehicle Operations

Coaches identified several critical practices in vehicle operations as measures for competency in vehicle operations. These practices relate to:

1. Vehicle safety (e.g., collision avoidance, lights and sirens, pursuits)
2. Multitasking (e.g., radio, information, plates while driving)
3. Vehicle reversing (i.e., mirrors, back window, and cameras)
4. Patrolling the environment
5. Strategic traffic stops (i.e., positioning)

Proficiency in these areas requires acute driving skills, sharp observation and attention to detail, coordination, composure under pressure, adaptability, quick decision-making, effective patrolling techniques, and precision maneuvers.

Motor-vehicle-related events (MVEs) are the leading cause of on-duty deaths among law enforcement officers[2]. In the past decade, fatal MVEs, including crashes and roadside incidents, have surpassed intentional acts of violence like shootings, strangulations, or stabbings[23]. Officers spend extensive hours behind the wheel during patrols, facing unique risks such as adverse weather, high-speed situations, in-car distractions, and exposure to speeding vehicles along highways[24].

Despite the prevalence of MVEs, collisions, and roadside incidents, officers often display complacency toward their elevated risk[25]. The US national officer-safety survey highlighted the necessity of aligning officer training with the real risks they encounter[2]. Research indicates that officers become more aware of the likelihood of on-duty MVEs when their departments prioritize reducing such incidents. The adoption of protective measures and equipment depends significantly on officers' perception of MVE-related hazards. For instance, officers are more likely to accept speed restrictions and restrictive driving policies when well informed about the risks associated with vehicle operations[26].

Vehicle safety

Officers must hone their keen observational skills and meticulous attention to detail, particularly during pursuits or searches, to expertly identify and monitor vehicles. Composure is vital, especially in intense situations like dealing with stolen vehicles, ensuring clear radio communication.

PHOTO 5.3 Mastering safe driving in all conditions: prioritize space, exercise caution, and anticipate hazards. A Traffic Escort method for traffic and intersections: Scan, study, select. Credit: Columbus Indiana Police, Bing, 2024

Prolonged chases demand fluctuating levels of concentration with brief moments of relaxation while waiting for backup. These events highlight the importance of preparedness, organization, and efficiency. Rapid decision-making is imperative for public safety. Daylight pursuits and the unpredictability of suspects further complicate these situations. Termination of pursuits due to safety concerns is common, causing frustration and emotional strain. Emotional resilience and effective coping strategies are essential. Previous successes influence an officer's mindset, emphasizing the importance of maintaining a positive attitude during difficult moments in a chase.

Collision-avoidance strategies

While 57% of officers noted car collisions as being problematic, most (73%) reported having effective controls in place. The officers who have built up the most comprehensive list were males and those with Patrol-only experience (97%, p = 0.065; 97%, p = 0.089, respectively). Officers with CRO experience (97%, p = 0.046) have the fewest reported strategies (Table 5.3).

Prevention is most often stated as an important rule to follow by excellent officers. They are advocates of properly allowing space, intelligently assuming the risk of becoming a liability, and carefully approaching a scene right the first time. Traffic Escort officers were particularly articulate in describing what they observe. For example, in their scan of an intersection, they study traffic patterns anticipating the flow and hazards before choosing a position.

Safety: "I was told, 'You can't do anything if you're dead.'"

Efficiency, safety—*I was told, "You can't do anything if you're dead." If you get into an accident and kill somebody or get killed, you're not going to the call. There's always somebody closer than you. Why put other people in jeopardy?*
—Neighborhood Resource

Accept the inevitable—*Sometimes you just can't avoid it—it's out of your hands. One accident I had was in bad weather where another guy lost control and I couldn't stop. He hit me. They're just unforeseen circumstances.*
—Canine

Inherent consequences—*Other drivers have been charged in accidents. It's part of driving eight hours a day. Anybody who drives eight hours a day, you always want to be alert—especially patrol officers who drive at odd hours with lack of sleep. It's really not an easy thing to do. Unfortunately, if it happens and it's your fault, you suffer the consequences.*
—School Resource

TABLE 5.3 Car Collision-Avoidance Strategies

	TOTAL RESPONSES Ranked by %
Car collision block	57
Car collision-avoidance strategies	73
Defensive: space, lead eye, don't assume, safe	
Efficiency: accident won't help, steady and smart is faster, slow and watch for persons fleeing	
Accept: statistical odds, inevitable, going to happen, minor damage, don't stress	
Minimize frequency: judgment, read into call	

Autopilot—*I can be driving, looking at my computer, and not even looking out my windshield (God forbid, because that's careless) and for some reason I put my foot on the pedal to slow down. I look, and I'm at an intersection. I am so comfortable behind the wheel of a car. That's my office, that's what I do ten hours a day!*

—Female Patrol

V8 inexperience—*I've probably had three collisions in my career… I've had a view as to why more are happening these days. Fifteen years ago, V8s with rear wheel drive were common vehicles. For the youth coming into policing, that's not a common car to drive. With mass transit, even though they've had their license for 10 years, maybe driving is not a normal thing for them.*

—Patrol

10-second difference—*"Police cars, take your time." We're more scared of getting hit by cruisers. They put you through the big stress driving test, and you always find that your time is within 10 seconds. With newer people out there, they want to be there in a hurry.*

—Tactical

Lights and sirens

Activating lights and sirens depends on the perceived urgency of the call, the need to adapt en route, and the risk of alerting suspects. This adaptability and adrenaline rush are integral to policing. However, a measured response, especially for firearm-related priority calls, prioritizes information gathering over haste. Not all "Priority 1 calls" require lights and sirens. Maintaining situational awareness while navigating traffic, including monitoring pedestrians, road conditions, and communicating with dispatch, remains paramount. During pursuits, balancing fight or flight instincts with strategic thinking is essential, emphasizing the need for frequent practice focused on tactical maneuvers.

> **Judgment**—*I'll drive fast, but I'm cautious in that respect, I won't go racing through a light—I'll stop and I'll look. Sometimes, I won't use the lights or siren going to a call, because you want to get the bad guy. If you're using your lights and siren, he's going to be gone.*
>
> —Neighborhood Resource

> **Read traffic**—*All of a sudden, a bunch of demonstrators stand up and start blocking the route. You can see the problem, you identify it, and you act on it. That's why they always have these primary routes and a secondary. You have to ad lib a lot. You have to see the opportunity, go for it, and drive crazy. Sometimes you do, you have to. And I love that. I get a rush from that. After 36 years now, I still take a lot of pride in wearing the uniform—I really do.*
>
> —Traffic Escort

> **Analysis**—*People see that Priority 1 come up and some think, "Hey man, that's my license to speed. Let's go." We have to reanalyze what a Priority 1 call is. Calls that are 911 misdials are entered as Priority 1s. You get these idiots driving lights and sirens to that. It says right on the call, 10-33 emergency, no voice contact, or voice contact, person says they misdialed—Priority 1. Why's it in there?*
>
> —Canine

> **Prioritize**—*I've always taken my calls as, "Is this call worth me killing somebody on the way there?" And I drive in that aspect. If I get into an accident, I'm not going to get to a two-year-old not breathing, and at the same time, that's a call where I need to be risking the lives of other people on the streets. There's*

often not a reason to be driving crazy, because the situation is de-escalated AND if you go racing to every call, how do you race to the priority calls? [laughs]

—School Resource

Urgency—*We get to know dispatchers' voices when they get excited and they get to know our voices as well. Without us asking for a specific emergency request, they know from our voice if there's an urgent matter.*

—Patrol

Call the boss—*Completely ready doesn't start for me until I give a guy the thumbs up that I'm here, geared up, got everything I need and I'm in position... It was windy, cold and we weren't ready until we called the boss on the radio and said, "We are in position, our optics are set up and we are ready to operate, right now."*

—Tactical

Tactics in pursuits—*During a chase, you can get very focused on the run. Sometimes I have to say to myself, "Whoa. Start thinking again." It's the difference between the basic fight or flight functions versus higher thought patterns that allow you to think despite danger, physical exertion and fatigue. We should practice vehicle pursuits much, much more, with a strong emphasis on using tactics, instead of just trying to keep the subject vehicle in sight. It's like chess moves.*

—Neighborhood Resource

Multitasking

Officers juggle various tasks while driving, including communication, assessing situations, and maintaining situational awareness, all while prioritizing safety and effectiveness. Multitasking requires skill, quick decision-making, focus on critical aspects, and practice. In such scenarios, officers emphasize the significance of managing their workload and emotions to ensure effective responses when challenged.

Officers rely on their radios for sharing information when responding to calls. Accessing prior knowledge and radio updates to assess potential risks are vital. Staying calm and speaking clearly are essential, even when excited or hurried. A good dispatcher–officer relationship helps to relay urgency from subtle radio voice-cues during intense situations. Good radio communication between officers facilitates their coordinated responses.

> **Assessment**—*You're trying to set things up, keeping it as brief as you can on the way to a call—that's the first thing… You're assessing the data you have from the call, from the laptop, then you hear people talking on the air as to what their responses are, or the lack of response. That's when you start making sure things are getting lined up… contain the scene and get another officer there available to backup… From repetition, you get with the process fairly quickly.*
> —Canine

> **Concentration**—*Going through those mental exercises affects your plan. You can imagine the amount of thoughts that are going through your mind at the same time you are concentrating on your driving… You're not driving one-handed at 100 plus km per hour, but you have to go through the same exercise.*
> —Neighborhood Resource

> **Little things**—*If you're going lights and sirens, be conscious of your speed. A pedestrian may be crossing the road. Remember to turn off your AM/FM radio in the car. Pay attention to what your dispatcher is saying, other traffic on the road, road conditions, the atmosphere, and the conditions. Those are a lot of little things before you actually get on scene that officers have to be aware of. Those are the multitasking things.*
> —Patrol

> **Multitask MVAs**—*Had two accidents early on in my career. I backed into a fire hydrant and poked out the red light on the cruiser. Fire hydrants normally have the flag up in the wintertime, this one didn't. Another one, I was actually responding to an emergency call and looking at my laptop at the same time. I bumped into somebody in front of me.*
> —Patrol

> **Multitask safely**—*I am so organized, multitasking is a cinch. It's not hard for me. I can literally be driving, on a cell phone, on*

the computer and the radio, all at the same time. If things are too hairy, I'll literally drop the phone or pull over, whatever I have to do. My prime objective is to get there but if I can multitask safely, I'll do it.

—Patrol

Composure—*It's funny. The last couple of times (it makes me laugh even thinking about it), I followed a stolen car, I grabbed the radio and felt my heart race… I find myself taking a deep breath before I make that first transmission on the radio, and get the message back that it's stole… The more excited you get, the more garbled it's going to be and that's not going to help the people in the area who are listening to the radio.*

—Canine

Radio considerations—*I really like it when my team does well… They are being professional like a well-oiled machine. They're not tying up the air, and they're not asking stupid questions. I teach, "Guys, if you're going to talk on the radio, think what you want to say, think what you want to do."*

—Patrol

Distress over airways—*You go over the air, "I hear screaming, there's a broken window. I hear smashing and banging going on in there." Somebody is saying, "Please don't kill me." You may radio that over the air, so that other officers arriving on scene have that information.*

—Patrol

Cruiser coordination—*This is how we're going to plan it out. A cruiser here, here, here, set up a perimeter, Canine's not too far, we'll get a track if we can't find this guy. He's already running from security so we know he's on the run.*

—Patrol

Navigation—*When I drive to a scene, I try to visualize where I'm going. I'll think, "I remember that building. Where am I going to park? There's an oak tree 50 feet away with a path. I'll park there and then come in on foot." It just runs through my head.*

—Neighborhood Resource

Vehicle reversing

Officers emphasize the importance of using mirrors to prevent accidents when backing up into parking spots and maintaining awareness of suspects in their vehicle. In high-speed emergencies, mirrors offer reassurance by showing multiple cruisers responding together with their lights on.

However, using the back window, rather than relying solely on mirrors when reversing or making precise maneuvers, is crucial for safety and precision. Mirrors have blind spots and limited depth perception, while the back window offers a direct line of sight, helping officers avoid obstacles and judge distances accurately. Backup cameras further enhance safety. Combining mirrors, the back window, and backup cameras ensures a comprehensive view, reducing accident risks

> **Defensive**—*Before I came here, I drove professionally for the military. Big trucks, little trucks, and I learned the respect of knowing your surroundings… Tactically, we see a lot of our accidents are backing up into the parking spot. People don't know how to use the mirrors. If you see you are going to hit something, stop! [laughs]*
> —Tactical

> **Tracking**—*I had the rear-view mirror on him. I knew what was happening in my surroundings, for sure.*
> —Canine

Patrolling the environment

Effective police driving in neighborhoods requires building positive community rapport, remaining vigilant despite fatigue, and slowing down to enhance visibility and reaction time. Officers must identify unusual behavior from other drivers who may react differently to a police cruiser. Experience in a patrol car, even in less challenging areas, lays the groundwork for developing safe driving in dynamic situations.

Solo patrol offers autonomy, but experienced officers stress responsible driving, balancing caution with urgency. Newer officers may rush to incidents, increasing road risks and liabilities.

Experienced officers underscore continuous practice, mastery of defensive driving techniques, and confidence are vital. Familiarity with surroundings and stress management behind the wheel are essential for safe and effective police driving.

> **Cautious**—*I'm cautious when I drive. I realize that I drive a police car, but it's not a ticket to speed. I take my time. Yeah, I do take my time. I'm safe for myself and I'm safe for others on the road.*
>
> —School Resource

> **Honed skills**—*If traffic permits, I will still drive somewhat in a harder or more aggressive manner, without putting the public at risk… The day that someone calls for a 10-78 or for assistance now, it's not a good time to experience driving fast and driving aggressively for the first time… I want my skills to be up in all types of weather. Even if the traffic is a bit denser, if the conditions are not the best, I want to be in control of that car… You can only achieve that by practicing periodically… I'm glad to show up quick when someone asks for help. I like to be there.*
>
> —Patrol

> **Observation**—*I always say to my recruits, "Why all of a sudden did that car turn for no reason? It looked like he was going to go left and now he went right. How come? Let's go check him out. He's done something."*
>
> —Canine

> **Autonomy**—*I enjoy it. You get used to being by yourself in your cruiser, and you just don't want to be with someone else. It's nice being in your little mobile office by yourself, cruising along, taking your calls, and doing your own thing.*
>
> —Patrol

Strategic traffic stops

During traffic stops, police officers strategically position their vehicles to achieve optimal visibility for passing traffic, provide a protective buffer, and ensure a clear line of sight to the occupants of the stopped vehicle. This positioning enhances safety and enables officers to vigilantly monitor potential dangers. Officers may take proactive steps to document their location, even during routine traffic stops, to avoid complacency and enhance overall situational awareness.

PHOTO 5.4A AND B 24-7, maintaining visibility and situational awareness is crucial, even during seemingly routine stops. Credit: Ottawa Police Service, 2024

Precautions—*They'll say, "Yeah, what do you want?" "Well sir, the reason I'm stopping you is blah, blah, blah." The exact same script but mentally, I'm in a different place. I'm watching everything, whereas the grandmother may have been by herself. I'm still watching her hands, what she does, the way her eyes move and where she's looking… But prior to stopping the four guys, I would have booked myself over the air, letting everybody else know that I have four guys in a car I'm stopping at this intersection. It doesn't mean I'm calling for help, but all of a sudden everybody knows where I am. Perhaps a car will slide by. Even a cruiser driving by while you're in a traffic stop is a show of force. It makes someone think twice about doing something.*
—Traffic Escort

Accusations—*So, if it got the language like, "You can't f---ing do this" and "You don't know what the f--- you're doing, you're always f---ing harassing me." "I've never met you before in my life." "Oh, you're stopping me because I'm black." "Well, you're only saying that because I'm white" [laughs]. I mean, white people, black people, Chinese people, Polish people, all go through red lights and everyone tells a different lie, or reacts to*

you differently. Sometimes the most affluent people are the biggest a--holes, when you're dealing with them.
—Traffic Escort

D. 20 Key strategies for physical readiness in policing

The following 20 key strategies summarize physical readiness in policing.

1. **Assess physical competency:** Coach officers have defined three key performance indicators for assessing physical competencies in policing: Officer Safety, Use of Force, and Vehicle Operations.
2. **Hone safety, proficiency and defense skills:** These physical-competency markers emphasize safety protocols, equipment proficiency, defensive tactics, and skilled driving.
3. **Customize yearly updates:** California's Perishable Skills Program mandates annual police training, covering tactical firearms, arrest and control, driver training, and tactical interpersonal communication.
4. **Modify use of force:** Current research on use of force primarily focuses on defensive tactics, force in mental-illness calls, equipment proficiency, and cultural and gender challenges.
5. **Stay fit:** Officers highlight the importance of consistent physical conditioning, wellness and proper nutrition for stress relief, frontline readiness, and preventing on-the-job injuries.
6. **Value team workouts:** Officers transferring from other services place a high value on fitness for handling situations and building team camaraderie.
7. **Experiment with shift-work life:** Police shift work creates both flexibility and exhaustion, necessitating diverse strategies to maintain the healthiest life balance.
8. **Think long-term:** Combating officer fatigue is complex and important, and must involve multiple strategies for maintaining readiness and long-term health.

9. **Respect good containment:** Successful containment operations demand resilience, teamwork, and safety awareness in various environmental conditions.
10. **Practice vigilance:** Officers stress the need for continuous training, threat assessment, and rapid decision-making, whether facing firearms, high-speed pursuits, or routine traffic stops.
11. **Prepare equipment:** Officers meticulously perform daily gear checks and organization, from firearms to non-lethal tools, for equipment readiness and boosting confident and preparedness.
12. **Grasp defensive maneuvers:** Defensive tactics training equips officers to safely control suspects while maintaining awareness and adhering to policies, emphasizing the importance of physical fitness and continuous training.
13. **Execute skills training with rapid judgment:** Use of force combines physical skills and judgment, demanding rapid decision-making, problem-solving, and vigilance in high-stress situations.
14. **Advocate for mental-health support:** Addressing mental-illness calls requires specialized training, including Crisis Intervention Teams to divert individuals to mental-health support.
15. **Follow reasonableness:** Officers navigate ethical considerations and accountability when assessing behavior and circumstances, ensuring justifiable actions in the face of public scrutiny.
16. **Master precision driving in all conditions:** Police vehicle operations require exceptional skills to manage high-risk scenarios with precision and expertise, ultimately ensuring public safety.
17. **Prioritize safe driving:** Multitasking becomes an art when officers juggle information, communication, and driving while prioritizing safety and effectiveness.
18. **Perfect reversing:** Mastering reversing techniques is vital to prevent accidents, with effective use of mirrors, back windows, and backup cameras reducing road risks.

19. **Be both positive and alert:** Officers engaged in community policing adopt a vigilant approach, fostering positive relationships with residents while remaining alert to suspicious behavior in their neighborhoods.
20. **Execute safe t-stops:** Strategic traffic stops are a cornerstone of effective policing, involving the strategic positioning of vehicles to enhance safety, maintain visibility, and ensure situational awareness during interactions with the public.

Notes

1 The Academy*, "Perishable skills program: South Bay regional public safety training." Retrieved from https://theacademy.ca.gov/event/perishable-skills-program-7/, 2022.
2 J. Rojek, Grieco, J., Meade, B. and Parsons, D., "National survey on officer safety training: Findings and implications," National Police Foundation, Washington, DC, 2020.
3 K. Lyons, Radburn, C., Orr, R. and Pope, R., "A profile of injuries sustained by law enforcement officers: A critical review," *International Journal of Environmental Research and Public Health,* vol. 14, no. 2, pp. 142–162. https://doi.org/10.3390/ijerph14020142, 2017.
4 H. Jain, Singh, P. and Agocs, C., "Recruitment, selection and promotion of visible-minority and aboriginal police officers in selected Canadian police services," *Canadian Public Administration,* vol. 43, no. 1, pp. 46–74. https://doi.org/10.1111/j.1754-7121.2000.tb015, 2000.
5 E. Marins, David, G. and Del Vecchio, F., "Characterization of the physical fitness of police officers: A systematic review," *Journal of Strength and Conditioning Research,* vol. 33, no. 10, pp. 2860–2874. https://doi.org/10.1519/JSC.0000000000003177, 2019.
6 C. Crifasi, Pollack, K. and Webster, D., "Effects of state-level policy changes on homicide and nonfatal shootings of law enforcement officers," *Injury Prevention,* vol. 22, no. 4, pp. 274–278. https://doi.org/10.1136/injuryprev-2015-041825, 2016.
7 J. Helsby, Carton, S., Joseph, K., Mahmud, A., Park, Y., Navarrete, A., Ackermann, K., Walsh, J. and Haynes, I., "Early intervention systems: Predicting adverse interactions between police and the public,"

Criminal Justice Policy Review, vol. 29, no. 2, pp. 180–209. https://doi.org/10.1177/0887403417695380, 2018.
8. C. Tomes, Orr, R. and Pope, R., "The impact of body armor on physical performance of law enforcement personnel: A systematic review," *Annals of Occupational and Environmental Medicine,* vol. 29, no. 1, p. 14. https://doi.org/10.1186/s40557-017-0169-9, 2017.
9. C. Gutshall, Hampton, D. P., Sebetan, I. M., Stein, P. C. and Broxtermann, T. J., "The effects of occupational stress on cognitive performance in police officers," *Police Practice & Research,* vol. 18, no. 5, pp. 463–477. https://doi.org/10.1080/15614263.2017.1288120, 2017.
10. M. Plat, Frings-Dresen, M. and Sluiter, J., "A systematic review of job-specific workers' health surveillance activities for fire-fighting, ambulance, police and military personnel," *International Archives of Occupational and Environmental Health,* vol. 84, no. 8, pp. 839–857. https://doi.org/10.1007/s00420-011-0614-y, 2011.
11. P. Dick, "Dirty work designations: How police officers account for their use of coercive force," *Human Relations,* vol. 58, no. 11, pp. 1363–1390. https://doi.org/10.1177/0018726705060242, 2005.
12. P. Di Nota and Huhta, J., "Complex motor learning and police training: Applied, cognitive, and clinical perspectives," *Frontiers in Psychology,* vol. 10, p. 1797. https://doi.org/10.3389/fpsyg.2019.01797, 2019.
13. J. Preddy, "Building a cognitive readiness construct for violent police-public encounters," Doctoral dissertation, Old Dominion University, 2018.
14. E. Jefferis, Butcher, F. and Hanely, D., "Measuring perceptions of police use of force," *Police Practice and Research,* vol. 12, no. 1, pp. 81–96. https://doi.org/10.1080/15614263.2010.497656, 2011.
15. T. Prenzler, Porter, L. and Alpert, G., "Reducing police use of force: Case studies and prospects," *Aggression and Violent Behavior,* vol. 18, no. 2, pp. 343–356. https://doi.org/10.1016/j.avb.2012.12.004, 2013.
16. M. Rogers, McNiel, D. and Binder, R., "Effectiveness of police crisis intervention training programs," *The Journal of the American Academy of Psychiatry and the Law,* vol. 47, no. 4, pp. 414–421. https://doi.org/10.29158/JAAPL.003863-19, 2019.
17. K. Chidgey, Procter, N., Baker, A. and Grech, C., "Police response to individuals displaying suicidal or self-harming behaviours: An integrative review," *Health & Social Care in the Community,* vol. 27, no. 3, pp. e112–e124. https://doi.org/10.1111/hsc.12668, 2019.

18 R. De Similien and A. Okorafor, "Suicide by cop: A psychiatric phenomenon," *American Journal of Psychiatry,* vol. 12, no. 1, pp. 20–22. https://doi.org/10.1176/appi.ajp-rj.2017.120107, 2017.
19 S. Bresler, Scalora, M., Elbogen, E. and Moore, Y., "Attempted suicide by cop: a case study of traumatic brain injury and the insanity defense," *Journal of Forensic Sciences,* vol. 48, no. 1, pp. 1–5. https://doi.org/10.1520/JFS2001045, 2003.
20 F. Mastison, "On target: 20 police marksman facts," *Tactical Life.* https://www.tactical-life.com/lifestyle/tactics/target-20-police-marksman-facts/, February 16, 2015.
21 C. Torres and Kim, Y., "The effects of caffeine on marksmanship accuracy and reaction time: A systematic review," *Ergonomics,* vol. 62, no. 8, pp. 1023–1032. https://doi.org/10.1080/00140139.2019.1613572, 2019.
22 K. Adams and Jennison, V., "What we do not know about police use of Tasers™," *Policing: An International Journal,* vol. 30, no. 3, pp. 447–465. https://doi.org/10.1108/13639510710778831, 2007.
23 National Law Enforcement Memorial Fund, Causes of law enforcement deaths: Over the past decade (2014-2023), 2014. Available at https://nleomf.org/memorial/facts-figures/officer-fatality-data/causes-of-law-enforcement-deaths/ Updated April 29, 2024.
24 H. Tiesman, Hendricks, S., Bell, J. and Amandus, H., "Eleven years of occupational mortality in law enforcement: The census of fatal occupational injuries, 1992-2002," *American Journal of Industrial Medicine,* vol. 53, no. 9, pp. 940–949. https://doi.org/10.1002/ajim.20863, 2010.
25 K. Wehr, Alpert, G. and Rojek, J., "The fear of the ninja assassin: Understanding the role of agency culture in injurious and fatal on-duty vehicle collisions," *Journal of California Law Enforcement,* vol. 46, no. 2, pp. 18–26, 2012.
26 H. Tiesman, Heick, R., Konda, S. and Hendricks, S., "Law enforcement officers' risk perceptions toward on-duty motor-vehicle events," *Policing,* vol. 38, no. 3, pp. 563–577. https://doi.org/10.1108/PIJPSM-03-2015-0028, 2015.

6

Technical readiness in policing

> **SPOILER ALERT**
>
> Harnessing technology and building community trust can keep streets safer.

Abstract

This chapter defines technical readiness in policing as know-how and application in the law, speaking well, writing reports, and understanding the community. This entails detailed proficiency in legal authorities, verbal and written communication, and knowledge of police service and community dynamics. As policing evolves, technical competencies become vital for managing risks and reducing crime proactively, with support from new technologies on the frontline. Enhanced articulation training fosters clear communication, facilitating de-escalation and peaceful resolutions. Emphasizing collaboration and information-sharing builds trust and effectiveness in policing efforts. However, challenges such as hate crimes and counterterrorism highlight the importance of robust mental-health support for officers. Community policing, focusing on community involvement, improves public perceptions and trust, ensuring communication stays strong. The chapter concludes with 20 strategies aimed at enhancing technical readiness in policing.

DOI: 10.4324/9781003145493-6

This chapter discusses peak performance in policing in five sections:

A. Proficiency in law
B. Verbal communication
C. Written communication
D. Knowledge of police service and community
E. 20 Key strategies for technical readiness in policing

Coach officers have defined four key performance indicator categories for assessing technical competencies. To efficiently evaluate overall technical competency in real-world scenarios, they identified specific practices for each indicator. These coach-officer performance indicators and informed practices were combined with current research findings as follows:

A. **Proficiency in law**: Has knowledge and application of local, provincial, federal laws; understands court procedures and processes; knows arrest authorities; knows and applies use of force principles; conducts effective apprehensions.
B. **Verbal communication**: Prevents conflicts; de-escalates (Tac com); exhibits good articulation; uses appropriate tone; demonstrates active listening; builds community rapport; shows effective interviewing.
C. **Written communication**: Follows systematic note-taking (according to policy); submits timely reports; completes suitable report writing (i.e., general occurrences, arrest reports, use of force reports).
D. **Knowledge of police service and community**: Understands the police service (organizational structure, reporting relationships, vision and mission); knows and complies with policies and procedures; understands community composition (geographic locations, landmarks, diversity); accesses applicable community resources.

These technical-competency markers collectively emphasize the comprehension and application of governing authorities and principles, the role of verbal and written communication, and the importance of organizational structure and community relations in modern policing.

Police organizational research accounted for 40% of current technical publications, with a focus on philosophy, policies, culture, and the impact of terrorism. This was followed by research related to community understanding (27%), the application of laws (25%), and verbal-written communication (8%). For a more detailed literature review see Appendix F: Technical Competencies in Policing.

A. Proficiency in law

Coach officers identified essential practices among a wide range of practices aimed at having a deep applied understanding of the law. These practices relate to:

1. Knowledge and application of laws
2. Court procedures
3. Arrest authorities
4. Use of force principles
5. Effective apprehensions

A deep understanding of the law is the cornerstone of effective policing. It encourages informed decision-making, professionalism, and superior job performance. Impacts of legalized cannabis for recreational use are a notable example where responding effectively requires specific knowledge and abilities[1,2]. While physical skills are important, a firm grasp of legal principles, combined with a balanced approach, is paramount. Police officers who excel in preparing for court appearances, respecting legal boundaries, and employing adaptable tactical strategies are better equipped to handle complex situations. Their ability to mediate, de-escalate, and prioritize assertive action during arrests not only ensures safety but also upholds legal standards.

Several information technologies are now integral to law enforcement, including: body-worn cameras[3,4,5,6,7], crime mapping[8,9,10,11], social media[12,13], data-mining software[14,15], car cameras[16,17], and license-plate readers[18]. Technology "adoptability appetite" depends on agency size. Computer software can forecast when and where crimes may occur, and virtual simulations can train officers in real-time decision-making[14,19].

PHOTO 6.1 Tech-savvy policing: From body cameras to crime mapping, the digital transformations of modern law enforcement. Credit: Ottawa Police Service, 2024

Adapting to legal and technological changes can be overwhelming, but accessing up-to-date resources makes it manageable. Ethical considerations like transparency and accountability are paramount.

> **Resources**—*We're responding to calls first hand, which can go in any direction. Mentally and physically we have to be at peak performance, and prepped for what's about to happen, or if something changes, we can adapt. Technically, as long as we have other resources, we don't have to have it all implanted in our brain.*
>
> —Patrol

Knowledge and application of laws

A strong grasp of the law is essential for officers to make informed, professional decisions. Balancing reasonable justification, a clear understanding of legal principles, and continuous training preserves the integrity of law enforcement. While physical fitness is important, a deep comprehension of the law and mental sharpness elevate an officer's authority and influence beyond mere physical prowess.

Knowledge of the law can be leveraged by sharing resources and learning from colleagues, valuing educational and academic resources to enhance professionalism, deriving enjoyment from legal expertise, focusing on reasonable grounds for searches, and emphasizing a solid understanding of basic offenses despite the evolving nature of the law.

> **Enforce the law**—*If the bad guy is a career bad guy, he's going to be caught somewhere down the line because I'm a career police officer. Getting the bad guy is important but not at the sacrifice of someone. My job is to use my role to enforce the law. I look at it as using my career to help people.*
> —School Resource

> **Shared resources**—*When I joined, I learned the legal aspect of being a police officer. I also learned a lot from coworkers. I will attend a call with another officer, who will make reference to a certain Section in a certain Act, and I'm thinking, "Oh my God, I did not remember that… I never underestimate my coworkers. I know that if I don't have the answer, they probably do have it.*
> —Patrol

> **Officer intellect**—*I would put a lot more emphasis on educational and academic resources, and encourage the officers to use them. I've already talked to the civilian lawyer attached to the police service. It's a matter of putting material on the intranet site, like documentation case law, interesting stories. Or on training days (everybody has an hour), "Read this excerpt from this recent case law. We're going to discuss it for the next three hours and debate about it" or something. Professionalism, you have to be thinking about it all the time. You have to keep up with current developments.*
> —Neighborhood Resource

> **Knowledge is fun**—*Knowledge of the law is so incredibly important. If you know all your authorities… Are you aware that I could probably arrest you for something right now? Seriously,*

if I had to, I could find something... Knowledge is FUN out there. Someone says, "You can't do this!" Well, "Guess what? Yeah, I can." You won't find me making false arrests. It's just so much fun when you know.

—Patrol

Reasonable grounds—*People overcomplicate this job. I've never had difficulty searching vehicles or people. I never think, "What if this person complains?" If I have reasonable grounds that apply to an actual Section of the Criminal Code, that gives me the authority to apply the legislation.*

—Patrol

Basic offenses—*Not everyone's going to know everything about the law. The law changes so you can't be always be all-knowing. But you have got to know what the facts in issue are for basic offenses—for trespass to property, liquor license acts, impaireds, assaults, and domestics. You have to know what you're doing with the Landlord & Tenant, traffic stops, speeding, and red lights. You have to know the basics of what you're doing.*

—School Resource

Court procedures

Court appearances can involve rigorous scrutiny of an officer's actions and decisions. Insufficient legal understanding while testifying can be embarrassing, but officers can mitigate stress with meticulous preparation. To maximize efficiency, officers prepare their notes, read case reports, and collaborate with colleagues and schools in investigations. Submitting reports in advance, reviewing them multiple times, and ensuring full preparedness for court proceedings eases stress, boosts confidence, and guarantees all essential documents are readily available. Officers stress the significance of learning from court experiences, despite potential challenges.

Court appearance strategies

Officers are divided on whether or not court appearances are a stressor to performance (47% report it as a stressor). Regardless, most (72%) have a plan going into court, taking the responsibility seriously in thoroughly preparing before having to potentially testify. It is also recognized that "the system" does not allow for control so it is not worth becoming aggravated. Some officers expressed simply that "it's a game," an opportunity for overtime pay, or a social event with other officers. Refocusing strategies for court are influenced primarily by education. All officers with college education, most with university, and significantly less with high school only use refocusing strategies for court appearances (100, 94, and 75%, $p = 0.081$, respectively). Most officers with frontline-only experience also use these strategies more frequently (96%, $p = 0.084$) than those with training beyond frontline. Table 6.1 provides details on court appearance strategies.

TABLE 6.1 Court Appearance Strategies

	TOTAL RESPONSES Ranked by %
Court appearance block	47
Court appearance strategies	72
Prepare: anticipate, duty book entries, reports represent you, track, thorough, timely	
Focus: listen, take your time, honesty	
Accept: "it's a game," low anxiety, all relative, can't win	
Good money	
Win: a challenge, closure to justice	
Social: opportunity to socialize, network with other officers	

Accept, calm—*Once, I realized the defense had got me saying "I don't know." As soon as you say "I don't know," then all of a sudden, it's boom-boom-boom. Now the judge is looking at what you just said five minutes ago. Don't get rattled. Be calm. Take your time. Know that [the defense] will try to do this and just let it roll off you.*

—Tactical

Opportunity—*Court is your chance to bring some life to it. A Crown Attorney told me, a policeman is the best witness because we can quantify and qualify every- thing. The average person doesn't necessarily have the attention to detail but* it's expected of us. If you can break it down and put it in detail when you're talking to a Justice of the Peace, he'll turn around and look at you. He knows that everything he's heard from everybody else is probably 50% true, whereas what he gets from you is from a statement made at the time.

—Neighborhood Resource

Court: Winning—*There's a certain methodology to it. You've done all this work to do something, it gets to court and sure enough the fruits of your efforts are realized.*

—5 to 10 years on

Reward—*You know what puts me in a good mood for work? When I sign on for email and there are court subpoenas waiting from an arrest I made. Now I've got paid court appearances and I'm going to get a little extra for working hard. That gives me incentive to go out and do it again.*

—Canine

Get the experience—*I do what I can with what I've got. The training I've got, the experience I've got. Am I happy that something goes to court and it's tossed out? No. Did I learn from that experience as to maybe a piece of evidence that I missed or didn't say the right thing in court? Yes. But oh well. You learn from that experience. Hopefully it's not going to be at a murder level.*

—Neighborhood Resource

The admin—*After I make the arrests, when I got them all done, no problem [snaps fingers]! Now I've got to fight with that computer to get my court folder done. It's not a quick clear-off on the page. But the bottom line is that these guys needed to get charged. Dealing with people and that kind of thing, no problem, but the paperwork, and dotting the i's… [laughs and sighs].*

—School Resource

Visualize notes—*I feel confident with court appearances. I feel confident with the notes I take and my recollection of situations based on my notes. I review my notes. I'll dig up all the paperwork I need… Skim through the first time, and then the second day leading up to the court appearance. A whole week* *ahead of time I'll go over it. Then I'll visualize what the situation was at the time.*

—Neighborhood Resource

Stressful critique—*I take them seriously. It can be stressful because you can see a court appearance as a critique of how you did. They're looking at everything you did at that time. You may have felt confident when it happened but they'll see how sure you really are. Court situations can be stressful.*

—Patrol

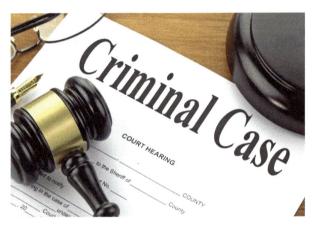

PHOTO 6.2 Facing the bench: Officers undergo rigorous preparation for court appearances. Credit: Nick Youngson, Picdedia, Bing, 2024

Preparation—*I don't find court overly stressful. You need to do a good job in your preparation and your note taking. The way you write your notes at the time, paying attention to detail, knowing what you have to write. Lawyers are going to be SOB's, and try to get under your skin. I look at them and say, "I've had worse guys, try to get under my skin, you're not going to win." Everything is methodical. If you're dealing with this type of a case or this type of a call, you know that in court you're going to have to say that I saw these bruises… You have to read your reports and know them inside out.*

—Patrol

Breath-tech savvy—*As a breath-tech, I used to do a lot of court. I was prepared. I had a mental checklist and a physical checklist—and I made sure that I had everything checked off. I would go over each case—I wouldn't just show up. I would have gone over it a few dozen times before.*
—Tactical

Arrest authorities

Officers are entrusted with the responsibility and authority to ensure public safety and maintain peace. Depriving someone of freedom demands intelligence, professionalism, adaptability, effective communication, and a strong knowledge base for handling diverse individuals and complex situations. Treating people with respect and empathy, even in difficult scenarios, often yields better results than relying solely on authority. Technical preparedness, confidence, and focus are vital for making sound on-the-spot decisions. Confidence is gained by knowing authorities, feeling valued, trusted, and mandated to do your job. However, it is crucial to manage the unique experience and confidence gained from policing appropriately to avoid impacting their personal relationships.

Paid to win—*You're taking somebody's freedom away from them. It doesn't sit well with people and you can't blame them. And if there's a physical confrontation—I'm not losing. I don't get paid to lose… We're here for the public peace and public security. If we drop the ball, everybody knows.*
—Neighborhood Resource

Authority—*We had all of our less-lethal munitions with us now. We're prepared to use it, we've been given authority to use it, and we know how to use it. The only problem, now we're going down into the basement—to the unknown. The troops were committed in the same thought process as me, "Let's get the hell down there and get this guy. Let's get it over with."*
—Tactical

Job functionality—*When you pull someone over, you need to know what your authorities and definitions for motor vehicle* *and vehicle are in the Criminal Code, which differs from the Highway Traffic Act. These are the basic things for basic job functionality. If you end up making a stupid decision because you neglected to learn what you're supposed to know, you could open yourself up to a lawsuit for overstepping your bounds. But you don't necessarily have to know all aspects of traffic. If you pull somebody over and you want to check their tires, you can always leaf through the book and say, "OK, bald tires are this, this, this, this." Does it match? The vehicle's already stopped. I know my authority.*

—Traffic Escort

Authorities—*Gain confidence by: knowing authorities, and knowing you are valued, trusted, and mandated to do your job. Along with authority comes responsibilities.*

—Police Executive

PHOTO 6.3 Every police arrest requires intelligence, professionalism, adaptability, and confident authority. Credit: Ottawa Police Service, 2024

Uncertainty—*I always like to do traffic stops. I stopped this guy who was a big muscle, steroid biker enforcer, and I stopped this guy for a misuse of plates. He drove it up on private property. He got off the bike and said, "You can't do anything, it's on private property." I was uncertain of my authority. I was pretty sure that it was arrestable, even on private property, which it* *turns out it was. But I didn't know at the time—I knew, but I wasn't positive. It was a lack of knowledge.*

—Neighborhood Resource

Comfort with authorities—*The job, like any job, will change you. Especially when you give someone a job where you carry a gun and you have the authority to take people off the street, chain them up and throw them in a cage. After you've done that a few times, the first few times you're all nervous, but then when you realize you're doing it properly and you're doing it right, now you start to develop a lot more confidence when you're dealing with people.*

—Patrol

Use of force principles

Tactical law enforcement relies on adaptability, diverse skills, and continuous learning for handling dynamic situations such as sensitive domestic calls and providing security at high-profile events. Officers prioritize containment in dealing with armed individuals but may face the frustration of downtime when awaiting higher-level decisions. This underscores the importance of policy adherence, unit coordination, preparation, and proactive incident prevention through community engagement. The ability to envision various scenarios is crucial, particularly for drug-related and high-risk calls. Effective cooperation between Tactical and Patrol officers, along with ongoing, realistic, and rigorous training and leadership development, is vital for confronting extraordinary crises.

Standards—*We don't stand back and let people get hurt but we have policies and procedures to follow. If we hear, "Put the gun down," we're going to back away and wait for Tactical—that's their job. That's our policy. If you don't follow policy, you'll end up getting hurt and causing a bigger situation that won't help anyone.*

—Patrol

Assessment—*Depending on what type of call it is, never walk into a call alone. I don't care how big a cop you are or how good* *a fighter you are, it just takes one bullet to take down any size person. If it's a high priority call—it could be threats of violence, weapons involved. You assess it right at the beginning. "Well buddy, the man said he had a gun. We're not going to walk into that alley. It's got to be Tactical that takes it. We're going to set them a perimeter, hold the perimeter and they're going to do their job." That's what it's all about.*

—Patrol

Training confidence—*Technical, I knew that I've trained for these situations. I'm not going into something where I don't have a plan or idea what I'm doing. I was proficient with the equipment I had.*

—Tactical

Justification—*Whether you do something physical to a person, or you lip off, you have to justify doing what you're doing. You can't go whacking guys for no reason, or shouting and screaming at people. Somebody called two people "retards" who were probably mentally challenged. He lost 3 days pay for it. How do you justify saying something like that? You can't. If I do something, I'm going to be justified in doing what I'm doing. You have to know how to handle the situation.*

—Canine

Training versus real—*The training at the Police College, "What am I going to do if a guy comes with a gun?" Right now, who knows? But once you've gone through the training, you have a gun, you have pepper spray, you have an asp, you have tactical communication. You'd surprise yourself at what you could do.*

—Female School Resource

Anticipate—*I looked at my partner and my partner looked at me and we said, "We may have to kill somebody tonight." That was a look that we both acknowledged and knew that once we heard that, we were thinking, "OK, what do we have to do, what are we going to do, where are we going to be?"*

—Tactical

Back-up—*I'll read the call to try to give me more details as to what's going on. The first time I read the call, if I hear that there's a weapon involved, I WANT Tactical to be there as well. And if there's a weapon involved, I'll WAIT for Tactical. If there's not a weapon involved, then I can take a patrol officer with me. We can enter.*

—Canine

Harder training—*I would make the training hard (harder than what it is now), more realistic at all levels. There doesn't seem to be very much past at any rank level. There's no structured, formal leadership training. There are leaders on the road now responsible for evacuation. Think of the complexity of the situation of: containing; dealing with casualty evacuations; controlling the additional resources that you need… and just trying to contain it all—you don't get touched by a magic wand. You don't get anointed as soon as that breaks out and become an effective leader. You have to be trained.*

—Neighborhood Resource

Effective apprehensions

Prioritizing assertive action in arrests is crucial to mitigate risks and avoid hesitation. Officers can mediate effectively, utilizing empathetic communication to potentially prevent charges. Successful arrests involve maintaining control, following procedures, and using handcuffs as a precaution. Ensuring police searches adhere to legal rights is imperative, and seeking backup in confrontational situations is prudent. Post-arrest, de-escalation becomes essential for safety and resolution, encompassing various tactics such as assessing aggression, controlling personal space, calmly explaining procedures, and emphasizing communication to effect positive change.

Settling down—*He was sitting out in the office and he was being physically aggressive. He wasn't in my face or anything but you could tell that he was a little unpredictable. So I put him in handcuffs and I arrested him for the assault, because I had the grounds to do so. Afterwards, once he settled down in*

his seat and you know he's not endangering himself or anybody else, that's when you can start bringing things down a little bit.
—School Resource

Space and authority—*You're not allowed in my space, you can't get in closer than that. So if you are going to hurt me, all you're going to do is hurt my leg. If you move over here, I can go over here. And then if you invade my space, I'm going to get you out of my space. If you're not going to listen, then I'm going to take charge of the scene. I give you very little time to do it my way. If I'm going to arrest you, you have probably 3 seconds, and then I'm going to take you forcibly, take you under control. I've done this for 25 years. I've never been hurt on the job.*
—Canine

Explain and wait—*There was no, "Shut up, listen to me, do what I say." Her ranting and raving does not hurt me physically and if it means that she's depleting her energy by doing this, then fine. "This is what I'm doing with you. I'm reading you your rights. You're under arrest. We're waiting for a patrol car. You're going be transported… By the time she got into the cruiser, I said, "Okay, you're ready to go. You're going downtown now and you're being charged." She said "Yeah, yeah, all right."*
—Neighborhood Resource

Our procedures—*One kid asked me if police officers are allowed to walk up, throw you on the hood of a car and search you. I told him what our procedure is and what I would do in that situation but that I can't comment on what somebody else did because I wasn't there. He said, "Oh, my friend said the police did that and that and that." I said, "Were you there?" He said, "No, but my friend said." I said, "Well, I'm thinking maybe there were a couple more little details. You should have been there to make a full commentary."*
—Female School Resource

Compliance—*Hopefully you've got the experience that says, "Hmmm, I'm not going to tell Stupid (even though I think he's stupid) that he's under arrest. We're going to talk and I'm going to calm down the situation and then he's going to be a little more* *compliant to being arrested because of the fact that you're talking to him and you're explaining to him."*

—Neighborhood Resource

Change approach—*I don't know how many times we get calls, and then by the end of the call the guy says, "Look, I don't want the guy arrested, I don't want the guy charged, but maybe you could just talk to him." Sometimes that's all they need… Sometimes we can make a difference. I've spoken to some guys after I've arrested them four or five times, that have changed their lives.*

—Patrol

B. Verbal communication

Coach officers identified critical practices aimed at proficient verbal communication. These practices relate to:

1. Prevention of conflicts and de-escalation (Tac com)
2. Good articulation and appropriate tone
3. Active listening
4. Community rapport and humor
5. Effective interviewing

Skillfully navigating confrontations is vital, particularly for rookies, in order to defuse volatile situations and establish connections and rapport. Officers must adapt and justify their communication styles for various scenarios, a practice recognized to be the most important for new recruits in good policing. Similarly, Special Constables, serving in roles such as court security and temporary custody, heavily rely on communication as their primary tool, given their limited personal protective equipment[20].

Effective interviewing remains a crucial verbal skill. Practicing active listening and giving individuals the opportunity to express themselves are essential for gathering information and preventing public complaints. Police must debunk misinformation while striving to maintain public trust and transparency, especially when dealing with youth.

Resources like de-escalation case studies[21] and *Police Talk: A Scenario-Based Communications Workbook for Police Recruits and Officers*[22,23] demonstrate effective and ineffective dialogue. This refined communication improves officer safety, interview skills, note-taking, conflict resolution, assertiveness, and sensitivity during calls related to domestic violence, sexual harassment, or disabilities.

Prevention of conflicts and de-escalation (Tac com)

A well-calibrated verbal approach can initiate open communication, even in dangerous encounters, facilitating de-escalation while waiting for backup. This is crucial for rookies building confidence addressing the public in uniform. Effective verbal communication balances passive control, allowing individuals to express themselves, and active control while avoiding a heavy-handed approach (Tac com). Maintaining a calm voice, and employing consistent tones, officers prevent conflicts and effectively de-escalate situations. Learning from officers with strong verbal skills is invaluable for training and teamwork, as even experienced officers acknowledge the need for self-control.

> **Passive control**—*I've seen the way rookies talk to people. They don't allow people an opportunity to talk. They come in doing what they're told—control, control—but they haven't learned that there's "passive control" and "active control." You can control a situation by stepping back, allowing the person to talk, vent or whatever, and then dealing with the situation with some compassion or sense of duty… Once it's done, you can deescalate back to normal, loosen up to a normal tone of voice.*
> —Traffic Escort

> **Voice control**—*A calm voice calms people down, and it calms me down as well. Once you start yelling and screaming, you're making yourself panic and you're not controlling the situation. More often than not, you don't get the results you would like. Other times, you may not get results by remaining calm but I feel much more in control when I keep a lower tone and a calm voice. It's also better for other officers who are either around*

or listening to what's going on over the radio. Remaining calm serves a purpose for the situation, for you and for your fellow officers.

—Patrol

Hand-off—Probably about the sixth or seventh car—the worst offender of the day. I mean, she just went right through and didn't even slow down. And she was yelling, "I have kids! I have a baby seat. I would never do this! I'm a Mom! Blah, blah, blah!"… I lost my cool and I wasn't happy that I was starting to get upset with her. My partner actually at one point stepped in and started talking to her. That seemed to calm her down, instead of dealing with me. So, I felt slighted. I wasn't mad at him or anything, I was just mad at the situation. Here I am putting in all this effort and she's talking to you and to me she's so abusive.

—Traffic Escort

Consistent tone—When I was coming into this world and I wanted to know exactly what to do and how to do it, I can reflect and remember conversations I've had with two officers. One was a massive man, but calm, soft-spoken and well mannered. He got the job done, all the time. The other guy I only rode with for two weeks. The tone of his voice never changed. He could be mad, he could be whatever—it never changed. He would lull people into handcuffs and I learned from him. I learned that if you talk a certain way and use certain words, you can get people to cooperate.

— Neighborhood Resource

Credibility—Word for word I told them what happened at the meeting and then I said, "I know you're a Staff Sergeant and you outrank me, but you have a responsibility to us and to the calls…" I said, "We're speaking right now frankly…" I guess the way I worded it, he didn't take it as an insult. He saw that I was heated because of the situation, and I was glad, because he put the wheels in motion to address it… I guess that's the one thing that always gets more credibility, is the accuracy of what you're saying. Sometimes we'll embellish but there's times *when you have to know that you have to put down exactly what somebody said.*

—Neighborhood Resource

Respect before reaction—*For the amount of situations I've been in, I've been in very few physical altercations. First of all, I believe that everyone meets their match out there—I don't care how big you are, how smart you are. And second, that everyone deserves respect—everybody—until they set their own course. Then I can do what I have to do to get a successful conclusion.*

—>10 years on

Good articulation and appropriate tone

An officer's ability to modulate tone and convey urgency is pivotal in asserting authority and commanding suspects. Equally, maintaining a composed voice and choosing words carefully can serve as a valuable conversational tactic in dealing with distressed individuals, reducing the need for force. Effective communication involves using appropriate language and adapting styles that resonate in the specific scenarios, be it irate individuals, suspects, or crowds. Professionalism relies on clear, respectful, and justifiable communication strategies. Using an assertive yet serious tone proves effective in situations requiring immediate compliance, and as an alternative to resorting to force.

Radio voice—*It's funny—it makes me laugh even thinking about it—but the last couple of times I followed a stolen car, I grabbed the radio and felt my heart race. I was right behind it, and thinking, "Great! This is going to be fun!" But I was also thinking, "OK, time to get going here." I find myself taking a deep breath before I make that first transmission on the radio… The more excited you get, the more garbled it's going to be and that's not going to help the people in the area who are listening to the radio.*

—Canine

Respect—*It's just the way I talk to them. Instead of talking to them like they're sitting down and I'm standing up. I'm not yelling at them, I'm not saying anything rude. If you give somebody* *a ticket, and you say "Have a nice day," that's being condescending. I just say "Drive safe." I always have the same routine… I don't just get their documents, go back, write up the ticket, come back, present it, and say "It's a fine for this amount." "You went through this and you didn't stop." "Yes, I did." Well you know what, I'm not going to argue with you. You have your options on the back… It's tone of voice—not being rude to them.*

—Traffic Escort

Breathe—*I don't like panickers. When you talk on the air, nobody wants to hear panic in your voice because no one gets paid to panic. Take a deep breath and drop your voice one octave, and talk in a deep voice. Take the panic out of your voice. People will remember that.*

—Patrol

Tone, wording—*Negotiations by email are almost a "no-win situation." Negotiators look for tone of voice and the actual words used. When you do it by computer, it doesn't work.*

—Tactical Sergeant

Angry voice—*"Police! Drop the knife!"… then I leaned in. The first time, it wasn't a real yell. It was to get his attention. "You're going to get shot." And the second time was like, "I'm going to shoot you if you don't do it." He knew that I would. I just said in a more serious tone, [angry voice] "Drop the knife."*

—Patrol

Track record—*I've worked a rural area, downtown, and stuff where you're not frontline like Ident, Fraud, C.I.D. I use my verbal diarrhea, and talk my way out of situations as opposed to use of force. It doesn't always work, but in 19 years, I've never had to use my pepper spray, I've never had to use my baton, and the only time I've ever had to draw my firearm to shoot is for animals.*

—Patrol

Active listening

Active listening is indispensable in law enforcement training, enabling officers to gather essential information in high-stress situations. It helps prioritize data, shift attention from laptops to dispatcher updates, and capture critical details. It becomes a learned listening skill in discerning important information and filtering out irrelevant details. Listening and allowing individuals to express themselves can avert public complaints. During extended operations, officers must listen for changes when negotiators take over. In leadership roles, attentive listening emphasizes mutual respect, feedback, and situational awareness, serving as a sign of accumulated experience. Accepting feedback fosters a culture of continuous improvement, demonstrating a willingness to listen to constructive criticism, even from younger colleagues. Ultimately, listening and heeding one's inner voice and instincts is vital for self-awareness in assessing situations.

> **Show leadership**—*Have respect for the members. Show them how to do it. Be a leader and keep your cool, don't blow it, and listen. Be able to listen to other people, regardless of their sex, regardless of their seniority.*
> —Traffic Escort

> **Others' opinion**—*I love listening to other people's opinion on some things. If I screw up, I want you to say, "You f---ed up." "Okay. I did, I know I did." I'm my biggest critic. I listen, no matter who it is. Some guys are good. Some young kids call us in.*
> —Traffic Escort

> **Talk their language**—*I usually let the person vent, because they are going to stop sooner or later. Then they are going to realize what the heck they just said. And then you say, "Are you done? Why am I a f---ing a--hole? Why would you say something like that? You know, because right now you are the f---ing a--hole." It will depend a lot on who you are dealing with. If you're dealing with somebody who might want to kill you, and he's calling you that, then sometimes you have to lower yourself to his level, and talk his language. And THEN you start working on the communication. You say, "All right, this is what I can do for you, da da da da da."*
> —Patrol

Learned listening—*You're always listening on the radio to different calls to hear what's going on, whether it's a break-in in progress, a shooting, an accident with injuries, a fight, or if another officer needs assistance. It's a multitude of things you learn to listen for. There's other stuff that you dial out—it's a learning thing over the years. You read between the lines or what could potentially happen, or what MIGHT happen.*
—Patrol

Self-awareness—*Telling yourself the truth is important. Take the time to analyze the energy within you and listen to that small voice. It makes a big difference in how you assess the situation. There's the book aspect and the technical aspect that we all learn, but there's energy in us that we have to just stop and listen to sometimes and acknowledge.*
—Neighborhood Resource

Community rapport and humor

In developing community policing, clear and empathetic communication strengthens ties and promotes a peaceful coexistence. Transparency is especially compelling with youth, as explaining consequences can deter risky behavior. Engaging children in interactive activities like handcuffing demonstrations reduces fear and builds trust. Casual interactions, like participating in creative activities with kids or responding spontaneously to public requests, contribute to positive community perceptions and mutual respect. Experienced officers pre-empt confrontations with effective communication and collaborative decision-making, drawing insights from regular community engagement. Even in the aftermath of physical altercations, maintaining an open dialogue while asserting authority can further trust and respect.

Debunking misinformation has become a societal obsession, evident in tools like fact-checking websites, social media fact-checking chatbots, computational propaganda detection, and technology to spot fake news[24,25,26]. Effective policing necessitates a proactive, balanced approach in questioning information while placing trust in reliable sources, to avoid simply doubting everything.

Building community rapport involves honing the ability to read people and situations, cultivating insights that improve preparedness. Maintaining a zero-tolerance stance for disrespect sends a clear message about the standards officers uphold. The essence of community policing lies in a proactive and respectful approach, fostering understanding and cooperation between officers and the public[27,28].

External communication

About half of the officers (51%) highlighted the importance of communicating and coordinating with external specialists (e.g., Fire, Paramedics, Housing, Aid Society, Public Health), public bystanders, and witnesses during the preparation phase. Further substantiation for this step comes from elite officers who list external communication as a significant preparation activity (85%; $p = 0.001$) more than the other officers. It is also valued more by female officers (73%, $p = 0.044$) and those from the Neighborhood Resource Team (NRT) and School Resource Officer specialty units (75%, $p = 0.065$). Officers with only patrol experience are less likely to identify external communication (20%, $p = 0.068$).

> **Human lie detectors**—*I know guys that spent 20 years on the street. It's where you learn how to do police work. We're walking talking lie detectors. Somebody say something to me and gives me a name. I'll just look at my partner, "You're kidding me, right? That's not your name."... The more contact I have with people on the street, the better feel you have, the better prepared you will be to taking care of calls, setting up a containment, dealing with unruly crowds and assaults of a serious nature, taking care of crime scenes.*
> —Neighborhood Resource

> **Stop and talk**—*It could be a hooker with AIDS, I always try to give the person the respect they deserve. I start off very fair at the beginning. The junkies learned that I was okay and not the big tough jerk. I would just stop and talk to them.*
> —School Resource

Disrespect—*I've passed three young teenagers walking on the sidewalk. As I drive by and they think I'm not looking anymore, they give me the finger. I will do a U-turn in traffic, and park halfway up on the sidewalk, and have a word with them. That's how little tolerance I have for that. I will ask for identity, and take their names down. I won't probably do anything or write a report, but I'm going to remind them that not every officer will tolerate that and that they have to be very careful about when and where they decide to do this. Some officers do say, "Whatever." I'm not at that point in my life or in my career where I turn and walk away. To me it's uncalled-for disrespect. Hopefully next time, the little light will come one before he does or says something.*

—Patrol

Creativity—*If you're not creative when you're working with kids, you're killing yourself. Working in the neighborhood with more hard-core clientele. Some of them have noticed their Dad or Mom being arrested by police. So, I also have to take that image away. If I just go in there and be a bad cop, no. I go in there on good days too. I go bowling, shoot basketball, and play bingo with them in the schools. There's a pajama day, I don't care, I go in pajamas. You have to be creative so the kids see through the uniform. I think that's one reason why I'm respected. I do my job and share what I've done with others.*

—School Resource

Impromptu responses—*I'm in the public and in uniform. They expect a certain level of service from me. So it's that "I want to do a good job" thing that kicks back in. What triggers it for me is past experience where I HAVEN'T done that, and something bad has happened or something not bad has happened. It's like, "I'm enjoying this conversation but you know what? I'll get back to you. I'm going to do this right now." It just pulls me, boom, and I go do it—just from knowing exactly what COULD happen.*

—School Resource

Comfort level—*I listen to colleagues. I show a lot of respect, even to a high-ranking officer, a bunch of rookies, young guys*

> *or whoever—even the public. I show a lot of respect when I go one-on-one. I'll treat higher-ranking Officers, even joking wise and teasing the same. I'm comfortable with everybody.*
> —Traffic Escort

> **Dedication, networking**—*At a community meeting you're going to find out that neighbors know what's happening in their area. You might find out about a crack house that hasn't appeared on the radar screen yet. Listen to the public. Cops who used to walk the beat could hear the public talking.*
> —Neighborhood Resource

> **External network**—*If I don't have the answer, I know where to find it. I've worked hard to maintain solid working relationships with the people that I work with, my stakeholders—people that I trust. In the event I need an answer, I can call them and get a solid, straight-up answer.*
> —Patrol, >10 years on

Effective interviewing

Credibility is foundational in policing, influencing interviews, and trust-building within the community. Successful interviewing demands persistence and a strategic, empathetic approach, emphasizing officer safety and comprehensive training to avoid common errors. Expanding the scope of effective interviews can include providing emotional support and comfort. Overcoming communication hurdles and employing strategic methods, such as guiding individuals beyond denial, are crucial for constructive interviews. Establishing credibility in initial interactions allows officers to swiftly build rapport and encourage open discussions. Integrating physical and investigative skills aids in successful apprehensions.

> **Perseverance**—*There are a lot of hurdles. It's work-in-progress. I've been to interviews where I just couldn't veer the people around. I just couldn't. You've got to keep on trying. Hopefully, you ultimately get to your goal. "I'm not consuming" and denial, at one point you put their back against the wall. You've got so much ammo that you keep on bombarding them…*

Technical readiness in policing ■ 195

PHOTO 6.4A-C Strategic conversations infused with credibility, persistence, and empathy lay the groundwork for trust in policing from the first seconds of an interview. Credit: Anna Collins, Femanin, Bing, 2023; Pexels, Bing, 2024; Ed Vulliamy, The Guardian, Bing, 2015

"How do you pay for your dope?" If you start an interview by telling someone that they're a stripper or they're going to become a prostitute, you're going to get a slap in the face and that's going to be the end of the interview. I probably mentioned those words 40 times in the interview. I didn't get a single slap in the face. She disagreed, she strongly disagreed on some of the things, but at least it was constructive. It was because I brought her to the hurdle, and brought some ladders to get over it. I showed her—this is what I've got.

—School Resource

Credibility—*Credibility can be established in the square root of one second—how you present yourself. I think that particular day my credibility did help me. She wasn't very happy when she saw me. Her first words were "Holy sh--. What are the cops doing here?" Then I stepped down and I said, "There are things we need to discuss." We went downstairs and we started the interview process.*

—School Resource

Combined skills—*I like the physical skills, then, apply that to investigation—knowledge, interview skills, and stuff like that to catch the bad guy. That's a good job. You know you've helped out someone to get that bad guy—the one who is breaking into that house and, "Got him!" But everybody is happiest when you can see the patrol guys made the good scoop.*

—Tactical

C. Written communication

Coach officers identified critical practices aimed at proficient written communication. These practices relate to:

1 Systematic note-taking (according to policy)
2 Timely reports
3 Suitable reports (General occurrences, Arrest, Use of force)

Efficient police written communication relies on judicious note-taking, balancing capturing key details and avoiding excess during active situations. Notes form the basis for clear, transparent incident narratives, aiding rapport-building, court preparation, and addressing public complaints[22]. Crafting a standout police report, a symbol of professionalism, requires meticulous detail. The challenge is submitting comprehensive reports promptly amid multiple job demands.

> **Observe and remember**—*There's this thing where they have to write everything in a notebook while the situation is still going on. Instead of observing what's going on and getting it up here in your head, they flip open a notebook. It's a safety concern.*
>
> —Patrol, <5 years on

Systematic note-taking

Efficient note-taking, according to policy, involves promptly documenting essential details, particularly after significant events, avoiding excessive note-taking during active situations, which can be counterproductive and pose safety concerns. Maintaining situational awareness while writing is achieved by periodically scanning and staying vigilant. Prioritizing crucial details contributes to incident narratives and relevant background information. Consistency between notes and reports is vital. Maintaining notes supports officers in tactical situations and court testimonies, serving as an aid in rapport-building. Detailed notes uphold transparency and accountability. Even if specific notes are not admissible in court, capturing context and demeanor is essential. Some officers create cheat sheets in their duty books for swift reference in specific scenarios. In traffic stops, officers use the actual ticket to document their account of any perceived potential disputes.

> **Notes versus reports**—*[Laughs] My reports are VERY detailed. My note-taking is actually not that good. I learned old-school where you do your notes, but don't write your report in the notebook. Let's say you put "on" instead of "the" in the report, they're going to compare it to your notebook. I say to my recruits, "Notes, notes, notes, notes, notes." I want to teach best practice. The report should be extremely detailed. If you write in your notes, "grey car," and start your report and write "beige car," it's just a little variation but, "Uh, officer, was it grey or was it beige?" If you say, "I'm not sure, maybe in between," they just have a field day. Put your basic, vital information in your notes and then do your report as soon as possible. If you are not able to do your report right away, then put as much detail as possible in your notes. Keep it simple in the notebook. You can question me on my report. It just makes life easier.*
>
> —Patrol

> **Note-taking safety**—*Recruits have this thing where they have to write everything in a notebook. Instead of observing what's going on and getting it up here in your head, they flip open a notebook. They're writing while the situation is still going on. It's a safety concern.*
>
> —Patrol, <5 years on

> **Scanning habits**—*The tendency of a lot of officers is to be buried in their duty book, writing and writing, and they don't have a clue what's going on out there now. Every couple of words, look up. Keep scanning, just like you're driving a car. As you're walking back to your cruiser, same thing. Give a look back to make sure that this guy's not getting out of his car, or*

pointing a hand gun at you. Get in your car, start writing your notes. Sometimes I'll write, and not even look at the page.

—Patrol

Cheat sheet—*When I first came out as a Supervisor on the road, I made a little cheat sheet—like Cole's Notes right in my duty book. "If I get a major crime, what are the six things I have to do immediately: Set up containment, call Duty Inspectors, set up Command Post, etc."*

—Patrol Sergeant

Ticket notes—*If somebody at a traffic stop said that I was rude with them, if I did make a specific comment, I usually write it down on my ticket. I'll give the court a photocopy of my notes. I'll indicate this is what happened. "OK, if that's rude. So be it." I have only had three or four over the years.*

—Traffic Escort

Evidence—*I've learned in court: it's not about the truth, it is not about justice, it's just, present the evidence… Catch-22. It doesn't matter what you write in your notebook, you write a certain phrase there, or change a word in your report, oh my God! "It's the same thing!" "No, it's not." All of a sudden, you're being criticized… I always kick myself in the butt, "I should have said this, or said it this way, or I didn't come across correctly." But I don't worry about it. I prepare, I go through my notes and my reports. I don't read anybody else's report, because I don't want their information to influence mine. "Where did I get that?" I'm a note-taker. If I don't know, I don't know or don't remember.*

—Patrol

Testimony notes—*You make good notes as to the attitude of the person. What specifically was said… I can't say, "And Your Worship, the driver told me that I was an 'f-ing idiot' and that 'why don't I go stick it up my hat.'" But I will say, "And Your Worship, the driver gave me a specific quote that day as to what I could do with my…" So I can't say it verbatim but I can give him a general idea as to what he said.*

—Traffic Escort

Timely reports

Timely report submissions can be challenging due to competing demands. Law enforcement uses electronic autofill features and text options for quick data entry to expedite report writing, enhance efficiency, and maintain consistency, but excessive reliance can oversimplify complex cases. Nonetheless, there is often still a need to repeatedly re-enter basic information. Striking a balance is crucial to preserve report integrity. Collaborative efforts, such as delegating initial investigations to schools, streamline reporting processes and enhance efficiency. However, completing an internal group file can become frustrating when team members fail to meet standards, affecting the submission for court or program purposes.

Officers prioritize timely completion of notes and reports during downtime, ensuring accuracy and aiding memory retention. A well-crafted report minimizes court appearances, fostering a reputation for consistency and reliability. The balance between working efficiently and maintaining comprehensive documentation is highlighted, emphasizing the need for practical approaches like settling issues on the spot when appropriate. However, officers express frustration with administrative requests that seem redundant, labeling them as time-wasters and hindrances.

> **School reports**—*I ask the schools to do as much of the initial investigation as they can… I'll ask them to take statements and write everything out for me. When I get there, everything's together and then we work together. That way it's a good report, saves time for us and it takes less time to get it down. You work in partnership to make the school safer and it's a good way of dealing with things on both sides.*
> — >15 years on

> **Note completion**—*During the downtime, I catch up. Notes, reports, and stuff like that. After a call, I'll do my notes unless I get an emergency call, and then I'll have to go back to it. I rarely leave my notes 'til another time, if ever.*
> —Patrol

Less court time—*I take pride in the fact that I have had a number of officers say, "Do you know why you don't go to court that much? Because you write a good report." There's no ambiguity, you're not contradicting yourself anywhere in the report. You said the same thing at the beginning as you did at the end. You presented your information, your observations, and what conclusions that you drew from that. I'd rather be known as an officer who does a good report. Defense lawyers don't want me to come to court because you're not going to help this case any. Rather than "Hi, my name's Officer Bob, I go to court all the time because defense lawyers love talking to me!"*

—Neighborhood Resource

Ways and Means Act—*It's nice to work with the young kids. They've got some good ideas too. But the older guys can show them some shortcuts—The Ways & Means Act... With a lot of the younger ones now, it's out comes the notebook and they make a report. But WHY should you make a report if you can settle it on the spot? A lot of people stop communicating with the public because they're busy doing their reports. Some will say, "Geez, I thought I was going to have to make a report. I'm going to have to remember how you did that!"*

—Patrol

Time waster—*We are constantly being sent messages and requests for administrative things that are not always consistent. I got this request to create a civilian witness list as to what that civilian has contributed. It's in three independent places in the report and I still have a critique saying, "Could you please create a civilian witness list."—some abstract computer creation on that file. This is surreptitious—just ridiculous. This is the kind of stuff that I hate. It just adds to the extra time.*

—Neighborhood Resource

Group files—*If I take the sweep, there's a lot of things that go into making, creating and completing a file. A problem I would have is if somebody else wouldn't submit what they're supposed to submit (like say notes or something like that) to put together this file. At the end of the night, that goes off to courts or to John School or what-have-you. Everybody's got to work together to* *make sure the file's complete. If you have somebody who's not or who would rather just go home that is a frustration for me, for sure. I hold people to a certain standard.*

—Neighborhood Resource

Suitable reports (General occurrences, Arrest, Use of force)

A well-crafted police report is an unmistakable hallmark of exemplary law enforcement, showcasing an officer's professionalism and competence. Grammar proficiency is crucial, as a poorly written report can influence how individuals perceive an officer. Achieving a balance between thoroughness and avoiding overwhelming detail is especially crucial in domestic reports. The importance of articulation encourages officers to provide precise and descriptive accounts in their reports. Properly documented evidence, as seen in traffic cases, is vital to prevent cases from being dismissed due to inadequate reporting. The ability to convey information chronologically and comprehensively remains a revered skill in law enforcement reports.

PHOTO 6.5 Mastering the balance between detailing incidents with evidence and ensuring thorough documentation without overwhelming is essential. Credit: Ottawa Police Service, 2024

Grammar—*The most important thing is report writing. You can't have a Coach Officer who doesn't know how to write reports, doesn't know the English language properly to write it. That's how people see you. If you're writing a report that's not easy to read, doesn't make any sense, and has poor grammar, it's a reflection of who you are.*

—School Resource

Premises search report—*Once the victim is evacuated by ambulance, we still had to search the residence, because we heard there were more weapons in the house. It's downtime when you are doing a proper search of the premises and securing the scene. We have to maintain the scene. Everything has to be properly documented.*

—Patrol

Domestic reports—*The key to report writing is detail, but not too much detail. For a domestic report, always give a background. There's always something that happened before your start telling the story. Do they have children together? Is there a history of assaults? Because of my Coach Officer, I received a commendation for my report writing.*

—Neighborhood Resource

Resisting arrest—*It's the end of your shift, it's a late call, it's 4:45a.m., you're done at 5:00 but you're still on the street. Everybody else is gone and we're still there. You'll give them, "C'mon." And it's "Oh, yeah…" and they just don't want to. The next thing you know, it's a physical confrontation. What an idiot. This guy's a f---ing ar--hole for doing this. You could have just got in the car and we would have gotten it done and over with, literally. Now, you've got a guy who hates you now because he lost. He's not too pleased with that. Now he's going to face more charges because it's resisting arrest and whatnot. There's three or four hours of paperwork for me, and I'm not getting home. When this could have all just been, handcuff, search, "Nothing on ya. Get in the car and let's go."*

—Neighborhood Resource

Articulation—*Report writing is a lost art. You used to have to put everything in—the guy's name, the description, the car. People won't walk around a car to look at the damage on a car anymore. I still put it in somewhere. I was taught how to write a report properly and chronologically. Even the back and forth, "This information was received after this but it corroborates with this." If you see a guy with a clenched fist and he's hitting a guy... Yeah, "fighting" but why not say, "Hit him with a closed fist on the left side of the face with his right hand." Break down what you saw. Describe the type of driving, his actions and how he spoke.*

—Neighborhood Resource

Traffic evidence—*When you don't do reports properly and you're not prepared, a lot of your cases can get thrown out. Say, somebody runs a red light. If you don't give the proper evidence supports—that you went back to make sure that the traffic lights were cycling properly—that could be a big issue.*

—Traffic Escort

D. Knowledge of police service and community

Coach officers identified critical practices aimed at determining proficient knowledge of the police service and the community being served. These practices relate to:

1. Police service (i.e., organizational structure, reporting relationships, vision and mission)
2. Policies and procedures
3. Internal communication
4. Community composition (i.e., geographic locations, landmarks, diversity) and resources

Understanding frontline policing dynamics involves acknowledging the complexities, career demands, and internal motivations to deliver exceptional service. Policing mandates adaptability, composure, and unwavering commitment to manage shift work, high-stress scenarios, and maintain professionalism in community interactions. Frontline sergeants prioritize supervision qualities such as competence, empathy, self-awareness, and responsibility, maintaining strong connections with officers and the community.

Strong community relationships and community-oriented policing contribute to a safer, more cohesive community, where officers extend their roles to assist and connect with community members, accessing valuable resources.

Police service

Modern police organizations face evolving challenges, blending hierarchical structures with community-oriented, transparent models, largely due to "big data" analytics[29]. Reporting relationships extend beyond the chain of command to diverse stakeholders, emphasizing Community-Oriented Policing (COP) and Problem-Oriented Policing (POP). COP has been adopted by 90% of US agencies alongside new communications training[30]. POP prioritizes chronic issues over acute events[31].

Private police growth in Canada raises concerns about governance and accountability, especially in investigative and arrest powers[32]. The NYPD Shield program exemplifies public-private partnerships for information sharing and counter-terrorism training[33,34].

Computer-mapping and crime analysis systems enhance departmental proactivity, accountability, and information-driven operations[35]. However, adapting policies and procedures to social changes and new technologies often faces a high-failure rate, influenced by organizational culture[36,37]. Organizational culture and training are shifting toward officer-centered education, although adoption is hampered by a lack of evidence for active-learning strategies[38].

Diversity remains a challenge in law enforcement, with underrepresentation of minority groups. Efforts to reflect community diversity are hindered by concerns of racism and discrimination. Diversity in Europe has improved, but decreases with higher ranks. Data on recruitment and retention policies is limited[39,40].

Effective leadership means balancing public safety, individual rights, ethics, and public trust, especially when addressing hate crimes and terrorism[41]. Counter-terrorism poses unique challenges and mental-health risks, contributing to depression, trauma effects, and post-traumatic stress disorder among officers[42]. Protective factors are under-researched[43], while efforts like the "Road to Mental Readiness" (R2MR) aim to address mental-health challenges[44,45]. Police organizations navigate complex considerations to safeguard society, uphold justice, and protect human rights.

The police organizational structure and associated challenges are diverse. Shift work significantly impacts both the professional and personal lives of officers. The importance of utilizing power and authority judiciously in law enforcement is a central message. The significance of adhering to policies, coupled with providing support after traumatic incidents, is underscored for frontline personnel. Frontline policing has undergone a noticeable shift toward reactive, quantity-focused work. Inter-organizational politics can have a negative impact on practical police work. Fostering informal leadership in upholding order and respect is invaluable. Similarly, senior leaders who can adapt while remaining relatable retain frontline respect. The rise in hate crimes has sparked rapid engagement from both media and the community. Together, these insights offer an understanding of the complexities within police organizations from a frontline perspective.

> **Shift work**—*Well, if you're just coming on, are you familiar with shift work? Are you married or have you got a family? Your social life is gonna take a beating the first few years. Maybe five years, you're going to be working a lot of statutory holidays. You won't be getting summer holidays for a while—unless you get on the right team or you've got some special trade or some special gift. Then it depends on what YOUR interests are… There are different fields.*
> —Traffic Escort

> **Power**—*The Former Chief gave an address and he mentioned something that really stuck in my mind. He said, "In this job,*

you're going to have a lot of power over people. You have to use it wisely. Don't become a power-monger. You have to remember to use your power judiciously, wisely and remember who you're dealing with."

—Neighborhood Resource

Reassurance—*I'm more like a robot. Some people find the old school strict, but I am more robotics. I find it's the best way. Officers, the ones that talk to me, respect me because I know what I'm doing and I get things done. My most useful application in my role as Sergeant is to be able to keep a level head, follow procedures and policies, and (in the back of my mind the whole time) reassure them that I am the officer who offers the assistance they require.*

—Neighborhood Resource

Timely support—*Our officers were involved in a high-speed chase and an elderly couple was killed. I was working the front desk, which was very challenging, fielding everybody from the chief down. I felt that I did a really good job that day, but the most gratifying part was that I recognized when the officers came in, what they'd been through. I remember holding one officer while he cried. Nobody knows that. But that's all it took. "You take your time. You come back to work when you want to." What that officer needed to hear right there, is that no matter what, we are here. Some would say, "You can't go home sick, are you using holiday time?" Sh-- like that. That's not what that officer needed at that time—It's just common sense.*

—Patrol Sergeant

Politics—*I knew right when that happened (I had that feeling again, just boiling, the heat in my body)—I didn't want to be there. I wasn't focused. I had another hour and nobody helping me. I remember there was a [provincial police officer] who came by. He knew I was alone there. He saw that I was in trouble… But he told me, "I can't stay, because I was told by your supervisor that [provincial police] weren't welcome here"—politics.*

—Traffic Escort

Informal leadership—*I AM a "Coach Officer" in a sense. I'll say what I like and don't like. It's also about offering "that*

calm voice." *If I show up at a situation and get as excitable as them, then the leadership is diminished. Officers need "that calm voice." It identifies the senior or at least a respected officer on a platoon. Informal leaders are big. They have a role to play.*
—Patrol

Still relatable—*Some in management do have respect because of the fact that they never lost contact. They come in now, maybe as a Deputy Chief, hasn't changed too much, and still remembers who was their Sergeant on patrol. There's certain things have to change as you climb the ladder of success, because you have to adapt. But you still have to come down and relate to the troops and talk about certain things.*
— Neighborhood Resource

Perceived hate crime—*There was misconception on the part of the media, it was not a hate crime, it wasn't a gay bashing. It was a robbery that went bad. I had to assist because the Hate Crime Section was very busy. At the same time, the community wanted posters delivered, so I was doing both. I was the mailman and I would strike up a conversation… It wasn't planned, but it was effective. The response that came back to the Hate Crimes Section was very good in the sense that the community appreciated the police assistance. It wasn't a grandiose plan, it was low key. Service was provided, and police were there responding to their needs.*
—Neighborhood Resource

Policies and procedures

Excellent officers approach the challenges and expectations around policies and procedures by striking a balance between policy compliance, ethical considerations, and practical judgment[46]. In the dynamic and often unpredictable field of policing, technical readiness with adaptability and ongoing learning is needed.

Some officers adopt a methodical approach, routinely reviewing policies during downtime to maintain constant awareness, despite the dry but necessary content. They recognize that well-intentioned actions may require follow-up related to adherence to policies and procedures. In dynamic situations, reliance on Standard Operating Procedures (SOPs) becomes automatic. Policy awareness extends to available resources, such as compassionate trauma support. The commitment to ongoing preparedness is evident through the continuous assimilation of knowledge from peers and training

Review and interpret internal resources

Half the officers (50%) highlighted the need to regularly review policies and procedures. The importance of internal resources is highly regarded by officers with NRT experience (70%, $p = 0.063$), and of least importance to officers with Traffic Escort and or rural experience (13%, $p = 0.058$; 31%, $p = 0.051$, respectively). Many officers (44%) value reviewing and interpreting internal resources such as policies, special reports (e.g., vehicle theft), procedures, and laws (e.g., traffic searches, Young Offenders Act [YOA]). Ironically, these same conscientious officers also attribute luck and faith to their success (correlation = 0.375, $p = 0.009$). Good review habits show additional benefit. Officers who report habitually making inferences from internal resources also acknowledge the benefit of formal evaluation methods such as debriefing with supervisors and having written goals (correlation = 0.408, $p = 0.004$).

> **Policy and "what's right"**—*The problem with policing is that "policy" and "what's right" can be two separate things...I will continue to do the "right thing," as opposed to what policy states. At least I can sleep...*
> —School Resource

> **Downtime reviewing**—I prepare all the time. When I have downtime or it's quiet in the car, I'll bring the policies up on the laptop and review them. I make a point of reviewing them about every three months. They change all the time, but even when they don't it's very dry and your ability to remember is probably about 30%. I review constantly so I remember.
> —"Elite" Patrol Sergeant, >10 years on

Knowledge: "I feel that I'm prepared, but there's always room for more."

Absorbing knowledge—*I try to review policy and procedure about this job. I try to absorb all the knowledge that's being imparted to me by officers around me and through training. I can only absorb as much as they're giving me. I feel that I'm prepared, but there's always room for more.*

—Tactical

PHOTO 6.6 Walking the fine line between protocol and practice is crucial for staying current and upholding what's right while navigating evolving policies. Credit: Ottawa Police Service, 2024

In good faith, policy-debrief—*If you don't follow policy and procedure when you're operating in good faith and for the better good, it's not harmful to anybody. It can actually prevent harm. In this particular instance, I revisited the officers and said, "Here's the policy. This is what I should have done. We probably went a little heavy handed based on previous experiences with this type of thing. Be aware that this is what the policy says."*

—Patrol Sergeant, >15 years on

Road-side preparation—*I always want to be prepared before I get to a scene. If I have a long distance to travel or if it's not pressing at the scene, I'll pull over and read the policy book. I'll check my "cheat sheet" real quick.*

—"Elite" Patrol, >10 years on

SOPs—*On the way there, because we don't know the situation, you're not sure what you need to do until you get there. Yes, I have all my equipment. Yes, I know it's a barricaded person. Yes, I know that they're going to whatever, and Standard Operating Procedures kick in at that point. I really don't have a choice in the matter—that's what we have to do—Containment, IAT, and then, try and talk to them.*

—Tactical

Service resources—*First thing you do is to reassure them that you are going to assist and make sure they know that you know what you are doing. That requires being familiar with policies, procedures and what resources are available to assist them in their physical or emotional trauma... They come up to you and say, "Serge, we know you are going to get it done, one way or another."*

—Sergeant, Neighborhood Resource

Procedures—*I'm chasing it around and part of me was just so focused on following this car and getting this person, that I realized that I hadn't gone over the air to say what I was doing. That is SO WRONG. [Laughs]*

—Neighborhood Resource

Assimilate—*I try to review policy and procedure about this job to absorb all the knowledge that's being imparted to me by officers around me and through training. I can only absorb as much as they're giving it to me. I feel that I'm prepared, but there's always room for more.*

—Tactical

Internal communication

In detailing best performances, the majority of officers (82%) identified some form of internal interaction as having contributed to their successful outcome. The nature of this communication includes discussions with peers, coordinating and prioritizing resources, receiving strong patrol support, having an insightful dispatch, contacting a Specialty Unit, and informing a supervisor (see Table 6.2).

TABLE 6.2 Internal Communication Strategies

	TOTAL RESPONSES Ranked by %
Communicating internally	82
Rely on team: peer advice, backup, emotional support	
Coordinate others and resources: prioritize, organize, determine	
Rely on patrol support: proper containment done, information collection, overall presence	
Have proficient dispatcher, assistance, insight	
Call in specialty units: Canine, Tactical, Identification, national police	
Inform and involve supervisor; i.e., Sgt, S/Sgt, Duty Insp., management	

This intra-organizational skill is most common to all officers with Tactical experience and for most with only Patrol experience (100%, p = 0.091; 89%, p = 0.004, respectively).

Communication, gossip—*Police are the worst gossips because it's the only way to tell other colleagues what you think.*
—Patrol, >15 years on

Team, advice, trust—*My biggest ritual is depending on the guys. I won't remember everything, but they know their stuff and will tell me if I forget something. I always double check: "What have I missed here?" And the guys will tell me. That's what you want from the guys you work with.*
—Tactical

Team input: "Others come from different backgrounds and look at things from a different angle, and I want that input."

Team input, background—*I like being analytical and involving other people. I can be a dictator and say, "This is how we're doing it," but I don't have all the knowledge, skills or abilities. Others come from different* backgrounds and look at things from a different angle, and I want that input.

—>15 years on

Coordinate, organize resources—*"Ready" doesn't start until I give the thumbs-up: I'm geared up, got everything I need, in position and ready to operate—right now.*

—Tactical

Contain, coordinate, safety—*Arriving on the scene of a person held up in a home with a weapon, never knock on the front door and say, "Police, come on out." NO-O-O! First and foremost, contain the residence. Ensure that if someone else is in the home, you get them out. There are a number of things. You have to get all the players lined up.*

—Patrol, >10 years on

Information sharing, networking—*When I first started as a police officer, officers [would meet] at Tim Horton's during shift overlaps. If one officer was working afternoon shift and I was working midnight shift, we'd sit and have a coffee for one hour. We talked about the crack house down the street and what names she'd been dealing with. Information sharing. That was a different era. Now police officers are busier. We are short-staffed, with fewer officers on the street.*

—>15 years on

Dispatchers, voices, insight—*Dispatchers also get excited, and sometimes you can tell by their voice. We get to know dispatchers' voices and they get to know our voices as well. Without us asking for a specific emergency request, they know from our voice if there's an urgent matter. When they're dispatching a certain type of call where someone is injured or it's violent or weapons are involved, they will tell us if they can hear screaming in the background on the telephone.*

—Patrol, <5 years on

Dispatch, perspective—*The dispatchers are very helpful and they may make suggestions. You're in the thick of things and it may not cross your mind to think of Tactical or Canine.*

—5 to 10 years on

Supervisor support—*We had a supervisor who was knowledgeable about how to deal with different situations. You could call him anytime, and he was really supportive.*
—School Resource

Specialty roles, responsibilities—*Know what resources you need—Tactical, Canine, Explosive Disposal. Be very cognizant of their abilities and when you call them—and when you don't. They enjoy having someone like me out there because they know they're not going to get called unnecessarily. And they know that when they arrive, the scene is going to be set up so that they are able to slide in seamlessly.*
—Patrol, >15 years on

Community composition and resources

Familiarity with landmarks and streets is crucial for police navigation, especially in unfamiliar areas, to reduce the risks of complacency during routine patrols and prevent getting lost during pursuits or critical responses. Officers' geographic awareness significantly influences their situational tactics, decision-making, and swift and precise responses to emergencies, incidents, or calls for help[14]. By leveraging local knowledge and community awareness, officers can adeptly identify and address crime-related issues within specific areas. This often involves increasing police presence in problem areas based on the consistent identification of sites or properties linked to disorder-related calls[47].

Special-interest groups have a notable impact on law-enforcement practices. For instance, advocacy groups pushing for alternatives to School Resource Officers in schools often succeed in their efforts to remove these officers. Police are exploring options for enhancing school safety, including having officers present without uniforms[48].

Deinstitutionalization, coupled with gaps in police training, has contributed to an upsurge in arrests of individuals with mental illnesses, often for behavior management[49]. Mental-health advocacy groups have lobbied to ensure subsequent care for these individuals[50]. The influence of anti-racism efforts on policing is well documented, affecting public perceptions of police racism and strategies to address criticisms[51,52,53,54].

Persistent hate crimes against the LBGTQ2S+ community sometimes reflect bigoted beliefs within the police culture. This has resulted in under-policing of LBGTQ2S+ victimization and over-policing in leisure areas, straining community relations[55]. Debates over uniformed police participation in Pride Parades highlight the ongoing battle against homophobia[56].

Escalating concerns surrounding street-drug use have prompted changes in police training, emphasizing harm reduction, overdose recognition, occupational safety, and appropriate policing practices. However, the effectiveness of such training, its optimal design, and its impact on policing practices remain unclear, necessitating formal evaluations[57]. Collaboration between healthcare and law enforcement can enhance surveillance and injury control. Expanding these partnerships to other injury types can further improve prevention[58].

The media plays an increasing role in shaping public perceptions of law enforcement, often featuring reports of resisting arrest and assaults on officers making headlines. Misinformation from social and news media outlets can negatively influence individual perceptions, leading to threats and violent actions against police, subsequently heightening the dangers associated with police-community interactions[59].

Officers face public disrespect, disapproval, and complaints, which necessitate strategies for addressing this deep-seated criticism[60].

The uniform—*Once in a police uniform, the public is against policing and puts that on you. That affects members who see it every day. It is not easy to just push it aside. And, there are distressing calls that cannot be unseen. Officers need to find their personal resilience to remain in the game.*
—20-year reflection from one of the original "excellent" officers

Experienced officers strongly recommend ensuring that policing is a suitable and lasting character fit. Beyond conventional aspects like apprehending criminals, showing people respect, compassion, understanding, and patience is part of the job. Community engagement extends beyond identifying potential offenders.

Active connections with shop owners and residents foster valuable relationships contributing to crime prevention. Additionally, maintaining constant location awareness, including knowing landmarks and street signs, is vital. Positive feedback from community initiatives remains significant. Overall, effective policing is portrayed as dependent on community involvement and genuine interaction.

> **Not-typical feedback**—*We did an impaired driving project that meant a lot to me. Usually, Ride Programs are on highway off-ramps but, since we were getting complaints from the local community about drunk drivers, we set up in a residential neighborhood. That is definitely not typical but we got a lot of people, and the feedback was phenomenal. People were really thankful. They'd never seen that.*
> —Neighborhood Resource

> **Character fit**—*Make sure you're suited for this job. Make sure your basic human composition is conducive to you being a police officer. Be willing to make this a career, willing to take the responsibility seriously. It's not only about the job, arresting bad guys and catching them, there are a lot of other things that come into play. Treating people with respect, sometimes having a bit of compassion, a bit of understanding, and some patience.*
> —Patrol Sergeant

> **Community Contacts**—*When I was on Platoon, I focused on knowing who my bad guys were. That's fantastic, but take the time to go into that store to get to know that shop owner. Get out there and get to know people. That's valuable—a lot of times they know who's doing the robberies up the street. I never took the time to do that and it's the biggest thing I learned. On Patrol, make time. Take that 5 minutes, walk into that store and just say, "Hello, this is who I am." That way, they'll know your name and face, and the next time there's an issue, maybe they'll come to you.*
> —Neighborhood Resource

> **Informants**—*As a Neighborhood Resource Officer, your most valuable tool is your community contacts. If you don't nurture a*

relationship with the community, you're not getting anywhere. You have to have sources and informants from relationships and with different agencies—Property Standards, Alcohol & Gaming and all of those places. You have to have that ability to get along and network with these people.

—Neighborhood Resource

Location—*You have to know where you are at all times. That is HUMUNGOUS. Glance up at every corner and if you can't see the street signs, then you'd better know a landmark. That night, we were looking for someone who had taken off from another officer. I found him and they said, "Where are you?" I didn't know because I had never worked that area before and I wasn't paying attention. I should've known better because my Training Officer used to drive down the street, stop the car and say, "Where are you?" If I didn't know, I'd suffer some serious embarrassment.*

—Neighborhood Resource

Community engagement—*When I came on the job, I thought I am going to just catch all these bad guys. Now I think, "OK, wait a second, there is a community involved here, never mind just all these bad guys." So I'll drive through my neighborhoods, see a guy out shoveling snow, and I'll get out of the car. "How are you doing, is everything OK in the neighborhood?" "As a matter of fact, officer, there are these kids hanging out in the park on Friday nights, doing this and this and this." "Thank you very much." When I leave here, that guy will think "Holy crap, this guy got out of his car and actually talked to me?"*

—Patrol

E. 20 Key strategies for technical readiness in policing

The following 20 key strategies summarize technical readiness in policing.

1. **Understand basic law:** Proficiency in law is a police cornerstone, requiring a basic understanding of legal principles for informed decision-making and elevated professionalism.

2. **Access updated resources:** Keeping up with legal changes comes with up-to-date resources, ensuring frontline responses are at their best and able to adapt.
3. **Integrate technology:** From body-worn cameras to crime mapping, technology in policing enhances real-time decision-making and boosts officer training effectiveness.
4. **Prepare for court:** Officers gain confidence and success in court appearances through meticulous preparation, administrative diligence, and effective stress management.
5. **Meet responsibilities with new skills:** Entrusted with authority, officers combine intelligence, adaptability, and clear communication, while continually learning to keep their skills sharp.
6. **Design quality training:** Balancing training scenarios with real-life situations equips officers with confidence, justifiable actions, and effective crisis-handling practices.
7. **Be tactical in crises:** Effective crisis management in tactical law enforcement demands adaptability, policy adherence, and proactive community engagement.
8. **Aim for a positive arrest:** In arrests, officers prioritize assertive action, using empathetic communication, control measures, and post-arrest de-escalation for positive resolutions.
9. **Use verbal de-escalation:** Mastery of tone and word choice helps officers calmly handle and defuse conflicts, minimizing the need for force and improving public trust.
10. **Listen first:** Active listening underpins law enforcement, helping officers prioritize information, build mutual respect, and enhance situational awareness.
11. **Inject humor for rapport:** Community rapport and humor disarm tension, evoke empathy, and further positive relations and trust.
12. **Conduct effective interviews:** Interviews grounded in credibility and empathy improve an officer's chances of overcoming arduous conversations and building rapport for a successful apprehension.
13. **Balance verbal and physical skills:** A blend of verbal finesse and physical wisdom builds community leaders, promoting safety, understanding, and a culture of continuous improvement.

14. **Prioritize situational awareness:** Note-taking safety is a concern as officers balance the need for documentation without compromising situational awareness.
15. **Learn to write consistently:** Efficient police written communication is an art, capturing crucial details and maintaining consistency in reports, court appearances, and addressing public complaints.
16. **Navigate report writing:** In law enforcement, timely reports are a constant juggling act—balancing electronic shortcuts for efficiency while preserving the integrity of complex cases.
17. **Look for time savers:** Collaborative efforts and maximizing downtime emerge as key strategies for timely note completion.
18. **Compile checklists:** Cheat sheets and ticket notes are practical solutions to ensure accurate and reliable reports.
19. **Write professionally:** Navigating thoroughness and overwhelming detail, the well-crafted report stands as a testament to an officer's professionalism, showcasing grammar proficiency and chronological precision.
20. **Include the background:** In domestic reports, key background details before articulating "the story" can make or break a case.

Notes

1 S. D. Perea, "Marijuana, law enforcement, mental health: a dangerous social experiment." https://www.policechiefmagazine.org/marijuana-law-enforcement-mental-health/?ref=6a709f431039dddb4f1512a2a1f010d8, March 2019.

2 L. P. A. Ward and Murphy, A., "The impact of Marijuana legalization on law enforcement in states surrounding Colorado," *Police Quarterly*, vol. 22, no. 2, pp. 217–242. https://doi.org/10.1177/1098611118819902, 2019.

3 B. Ariel, Farrar, W. A. and Sutherland, A., "The effect of police body-worn cameras on use of force and citizens' complaints against the police: A randomized controlled trial." *Journal of Quantitative Criminology*, vol. 31, no. 3, pp. 509–535. https://doi.org/10.1007/s10940-014-9236-3, 2014.

4 M. D. White, Gaub, J. E., Malm, A. and Padilla, K. E., "Implicate or exonerate? The impact of police body-worn cameras on the adjudication of drug and alcohol cases," *Policing: A Journal of Policy and Practice,* vol. 15, pp. 759–769, 2019.
5 J. M. Phelps, Strype, J., Le Bellu, S., Lahlou, S. and Aandal, J., "Experiential learning and simulation-based training in Norwegian police education: Examining body-worn video as a tool to encourage reflection," *Policing: A Journal of Policy & Practice,* vol. 2, no. 1, pp. 50–65. https://doi.org/10.1093/police/paw014, 2018.
6 L. Grossmith, Owens, C., Finn, W., Mann, D., Davies, T. and Baika, L., "Police, camera, evidence: London's cluster randomised controlled trial of Body Worn Video," College of Policing and the Mayor's Office for Policing and Crime (MOPAC), London, 2015.
7 T. N. White and Gaub, J. E., "Examining body-worn camera integration and acceptance among police officers, citizens, and external stakeholders," *Criminology & Public Policy,* vol. 17, no. 3, pp. 649–677. https://doi.org/10.1111/1745-9133.12376, 2018.
8 C. S. Koper, Lum, C. and Hibdon, J., "The uses and impacts of mobile computing technology in hot spots policing," *Evaluation Review,* vol. 39, no. 6, pp. 587–624. https://doi.org/10.1177/0193841X16634482, 2015.
9 A. G. Ferguson, "Policing predictive policing," *Washington University Law Review,* vol. 94, p. 1109, 2016.
10 G. O. Mohler, M. B. Short, P. J. Brantingham, F. P. Schoenberg and G. E. Tita, "Self-exciting point process modeling of crime," *Journal of the American Statistical Association,* vol. 106, no. 493, pp. 100–108, 2011.
11 A. K. Jain, D. Deb and J. J. Engelsma, "Biometrics: Trust, but verify," *IEEE Transactions on Biometrics, Behavior, and Identity Science,* vol. 4, no. 3, pp. 303–323, 2021.
12 M. Beshears, Beshears, M.L. and Bond, M., "Improving police social media use practices," *International Journal of Social Science Studies,* vol. 7, no. 5. http://ijsss.redflame.com, September 2019.
13 C. Sanders and Condon, C., "Crime analysis and cognitive effects: The practice of policing through flows of data," *Global Crime,* vol. 18, no. 3, pp. 237–255. https://doi.org/10.1080/17440572.2017.1323637, 2017.
14 L. B. Moses and Chan, J., "Algorithmic prediction in policing: Assumptions, evaluation, and accountability," *Policing and Society,* vol. 28, no. 7, pp. 806–822. https://doi.org/10.1080/10439463.2016.1253695, 2018.

15 S. Raaijmakers, "Artificial intelligence for law enforcement: Challenges and opportunities," *IEEE Security & Privacy*, vol. 17, no. 5, pp. 74–77, 2019.
16 E. L. Piza, Caplan, J. M., Kennedy, L. W. and Gilchrist, A., "The effects of merging proactive CCTV monitoring with directed police patrol: A randomized controlled trial," *Journal of Experimental Criminology*, vol. 11, no. 1, pp. 43–69. https://doi.org/10.1007/s11292-014-9211-x, 2015.
17 E. Groff, Haberman, C. and Wood, J. D., "The effects of body-worn cameras on police-citizen encounters and police activity: Evaluation of a pilot implementation in Philadelphia, PA," *Journal of Experimental Criminology*, vol. 16, pp. 463–480. https://doi.org/10.1007/s11292-019-09383-0, 2020.
18 J. A. Hendrix, Taniguchi, T., Strom, K. J., Aagaard, B. and Johnson, N., "Strategic policing philosophy and the acquisition of technology: Findings from a nationally representative survey of law enforcement," *Policing & Society*, vol. 29, no. 6, pp. 727–743. https://doi.org/10.1080/10439463.2017.1322966, 2019.
19 T. Söderström, Åström, J., Anderson, G. and Bowles, R., "A framework for the design of computer-assisted simulation training for complex police situations," *Campus-Wide Information Systems*, vol. 31, no. 4, pp. 242–253. https://doi.org/10.1108/CWIS-10-2013-0060, 2014.
20 S. Charman, *Police socialisation, identity and culture becoming Blue*. New York: Palgrave Macmillan, 2017.
21 L. L. Charles, "Disarming people with words: Strategies of interactional communication that crisis (hostage) negotiators share with systemic clinicians," *Journal of Marital and Family Therapy*, vol. 33, no. 1, pp. 51–68. https://doi.org/10.1111/j.1752-0606.2007.00006, 2007.
22 J. Reynolds, Mariani, M. and Goodman, D., *Police talk: A scenario-based communications workbook for police recruits and officers*, 1st ed. Upper Saddle River, NJ: Pearson, p. 128 , 2001.
23 D. Faggiani, "Police talk: A scenario-based communications workbook for police recruits and officers," *Criminal Justice Review*, vol. 31, no. 4, pp. 381–382, 2006.
24 I. Miyamoto, "Disinformation: policy responses to building citizen resiliency," *Connections: The Quarterly Journal*, vol. 20, no. 2, pp. 47–55. https://doi.org/10.11610/Connections.20.2.05, 2021.
25 J. A. Banas and Bessarabova, E., "Debunking and preventing conspiracies," in *The social science of QAnon: A new social and political phenomenon*, p. 252. https://www.cambridge.org/core/books/abs/social-science-of-qanon/debunking-and-preventing-conspiracies/F3B0959F99F30999F0CEEB6404DC9579, 2023.
26 R. Buluc, Stoian-Iordache, V. and Mato, C. A., "3.2 debunking, fact-checking, pre-bunking." Project: DOMINOES Digital cOMpetences

INformatiOn EcoSystem ID: 2021-1-RO01-KA220-HED-000031158, p. 160. https://wordpress.projectdominoes.eu/wp-content/uploads/2023/07/DOMINOES-Handbook.final_.pdf#page=160.

27. T. Carrique, "Recruiting with vision: Cultivating a police service that reflects the community." ProQuest Dissertations Publishing, Masters Dissertation, Royal Roads University, 2005.

28. C. Gill, Weisburd, D., Telep, C., Vitter, Z. and Bennett, T., "Community-oriented policing to reduce crime, disorder and fear and increase satisfaction and legitimacy among citizens: A systematic review," *Journal of Experimental Criminology,* vol. 10, no. 4, pp. 399–428. https://doi.org/10.1007/s11292-014-9210-y, 2014.

29. M. Kaufmann, Egbert, S. and Leese, M., "Predictive policing and the politics of patterns," *The British Journal of Criminology,* Vol. 59, no. 3, pp. 674–692, https://doi.org/10.1093/bjc/azy060, 2019.

30. C. Massinger and Wood, N., "Improving law enforcement cross cultural competencies through continued education," *Journal of Education and Learning,* vol. 5, no. 2, pp. 258–264, 2016.

31. A. F. Dias and Hilgers T. Community oriented policing theory and practice: global policy diffusion or local appropriation?. *Policing and Society*, 5:1–9, Jun 2020.

32. S. Burbidge, "The governance deficit: Reflections on the future of public and private policing in Canada," *Canadian Journal of Criminology and Criminal Justice,* vol. 47, no. 1, pp. 63–86. https://doi.org/10.3138/cjccj.47.1.63, 2005.

33. N. Basu. Learning lessons from countering terrorism: The UK experience 2017–2020. *Cambridge Journal of Evidence-Based Policing*, 5:134–45, Dec 2021.

34. V. Amadeo and Iannone, S., "Successful public-private partnerships: The NYPD shield model," *Journal of Business Continuity & Emergency Planning,* vol. 10, no. 2, pp. 106–117, 2007.

35. W. J. Bratton and Malinowski, S. W., "Police performance management in practice: Taking COMPSTAT to the next level," *Policing: A Journal of Policy and Practice,* vol. 2, no. 3, pp. 259–265. https://doi.org/10.1093/police/pan036, 2008.

36. L. Lewis, *Organizational change: Creating change through strategic communication*, vol. 2. Hoboken, NJ: John Wiley & Sons, 2011.

37. Y. Yuksel, "Understanding the role of culture and communication in implementing planned organizational change: The case of compstat in police organizations," PhD Dissertation, Rutgers University, New Brunswick, NJ, 2013.

38 R. L. Norris, "Training for community policing: Constructing effective police education (Order No. 10846444)," ProQuest Dissertations & Theses Global (2124408064). https://eric.ed.gov/?id=ED590199, 2018.
39 A. Van Ewijk, "Diversity within police forces in Europe: A case for the comprehensive view," *Policing: A Journal of Policy and Practice,* Vol. 6, no. 1, pp. 76–92. https://doi.org/10.1093/police/par048, 2012.
40 S. P. Jain and Agocs, C., "Recruitment, selection and promotion of visible-minority and aboriginal police officers in selected Canadian police services," *Canadian Public Administration,* vol. 43, no. 1, pp. 46–74, 2000.
41 Nagengast, "Countering digital terrorism: A qualitative study on information sharing to deny digital radicalization and recruiting," Doctoral dissertation, Colorado Technical University, 1–120, 2021.
42 D. Paton and Violanti, J. M., "Policing in the context of terrorism: Managing traumatic stress risk," *Traumatology,* vol. 12, no. 3, pp. 236–247. https://doi.org/10.1177/1534765606294990, 2006.
43 F. Losel, King, S., Bender, D. and Jugl, I., "Protective factors against extremism and violent radicalization: A systematic review of research," *International Journal of Developmental Science,* vol. 12, no. 1–2, pp. 89–102. https://doi.10.3233/DEV-170241, 2018.
44 R. N. Carleton, Korol, S., Mason, J. E., Hozempa, K. and Anderson, G., "A longitudinal assessment of the road to mental readiness training among municipal police," *Cognitive Behaviour Therapy,* vol. 47, no. 6, pp. 508–528. https://doi.org/10.1080/16506073.2018.1475504, 2018a.
45 D. Fikretoglu, D'Agata M. T., Sullivan-Kwantes W., Richards K., Bailey L. S. Mental health and mental health service use attitudes among Canadian Armed Forces (CAF) recruits and officer cadets. DRDCRDDC-2017-R027. Toronto, ON: Defence Research and Development Canada (DRDC); Feb, 2017.
46 L. K. Lewis and Seibold, D. R., "Reconceptualizing organizational change implementation as a communication problem: A review of literature and research agenda," *Annals of the International Communication Association,* vol. 21, no. 1, pp. 93–152. https://doi.org/10.1080/23808985.1998.11678949, 1998.
47 G. Bichler and Gaines, L., "An examination of police officers' insights into problem identification and problem solving," *Crime and Delinquency,* vol. 51, no. 1, pp. 53–74. https://doi.org/10.1177/0011128704265936, 2005.
48 D. C. Gottfredson, Crosse, S., Tang, Z., Bauer, E. L., Harmon, M. A., Hagen, C. A. and Greene, A. D., "Effects of school resource officers on school crime and responses to school crime," *Criminology & Public Policy,* vol. 19, no. 3, pp. 905–940. https://doi.org/10.1111/1745-9133.12512, 2020.

49 M. S. Morabito, "Horizons of context: Understanding the police decision to arrest people with mental illness," *Psychiatric Services,* vol. 58, no. 12, pp. 1582–1587. https://doi.org/10.1176/ps.2007.58.12.1582, 2007.
50 R. D. Borschmann, Gillard, S., Turner, K., Chambers, M. and O'Brien, A., "Section 136 of the Mental Health Act: A new literature review," *Medicine, Science and the Law,* vol. 50, no. 1, pp. 34–39. https://doi.org/10.1258/msl.2009.009004, 2010.
51 C. Chaney and Robertson, R. V., "Racism and police brutality in America," *Journal of African American Studies,* vol. 17, no. 4, pp. 480–505. https://doi.org/10.1007/s12111-013-9246-5, 2013.
52 K. D. Hassell and Archbold, C. A., "Widening the scope on complaints of police misconduct," *Policing: An International Journal of Police Strategies and Management,* vol. 33, no. 3, pp. 473–489. https://doi.org/10.1108/13639511011066863, 2010.
53 S. King, "'Ready to shoot and do shoot': Black working-class self-defense and community politics in Harlem, New York, during the 1920s," *Journal of Urban History,* vol. 37, no. 5, p. 757–774. https://doi.org/10.1177/0096144211413234., 2011.
54 P. Muennig and Murphy, M., "Does racism affect health? Evidence from the United States and the United Kingdom," *Journal of Health Politics, Policy and Law,* vol. 36, no. 1, pp. 187–214. https://doi.org/10.1215/03616878-1191153, 2011.
55 L. Dario, Fradella, H. F., Verhagen, M. and Parry, M. M., "Assessing LGBT people's perceptions of police legitimacy," *Journal of Homosexuality,* vol. 67, no. 7, pp. 885–915. https://doi.org/10.1080/00918369.2018.1560127, 2020.
56 A. Holmes, "Marching with pride? Debates on uniformed police participating in Vancouver's LGBTQ pride parade," *Journal of Homosexuality,* vol. 7502386, no. id5, pp. 1–33. https://doi.org/10.1080/00918369.2019.1696107, 2020.
57 T. Khorasheh, Naraine, R., Watson, T. W., Wright, A., Kallio, N. and Strike, C., "A scoping review of harm reduction training for police officers," *Drug and Alcohol Review,* vol. 38, no. 2, pp. 131–150, 2019.
58 S. F. Jacoby, Kollar, L. L. M., Ridgeway, G. and Sumner, S. A., "Health system and law enforcement synergies for injury surveillance, control and prevention: A scoping review," *Injury Prevention,* vol. 24, no. 4, pp. 305–311. https://doi.org/10.1136/injuryprev-2017-042416, 2018.
59 S. Morrow, "Social and news media's effects on law enforcement," *Global Journal of Forensic Science & Medicine,* vol. 1, no. 4, p. GJFSM.MS.ID.000516. https://doi.org/10.33552/AJGH.2019.01.000516, 2019.
60 J. McDonald, *Gold medal policing: Mental readiness and performance excellence.* New York: Sloan Associate Press, 2006.

7

Mental readiness in policing

> **SPOILER ALERT**
>
> There are no "Take 2s," so have a packing ritual
> to consistently organize your gear
> for instant readiness, focus, and precision.

Abstract

This chapter delves into evidence-based mental-readiness competencies for police officers, based on Orlick's "Wheel of Excellence" grounded in work with Olympic athletes. Seven key elements—Commitment, Confidence, Positive Imagery, Mental Preparation, Full Focus, Distraction Control, and Constructive Evaluation—are outlined for achieving excellence in challenging police scenarios. Frontline officers prioritize communication and empathy, upholding professional standards while embracing the diverse challenges of their role. Confidence, derived from maintaining calmness, clarity, and strong support systems, is paramount. Quality training, mental rehearsal, visualization, and adaptive coping mechanisms prepare officers for diverse and stressful situations, allowing them to maintain focus during crises. Self-evaluation, feedback, and adaptive coping mechanisms are vital for professional growth. The chapter explores how factors like background, specialty-unity training, and police distinctions impact mental-readiness skills, concluding with 20 strategies for mental readiness in policing.

DOI: 10.4324/9781003145493-7

This chapter discusses mental readiness in policing in 10 sections:

A. Assessment of mental success elements
B. Commitment
C. Confidence
D. Positive Imagery
E. Mental Preparation
F. Full Focus
G. Distraction Control
H. Constructive Evaluation
I. Influential factors and trends for success practices
J. 20 Key strategies for mental readiness in policing

A. Assessment of mental success elements

As a standardized assessment tool, the Orlick's "Wheel of Excellence"[1,2] was used to determine the quantity and quality of mental readiness for achieving excellence in policing. It provides psychological attributes that allow individuals to excel, or to become the best that they can possibly be in a chosen pursuit. This heightened level of consistent, personal excellence can be attained through dedicated practice of mental readiness. The "Wheel of Excellence" (see Figure 7.1) outlines seven success elements of excellence. Some adaptations were made to the original terms to enhance their relevance to policing, as indicated in parentheses. They are: Commitment, Self-Belief (or Confidence), Positive Images (or Positive Images), Mental Readiness (or Mental Preparation), Full Focus, Distraction Control, and Constructive Evaluation (and Coping).

Interview quotes are provided to highlight the most interesting practices.

This study verifies the presence of the seven mental success elements in "excellent" frontline officers and coach officers during challenging policing situations (as defined in Chapter 1).

The findings are reported in three ways:
- discussions of each success element with profiling practices and percentage frequencies tailored specific to policing
- representative interview quotes highlighting the most interesting practices
- identification of relationships between mental readiness traits and factors related to officer demographics (through chi-square analysis)

FIGURE 7.1 Orlick's Wheel of Excellence
Source: Adapted from Orlick (2003) http://www.zone-ofexcellence.ca/free/wheel.html

Orlick's seven success elements[2] or Performance Indicators (see also Appendix N: Orlick's Wheel of Excellence: Mental success elements) are described generically below. Some terms were modified to better suit policing, as shown in parentheses:

Commitment and Self-Belief (Confidence) form the core of excellence, emphasizing a strong personal drive to excel without being the sole focus. This involves mental readying skills that produce a superior performance at critical events.

Positive Images (Positive Imagery) enhances mental rehearsal, skill refinement, technical corrections, and envisioning success, crucial for effective daily visualization.

Mental Readiness (Mental Preparation) involves systematic procedures, including rituals and positive thoughts, ensuring a well-developed and consistent pre-event plan for focus and success.

Full Focus centers on the present task, excluding irrelevant thoughts, and refining a focused plan.

Distraction Control handles expected and unexpected disruptions swiftly, avoiding them and quickly refocusing in high-stress situations.

Constructive Evaluation extracts key lessons from events to refine mental approaches for continuous personal excellence. See Appendix N: Orlick's Wheel of Excellence—Mental Readiness Success Elements for more details.

B. Commitment

What moves you? What is your "Why?" It is this unselfish core quality that motivates a weary officer to go back to work during a crisis to replace a fatigued team member.

Commitment is a crucial factor in coaching decisions and in assessing Olympic athletes. Though it may manifest differently on the ice, it remains a critical element for success.

> **Courage and physical commitment**—*Judges look for a conviction of edges.*
> —Tessa Virtue, Canadian Olympic Figure Skater[3]

However, "Commitment" often resonates differently across generations and can even strike a nerve. Years ago, officers worked tirelessly, socialized with colleagues, and prioritized work over personal health and time off, fearing they might miss something important. Today, dedication occurs during work hours. They value their well-being and understand the importance of work-life balance. This shift reflects a change in perspective, not a lack of commitment.

> **Pride of uniform**—*Honestly, that's why I joined. That's the glue of this Police Department. That's Patrol.*
> —Neighborhood Resource

> **Initiative**—*Friday afternoon—I got hockey tickets (I'm a die-hard junior hockey fan). I heard a call—once, twice, three times. I waited—no response. I wasn't far and I said, "I'm doing it."*

I flew down the street and scooped the guy, threw him in the cuffs, gave him the charter, did the statements, talked to fraud, did the report. I phoned my wife, "Listen, I'll be late for the game. I'm tied up with this call." We missed the first period. No big deal. Somebody's gotta do it.

—Patrol, 5 to 10 years on

Proactive—*You have an officer who will drive 1000 miles per hour, safely, to go help another officer. You have the one who is going to have 100-200 criminal arrests per year.*

—Neighborhood Resource

Police Commitment is defined by nine practices ranging from Empathy and Professional Discipline to Pride of Uniform. Their exceptional commitment is evident given the consistency where on average, officers report seven of the nine practices (77%). Excellent officers clearly express a genuine "love for the road," expressed in multiple ways (see Figure 7.2).

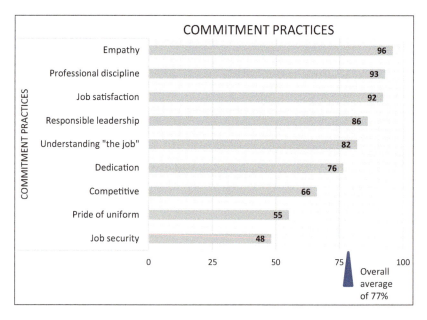

FIGURE 7.2 Commitment Practices

All excellent officers had an overall average of 77% Commitment practices (7 out of 9 practices per officer).

These Commitment Practices are presented as:

1. Empathy
2. Professional Discipline
3. Job Satisfaction
4. Responsible Leadership
5. Understanding "the Job"
6. Loyalty: Dedication and Pride of Uniform
7. Motivated to succeed: Competitive and Job Security

Officer commitment has become a focal point in current research and among coach officers. Empathy for the public and colleagues remains fundamental to exceptional officers—a trait sought after by both coaches and management. Programs like California's Perishable Skills Program now emphasize that officer standards and discipline training should include professional ethics training[4], aimed at improving decision-making, adherence to protocol, and stronger leadership in ethically challenging situations[5]. Ethical decision-making now considers personal and organizational biases, such as victimization, racism, and priorities. Self-esteem, maturity, and comfort with cultural diversity are influential[6,7,8,9].

The dilemma between how you feel and how it "looks" is an ethical challenge to flush out. Can one bad experience shape an officer's future outlook and actions? Also, there is a prevalent undercurrent that the perceived status of patrol ought to be elevated[10]—an even stronger sentiment of coach officers.

We need to enhance the pride and recognition of being on platoon.

—Patrol, >15 years on

Over 75% of officers and coaches showed their commitment by
- feeling empathy and compassion
- setting high standards in their professional discipline
- experiencing job satisfaction and overall enjoyment
- recognizing the risk and their responsibility for safety
- dedicating extra time and resources to their profession

"Elite" officers (81%, p = 0.022), Canine officers (90%, p = 0.007), and officers with over 10 "years on" experience (79%, p = 0.032) show the highest levels of Commitment. Officers with less than 10 years on (65%, p = 0.032) and those with Traffic Escort experience (63%, p = 0.059) have somewhat lower ratings.

Empathy

Empathy is having the courage to armor-up, be vulnerable, and connect with other people[11]. Almost all experienced officers (96%) demonstrate empathy and compassion through acts of kindness, the need to protect others, and support for "the team." Officers illustrate the impact of prioritizing communication and alternative solutions over punitive measures.

> *Great to see compassion flagged as a public value—undervalued and taken for granted in my opinion.*
> —Chief Andy Rhodes, Lancashire, UK

> **Presence, listen, respond**—*I thought, "You know what? Screw it. I don't pull numbers at bingo. You broke the law and I'm gonna charge you." I came down on this kid. Then this hard-ass kid (who had been telling me to "f--- off," "f--- the school") says, "I just don't care anymore." All of a sudden, my spider senses kicked in and I thought, "Whoops! He doesn't care about whether there are charges. He doesn't care about getting kicked out of school. What else doesn't he care about?" I poured on the caring and he just lost it—just started bawling. I had turned it around.*
> —School Resource

> **Caring, communication**—*A young guy I had dealt with many times came up to me. He said, "I want to shake your hand. I've been clean for six months and I'm back at my mom's place." I shook his hand and he introduced me to his mom. That came from the fact that we stop and engage people in conversation. We challenge people.*
> —Neighborhood Resource

Compassion: "Somebody said that I am too compassionate. I said, 'Well, the day that I'm not is the day I should leave.'"

Same end result, another way—*I'm not getting paid by how many charges I lay per month. Maybe the better police officer is the one who doesn't lay the charge and finds another way to get to that same end result.*

—School Resource

Compassionate, success—*You really have to push me to make me mad. Somebody said that I am too compassionate. I said, "Well, the day that I'm not is the day I should leave." I was also told that I give people too many chances. Yeah, 99% of the time, I do—I want people to make decisions for themselves, especially when it comes to being physical with somebody.*

—5 to 10 years on

Helping others, reward—*I can be having the worst shift imaginable, and all it takes is for one person to say, "Officer, you did a wonderful job. You helped me and I don't know how to thank you." It's sweet and touching and it's all I need. I don't need letters and commendations. You feel like, "Wow, now I know why I'm out there. I put my uniform on because people like that and need me. I want to help those people—that's what makes it all worthwhile.*

—Patrol, >10 years on

Professional Discipline

Consistently, most excellent officers (93%) value high levels of discipline, as evidenced through their work ethics, efficiency, honesty, and self-initiated calls. Appearance was highlighted by officers in detailing a conscientious approach to dress, personal hygiene, and respectful manner. Notably, Pride of uniform and Job security were said to contribute more to Commitment now than 20 years ago.

A description of Professional discipline is captured in Table 7.1.

TABLE 7.1 Professional Discipline Practices

	TOTAL RESPONSES Ranked by %
Professional discipline	93
High standards: plan well, do your best, meticulous, work ethics, best effort	
Time management: prioritize, quick and efficient, finish one at a time	
Honesty: be yourself: do the job, be true to you	
Discipline look: uniform, shoes, hair, respectful, professional attitude	
Self-initiated: proactive, digging, take your calls (do them quickly, find out information)	

High standards, honesty—*Don't be so macho that you put somebody's safety in jeopardy; recognize when something's not kosher. You have a shitty day. You may bring it to work, so your thought processes won't be up to par. Or you could have twisted your knee from running. You may need to make some quick movements for the safety of the team. If there is something wrong say, "I don't know if I can do it. Put me on containment." You want to be in the heat, but somebody has to do containment.*

—Tactical

Work ethics, professionalism—*I'm a hard-nosed officer. I'm pretty much by the book. I deal with my job very seriously. Everything is done professionally. I try to be as professional as I can with everybody I encounter.*

—>10 years on

Time management, prioritize—*You don't turn them off. We live by the agenda. We keep the agenda with us and, "Okay, tomorrow two o'clock…" It's just a matter of reorganizing everything and prioritizing it.*

—School Resource

Mental time management—*I think mentally you need to be able to manage your time.*
—School Resource

Honesty, be true to yourself, seriousness—*When something drags on, I just grin and bear it. Unless I've got a thought bubble: "Have you done this? Thought of this?" Sometimes it seems foolish, but then you find out they HADN'T thought of it and you go, "Ahhh, sh--. I should've said something."*
—Tactical

Discipline, appearance, confidence—*On the street it comes down to a lot of things. First, what they see when you approach them has an impact. I don't care what anybody says, appearance has an impact. If your shirt's creased, your pants are pressed, your stuff looks clean, you carry yourself well and you walk with confidence—right away it sets a tone. It's visibility—what they see.*
—5 to 10 years on

Proactive, disciplined, honest—*This is my job and my responsibility—I get paid for it, and I get paid until the end of the day. That person could be your mother, brother or sister. A lot of people say I get too emotional and I personalize—but that's what motivates me. If you're fed up with the job, go elsewhere.*
—Neighborhood Resource

Moral goodness in policing requires openness, honesty, following the values of service, and maintaining public trust. The high standards these proficient officers set for themselves are characterized by:
- striving for a high work ethic and best effort
- being yourself and doing the job
- managing your time with punctuality
- maintaining a disciplined look in uniform, shoes and hair
- self-initiating

However, ethics or morals are complicated. Officers are often called upon to do things that border on their ethical compass. Few, and in law enforcement nobody, should ever want to shoot another human being, no matter the circumstance. They want to help, not harm. And yet, sometimes it is necessary. There are always consequences. *What will happen to "me" and "my" family, if I pull the trigger?*

Biases too are complicated and can prevent ethical behavior. They are impacted by officer maturity, camaraderie, rank, personality, race, and gender[12]. Contemporary ethics training presents real-life ethical risks and the best possible response options in these difficult situations[13,14]. While understanding does not guarantee application, legal versus questionable actions are mapped out.

> **Time management**—*You can't plan for what you can't control. I plan my days around an agenda I can work with. I won't try to fit two liters into a one-liter jar. It can't be done, but I try to please as many people as I can. Sometimes you don't have a choice. It's not in your agenda but you have to go deal with your emergency.*
>
> —School Resource

> **Appearance, confidence**—*I made sure my boots were shined and my appearance was good—I felt comfortable. Once my appearance is up to a good standard, then I feel confident. Not overconfident, but confident.*
>
> —>15 years on

Do your best: "After every incident, you can say, 'I did the best I could at that particular time, with the skills, equipment and training I had.'"

Do your best, learn—*Dwell on your disappointments and you'll never get through this job. The road is full of disappointments, but you've got to move on—it's a learned coping mechanism. Just believe in your skills and training and do your best. After every incident, you can say, "I did the*

best I could at that particular time, with the skills, equipment and training I had."
—Neighborhood Resource

Work ethic, knowledgeable—*I go out there and I find things. I am fairly respected because of my work ethic. I'm not a lawyer by any means, but I am knowledgeable about police practices. You've got to have somebody like that to speak to when you're not sure, and I have a fair bit of experience. People come to me with questions.*
—Patrol, >10 years on

Self-initiate, keep busy—*I went out and sought people out. If I had spare time, I'd go to drug houses and sit outside or go up the stairs and stand by the door to listen in on what was being said. Once a fight occurred, and somebody barged out—I was standing right there. I said, "No. Come on, let's go back inside and figure this out." I started taking names and seizing drugs. You have to get out of the police car in order to get these things done.*
—5 to 10 years on

Job Satisfaction

Job satisfaction is considered critical to attract, engage and maintain the commitment of well-qualified officers[15,16]. Positivity in policing today is connected to ethical leadership and openness to using new innovative online-training methods[9,17]. In fact, increasing organizational commitment and job satisfaction has been proven to reduce turnover[15].

Almost all excellent officers speak about enjoying the challenge, the thrill of getting "a good high," and "a bit of a rush" from responding to calls. In short, they like patrol. As many as 46% specifically identified that they enjoy the diversity and freedom, "being your own boss," the physical skills, and the environment that policing offers.

While 92% of officers identify job satisfaction, all non-patrol specialty unit ratings are at 100%. A significant drop is noted among Patrol officers (83%, $p = 0.073$), Sergeants (80%, $p = 0.024$),

Visible Minority-Aboriginal officers (78%, p = 0.03), and "New School" males (<10 years on; 67%, p = 0.015).

> **Smiling, fun**—*My wife says to my sons, "Why the hell do you want to be a cop? You have to work midnights… blah, blah, blah." "Because Dad is always smiling. He's always talking about how much fun he had at work." Especially for kids, it's "Cool. I want that job."*
>
> —>15 years on

> **Likes nights, fun**—*I like working nights, but it doesn't matter—it's the job itself I really like. Coming to work is all fun.*
>
> —>10 years on

> **Different calls, fresh air**—*This job is wonderful. You don't sit behind a desk all day—you go out and enjoy the fresh air. You help people, every call is different and the group of people you work with can all relate—you're a family. In what other job do all those things come together?*
>
> —Neighborhood Resource

Responsible Leadership

Being responsible in police work means understanding the risk that you may get hurt and having the courage to face that challenge. For most officers (86%) this was possible by:

- taking a cautious approach and attending to officer safety
- maintaining a positive attitude toward the seriousness of the job
- often accepting that things are going to happen as part of the job
- being honest when not 100% to not jeopardizing people's lives

This sense of leadership improves officers' enthusiasm, performance, development, and overall commitment to organizational culture and its vision[18,19]. *All* officers between 10 and 15 years-experience (100%, p = 0.033) reported this trait, while Neighborhood Resource Team (NRT) and School Resource Officer (SRO) ratings are significantly less frequent (67%, p = 0.098). A quote from a seasoned officer with over 15 years on emphasizes the importance of honesty when impaired to avoid endangering others. The use of alcohol as a coping mechanism is not explored in depth and may be worth flagging as a gap in fully understanding this issue.

> **Responsible, vigilant**—*I believe and treat every situation as if there is a knife on the front seat of the car or a bad guy waiting with a two-by-four around the corner of the building. It's not just an alarm, it's my life or the life of the officer behind me. It's the life of the citizen down the street. It's not a matter of pumping yourself up.*
> —5 to 10 years on

> **Risk, threat**—*The guy was in the immediate area with a shotgun. If he'd wanted to kill one of us that night, one of us would be dead. That's sobering to think about. Those calls change you.*
> —Patrol, >10 years on

> **Officer safety, "toute la gang"**—*I'm very strong on officer safety, and I don't mean just my guys—it's "toute la gang" and right across the board. The bottom line is, we're all going home. No matter what the hell happens. That's my responsibility as a supervisor and that goes for the Patrol guys too.*
> —Tactical

Honesty: "Be prepared to say you're not 100%. If you've had a couple drinks, just tell us. You know yourself."

> **Officer safety, honesty**—*You can't take chances or jeopardize people's lives. Be prepared to say you're not 100%. If you've had a couple drinks, just tell us. You know yourself.*
> —>15 years on

> **Fear advantage, alertness**—*Fear works for you; it keeps you on your toes. Fear brings me to life and awakens my every sense—my being. It makes me more alert and more aware. I use fear to my advantage. I don't let it overtake me, but I do use it to my advantage.*
> —Patrol, >10 years on

> **Safety, coach officer responsibility**—*If I can help someone along and teach them well, so that when they're on their own they'll feel good and turn into a good police officer, I've got to*

do it. As police officers we owe it to ourselves, because we'll be working with them someday. We owe it to the rookies, the department, and society as well.

—Patrol, >15 years on

Understand "the Job"

Having a clear understanding of policing before choosing it as a career path was paramount for these officers. Job awareness was described with the diversity of seven issues, ranging from personal reality checks to shift-work demands to the acceptance of gender conflict (see Table 7.2). All Elite officers see this attitude as being critical to high performance (100%, p = .007).

Regardless of the issue, 82% of the officers interviewed believe that a level of tolerance to the terms and conditions of employment is required. However, no one issue gains full support from the officers, which may suggest that job expectations

TABLE 7.2 Understanding "the Job" Practices

	TOTAL RESPONSES Ranked by %
Understanding "the job"	82
Reality checks: step back from the uniform, confront in advance, accept the realities	
Jaded and skeptical: bad side of community, "victims," alcohol/drugs/anger, irate parents	
Personal anxiety: perfect image, "life in a bubble," decisions analyzed, accountability	
Shift work: part of the job, fatigue, scheduling, family logistics	
Family conflict: spouse's fear, lateness, isolated/misunderstood, failed marriages	
Work volume: hard, long hours	
Female policing issues: macho workplace, rejection, stereotyping, morale, retention	

are undergoing substantial internal scrutiny. For example, high work volume and female-policing issues may now be either less tolerated or are less of an issue upon entering policing. Setting boundaries, maintaining integrity, exercising judgment, refraining from negative assumptions, and showing generosity, rather than assuming *"people are intentionally trying to piss me off,"* can build operational effectiveness and positive relationships—says TED Talk speaker Brené Brown[11].

> **Reality, skeptical, family**—*I don't drive to work in my uniform. When I'm in my personal vehicle, I don't need people knowing that I'm a police officer. That vehicle is driven by my wife. That vehicle is parked in front of my house. I like a little bit anonymity because you don't know the people you're dealing with. There are a lot of people in this world who respect police officers, and there are a lot who hate them. That probably hit me hardest when I first started. I didn't realize how many people actually hate police, as opposed to knowing that we're there to help people.*
>
> —Patrol, >10 years on

> **Reality, boring, monotonous**—*It's monotonous work at times. Pushing a police car is pretty boring, until something happens. You can make it as exciting as you want to—you can stop every car that ever drove through your area. Or you can choose to do nothing. For the most part it's fairly monotonous.*
>
> —Tactical

> **Accountability**—*Most officers know they're being watched by many different bodies, especially when they're at fault. There are professional standards, the Chief, the supervisors, the internal review board, SIU—everybody is ready. That's a reality of frontline policing.*
>
> —Patrol Sergeant

> **Reality, anger, danger**—*When you first start, you're not going to understand how much you are hated by the public. People out there want to kill us. It'll floor you, because we're decent people, and it doesn't make sense to us. That's really hard to deal with.*
>
> —Female Patrol

> **Cynical, sick humor, step back**—*You become cynical and develop this sick sense of humor. You have to watch out, because it grows around you. You need to be able to identify it and step away.*
> —Neighborhood Resource

> **Anxiety, family, skeptical**—*If you don't meet or talk to someone when you're out, it's a rare thing. If I'm with someone (like my wife), and I say to them to keep walking, then I mean, "KEEP WALKING!" [The guy might say,] "Is this the little wife? Hi, Mrs. [So and so]." He's letting you know he knows.*
> —Patrol, >15 years on

> **Family considerations**—*Have you thought about how mentally taxing this is going to be on your family?*
> —5 to 10 years on

Loyalty: Dedication and Pride of Uniform

Experienced officers identified the importance of giving extra time to review internal resources and seek extra training. For 31% of officers interviewed, this means a dedicated lifestyle in which they need to make sacrifices.

Dedication skills are notably higher among all female officers compared with 70% of male officers (p = 0.042). This full dedication is also seen among NRT and SRO specialty units (100%, p = 0.049). Lower ratings are noted within officers with military (55%, p = 0.045) and Traffic Escort experience (50%, p = 0.048).

> **Preparation: home, bureaucracy**—*It's frustrating because it's a passion, and ten hours of work is not enough to get this job done. I get sh-- at home all the time [laughs] 'cause I take the laptop home. I'm always on it. I'll get on the laptop if I'm going to sit in front of the TV. It saves me time at work—I get to go with the guys rather than doing the crap stuff.*
> —Tactical

Cope: "Be with your family. Do stuff outside of work."

> **Dedication, personal time**—*Friday afternoon I had tickets for the 67s (I'm a die-hard junior-hockey fan). I heard a call—once, twice, three times. I waited—no*

response. I wasn't far, and I said, "I'm doing it." I flew down the street and scooped the guy. I threw him in the cuffs, and gave him the charter. I did the statements and talked to the fraud guy. Did the report, everything. I phoned my wife and said, "Listen, I'll be late for the game. I'm tied up with this call." We missed the first period. No big deal. Somebody's gotta do it.

—Traffic Escort

PHOTO 7.1 Missing moments and making sacrifices to serve others in the name of community protection. Credit: Cape Charles Wave, Bing, 2012

Opinions exist of a generational shift from absolute devotion to a lifestyle that distributes time more evenly between work and personal priorities. It is also now counseled that demanding lives need to establish a pattern of time away as "expansion gaps" for other interests. Professional commitment is then put second to family, greater education, and relaxation. Over the years, regardless of differences, this longitudinal study shows that the view of "dedication" remains consistently high in policing.

Coping, family—*With four young kids, I try to do my eight to ten hours a day and the rest is for family. Policing is the part time job—I come to work to relax! [Laughs]*

—Patrol

Cope, external support—*In this career, you tend to associate with people from work. When you're with other cops, you*

> *talk cop. It's policing, policing, policing. Use your brain. Be with your family. Do stuff outside of work.*
>
> —Patrol, 5 to 10 years on

Uniformed policing contributes to a sense of loyalty and pride in the role of protecting the community. This identity was noted more frequently by those over 15 years on (59%, p = 0.04) and officers with military experience (64%, p = 0.044). In contrast, it was mentioned less by Visible Minority-Aboriginal officers (11%, p = 0.073). Pride of uniform currently contributes more to Commitment than 20 years ago.

> **Pride, glow**—*Throwing on a uniform is a great experience—get a good night's sleep and you get a glow on when you go to work.*
>
> —Traffic Escort

> **Trusted, identity, feeling**—*Getting out there and being trusted by your peers and supervisors is great. In Traffic you're trusted—you don't have a leash. You take the ball and run with it, however you want to do it. It's your bike—you do what you want and go where you want. If someone makes a complaint, we'll deal with it.*
>
> —5 to 10 years

Motivated to succeed: Competitive and Job Security

The majority of officers expressed either that they "want to win" or at least that they "do not like losing." They spoke of "scooping the bad guy," "not wanting to get burned," and "finding closure to justice." Only 23% of the officers clearly identified aspirations for a promotion.

Competitiveness is an outstanding quality of all the Elite officers (100%, p = 0.0023) and all officers with NRT experience (100%, p = 0.055). The lowest scoring is among officers with previous SRO, Traffic Escort, and Rural experience (43%, p = 0.021; 50%, p = 0.048; 65%, p = 0.038, respectively).

Financial security and the opportunity for overtime pay.

Financial security and the opportunity for overtime pay are also valued in feeling professional accountability for performing well in policing duties. Job security is most important to officers with Canine (90%, p = 0.005) and those with External Police Experience (50%, p = 0.041). No officer with less than ten years on identified value in job security (0%, p = 0.049). Overall Job security contributes more to Commitment now than 20 years ago.

> **Security, good deal**—*If you are truly interested in being a police officer, there aren't too many other professions that could treat you as well. I've never had to worry about losing my job. If you want to give to the profession, it's a good deal.*
> —>15 years on

> **Get bad guy, achievement**—*The best thing is getting the bad guy, but that can't be the only way you measure success, because we don't deal with bad guys every day. We have other successes—solving a problem, camaraderie in the unit, going out and achieving something, not feeling like you've come to work and done nothing.*
> —>15 years on

> **Catch the bad guy, team atmosphere**—*Catching the bad guy is important— that's why we all get into it. In patrol you have a chance to go and get the bad guy, and it's great to be able to do that. But it's not the driving issue… There are times where you might not catch a person, but the quality of your report might get them caught down the road. It is a team atmosphere.*
> —Patrol, >10 years on

Don't want to lose: "I don't want to lose to bad people. Call me chicken, but I'm going to bring some friends with me."

Don't want to lose—*There's a bit of pride involved, particularly when it comes to being injured by another human on purpose. I don't want to lose to bad people. I'll do everything I can to prepare beforehand so that I'm going in with the best knowledge,* *preparedness and backup. Call me chicken, but I'm going to bring some friends with me.*

—Patrol

C. Confidence

To accomplish any daunting, overwhelming, or seemingly impossible task, Desmond Tutu wisely said, "There is only one way to eat an elephant: a bite at a time." In the moment, steps to amass confidence:
- chill out and take a deep breath
- gain perspective on your desired results
- break it down into smaller pieces
- assess the effort and gains
- start eating the elephant

All officers interviewed project a strong belief in themselves and their ability to carry out their duties. However, this is qualified with an acknowledgment that their level of confidence is achieved through Quality training and specific repetition (98%). A take-charge attitude in confronting situations is equally valued by almost all experienced officers (95%). The majority of officers (85%) also credit having Police mentors for their own abilities to succeed. Garnering Family support (67%), and appreciation from their organization and the public (62%), is ranked high in building Confidence by many of these very competent officers. Notably, not all officers (64%) mention Camaraderie as a contributor to confidence. Educational backgrounds (30%), and the belief in Faith or luck (20%) also contribute to officer Confidence. Like their Commitment, maintaining Confidence is evident given that on average, officers report five of the eight Practices (77%). (see Figure 7.3).

These Confidence Practices are presented as:

1. Quality training
2. Control environment
3. Police mentors
4. Seek support: Family and Camaraderie
5. Grounded: Recognition, Thanks, Education, Faith, and luck

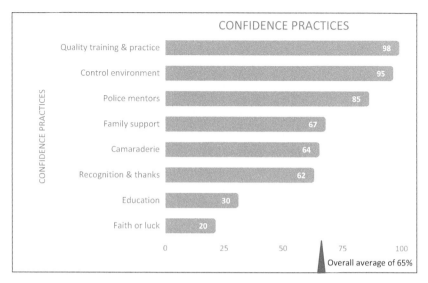

FIGURE 7.3 Confidence Practices

All excellent officers had an overall average of 65% Confidence practices (5 out of 8 practices per officer).

Quality Training

Training builds confidence, reducing doubt and preparing officers for challenges[20]. Acquiring specialty police training, unrelated external courses, regular visual rehearsals, and an effort to maximize equipment competence are viewed as critical resources for building personal comfort in situations. Although officers feel that previous successes, a sixth sense, and gut feelings could account for much of their confidence, almost all (98%) agreed that confidence is fundamentally something learned through actively seeking opportunities for improvement to know your strengths and limitations[7].

Training: "The more tools you have the more confident you feel."

Knowledge, skill, ability, equipment—*It's all based on training and preparation. You need that matchable four, no matter what section you're in. If your equipment (especially) is not ready, you're euchred. For the frontline patrol guy: What's the condition of your* *firearm? Have you been to the range in the last year? That's one of my personal beefs—being prepared. We inventory our trucks to make sure the equipment is there because the last thing I want to do is arrive at a scene, need a crucial piece of equipment and it's not there because somebody didn't put it back. It ends up costing lives.*

—Tactical

Training, interviewing—*I've been doing my interviewing course, and now I've got some new tools. The more tools you have, the more confident you feel.*

—5 to 10 years on

Training, controlling drunks—*There's no one secret for drunks. You've got to see where they're at. You can't get into an argument. Start yelling at a drunk, and he'll do the same thing to you and you'll never resolve what you're trying to resolve. Sometimes, if they're way up here, you have no choice. Nobody likes to be laughed at, and you can easily escalate a drunk by making fun of him. At some point you've gotta cut your losses and decide—cut them loose or make an arrest.*

—Patrol

Practice 1,000 times—*Training allowed me to do it a thousand times before I had to do it critically. Play it through, play it through, practice, practice, practice. Now, let's go do it.*

—Tactical

Personal happiness versus rank—*Everyone thinks that to be a success, you have to move up the ranks. I think success is being happy with what you do.*

—Neighborhood Resource

They got you—*You're driving down the street in your cruiser and somebody gives you the finger and it's three teenagers and they laugh. You go, "Why are you doing that? Grow up, for Christ's sake." I've seen other officers who will screech into reverse, come back, get out of the car, the finger to the chest and so on. Are you going to win? What are you winning in that situation? They got you. They put out the fishing rod, reeled* *you in and they got you. Be professional. Come back and say, "What's that about?"*

—Tactical Sergeant

Personal comfort—*You've done okay if you can go home at the end of the day and sleep. If you can't sleep at night, you're doing something wrong—you've gotta change something.*

—Patrol

Control Environment

The majority of officers (95%) enhance their belief in themselves by seeking ways to gain control of a situation by taking charge, forcing an outcome, or confronting a situation. This skill is used predominantly in controlling a crisis, as well as in challenging street disrespect, ending a lull or complacency and, for women, handling female-officer challenges. Maintaining control of situations relies heavily on being independent, projecting credibility, and fostering public trust, particularly when your actions are constantly being recorded.

Control: "You want the balance of control on your side—no matter what. We don't get paid to lose."

Control, identity, power—*Once you know somebody's identity, you have power over them.*

—Neighborhood Resource

Video records—*You are being watched and recorded all the time. Today everything is on video. Even at a hockey game, if a police officer is spotted, everyone's eyes shift to the officer to see if anyone's hurt, if there's danger or if someone is being taken away.*

—>15 years on

Control, physical factors—*First and foremost is control. The second you lose control, things start to happen. Your mouth has everything to do with it, but there are physical factors. Some people will not be told what to do. Some people will not listen, and that's where other factors come in. If you are physically*

imposing, it changes the situation. You want the balance of control on your side—no matter what. We don't get paid to lose.
—5 to 10 years on

Control, talk, handcuffs, backup—*I don't search anyone until after he's handcuffed and under arrest. I tell him, "You're under arrest, sir. Turn around." If he turns around, I say, "Look, we'll make it easier. I'll just handcuff you, then we'll talk about it" (to make them feel relaxed). Once you have them in the handcuffs, they're under your control. If he starts jerking around when you go to handcuff him, get dispatch to send another unit. That's when the troops will come.*
—Neighborhood Resource

Take charge, lead—*"I wish you'd come in when I called you in!" That was a big lesson for me. Sometimes you have to step across the line, and instead of being their coach, just tell them, No. Get in here, because I need you again."*
—Tactical

Crisis control, procedures—*First, reassure the victim that you are going to assist and let them know that you know what you're doing. That requires being familiar with policies, procedures and what resources are available to assist them in their emotional or physical trauma. Officers respect me because I know what I'm doing and I get things done. My most useful application in my role as an officer is to keep a level head and to be able to follow procedures and policies.*
—Neighborhood Resource

Credible with kids—*Credibility can be established in the square root of one second and how you present yourself. I have a good, friendly working relationship with the student body in all my schools. The 2% that don't like me, see me as a nuisance to their drug trading or stuff like that. That I can live with… Sometimes principals make me look like an enforcer, and that takes away from my credibility. I'm there in a helping, working relationship.*
—School Resource

Police Mentors

Police role models, whether a coach officer or valued police mentor, benefit individuals' careers[21,22]. Likewise, role modeling has been depicted as an important influence in other professions such as in medicine[23,24] relating to bedside manner and technical skills. Questions can arise on mentors' suitability for addressing racial diversity challenges[25,26]. Research shows that senior officers exhibit greater self-esteem and positive interactions across diverse cultures[6].

> **Two coach officers**—*I took a little from both of my Coach Officers. One was extremely strong administratively. He had a certain way of doing his notes. He knew what reports had to be done and who to contact. The other was very, very personable—he could talk to absolutely anybody.*
>
> —Patrol

> **Best coach**—*My best Coach Officer knew pretty much everything. He was calm. He knew where the paperwork was. He wasn't someone on patrol who was relegated to patrol. He was there by choice. He really liked patrolling. He was down to earth and able to tell me, "This is not for you right now. This is maybe the way you should follow."*
>
> —Patrol Sergeant

> **Valued sergeant**—*This Sergeant is very intelligent—I feel good about his capabilities, his knowledge, his intuition. They say he's one of the best operators. If he criticizes me, I know that it is well meaning and for my own benefit. Whereas I would get my hackles up if some other guys said something, and it was not the right place or the right forum.*
>
> —Tactical

Seek support: Family and Camaraderie

Having a range of support systems plays a significant part in nurturing confidence among high performers. Likewise, relationship building within one's immediate and extended family creates balance and peace of mind[27]. The "police family" was highlighted by 62% of officers. Generally, this unique bonding is patterned through sharing street contacts, razzing, and informal networking, as seen, for example, in "wings and beer nights."

Family support, from spouse, kids, parents or siblings, was rarely mentioned by officers with Canine experience (20%, $p = 0.021$). In contrast, family was raised by all Visible Minority-Aboriginal officers (100%, $p = 0.086$), whereas Camaraderie was not mentioned at all (0%, $p = 0.001$). Conversely, Camaraderie is clearly a source of Confidence for Caucasian officers (62%, $p = 0.001$), those with over 15 years' experience (72%, $p = 0.059$), or officers with prior police-related experience (72%, $p = 0.089$).

> **Family, shift work**—*It makes it that much easier if your partner understands that shift work comes with the career. It may be an issue when kids arrive, but you work around that. It is stressful on the body, and we see stuff that 90% of the public doesn't see. That creeps up on you once in a while but you deal with it by talking about it.*
>
> —Patrol

> **"Society sucks" belief**—*Getting married and having a family helped. That was a big issue for me. Before that, I went through a "society sucks" stage. I'd think, "Is everybody a*

PHOTO 7.2 Evolving one's frame of mind from "society sucks" to empathy and understanding is a journey supported by home and uniform. Credit: AI NOW Institute, Bing, 2019

criminal? What's going on?" After a while you realize this is just a small piece of society, and most of society is good. Leave it in the locker room; go home and enjoy life. You have to be healthy as a person.

—School Resource

Caring, venting, listening—*If I care for a person and he comes to me with a problem, I'll offer suggestions to open up other avenues. I'll say, "let's go for a beer and we'll talk." I let them vent. Listening is the key. I know what it's like when somebody else does all the talking.*

—Traffic Escort

Camaraderie, memorial parades—*Camaraderie makes a big difference. The camaraderie in the Police Service is amazing—get to know the people you're with. I went to the Police Memorial, and if you don't have tingles down your spine marching in that parade, there's something wrong with you. It's the "all for one" thing—because people have given their life.*

—Patrol

"How are you doing?"—*One of the officers I went to that call with called a couple of days later and said, "How are you doing?" I said, "Oh, I'm okay." He said, "no. How are you doing?" He knew. He actually cared, and it brought a human aspect back into it, as opposed to a job aspect.*

—Patrol, >10 years on

Grounded: Recognition, Thanks, Education, Faith, and Luck

Feeling grounded in policing can derive from various sources equally from internal recogniton, a public thank you to one's education or faith. Recognition was mentioned as frequently as camaraderie and family support by officers. An officer's personal outlook is positively influenced by "atta boys" or "atta girls" from the Chief, being seen as a valued leader or trainer, and the Staff's (Staff Sergeant's) recommendations and public feedback. Spiritual belief or religion was indicated by 20% of officers as a factor in enhancing their self-confidence. Not so coincidentally, those having a strong faith or belief in luck also score higher than most in reviewing and interpreting internal resources such as policies, special reports, procedures, and laws (correlation = 0.375, p = 0.009**).

Faith and luck were mentioned more often by Visible Minority-Aboriginal officers (44%, p = 0.056) and officers with frontline-only experience (33%, p = 0.035). Sergeants never mentioned faith (0%, p = 0.071) but are among the few (13%) to acknowledge confidence from education (30%, p = 0.063).

> **Remember, recognition**—*They say that as people move up in the ranks, they change. They forget what life on the road is like and make decisions that negatively impact officers on the road. I'm a Sergeant and [a certain] Constable constantly reminds me, "don't forget. Don't lose a sense of who you are. Recognize extra hours. Be nice—don't power trip." It's a reality check for me. It helps me do a good job. I'm still the person I was, but [it's easy to] start forgetting, because your responsibilities shift to budget and staffing issues.*
> —Patrol Sergeant

> **Recognition, fairness**—*The things they worry about on the street are: Being recognized for what they've done, finishing their shift on time, getting extra hours back in some form, getting the time off they deserve.*
> —Female Patrol

> **Education, psychology**—*There is a new breed of people who come into this job highly educated. There's nothing wrong with that. In fact, education should be even higher for police officers because of the tasks being assigned to them. There are people on this job who change people's lives. In different sections, like Sexual Assault, there is certainly more education needed in how people tick.*
> —Traffic Escort

> **Faith**—*At the end of the day it's all in belief. It doesn't matter what or who you believe in, it's the belief that's important. If it makes you feel good, who are you hurting?*
> —Patrol

Belief, luck—*I have my guardian angel. My mom gave me a little guardian angel when I started the job, and it's always in my jacket. Maybe it's that [laughs].*
—5 to 10 years on

Training omens—*A couple of people had shot no-shoot targets. I don't know if it was a bad omen or what*
—Tactical

D. Positive Imagery

Positive Imagery, often referred to as visualizing, is a common practice before, during, and after a call or when faced with having to recall information under stressful situations. Policing lends itself well to role-playing hypothetical scenarios, developing mental checklists, and trying to enhance memory.

Positive thinking plays an important role in visualization. However, criteria for determining if officers utilized positive imagery or visualization were very stringent, requiring statements about visualizing, imagining, or creating mental pictures, not just positive thinking.

All officers (100%) picture images with varying degrees of vividness and quite often involve visual triggers or rituals with equipment. These mental pictures appear to be of special value to officers in terms of:
- anticipating potential hazards and corresponding courses of action
- memorizing the "perfect" sequence of events
- developing a personalized mental checklist for use en route to a call
- debriefing a call individually or one-on-one with a supervisor
- practicing "mentally" while injured
- visualizing during team briefings or at parade
- anticipating cross-examination in court

254 ■ Mental readiness in policing

- ♦ recalling duty-book entries or reflecting on notes for court
- ♦ rehearsing tense situations using other officers' calls
- ♦ relieving anxiety or gastric and general pain
- ♦ relaxing before trying to sleep
- ♦ planning a "recce" (reconnaissance) in advance
- ♦ visualizing as a form of an improvised training exercise
- ♦ rehearsing procedural steps to develop more fluid movements with firearms marksmanship

Collectively, seven Positive Imagery Practices were identified by these excellent officers, which related to imagery techniques and opportunities to use this skill (see Figure 7.4). However, on average, they individually utilize only three out of the seven practices. Overall as a group, their approach is therefore diverse and inconsistent. The most prevalent strategies are vivid imagery en route to or on scene at calls (91%) and pertinence to court preparations (68%). Less common imagery skills include complementary visual triggers (46%), visualizations at debriefs (38%), impromptu rehearsals (37%), and instructor (19%) or supervisor

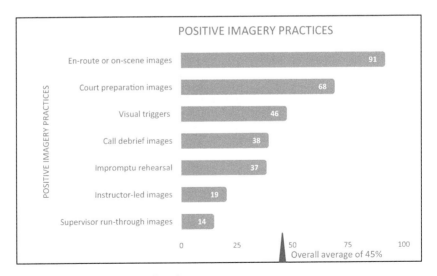

FIGURE 7.4 Positive Imagery Practices

All excellent officers had an overall average of 45% Positive Imagery practices (3 out of 7 practices per officer).

(14%) role-playing sessions. This may indicate that there are several fundamental visualizing strategies in policing; however, there is room for personalizing their application.

Visualizing is noted most often by those with Tactical experience (50%, p = 0.056) and officers with college education (50%, p = 0.047). Both positive thinking and visual imaging are significantly less noted by officers with Canine experience (80%, p = 0.064; 60%, p = 0.062, respectively).

These Positive Imagery Practices are presented as:

1. Techniques: Vivid images and visual triggers
2. Opportunities to visualize
    - En-route or on-scene images
    - Court preparation images
    - Call debrief images
    - Impromptu rehearsal
    - Instructor-led images
    - Supervisor run-through images

Techniques: Vivid Imagery and Visual Triggers

Vivid imagery was reported by all officers (100%) in various situations. Visualization in a policing environment is described as using mental pictures to rehearse procedures and potential outcomes en route to a call and tailor mental checklists. In recalling or hypothetically playing out a call, some officers often try to realistically imagine the sensory details of situations. Sounds, smells, interpersonal tensions, and personal reactions are anticipated using imagery. See Table 7.3 for a detailed description of Vivid Imagery.

Visual triggers (46%) further enhance visual recall for some officers through self-initiated practices such as taking photos or making special notes, records, sketches, or entries into a duty book or "career diary." Officers who reported the use of these visual triggers correlate high with those stating the importance of electronic aids in preparation (e.g., car computer, cell phone; correlation = 0.296, p = 0.041). Officers using visual triggers are

TABLE 7.3 Vivid Imagery Practices

	TOTAL RESPONSES Ranked by %
Vivid Imagery	100
Pictures: mental role-playing, hypothetical scenarios	
Checklist: personalized mental list (often on paper too)	
Senses: hear, smell, taste, tension, feelings	
Imagery relief from: anxiety, gastric/general pain, stress, sleeplessness	

also highly associated with reporting the importance of equipment checks in preparation (correlation = 0.375, p = 0.009).

Anticipate danger, worse-case scenarios—*I'm constantly visualizing the worst-case scenario. Behind a car at a red light, I'll think, "What happens if that guy jumps out with a shotgun?" It's paranoid, but there is a large degree of danger in my job. How do I respond? What would I do? So, I visualize.*
—Sergeant

Role-play with policy—*Especially with the policies always changing, you role-play: "Okay, what's the policy now? What do I have to do?"*
—Neighborhood Resource

Visualize equipment, safety—*Marijuana growers have been setting up booby-traps, like wiring doorknobs. You have to visualize—to be prepared. "Did I bring my circuit-tester?" That way you don't touch something that's going to kill you.*
—Tactical

Layout—*Multitasking isn't easy. If I'm going to a violent call, for example, I picture the layout of the entire area in my mind.*
—Traffic Escort

Visualize physical response—*I don't know if I would actually see it. I work with the scenario that I'm presented with at that second. Let's say it's happening right now. Okay, what have I got around me? Visualize? So I visualize what's physically*

there, and then how would I respond based on my surroundings, my environment at that point.
—Patrol, >10 years on

Partner rehearsal—*My sniper partner and I, we'll talk to each other. He's my observer or I'm his observer—whoever is in the position at the time. We mentally rehearse and we'll go, "What if he comes out the side door? How much farther is that than the front door?" "Well, with the laser, the side door is 255 meters. So it's 55 meters more. You'll have to hold at the top of his head or adjust your elevation." "Well, what if he comes out the door, and he starts to walk to his car? How much lead do I need? Is he walking perpendicular to me, or is he walking oblique to me?" We'll mentally rehearse where we could potentially get the shot.*
—Tactical

Pictures, checklist—*I have a mental picture of my physical checklist. It's in-and-out visualizing. "Where are the other officers coming from? How are we going to set up?" If I'm missing something, there'll be an empty space—I can SEE it. Then it'll take me a few minutes to figure out what I'm missing. If time permits, I'll refer to the physical checklist, but usually it doesn't.*
—Female Patrol

> *Thinking back: "I start going through my mental checklist. 'I'm going to need this, I'm going to need that...'"*

Mental checklist—*Say, I'm going to a hostage taking. Now I start thinking back, "What are the things that we're going to need step-by-step?" Now I start going through my mental checklist. "I'm going to need this, I'm going to need that, I'm going to need this."*
—Tactical, >15 years on

Approach, emotional awareness—*It's best if you know the building. A lot of times you're going to places you know like the back of your hand. You know the mentality of the people, and you know what you're getting into—not a whole lot of "friendlies." That's visualization right there—knowing that you're going into a den of iniquity.*
—Tactical

Winning—*We were ready. We didn't envision defeat. You can envision getting hurt and still winning. You can envision a slight advantage to the bad guys at one point and still winning. You are envisioning all your contingencies and how to shut this down, make the arrest, and end it positively and safely. We always win in most of our experiences.*

—Neighborhood Resource

Visual trigger notes, sketches—*I follow a chronological sequence. I let him write it in: "Give me your last name, your first name, your middle name, your address. Your phone number?" I write in a time. I sketch a picture, in case he takes off—which happens. He's got a mole here and he's got a scar here. Use everything you can. It's 13h56, so six minutes later he's under arrest. And you have to be able to justify that in court.*

—Neighborhood Resource

Visual cheat sheets, personal indexing—*I carry cheat sheets called the "notebook companion." It's got short-form wording for everything in Traffic—like your Off-road Vehicle Act, Motorized Snow Vehicle Act, Trespass Property Act, Mental Health Act. If I stop somebody for something silly, you go, "Oh, man, what would be the Section for that?" If they lost THAT, a lot of officers would cry (I'd be lost without it). I've personalized the indexing to my needs too. It's just fingertip stuff that is so valuable.*

—Traffic Escort

Opportunities to Visualize

Opportunity "to see in the mind's eye" is most dominant (91%) en route to, or on scene at, a call. It also presents itself in anticipating court appearances (68%). These visualized court rehearsals were mentioned by all Visible Minority-Aboriginal officers (100%, p = 0.066) and "New School" males (<10 years on, 100%, p = 0.065).

Further use of imagery used outside of regular responses to calls occurs during a debrief. Recalling and evaluating the details from a call was also reported by officers. Female officers and those with experience beyond the frontline practice this post-visualization technique more frequently than most (36%, p = 0.092; 29%, p = 0.067, respectively).

Less common visualization opportunities include:
- spontaneously running through another officer's call (37%)
- improvising at instructor-led training or special lectures (19%)
- improvising while meeting with a supervisor on parade or in team briefs (14%)

Officers with Tactical experience promote run-through visualizing with supervisors and impromptu rehearsal (30%, p = 0.013; 33%, p = 0.013, respectively). The spontaneous mental rehearsal may be a separating quality, since it was an uncommon skill also reported by Elite officers (23%, p = 0.083).

Training instructors and supervisors may be a strong influence on officers' tendency to electively perform impromptu imagery in their downtime. Officers who reported participating in instructor-led visualization scenarios also stated that in downtime they often run through situations while listening to other officers' calls (correlation = 0.553, p = 0.000). In addition, officers who reported having visualization instruction stated the importance of using imagery in supervised briefings (team or individual: correlation = 0.391, p = 0.006).

A final connection occurs between those who reported using imagery with supervisors and those who recognize value from informal social debriefing, such as in the gym or going out after a shift (correlation = 0.516, p = 0.000). Guided-imagery training has been shown to enhance relaxation and stress reduction[28,29], performance, attention, confidence, and emotional control[30,31]

> **Visualized debrief**—*If I wasn't successful or I was frustrated with a call, I'll go through what happened in my head: "Where did I go wrong?" Sometimes I will visualize, rethink it and remember what happened.*
> —Canine

> **Court checklists, repetitions**—*As a breath tech, I used to do a lot of court. I was prepared. I had a mental checklist and*

Court checklists: "As a breath tech… I was prepared. I had a mental checklist and a physical checklist."

a physical checklist—and I made sure that I had everything checked off. I would go over each case—I wouldn't just show up. I would have gone over it a few dozen times before.

—>15 years on

Court prep, notes, order—If you go to court and you're not prepared, you lose confidence in yourself. I like to be prepared. I go over my notes and try to get everything in order. I bring all the stuff I have to bring.

—Traffic Escort

Visualize: "A lot of times there's no preparedness, and I just visualize what may be there."

Visualize, team brief—A lot of times there's no preparedness, and I just visualize what may be there. Other times we have mini-briefings—your specific function in the line may be breaching a door or carrying a taser. But as soon as you go through the door, everything can change. If the front door doesn't go in, all of a sudden, the back door is the main entry.

—Tactical

Parade, supervisor prep—The mental readiness has to be there when the officers walk out the door. So we do a briefing every day before they go out. They sit down at the table—the kids, the husband or the wife are gone. You are here. I have 15 minutes to prepare them and get them going.

—Sergeant

Appropriateness en route, team—You try to visualize on the way to a call, but it's hard because there's so much going on—you can't just sit there like a friggin' zombie.

—Tactical

Scenarios, training practice—It was an "active shooter"—somebody in a large-volume area, gone crazy and shooting people. We'd played that a thousand times, and acted through every different scenario—he comes out with a gun, a hostage, a bomb.

> *It was the real deal, but we'd been through it a thousand times. We got there and—to use athlete's terminology—the "game face" came on.*
> —Tactical

E. Mental Preparation

Officers were asked to recall their preparation activities prior to a recent successful performance in policing. The intent was to determine what precedes top performances that allows them to feel ready. Collectively, officers show a high level of consistency by on average choosing six planned Mental Preparation Practices from their combined list of seven. This pattern of consistent mental preparation is quite outstanding suggesting influential training of officers in this area. These practices are skillfully used in setting the tone, understanding realities, and managing consequences.

> **Shift ritual**—*Before every shift I do the same thing. As soon as I get in my own personal vehicle, I turn the radio off and I run through three things: A high-speed pursuit, first aid/CPR and a barricaded person scenario. For example, I go through when high-speed pursuits are permitted, what you can and cannot do, what questions I would ask, etc. I do that every shift. I've done one high-speed pursuit in the last two years. They don't come around a lot, but it's very important to me to have the answers because of the probability of an inquest.*
> —Patrol Sergeant

Nearly all officers adhere to three key practices: strategically planning en route or on-site (100%), thinking positively arriving on scene (96%), and setting clear objectives (91%). They accomplish this by collecting information and running through personal checklists. Before carrying out their duties, they minimize interruptions (83%) and recognize the risks (75%). Officers commonly designate a specific location (60%) to prepare—be it from their patrol car, the gym, home, or elsewhere—often with rituals (56%) to set the right tone (see Figure 7.5).

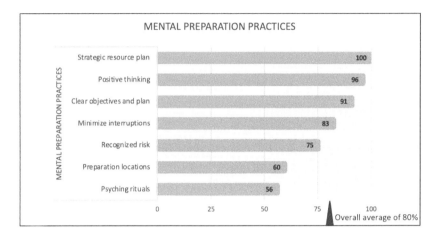

FIGURE 7.5 Mental Preparation Practices

All excellent officers had an overall average of 80% Mental Preparation practices (6 out of 7 practices per officer).

Overall, the groups demonstrating the greatest number of preparation practices are Elite officers and officers with Canine and Tactical experience (50%, p = 0.024; 90%, p = 0.072; 49%, p = 0.029, respectively). A significantly lower-than-average practice range was reported by officers with Patrol-only training (80%, p = 0.044).

Furthermore, as part of their standard approach to taking calls, excellent officers convey several basic principles and attitudes—also serving as personal long-term coping strategies (see Constructive Evaluation). Most significant is their commitment to Professional Discipline (93%) and Understanding of "the Job" (82%) which lays the groundwork for executing their duties effectively. A series of basic strategies for resting (75%) and maintaining physical fitness (52%) exist among these excellent officers.

These Mental Preparation Practices are presented as:

1. Strategic resource plan
2. Positive thinking
3. Clear objectives and plan
4. Minimize interruptions

5. Recognize risks
6. Psyching: Rituals and preparation locations

Strategic Resource Plan

When faced with complexity and pressure, sometimes it is the basics that ground you. Golf Digest's No. 1-ranked teacher Butch Harmon is coach for tour players like Tiger Woods, Phil Mickelson, Jordan Spieth, and Justin Thomas. He emphasizes that every part of the swing is only as good as the parts that come before it[32]. Tiger Woods reportedly started each season with his coach reviewing his grip.

> **Review fundamentals**—*One simple way to keep your swing on track is to review the fundamentals in step-by-step order. It allows you to check your technique in small pieces and identify where you might be getting out of position.*
> — Butch Harmon, Pro-golf coach[32]

Strategically planning resources in advance, whether it is days, hours, or mere moments before crucial activities, is a consistent practice for all exceptional officers (100%). This preparation entails strategically reviewing physical and technical aspects, with a focus on ensuring internal communication (82%) and officer safety (82%). Additionally, officers run equipment checks (55%), liaise with external resources (51%), review internal procedures (50%), and utilize electronics as aids (25%). Continuously anticipating scenarios, addressing victims, securing scenes, and allowing access for emergency services, all while maintaining adaptability and relying on organizational skills, are critical steps. See Table 7.4 for a detailed description of Strategic Resource Plan.

> **Scene management**—*I'm constantly reviewing the scenario, thinking about all the options. I can't stop the cruiser in an emergency situation, pull up the policies and start to read. I'm doing scene management, ensuring that victims are tended to, the scene is shut down, fire and ambulance have access to everybody, witnesses are being checked into. Those are the cores I'm*

TABLE 7.4 Strategic Resource Plan Practices

	TOTAL RESPONSES Ranked by %
Strategically Plan Resources	100
Communicate internally: talk to peers, inform supervisor, specialty unit back-up, contain	82
Ensure officer safety: safety sense, cautious approach, proper search	82
Run equipment checks: check force options, gun taps, stock duty belt, before shift/call	55
Communicate externally: external specialists, bystanders, witnesses	51
Review policies and procedures: interpret policies, balance compliance, ethics and judgment	50
Value electronics: importance of car laptop, run dates, cell phone	25

very comfortable with… Confidence comes with the Inspector showing up after the fact with a checklist and supports me by saying "Have we done this?" "No we haven't, let's do that now." I found that extremely helpful.

—Patrol Sergeant

Close as I can—*Other people are relying on you. You can't coast. Tactically and mentally, you have to be fundamentally sound. It would be nice to be 100% [pause]. I can't say that I am, because unless you've actually been in that situation, you can't really say, but I'm as close as I can possibly get to 100%. I try to do that.*

—Tactical

Weapon check—*You're absolutely, always, always checking for your weapon. As soon as that Dispatch happens, it's instinctive—you make sure your gun is on your side. I go nowhere without checking my weapon. I will touch my gun, or elbow my gun. If you watch, I think everybody does it. They teach you* *that every call's a gun call. And they're right, because you're bringing a gun [laughs].*

—5 to 10 years on

Flexible—*You may want it to run this way, but it probably doesn't. So, you have to be flexible. You have to go with the flow, and be able to deal with it. You can't go into a domestic, thinking, "I'm going to arrest the husband, cuff him, get a statement off the wire, take him downtown, get pictures of the wife, do my report and that's the end." But it doesn't always run that way. The husband doesn't want to be arrested, so you fight with him. The wife doesn't want to give you a statement, so you've got to beg her to give you a statement. Maybe there are kids there, so you have to be very flexible.*

—Tactical

Organizational skills—*Many of the skills I have, I brought in or acquired before I came on. There are a few things I have learned in the military that still serve me here today—organizational skills, like leadership and decision making… These are things I brought to the table before I joined the police, as well as physical and technical skills.*

—Patrol

PHOTO 7.3 The mindset: Safety first, scene managed, support each other. Need to plan resources well ahead, run equipment checks, review procedures, liaise with external resources—always ready to adapt as required. Credit: Unison, Bing, 2017

Positive Thinking

Positive thinking relates to an officer's capacity to perform and the feelings associated with "perfect" execution of a procedure. Positive thinking on scene is among the most common practices among these officers (96%). Overwhelmingly, most enjoy their job for the "thrills," the diversity and freedom it presents, as well as seeing benefit in the physical demands, outdoor environment, and flexible time. Research corroborates that a positive attitude emerged as one of the "most impressive" traits among the highest-performing officers[33].

> **Olympic perspective**—*Positive thinking is one of the most important skills to reinforce in Olympic training. One of the reasons this is such a valuable skill is because "negative thinking" is so common under pressure. Under pressure we tend to be negative thinkers; get psyched-out; and have doubts. The focus you want is best-performance thinking.*
> —Dr. Yoshinori Okazawa,
> four-time Olympic sport psychologist, 2020

A source of frustration in policing is the shift in focus. Instead of fighting crime and catching criminals, policing roles now emphasize protecting vulnerable communities, resolving neighborhood conflicts, initiating community-engagement programs, and addressing the modern threats of terrorism and cyber-enabled crime[34,35].

Less than half of the officers reported various specific means of encouraging a positive attitude in arriving on scene—for example, getting "psyched," using creativity to refocus, adding humor in tense situations, and having faith in "what will be." Details for Positive thinking are listed in Table 7.5.

Enjoyment: "You have to want to be a police officer."

Enjoyment, thrill, diversity—*You have to want to be a police officer—the thrill of the chase, the challenges of different calls, meeting different people, helping people. There's always something new, and it's always interesting.*
—Patrol, >15 years on

TABLE 7.5 Positive Thinking Practices

	TOTAL RESPONSES Ranked by %
Positive thinking	96
Job satisfaction: enjoyment, thrill, diversity, freedom, physical, outdoors, flexible time	
Psyching: positive talk, rituals, quiet time to prepare	
Positive refocus: "it's a game," all relative, "nothing compares," improvise, have some fun	
Humor: keep things light	
Faith: luck, spiritual, external faith, pray, "it's meant to be"	

Game, puzzle—*Fraud suspects are intelligent, and they love to lie. When you make a deal with them, it's a game—like solving a puzzle. Let them talk, and then put it all together. When they know you know, then they play dumb [laughs].*
—Neighborhood Resource

Readiness—*I'm at work a half-hour before my shift starts. I don't like being rushed. Sometimes you get a serious call, where you're literally running out of the police station, and you can't be ready for that. There's a certain readiness that's gotta be done by the time you start your shift, before you get that serious call. You've gotta know your work.*
—Patrol, >10 years on

Joking, sanity—*I start talking about what and where we're going. We're always joking. You need to, just to keep yourself sane. (If we're responding to a crisis situation, there's a little bit less.)*
—Tactical

Humor, quickness—*They call me "The King of One-Liners." It's one of my outlets—I snap right back with a comment, just as quick.*
—>15 years on

Fun, differences, talk—*One of the fun things about this job is your style. Everyone has a different style. Somebody may do it differently and get to the same result. My partner was very* *different, and it was frustrating. But I'd bite my tongue and watch him, and I'd learn something. We had a little debriefing because we both felt this way. Meanwhile, we learned something. It was a really good environment that way.*

—Traffic Escort

Positive talk, focus, game—*My partner and I mentally rehearse during downtime in a sniper position. We'll say, "If he comes out, I need a half a mil dot lead on the front of his skull, and I'll put the bullet in his ear." It's a game. It probably sounds sick, but it's focus training.*

—Tactical

Practice, luck—*We had done it before in other areas—but sometimes it won't work. You sort of cross your fingers.*

—Traffic Escort

Clear Objectives and Plan

Nearly all officers (91%) in their preparation stage listed setting Clear objectives, developing Action plans, and collecting facts for their "mission." Actions without a meaningful goal make for wasted effort. Police are in life-and-death situations and are trained to expediently and cautiously assess before acting. In particular, Tactical officers have an uncanny ability to "buy time" in situations that most would think are staggeringly urgent and time-sensitive. Yet they conduct their "mission" in a very controlled and methodical manner.

Think, plan—*There's no sense rushing to your death. Why go in there not thinking, not having a plan? All you're going to do is get killed or kill or get somebody else killed. Everybody else is lighting his hair on fire thinking there's only seconds to spare. [I don't think that way] because there isn't. There are not seconds to spare. If you go in running, you're going to make the situation worse. My job is to go up to a situation where people don't have the training, go in and make sure that everybody comes out safe. That means the victim, the bad guy and me (… not in that order). If I go in there, precipitate something and somebody gets hurt—well, I haven't done my job. I know I can't do it all the time—there are going to be situations where it can't*

be helped. [It's my job to see that] my actions should not be the cause of somebody getting hurt.
—Tactical

A good game plan provides an officer with clear direction. An open mind ensures that the unknown and the unpredictable will be dealt with effectively. These officers reported that planning a series of activities leads to a state of mental preparation before beginning their shift or taking the call that resulted in best performances.

Information, speed, awareness—*You're hungry for information—it will dictate your next move. As soon as the computer dings or you hear the dispatcher, it's like, "What? C'mon, let's go." The more information you get the better—but there's a fine line. You might miss what's going on around you.*
—>10 years on

Planning:
"Having no plan and not knowing what you're getting into—that's where people get hurt."

Speed, planning, knowing—*Speed is everything when you're going through the door. If you know what you're doing, speed is good. But when you act before you have a plan, things start to go wrong. Doing things with speed when you first arrive, having no plan and not knowing what you're getting into—that's where people get hurt.*
—Tactical

Plan en route, control—*What's the first thing I've gotta do? If I don't get my planning prepared in advance, I will pull over. Some people will ask for a second to figure out what they're going to do. I like arriving calm, cool and collected—to show my guys that I am in control.*
—Sergeant

Minimize Interruptions

Strong officers are able to put things on hold and isolate themselves to deal with issues, and then get back on track. Driving defensively, choosing arterial routes, and slowing down to watch for people fleeing are seen as minimizing interference. This practice was noted by 83% of officers, which included all Tactical, Canine, and Traffic Escort officers (100%, p = 0.011). In comparison, it is less common among excellent female officers (73%, p = 0.039) or those with NRT or SRO experience (70%, p = 0.024; 71%, p = 0.092, respectively).

> **Shut out interruptions**—*One of the techniques I learned as a negotiator was to shut all the other crap out. The only thing that matters is what you and him are talking about. I'll put my head down when I'm on the phone so I don't see the crap around me—"It's just me and you, buddy. None of this other shit matters."*
>
> —>15 years on

> **Turn down interference, relax**—*We're there to identify the problem and find a solution. Try to take everything in. Turn down the outside interference—you don't want distractions. If there's a stereo going and people are drunk, just relax. Try to get other people involved in the call.*
>
> —>15 years on

> **Driving control, plan, alternatives**—*I don't know. I just think I drive properly. There's no need to drive like a lunatic. I am certainly far from the last car on-scene—if not the first, one of the first, for sure. If there's a call that I need to go to lights and sirens, I'm there, but I'm not going to run over four or five kids to get there. Rather than blowing lights, I scoot along side streets that run parallel—less traffic, fewer people on the road. You plan: "What's going to be the quickest and safest way to get there?" For the people who are having accidents, I would just try to think of some alternate routes.*
>
> —>15 years on

Recognize Risks

The need to Recognize risks was highlighted by 75% of officers. This principle is summarized by these statements:
- recognize and respect the risks
- live with the personal fear that you might get hurt

- acknowledge that not all the work is fun, but it's part of the job
- maintain a positive attitude for the responsibility and seriousness of the work
- accept the statistics as indicators of the level of incidents that are reasonable

This reality check for anticipating risk was more frequently noted by officers with over 15 years on and those with university education (85%, p = 0.088; 87%, p = 0.065, respectively).

> **Anticipate the worst**—*At any given time you have to be ready for those worse case scenarios—the shooting, the vehicle pursuit, the foot pursuit, the fight—the Hollywood action-type scenario.*
>
> —Neighborhood Resource

> **Courage, risk, fear**—*I was preparing myself for a firefight. I was preparing to get shot and how I would react to that—I wasn't going to quit. No way I was going to stop or do anything but press on and get the job done. There wasn't "paralyzing fear" but there was fear.*
>
> —Tactical

Psyching: Rituals and Preparation Locations

Psyching Rituals

Rituals like tactical breathing and squad meetings aid clear thinking, relaxation, bonding, and handling stress[27,36]. Chief Robert Lunney, an icon of Canadian policing, compared street policing and hockey performance rituals.

> **Performance rituals**—*Watch a hockey team emerge from the locker room prior to the start of a game. They exit in a pre-determined order, often led by the goaltender. The captain stands by the door, recognizing each player in turn with a nod or touch on the shoulder. All rituals are part of the preparation for action. It is the same in all premier sports.*
>
> —Chief Robert Lunney[27]

Officers attempt to increase predictability by engaging in self-encouragement, pre-shift rituals, respect for the parade room environment, and personal equipment-check routines. This trait is highest among all Canine officers (100%, $p = 0.048$), most officers with Tactical experience (89%, $p = 0.041$), and those with more than frontline experience (75%, $p = 0.02$). It was least mentioned by officers with SRO experience or with only patrol experience (29%, $p = 0.067$; 30%, $p = 0.043$, respectively).

A coach officer shared a story about dieting. If he caught himself reaching, he simply told himself, "Do not eat that!" and that was enough to change course. He asks his trainees, "What are *your* words [when taking a tough call]?" One trainee's response, "I'm ready NOW!"

> **Getting psyched**—*In [former large city police service] I used to make sure everything was in order before I left home. While I was driving to work, I'd have a cup of coffee and listen to rock music to pump me up. The time in the car was my constant. I knew I had a whole night ahead and I was getting myself in tune. In the locker room, it was a miniature war. We would play rock and metal-type music... all you'd hear was guys loading their guns.*
>
> —Patrol, >10 years on

> **Music rituals**—*Movie sound-tracks are a great choice to set a mood since they have been researched to evoke specific emotions. For example: Titanic (resiliency in desperate times), Gandi (innovation and change), Mission Impossible (do the impossible), Rocky's Eye of the Tiger (motivation), and Brave Heart (bravery).*
>
> —Isabelle Fontaine, Neuroscience researcher[37]

> **Community mindset**—*For a School Resource Officer, it's important to be time-management oriented, ready to work with kids and ready for partnerships with communities and services. You have to have that mindset.*
>
> —School Resource

> **Equipment, preparation**—*There's nothing worse than being last guy in the truck. When I put my stuff away, I know where*

everything is—I don't have to hunt around. If you were lazy the night before and didn't do that, then you're taking extra time.
—Tactical

Parade, sharing, social—*Parade is a big deal. You get a room full of people sharing information. Things like, you pulled over someone dangerous the night before. The guys beside you might not even know that. There's a lot of information to be shared in a group of people like that, let alone a police service of 1500 people. Parade is invaluable. Plus, it's as social as it is work. You've gotta get along with the people you work with—you're a team.*
—>10 years on

Preparation Locations

Careful analysis of the police officers' transcripts reveals that many officers (60%) show a preference for the place they engage in mental rehearsal. Designated locations for preparation include the officer's patrol car, the station, and the home. SME officers favored the spontaneity and improvisation of using command posts, the gym, or elsewhere. Details for Preparation Locations are listed in Table 7.6.

TABLE 7.6 Preparation Location Practices

	TOTAL RESPONSES
	Ranked by %
Preparation Locations	60
Car: "my office," while driving	
Station: parade, locker room, equipment prep, listen to orders Home: night before, pre-shift rituals, review court notes	
Command post: car, trunk, light post	
Gym: workout, think through, workout prior to shift	
Anywhere: watching TV, restaurant, always what ifs	

Car-office investigation—*I took the investigation back to my office—my car is my office.*
—Neighborhood Resource

> **Drive, think, plan**—*I think about all that I need to do while I'm driving.*
> —Female Patrol, >10 years on

> **Home, plan**—*I plan specialized training weeks at home. I need time away from these clowns sometimes—just to sit back and put it together. Then I bring it all back and delegate things out.*
> —>15 years on

> **Home in bed, scenarios**—*Every scene is different. I could actually be lying in bed thinking about that same scenario. Someone jumps out at a red light.*
> —>10 years on

> **Gym thinking**—*I'll think and visualize stopping a car. What I want to do and the steps I want to go through. I'll think about it in the gym.*
> —Neighborhood Resource

F. Full Focus

All officers described experiencing a fully focused state during their best performances. This focus is marked by the ability to command a presence of mind (93%), anticipate the next step (92%), derive confidence from their equipment (89%), and work on a team trusting their peers (88%). Most often the fully focused state is accompanied by a lack of anxiety. For the majority, the call or situation is a very connected, enjoyable challenge (78%) that is relaxed (65%) and takes on a rhythm and flow of its own (72%). On average, officers employ six of seven reported Full Focus Practices demonstrating their consistency in attaining this focus (see Figure 7.6).

> **No "Take 2"**—*With challenges, you need to focus and follow directions. Some people exhibit attention deficit when assigned a series of tasks, jumping from one to another without completing anything. In policing, a lack of focus has consequences; there's no room for saying, "Oh, I forgot this." There is no "Take 2."*
> —Police Executive

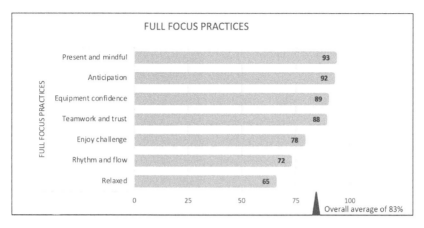

FIGURE 7.6 Full Focus Practices

All excellent officers had an overall average of 83% Full Focus practices (6 out of 7 practices per officer).

> **One thing**—*You cannot be 100% all the time or you'll burn out. But there are times where you have to be focusing 110% of your attention on one thing.*
> —Traffic Escort

Guidance on narrowing attention and excluding distractions through imagery, relaxation, and deep breathing has been extensively used in marksmanship training[31]. However, achieving and applying this focus can extend beyond this context. Officers consistently experience full focus in challenging situations.

These Full Focus Practices are presented as:

1. Present and mindful
2. Anticipation
3. Equipment confidence
4. Teamwork and trust
5. Emotional intelligence: Enjoyment, Rhythm, and Relaxation

Present and Mindful

Officers are constantly confronted with risks that require ongoing assessment. A traffic cop will quickly clarify that what seems like a simple activity in an urban intersection involves risk assessment, decisions based the appraisal of risk and risk management. In an ideal performance state, an athlete speaks of "being in the zone." For 93% of the officers, this same "presence" is experienced as:
- being mindful and alert with heightened observation
- having a sixth sense, or gut feeling
- being "on"
- reading people
- gauging space and proximity
- ramping up
- exercising good judgment

Focusing in this way appears to be a trait common to Anglophone officers (100%, p = 0.000).

An officer's heightened alertness in a challenging call is akin to the unwavering concentration of surgeons performing an intricate operation, or the situational awareness training for air traffic controllers managing air and ground conditions, or the deliberate movements of a Sherpa guide rehearsing the safest path up the mountain. "Mindfulness" describes this intensified awareness of thoughts, feelings, and sensations, like viewing life in slow motion. This acute awareness can improve decision-making, detecting and adjusting to errors, and debriefing after a shift[38,39].

> **Watch and listen**—*A domestic is the worst call—it's the unknown factor. I'll try to identify the problem by watching and listening. I'll watch the body language and the eyes. I'll look around the room for any possible signs. Like a glare or a blank stare—maybe they're thinking of something else, or there are drugs involved, or they're lying. You can tell. Just watch the hands. That's old-school sh--. It's no big deal—you can pick up on that.*
> —>15 years on

Stop reading—Sometimes you're inundated with information. You have to just close the laptop down and listen to what the dispatcher's saying on the air. If it is a big call, everything that you're updated on (on the laptop) is also articulated over the air. So, there are times where I'll say, "Okay, I'm not reading any more. I'll just listen to what she's saying." When it's a medium-priority call, then you're doing both.

—Neighborhood Resource, 5 to 10 years on

Anticipation

One predominant strategy used by almost all officers (92%) is anticipating complications and solutions. By answering, "What would I do if… ?" the officers develop a plan for dealing with the unknown and the unpredictable. Officers prepare by verbalizing potential complications, listing their checklist of procedural steps and reviewing their plans (often while driving to the scene).

This ability to be present in a situation yet be thinking ahead is a highly sought-after skill in mental training. Perhaps the consistency of the police approach can be attributed to the high-level specialized training, practice, and discipline in policing. Details for Anticipation are listed in Table 7.7.

TABLE 7.7 Anticipation Practices

	TOTAL RESPONSES Ranked by %
Anticipation	92
Plan for what ifs, nothing normal, options	
Prepare for court: anticipate, duty book entry, notes	
Prevent public complaints: don't get them, respectful	
Prevent public disrespect: treat respectfully, think fast	
Prevent lulls: anticipate the situation	
Minimize collision frequency: judge, read into call	
Proactive with public disrespect (long-term): public promotion, demos, talks in school	

Readiness, action—*At any given time you have to be ready for those worst-case scenarios—the shooting, the vehicle pursuit, the foot pursuit, the fight—the Hollywood action-type scenario.*

—Patrol, <5 years on

Anticipate approach, information—*Just because a call comes to you as a priority one, it doesn't mean lights and sirens. My experience tells me that I'm going to get a lot more information if I have officers on the scene, approaching the situation cautiously, and listening to the airwaves. You're thinking about the area, location. In a high-risk situation, such as a gun call, the direct route may also be the line of fire for somebody.*

—Patrol, >15 years on

Complacency, "you never know"—In policing, complacency is dangerous. It also depends on the people you're dealing with. If you're dealing with a drug-addicted person, for example, repetition will happen. But even if you deal with them on a daily basis, never assume that everything's going to be fine. You never know.

—Neighborhood Resource

Anticipate, danger—*I was preparing myself for a firefight. I thought, "This person wants to kill more people. We're going to get shot at." I was convinced that he was going to shoot at us and we were going to have to shoot at him. I think any of the guys going there had the same thought.*

—Tactical

Identify, assist—*When the situation is confirmed, I establish how I can safely assist. It means a lot if I can identify who else is going. If I've been to the area before, I'll try to identify who the actors are, "Oh yeah, I've dealt with this guy before. He's got* weapons," or, "This guy's on drugs all the time, he's a problem," or, "This guy isn't so bad." There are a lot of factors.

—Traffic Escort

Prepared: "My thought process is that if you're prepared for the worst, then everything is so much easier to handle."

Prepared for the worst—*My thought process is that if you're prepared for the worst, then everything is so much easier to handle.*

—Patrol

Equipment Confidence

For most uniformed police officers (89%), the use of and feel for equipment plays a major role in boosting confidence and concentration. Equipment is a leading factor in effective police communication, protection, and performance. Bantering across radio

PHOTO 7.4 Confidence with equipment is non-negotiable—it's typically just you and your gear sometimes. A "packing ritual" ensures you know where everything is—no thinking, just action. Credit: Chris Yarzab, Action Alliance, Bing, 2015

frequencies, cellular airways, and on-line terminals is a testament to the complexity of police e-communications. Internal and public demands for responsible "force options" impose high equipment standards on a frontline officer. Persistent gun checks and duty-belt habits reinforce comfort and fluency while in uniform (also detailed in Mental Preparation—Strategic Resource Planning; and Chapter 5. Physical readiness in policing—Use of Force). The way officers interact with their equipment is influenced by human factors. This idea is seen as a "Judgment Continuum"[40], which also involves perception, ethics, and biases in how officers decide when to use force[41,42,43].

> **Packing ritual**—*After every call and every training day, my bag gets emptied the same way and put back the same way. I know where everything is in my bag. I don't have to think about it.*
> —Tactical

> **Radio communication**—*I'm alone, yes, but I've got the radio. I'm able to communicate to the other Sergeant or to whomever else. Everyone else knows enough to shut up, let us take the radio, and not ask for anything silly.*
> —Patrol Sergeant

> **Equipment 100%**—*Mentally, that's the most important. If you're running not at 100% physically, and you're not at 100% in terms of knowledge, you have to be 100% confident with your equipment. It's just you and your equipment sometimes.*
> —Neighborhood Resource, 5 to 10 years on

> **Equipment prep, ready**—*Next time you won't have time to fart around getting ready—it'll be in your face. So be prepared.*
> —Tactical

> **Equipment, safety**—*We had a situation with some drug dealers who said they wouldn't be taken alive. Guys who say, "I won't be taken alive" are usually the first to crap their pants—but you can't always depend on that. To prepare, we made sure we had heavy rifles and we got an Armored Suburban. It weighs about 10 tons—you can fire a rifle into it and it won't hurt it.*
> —Senior Constable, >15 years on

Updates—*I try to read the laptop, but that's tough to do sometimes, depending on traffic. I listen for updates on the air.*
—Canine

Teamwork and Trust

For most officers (88%), achieving full focus is accompanied by a deep loyalty for and trust in partners and teams. Officers impose a strict code about the expectation of "being there for each other" and "sticking together." This is often casually reinforced with a friendly drive by at another member's traffic stop. However, this peer trust is significantly more present among Caucasian male officers (94%, $p = 0.056$).

Team, empathy—*When we left I said, "I'm sorry I talked. It was your call." He said, "No, Jesus. You really tapped in. I couldn't have come up with that." I seem to have a skill of drawing things out of people. They can sense that something's coming back to them.*
—School Resource

Team, safety—*I've gotten into fights on busy streets and friends have happened to drive by and come to give me a hand. You're safe in the public venue.*
—Neighborhood Resource

Reassurance—*I've never forgotten. The first 6 months I was on the job, a 10-78 came in. I was driving down a main road at some pretty frightening speeds at one o'clock in the morning. I looked over my shoulder through the mirror and saw, as far as the eye can see (we're talking an 8-10 block stretch) just car after car with all their lights on. It was reassuring. That's the way it should be.*
—Neighborhood Resource

Community team—*You work as a team. It's a partnership with them to make the school safer and it's a good way of dealing with things. It saves time for us and it also gets a good investigation done on both sides.*
—School Resource

Interdependence—*It's interdependency—the guys I'm with know what they're doing. I know that. We're all trained together. I have complete faith in them. If I didn't think the guy next to me could do the job or that I couldn't put my life in his hands… then, I couldn't do this job.*

—Tactical

Emotional Intelligence: Enjoyment, Rhythm, and Relaxation

"Emotional Intelligence" means understanding your own feelings, controlling them, staying motivated, showing empathy, and having good relationships. It stands apart from personality traits and serves as a predictor of job performance[15]. When staying focused, officers say they feel content, notice the rhythm and pace of things, and remain calm and comfortable.

Enjoyment during best performances was captured by most officers (78%) as a thrill, a good high, a bit of a rush, and a love for being busy responding to calls.

Rhythm: Officers must go beyond being fully able to focus at any time. Calls can be very lengthy, with many fluctuations in tempo, and officers need to flow between intense and more relaxed moments. In the emergency-response world of policing, it is important to remain alert. The slow routine periods demand a different type of mental control, which is also vital to the success of the call. When the tempo is faster, the situation becomes more fluid and automatic, with a frenzy of multitasking. Officers need to know when to grab a quick break before starting up again. Establishing a rhythm or pace was important to 72% of all officers, but less common among officers with SRO experience (29%, $p = 0.047$).

Relaxation: Many officers (65%) find it essential to take time to relax and prepare themselves mentally before a call, regardless of how briefly. This practice is most common among officers with university and college educations, and used less by those with high school education only (94%, 75%, and 40%, respectively, $p = 0.003$). Establishing a calm state is done through personally planned rituals for staying relaxed such as:

- ♦ keeping things light with humor

- taking a quiet focus time to regain a level head
- following a quick breathing technique (e.g., Grossman's tactical breathing technique)
- pitching the voice an octave lower
- visualizing "calmness"
- progressively relaxing muscles while taking some deep breaths
- narrowing attention to exclude extraneous thoughts and noise

Enjoy, challenge, fun—*I love nights. That's when the kooks come out and all the bad guys are rolling around. That's when everything happens. It's fun. I look forward to it.*
—Patrol, >10 years on

Enjoy, excitement—*I love coming to work. There's no job that I think is below me. Some guys think, "Let somebody else do it," but I take whatever they give me. I enjoy it, right to this day. The job itself is appealing—no two days are the same. It's exciting and it gets the adrenaline going… If it doesn't, something's wrong!*
—Senior Constable

Enjoyment, major accidents—*I'm not one to back down from a call. If there's a serious accident or a major crime call, I'll go. I love that shit. I never turn one down. I've been doing it for years and I still like it.*
—Patrol, >15 years on

Rhythm, pace, complacency—*At first, you're up there—everybody's up there. As time progresses, it slides down and plateaus. You have to let yourself down to a certain degree but there's complacent, and then there's TOO complacent. You can't let it slide too far.*
—Tactical

Rhythm, prioritizing tasks—*Multi-tasking isn't easy. If I'm going to a violent call, for example, I picture the layout of the entire area in my mind. Are the suspects in a vehicle? Where's a good cut-off point? Who else is going? Do I know that guy? You're concentrating on these things—plus you're driving. I* *don't close everything down, but I don't respond to it. I'll glance at [the computer] or listen to the radio but I just concentrate on my driving because getting there as fast and safely as possible without having an accident is the most important thing.*

—Traffic Escort

Relax, physiological effects—*You're driving down the road and you catch a moving stolen vehicle. If you just jump on the radio, your voice is all over the place. Your emotions get up, your heart rate gets up—it affects your whole physiological being. When I was a sniper, I learned to take deep breaths. You deepen in, cleansing out, in, hold it for two seconds, and out. It makes a BIG difference.*

—>10 years on

G. Distraction Control

This section concentrates on the success element Distraction Control. More information about the specific blocks that affect performance can be found in Chapter 3: Police under Pressure—Performance Blocks.

Reacting to disturbances can easily interrupt concentration. Distractions that prevent an officer from being alert, relaxed, and meticulous can quickly create a performance disadvantage. In high-performance situations, this success element is highly regarded. Emotional control is important for de-escalating situations, managing distractions, being a good leader, preventing mental-health issues, and sustaining interpersonal skills[44].

Distraction Control has the largest inventory of practices (14) of all the elements. These practices exist for both generic and specialized hindrances on the job. Out of the 14 Distraction Control or refocusing practices, only three are consistently used by most officers (over 75%) in varying degrees. These core practices include De-escalation (90%), Involvement of others (89%), and Crisis refocusing (79%). The other 11 practices mainly target specialized controls strategies, addressing issues such as fatigue (75%), downtime (71%), and female policing (45%). Being task orientated was a generic practice that was only reported by 39% of officers. Overall, the Patrol unit (87%, p = 0.026) is significantly higher in Distraction Control Practices than any of the other five specialty units (NRT-SRO units at 79%, Tactical-Canine-Traffic Escort units at 80%).

In recalling distractions that occurred during successful performances, all officers reported generally getting back on track quickly—although not for all types of distractions. They excel at concentrating in high-action periods during a call involving a "crisis." Many officers (70% to 75%) have developed practices to address fatigue, overcome street disrespect, drive safely, appear in court, and refocus during downtimes or routine tasks. However, as a group, they were not as effective at counterbalancing distractions from shift work, public complaints, work volume, not being promoted, or female-policing issues. (see Figure 7.7).

Shift-work fatigue is rated by the majority of officers (80%) as a common distraction yet it had one of the lowest scores (69%) with respect to officers' skill at handling this distraction effectively.

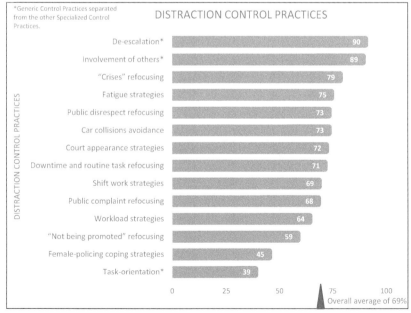

FIGURE 7.7 Distraction Control Practices

All excellent officers had an overall average of 69% Distraction Control practices (10 out of 14 practices per officer).

Dealing with the inherent on-the-job consequences of shift work is perhaps the first step in an area that needs further attention.

Another source of imbalance occurs when a distraction is outside an officer's control and where supervisor intervention may be required. The aggressive nature of Rookie Patrols was identified by most officers (80%) as a serious block. None of the Specialized Control Practices directly address this issue and the Generic Control Practices would be only marginally effective. The same disparity exists between the distractions created by workload volume (75%) and the limited depth in the solutions contributed by officers (64%). Creating control skills to target personal anxieties between experienced and inexperienced officers is a predominant need. The complete list of officer Distraction Control Practices is included in Figure 7.7.

These Distraction Control Practices are presented as:

Generic Control Practices

1. De-escalation
2. Involvement of others
3. Task orientation

Specialized Control Practices

1. "Crises" refocusing
2. Fatigue strategies*
3. Public disrespect refocusing
4. Car collisions avoidance*
5. Court appearance strategies**
6. Downtime (lulls) and routine task refocusing
7. Shift-work strategies*
8. Public complaint refocusing
9. Workload strategies
10. "Not being promoted" refocusing
11. Female-policing coping strategies

* These Distraction Control Practices are described in Chapter 5: Physical Readiness in Policing.
** These Distraction Control Practices are described in Chapter 6: Technical Readiness in Policing.

General Control Practices

Officers have developing three generic methods to varying degrees for controlling blocks to performance with excellence. They include the following skills:

1. De-escalation
2. Involvement of others
3. Task orientation

De-Escalation

Officers are well versed in de-escalating situations (90%), successfully diffusing aggressiveness in multiple scenarios. They prioritize maintaining emotional control and accepting what cannot be changed to de-escalate a situation. Other effective practices are employed such as pausing to gain perspective on the situation or task at hand, adjusting their approach, or minimizing interruptions. Practice details for De-escalation are listed in Table 7.8.

TABLE 7.8 De-escalation Practices

	TOTAL RESPONSES Ranked by %
De-escalation	90
Emotional control: relax, calm down, pause, breathe, walk, talk, joke, go easy, think	
Accept: it's a "game," statistical odds, inevitable, part of the job, can't change it, rise above	
Big picture: step back, whole, perspective, fair judgment	
Avoid promotional process: don't apply, other internal interest (e.g., training), no ambition	
Adapt: change approach, conform, open-minded, take orders, be "one of the guys"	
Security and pay: perspective on financial and job security, appreciate the overtime	
Minimize interruptions then get back on track: put things on hold, isolate yourself	

Refocus, tactics—*During a chase, you can get very focused on the run. Sometimes I have to say to myself, "Whoa. Start thinking again." It's the difference between the basic fight or flight functions versus higher thought patterns that allow you to think despite danger, physical exertion and fatigue. We should practice vehicle pursuits much, much more, with a strong emphasis on using tactics, instead of just trying to keep the subject vehicle in sight. It's like chess moves.*

—<5 years on

Biggest fears, assess—*One of the biggest fears on the job is a 10-78 [request assistance]. Talk about a jolt of energy. You can't go crazy because you're no help if you don't get there. You look around and you assess. You've really got to pull the reins back, control, and get there as quickly and safely as you possibly can.*

—Female Patrol

Calm: "An old, old, old officer taught me to never run to a fight."

Calm equals calm—*An old, old, old officer taught me to never run to a fight. I walk and I watch because if there's a knife or anything going on, I'm going to see it. If you're running, everybody runs with you and it gets their anxiety up. Calm equals calm and panicky equals panicky.*

—School Resource

Fatigue, rest—*Do I use coffee to fight fatigue? Not necessarily. I'll nap. I'll take a lunch hour, and lie down. I'll sleep for one hour, either in my car or the couch here at the station, because in the end, it could affect me. It could be the last hour of your shift when the big call comes in. If you are dead tired, you'll either end up dead, hurt, or affect your partner—it affects your mental readiness, big time.*

—Patrol 5 to 10 years on

React, whistle, reassess, go—*"One thing when I get that initial shock, I've noticed that I whistle. It might sound silly, but* *probably it's a sense of calm. I say that because that's my time out. Then I reassess and let's go."*

—>15 years on

Humor—*I try to deal with everything with a little wit and humor. I'm just my typical obnoxious self—which is apparently quite funny to some people. One kid said, "Ah, Miss? Are Police Officers allowed to just walk up and call you a cocksucker?" I said, "I don't know. Are you a cocksucker?" The whole class just LOST it. At that point they're thinking, "Oh, she's kind of funny."*

—School Resource

Involvement of Others

Officers are keenly aware of the importance of others in managing distractions. This often entails placing trust in others to help control the situation. The interaction may require:

- trusting and staying committed to the team
- taking charge and leading others
- sympathizing and apologizing when wrong
- looking to internal support
- responding promptly to resolve problems

Practice details for Involvement of Others are listed in Table 7.9.

TABLE 7.9 Involvement of Others Practices

	TOTAL RESPONSES Ranked by %
Involvement of others	89
Peer trust: support and advice partner and team, team commitment, stick together	
Control environment: take charge, manipulate, force the outcome, confront	
Apologize: admit when you've erred, sympathize with others	
Confidence in internal support: trust supervisor, just respond and problem goes away	

PHOTO 7.5 Leading others requires a firm commitment to the team and the mission. Internal support and quick problem resolution are key to maintaining order and focus. Credit: Russ and Tiña De Maris, RVTravel, Bing, 2022

Dynamic trust—*I have an enormous amount of faith in my partner. I can commit to action very quickly in a dynamic situation, like clearing a house at gunpoint—I don't have to look over my shoulder to know what she is doing.*

—Neighborhood Resource

Procedures: "My most useful application in my role as an officer is to keep a level head and to be able to follow procedures and policies."

Crisis control, procedures—*First, reassure the victim that you are going to assist and let them know that you know what you're doing. That requires being familiar with policies, procedures and what resources are available to assist them in their emotional or physical trauma. Officers respect me because I know what I'm doing and I get things done. My most useful application in my role as an officer is to keep a level head and to be able to follow procedures and policies.*

—Neighborhood Resource

Refocus, reliance—*You have to refocus on your target, your main principal. It could be a distraction for an ambush, or just a*

screw up or a near miss—you don't know. Get back in the game because if you don't, you're going to leave a gap in which everybody else relies on you. Stay focused and get to where you're getting to.
—Traffic Escort

Reciprocal respect—*I don't tolerate disrespect. My rule of thumb is to treat people like I would want to be treated. We start on an even keel but if a person escalates, then it goes up. That's only fair.*
—Female Patrol

Teamwork—*It's not one person doing something extraordinary. It's a team.*
—>15 years on

Task Orientation

Managing distractions often involves officers becoming more efficient, more persistent, more knowledgeable, or more alert. Refocusing on the task at hand requires a clear goal, concentration, and judgment. Excellent officers highlight these essential principles for efficiency (see also Table 7.10 for more details):

♦ simplify tasks, adapt goals
♦ stay persistent and dedicated

TABLE 7.10 Task Orientation Practices

	TOTAL RESPONSES Ranked by %
Task orientation	39
Common sense: practical, keep it simple, street smarts, "Ways and Means," protect, defend	
Shift task: do other work, change goal, get up from desk/car and walk, talk or interact	
Persist: consistent, commit, just do it, keep trying, dedicated lifestyle, extra time, sacrifice	
Time management: prioritize, quick, efficient, finish one at a time	
Stimulant drinks and fast food: coffee/hot beverage/pop, fight fatigue, stay cool	
Assess: possible options, refocus in a crisis, briefly plan	
Update: get information, filter cues, check the obvious, briefings, focus, listen and take time	
Policy: refer to policies, procedures, becomes robotics	

- prioritize time management
- combat fatigue with stimulants
- assess and adapt quickly
- stay informed and follow policies

Current research[45] confirms and offers additional steps for eliminating extraneous thoughts to accomplish tasks:
- focus limited energy on only vital tasks
- eliminate habits that add to fatigue like worry, procrastination, gossip, and not setting boundaries
- address issues separately since they may be unrelated
- tailor actions to the challenge: complete tasks, solve obstacles, and allow time to process setbacks

Confidence: laws, authority—*People overcomplicate this job. I've never had difficulty searching vehicles or people. I never think, "What if this person complains?" If I have reasonable grounds that apply to an actual Section of the Criminal Code that gives me the authority to apply the legislation. I encourage that kind of education. It builds confidence.*
—Neighborhood Resource

Perspective—*My biggest thing is keeping perspective. Yes, you saw a bad thing but it's part of life. Babies die, people get killed in car accidents or by other people. Keep perspective of what your role is.*
—Patrol Sergeant

Persistence—*They were ready to quit, they didn't know what else to do. I divided the map and gave everyone assignments over the same streets they'd gone over before. Half an hour later one of the Officers found her. He went back to a street he had already checked, but this time found someone who had seen the missing woman. We saved her life.*
—Patrol Sergeant

Specialized Control Practices

In policing, excellent officers generally hold a strong, logical, personal opinion about what works in controlling the most typical Performance Blocks. Candid frontline solutions now exist associated with the following 11 practices to address 11 traditional stressors commonly reported by excellent officers, with the percentage of officers identifying them as a Performance Block indicated (see Table 7.11).

However, not all these blocks have comprehensive or necessarily effective solutions. Gaps are suspected when the block is consistently ranked high by the majority or when the Distraction Control strategies do not exist for most officers. In these cases, either the Distraction Control strategies are too few or only partially or temporarily effective. This gap is particularly evident in dealing with Crises, Fatigue, Shift work, Workload volume, and specific to Female policing issues.

TABLE 7.11 Performance Blocks and Specialized Related Control Practices

Performance Blocks*	%	Specialized Control Practices	%
"Crises"	90	"Crises" refocusing	79
Fatigue	80	Fatigue strategies**	75
Public disrespect	70	Public disrespect refocusing	73
Car collisions	57	Car collisions avoidance**	73
Court appearance	47	Court appearance strategies***	72
Downtime and routine tasks	66	Downtime and routine task refocusing	71
Shift-work fatigue	80	Shift-work strategies**	69
Public complaints	53	Public complaint refocusing	68
Workload volume	75	Workload strategies	64
"Not being promoted"	34	"Not being promoted" refocusing	59
Female-policing issues	52	Female-policing coping strategies	45

*All Performance Blocks are described in Chapter 3: Police Under Pressure—Performance Blocks.

**These Distraction Control Practices are described in Chapter 5: Physical Readiness in Policing.

***These Distraction Control Practices are described in Chapter 6: Technical Readiness in Policing.

Alternatively, some blocks and controls appear balanced, and some having proportionately greater controls, such as car collisions, court appearance, public complaints, and not being promoted.

"Crises" Refocusing

Police officers are well trained to take quick, strategic, alternative actions in response to a "crisis." However, all officers admit that feeling emotionally startled, either aloud or internally, is a common reflex. This reaction can work for or against the officer. Less obvious are the details that allow a compassionate officer to enter an ideal focus state to perform under these high-stress conditions. The key is a brief pause before choosing an alternative action. While 90% of officers identified a "crisis" as an issue, 79% reported having refocusing strategies, suggesting a need for additional training in managing emotions in high-stress situations. Details for Crises refocusing are listed in Table 7.12.

TABLE 7.12 "Crises" Refocusing

	TOTAL RESPONSES Ranked by %
Crisis reaction	90
Crisis refocus strategies	79
Brief pause: breathe, calm down, relax, and slowly move back, personal mindset, whistle	
Preferred alternative actions	
Act: responding with necessary action to protect	
Take charge: instructing others, influence team mindset, psyche, or calm them	
Assess: briefly assessing possible options, plan, "Think then act"	
Request backup	

Brief pause

Excellent officers insist on a brief pause for composure. This personal moment allows them to think positively either by recalling past successes, using positive self-talk, taking deep breaths, whistling, counting, or saying a quiet prayer. This short time-out appears to be key in successfully refocusing to ensure calmness and good judgment before taking the necessary alternative actions.

The steps taken after successfully overcoming a crisis may also have relevance. Taking a break at this point can help to reduce tension before proceeding further.

> **Pause, assess**—*I breathe and look around. The voice in my head says: "Have a look around. Assess the situation—what do you have?"*
>
> —Neighborhood Resource

> **Crisis, pause**—*When you hear 10-78, it's very easy to just GO! When you first start and you get that 10-78, you drive like an idiot trying to get there. You almost get tunnel vision but over the years you learn to draw yourself back.*
>
> —5 to 10 years on

> **React-pause-assess-act**—*It's the deep breath. The mental flush. "Okay, cool, let's go on."*
>
> —Tactical

> **Counteract freezing**—*For a second, I froze, and the Sergeant grabbed my arm. As soon as the Sergeant made the motion to grab, the motion was enough for me. I pounced on the guy too and we got control. Somebody else initiated the action and then I reacted to his reaction.*
>
> —>15 years on

> **Breathe, analyze**—*When new recruits query a plate and it comes back stolen, a lot of them will get on the air and scream when it might just be a pointer vehicle. I always told my recruits to take a breath when they see something that doesn't look right. Take a second to think about what the hell is going on. Sometimes that breath has to be a quick one, but take that second to analyze as opposed to making a hasty decision.*
>
> —Canine

> **Crisis Control: a 'four-breath'**—*"Had there been time, I would have taken a few minutes. No… I think I was too wound*

up at that point (laughs). Now that I know 'Tactical-breathing'—that's all you have time for. That 'four- breath': Take a breath in for a count of four, hold it in for four, breath out for four, and hold it out for four."

—School Resource

Crisis refocusing ritual—*I just focus in. I usually always say, "Here we go"—like I'm getting ready. It's something I always say in hockey, "Here we go, boys. Here we go!"*

—Patrol, >10 years on

Preferred alternative actions

Officers show preference in choosing alternative actions in a crisis, prioritizing immediate action and taking control quickly and quietly as important steps. In the heat of an emergency, many officers continue to assess possible options. Finally, as needed, officers request backup.

This combination of personal and strategic inventories translates into an ideal performance state for managing highly irregular and volatile conditions.

Public Disrespect Refocusing

Disrespect on the street toward an officer is alarming and taken as a serious hindrance to performance by most officers (70%) and equally balanced (73%) with personal strategies. The decision to confront or ignore disrespect is equally defended as a solution. Consciously trying to prevent it through respectful conduct and

TABLE 7.13 Public Disrespect Refocusing

	TOTAL RESPONSES Ranked by %
Public disrespect block	70
Public disrespect refocusing	73
Confront: challenge comment, end it, demand respect	
Accept: ignore, consider source, can't change, give no attention, stay above it	
Prevent: treat respectfully, think fast	
Proactive: public promotion, demos, talks in school	

quick wit are also strategies. Some merit is given to the positive long-term impact of public promotions and school presentations. All Anglophone officers and most Caucasian officers have significantly more strategies than other officers (100%, p = 0.054; 97%, p = 0.03, respectively). Details for Public Disrespect Refocusing are listed in Table 7.13.

Diplomacy—*I was trained in the city, where you're able to call the shots and be upfront with people. I was always fair but I said it like it was. Out in the suburbs, there was just no way could I win like that. It was different out there and it taught me to be much more diplomatic. It was good for me, but frustrating because I do not want to tell somebody what they want to hear. I'm a person who wants to always tell it like it is.*

—School Resource

Know your policies—*If you don't know your policy and you don't know your laws, they'll say, "He doesn't know what he's doing." It's about professionalism. I mean, that's why I do it.*

—Patrol

Ignore disrespect: "I know who I am and what I do. They have no idea who I am."

Accept, ignore—*People can say or call me whatever they want. It just doesn't bother me. You want to be ignorant, go ahead and be ignorant. I know who I am and what I do. They have no idea who I am.*

—>15 years on

Support, accept—*My partner saw what the guy was doing and how he was talking. It changed everything. I was watching my partner and surviving off of his cues. He was not involved in the situation like I was. He was calm, so I was calm. This guy wants to be an a--hole, no problem.*

—5 to 10 years on

Avoid argument, accept—*You might want to say something, but it's not worth getting in an argument—you're not going to win that argument. No matter what you say to these people, you're not going to change them. Just take it. Let it bounce off* *you. They may be saying it just to get a reaction out of you. You have to see beyond the verbal comments.*

—Traffic Escort

Public Complaint Refocusing

Approximately half (53%) of the officers expressed a concern over the public complaint process. Most avoid them. Those receiving complaints recommended strategies ranging from accepting them without overly personalizing or clearly defending them with honest, documented information. Details for Public Complaints Refocusing are listed in Table 7.14.

TABLE 7.14 Public Complaint Refocusing

	TOTAL RESPONSES Ranked by %
Public complaint block	53
Public complaint strategies	68
Prevent: don't get complaints, respectful	
Accept: statistical odds, inevitable, going to happen, related to arrest volume	
Defense: collect evidence, duty book entry, prepare	
Confidence in system: supervisor support, just respond, went away after response	

Unexpected cooperation—*In talking about how people are people and everybody has their reasons, if you treat people decently, sometimes they're not expecting it because their lives are, in some circumstances, pretty shi--y. They'll like you.*

—Female Patrol

Communication—*You're going to get complaints here and there. It depends on what type of people you're dealing with. In 99% of cases, you can avoid a complaint with a little communication. A lot of times that person wants to vent. Let them. Don't try and control every situation or every person. Rather than always telling them to shut up, let them vent.*

—Patrol, 5 to 10 years on

Validation, support—*My old Staff Sergeant had four kids come in to complain about me. He called me into the office. I said, "Four teenagers driving around in a suburban community at 3:00 a.m., I ran the plate, made sure it wasn't stolen, and that was the end of it." He turned to them and said, "The officer was doing his job. F--- off." That's what should happen.*

—Sergeant

Part of the job—*Some people say if you're not getting public complaints, you're not doing your job.*

—Traffic Escort

Control—*If you're handling yourself properly and doing the call properly, you shouldn't get a public complaint.*

—>15 years on

Downtime (Lulls) and Routine Tasks Refocusing

Downtime and routine phases are considered a distraction by the majority of officers (66%). Officers' concentration and attentiveness are often interrupted by procedural lulls and routine in responding to calls. Of all the distractions in policing, downtime presents the potential danger of drifting and inadvertently becoming complacent. While the ability to get back on track after a lull was successfully reported by 71% of officers, there is no

TABLE 7.15 Downtime and Routine Task Refocusing

	TOTAL RESPONSES Ranked by %
Downtime and Routine Task block	66
Downtime and Routine Task Refocusing	71
Shift task: do other work	
End lull: take control, insistent, put pressure to end, avoid complacency, be cautious	
Positive attitude: responsible, serious job, part of whole	
Relax: stay calm, leave, talk, walk, read, joke	
Prevent: anticipating situation	
Updates: regular updates, briefings, get information	
Socialize: opportunity to socialize, network with other officers	

pattern of consistency in their responses. It is possible that more skills for dealing with passive distractions need to be developed.

Being flexible in completing tasks helps to prevent boredom. Shift tasks was a common way to avoid complacency. Officers also try to control the situation and prevent frustration by putting an end to the routine or relaxing or even leaving the area.

This refocusing practice was not more prevalent among any one group of officers. The types of distraction control strategies found to be effective in dealing with lulls are detailed and individualized. Details for Downtime and Routine Task Refocusing are listed in Table 7.15.

> **Take action**—*Get yourself into the mindset by action. I used to play a game with myself: If I'm getting into that lull, sitting there… All right, let's make something happen. I'll turn off the lights and start driving slowly through a neighborhood. That way, if there's someone on the next street, they don't see the car lights coming. A lot of times I'll let it roll and use the mercy-brake pedal because it doesn't illuminate the red lights in the back. There may be NOTHING for miles, but you're getting back in that mode again. You scan and you're back in it. You have got to push yourself to do it. You have got to do whatever it takes. The last couple of hours of a 12-hour shift—at 4:00 a.m.—you know there's stuff going on, somewhere. You just have to FIND it.*
>
> —Patrol, >10 years on

> **Stillness**—*Use the quiet moments—be still for just a second. Make stillness work for you.*
>
> —Patrol

> **Live with it**—*You start to turn it off after a while, especially when they drag on. Then they finally come on saying, "OK, he's not going to be here until 8:00." Here you are, ready to go at 6:00 o'clock, you've been sitting on your butt for two and a half hours in a police cruiser and… your body starts to shut down. You know to pack a book, but you can only read so much… And then, before you know it, they're yelling over the radio, "OK, he's landed! Everybody get out to your spots." So, it's, "Ooookay." You jump up and away you go. You learn to live*

Mental readiness in policing ■ 301

with it [laughs]. It's part of the ups and downs... We really can't say anything. It's not the place.
—Traffic Escort

Efficiency—*Down time is a good time to go to the washroom. If it's a long period then I'll get a bite to eat—because you don't know what kind of schedule you're going to have. There's nothing worse than a copper on an empty stomach! You get pretty grumpy. You have got to make sure you get your calories and your drink.*
—Traffic Escort

Family: "I look at my wife and children... I take everything seriously when I'm out there."

Family, responsibility—*I look at my wife and children. If something happens to me, who's looking after them? I use that frame of mind and I try to mentally go over what I have to do. I take everything seriously when I'm out there.*
—<5 years on

Change sections—*What tires me is the routine of the same thing over and over again. I'm a firm believer that you've got to change sections every three or four years. Then you'll come out with a good attitude. Before you know it, you're looking for that 25-year retirement—and away you go! What gets me tired is the routine of the same thing over and over again.*
—School Resource

Workload Strategies

Among the organizational distractions, workload is rated as a block by a relatively large number of excellent officers (75%). Four effective workload strategies were identified: time management techniques such as prioritization and handling interruptions, finding enjoyment in the busy nature of the job, accepting the workload, and scheduling breaks for balance and pacing. These strategies were reported most by officers with Patrol-only experience (90%, p = 0.046) and least mentioned by Traffic Escort officers (25%, p = 0.018). Details for Workload Strategies are listed in Table 7.16.

TABLE 7.16 Workload Strategies

	TOTAL RESPONSES Ranked by %
Workload block	75
Workload strategies	64
Time management: finish one at a time, prioritize, manage time/interruptions	
Enjoyment: love busy, respond to call, like patrol	
Acceptance: put in a day's work, won't change, no one listens	
Scheduling: take break, balances out, pace	

Day's work—*Seriously, we look at it as: Just go, go, go, go. Don't stop.*

—Neighborhood Resource

One at a time—*It's huge and it probably took me five years to learn—you can only take one call at a time. Finish your paperwork. You get interrupted so many times. As the day goes on, you stack reports—by the time you start, they're garbage compared to what you would have written at the time. Complete the call. Finish it off right in the car and send it through.*

—Patrol, >10 years on

Flex times—*We were so busy that my partner and I would work late, if we could. Or we'd just try to squeeze it in. Since our particular area was busier during the late-evening, we would switch our shifts. If we worked Monday to Thursday we would come in during the day on Monday and Tuesday to focus on our follow-ups and assigned cases. Then, on Wednesday and Thursday we would switch to afternoons.*

—Female, Neighborhood Resource

Balance—*It balances out. Sometimes it just seems that it never rains but it pours. Yet the other day, you thought, "It's so quiet. What we need is a running gun battle." You have to watch what you wish for and just take it as it comes.*

—Tactical

"Not Being Promoted" Refocusing

Only 34% of officers identified the inability to advance in the organization as a performance block. This is rather surprising given that this is a selected sample of excellent officers. However, this does not indicate that the other 66% are satisfied if we consider how they refocus from "not being promoted." Their rationale includes avoiding the process, prioritizing other internal or external avenues, and setting new goals. While 59% listed their reasons for not viewing this as a problem, only a small percentage believed that through effort (10%) and confidence (6%) they could succeed in the promotional process. Most officers deal with the frustration by either avoiding the competition or seeking out alternative career goals. Officers with SRO experience listed the least number of strategies.

Clearly, outstanding officers show creativity in developing their careers laterally. The dilemma arises when highly capable individuals do not want to progress, while those with lesser competence do. Consequently, if the exceptionally competent individuals are staying in their current positions, it means that those less competent are advancing in larger numbers. This might contribute to certain police-cultural issues where frontline personnel neither respect nor trust their superiors.

TABLE 7.17 "Not Being Promoted" Refocusing

	TOTAL RESPONSES Ranked by %
"Not being promoted" block	34
"Not being promoted" refocusing	59
Avoid process: can't complain, other internal interest (e.g., training), no ambition	
Effort: keep trying, finally got it, hard, persistence	
Alternatives: other external avenues, other interests, set new time limits, change goals	
Confidence: be yourself, comfortable with your answers, not just "right" answer	

This particular issue must be distinguished as an important item for change if succession planning is to be effective. Details for "Not Being Promoted" Refocusing are listed in Table 7.17.

Personal satisfaction—*When I first came on, if you weren't promoted, it was a big deal. You were considered a failure. The feel in police work now is if you find something that is personally satisfying, then you do it. You take tactical guys and canine guys: They're probably some of the best people you have in the police service and 80% to 90% of them aren't qualified to be promoted. And they don't want to be promoted. They want to be left alone. They're happy.*

—Canine

Promotional interviews—*Positive thinking and perseverance… You may not be successful the first or second time. Remember, you're being interviewed by humans. For whatever reason, they may just find the next guy a better applicant than you… The main thing is, do not be discouraged, go for it again… a lot of people give up. You're going to learn something from that interview. You should do that much better next interview… I'm not a super brain. I consider myself the average Joe Schmo. You have to have the willpower inside of you. You have to want to do it. Have a positive attitude. You have to persevere. "I can do it. I'm going to do this. I WILL do it."*

—Patrol

Sense of accomplishment—*A job I really enjoy, working with a good bunch of people, and having time off for my family. And if I can have that, then I'm a happy guy. I don't have to have a book or a stripe or a crown on my shoulder to make me feel like I'm accomplishing what I have to accomplish in policing.*

—>10 years on

Alternatives—*As a Constable I have more options. I can go into different Departments and have different experiences. Being a Sergeant (and I've been asked) limits the experiences I can have as a Police Officer. I wouldn't be able to tap into that sixth sense and listen to that inner voice because I'd be busy dealing with administrative duties.*

—Neighborhood Resource

Female-Policing Coping Strategies

About half of all the officers (52%) expressed their belief that female gender remains a performance issue in policing, while acknowledging a significant improvement in acceptance over the years.

In addressing female challenges, 45% employ coping strategies such as embracing improvements, adopting diverse approaches to balance services, relying on peer support, adapting and making personal adjustments, and confronting issues through education and organizational avenues. These strategies were raised most frequently by officers with Patrol-only experience or with only frontline experience (50%, p =0.042; 38%, p = 0.048). While issues and strategies are presented, the inability to separate female-only responses limits the full interpretation. Details for Female-Policing Coping Strategies are listed in Table 7.18.

TABLE 7.18 Female-Policing Coping Strategies

	TOTAL RESPONSES Ranked by %
Female-policing block	52
Female-policing coping strategies	45
Improved: not like past, not a problem	
Much needed approach: different styles and approaches, balances services, reasonable	
Peer support: stick together, be a team	
Personal change: open, adapt, conform, be "one of the guys," reorganize	
Confront: educate, seek organization support, harassment option	

Note: Female respondents represented 14 of the 76 officers in this sample.

Confidence—*If they hired me for my life experience and the pre-requisite is to keep my mouth shut and work 25 years, then they should have hired me when I was 21. I've got life experience and I've got an opinion… they hired me because I've been places. I've got a sense of what works and what doesn't work. If* *you can't take someone with six years on respectfully giving a suggestion, that's not my problem. It's about you.*

—Female Neighborhood Resource

Prove yourself: "I don't care if you're pink, polka-dotted, or six foot tall. If you can prove yourself out on the street, you're tops in my books."

Prove yourself—*I don't think there really is a female issue anymore. It has everything to do with intelligence. If you're a hundred pounds soaking wet, but can talk a bad guy out of his weapons, I'll have you there in a second. Imagine how hard it is for a rookie who is smaller in stature and not sure what to do. You've got to have a lot of heart and maybe that's the type of intestinal fortitude you need. Bottom line, proof's in the pudding. I don't care if you're pink, polka-dotted, or six foot tall. If you can prove yourself out on the street, you're tops in my books. If you're nothing but a knuckle-dragger, I'm not interested. This is my career and you're not going to put that in jeopardy.*

—Patrol, >10 years on

H. Constructive Evaluation

Every officer has a way to check how well they are doing. While evaluation is viewed as important, this success element (SE) lacks the same depth of detail and breadth as the other six SEs. Much like Positive Imagery Practices, this SE has one of the fewest core practices, therefore allowing for greater individual differences. On average, each officer practices four Constructive Evaluation Practices from a list of eight. This may be related to the consequences associated with error.

Inversely, research on evaluation and coping in policing dominated publications, accounting for 22%, second only to publications on Commitment at 30%[46]. The existing literature emphasizes the scrutiny officers receive from the organization, the public, and the officers themselves. With this level of accountability, officers would understandably be very reluctant to obtain open feedback (Figure 7.8).

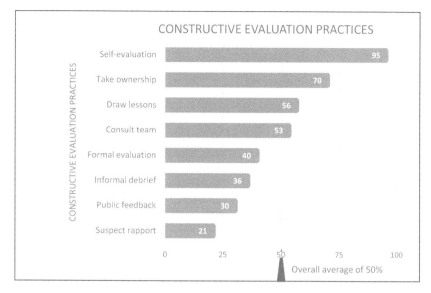

FIGURE 7.8 Constructive Evaluation Practices

All excellent officers had an overall average of 50% Constructive Evaluation practices (4 out of 8 practices per officer).

These Constructive Evaluation Practices are presented as:

1. Self-evaluation
2. Feedback from others: Team, Formal, Informal, Public, and Suspects
3. Coping: Take Ownership and Draw Lessons

Self-Evaluation

Self-evaluation and reflection of results are preferred by almost all officers (95%). Their decisiveness and willingness to improve dominates their responses. Their personal assessment methods include:

- assessing during calls
- visually referencing with notes, sketches, and/or photographs
- visualizing to remember the call
- writing a timely report
- asking: "What am I contributing?"

Self-critique—*I critique my own behavior, "What did I do there that I could do better?" I pay attention to other people—I don't critique them openly but I may critique them to myself. I do my best to keep my mind open and learn something new every day.*

—5 to 10 years on

Visualize, practice—*I'll run through most calls—even if it's not mine. I'll hear a weird call and not know what I would do. I'll talk to the officer or I'll learn by reading through the call afterwards.*

—Female Patrol

Assess during calls—*You have to hold back a little bit, even if it's just for a little while. Just slow down, take a breath and then have a look around, so you can let the energy process through you in terms of breathing and assessing. That's where you've got to listen for that inner voice.*

—Female Neighborhood Resource

Abilities: "Different officers have different skills. Some have great memories… I refer to my notes."

Personal process, reflection—*You switch into different modes at a moment's notice. You're not even conscious of it until afterward. There are so many nuances. You bring a certain number of personal and professional qualities when you step into policing. You nurture and hone in on those qualities when you're doing your job. I can be in one mode and still be aware of other things.*

—School Resource

Seek training—*We don't get half the training we should as police officers. We should be aware of it and seek it out on our own.*

—5 to 10 years on

Recognize abilities—*Different officers have different skills. Some have great memories. They remember faces, names, where you were. I'm not like that. I refer to my notes.*

—Neighborhood Resource

Feedback from others: Team, Formal, Informal, Public, and Suspects

Officers seek feedback in different ways like from their team, supervisors, and even the public, and they use it to learn and improve for next time. These evaluation styles include:
- seeking and accepting feedback
- not getting defensive in debriefs
- consulting the team (e.g., colleagues' feedback, debrief on-site)
- learning from formal evaluation (e.g., parade, supervisor/duty inspector debrief, written goals, investigation)
- listening to public feedback (e.g., public comments, involvement, role, reaction, thanks, victim reaction)
- conducting informal debriefs (e.g., socials, gym workout, wings and beer night, razzing, nothing is sacred)
- developing suspect rapport (e.g., understand suspect attitude for next time, address being "spooked")

Team advice (53%) and *formal evaluations* (40%), while low, were the most dominant feedback methods with others. Consulting with the team was most common among Sergeants (70%, p = 0.018), and *not* practiced by any officers with SRO experience who tend to work solo (67%, p = 0.028). Generally, evaluation practices were mentioned more by Sergeants than Constables. Formal evaluations remain a priority by services as a means of monitoring and predicting future officer performance[47,48].

Informal debriefs (36%) generally take place spontaneously after a call, especially after violent events, and are shown to reduce stress and enhance strategic reflection[49]. Video-cued debriefs utilize footage for evaluation[50,51,52]. Tactical and Canine officers are encouraged to debrief *all* calls, serving as training to analyze what an officer did at a call and reinforce desired behavior. Debriefs are also common with Traffic Escort units and officers with prior police-related experience (28%, p = 0.096; 36%, p = 0.021, respectively). However, they are never mentioned by NRT officers (0%, p = 0.096).

Debriefing?—*What debriefing? Officers on the road get together for coffee. We move creamers around the table—that*

would be our debriefing. Actually, having supervisors come around for debriefings just started—to the organization's credit.
—Neighborhood Resource

How'd it go?—*"Anything for the debrief?" "No, nothing, nothing." Or "This piece of equipment didn't work—no batteries. Let's take care of that now." "You five that went on the track, how did it go?"*
—Canine

Commendation—*"You did well when you did x, y. z. That was really solid. Well done."*
—Tactical

Public feedback in listening to residents' concerns is important for maintaining community trust, as emphasized by research[47,53]. However, only a few officers (30%) prioritize public feedback. Notably, Elite officers and those with Tactical experience mention public feedback the least (8%, p = 0.095; 0%, p = 0.057), while a majority of officers with SRO experience (57%, p = 0.035) demonstrate well-developed engagement with public feedback. Although officers often express surprise at negative public perception of the police, openness to public feedback is not highly regarded.

Suspect rapport. It is worth noting that rapport with suspects is sought after by a small group of officers (21%), primarily Elite officers and those with NRT experience (23%, p = 0.083; 40%, p = 0.001, respectively).

Reflect, apologize—*I made the decision to send him alone. The info we got was a kid playing with the phone. 99.9% of it is always that reason. But there's always that 0.01% where, "Geez, if he walks into a domestic, or something, he's alone." That bothered me and I apologized to him later. I said, "I'll never put you in that position again. Officer safety, you're Number One and I forgot it." As good as we did, there was a shortcoming somewhere else.*
—Sergeant, >15 years on

Debrief incidents—*The value of debriefing incidents right after they happen is enormous—I can't speak enough about it.*

Mental readiness in policing ■ 311

It shouldn't only happen at the individual patrol officer's level, or at the Community-Resource team level. For all operations, always, there should be a debrief because that is how we learn and improve.

—<5 years on

Public feedback: "Somebody saying 'Thank you,' is all I need."

Public feedback—*Every time somebody says, "Great job, Officer. You really helped me," that's pure success. Somebody saying, "Thank you," is all I need. That's a success right there—it means I've done my job for that person. If I can do it for that person, I can do it for a whole lot of other people.*

—Patrol, >10 years on

Desired feedback—*If I screw up, I want you to say, "You f---ed up." I love listening to other people's opinions, no matter who it is.*

—>15 years on

Parade debrief—*If the call was potentially high risk or high profile, my ritual is to sit down and talk about it afterward with the officers. If young officers don't have the opportunity to see what other people are doing, it's an opportunity to sit in a group. I invite those who weren't involved to stay. It usually happens the next shift at parade.*

—Patrol Sergeant

Informal debrief—*The Patrol Officers might debrief after work when they go for a beer. They won't talk in the parade room. But if Officers go for a beer, they might say something. As soon as one says something, the others will start listening and then it all comes out. The more the officers talk, the better it is. It's off their chest.*

—>10 years on

Suspect/Victim: "Make sure that person wants help for the right reasons, not just to get you in their corner."

Understanding suspects/victims—*You have a responsibility to offer help—period. But before you allow yourself to go further, be aware. Make sure that*

> *person wants help for the right reasons, not just to get you in their corner.*
> —Neighborhood Resource

> **Consult team, debriefs**—*In negotiating, we're making notes all the times—debrief, debrief. When we're off the phone, we debrief very quickly: "What have we got? Where are we at? Here's what he said. Here's what's happened. Here's what I'm thinking. Is this the proper time to introduce the hook? He's mentioned about the grandfather. Is this the proper time to introduce the grandfather? Did he say 'my grandfather'? or did he say 'my GRANDfather'?" We're listening to the tone for what's he really saying here. "Is this love or hate?"*
> —>15 years on

Coping: Take Ownership and Draw Lessons

> **Readiness versus resilience**—*The notion of "readiness" as opposed to "resilience" captures a greater strength-base and positive description of being "psyche-fit" for such strenuous work. Resilience can be seen as "shutting down" mentally.*
> —Police Chief

Whether focusing on "readiness" or "resilience," dealing with terrorism, preventing stress injuries, and improving performance are now both an individual and organizational responsibility[54,55]. Traditionally, supports include on-scene mental wellness, regular drills, peer debriefs, and learning from body-cam footage[56]. Self-confidence, self-directed learning, social support, and job satisfaction have been linked to well-being and lower post-traumatic stress disorder risk[54,57]. There is ongoing debate whether police should undergo mandatory or optional annual wellness check-ups[56].

Taking ownership (70%) was reported as a sign of independence, leadership, and confidence in one's abilities. Drawing on lessons learned (56%) permits learning from mistakes, adapting to or salvaging a situation, identifying gained experience—or simply starting over. Current police research supports these approaches, whether expressed as protective factors[58], well-being[59], "stress shield"[60], trauma resilience[61], mental toughness[62], or grit[63].

> **Tears**—*I'll tell you one thing, when you have young men and women in combat operations and they lose their friends, one thing you quickly learn not to be ashamed of is tears.*
> —Rick Hillier, Chief of Defense, Canadian military[64]

> **Energy release**—*Many calls are not fight or flight but rather high alert requiring control through diplomacy, communication and personal restraint. A good laugh, a good cry and/or a good workout can provide the necessary, natural and needed release of energy to complete the cycle and stay healthy.*
> —Patrol

> **Learn from mistakes, humble**—*People who are good at their job learn from their mistakes. I can't stand working with officers who never learn from their mistakes—they're always right. You're going to make mistakes. I've made hundreds of mistakes—and some pretty serious ones—but I learned from them. I accepted the ribbing and the lumps, and I moved on. That's what makes the difference in good students, parents… people. You have to be humble and know that you are going to make mistakes—some of them serious.*
> —5 to 10 years on

These officers also apply standard practices[65] before and after calls to facilitate long-term coping. Most significantly, they exhibit positivity (96%) and professional discipline (93%). Understanding job demands (82%), including shift work, workload, and its impact on family life, prevent frustration, leading to greater calmness. Recognizing risks (75%) promotes astute courage for frontline duties. Basic practices such as resting (74%) and maintaining physical discipline (63%) contribute to coping and excellence.

Current research also promotes "mindfulness" as a way to slow down and become more intensely aware of thoughts, feelings, and sensations during everyday tasks such as showering (noticing temperature and sensations), eating (taking measured bites, savoring taste), or dressing (making choices reflecting mood). Accepting the present moment can alleviate pressure[66].

I. Influential factors and trends for success practices

A total of 22 detailed demographic factors were originally collected and analyzed. These factors were grouped as: Background factors (such as gender, language, ethnicity, and military experience), Developmental factors (experiences such as patrol-only, tactical, canine, and rural), and Police Distinction factors (such as "elite," specialty unit, rank, and years on). All 22 factors exhibit varying degrees of influence on the 60 mental-readiness practices for policing performance excellence. See Appendix A: Evidence-Based Rigor: Study Design, Figure A.1. Influential Factors in Policing for more details.

Overall influence by factor groups

On average, all three factor groups have a similar degree of impact on practice development. They have relatively the same average number of practice differences per group (6 to 8), with the same upper (10 or 11) and lower (5 or less) limits. However, the total practice differences within each group range widely from 38 to 63. Whether an officer views a challenging situation as complex and unfamiliar is strongly influenced by the most factors (Table 7.19).

> **Background factors**: In total, the eight factors within this group collectively impacted the total mental-readiness success practices 47 times. Gender scored highest, with an impact on 10 out of 60 mental-readiness success practices. Language and ethnicity show moderate influence (affecting 6–7 practices). Prior police-related experience

TABLE 7.19 Practice Tendencies by Factor

FACTOR	NUMBER OF PRACTICE DIFFERENCES	% OUT OF 60 PRACTICES
Background factors: Total = 47 / Mean = 6		
Gender	10	17
Primary language	7	12
Male ethnicity	7	12
Multiple languages	6	10
Ethnicity	6	10
Prior police-related experience	5	8
Military experience	3	5
Education	3	5
Developmental factors: Total = 63 / Mean = 7		
Patrol-only experience	10	17
SRO experience	9	15
Tactical experience	9	15
Canine experience	8	12
CRO experience	7	12
External police experience	7	12
Traffic Escort experience	6	10
More than frontline experience	5	8
Rural police experience	2	3
Police distinction factors: Total = 38 / Mean = 8		
Elite (by group and scoring)	11	18
Frontline specialty unit	11	18
Rank	7	12
Total years of experience	5	8
"Old/New School" males	4	7

(5), military experience (3), and education (3) have an unexpected lower influence on success practices compared to other factors.

Developmental factors: Officers with Patrol-only experience impacted the greatest number of practices (10) both positively and negatively compared to those with additional frontline specialty unit training (6–9) or with external police experience (7). The least influential Developmental factors were those having experience beyond the frontline (5) or rural experience (2). In total, the nine factors within this group reflect that training and experience within the various frontline units collectively have a very significant impact (63 times) on the total success practices.

Police Distinction factors: In total, the five factors within this group collectively impacted the total mental-readiness success practices 38 times. "Elite" versus non-Elite officers influenced the greatest number of practices (11 out of 69), as did the specialty unit factor (11), which was divided between three sub-units (i.e., Patrol unit versus Tactical-Canine-Traffic Escort units versus NRTO-SRO Uuits). An officer's rank had a moderate impact (7), while total "years on" experience (5) and old/new school males (4) had relatively lower scores than might be expected.

Most influential factors

All three groups have high scoring factors that influence a relatively identical number of practices. The Police Distinction group has two factors (elite and specialty units) while Background and Developmental groups each have one (gender and Patrol-only experience) that influence the greatest number of success practices (10 or greater). These four specific factors are considered the most influential and can have either a positive or negative impact on practice development. The following profiles describe in detail the characteristics of these four most influential factors.

"Elite" officer distinct practices

The "Elite" officer factor relates to the 13 officers who were identified as "the very best" by both their peers and supervisors, and ultimately have the highest success practice scores compared to other officers within the sample. Similarly, while all athletes at the Olympics are excellent, only a few are "elite" medal winners. Interviews with these individuals leave several immediate impressions. The "Elite" officers are consistent in providing intimate details in all areas of mental preparedness. They are also the most open and/or least inhibited in the disclosure of sensitive

TABLE 7.20 Elite Officers' Distinct Practices

SUCCESS PRACTICES	ELITE %	NON-ELITE %	P-VALUE
Physical Competency	50	39	0.024
Fitness and Wellness			
Rest*	54	71	0.093
Officer safety	85	57	0.040
Electronic aids	46	17	0.077
Technical Competency	50	39	0.024
Verbal Communication			
External communication	85	31	0.007
Mental Competency	50	39	0.024
Commitment	81	71	0.022
Competitive	100	69	0.023
Understand "the job"	100	60	0.016
Positive Imagery			
Impromptu rehearsal	23	6	0.083
Distraction Control			
Fatigue strategies*	46	91	0.001
Constructive Evaluation			
Suspect rapport	23	6	0.083
Public feedback*	8	31	0.095

Note: * Practices where Elite officers have a lower practice level than non-Elite.

information. These qualitative impressions are confirmed below through statistical factor analysis of the interview transcripts. The list of the success practices that are significantly different for the "Elite" officer factor is given in Table 7.20.

The expertise of the "Elite" factor officers is unmistakable. Elite officers view External Communication, Understanding "the Job," Officer Safety, and use of Electronic Aids in preparation as having an important influence in their mental readiness. The significantly superior Commitment was exhibited through their Competitiveness and Understanding "the Job." In addition, compared with non-Elite officers, they show higher levels of Impromptu Rehearsal, and a unique Suspects Rapport through better understanding the criminal perspective. Public feedback was however acknowledged less by Elite officers as a means of evaluation.

They are further differentiated in not acknowledging fatigue to the same detail as other officers. They demonstrate a lack of awareness for needing Rest and report significantly less practices related to developing Fatigue Strategies. Military research on informed decision-making among high-risk personnel highlights their job-specific skills, including effective teamwork, adaptability, judgment, and physical endurance[67]. Greater physical endurance may account for a higher tolerance to fatigue. However, this study did not find teamwork to be a differentiating factor. Collaboration, adaptability, and judgment could be implied by a superior sense of Officer Safety, Understanding "the Job," and External Communication skills both within agencies and with suspects.

"Patrol-only experience" distinct practices

Officers with Patrol-only experience, versus those with additional frontline specialty unit experience, show a slightly greater influence on success skills (10). Interestingly, their scores are significantly lower on certain skills within the Mental Preparation, Commitment, and Full Focus success elements but higher on Distraction Control, Self-Belief, and Constructive Evaluation. The list of the success practices that are significantly different for officers with Patrol-only experience is given in Table 7.21.

TABLE 7.21 Patrol-Only Experience Distinct Practices

SUCCESS PRACTICES	PATROL-ONLY EXPERIENCE	OTHER FRONT-LINE EXPERIENCE	P-VALUE
Mental Competency			
Distraction Control	90	80	0.006
Fatigue strategies	100	74	0.071
Workload strategies	90	55	0.046
Female-policing strategies	50	18	0.042
Self-Belief			
Education	30	8	0.063
Constructive Evaluation			
Formal evaluation	38	14	0.056
Mental Preparation*	36	44	0.044
Physical discipline*	10	63	0.003
Psyching*	30	66	0.043
External communication*	20	53	0.068
Commitment			
Job satisfaction*	80	97	0.046
Full Focus			
Equipment confidence*	80	97	0.046

Note: * Practices officers with Patrol-only experience have a lower practice level.

All specialty-unit training an officer receives, through being currently or formerly active in a given frontline unit, has an influence on their mental-readiness success practices. Consistently, Patrol, SRO, Tactical, and Canine training has a slightly higher impact on success practice than Community Resource Officer (CRO) and Traffic Escort. Overall, experience from any of the specialty units (Developmental factors) has a greater influence on success skills than the impact of total "years on" experience.

Gender factor profiles

Within the group of Background factors, gender has the highest influence on performance success by impacting 10 skills.

Female dominant practices: Being dedicated to policing is reported by 100% of female officers interviewed, compared with only 70% of male officers. Debriefing with visualization is more dominantly used by female officers. Female officers demonstrate their flexibility as they are less prone to use a specific location for their preparation routine(s). Personal coping strategies for surviving in a male environment are a conscious set of female skills beyond their duties as an officer.

Male dominant practices: Male officers use camaraderie as a basis for their confidence more than female officers. More males report strategies for minimizing interruptions, ensuring officer safety, avoiding car collisions, and handling public complaints. Preparation rituals associated with locations are also more prevalent with male officers.

Language and ethnicity

While the four language (primary and multiple) and ethnicity (all and male-only) factors independently appear to have a moderate impact on success skills, their interrelationship and combined influence can be considered high to merit further investigation.

Least influential factors

Although still significant, there are several factors that have a relatively lower impact on success skills (scores of 5 or less) within the sample. Surprisingly, two intuitive beliefs for policing success—education and years on—have substantially less impact on success compared to the specific police training factors.

Background factors: Three factors had the least influence within this group and include: prior police-related experience (5), military experience (3), and education (3). Clearly, these factors associated with education and other experience have lower influence on the success skills relating to policing excellence.

Developmental factors: Of these factors having more than frontline experience (5) and rural experience (2) have relatively low influence on success skills when compared to the various specialty unit training. Military and rural experience factors influence only a very small number of skills (3 and 2, respectively); however, they do suggest that certain success skills may lend themselves to certain Background and Developmental factor tendencies. Thus, there is an opportunity for predisposed internal experts to be identified.

Police Distinction factors: Performance skills are not highly influenced by the total "years on" experience (5) factor. A range of scenarios were tracked based on less than 5, 5 to 10, and over 10 years of policing experience among excellent officers. As an example, attitudes and behaviors relating to police commitment inconsistently evolve as follows:
- the importance for job security peaks between 5 and 10 years on
- a sense of responsible leadership peaks between 10 and 15 years on
- risk recognition increases steadily with more years on

Similarly, the old/new school male factor shows little influence on success skills. Given the relatively low influence of total "years on" experience, which might be associated with the "old school" generation, this result is not surprising. It is somewhat unexpected to note that there is no apparent independent advantage on success skills of either of these factors.

While it is possible to generate profiles of all 22 factors influencing success, this analysis is beyond the scope of this project.

Trends in mental-readiness practices

Changes in police mental-readiness practices reporting over time provide insights into potential emerging trends.

Figure 7.9 illustrates temporal changes in mental-readiness practices over 17 years, with analysis available in Appendix N. Significant decreases over time are depicted across the seven

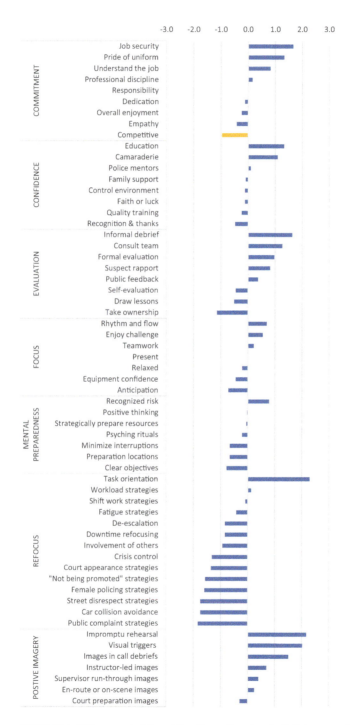

FIGURE 7.9 Differences in Mental-Readiness Practices in Policing over 17 Years

success elements. At the top, Job security shows the greatest increase within Commitment. At the bottom, Positive Imagery, Court-preparation images have seen a slight decrease in reported use.

Commitment: Job security, Pride of uniform, and Understanding "the job" are reported as moderately greater sources of Commitment than in the past, while Competitiveness is slightly less influential. Efforts to increase internal mentoring may account for a more realistic view of the job, lateral career options, and a stronger internal bond, as evidenced by an increase in Camaraderie.

Confidence: Over the years, Education and Camaraderie have become more influential factors in building confidence.

Constructive Evaluation: There are marked differences in how officers evaluate their work. Taking personal ownership has shown a moderate decrease. In contrast, Informal debriefs, Team consultations, and Formal evaluations are all rated higher, suggesting a more team-oriented approach to evaluations, and possibly a result of involving coach officers. Additionally, developing Rapport with suspects shows a slight increase, possibly due to the shift toward community policing.

Full Focus and *Mental Preparation* practices remain the most consistent over time. While the ability to Anticipate, Minimize interruptions, and Set objectives has diminished slightly, there is a slight rise in enjoying the challenges and flow of the job.

Distraction Control: There appears to be a shift away from multiple specialized practices for controlling distractions toward a greater emphasis on being Task-oriented to refocus. Given the vast differences in managing Crises, Court appearances, and Public complaints this decline may be a point of concern. Strategies for Workload, Shift work, and Fatigue remain unchanged and continue to challenge most officers.

Positive Imagery: There has been a significant increase in the use of Positive Imagery techniques. This could be due to initiatives such as debriefing, imagery in marksmanship, mindfulness training, and mental-health programs such as the "Road to Mental Readiness." Visualization is a proven skill separator in elite sport.

J. 20 Key strategies for mental readiness in policing

The following 20 key strategies summarize mental readiness in policing.

1. **Follow a reliable roadmap:** Orlick's "Wheel of Excellence" offers a roadmap to personal excellence, emphasizing commitment, confidence, and mental-readiness skills crucial for success in policing.
2. **Be committed to succeed:** Officers demonstrate unwavering dedication, often prioritizing duty over personal plans, driven by a pride of uniform.
3. **Find compassionate solutions:** Officers excel at connecting with others, prioritizing communication, and displaying compassion in seeking alternative solutions over punitive measures even in difficult situations.
4. **Maintain high standards:** Professionalism is upheld through high standards, honesty, and proactive approaches, evident in punctuality and disciplined appearance.
5. **Find job satisfaction:** Frontline officers find fulfillment in the diversity, freedom, and camaraderie in a demanding job, fueled by positivity and strong leadership.
6. **Advance self-belief:** Confidence in policing grows step-by-step, starting with staying calm, gaining perspective, assessing, and acting, drawing from training, mentors, recognition, education, and other support systems to remain grounded.
7. **Make all training purposeful:** A commitment to quality training equips officers to handle diverse situations effectively, boosting personal comfort, confidence, and overall success.
8. **Incorporate visualizaton:** Vivid mental imagery, mental checklists, and visual triggers (like picturing gear, recalling building layouts, and rehearsing court appearances) aid in preparing for stress, anticipating dangers, planning responses, maintaining confidence, and debriefing.
9. **Mentally rehearse anywhere:** Elite officers engage in spontaneous or structured mental rehearsal before calls, combining

strategic planning, positive thinking, and pre-shift routines such as rehearsing dynamic scenarios in the station, their patrol cars, or at home.
10. **Have a goal:** Clear objectives, recognized risks, and minimal interruptions ensure readiness to act effectively in critical situations.
11. **Plan to be focused:** Fully focus involves heightened awareness, thinking ahead, and trust in equipment and team.
12. **Predict and manage risks:** Predicting what might go wrong and planning for it shows adaptability and strong risk management skills in unpredictable situations.
13. **Use tactical breathing:** Emotional intelligence with tactical breathing aids in enjoyment, maintaining pace, and staying calm and focused.
14. **Multitask to handle distractions:** Navigating distractions requires de-escalating situations, involving others, completing tasks, while staying calm to make smart decisions and manage crises effectively.
15. **Develop specialized control practices:** Officers commonly face issues like shift work, public disrespect, and public complaints, underscoring the need for targeted control skills—such as dealing with public disrespect through either confronting it head-on or brushing it off, each for different reasons.
16. **Anticipate complacency:** Managing downtimes or routine tasks successfully means engaging in different activities or maintaining a positive and non-complacent attitude.
17. **Have a fulfilling career plan:** Excellent officers often prioritize lateral moves or job satisfaction over promotions.
18. **Accept feedback and grow:** Self-evaluation, gathering feedback, taking ownership, learning from mistakes, and finding ways to relax are essential for professional growth, coping with pressure, and becoming a better cop.
19. **Understand mental-readiness influencers:** Demographic factors like specialty-unit training, gender, and patrol-only experience strongly influence mental-readiness practices, while others like education, military experience, rural-patrol background, and years of service have minimal impact.

20. **Particpate responsibly in preparedness:** Law enforcement emphasizes both physical and mental preparedness for duty, highlighting the responsibility of individuals for self-care and the organization for professional development.

Notes

1 T. Orlick, "The psychology of personal excellence," *Contemporary Thought on Performance Enhancement,* vol. 1, pp. 110–122, 1992.
2 T. Orlick, "Wheel of excellence," http://www.zoneofexcellence.ca, October 25, 2003.
3 T. Virtue and S. Moir, "Tessa Virtue and Scott Moir commentate RD at Beijing 2022," Olympic Broadcasting. https://twitter.com/wheelsofadream/status/1492526971225575425?lang = en, February 12, 2022.
4 K. M. Markos, "A conduit from public trust to legitimacy: Continuous ethics training in law enforcement." ProQuest Dissertations Publishing, *Doctoral dissertation, University of La Verne, 1-152,* 2017.
5 H. Wyatt-Nichol and Franks, G., "Ethics training in law enforcement agencies," *Public Integrity,* vol. 12, no. 1, pp. 39–50. https://doi.org/10.2753/PIN1099-9922120103, 2009.
6 S. Charles, "Professional integrity, modern racism, self-esteem, and universality-diversity orientation of police officers in a large urban police agency." ProQuest Dissertations Publishing, Doctoral Dissertation, Education of Fordham University, 2009.
7 P. O. Dissmore, "Ethics for the military officer: Teaching ethics at the maneuver support center for engineer officers." ProQuest Dissertations Publishing,, Doctoral Dissertation, Assemblies of God Theological Seminary, 1–251, 2009.
8 P. A. Lasiewicki, "Achieving congruence between individual commitment to policing and organizational objectives in police departments." ProQuest Dissertations Publishing, Doctoral Dissertation, University of Phoenix, 1–435, 2007.
9 R. B. Gaither, "Ethical leadership and its impact on role modeling, strictness, openness, and job satisfaction of law enforcement officers." ProQuest Dissertations Publishing, Doctoral Dissertion, Keiser University, 1–113, 2017.

10 S. Charman, "Making sense of policing identities: The 'deserving' and the 'undeserving' in policing accounts of victimisation," *Policing & Society,* vol. 30, no. 1, pp. 81–97. https://doi.org/10.1080/10439463.2019.1601721, 2020.
11 B. Brown, "The power of vulnerability." http://TED.com, https://www.youtube.com/watch?v = iCvmsMzlF7o, 2011.
12 R. Martin, "Police corruption: An analytical look into police ethics," *FBI Law Enforcement Bulletin,* vol. 80, no. 11, pp. 11–17, 2011.
13 J. Edwards, "Ethical decision-making: A treatise into the role of ethics in 21st century policing." ProQuest Dissertations Publishing, Doctoral Dissertation, London Metropolitan University, 2012.
14 B. English, "'Climate for ethics' and occupational-organisational commitment conflict," *Journal of Management Development,* vol. 27, no. 9, pp. 963–975. https://doi.org/10.1108/02621710810901309, 2008.
15 Y. Brunetto, Teo, S., Shacklock, K. and Farr-Wharton, R., "Emotional intelligence, job satisfaction, well-being and engagement: Explaining organizational commitment and turnover intentions in policing," *Human Resource Management Journal,* vol. 22, no. 4, pp. 428–444, 2012.
16 A. A. Escamilla, "Are you in or out? A study of law enforcement officers' perceived quality of relationship with their leader and its effects on organizational commitment." ProQuest Dissertations Publishing, TX, Doctoral Dissertation, Our Lady of the Lake University Strange, 2015.
17 M. B. Halicioglu, "Examination of the relationship between self-directedness and outcomes of the online COP training program in the Turkish National Police context." ProQuest Dissertations Publishing, Doctoral Dissertation, Michigan State University, 2010.
18 British College of Policing, "Integrity and transparency." https://www.college.police.uk/What-we-do/Ethics/integrity-and-transparency/Pages/Integrity-and-Transparency.aspx, February 12, 2022.
19 K. Breevaart, Bakker, A. B. and Demerouti, E., "Leader-member exchange, work engagement, and job performance," *Journal of Managerial Psychology,* vol. 30, no. 7, pp. 754–770. https://doi.org/10.1108/JMP-03-2013-0088, 2015.
20 M. Bettschart, Herrmann, M., Wolf, B. M. and Brandstätter, V., "The seed of goal-related doubts: A longitudinal investigation of the roles of failure and expectation of success among police trainee applicants," *Frontiers in Psychology,* vol. 10, p. 2151. https://doi.org/10.3389/fpsyg.2019.02151.
21 H. Sprafka* and Kranda, A. H., "Institutionalizing mentoring in police departments," *Police Chief,* vol. 75, no. 1, p. 46, 2008.

22 H. Sprafka and Kranda, A., "Best practices for institutionalizing mentoring into police departments." International Association of Chiefs of Police, 1-7. https://www.ojp.gov/ncjrs/virtual-library/abstracts/best-practices-institutionalizing-mentoring-police-departments, 2003.
23 F. Dalgaty, Guthrie, G., Walker, H., and Stirling, K., "The value of mentorship in medical education," *The Clinical Teacher*, vol. 14, no. 2, pp. 124–128. https://doi.org/10.1111/tct.12510, 2016.
24 N. Henry-Noel, Bishop, M., Gwede, C., et al., "Mentorship in medicine and other health professions," *Journal of Cancer Education*, vol. 34, pp. 629–637. https://doi.org/10.1007/s13187-018-1360-6, 2019.
25 L. W. Bewley, "Seasons of leadership development: An analysis of a multi-dimensional model of mentoring among career groups of United States Army officers." ProQuest Dissertations Publishing, Doctoral Dissertation, University of Alabama at Birmingham, 1–115, 2005.
26 O. A. Graves, "Phenomenological study exploring mentoring received by Black Army officers to improve promotions." ProQuest Dissertations Publishing, Doctoral Dissertation, University of Phoenix, 1-259, 2016.
27 R. Lunney, "Performance ritual for street policing," *Blue Line Magazine*, January 28, p. 17, 2015.
28 J. P. Andersen and Gustafsberg, H., "A training method to improve police use of force decision making: A randomized controlled trial," *SAGE Open*, vol. 6, no. 2, p. 215824401663870. https://doi.org/10.1177/2158244016638708, 2016.
29 R. L. Krakauer, Stelnicki, A. M. and Carleton, R. N., "Examining mental health knowledge, stigma, and service use intentions among public safety personnel," *Frontiers in Psychology*, vol. 11, p. 949. https://doi.org/10.3389/fpsyg.2020.00949, 2020.
30 J. W. Page, Asken, M. J., Zwemer, C. F. and Guido, M., "Brief mental skills training improves memory and performance in high stress police cadet training," *Journal of Police and Criminal Psychology*, vol. 31, no. 2, pp. 122–126. https://doi.org/10.1007/s11896-015-9171-8, 2016.
31 G. R. Mount, "Mental practice: Police performance in hostage negotiation," *Journal of Police Crisis Negotiations*, vol. 7, no. 2, pp. 141–143. https://doi.org/10.1300/J173v07n02_11, 2007.
32 M. MacClurg, "Back to basics with Butch Harmon," *Golf Digest*. https://www.golfdigest.com/story/back-to-basics-with-butch-harmon], June 3, 2020.
33 S. Charman, *Police socialisation, identity and culture becoming Blue*. London: Palgrave Macmillan, 2017.

34 R. Peace, "Probationer training for neighbourhood policing in England and Wales: Fit for purpose?," *Policing: An International Journal of Police Strategies and Management,* vol. 29, no. 2, pp. 335–346, 2006.
35 P. Manning, *Policing contingencies.* Chicago, IL: University of Chicago Press, 2003.
36 P. Bury, "Barossa night: Cohesion in the British Army officer corps," *The British Journal of Sociology,* vol. 68, no. 2, pp. 314–335. https://doi.org/10.1111/1468-4446.12236, 2017.
37 I. Fontaine, *Neuroscience in support of resilience: Recommendations for self-care,* University of Ottawa Employee Webinar, Ottawa, Dec 9, 2020.
38 R. Z. Bondar, Bertollo, M., di Fronso, S. and Robazza, C., "Mindfulness to performance enhancement: A systematic review of neural correlates," *International Review of Sport and Exercise Psychology,* vol. 17. https://doi.org/10.1080/1750984X.2021.1949742, 2024.
39 A. Baltzell, "Mindfulness and performance," in *Mindfulness in positive psychology.* Routledge, pp. 64–79. https://assets.cambridge.org/97811070/74699/frontmatter/9781107074699_frontmatter.pdf, 2016.
40 R. K. Wortley, Measuring police attitudes toward discretion. *Criminal justice and behavior,* 30(5), 538–58, Oct 2003.
41 K. McLean, Alikhan, A. and Alpert, G. P., "Re-examining the use of force continuum: Why resistance is not the only driver of use of force decisions," *Police Quarterly,* vol. 26, no. 1, pp. 85–110, 2023.
42 S. N. Knights Jr, "Ethical decision-making framework in police officers' use of the force continuum," Doctoral Dissertation, Capella University, 1-179, 2021.
43 C. Frank Klahm IV, Frank, J. and Liederbach, J., "Understanding police use of force: Rethinking the link between conceptualization and measurement," *Policing: An International Journal of Police Strategies & Management,* vol. 37, no. 3, pp. 558–578, 2024.
44 B. H. Johnsen, Espevik R., Saus E. R., Sanden S., Olsen O. K., Hystad S. W. Hardiness as a moderator and motivation for operational duties as mediator: The relation between operational self-efficacy, performance satisfaction, and perceived strain in a simulated police training scenario. *Journal of police and Criminal Psychology,* , 32:331-9 Dec 2017.
45 A. Graham, *Take back your weekends: Stress less. Do more. Be happier.* Elevate Press, pp. 148, 2021.
46 M. Abu-Alhassin, McDonald, J., Kirkwood, T., Williams, M. and Cheng, C., "Police mental competencies," in *Gold medal policing*, 2nd ed. Routledge, pp. 537–550, 2025.

47 M. P. DeRosia, "Ethics training and practice within the Central Valley Police Department." ProQuest Dissertations Publishing, 2012, Doctoral Dissertation, Walden University.
48 M. J. Cuttler and Muchinsky, P. M., "Prediction of law enforcement training performance and dysfunctional job performance with general mental ability, personality, and life history variables," *Criminal Justice and behavior,* vol. 33, no. 1, pp. 3–25, 2006.
49 Gutshall, C., Hampton, D. P., Sebetan, I. M., Stein, P. C. and Broxtermann, T. J., "The effects of occupational stress on cognitive performance in police officers," *Police Practice & Research,* vol. 18, no. 5, pp. 463–477. https://doi.org/10.1080/15614263.2017.1288120, 2017.
50 L. Grossmith*, Owens, C., Finn, W., Mann, D., Davies, T., and Baika, L., "Police, camera, evidence: London's cluster randomised controlled trial of Body Worn Video," London. https://www.london.gov.uk/sites/default/files/bwv_report_nov_2015.pdf, 2015.
51 Blackhall, V., Walker, K. G., Whiteley, I. and Wilson, P., "Use of head camera-cued recall and debrief to externalise expertise: A systematic review of literature from multiple fields of practice," *BMJ Simulation & Technology Enhanced Learning,* vol. 5, no. 3, pp. 121–129. https://doi.org/10.1136/bmjstel-2018-000341, 2019.
52 M. D. White, Gaub, J. E., Malm, A. and Padilla, K. E., "Implicate or exonerate? The impact of police body-worn cameras on the adjudication of drug and alcohol cases," *Policing: A Journal of Policy and Practice,* vol. 15, pp. 759–769, 2019.
53 A. Armenta, "Between public service and social control: Policing dilemmas in the era of immigration enforcement," *Social Problems,* vol. 63, no. 1, pp. 111–126. https://doi.org/10.1093/socpro/spv024, 2016.
54 M. Andrew, Violanti, J. M., Gu, J. K., Fekedulegn, D. and Li, S., "Police work stressors and cardiac vagal control," *American Journal of Human Biology,* vol. 29, no. 5. https://doi.org/10.1002/ajhb.22996, 2017.
55 D. Paton and Violanti, J. M., "Policing in the context of terrorism: Managing traumatic stress risk," *Traumatology,* vol. 12, no. 3, pp. 236–247. https://doi.org/10.1177/1534765606294990, 2006.
56 L. Cohen, Dahlen, G., Escobar, A., Fejerskov, O. and Johnson, N., "Why a radical overhaul of dentistry is needed," *Indian Journal of Dental Research,* vol. 28, pp. 471–474, 2017.
57 H. A. Smith, Wolfe-Clark, A. L. and Bryan, C. J., "An exploratory study of the mental toughness psychological skills profile psychometrics, and the mediating effect of social support sources on mental toughness and suicidal ideation among military police," *Journal of Police and*

58. J. K. Lee, Choi, H. G., Kim, J. Y., Nam, J., Kang, H. T., Koh, S. B. and Oh, S. S., "Self-resilience as a protective factor against development of post-traumatic stress disorder symptoms in police officers," *Annals of Occupational and Environmental Medicine*, vol. 28, pp. 1–7. https://link.springer.com/article/10.1186, 2016.
59. K. C. Burke, "Democratic policing and officer well-being," *Frontiers in Psychology*, vol. 11, p. 523876, 2020.
60. J. M. Violanti, Paton, D., Johnston, P., Burke, K. J., Clarke, J. and Keenan, D., "Stress shield: A model of police resiliency," *Emergency Mental Health*, vol. 10, no. 2, pp. 95–108. https://ovc.ojp.gov/sites/g/files/xyckuh226/files/media/document/res_stress_shield_resilience-508.pdf, 2008.
61. A. Paterson, *Trauma and resilience in contemporary Australian policing: Is PTS inevitable for first responders?* Singapore: Springer Nature, 2021.
62. L. Crust and Clough, P. J., "Developing mental toughness: From research to practice," *Journal of Sport Psychology in Action*, vol. 2, no. 1, pp. 21–32. https://doi.org/10.1080/21520704.2011.563436, 2011.
63. A. Duckworth, *Grit: The power of passion and perseverance*, vol. 234. New York: Scribner, 2016.
64. R. Hillier, "Rick Hillier Quotes." AZ Quotes. https://www.azquotes.com/author/64129-Rick_Hillier.
65. J. Kinley, "The 8 steps to resilience," Atlantic Institute for Resilience Inc. https://pans.ns.ca/sites/default/files/8steps_to_resilience.pdf.
66. J. D. Creswell, "Mindfulness interventions," *Annual Review of Psychology*, vol. 68, pp. 491–516, 2017.
67. J. J. Picano, Roland, R. R. and Williams, T. J., "Assessment and selection of high-risk operational personnel," in *Military psychology: Clinical and operational applications*, pp. 326–343.https://books.google.ca/books?hl=en&lr=&id=3LtzEAAAQBAJ&oi=fnd&pg=PA326&ots=8wCTxIy4Tu&sig=nXzekuuaIHIrDGWTbP0V6fONc50&redir_esc=y#v=onepage&q&f=false, 2022.

8

Police leadership at all levels

> **SPOILER ALERT**
>
> Successful leadership emphasizes teamwork and a balance between intellect and emotions.

Abstract

Effective senior leadership in policing requires clear ethics, talent mobilization, and making informed decisions. True leaders prioritize people, showing courage, optimism, and clear communication, ensuring success even in the face of adversity. Senior police management faces unique challenges such as terrorism, politics, and media attention, needing emotional intelligence and adept crisis management skills. Frontline leadership is vital for effective law enforcement, with sergeants and informal patrol leaders guiding and mentoring others. Successful police leaders inspire commitment by setting examples, being open and accountable, and building strong relationships with their teams. Trust, communication, and humility are key for successful partnerships in achieving organizational goals.

This chapter discusses peak performance in policing in five sections:

A. "Gold-medal" senior leadership
B. Management under pressure
C. Effective leadership tactics
D. Leadership in the field
E. 20 Key strategies for police leadership

As part of the Gold Medal Policing studies, data was collected on the parallel needs of police executives, superintendents, and inspector-level policing. Information on senior police management was collected through various means. First, 11 one-on-one interviews were held with senior police members of the Ottawa Police Service, including all four command executives and seven other senior officers at the superintendent and inspector levels. Over the years, interviews were conducted with senior executives from various policing and security sectors, such as the Royal Canadian Mint, border patrol and security services. Additionally, valuable insights were gained from presentations and discussions at conferences, providing inspiration for leadership at all levels within organizations.

This chapter underscores the demands placed on senior leadership, emphasizing the need to be clear about what's right, good at getting the best out of their team, and able to make smart decisions. These leaders must navigate unique challenges like terrorism, political pressures, and media scrutiny. They require emotional intelligence and adept crisis management skills. Examples illustrating how true leaders put people first, demonstrate moral courage, are optimistic, and communicate well are highlighted through quotes by exceptional leaders at all levels.

A. "Gold-medal" senior leadership

Ethical leaders understand their values clearly. Senior leadership in policing demands ethical clarity, mobilization of talent, modern thinking, and informed decision-making. Leaders must embody integrity, accountability, and reliability, inspiring their teams to believe in a shared vision. They mobilize talent, embrace paradoxes, and make informed decisions. True leaders prioritize people, demonstrating moral courage, optimism, and clear communication, ensuring success even in the face of adversity. They hold themselves accountable for their actions and stick to their principles, inspiring others to believe in their vision[1,2].

> **Mobilize talent**—*A leader does not have to be a subject matter expert; rather, they must mobilize talent and get the team as productive and enthused as possible. A talented leader can be taken out of their comfort zone and still be effective.*
> —Gaither (2017)[1]

Blair Sheppard, a global leader, emphasizes the need for modern thinking to address 21st-century challenges. To solve urgent problems, leaders should embrace paradoxes like being tech-savvy and caring, thinking globally but acting locally, being both strategic and hands-on, humble yet heroic, traditional yet innovative, and always honest[3].

> **Informed decision-maker**—*You don't have to be a subject matter expert but you need to recognize what you don't know before making decisions. Pretending to know is the worst. Don't let your ego interfere with making the right decision for the organization.*
> —National Police Executive

A good leader quietly gets things done and motivates their team. They communicate clearly, delegate tasks, and trust their team. They admit when they don't know something and stay positive during tough times. They treat everyone fairly, take risks, and recognize their team's efforts.

Executives interviewed defined a good leader this way:
- is understated, quietly getting things done gaining people's support and buy-in
- motivates, making people feel confident, valued, and good about coming to work
- creates partnerships, so when away, someone trusted takes over responsibilities, reciprocating when needed

- gives clear instructions, then lets people get the job done, without meddling
- conducts regular updates, ensuring work is on time, on track, and on budget
- articulates priorities clearly, displaying company values in their behavior
- surrounds themselves with the right skilled people, admitting what they don't know
- isn't risk averse, staying positive when things get bad, owning failures—eventually you'll find a flower growing out of a crack in the concrete
- prioritizes one-on-one time with direct reports, despite a full schedule
- treats all employees fairly, although not necessarily equally
- quickly praises others for successes, recognizing that success is not only due to what they did but as a direct result of the team's effort

Never one to shy away from expressing his opinions, Rick Hillier, former Chief of Defense for the Canadian military, is known for his frank and straightforward approach. According to Hillier[4], leadership is primarily about people—embracing those you lead and winning over those you need to work with—rather than avoiding risks or following management trends. True leaders think ahead and have a clear plan. They demonstrate their leadership through actions, not just words, and they create their own luck. However, leaders also act with moral courage, leverage crises, accept failure, and maintain a perpetual sense of optimism.

> **Optimism** *can be more powerful than a battery of artillery or squadron of tanks. It can be contagious and it's necessary to being a leader.*
> —Rick Hillier, Former Chief of Defense, Canadian military[2]

Whether on the front lines of business or in any situation requiring strong communication and vision, leaders trust their instincts and make difficult decisions appear effortless.

B. Management under pressure

Senior police management faces unique policing challenges. For instance, complex and emotionally-sensitive matters such as audits, officer suicides, and combating corruption all require adept crisis management skills. How do senior management challenges and reactions differ from those on the frontline?

Senior police management challenges

Dealing with high-profile crimes, political risks, and media attention presents a unique set of challenges for police management compared to those faced by frontline officers. Management must be accountable, adhering to protocols, managing public expectations, and addressing internal and external issues. Mentoring employees is crucial for building relationships and competence, particularly during unfamiliar and unprecedented circumstances[5]. When the management team is frustrated, itaffects everyone.

Police leaders need emotional intelligence to balance the conflicting values and needs of their members and the ever-changing community they serve[6]. Ineffective leaders may overestimate their abilities, making the situation worse[2,7].

> **Dysfunctional**—*I left when I was clashing with the Commissioner. I understand that when top leaders have a dysfunctional relationship, it affects the organization's functionality and is very difficult for people below them.*

Below is a list of challenging situations identified by senior police members, which parallels the list provided by frontline officers. Management challenges can range from terrorism, media issues, and politics to audits, officer suicides, being the "hired gun," and corruption (see Chapter 3: Police under Pressure—Frontline Police Challenges).

Heightened risk: high profile crimes • political risks • accountability • terrorism (the new reality) • media storm… war (wrong story, misinformation, leaked info) • liability issues • serious operational error (someone is going to have to wear it)

Complex situation: bound by protocol/guidelines • complex documents/deadlines • public agendas • people in camps • "bureaucratic quagmire" • internal audit • political controversy • balancing operational-management needs • community partnership development • non-confidence vote

High-risk persons (internal and/or external): members' misconduct • special interest groups • racial and gender issues • new political administration • new Board • anonymous complaint • public expectations • suicidal officers • attitude problems • "Gen Now" issues • persons with unreasonable demands or expectations

Coaching/Leadership: mentoring high-level employees • department with a bad reputation • being "the hired gun" • leadership issues • team projects • officers seeking advice or support

Unprecedented circumstances: intensity of a "24/7-group" • extremes in work volume • overlapping or conflicting obligations • decisive under fire • organizational inertia • crimes for which there are no laws • leading the pack

Unfamiliar situations: leading in a new area • media in/media out—no control • where I haven't been tested yet • the unknown • making "uninformed" decisions

Emotionally-charged situations: incident with an officer • personal allegations • physical and mental fatigue • not looking foolish with peers • police corruption • media leaks • power struggle • internal aftermath • slander and character defamation • emotional relationship • being hung out to dry by the organization

"Crises"

A frontline patrol leader describes a crisis as feeling overwhelmed by many things beyond their control. They worry about patrol duties consuming them and ensuring officers handle calls correctly, especially when they resort to shortcuts due to their training.

Frontline officers define a "crisis" call as: officer requesting assistance, a child in danger, surprises, missing shots, things they can't control, their own panic reaction, feeling in trouble, new situations, and others taking shortcuts with serious consequences.

In contrast to frontline officers, when senior police management members were asked to define the term "crisis," it was most often described as *"perpetual and unstoppable situations"* such as the following:

- being under political fire
- having budget overrun dealing with terrorism
- living with media leaks… media wars
- damning portrayals
- coping with the 6th lawsuit this year
- taking on a Department with a bad reputation
- always redefining "a crisis"
- enduring bloodthirsty personal attacks
- managing never-ending crises
- lasting a battle promotion
- awaiting the aftermath

Senior management members admitted to having had an emotional "gut reaction," either aloud or internally, when first alerted to a "crisis." These immediate reactions are as follows:

- shaken to the core
- felt ill-prepared to deal with what's going on
- being squeezed little by little 'til the wheels come off
- I had dug a hole 10 feet deep
- like slings and arrows through my heart
- days where things couldn't get any darker
- social drinking
- impacting my family—my spouse, kids, and aging mother

While the sources of crises may differ, the emotional reactions from frontline officers, either aloud or internally, parallel those of senior management. Their immediate reactions are as follows:

- shock wave, gut-wrenching
- stomach just turns, sick feeling

- instant panic, terror, "I'm shaking"
- "Sh--!"…"God, where is he?"
- tunnel vision, dumbfounded, freeze
- the "Holy f---s" when you pull up
- body feels hot, sweaty palms
- breathing and heart rate changes
- unnerving feeling, heart in your throat
- emotions just go rampant
- can almost FEEL the adrenaline flow
- could make a mistake

Leadership pressures can cause stress and become a prolonged distraction during future high-performance situations. Similar to frontline staff, both groups experience emotional reactions when confronted with a crisis, ranging from feeling ill-prepared to panic and shock. Maintaining composure during and immediately after demanding situations is crucial to cultivating everyday resilience.

C. Effective leadership tactics

Learning from respected senior leaders provides seasoned, refined practices beneficial for leaders at all levels. These insights demonstrate how to overcome leadership hurdles through endurance, team building, engagement, and partnerships. Effective leadership requires interpersonal and motivational skills, focusing on both performance and potential. Successful police leaders inspire commitment by setting a good example, being open and accountable, and building strong relationships with their team. The significant influence of a police chief underscores their responsibility in assessing and making determinations regarding officer conduct, profoundly impacting individuals' careers and lives. Additionally, partnerships built on trust, constant communication, humility, and lack of competitiveness are essential for achieving organizational goals.

Endurance

Leaders can begin by encouraging open discussion and learning from the past. This can evolve to building confidence for change[8,9,10], evaluating performance versus potential, and implementing effective succession planning.

> **Baggage of understanding**—*The past is relevant. Know how things were by reading old files and talking to the person who held the job before you. Learn what changed, what failed, and why. This baggage of understanding is essential for effective leadership.*
> —Law Enforcement Executive

> **Executing good ideas**—*I typically speak last. If I say, "Go with color blue," I will get too much agreement. I like challenge, open discussion, and push back—"Why blue, why not green?" It's not about my ideas always being adopted. Ideas are all around us, and anyone around the table could come up with the best one. Create a vision and discuss within your circle of direct reports. However, the leader ultimately makes the decision, and once made, others must line-up and execute.*
> —National Security Executive

> **Change**—*Sometimes the rank and file feel that change has to always come from the top. If this is the case, then the leadership isn't doing a good job. The responsibility for change lies with everyone, and employees should understand that they have a voice and that leadership will listen. An employee with good leadership potential will engage and make suggestions. When people feel confident enough to speak up, they can impact a lot of change. A good leader will create that opportunity.*
> —Police Senior Leader

Team building and partnerships

Effective leadership involves more than just job performance; it requires interpersonal and motivational skills. Executives distinguish between two separate indicators when evaluating employees: performance and potential[11]. Performance is the ability to do one's job, while potential refers to leadership ability. Succession planning focuses on identifying individuals with both performance and leadership potential. Immediate coaching and mentoring are crucial for developing future leaders and ensuring a smooth transition when vacancies arise.

> **Performance versus potential**—*An officer may excel at their day-to-day job, such as interviewing, but lack interpersonal or motivational skills. Saying, "Just leave me alone. Give me that file" and they may do a great job. However, they are not a good leader and will kill people working around them. On the other hand, you could have someone who has great leadership potential but does only adequate work.*
> —Law Enforcement Executive

> **Succession planning**—*Is someone exhibiting both performance and potential leadership skills for the next rank? If an individual scores 10/10 in Performance and 10/10 in Potential, then this is someone you keep an eye on to be identified for accelerated promotions. Our succession planning program is important for those showing leadership potential. In our program, an officer shadows a prominent community leader from various disciplines to gain exceptional leadership training.*
> —Police Senior Leader

> **Employee "exit strategy"**—*If an employee scores poorly in both Performance and Potential, then it's time for an exit strategy. Of course, they would be coached, mentored and allowed the opportunity to improve before being shown the door.*
> —National Security Executive

> **Immediate coaching** *is crucial for leadership succession. When I promote someone, I ask them to identify two or three potential replacements right away. You should not start looking for a replacement when the incumbent leaves. That coaching and mentoring process should start immediately and be ongoing to develop individuals with leadership potential.*
> —Police Executive

Police chiefs recognize that leadership principles are universal across professions, demanding accountability and excellence. *Working Together* delves into the successful partnership of Frank

Wells and Michael Eisner at the Walt Disney Company. Their unbreakable bond, built on trust and constant communication, highlights the importance of a supportive, passionate, and humble partnership in achieving organizational goals.

Effective partnerships, like those between Warren Buffett (the visionary) and Charlie Munger (the day-to-day "architect") of Berkshire Hathaway Inc., are essential for success. These partnerships foster trust, teamwork, and a balance between intellect and emotion. The best partnerships thrive on trust and understanding, with each partner embracing their role[12]. True partnerships, as Warren Buffett emphasizes, don't keep score, encouraging humility and intelligence to prevail. Fostering partnerships devoid of envy, jealousy, and rivalry is crucial for a better way of working, applicable at all levels in any organization, including policing.

Engagement

Leadership research[13,14] suggests that various factors throughout the day can trigger changes in individuals, influencing their thoughts and actions, leading to a sense of engagement. To keep officers engaged and performing well, it is essential to understand what motivates them[15]. Successful police leaders inspire officer commitment by setting a good example, being open and accountable, and building strong relationships with their team. The significant influence of a police chief in clearing officers of wrongdoing underscores their power and responsibility in assessing and making determinations regarding officer conduct. Such decisions can profoundly impact individuals' careers and lives.

> **Morale**—*Build opportunities. You can't always have the best, but but don't fall below a critical level. Focus efficiently on the resources you have. Ensure people understand what you're trying to accomplish. Make sure your actions are seen and heard. Believe in the mission and avoid unnecessary risks.*
> —Police Chief

Universal humanity—*New military officers learn ethical guidelines at the Maneuver Support Center for Engineer Officers. They study basic ethical principles universal to humanity and specific to the profession of arms. Understanding the reasons for which they fight is crucial; otherwise, they may go after the wrong objectives. The Ten Commandments provide valuable guidance for soldiers navigating life's complexities. Chaplains undergo extra ethics training before becoming instructors.*

—American military ethics training[16]

Ethical issues—*Leaders set an example. Education doesn't change values but is necessary to set a clear standard. Hold people accountable with common-sense ways rather than punishing everyone. Invest in young people so that values become part of their life.*

—Police Chief

Power—*The Chief cleared everybody saying there was no intention to hurt anybody, that the officers didn't purposely or willfully do anything to hurt anybody and that he can't find any negligence on their part.*

—Patrol Sergeant

Support—*It starts from the top… If somebody up there says, "I know my officers. They do a great job, until proven otherwise… They did what they needed to do in that incident, and all the rules were followed, according to our use of force measures. Until I see otherwise, that's where I stand. Thank you very much."*

—Patrol, > 10 years on

D. Leadership in the field

Frontline leadership in policing is crucial for effective law enforcement. Sergeants play a big role, putting the team first and ensuring tasks are done well. Beyond formal ranks, there are informal patrol leaders who guide and mentor others.

Supervisors constantly strive for improvement, supporting their team, even when things change quickly in the field. In crises, good leadership means maintaining optimism and providing unwavering support to officers. Police chiefs also play a vital part, making sure officers feel valued and supported in their roles, especially during challenging situations.

Sergeants' perspectives

The police structure allows for fluidity in frontline leadership roles and responsibilities, even if it is not their typical assignment. Passion is paramount, with a sense of responsibility and empowerment. The importance of making critical decisions rests on the frontline. Negative consequences arise when leaders prioritize their own interests over those of their team members, emphasizing the need for selfless leadership and sacrifices for the team's well-being. Autonomy ensures efficient task management and team well-being.

> **Passion**—*Be prepared. For me this is not a job. I love doing this; it's a passion. Last night, although we were supposed to leave at 4:00, we left at 5:30 just because the calls kept rolling in—big deal, especially as a Sergeant.*
> —Tactical Sergeant

> **Empowered**—*I am probably in one of the most powerful positions in this department. It's not the chief who's making those decisions about what's happening in this end of the city. While the chief is the most powerful person administratively, I am the most prominent in this area. Not even the Staff Sergeant, holds as much influence as I do. That's a rush, keeps me young, keeps me going.*
> —Patrol Sergeant

> **Don't interfere**—*It's really hard to step down sometimes from thinking "I'll take care of this." As a Sergeant, my biggest faux pas is interfering with the officers who were already handling the situation. I should have just shut my mouth. But I didn't—I had to stick my nose in, and that's where I went wrong.*
> —Patrol Sergeant

Selfless leadership—*Team leaders who put themselves above their followers... One or two individuals I see it, but not the majority.*
—Tactical, > 10 years on

Autonomy—*When I assign a task, I don't tell them how to do it. I just tell them what I want done, give them a timeline, and let them do it. If you continually tell people how to do their job, they'll start feeling like a monkey could do it. If done well, you stroke them, and they feel good about doing it. Working with people just makes me feel good.*
—Traffic Escort Sergeant

Leadership beyond ranks

Frontline officers in policing understand the significance of informal patrol leaders within the Platoon's management hierarchy. While sergeants adhere strictly to established processes, there exists an informal leadership structure that is often lacking. Experienced officers have learned the importance of spontaneous leadership, mentoring, and offering training opportunities. Identifying natural leaders within the team and empowering them as coach officers is essential for effective leadership development.

Informal patrol leaders—*There are different tiers of informal management of the Platoon. Sergeants are expected to follow the process—right to a "T." But there is an informal process where a good Senior Officer will behave and respond a certain way. It's missing right now and we need to bring it back.*
—Patrol Sergeant

Spontaneous leadership—*I was done day shift, and it was the afternoon guys going out. They didn't have a Sergeant or a TLT [Transactional and transformational leadership] lead. So, they asked me to join them and run the call. Actually, the guy who had asked me was perfectly capable. Sometimes it's just because he hasn't done it before. So, I said, "OK, I'll go along."*
—Tactical, > 10 years on

Mentoring—*You learn from other's mistakes too, and you try to pass on those lessons. My philosophy is, "If I screwed up on something, whether it's small or major, I never want anybody to go through the anxiety that I went through." So, I make sure I share that, even at my own embarrassment. And I ensure they only have to hear it once.*
—Female Sergeant

Offer training—*As soon as I stepped onto the Platoon as an active Sergeant, they knew I was from Tactical with all this additional training. I've been on three Platoons, and on each one, I planned training sessions on location. We did high-risk takedown during the shift, and on quiet night shifts, we'd sneak away to the range to shoot. They loved it. Who wouldn't want to improve their tactical response to calls?*
—Patrol Sergeant

Natural coaches—*Some people are natural leaders—people whom others want to follow. Then there are positional leaders—people others have to follow because they're positioned in an organization. A good Sergeant or Staff Sergeant should be able to identify these natural leaders who could positively influence their peers, especially recruits. These individuals should be selected as Coach Officers.*
—Patrol, 5 to 10 years on

Coach officers—*Identify effective police officers willing to become teachers for young officers. Implement teaching roles at all levels, fostering leadership by example. This is crucial for our profession's development.*
—Neighborhood Resource

Supervisors' dilemma

Supervisors constantly engage in self-criticism and strive for improvement. They take pride in their team's accomplishments and their role in guiding and supporting their officers to ensure team success. They must also ensure the safety of their team members while carrying out the mission, adapting to changing circumstances and challenges in the field.

Teamwork pride—*No matter how well I perform, I still criticize my actions rarely acknowledging excellence, always seeing room for improvement. For instance, I just supervised a situation, taking some statements, and obtaining information, I often think, "Okay, I should have done this differently, I could have done that better." Nevertheless, I take pride in the teamwork displayed.*

—Female Patrol Sergeant

Safety—*As the team leader, I found myself in a situation where our usual munitions didn't work at all. There was a high possibility of frying my own guys. I wanted to get my own people out, and everybody out as quickly as possible… Wearing a gas mask, they couldn't understand me very well. I had to yell, "Get out of the basement, get out now."*

—Tactical Sergeant

Resourceful—*I always say to my guys, "If I can't give you the answer, I'll get you the answer." I'll never leave them hanging with "I don't know" or "I'm not sure."*

—Female Patrol Sergeant

Vigilance—*My personality drives me to take calls. Beyond supervision, I take calls to remain fresh and deal with particular situations, so I'm up on things. I'm also keeping physically fit and ready.*

—Patrol Sergeant

Attitude and actions

In policing, leadership involves seizing opportunities in crises, maintaining optimism, and providing unwavering support to officers. Crises can be used as opportunities to achieve visions faster, emphasizing that actions speak louder than words.

Support originates from leadership at the highest levels within a police department, highlighting the importance of following established rules and use of force measures. It demonstrates the role of leaders in supporting fellow officers during challenging situations and maintaining confidence within the team.

Never waste a crisis—*Make it an opportunity to achieve your vision more quickly. Watch how you perform in the face of failure… Action articulates your values loudly.*
—Rick Hillier, Former Chief of Defense, Canadian military[4]

Upbeat before pessimism—*As bad as things can get sometimes, you cannot communicate pessimism to your employees. You need to stay up-beat and keep everyone motivated.*
—Police Executive

Support—*It starts from the top… If somebody up there says, "I know my officers. They do a great job, until proven otherwise… They did what they needed to do in that incident, and all the rules were followed, according to our use of force measures. Until I see otherwise, that's where I stand. Thank you very much."*
—Patrol, > 10 years on

Be confident—*There's a realization that I can't be everything to everybody out there. Ensuring that this is taken care of, I'm confident that they're going to be there. I assigned an officer to the injured officer—"No matter where he goes, stay with him, comfort him, and do what you have to do." And I did the same thing assigning officers to the victims.*
—Patrol Sergeant

Police leaders must remain upbeat, supportive, and confident, ensuring officers feel valued, supported, and empowered in their roles, especially during challenging situations.

E. 20 Key strategies for police leadership

The following 20 key strategies summarize police leadership at every level.

1. **Be ethical:** Ethical clarity is fundamental for senior police leaders, inspiring talent, modern thinking, and good decision-making from their teams.

2. **Value people:** True leaders in policing prioritize people, showing moral courage, optimism, and clear communication, even in adversity.
3. **Demonstrate optimism:** Effective leadership in policing involves seizing opportunities in crises and maintaining optimism.
4. **Model excellence and humility:** Police chiefs recognize the universal importance of accountability and excellence, emphasizing trust, talking, and humility in reaching goals.
5. **Encourage dedication:** Effective senior police leaders inspire commitment, set examples, and build strong team relationships.
6. **Confront challenges with courage:** Police executives face unique challenges like terrorism, political pressures, and media scrutiny, demanding emotional intelligence and adept crisis management.
7. **Inspire and mobilize others:** Senior police executives understand the importance of clear ethical thinking, mobilizing talent, and informed decision-making in today's policing.
8. **Balance internal and external expectations:** Leadership in policing demands accountability, adherence to protocols, and managing public expectations during tough times.
9. **Build strong teams:** Building relationships and competence are crucial in management, especially when dealing with complex issues like audits and combating corruption.
10. **Nuture leadership:** Frontline leadership, with sergeants and informal patrol leaders, plays a vital role in guiding and teaching others.
11. **Highlight the team:** Honorable police leaders prioritize their team's well-being over personal interests.
12. **Strive to be your best:** Strong supervisors in policing constantly self-evaluate and strive for improvement.
13. **Offer untiring support:** Good supervisors maintain optimism, and provide unwavering support to their teams, even when things change quickly.
14. **Interact with the team:** Successful police leaders inspire commitment by setting good examples, listening, and building strong relationships with their teams.

15. **Prepare for profound issues:** Senior police bosses face complex, sensitive issues like officer suicides, requiring sensitivity and strength.
16. **Inspire a vision:** Effective policing leadership involves endurance, team engagement, and partnerships to inspire belief in a shared vision.
17. **Notice performance and aptitude:** Leadership that focuses on both performance and potential inspires commitment and fostering a positive work environment.
18. **Build sound partnerships:** True partnerships thrive on trust and understanding, without keeping score or feeling envy and rivalry.
19. **Appreciate the frontline:** Police chiefs empower officers, ensuring they feel valued and supported, especially during challenging times.
20. **Acquire valued insights:** Learning from respected senior leaders provides valuable insights for leaders at all levels in policing.

Notes

1 R. B. Gaither, "Ethical leadership and its impact on role modeling, strictness, openness, and job satisfaction of law enforcement officers." Keiser University, Doctoral Dissertation, 1–113, 2017.
2 R. Hillier, "Rick Hillier quotes," AZ Quotes. https://www.azquotes.com/author/64129-Rick_Hillier.
3 Y. Tay, "Can't solve 21st century problems with 20th century ways of thinking: PwC Network's Blair Sheppard," *People Matters*. https://www.peoplematters.in/site/interstitial?return_to=%2Farticle%2Flife-at-work%2Fcant-solve-21st-century-problems-with-20th-century-ways-of-thinking-pwc-networks-blair-sheppard-27708, November 26, 2020.
4 R. Hillier, *Leadership: 50 points of wisdom for today's leaders.* Toronto: HarperCollins, 2010.
5 H. Sprafka and Kranda, A., "Best practices for institutionalizing mentoring into police departments." International Association of Chiefs of

Police, pp. 8. https://www.ojp.gov/ncjrs/virtual-library/abstracts/best-practices-institutionalizing-mentoring-police-department, 2003.
6. S. Terrell, "Executive coaches who use Eq-i 2.0 in leadership development: A qualitative study." ProQuest Dissertations Publishing, Doctoral Dissertation, Capella University, 1–137, 2020.
7. E. Pallas, "The relationship between emotional intelligence, transformational leadership style, and effectiveness among police supervisors," Wilmington University, New Castle, DE, 2016.
8. L. K. Lewis and Seibold, D. R., "Reconceptualizing organizational change implementation as a communication problem: A review of literature and research agenda," *Annals of the International Communication Association,* vol. 21, no. 1, pp. 93–152. https://doi.org/10.1080/23808985.1998.11678949, 1998.
9. L. Lewis, *Organizational change: Creating change through strategic communication*, vol. 2. Hoboken, NJ: John Wiley & Sons, 2011.
10. Y. Yuksel, "Understanding the role of culture and communication in implementing planned organizational change: The case of compstat in police organizations." PhD Dissertation, Rutgers University, New Brunswick, NJ, 2013.
11. N. K. Steffens, Fonseca, M. A., Ryan, M. K., Rink, F. A., Stoker, J. I. and Pieterse, A. N., "How feedback about leadership potential impacts ambition, organizational commitment, and performance," *The Leadership Quarterly,* vol. 29, no. 6, pp. 637–647, 2018.
12. M. D. Eisner and Cohen, A. R., *Working together: Why great partnerships succeed*. New York: HarperCollins, 2010.
13. M. Goldsmith and Reiter, M., *Triggers: Becoming the person you want to be*. New York: Crown Business, 2015.
14. M. Goldsmith, "The circle of engagement," *Leader to Leader,* vol. 81, pp. 31–35. https://doi.org/10.1002/ltl.20242, 2016.
15. S. Charman, *Police socialisation, identity and culture becoming Blue*. New York: Palgrave Macmillan, 2017.
16. P. O. Dissmore, "Ethics for the military officer: Teaching ethics at the maneuver support center for engineer officers," Doctoral Dissertation, Assemblies of God Theological Seminary, 1–251, 2009.

9

Knowledge transfer

Conclusions

> **SPOILER ALERT**
>
> Despite expectations, formal education and total years of experience have minimal influence on developing frontline success skills.

Abstract

The primary goal of this study was to assess operational readiness in policing, focusing on three key competencies: physical, technical, and mental readiness. A secondary goal was to update mental-readiness standards with input from top coach officers. Performance blocks and factors influencing performance excellence were evaluated for their impact on policing. The aim was also to create practical resources for law enforcement. The overall intention was to enhance frontline police performance by developing an Operational Readiness Index based on outstanding officers. This police-specific index seeks to improve training programs, ensure consistency, reduce errors, and increase efficiency in police operations. Building on existing research on policing performance, stress, and officer competencies, the Operational

Readiness Framework was applied to measure and assess frontline police readiness. Conclusions are drawn from qualitative and quantitative findings, covering the Police Operational Readiness Index, success elements, performance blocks, emerging "watch item" issues, and influential success factors.

Conclusions drawn from an integration of the qualitative and quantitative findings in this study are presented as follows:

A. Police Operational Readiness Index
B. Confirmation of mental success elements
C. Confirmation of technical and physical success elements
D. Performance blocks in policing
E. "Watch items" (emerging problems)
F. Influential factors on success skills
G. 20 Key summary conclusions

A. Police Operational Readiness Index

Overall measures for the relative importance of physical, technical, and mental readiness were assessed. "Excellent" officers and coaches identified mental readiness (44%), technical skills (30%), and physical fitness (26%) as crucial for peak performance. Mental readiness is clearly crucial to a police officer's performance. See detailed practices in Appendix P: Police field training assessment and progress report.

In fact, mental readiness shows the most significant change between successful and disappointing performances. In measuring police officer readiness during successful and disappointing performances, all three aspects of readiness (physical, technical, mental) were high during successful performances, with an average rating of 9 out of 10. However, during disappointing performances, mental readiness dropped the most (24% at 6.4/10), followed by technical readiness (10% at 7.8/10). Physical readiness remained relatively constant (8.8/10).

Finally, in comparing results from 2003 and 2019, mental readiness was found to increase by 10% during that time period, while physical and technical readiness decreased (4% and 6%, respectively). Despite advances in technology, use of force, and community policing, the greatest impact was on officers' mental preparedness.

B. Confirmation of mental success elements

Assessment of mental readiness

All of Orlick's seven success elements related to mental readiness are clearly evident to various degrees among all excellent officers and coach officers during best performances. The study confirms that there are many similarities in the mental readiness engaged in by top police, other high-performance professions, and top athletes. These success elements include: Commitment, Self-Belief/Confidence, Positive Imagery, Mental Preparation, Full Focus, Distraction Control, and Constructive Evaluation. For example, extraordinary discipline and distraction skills are essential. Success practices during best performances are uniquely prioritized and characteristic to the policing environment as described below. See Table 9.1 for a detailed summary of the mental success elements and practices.

Within the seven mental success elements, excellent officers identified a total of 60 mental practices, which were assessed based on skill range (number of skills per element), skill consistency (percentage used by officers), and skill classification (categories to distinguish skill needs). Table 9.2 provides a detailed tally of the mental success elements.

Seven distinct practices separate the "elite" from the "excellent" officers (i.e., similar to the analogy between gold medalists and Olympians). These practices are: Commitment, Positive Imagery, Distraction Control, and Constructive Evaluation within mental readiness; Fitness and Wellness within physical readiness; and Verbal Communication within technical readiness (see Table 7.20 in Chapter 7).

In summary, based on 75% of the officers, the greatest consistency and relative weight for practices is in Full Focus (83%), Mental Preparation (80%), and Commitment (77%). While

Distraction Control has the greatest range of practices (14 of the 60 practices), officer consistency of core practices is low (21%). This indicates that policing allows for some individual differences in Distraction Control, likewise for deriving Confidence. Constructive Evaluation and Positive Imagery are highly personalized with the lowest number of core practices.

> **Full Focus**: The ability to focus proves to be the strongest and most consistent (83%) of the success elements in policing. Officers show the same high degree of consistency with Mental Preparation (80%) and Commitment (77%). The ability to be present and mindful, yet still anticipate, is a highly sought-after skill in performance and, remarkably, shared by the majority of officers. Having equipment confidence, trusting peers, and enjoying the challenge are also recognized as critical skills. Five of the seven focus practices are shared by the majority of officers, making individual differences inappropriate to be effective.
>
> **Mental Preparation**: Mental Preparation is exhibited with an equally high degree of consistent practice (80%) as seen with Full Focus. Officers share four of the seven core practices. They are able to adapt individually, allowing for some differences in their approaches to recognizing risk, where they prepare, and how they get "psyched." However, strategic-resource planning and positive thinking are fundamental principles. Setting clear objectives and minimizing interruptions are shared as essential planned preparation procedures.
>
> **Commitment**: Like their ability to focus and mentally prepare, Commitment is demonstrated with consistent practices (77%). Empathy, Professional Discipline, Job Satisfaction, Responsible Leadership, Understanding "the Job," and Dedication are shared to an outstanding extent. Given that six of the nine practices were reported by most officers, it is important to recruit and encourage a shared and broad motivational approach.
>
> **Distraction Control**: On average, each officer has an exceptionally large range of practices (10 out of 14) for addressing

many different distractions, however only 21% (3 of the 14) are core practices shared by over 75% of officers. These key practices are De-escalation, Involvement of Others, and Crises Refocusing. Even the best officers vary in their ability to manage specific distractions such as fatigue, public disrespect, car collisions, court, downtime and routine-tasks, workload, and the promotional process.

Confidence: Officers' self-belief comes from multiple sources. There is a high dependency on quality training and practice (98%) and controlling the environment (95%). Fostering police mentors are also considered essential for self-confidence. However, individuals derive confidence differently related to family support, camaraderie, and recognition and thanks.

Constructive Evaluation: This element has limited consistency in how officers evaluate and cope with their performance. Self-evaluation is unanimously preferred by all officers for ongoing learning. Officers generally supplement their self-evaluation with three additional practices that vary from officer to officer. For example, Tactical officers are more inclined to use informal debriefs, whereas School Resource Officers (SROs) tend to seek public feedback, and Neighborhood Resource Team (NRT) Officers develop rapport with suspects. This element has a very narrow window for achieving success. Coping practices range from taking ownership and drawing lessons to consulting peers.

Positive Imagery: Vivid imagery, coupled with the officers' positive perspective, is the essence of using this technique en route to a call or on scene. Court preparation is the most dominant secondary use of visualization. Officers showed many other creative individual differences and alternative uses for visualization in practicing and debriefing.

Table 9.1 provides a detailed summary of the mental success elements and practices.

Knowledge transfer ◆ 357

TABLE 9.1 Detailed Summary of Mental-Readiness Success Element in Policing

PRACTICE CLASSIFICATION	SUCCESS ELEMENTS (contributors to future Performance Indicators)						
	Commitment	Confidence	Positive Imagery	Mental Preparation	Full Focus	Distraction Control	Constructive Evaluation
Core Practices >75% of officers 23/60 practices (38%)	Empathy Professional discipline Job satisfaction Responsible leadership Understanding "the job" (+) Dedication	Quality training & practice Control environment Police mentors	En-route or on-scene images	Strategic resource plan Positive thinking Clear objectives and plan Minimal interruptions	Present and mindful Anticipation Equipment confidence Teamwork and trust Enjoy challenge (+)	De-escalation Involvement of others Crises refocusing	Self-evaluation
Enhanced Practices 50-75% of officers 22/60 practices (37%)	Competitive (−) Pride of uniform (+)	Family support Camaraderie Recognition & thanks	Court preparation images	Recognize risk Preparation locations Psyching rituals	Rhythm and flow Relaxed	Fatigue strategies (−) Public disrespect refocusing (−) Car collision avoidance (−) Court appearance strategies (−)	Take ownership (−) Draw lessons Consult team (+)

358 ◆ Knowledge transfer

PRACTICE CLASSIFICATION	SUCCESS ELEMENTS (contributors to future Performance Indicators)							
	Commitment	Confidence	Positive Imagery	Mental Preparation	Full Focus	Distraction Control	Constructive Evaluation
						Downtime & routine task refocusing (−) Shift work strategies Public complaint refocusing (−) Workload strategies "Not being promoted" (−)	
Elective Skills <50% of officers 15/60 practices (25%)	Job security	Education Faith or luck	Visual triggers Call debrief images Impromptu rehearsal Instructor-led images Supervisor run-through images			Female-policing copings strategies (−) Task orientation (−)	Formal evaluation Informal debrief Public feedback Suspect rapport

Notes: (+) Elevated from lower practice classification.
(−) Reduced from higher practice classification.

Range and consistency of practices

Within the seven success elements, a total of 60 mental training skills were identified by excellent officers.

Skill range: The skill range within each success element varies from 7 to 14; the average is 9 practices per success element. Distraction Control (14 practices) had more than twice the breadth of five of the other elements. The most narrowly defined elements (7 practices each) are Positive Imagery, Mental Preparation, and Full Focus.

Skill consistency: Consistent skill use and opportunity for individual differences vary depending on the success element. On average, each officer reports consistently practicing 38 of the 60 practices (63% of the total practice range). The 60 mental training practices are classified under three areas of importance—practices performed by most (>75%) officers (Core practices); by 50–75% (Enhanced skills); and those more dependent on personal choice of less than half the officers (ndividual practices). These three practice classifications are as follows:

Core skills: Of the total skills, 23/60 (38%) are performed by over 75% of excellent officers and therefore considered essential or core to any high-performance police-training program. These skills define the most effective mental training techniques for policing. Using this measure, the greatest consistency among officers is evident with Full Focus, Commitment, and Mental Preparation.

Enhanced skills: A group of 22 practices (37% of total practices) is reported by more than half but 75% or less of the officers. This practice set is considered to enhance the core skills. Distraction Control contributes close to half (9 of the 22 practices) of the distribution of practices in this category, followed by Confidence and Mental Preparation (both 3 of 22).

Elective skills: There are 15 skills (25% of total practices) that less than 50% of officers identified as important in their mental readiness. These less-common skills are considered personal choices. Elective skills were further analyzed using factors to see whether there is any association between the less common practices and the various factors among officers—Background, Developmental, and Police Distinction.

TABLE 9.2 Mental Success-Element Practices Tally

Mental Success-Element Practices Tally

SUCCESS ELEMENT TYPE	RANGE of PRACTICES	AVERAGE PRACTICES Average # of practices per officer (%)	PRACTICE CLASSIFICATION CORE # practices (%) by >75% of officers	PRACTICE CLASSIFICATION ENHANCED # practices (%) by 50-75% of officers	PRACTICE CLASSIFICATION INDIVIDUAL # practices (%) by <50% of officers
Overall total Practices	60 (100%)	38/60 (63%)	23/60 (38%)	22/60 (37%)	15/60 (25%)
Commitment	9 (15%)	7/9 (77%)	6/9 (67%)	2/9 (22%)	1/9 (11%)
Confidence	8 (13%)	5/8 (65%)	3/8 (38%)	3/8 (38%)	2/8 (24%)
Positive Imagery	7 (12%)	3/7 (45%)	1/7 (14%)	1/7 (14%)	5/7 (72%)
Mental Preparation	7 (12%)	6/7 (80%)	4/7 (57%)	3/7 (43%)	0/7 (0%)
Full Focus	7 (12%)	6/7 (83%)	5/7 (71%)	2/7 (29%)	0/7 (0%)
Distraction Control	14 (23%)	10/14 (69%)	3/14 (21%)	9/14 (65%)	2/14 (14%)
Constructive Evaluation	8 (13%)	4/8 (50%)	1/8 (13%)	3/8 (37%)	4/8 (50%)

Using this measure, the success practices allowing for the high degree of individual interpretation to be effective are Positive Imagery and Constructive Evaluation.

Table 9.2 provides a detailed tally of the mental success elements. These parameters set clear, evidence-based mental-readiness competency measures to combine with the well-established technical and physical competencies in the right balance.

C. Confirmation of technical and physical success elements

With input from a Coach Officer Advisory Group, Performance Indicators (PIs) were modified based on occupational functionality definitions developed for physical and technical readiness. Trainees must demonstrate full competence in these PIs to ensure operational readiness for frontline duty. The PIs were designed to be integrated into a Field Training Assessment tool of 12 Performance Indicators, proportionately balanced to the Operational Readiness Index (technical at 30%, physical at 26%, mental at 44%). Thus, four benchmarks were set to approximate the weight for technical readiness (33%) and three for physical readiness (25%).

Benchmarks for technical readiness

Four key performance indicators and associated practices are essential to ensure technical readiness in policing. First, proficiency in law includes a thorough knowledge and application of laws, understanding court procedures, arrest authorities, use-of-force principles, and effective apprehensions. Second, verbal communication emphasizes preventing conflicts and de-escalation, using good articulation and appropriate tone, active listening, building community rapport, and conducting effective interviews. Third, written communication involves systematic note-taking, and producing timely and suitable reports. Last, knowledge of police service and community covers understanding police services, policies and procedures, and the composition and resources of the community. These indicators and practices ensure that officers are technically well prepared for their duties. These technical-readiness success elements are presented in Table 9.3.

TABLE 9.3 Detailed Summary of Technical and Physical Readiness Success Elements in Policing

Technical Readiness Performance Indicators	Proficiency in law	Verbal communication	Written communication	Knowledge of police service and community
Technical Readiness Practices	Knowledge and application of laws Court procedures Arrest authorities Use of force principles Effective apprehensions	Prevention of conflicts and de-escalation Good articulation and appropriate tone Active listening Community rapport and humor Effective interviewing	Systematic note taking Timely reports Suitable reports	Police service Policies and procedures Community composition and resources
Physical Readiness Performance Indicators	Officer Safety	Use of Force	Vehicle Operations	
Physical Readiness Practices	Proper handcuffing Body search (including sensitive areas) Health, wellness & fitness Containment in environmental conditions Strong safety sense	Firearms and gunpoint arrest Equipment readiness Defensive tactics Physical control with appropriate use of force "Reasonableness"	Vehicle safety Multitasking Vehicle reversing Patrolling the environment Strategic traffic stops	

Benchmarks for physical readiness

To ensure physical readiness in policing, three key performance indicators and associated practices are crucial. First, officer safety involves proper handcuffing techniques; conducting thorough body searches; maintaining health, wellness, and fitness; managing containment in various environmental conditions; and having a strong safety sense. Second, the use of force includes proficiency with firearms and gunpoint arrests, maintaining equipment readiness, practicing defensive tactics, exercising physical control with appropriate use of force, and adhering to the principle of "reasonableness." Last, vehicle operations covers vehicle safety, effective multitasking, skillful vehicle reversing, patrolling the environment, and conducting strategic traffic stops. These indicators and practices ensure officers are physically prepared for their duties. These physical-readiness success elements are presented in Table 9.3.

D. Performance blocks in policing

Identification of performance blocks

There are many blocks or distractions to achieving high-level performance in challenging situations. They fall under the following three categories: inherent, organizational, and external blocks. Within these categories, a total of 45 blocks were identified by excellent officers (see Table 9.4). On average, each officer reported 22 blocks (49% of the 45 blocks). The three block classifications rank as follows:

Operational blocks: Distractions directed at active, on-the-job situations are dominant, supplying more than half the total blocks (63%, 28/45 blocks). These blocks are further divided into two groups:

> General blocks: The top distractions can be typical, habitual, and usually considered very serious, ranging from dealing with a "crisis" and personal fears to shift-work fatigue. Other distractions vary in seriousness and are

TABLE 9.4 Performance Block Tally

Performance Block Tally

PERFORMANCE BLOCK TYPE	RANGE of BLOCKS	AVERAGE BLOCKS Average # of blocks per officer (%)	IMMEDIATE NEED # blocks (%) by >75% of officers	BLOCK CLASSIFICATION SERIOUS # blocks (%) by 50-75% of officers	INDIVIDUAL # blocks (%) by <50% of officers
Overall total blocks	45 (100%)	22/45 (49%)	4 (9%)	17 (38%)	24 (53%)
Operational blocks	**28 (63%)**	**14 (49%)**	**4 (9%)**	**10 (22%)**	**14 (31%)**
General blocks	16 (36%)	9 (53%)	3	6	7
Rookie errors	12 (27%)	5 (44%)	1	4	7
Organizational blocks	**15 (33%)**	**7 (46%)**	**0 (0%)**	**7 (16%)**	**8 (18%)**
External blocks	**2 (4%)**	**1 (40%)**	**0 (0%)**	**0 (0%)**	**2 (4%)**

usually more discreetly discussed. There are 16 blocks in total (36%), ranging in severity from feeling jaded, dealing with public disrespect, and mistrusting the team to having a lack of information, facing court appearances, and dealing with others' complacency.

Rookie errors: The list of rookie errors is among the most numerous (12/45 blocks; 25%) and quite individualized from officer to officer—with one exception. There is high agreement that aggressiveness, such as overreacting and acting too quickly, is very problematic, needing immediate action.

Organizational blocks: Management-related issues make up 33% of the total blocks (15/45 blocks). The majority of officers identified workload (75%), lack of leadership (63%), bureaucracy (61%), and fewer resources (60%) as the dominant concerns in organizational effectiveness. The remaining 11 out of 15 organizational complaints are more individual in nature. However, of particular significance, only 34% of these excellent officers are concerned with "not being promoted," and very few believe advancing is due to effort (10%) and confidence (6%). These results are quite noteworthy given that this is a selected sample of excellent officers.

External blocks: Blocks occurring before or after a call or outside the workplace make up only 4% (2/45 blocks) of the total blocks. As noted in reviewing previous research[1,2], these issues seem generally under-stated and may require more attention than projected. The issues are family conflict (48%) and day-to-day pressures (31%).

Impact of performance blocks

The 45 blocks are further ranked based on the number of officers who reported them (see Table 9.5). They are ranked into the following three groups:

TABLE 9.5 Summary of Performance Block in Policing

DETAILED SUMMARY OF PERFORMANCE BLOCKS IN POLICING

PERFORMANCE BLOCKS

BLOCK CLASSIFICATION	Operational — General	Operational — Rookie Errors	Organizational	External
Immediate Needs >75% of officers	Crisis* Personal fears Shift work fatigue*	Aggressiveness		
Serious Stressors 50–75% of officers	Jaded and skeptical (−) Public disrespect* (−) Lulls and routine work* (−) Climate conditions (+) Car collisions* Peer mistrust	General patrol issues (+) Lack of safety (+) Poor reports (+) Unrealistic expectations (+)	Workload volume* Lack of leadership (+) Bureaucracy Fewer resources Public complaints* (+) Female policing issues* (−) Training issues	
Individual Stressors <50% of officers	Lack of information Court appearances* Work conflict Others' complacency Previous call External specialist attitudes Getting lost	Poor containment Rookie anxiety No action plan Discipline problems Negativity No basic law Lack community contacts	Changes Poor support Lack of management feedback Equipment limitations Politics Not being promoted Coaching issues Ethnicity issues	Family conflict Day-to-day pressures

Notes: (+) Elevated from lower stressor classification.

(−) Reduced from higher stressor classification.

* These blocks have specific refocusing strategies associated with them (see Chapter 7: Mental Readiness in Policing—Distraction Control).

Immediate needs: When performance blocks were identified by over 75% of excellent officers, they are considered to have immediate and very serious implications for the general workforce and to require immediate attention. If the greater majority of excellent officers, who have exceptionally developed skills to minimize blocks, find an issue problematic, then it must be profoundly more difficult for the average officer.

For example, shift work is a chronic distraction identified by most officers (80%) but it has the fewest number of control strategies (69%) for resolving it. In particular, officers with Patrol-only experience show a noticeable lack of shift-work strategies. There are four blocks out of 45 (9%) with this high level of importance, most of which (3 out of 4) are inherent to the job and unlikely to go away. This explains the dominant need for such broad and consistent distraction control strategies.

Serious distractions: Blocks raised by 50% to 75% of the officers are considered "serious." If they were simple issues, this group of excellent, experienced officers would have resolved them. Since they did not resolve themselves, and are not simple for more than half the group, they must be addressed as serious for these and probably an even greater number of the other officers. There are 17 blocks out of 45 (38%) considered serious, distributed between operational and organizational blocks. The operational ranged from feeling jaded (75%), downtime and routine-tasks (66%), to peer mistrust (55%). Rookie errors included general patrol issues (60%), poor reports (53%), and unrealistic expectations (51%). The organizational concerned effectiveness, namely workload (75% of officers), fewer resources (52%), and training issues (50%).

An unfortunate discrepancy is while a third (33%) of officers identified coach issues as blocking performance, early police mentoring is perceived as a highly valued service (85%) building confidence (see Chapter 7: Mental Readiness in Policing—Confidence).

Individual distractions: When less than 50% of excellent officers reported a block, it is considered an important "individual" block. This group contains an overwhelming 24 of the 45 blocks (53%) distributed heavily across all three block categories—operational (general and rookie errors), organizational, and external. This strongly indicates the need to develop personalized distraction-control plans to ensure appropriate individual responsibility in managing these blocks.

E. "Watch items" (emerging problems and initiatives)

Fluctuations in the reporting of police performance blocks over time offer insights into potential emerging trends and "Watch Items."

Potential impact of teamwork on individual accountability

The increased emphasis on teamwork in officer evaluations, alongside a decrease in personal ownership, suggests potential tension between these aspects. While a team-oriented approach can foster collaboration and communication, it is important to ensure individual accountability does not diminish entirely. Future monitoring of this balance is vital for effective policing.

Potential downside to generalized strategies

A rise in a task-oriented approach to refocus was reported. This combines with De-escalation and Involvement of Others remaining as core practices. However, specialized practices for fatigue, public disrespect, avoiding car collisions, managing downtime and routine tasks, public complaints, and navigating the promotional process are no longer categorized as core skills. While a generalized approach might seem efficient, it could be short-sighted given the varied nature of policing scenarios. Specialization in handling distractions could be key in high-pressure scenarios, and a more nuanced approach might be necessary. Both specialized and general approaches are utilized by excellent officers, but possibly applied differently. Monitoring and evaluating when and how these controls are used may be necessary for a positive outcome.

Shift in workload dynamics

Over 17 years, there has been a 25% increase (65% in 2003 to 90% in 2019) in reporting workload as a performance block, with a relatively low usage of workload strategy (64%), highlighting a potential gap. This imbalance could lead to burnout and decreased officer effectiveness if coping skills do not keep pace. Additional leadership support, workload checks, open communication, and team-building may help address this gap.

Artificial intelligence integration with mental training

Artificial intelligence (AI) is being integrated into policing through facial recognition, body cameras, video crime footage, and predictive policing, which analyzes data to identify patterns and hotspots[3,4,5,6]. Despite these technological advances, the importance of mental readiness increased by 10%, while physical and technical readiness decreased (4% and 6%, respectively) from 2003 to 2019. AI's controversy over biased decision-making and privacy violations demands greater transparency and accountability from officers[7]. This added stress is evident in the increased need for mental readiness.

Promotional realities

Only 33% of officers identified the inability to advance in the organization as problematic. Furthermore, only 10% believed they could succeed in the promotional process through effort and confidence (6%). Only 23% identified competitive aspirations for promotion, surprising given this sample of excellent officers. The lack of motivation in advancement is concerning for future succession planning. Leadership strategies recommend proactive career-planning measures.

"Not being promoted:" Most deal with the disappointment by either avoiding the promotional process or seeking out alternative career goals.

It also goes against previous evidence of their basic competitiveness and high standards. Most of those who responded deal with the disappointment by either avoiding the promotional process or seeking out alternative career goals.

Recruit selection and training

Performance blocks related to rookie officers, such as "No action plan," "Discipline problems," and "Negativity," have seen significant increases (ranging from 56% to 74%). This may reflect new recruitment procedures and factors such as inexperience, training gaps, stress, cultural adjustment, lack of support, and confidence issues. This reinforces the need for ongoing updates in recruitment, quality coach-officer selection, comprehensive training, and mentorship programs.

Proven initiatives for women, public protocol, and offense-defense mastery

Blocks like "Female-policing coping issues" (–76%) and "Public disrespect" (–51%) indicate a decreasing trend, suggesting developed strategies (45% and 68%, respectively) and positive organizational initiatives over the years. Personal fear (–43%) is also lower, possibly influenced by initiatives like Active-Shooter Training for all frontline officers for mastering offensive and defensive maneuvers.

F. Influential factors on success skills

All 22 factors examined for their influence on the 60 success practices within the seven elements were found to be significant, although the degree of influence varied substantially. The factors were classified into three groups: Background, Developmental, and Police Distinction. Interestingly, the four with the highest impact are within all three groups—the most dominant being Elite officers. Developmental factors related to frontline specialty-unit experience are ranked as moderately influential factors. Language, ethnicity, and rank (Background and Police Distinction factors) also have moderate influence. The seven factors with relatively low influence were also divided between the three factor groups. The education and total year on experience factors seem counterintuitive having less influence than expected on the development of success skills for performance excellence.

Most influential factor profiles

Predictors—"Elite" officer profile: Elite factor officers were selected by both their peers and supervisors as "the very best" and ultimately demonstrated the highest scores among the success skills compared to other officers. The corroboration between the qualitative real-life experience and quantitative transcript data analysis is a true testament to the accuracy of identifying highly respected officers through an anonymous internal cross-checking method. Similarly, this methodology could be applied to identify coaches, mentors, or individuals for other positions with top skill requirements.

"Elite" officers project intense competitiveness and commitment to be the best… creating impromptu mental-rehearsal opportunities.

While Elite factor officers have a high number of success skills in each of the seven success elements, they have an exceptional degree of refinement within the elements of Commitment, Positive Imagery, Mental Preparation, and Constructive Evaluation.

These Elite officers project intense competitiveness and commitment to be the best. For example, they demonstrate extra effort in creating impromptu mental-rehearsal opportunities. From the onset of going into policing (more so than others), these officers had a clear job awareness.

During challenging situations, their preparation skills are notably distinguished compared with all others. More consistency is identified among these officers in liaising with external specialists, officer safety practices, physical discipline, and deficiency with electronics.

In Constructive Evaluation, the Elite officers have more skills to build rapport with suspects implying empathy and good communication skills that can enhance their ability to deal with difficult, dangerous, and unpredictable people. However, within Mental Preparation and Distraction Control, the skills related to Rest and Fatigue Strategies, respectively, were significantly less developed than the non-elite group. This result implies a distinctive heightened resistance to fatigue in Elite officers with less need to dwell or focus on rest strategies. Additionally, in Constructive Evaluation, the skills related to Public Feedback were decidedly less than among non-elite officers. It is evident that Elite factor officers are well trained, respected, confident, and very accomplished top talent within their specialty units. Therefore, at their level of competence, they may find little value in seeking out public feedback.

It is strongly believed that the Elite factor officer, with unique and distinctive characteristics and skill sets, may be a critical indicator for achieving the highest levels of performance in policing.

Patrol-only profile [have exceedingly more] control strategies for fatigue, workload, and female-policing issues

Patrol-only experience profile: Subjects in the Patrol-only experience group reported a higher level of skills related to Distraction Control. In particular, they exceeded other officers in control strategies for fatigue, workload, and female-policing issues. It is not clear but plausible that Patrol-only workload exceeds that of other specialty units and is therefore a driver for increased strategies for fatigue and workload management. Enhanced successful Practices were also found in their Confidence related to Education, which may simply reflect the current recruiting practices with a preference to hire college and university graduates. Patrol-only officers, who are generally newer officers, tend to seek out Formal Evaluation (within Constructive Evaluation) to a higher degree than other officers. They appear to value their supervisors' influence at the early stage of their career in validating their performance.

In contrast, these officers scored lower than the others in their skills related to the performance excellence elements Mental Preparation and Full Focus. Specifically, their lesser reported skills included Physical Discipline, Psyching, External Communication, and Equipment Confidence, which are also strong indicators of physical and technical competencies. Their Overall Enjoyment of the job is also lower, which impacts their skills related to the Commitment element. It is believed that engaging frontline Patrol-only officers in developing specific Mental Preparation and Full Focus skills will heighten their confidence and impact overall enjoyment of the job.

Specialty unit profiles: Insight and opportunity for targeting recruitment… and guiding career paths.

Frontline specialty-unit profiles: Training and experience outside of Patrol accelerates valuable success skill development. Each specialty unit demonstrates a unique predisposition to certain performance success skills. This in-depth knowledge can contribute to targeting internal subject-matter experts for training and mentoring. Specifically, the different success skill profiles generated from the various frontline units create insight and opportunity for targeting recruitment, developing highly tailored training programs, establishing criteria for promotion, and guiding career paths.

Background factor profiles: Individuals come to policing with personal traits that can clearly influence the path of their skill development. Recognizing the highly competitive environment for recruiting good officers, a comprehensive understanding of the impact of Background factors on performance excellence may provide a significant advantage for a police service. Different inherent traits (such as gender, language, and ethnicity) can be considered in relation to desired performance skills while screening and training. Understanding these different skill tendencies can also create a broad skill base for team building.

> *"Macho:"* Female officers believe that the environment has improved.

Gender differences: Gender differences are evident from this study across 10 of the 69 success skills (15%) both as hindrances and preferred skill development. Female-policing hindrances around the "macho" environment, rejection, perceived physical limitations, and the need to overachieve are shared by 82% of female officers interviewed. Optimistically, almost half the female officers believe that the environment has improved.

Other individual traits: Language, ethnicity, and prior police-related work experience were shown to influence skill preferences. While military and rural experience have minimal impact, they too lend themselves to the potential for internal experts.

Less influential factors

Education: In general, from the outcomes of this study of excellent officers, the 69 success skills are minimally influenced by (formal) education levels and other non-specialty experience (e.g. military, rural, more than frontline). For example, one might expect that higher education would produce a more well-rounded and capable frontline officer and therefore influence the development of performance excellence skills. The following explanations may account for the relatively low influence of education on success skill development in a policing environment. First, the recruitment and selection process may successfully identify individuals with desirable learning potential for the required policing skills—thus limiting the influence of previous educational or non-specialty experience. Second, police training is highly effective, especially frontline specialty-unit training, and has greater impact than formal education on skill development.

This study indicates that frontline officers are neither advantaged nor disadvantaged by education (as a factor) in their success skill development. This contradicts research that has identified education as a significant factor in a lower number of disciplinary problems and in promoting high achievers (Truxillo et al., 1998). Since this study focused on a select group of excellent officers, and did not fully investigate the issues of disciplinary problems and promotion related to level of education, it would be remiss to draw any specific conclusions.

"Years on" experience alone has low influence as a factor on skills development.

Total "years on" experience: "Years on" experience alone has low influence as a factor on skills development. Developmental factors, especially exposure to various specialty-unit training versus simply "years on," have a much more dynamic influence on success skill development. Success skills peak and flatten throughout the career of excellent officers. For example, as the officers mature with increasing years of experience, their motivation and commitment progress from wanting job security to feeling a greater sense of responsibility to having an increase awareness of job risks. These particular attributes of "Total Experience" are not unexpected and should be acknowledged as normal career development. The wisdom of experience can be valued, harnessed, and shared with young officers in a systematic fashion interrelated with other factors specific to performance skills, so that organizational knowledge is not lost.

Factors profile development

The officers in this study were recognized as being the top performers in their police service. They possess highly refined sets of skills that allow them to excel in their work environment. These skills are influenced by specific factors, both inherent and learned, which allow unique profiling by factor. Sharing of advanced skills and teaching others in areas of lower skill competency will support a culture of continuous improvement and drive performance excellence.

There is considerable research opportunity for further detailing of individual factor profiles. Additionally, insight into the complex interdependencies between factors is yet to be developed. These detailed profiles would permit a better customized training and career path development for maximizing individual success.

G. 20 Key summary conclusions

The following 20 key points summarize the study conclusions.

1. **Police have a specific readiness profile:** The Operational Readiness Index reveals that excellent officers identify a balance of mental sharpness (44%), technical know-how (30%), and physical ability (26%) for operational readiness in challenging frontline situations—mental readiness standing out as distinguishing between successful and disappointing outcomes.
2. **Today, mental still trumps technical and physical preparedness:** Between 2003 and 2019, mental readiness increased by 10%, highlighting its growing importance, despite advances in technology and physical techniques.
3. **Focused attention is a strong predictor of police performance:** The ability to maintain full focus is the strongest and most consistent mental-readiness performance indicator in successful policing.
4. **Systematic mental preparation improves adaptability:** Consistent mental preparation allows officers to strategically plan resources, think positively, set clear objectives, minimize interruptions, and be readier to adapt.
5. **Highly respected officers exhibit dedication:** Commitment is consistency demonstrated through empathy, professional discipline, and job satisfaction by 77% of excellent officers.
6. **Effective distraction control varies:** The use of specialized practices to control distractions, such as fatigue, public disrespect, car collisions, court, downtime and routine tasks, workload, and the promotional process, is declining in favor of more general strategies.
7. **Police confidence can be learned:** High self-confidence in officers stems from quality training, controlling the environment, and mentor support, while external supports vary.
8. **Specialty units influence personal evaluation methods:** Officers prefer self-evaluation but supplement it with informal debriefs, rapport with suspects, and public feedback tailored to their roles.

9. **Visualization is used before, during and after calls:** Using vivid imagery and positive visualization techniques, officers prepare for calls and court for better performance and readiness.
10. **Technical markers bridge knowledge and application:** Technical-readiness benchmarks include law proficiency, verbal and written communication skills, and comprehensive organization and community knowledge.
11. **Detailed practices create technical competency:** Arrest authorities, verbal de-escalation skills, report writing, and understanding of police procedures and community resources are major contributors to full technical readiness.
12. **Physical markers advocate for safety and control:** Physical readiness benchmarks include officer safety, proficient use of force, and skilled vehicle operations.
13. **Muscle-memory rehearsal creates physical competency:** Proper handcuffing techniques, thorough body searches, maintaining health and fitness, proficiency with firearms, defensive tactics, and vehicle safety build confidence and contribute to full physical readiness on the frontline.
14. **Teamwork pros and cons:** Emphasizing teamwork may reduce personal accountability, necessitating careful monitoring to sustain confidence and independence in policing.
15. **Workload is impacting changes:** A significant increase in workload as a performance block highlights the need for improved coping strategies, leadership support, and team-building to prevent burnout and maintain effectiveness.
16. **AI gains may impose greater frontline culpability:** The integration of AI in policing has increased the importance of mental readiness, rather than technical readiness, demanding greater transparency and accountability to address the associated stress and potential decision biases.
17. **Leadership and succession-planning notification:** The low percentage of "excellent" officers motivated by promotion underscores the need for proactive career-planning measures to enhance future succession planning and leadership development.

18. **Updates needed in recruitment and rookie training:** Significant increases in performance blocks due to rookie errors highlight the need for ongoing updates in recruitment, coach-officer selection, training, and mentorship programs to address inexperience and support integration.
19. **Targeted initiatives influence change:** Decreases in blocks related to female-policing issues and public disrespect suggest that positive organizational initiatives and targeted training have successfully addressed these challenges.
20. **Training can breed greater improvement than years of service:** Despite expectations, formal education and total years of experience have minimal influence on the development of success skills among frontline officers, with specialized police training and other developmental factors playing a more significant role.

Notes

1 E. Wilson, McDonald, J. and Allen, J., "Sources of police stress," in *Gold medal policing: Mental readiness and performance excellence*, pp. 216–222. New York: Sloan Associate Press, 2006.
2 J. McDonald, 2006. *Gold medal policing: Mental readiness and performance excellence.* New York: Sloan Associate Press, 2006.
3 A. G. Ferguson, "Policing predictive policing," *Washington University Law Review,* vol. 94, p. 1109, 2016.
4 S. Raaijmakers, "Artificial intelligence for law enforcement: Challenges and opportunities," *IEEE Security & Privacy,* vol. 17, no. 5, pp. 74–77, 2019.
5 A. K. Jain, Deb, D. and Engelsma, J. J., "Biometrics: Trust, but verify," *IEEE Transactions on Biometrics, Behavior, and Identity Science,* vol. 4, no. 3, pp. 303–323, 2021.
6 G. O. Mohler, Short, M. B., Brantingham, P. J., Schoenberg, F. P. and Tita, G. E., "Self-exciting point process modeling of crime," *Journal of the American Statistical Association,* vol. 106, no. 493, pp. 100–108, 2011.
7 K. M. Markos, "A conduit from public trust to legitimacy: Continuous ethics training in law enforcement." ProQuest Dissertations Publishing, Doctoral dissertation, University of La Verne, 1–152, 2017.

10
What's next?

Recommendations and leadership directives

> **SPOILER ALERT**
>
> Implementing a structured curriculum that covers physical, technical, and mental success practices ensures comprehensive officer training.

Abstract

This chapter outlines 10 key recommendations to enhance frontline policing. These include customizing recruitment, selection, and retention guidelines; creating self-assessment tools; and focusing on career and succession planning. It also suggests developing web-based learning programs and promoting recognition plans. Additionally, the chapter covers establishing a corporate curriculum, mental-training programs, and enhancing the coach-officer function. It emphasizes pursuing publication opportunities and promoting further research. Practical tools and strategies provided include trainee field assessments, criteria for training exercises, simulation evaluations, performance reviews, and evidence-based resources. The chapter concludes with 20 summary recommendations focused on recruit assessment,

DOI: 10.4324/9781003145493-10

strategic tools, aligning expectations, self-evaluation, and skill profiles. Other key areas include mental training, e-learning, AI use, case studies, emotional control, customized coping strategies, and empowering rookies.

The recommendations to strengthen frontline policing are captured under the following categories:

A. Customize recruitment, selection, and retention guidelines
B. Create multilevel self-assessment tools
C. Target career and succession planning
D. Develop a web-based learning program
E. Promote a frontline-recognition plan
F. Establish a corporate curriculum
G. Create a high-performance mental training program
H. Enrich the internal role-model function: Coach officers, trainers and mentors
I. Pursue publication opportunities
J. Promote further related research
K. 20 Key summary recommendations

A short summary has been provided for each area. Numerous applications such as a Field Training Assessment, Coach Officers' teaching tips, Top 10 Quotes and Lessons, and Simulation-Training Focus Assessment are shared in this chapter.

A. Customize recruitment, selection, and retention guidelines

When choosing recruits, prioritize those committed to "duty of care," using the top core practices defined by the best: Empathy, Professional Discipline, Job Satisfaction, Responsible Leadership, and a realistic Understanding of "the Job." Like a coach selecting an Olympian, assessing long-term commitment is paramount.

Who's resilient? *Recruitment is looking for the individuals who are resilient, and hoping they are not just dipping their toe in to see what it's like. If not a long career, then getting the best out of them in the five years. When I joined, I knew this was it.*
—20-year reflection from a Commissioned officer, one of the original "excellent" officers

The results of this study demonstrate that recruiters can now systematically target recruits based on specific skill areas of high performers. Not only are tools possible for improving existing officers' performance, but the investigation also discovered that many of the characteristics of high performance come from the background and personality traits of the individual. In other words, increasing the number of high-performing officers can be achieved not only through on-the-job training of existing officers, but also through new targeted recruitment efforts.

Recruiting and in-service tool—*One of the biggest opportunities is to introduce Gold Medal Policing concepts and tools into new recruit assessment as opposed to "testing" once in-service (which of course is still a priority).*
—Reviewer, Police Chief

Individuals who have some or many of the characteristics for high performance can also be identified through the interview and hiring process. Although there are certainly no guarantees that selecting such individuals will automatically produce high-performance officers at the outset, the probability of finding such candidates is significantly increased by looking for these specific success factors.

To maximize these opportunities for recruitment, selection, and retention, the following tools should be customized:
- enhance "Outreach Messaging" by using detailed front-line terminology
- format a "Self-Screening Manual" for police applicants
- outline "Job Awareness Tips" for police applicants
- create an "Interview Question-Answer Grid" based on desired high-performance success skills

- develop a "Preferred Skills Screening Guide" based on individual factor tendencies
- determine "Coaching Benchmarks" based on core skills for high performance
- see Appendix P: Field Training Assessment and Progress Report
- see "Recommendations: Enrich the internal role-model function"
- align a "Supervisor's Guide" to address sequential planning

Outreach Messaging: A detailed collection of frequently used terminology and police "banter" was compiled during the course of this study. For example, the first 100 new words heard on a Ride Along or a Group Training Day provide a good sample of daily operational activities and priorities within that given specialty unit. This unique frontline perspective may provide the candid insight that potential applicants seek.

> **Expectations**—*On patrol, these are your responsibilities. If you're good at what you do, there's a process for advancement. Just be honest with them; don't create unrealistic expectations. Some feel, "I don't really have to try here because I won't be here that long." That's difficult for frontline supervisors to establish a responsible outlook.*
>
> —Neighborhood Resource

Self-Screening Manual: Realistic policing situations, success skills, and performance blocks are detailed in this report for individuals to self-screen. Based on an intelligent understanding of policing as a chosen career, candidates can be better educated on job expectations.

A clear understanding of policing as a career helps candidates know what to expect on the job.

Job awareness tips: Job awareness is rated by the best officers as fundamental to mental preparation.

The top five issues they recommend to be brought to the candidates' attention, before applying for police work, are to:
- do a reality check concerning personal lifestyle
- expect the probability of becoming jaded and skeptical toward society
- have to deal with personal anxiety from unrealistic expectations for image and accountability as a uniformed officer—"life in a bubble"
- understand the demands of shift work
- recognize the regularity of family conflict and spousal fears

Hiring practices, motivation—*It all starts at the ground level. We have to be very aware of what the motivation is for people we hire. If it's money, there are a lot of other places you can go to make money. We have to have people who are truly interested in serving the public.*

—Traffic Escort

Interview Q & A: Where have you demonstrated competitiveness in your life?

Interview Question-Answer Grid: Based on the major-skill predictors associated with police high performance, preferred life skills can be assessed using general knowledge questions.

To ensure a propensity for commitment, randomized questions can be derived based on the related indicators such as:

- Where might you show empathy and compassion as an officer toward the public and your peers?
- What would you find enjoyable about frontline policing?
- What standards do you set for professional discipline?
- What skills have you developed in managing high levels of responsibility?
- Where have you demonstrated competitiveness in your life?
- How will you demonstrate short- and long-term dedication to policing?

- Ask questions that highlight General Distraction-Control traits (e.g., being task-oriented; having the ability to de-escalate situations; directing leadership for involving others).
- Candidates can be given the "Top 10 Quotes and Lessons" exercise to complete prior to an interview (see Appendix Q: Top 10 Quotes and Lessons).

Performance results are not primarily a function of education.

Preferred Skills Screening Guide: Given the limited resources in hiring new officers, ensuring a strong profile of expected strengths and complementary skills for potential deficiencies would improve selection choices. Awareness of candidates' predisposition for certain skill preferences may allow a more thorough screening process. Some traditional factors may not be as influential as originally predicted—education for example.

Influential factors: Certain Background and Developmental factors may predispose officers to certain skill preferences. Skill preferences were found to exist within certain factors such as: gender, language, and prior police-related experience.

Non-influential factors (e.g., Education): Performance results are not primarily a function of education level. Generally, performance based on education is a flat line without trends in either direction. One might expect that higher education would produce a more well-rounded and capable frontline officer. This study indicates that frontline officers are not advantaged or disadvantaged in their skill development based on education. Some of the relatively low influential factors include: military experience, rural police experience, and old/new school males. However, for screening purposes, these factors do have prominent skill traits.

Coaching Benchmarks: The development of these Benchmarks is intended to enhance the Coach Officer Program; see "Recommendations: Enrich the Internal Role-Model Function."

Supervisor's Mental Training Guide: This Guide is intended to address training and target career and succession planning issues for supervisors; see "Recommendations: Target Career and Succession Planning."

B. Create multilevel self-assessment tools

"Performance Excellence Index" for officers to compare themselves with "the best."

One of the unique aspects of this study is the focus on "excellent" high-performance officers as identified by their peers and supervisors. This special set of officers formed a valuable source of role models. Their attitudes, work techniques, and approaches to difficult and routine situations alike can serve as an inspiration and guide for anyone within the organization who wishes to improve his/her own performance.

To formalize this opportunity, the following ideas could be developed into easily accessible reference guides and self-improvement instruments.

1. *Design a "Performance Excellence Index"* for officers to compare themselves with "the best." A personal profile would result to detail the officer's mental-readiness skills that contribute to excellence.

2. *Create a self-directed "Diagnostic Inventory."* For example for *"Personal Blocks and Coping Strategies for High-Performance Readiness."* While formal evaluation serves as a means of monitoring and predicting performance, excellent officers predominantly engage in self-evaluation, emphasizing ownership and drawing lessons. Their daily habits, focusing on positivity, discipline, and understanding job demands, develop effective independent practices as leaders confident in their abilities. Excerpts from excellent officers can inspire new learning strategies (see Chapter 7: Mental Readiness in Policing—Constructive Evaluation). For example:

Self-critique—*I critique my own behavior, "What did I do there that I could do better?" I pay attention to other people—I don't critique them openly but I may critique them to myself. I do my best to keep my mind open and learn something new every day.*

—5 to 10 years on

Find insights from a checklist informed by current research for coping in high-stress situations[1,2,3]:
- Unwind from having to be resilient.
- Break daily cycles; changing your setting changes your learning.
- Focus on meaningful issues—prioritize your energy.
- Avoid energy draining habits like worrying and gossiping—approach challenges positively.
- Address each issue separately; they may be unrelated.
- Believe that there is a lid for every pot.
- Seek and accept feedback from others.
- Learn from mistakes: adapt, salvage the situation, identify gained experience—or simply start over.
- Ask: will this matter in a month, a year, on your deathbed?
- Hope when you die, you have an ounce of fun left.

3. *Supply candid "Frontline Mentoring Stories"* easily accessible to other officers' that demonstrate the scope of options available to respond to various challenging situations.
4. *Produce a "Training Self-Assessment"* to help officers customize their professional development needs. This could be used to complement the existing corporate-training needs assessment. Presence of mind is often challenging in simulation training. The "Simulation-Training Focus Assessment" provides preparation and self-reflection on focusing during simulation training (see Appendix R: Simulation-Training Focus Assessment).
5. *Encourage Health and Wellness (amid shift work, fatigue and injuries).* In policing, being healthy means more than a medical check-up and a workout. Optimal performance must

also include physical discipline, strategies for shift work, fatigue and long-term rest, and injury management.
- Adapt to a shift-work lifestyle finding ways to lessen the impact on family life.
- Go easy and be realistic during high fatigue.
- Set lifestyle goals and begin with small steps.
- Revisit the basics: self-care and discipline (get up, make bed, eat right, get ready).
- Guard against burnout by setting personal time to refresh.
- Be mindful of physical and emotional accommodations when injured.
- Separate work from home.
- Express gratitude to those who provide support.
- Attend to your face and feet with care.
- Find a common-sense approach—not too aggressive nor absurdly cautious.

6. *Develop a "Progressive Career-Planning Guide"* that assists officers in identifying future career interests and the training or path that is required to achieve that objective. The Guide should also clearly identify—beyond the job description—what is realistically involved in the various officer positions.

C. Target career and succession planning

Specialty-unit skill profiles

Development of "Specialty-Unit Skill Profiles" would outline the skill preferences and tendencies of the various frontline operations. For example, Tactical officers show elevated skills in eight different areas. Likewise, profiles can be drawn for Patrol, Neighborhood Resource Team, School Resource, Canine, and Traffic Escort Units. Ambitious officers can thus direct their training and experiences to areas that will match their career goals. Conversely, officers might also recognize areas they do not wish to pursue based on the skill profile demands.

Align mental training to address sequential career planning for officers, as well as "Watch Items"

Early detection and sensitivity in personal career planning will be immediately relevant to personal choices in the Elective Skills area of the training. Proactively involving officers in career skills development will also encourage more effective succession planning.

Supervisor's Guide

Creating a "Supervisor's Guide" for mental training will help with career planning for officers, and address "Watch Items" like Visible Minority-Aboriginal alienation, promotional complacency, and job satisfaction.

D. Develop e-learning programs

"Anonymous Testimonial Database" from exceptional officers across all front-line specialty units

With the growing popularity of the Internet in everyday activities, ranging from personal entertainment to business transactions (particularly among the younger population), it is strongly suggested that the recommended initiatives also be developed and provided through a website. Not only will this address the new learning interests of future recruits and younger officers, but it will also allow for 24-hour, seven-day-a-week access to important training and self-improvement material to meet the needs of the shift-work environment. This is seen as a longer-term priority and one that can be developed incrementally over time. But as with all technological changes, the sooner this concept is embraced and developed, the easier it will be to develop and expand in the future.

The following is recommended as a starting point for e-learning programs:

- artificial intelligence and mental training to advance technical competencies, and address controversies in biased decision-making and privacy violations, and demands for greater transparency and accountability
- "Anonymous Testimonial Database" from exceptional officers across all frontline specialty units to enable searches for targeted knowledge transfer
- focused e-sites on managing issues such as counter-terrorism, hate crimes, fatigue, public disrespect, shift work, court appearance, public complaints
- "High-Performance Tools" for training and evaluation
- establish links to "Relevant Resources" for operational readiness

E. Promote a frontline-recognition plan

Officer recognition is a powerful tool linked to confidence for 62% of officers and ultimately to high performance. Specifically, officers base their need for respect and gratitude on

- internal recognition: something from the Chief, supervisor acknowledgment, and peer respect
- public feedback and appreciation
- status as a valued leader or trainer

Patrol officers have a uniquely greater vocabulary of refocusing and time-management skills than other specialty officers.

Generate foresight—*Services often shy away from some of the entrenched frontline attitudes, that can generate unhelpful defensive mindsets, which Gold Medal Policing flushes out. It doesn't shy away from saying, "These people have something to offer." Their hindsight is the next generating foresight. Okay, maybe some of their attitudes are not consistent with where policing needs to be but that doesn't mean we can't learn from them.*

—Reviewer, Police Chief

One of the most repeated concerns expressed by frontline officers is the lack of appreciation by various segments of the Service and community in regard to their efforts and dedication. When one speaks of morale in any workplace, recognition or the lack thereof is typically cited as the primary cause of poor morale. If left unchecked, this situation leads to poorer on-the-job performance, increased sick leave and other minor system abuses, and continual staff turnover. Altogether, this puts additional pressure on an organization already under considerable stress. To help address this situation, a variety of suggestions are made, many of which originate from the initial interviews. They include the following:

Formal recognition
Recognition is clearly sought by officers, and it is required to address individual and group morale needs. Ways in which this may accomplished include:
- Public recognition: Publicly acknowledge the results of this investigation, particularly those elements that identify police best practices.
- Reinforce high-performance: Highlight the readiness techniques as practiced by these high-performance officers.
- Recognize superior Patrol officer skills: Patrol officers have a uniquely greater vocabulary of refocusing (Distraction Control) and time-management skills than other specialty officers. Talents in controlling blocks are highly sought after in policing and require special acknowledgment and reinforcement. While the status of Patrol is in particular need of recognition, similar specialty-unit profiles would highlight their unique strengths.

Recognize unique skill sets: Go beyond traditional top-down or years-on notions of expertise and design team exercises to encourage sharing their different skill profiles and tendencies.
- Publish study results in professional and academic newsletters and journals.

Frontline organizational problem-solving

Leading organizational distractions: Workload, Coach Officer issues, bureaucracy, resources... [however, most DO NOT view] "not being promoted" as a problem.

- ◆ Propose international standards: Ottawa Police Service high-performance skills as a starting point for developing international standards through presentation of study results at international police symposiums.

The frontline perspective is valid and important for developing and achieving high performance. Officers hold a strong, logical opinion about what works for good performance versus poor performance. When given new parameters for an issue, frontline officers are prepared to struggle with the problem and not just rearticulate their former point of view. For example, frontline officers were shown a senior police management list of "challenging situations" (see Appendix H), which was strikingly different from their counterpart's list of situations. The officers openly expressed a new level of awareness and surprise, and proceeded to allow this new information to empathetically affect their thought processes.

Organizational blocks, identified by more than half the officers, may be best addressed through a frontline problem-solving process. The leading five organizational distractions to frontline high performance are:
- ◆ workload (75%)
- ◆ lack of leadership (63%)
- ◆ bureaucracy (61%)
- ◆ fewer resources (60%)
- ◆ public complaints (53%)

Bridging tools for the management-frontline gap can be developed from the results that recognize and respect the differences and responsibilities of each.

Frontline "buy-in"

For 96% of officers, empathy and compassion contribute substantially to frontline commitment. Officers demonstrate a very clinical thought process for operational issues that directly affect their performance. Thus for "buy-in," they believe very strongly in providing input. The depth and candidness of officer transcripts are a clear indication of their desire to provide alternative approaches to classic issues. It is not always critical that their ideas be acted on but important that frontline fact-finding be built into the decision-making process. The equally significant role of providing feedback was identified as a deficiency by less than half (45%) of officers.

The depth and candidness of officer transcripts are a clear indication of their desire to provide alternative approaches.

Whichever ideas are accepted and developed, it should *not* be a one-time event but rather built into the annual administrative activities of the Service in order to obtain a continuous and sustained result.

F. Establish a corporate curriculum

"Officer Skill Profiles"… relating to background, training, and police-service experience to encourage succession planning

Probably one of the most interesting conclusions reached in this investigation is the fact that high performance can be achieved in a number of ways, depending on the officer's individual Background, Developmental, and Police Distinction factors. In spite of some of the apparent unique elements to high performance, a range of techniques emerged that can be transferred both generically in groups and specifically, to individuals, depending upon the objectives sought. To maximize the transferability of these skills, a series of training programs should be developed along the following lines:

1. *Use the physical, technical, and mental 60 success practices* (Core, Enhanced, and Elective) to reinforce the existing training curriculum and identify how gaps to performance will be addressed. The "Top 10 Quotes and Lessons" exercise brings evidence-based practices to the frontline in a meaningful way (see Appendix Q: Top 10 Quotes and Lessons).
2. *Detail a "Corporate Curriculum-Planning Guide"* directed at improving productivity based on high-performance success elements.
3. *Integrate responsible Artificial Intelligence (AI) use* in frontline policing, addressing ethical concerns to keep pace with technological advancements.
4. *Develop "Officer Skill Profiles"* based on the factors relating to background, training, and police-service experience to encourage succession planning and recognize diversity among groups.
5. *Create "Enhanced Case Study Modules"* by integrating detailed mentor quotes with existing critical-incident simulations. Frame case studies using court cases and current evidence on issues such as:
    - *counter-terrorism* impact on community policing, and strategic deployment of police resources[4,5]
    - *hate crimes* including assault, vandalism, harassment, hate speech, discrimination, cyberbullying, homicide motivated by hate or bias[6,7]
    - *mass protests* with democratic protest policing, and difference issues (such as climate-change strikes, women's marches, anti-COVID vaccine, Black Lives Matters, farming and fishing protests)[8,9]
    - *relationship building within racialized communities* through policing social work and youth relations[10,11]
    - *body-cam evidence* related to digital evidence storage, professional responsibility, public records, and private evidence[12,13]
6. *Develop "beyond-arrest thinking"*: Encourage problem-solving by working with the community, using technology, and fostering a police culture of innovation within departments. Neighborhood Resource Team officers show creative

problem-solving skills. Advanced predictive analytics and artificial intelligence algorithms can identify hotspots and emerging trends, for targeting resources. Community engagement can empower residents to report problems, share information, and cooperate with law enforcement to solve local issues.
7. *Use candid quotes on sensitive or unspoken issues* to initiate open dialogue at all levels where awareness and feedback are needed.
8. *Actively cultivate and support readiness and resilience* for coping with acts of terrorism, preventing operational stress injuries, and improving performance as both an individual and organizational responsibility.
9. *Develop a "Frontline Resource Dictionary"* to feature frontline values when addressing day-to-day issues such as outreach, diversity, preparation, and equipment-user interface.

G. Create a high-performance mental training program

Police officers could benefit from systematic training in specific high-performance mental training skills to take advantage of insights from this study. This approach has been effective in sports and other high-performance workplaces, and could likewise play a meaningful role in helping police officers improve their mental readiness for the challenges they face. Four stages for training are recommended, as follows.

Overview of police mental readiness
This study allows for a never-before-detailed perspective from highly respected officers representing all frontline specialty units. The first step is to create a basic understanding of police mental readiness in challenging situations and its links to the seven success elements in performance excellence. Appropriate emphases can be directed at the unique skill range, consistency, and allowance for individual differences in applying each success element to the policing environment. Comparative profiles of Olympic athletes and various high-performance workplaces

can be used to emphasize the overall importance of mental readiness. Decision-making training programs, which complement standard tactical training, have been highly appreciated by frontline police officers and perceived to enhance learning significantly beyond traditional training methods[14].

Full Focus with Use of Force training

Use of force is linked to how officers perceive and measure it. Officers require a full, composed focus for sound decision-making. Daily practices, informed by current research[1,3], can enhance officers' clarity of mind, equipment confidence, and teamwork.

> **Situational awareness**—*It can be blamed on focus but it could be the training. Ongoing training is essential to be aware.*
> —Police Executive

Three tools can be combined with Use of Force training to enhance Full Focus: quotes from excellent officers, self-directed checklist, and a Simulation-Training Focus Assessment (see Appendix R: Simulation-Training Focus Assessment).

a) *Excerpts from excellent officers* can provide novel strategies (see Chapter 7: Mental Readiness in Policing—Full Focus). For example:

> **Watch and listen**—*A domestic is the worst call—it's the unknown factor. I'll try to identify the problem by watching and listening. I'll watch the body language and the eyes. I'll look around the room for any possible signs. Like a glare or a blank stare—maybe they're thinking of something else, or there are drugs involved, or they're lying. You can tell. Just watch the hands. That's old-school sh--. It's no big deal—you can pick up on that.*
> —>15 years on

b) *Self-directed checklist* informed by current research for focusing in high-stress situations[15,16,17,18,19] can inspire new practices, such as:

- commit to being present, positive, and observant
- resist a knee-jerk reaction. Stay grounded, breathe, and quiet your mind
- tune into the information and the context. Make sense of yours and others' reactions
- anticipate the risks to avoid incidents and promote astute courage
- feel confident with your equipment
- extend empathy and respectful communication to others—your team, the public
- do your best with the resources you have
- tackle different challenges differently: complete tasks, resolve obstacles, and allow time to reflect
- hone a comfortable, common-sense approach—not too aggressive nor absurdly cautious—aligned with your values and the mission
- ask yourself what makes you a good cop

c) *Full Focus Simulation Assessment* can accompany an instructor-led debrief to provide awareness, detailed feedback, and improvement strategies. The assessment form can also be used for self-assessment and reflection. See Appendix R: Simulation-Training Focus Assessment.

Distraction Control training

In a policing environment, effective Distraction Control is the most dominant of all success elements for high performance. Short- and long-term training emphasis on the most critical officer distractions is fundamental. Officers' emotional control is central to: managing distractions, demonstrating good leadership, enhancing memory, preventing mental-health issues, and maintaining interpersonal skills for career growth[20]. Stressful situations like public disrespect, complaints, and court testimony would benefit from refocusing practices like visualization, controlled breathing, and positive self-talk, rituals commonly used in marksmanship.

Identification of blocks: *Instruction begins with understanding the categorization of policing performance*

> blocks—Operational, Organizational, and External—and the frequency of their occurrence. Immediate Needs and Serious Blocks will thus be addressed differently between individuals. Assessing and building a customized officer inventory of blocks will allow for an effective personal focus on Distraction Control practices.
>
> **Systematic Distraction Control training**: Effective distraction controls should be the primary focus—as practiced and detailed by over 75% of excellent officers and directed at the leading performance blocks.

For example, in relation to Crisis and Downtime and Routine Task (Lull) Control, the approach would be as follows:

> **Crisis Control**: *A personal inventory for regaining or maintaining emotional control in a crisis appears to be a significant skill set among high performers in irregular and volatile conditions. Developing dependable accessible strategies is a critical step for all officers.*
>
> **Downtime and Routine Task Refocusing**: *While the ability to affectively get back on track after a lull was reported by 71% of officers, the solutions are either not working well or provide only temporary amelioration. There is no pattern of consistency in their responses. There is a clear indication that external intervention is needed to augment the current solutions. More systematic skills for dealing with passive distractions and complacency need to be addressed. Downtime and routine task refocusing is required to manage this and other performance blocks that remain a high source of concern for most excellent officers.*
>
> **Tailored coping strategies**: *Solutions may come not necessarily through counseling, generic training, or a clearer*

Get back on track: More systematic skills for dealing with passive distractions and complacency need to be addressed.

Tailor-made inventory of frontline-specific coping strategies that result in high performance *articulation of problems, but rather from a tailor-made inventory of frontline-specific coping strategies that result in high performance. Highly focused solutions from exceptional officers now exist from the study results to address these issues. For example, the officers can augment their existing strategies by reviewing Mental Preparation practices and "Informal debrief" of calls (Constructive Evaluation).*

Career and succession planning

Chronologically sequenced career planning prior to "Progressive Success-Skills Training" provides opportunity and foresight in appropriately identifying Elective Performance Skills Training. See "Recommendations: Target Career and Succession Planning" for details.

Progressive success-skills training

Unique skills and tendencies linked to high performance should be sought during recruiting and in advanced policing training programs. If not already available, these skill sets should be developed to augment the current curriculum.

The 69 police-specific mental training success skills have been classified based on their overall use by excellent officers. Training priorities have been set up to delineate Core, Enhanced, and Elective Skills.

Benchmark for optimizing lessons learned from highly respected officer

Instruction can thus be planned generically or allow for greater individual focus. Officers can develop a personalized work plan using the corresponding success skills to suit their needs. The training progression and emphasis should be as follows:

Core-performance skills training: Compulsory high-performance training is a benchmark for optimizing lessons learned from the highly respected officers in this study. Generic content should be directed at:

- ensuring that the 23 Core Practices performed by over 75% of these excellent officers are detailed for all officers to emulate
- highlighting common separating skills of "Elite" officers performing at high levels across all frontline units

Enhanced performance skills training: These complementary practices will combine with the core skills to broaden the base to allow officers to have multiple options when facing a challenging situation. Distraction Control, Mental Preparation, Confidence, and Full Focus contribute most to this category of Enhanced Skills agreed to by 50% to 75% of excellent officers. This section would make an inventory of 22 additional high-performance practices available to officers.

Elective performance skills training: *This training is directed at elevating an officer's individual preferences. Some high-performance skills and blocks were reported with less frequency (<50%) among respected officers; that indicates that the skills do not come naturally and are not easily obtained through experience. Nevertheless, these practices and blocks have an important impact on success and productivity, and will contribute to how officers refine their training choices.*

Factor deficiencies: Background, training development, and police distinctions can predispose an officer to certain practice deficiencies. For example, School Resource Officers tend to score lower in team consulting compared with officers with no School Resource experience. Officers could thus direct their training to compensate for deficiencies in their personal profile.

H. Enrich the internal role-model function: Coach officers, trainers, and mentors

Role modeling is an effective approach for profiling excellence. There is a strong need to further integrate and recognize role

models for knowledge transfer within the organization. Three types of policing role models are strongly identified as influencing mental readiness. They are:
- coach officers at the rookie level
- trainers for instructional development
- mentors for career planning and consulting on personal blocks

The study shows "years on" experience alone is not a good indicator of performance. More influential indicators are:
- excellent officers mutually identified by peers and supervisors
- specialty-unit experience, such as Neighborhood Resource Team, School Resource, Tactical, Canine and Traffic Escort officers
- background factors (e.g., gender, language, military)

Enhancement of the Coach Officer Program

Recommended enhancements to the Coach Officer Program are as follows:
- **Quality coach officers**: Choose capable coach officers with strong policing, teaching, and assessment abilities to help trainees improve. Remember that the frontline IS the first line of defense. Co-coaching shares workload and effectively exposes trainees to diverse approaches. See Appendix S: Coach Officers' 25 Teaching Tips.

A guide for core skills can be used to assess trainees.

Core mental-readiness competencies: It is critical that coaches possess the compulsory high-performance practices to ensure their ability to train high performers. A guide for core skills can be used to assess trainees. A guide for core skills can be used to assess trainees.

Mutual-appointment process: This study demonstrates that a strict confidential and anonymous external polling of peers and supervisors produces an accurate

determination of "excellent" frontline officers, in addition to gaining:
- an enthusiastic disclosure by peers
- a 90% buy-in (30/33 completed forms) from supervisors
- an extraordinary commitment by 96% of interviewees to participate (48/50 voluntarily completed tape-recorded interviews) and 100% (33/33) of coach officers
- strong evidence of accuracy, given that the identified elite scores had the highest number of success skills by factor

Buy-in and internal admiration were key practices in promoting confidence and commitment to high performers. One would therefore expect it to be a transferable process for encouraging the participation of "excellent" coach officers. Peers, supervisors, and others affected by a coach officer's teaching and leadership abilities would be involved in recommending suitable candidates.

Coach officer issues: Officers reported that there are four blocks that discourage "excellent" officers from participating as coach officers. They are:
- low standards and expectations
- career implications in being held back, overworked, and burnt out
- no recognition for the importance of being a good teacher
- low pay

Having open discussions with frontline officers, using the approaches suggested in this book, may encourage new solutions.

Choose effective coach officers *who have qualities you want to pass on to subordinate officers, and who are willing to become teachers. This creates leadership by example. Leading young officers and teaching them these qualities is ideal for our profession. However, I want to stay where I am as an operational police officer. There are officers who would gladly embody,*

teach, and serve as an example, making a difference in teaching young officers.
—Neighborhood Resource

Identification of ideal trainers

Assets: Influential factors—Background, Developmental, and Police Distinction—should be considered when targeting and selecting training experts. Certain factors predispose an individual to proficiencies or deficits in high-performance skill levels. For example, explicit driving skills tend to be better articulated by Traffic Escort officers and preparation rituals are notably superior among Canine officers.

Driving skills tend to be better articulated by Traffic Escort and preparation rituals are notably superior among Canine officers.

Inherent high-performance problems: Sensitivity and awareness of high-performance conditions are important for trainers in motivating excellence.

Underlining issues among high performers include
- increased fatigue and absenteeism caused by high stress from high-level accountability, rotating shifts, and extensive overtime
- feelings of being misunderstood and undervalued among frontline staff, who are often uniformed in the field and away from administration. (Note: Being "uniformed" translates to being "easily identified by the public and superiors, permitting unguarded day-to-day scrutiny.")
- inconsistent performance and productivity because of a lack of proper preparation techniques in facing critical situations such as counter-terrorism, hate crimes, mass protests
- a limited and exiting number of experienced veteran staff available to mentor a young and inexperienced workforce
- insufficient knowledge-transfer mechanisms to instill operational savvy and confidence

- open strategic discussions framed with evidence on current issues such as:
  - *counter-terrorism* impact on community policing, and strategic deployment of police resources[4,5]
  - *hate crimes* including assault, vandalism, harassment, hate speech, discrimination, cyberbullying, homicide motivated by hate or bias[6,7]
  - *mass protests* with democratic protest policing and difference issues (such as climate-change strikes, women's marches, anti-COVID vaccine, Black Lives Matters, farming and fishing protests)[8,9].
  - *relationship building* within racialized communities through policing social work and youth relations[10,11]
  - *body-cam evidence* related to digital evidence storage, professional responsibility, public records, and private evidence[12,13]

Support mentor-officer skill-set matching

Informal patrol leaders operate within various tiers of Platoon. Sergeants adhere strictly to the formal process, but there is also an informal way of doing things. Right now, that informal part, often by senior officers setting the tone, is missing and needs attention.

Compatible skill sets: In matching mentors with seasoned officers, skill sets, not personality or training, will drive success. Two mentors may have very different skills that lead to Orlick's seven basic success elements. For example, one officer may deal with a situation using one set of skills and have success, while another may apply a different set of skills and have the same success. Therefore, experienced officers seeking mentors should match mentors with readiness skills most compatible with their style.

Skill-set profile: The best way for seasoned officers to enhance their success may not be rooted in choosing like-personalities for relationship building and team assignments. Common skill sets denote similar approaches to a problem—and why a relationship works. In contrast, opposing skill sets may be favorable in some circumstances for providing necessary breadth in problem-solving. This study provides details to quantify and profile success based on high-performance skill sets.

I. Pursue publication opportunities

The aim of this study was to draw from the vast experience and seasoned patterns of the highly proficient frontline police officers. As a result of this detailed investigation, many factors related to excellence in policing are now clearly defined, particularly as they relate to Commitment, Self-Belief, Positive Imagery, Mental Preparation, Full Focus, Distraction Control, and Constructive Evaluation. A framework of future publications has been identified to further detail specific findings of this study. These journal articles can be used as handouts and resource information to lend international credibility to this investigation.

Practical resource topics include the following:
- a supervisory guide to police mentoring and career planning
- upgrade to mental training strategies in policing
- recruitment and hiring practices in law enforcement
- police culture through a frontline perspective
- critique of the police Coach Officer Program
- teachable moments in policing: informal training on what matters
- challenges and solutions for female police officers
- creative approaches for police as school resources
- AI technologies and human factors
- teachable principles for counter-terrorism and hate crimes
- insights for understated issues within families of police officers
- knowledge transferability between emergency and protective services

This resource compendium should be of practical value to the participating officers, as well as to less experienced officers, and has the potential to enhance the police-training curriculum. Upon completion, it will both extend knowledge from a theoretical perspective and provide effective mental training techniques pertaining to performing with excellence in the policing environment. By expanding research with respect to the mental components of performance excellence, other professions and students within our secondary and post-secondary school systems may also one day benefit.

J. Promote further related research

Further investigation is recommended in the area of mental readiness for the policing profession and other emergency first-responder disciplines. Possible topic areas for related research beyond the scope of this study include:

Skill Profiles for Specialty Units, such as Patrol, Tactical, and Neighborhood Resource Team, to enable officers to align their career goals with their strengths.

Evaluation of Improvement to Police Mental Readiness: Conduct a follow-up assessment on the impact of implementing the police mental-readiness practices.

Senior Police Management Mental Readiness Study: Assess data collected as part of this study that related to the parallel needs of police executive, superintendents, and inspector-level policing.

Incident Command Decision-Making Mental Readiness Study: Use this research tool to investigate performance excellence of the major decision-makers in disaster response situations (e.g., Emergency Response Teams, Police Chiefs, Fire Chiefs, City Managers).

Visible Minority-Aboriginal Issues in Policing: Conduct a detailed investigation to address the specific internal ethnicity issues in policing identified as a "Watch Item" in this study;

Coach Officer Program: Blocks and Benefits: Create a more detailed report using this study data to promote greater effectiveness and status associated with the essential succession-planning service of coaching young officers. Early career planning and ongoing mentoring strategies can also be addressed.

K. 20 Key summary recommendations

The following 20 key recommendations summarize the suggested next steps.

1. **Craft interview questions**: Design interview questions to incorporate *Gold Medal Policing* concepts, shifting the focus from in-service training to initial recruit assessment to nurture "duty of care," which embodies empathy, professional discipline, job satisfaction, responsible leadership, and a realistic grasp of "the job."
2. **Use strategic tools**: Utilize outreach messaging, self-screening manuals, job-awareness tips, and preferred-skills screening guides to strategically identify recruits with high-performance potential, beyond their academic achievements.
3. **Align expectations**: Ensure prospective police officers confront five realities before applying to align personal expectations with professional responsibilities: lifestyle impact, potential societal cynicism, anxiety from public scrutiny, shift-work demands, and family conflicts.
4. **Discover the Operational Readiness Index**: Encourage officers to compare themselves with top performers through an "Operational Readiness Index" and self-evaluation to foster a culture of ongoing improvement, professional development, and well-being.
5. **Use skill profiles**: Develop detailed skill profiles for various specialty units, such as Patrol, Tactical, and Neighborhood Resource Teams, to enable officers to match their career aspirations with their strengths.
6. **Create Supervisor's Guide**: Create a comprehensive Supervisor's Guide focused on mental training and career

planning to help supervisors support their officers' career trajectories and create an inclusive and motivated workforce.
7. **Offer more e-learning**: Implement more e-learning programs to offer accessible, immediate training tailored to learning preferences of younger recruits.
8. **Recognize frontline talent**: Establish a recognition program that includes public acknowledgment, peer respect, and leadership opportunities, recognizing the unique skills of officers to boost morale, enhance performance, and reduce turnover.
9. **Revise training agendas**: Implement a revised curriculum that includes physical, technical, and mental success practices for a comprehensive, well-rounded approach.
10. **Integrate responsible AI use**: Incorporate responsible AI use in training programs to keep pace with technological advancements while addressing ethical concerns to maintain public trust and officer mental well-being.
11. **Test case studies**: Use detailed case studies incorporating real-life scenarios on complex situations, like counter-terrorism and hate crimes, to foster a culture of innovation, problem-solving, and beyond-arrest thinking.
12. **Recruit and train for emotional intelligence**: Screen for and develop emotional control with practices like visualization, controlled breathing, and positive self-talk to stay "in the zone," enhance memory, and prevent mental-health issues during high-stress situations.
13. **Tailor coping strategies**: Recognize and customize inventories of operational, organizational, and external blocks to performance, then develop personalized, accessible, dependable coping strategies drawn from the experiences of exceptional officers.
14. **Teach refocusing skills**: Refocus during downtime and routine tasks with systematic practices for managing complacency and ensuring readiness for the next task.
15. **Invest in coach officers**: Empower rookie officers by selecting coach officers with strong policing, teaching, and assessment skills to ensure a foundation of high standards and effective knowledge transfer to future leaders.

16. **Tailor curriculum**: Tailor the corporate curriculum by leveraging individuals who excel in specific areas, such as Traffic Escort officers for driving skills and Canine officers for preparation rituals.
17. **Address coaching barriers**: Address the barriers to coaching—low standards, career implications, lack of recognition, and low pay—with open discussions and innovative solutions to attract and retain the best role models.
18. **Spotlight understated issues**: Highlight understated issues, such as the challenges faced by female officers and the impact of policing on family dynamics, to emphasize areas needing ongoing support within the organization.
19. **Incorporate scientific publications**: Integrate evidence-based research in training exercises to bridge scientific insights and lend international credibility to on-the-ground policing practices, such as AI in policing.
20. **Use the Operational Readiness Framework**: Utilize the Operational Readiness Framework to benefit not only policing but also other emergency and protective services, contributing to broader advancements in high-risk professions.

Notes

1 J. McDonald, *Gold medal policing: Mental readiness and performance excellence*. New York: Sloan Associate Press, 2006.
2 A. Graham, *Take back your weekends*. Elevate Press, p. 150, 2021.
3 A. Kinley, "The 8 steps to resilience." Atlantic Institute for Resilience Inc. https://pans.ns.ca/sites/default/files/8steps_to_resilience.pdf.
4 S. Pickering, McCulloch, J. and Wright-Neville, D., *Counter-terrorism policing*. New York: Springer, pp. 91–111, 2008.
5 T. L. Quinlan and Derfoufi, Z., "Counter-terrorism policing," In R. Delsol & M. Shiner (Eds.) *Stop and search: The anatomy of a police power*. New York: Palgrave Macmillan, pp. 123–145, 2015.
6 G. Mason, Maher, J., McCulloch, J., Pickering, S., Wickes, R. and McKay, C., *Policing hate crime: Understanding communities and prejudice*. London: Routledge. https://doi.org/10.4324/9781315696508, 2017.

7. P. Giannasi, "Policing and hate crime," in *The Routledge international handbook on hate crime.* Routledge, pp. 331–342. https://doi.org/10.4324/9780203578988, 2014.
8. D. Baker, "Paradoxes of policing and protest," *Journal of Policing, Intelligence and Counter Terrorism,* vol. 3, no. 2, pp. 8–22. https://doi.org/10.1080/18335300.2008.9686911, 2008.
9. G. Martin, "Protest, policing and law during COVID-19: On the legality of mass gatherings in a health crisis," *Alternative Law Journal,* vol. 46, no. 4, pp. 275–281, 2021.
10. S. Giwa, "Community policing in racialized communities: A potential role for police social work," *Journal of Human Behavior in the Social Environment,* vol. 28, no. 6, pp. 710–730. https://doi.org/10.1080/10911359.2018.1456998, 2018.
11. N. J. Phillips and Cromwell, A., "Building bridges in police-youth relations through experiential peacebuilding: How reduced threat and increased humanization impact racialized structural and direct violence in Baltimore," *Journal of Peace Education,* vol. 17, no. 3, pp. 324–345. https://doi.org/10.1080/17400201.2020.1782181, 2020.
12. S. E. Wood, "Police body cameras and professional responsibility: Public records and private evidence," *Preservation, Digital Technology & Culture,* vol. 46, no. 1, pp. 41–51. https://doi.org/10.1515/pdtc-2016-0030, 2017.
13. M. D. Fan, "Body cameras, big data, and police accountability," *Law & Social Inquiry,* vol. 43, no. 4, pp. 1236–1256. https://doi.org/10.1111/lsi.12354, 2018.
14. B. H. Johnsen, Espevik, R. S., Saus, E. R., Sanden, S. and Olsen, O. K., "Note on a training program for brief decision making for frontline police officers," *Journal of Police and Criminal Psychology,* vol. 31, pp. 182–188, 2016.
15. G. R. Mount, "Mental practice: Police performance in hostage negotiation," *Journal of Police Crisis Negotiations,* vol. 7, no. 2, pp. 41–143. https://doi.org/10.1300/J173v07n02_11, 2007.
16. P. McCaffrey, "Judgement continuum," Ottawa Police Services, Ottawa, 1999.
17. K. McLean, Alikhan, A. and Alpert, G. P., "Re-examining the use of force continuum: Why resistance is not the only driver of use of force decisions," *Police Quarterly,* vol. 26, no. 1, pp. 85–110, 2023.
18. S. N. Knights Jr, "Ethical decision-making framework in police officers' use of the force continuum," Doctoral Dissertation, Capella University, 1–179, 2021.

19 F. I. C. Klahm, Frank, J. and Liederbach, J., "Understanding police use of force: Rethinking the link between conceptualization and measurement," *Policing: An International Journal of Police Strategies & Management,* vol. 37, no. 3, pp. 558–578, 2024.
20 B. H. Johnsen, Espevik, R., Saus, E. R., Sanden, S. and Olsen, O. K., "Hardiness as a moderator and motivation for operational duties as mediator: The relation between operational self-efficacy, performance satisfaction, and perceive," *Journal of police and Criminal Psychology,* 32, 331–339, 2017.

11

Executive summary

Gold medal policing: Operational readiness and performance excellence

Introduction

This easy-to-understand textbook provides practical tools for improving job performance, productivity, and morale in law enforcement. Building on the success of the first edition, *Gold Medal Policing* confirmed the importance of mental readiness in frontline policing excellence. Through strategic partnerships and extensive use spanning recruitment, multilevel training, web-based learning, and field assessment, these principles have been integrated into law enforcement practices.

The second edition consolidates two decades of peer-reviewed research and training lessons, addressing emerging trends, contemporary issues, and proven tools. It introduces an Operational Readiness Framework, rooted in scientific principles and insights from "excellent" frontline officers, including coach officers. This framework systematically assesses physical (P), technical (T), and mental (M) readiness, creating a detailed police-specific profile. A comprehensive literature review informs current police preparedness practices. By upholding mental readiness to measurable standards comparable to physical and technical readiness, the book isolates best practices and establishes operational benchmarks and strategies to empower law enforcement professionals.

The mission: Enhancing law enforcement excellence

The Mission serves as a comprehensive guide for law enforcement personnel, offering actionable strategies, evidence-based tactics to enhance police health and performance and to ensure community safety. By examining the consistent best practices of top frontline officers, and leveraging evidence-based tactics, this book aims to inspire and equip officers and leaders with tools for sustainable improvement. Comparative analysis of current data against historical trends helps predict future developments.

Police readiness is analyzed across physical, technical, and mental competencies, presenting updated readiness strategies and practical resources to enhance frontline operational readiness. The ultimate goal is to improve training effectiveness and consistency, reduce errors, and increase operational efficiency. *The Mission* aims to foster a safer community through empowered frontline officers and leaders.

Approach

To produce peak performers, we must develop the skills that distinguish the *best* from the *rest*. Achieving peak performance in frontline policing necessitates the development of skills akin to those of top athletes under pressure. Textbook solutions often fall short, and support can be limited. Frontline policing requires adaptive skills, combining technical expertise, physical abilities, and mental sharpness.

The book adopts a standardized "Operational Readiness Framework for High-Risk Professions" inspired by domains like athletics, surgery, and aviation. *Gold Medal Policing* draws insight from 81 distinguished officers, identified by both peers and supervisors, across seven uniformed specialty units: Patrol, Neighborhood Resource Team (NRT), School Resource Officers

(SRO), Tactical, Canine, Traffic Escort, and Coach Officers. The study examines optimal performance in high-stakes scenarios, including life-threatening situations.

Through quantitative and qualitative analysis, the book provides practical tips derived from the experiences of top officers, facilitated by collaborative efforts involving the University of Ottawa, Ottawa Police Service, Ontario Police College, Routledge Publishing Inc., and the Principal Investigator.

Knowledge transfer: Results and conclusions

Police Operational Readiness Index (ORI)

Research identifies mental readiness (44%) as the most influential factor in peak police performance, followed by technical readiness (30%) and physical readiness (26%). This weighted profile of competencies creates a police-specific ORI. Despite technology advances and changes in policing methods, physical and technical readiness showed a decline of 4% and 6%, respectively, from 2003 to 2019. Conversely, mental preparedness saw a notable 10% increase during the same period.

Confirmation of mental success elements

The study confirmed Orlick's seven mental success elements among top police officers: Commitment, Confidence, Positive Imagery, Mental Preparation, Full Focus, Distraction Control, and Constructive Evaluation. It identifies 60 police-specific mental-readiness practices, emphasizing Focus (83%), Mental Preparation (80%) and Commitment (77%) as consistently practiced elements. Confidence is derived from quality training, taking control, and mentorship, with differing impacts related to family support and camaraderie. Varied approaches to Distraction Control and Constructive Evaluation highlight individual and unit-specific preferences and challenges. For example, tactical officers favor informal team debriefs, while SROs seek public feedback.

Confirmation of technical and physical success elements

Technical readiness relied on law proficiency, effective communication (verbal and written), and knowledge of police service and community, comprising 16 technical-readiness practices (See Table 9.3). For example, verbal communication emphasizes preventing conflicts and de-escalation, using good articulation and appropriate tone, active listening, building community rapport, and conducting effective interviews.

Physical readiness benchmarks included officer safety, use of force proficiency, and vehicle operations, comprising 15 physical-readiness practices (See Table 9.3). For example, officer safety involves proper handcuffing techniques; conducting thorough body searches; maintaining health, wellness, and fitness; managing containment in various environmental conditions; and having a strong safety sense. Specific practices within these competencies underscore the diverse yet standardized preparedness among officers.

Performance blocks in policing

Forty-five performance blocks categorized as operational, organizational, and external contribute to challenges in law enforcement, affecting efficiency and morale. These include situational issues including rookie errors, administrative hurdles, and external pressures and conflicts, reflecting the complex dynamics of policing.

"Watch items" (emerging problems and initiatives)

Emerging trends and "Watch Items" in police performance variability include:

1. *Balancing teamwork and individual accountability*: Increasing collaboration may blur personal responsibility and lead to groupthink and reliance on others. Ensuring officers support each other while maintaining individual accountability responsible is essential for effective and safe policing.
2. *Monitoring general and specialized approaches*: While task-oriented practices gained prominence, the shift away from specialized skills for unique scenarios could impact response effectiveness in areas such as refocusing after public

disrespect, avoiding car collisions, and dealing with public complaints. Integrating both approaches offers a range of comprehensive strategies.
3. *Addressing workload and burnout*: Rising workload is identified as a significant performance block, signaling the need for improved coping strategies and leadership support to maintain officer effectiveness and well-being.
4. *Ensuring transparent AI integration*: The role of artificial intelligence (AI) in policing raises concerns about bias and privacy issues. Robust measures are essential to ensure transparent and accountable AI use, requiring enhanced mental readiness among officers to handle its implications and maintain public trust.
5. *Proactive career planning for leadership*: Despite high performance, many top officers show low concern for career advancement, potentially leading to future leadership gaps. Effective succession planning and leadership development are important for organizational stability and performance continuity.

Influential factors on success skills

Analysis of 22 factors across success practices within seven success elements reveals varying influences. The most influential factors, with either a positive or negative impact on practice development, were elite status, frontline specialty-unit experience, gender, and Patrol-only experience. Education and total years of service show minimal impact on skill development for performance excellence.

For instance, "Elite" officers were distinguished by their physical competency, officer safety, use of electronic aids, impromptu rehearsal, unique suspects rapport, and superior commitment reported through their competitiveness and understanding "the job." In contrast, officers with Patrol-only experience scored lower in physical discipline, psyching, external communication, job satisfaction, and equipment confidence, but showed higher levels in strategies for managing fatigue, workload, and female-policing issues, as well as formal evaluation methods.

Recommendations

Ten actionable recommendations aim to enhance frontline policing:

1. **Customized recruitment and retention**: Tailor recruitment processes to identify and address specific skill deficiencies and preferences through targeted self-screening and interviews.
2. **Multilevel self-assessment tools**: Develop tools based on exemplary officers' attitudes and approaches, including a performance index, diagnostic stress inventory, and mentoring stories, to enhance training and career planning.
3. **Align career and succession planning**: Match career paths with specialty-unit skill profiles in a Supervisor's Guide and provide comprehensive training aligned with career goals.
4. **E-learning for shift workers**: Implement accessible e-learning programs to accommodate shift schedules and facilitate ongoing professional development.
5. **Frontline recognition initiatives**: Establish collaborative problem-solving processes to address organizational morale and recognize frontline contributions.
6. **Tailor training curriculum**: Develop a flexible training curriculum catering to officers' backgrounds and experience levels, offering core and elective skills training.
7. **Mental training program**: Introduce mental skills training focusing on distraction control and career planning to enhance officer resilience and performance.
8. **Enhanced role model selection**: Select trainers based on relevant factors beyond traditional credentials to enhance mentorship effectiveness.
9. **Promote publication and research**: Encourage research on specialty-unit profiles, AI technologies, incident command decision-making, and counter-terrorism principles to advance policing practices.

10. **Focus on continuous improvement**: Foster ongoing research and evaluation to improve mental-readiness improvement, incident response, and effectiveness of coaching programs.

Summary

Gold Medal Policing provides a comprehensive framework for achieving excellence in frontline policing excellence through specific readiness practices. It serves as a benchmark for enhancing performance, recruitment, and organizational effectiveness. Indispensable for officers, leaders, scholars, and aspiring law enforcement professionals, this book underscores the importance of continuous improvement and strategic development of law enforcement practices.

Bibliography

* Not scientifically peer-reviewed publications

Abu-Alhassin, M., McDonald, J., Kirkwood, T., & Williams, M. (2025). Critical analysis of Road to Mental Readiness (R2MR) Program. In J. M. McDonald, *Gold Medal Policing: Operational Readiness and Performance Excellence, 2nd ed.* (pp. 505–514). Routledge.

Abu-Alhassin, M., McDonald, J., Kirkwood, T., Williams, M., & Cheng, C. (2025). Police mental competencies. In J. M. McDonald, *Gold Medal Policing: Operational Readiness and Performance Excellence, 2nd ed.* (pp. 537–550). Routledge.

Adams, B. D., Davis, S. A., Brown, A. L., Filardo, E. A., & Thomson, M. H. (2013). *Post-traumatic stress disorder (PTSD) in emergency responders scoping study: Literature review.* Project No. CSSP-2013-CD-1115, PWGSC Contract No. W7711-098155/001/TOR, Defence Research & Development Canada.

Adams, K., & Jennison, V. (2007). What we do not know about police use of Tasers™. *Policing: An International Journal, 30*(3), 447–465. https://doi.org/10.1108/13639510710778831

Agaibi, C. E., & Wilson, J. P. (2005). Trauma, PTSD and resilience: A review of the literature. *Trauma, Violence & Abuse, 6*(3), 195–216. https://doi.org/10.1177/1524838005277438

Alsabrook, C. L., Aryani, G. A., & Garrett, T. D. (2001). The five principles of organizational excellence in police management. *Law and Order, 49*(6), 109–114.

Amadeo, V., & Iannone, S. (2007). Successful public-private partnerships: The NYPD shield model. *Journal of Business Continuity & Emergency Planning, Dec, 10*(2), 106–117.

Amyot, S., McDonald, J., & Allen, J. (2006). Current measures of police mental training. In J. M. McDonald, *Gold medal policing: Mental readiness and performance excellence* (pp. 230–238). Sloan Associate Press.

Andersen, J. (2007). *The use of resilience programming to improve health and prevent PTSD and OSI among first responders.* University of Toronto, Doctoral dissertation.

Andersen, J. P., & Gustafsberg, H. (2016). A training method to improve police use of force decision making: A randomized controlled trial. *SAGE Open, 6*(2), 215824401663870. https://doi.org/10.1177/2158244016638708

Andersen, J., Papazoglou, K., Arnetz, B., & Collins, P. (2015). Mental preparedness as a pathway to police resilience and optimal functioning in the line of duty. *International Journal of Emergency Mental Health and Humience, 17*(3), 624–627.

Andrew, M., Violanti, J. M., Gu, J. K., Fekedulegn, D., & Li, S. (2017). Police work stressors and cardiac vagal control. *American Journal of Human Biology, 29*(5). https://doi.org/10.1002/ajhb.22996

AQR International. (2017). *Mental toughness questionnaire: A user guide.* Rossett.

Ariel, B., Farrar, W. A., & Sutherland, A. (2014). The effect of police body-worn cameras on use of force and citizens' complaints against the police: A randomized controlled trial. *Journal of Quantitative Criminology, 31*(3), 509–535. https://doi.org/10.1007/s10940-014-9236-3

Armenta, A. (2016). Between public service and social control: Policing dilemmas in the era of immigration enforcement. *Social Problems, 63*(1), 111–126. https://doi.org/10.1093/socpro/spv024

Arnetz, B., Nevedal, D. C., Lumley, M. A., Backman, L., & Lublin, A. (2009). Trauma resilience training for police: Psycho physiological and performance effects. *Journal of Police and Criminal Psychology, 24,* 1–9. https://doi.org/10.1007/s11896-008-9030-y

Arrigo, B., & Claussen, N. (2003). Police corruption and psychological testing: A strategy for preemployment screening. *International Journal of Offender Therapy and Comparative Criminology, 47*(3), 272–290. https://doi.org/10.1177/0306624X03047003003

Bailey*, S. (2019). Road to mental readiness programme. *2015 Medical International Forum. Feb.* Canadian Forces Health Services.

S. Bailey*, Smith, S. and Williams, K., "Strive to thrive: Resiliency training for all levels of healthcare," in 6th *Canadian Conference of Physician Health (CCPH)*, St. John's Newfoundland, October, 2019

Baker, D. (2008). Paradoxes of policing and protest. *Journal of Policing, Intelligence and Counter Terrorism*, *3*(2), 8–22. https://doi.org/10.1080/18335300.2008.9686911

Baltzell, A. (2016). Mindfulness and performance. In I. E. Ivtzan (Ed.), *Mindfulness in positive psychology, Mar 17* (Vols. pp. 64–79). Routledge.

Banas, J., & Bessarabova, E. (2023). Debunking and preventing conspiracies. In Miller, M. K. (Ed.), *The social science of QAnon: A new social and political phenomenon*, 252.

Barath*, I. (2017, January 11). Police officer wellness training: The road to mental readiness. *FBI Law Enforcement Bulletin*, pp. 1–9.

Basu, N. (2021). Learning lessons from countering terrorism: The UK experience 2017–2020. *Cambridge Journal of Evidence-Based Policing*, *5*, 134–145.

Bennett, M., & Chan, J. (2018). Algorithmic prediction in policing: Assumptions, evaluation, and accountability. *Policing and Society*, *28*(7), 806–822. https://doi.org/10.1080/10439463.2016.1253695

Berking, M., Meier, C., & Wupperman, P. (2010). Enhancing emotion-regulation skills in police officers: Results of a pilot-controlled study. *Behavior Therapy*, *41*(3), 329–339. https://doi.org/10.1016/j.beth.2009.08.001

Beshears, M., Beshears, M. L., & Bond, M. (2019). Improving police social media use practices. *International Journal of Social Science Studies*, *Sep., 7*(5). http://ijsss.redflame.com

Bettschart, M., Herrmann, M., Wolf, B. M., & Brandstätter, V. (n.d.). The seed of goal-related doubts: A longitudinal investigation of the roles of failure and expectation of success among police trainee applicants. *Frontiers in Psychology*, *10*, 2151. https://doi.org/10.3389/fpsyg.2019.02151

Bewley, L. W. (2005). *Seasons of leadership development: An analysis of a multi-dimensional model of mentoring among career groups of United States army officers*. University of Alabama at Birmingham, School of Health-Related Professions. ProQuest Dissertations Publishing.

Bichler, G., & Gaines, L. (2005). An examination of police officers' insights into problem identification and problem solving. *Crime and Delinquency*, *51*(1), 53–74. https://doi.org/10.1177/0011128704265936

Bishop, G. D., Tong, E. M., Diong, S. M., Enkelmann, H. C., Why, Y. P., Khader, M., & Ang, J. C. (2001). The relationship between coping and personality among police officers in Singapore. *Journal of Research in Personality, 35*(3), 353–374. https://doi.org/10.1006/jrpe.2001.2319

Blackhall, V., Walker, K. G., Whiteley, I., & Wilson, P. (2019). Use of head camera-cued recall and debrief to externalise expertise: A systematic review of literature from multiple fields of practice. *BMJ Simulation & Technology Enhanced Learning, 5*(3), 121–129. https://doi.org/10.1136/bmjstel-2018-000341

Blackler*, K., Fikretoglu D, Liu A. (2018). Feasibility findings from a pilot Group Randomized Control Trial on the Road to Mental Readiness (R2MR) program. Defence Research and Development Canada.

Blais, A. R., Thompson, M., & McCreary, D. R. (2009). The development and validation of the army post-deployment reintegration scale. *Military Psychology, 21*(3), 365–386. https://doi.org/10.1080/08995600902914727

Bondar, R., Bertollo, M., di Fronso, S., & Robazza, C. (2021). Mindfulness to performance enhancement: A systematic review of neural correlates. *Oct,* 1–29. https://doi.org/10.1080/1750984X.2021.1949742

Bordua, D. J., & Tifft, L. L. (1971). Citizen interviews, organizational feedback, and police-community relations decisions. *Law & Society Review, 6*(2), 155–182. https://doi.org/10.2307/3052850

Borschmann, R. D., Gillard, S., Turner, K., Chambers, M., & O'Brien, A. (2010). Section 136 of the Mental Health Act: A new literature review. *Medicine, Science and the Law, 50*(1), 34–39. https://doi.org/10.1258/msl.2009.009004

Box, G., & Draper, N. (2013). Essentially, all models are wrong, but some are useful. *Statistician, 3*(28), 1919.

Bratton, W. J., & Malinowski, S. W. (2008). Police performance management in practice: Taking COMPSTAT to the next level. *Policing: A Journal of Policy and Practice, 2*(3), 259–265. https://doi.org/10.1093/police/pan036

Breevaart, K., Bakker, A. B., & Demerouti, E. (2015). Leader-member exchange, work engagement, and job performance. *Journal of*

Managerial Psychology, 30(7), 754–770. https://doi.org/10.1108/JMP-03-2013-0088

Bresler, S., Scalora, M., Elbogen, E., & Moore, Y. (2003). Attempted suicide by cop: A case study of traumatic brain injury and the insanity defense. *Journal of Forensic Sciences, 48*(1), 1–5. https://doi.org/10.1520/JFS2001045

British College of Policing. (2022, February 12). *Integrity and transparency*. Retrieved from https://www.college.police.uk/What-we-do/Ethics/integrity-and-transparency/Pages/Integrity-and-Transparency.aspx

Brough, P. (2004). Comparing the influence of traumatic and organizational stressors on the psychological health of police, fire, and ambulance officers. *International Journal of Stress Management, 11*(3), 227–244. https://doi.org/10.1037/1072-5245.11.3.22

Brown, B. (2011). *The power of vulnerability* (http://TED.com). Retrieved from TED Talk: https://www.youtube.com/watch?v=iCvmsMzlF7o

Brown, G. P., & Hoffman, R. (2000). The redesign of Advanced Patrol Training for police constables in Ontario: Making use of evaluation to maximize organizational effectiveness and efficiency. *Canadian Journal of Program Evaluation, 5*(1), 83–100.

Brunetto, Y., Teo, S., Shacklock, K., & Farr-Wharton, R. (2012). Emotional intelligence, job satisfaction, well-being and engagement: Explaining organizational commitment and turnover intentions in policing. *Human Resource Management Journal, 22*(4), 428–444.

Bullock, K., & Tilley, N. (2009). Evidence-based policing and crime reduction. *Policing: A Journal of Policy and Practice, 3*(4), 381–387. https://doi.org/10.1093/police/pap032

Buluc, R., Stoian-Iordache, V., & Mato, C. (n.d.). 3.2 debunking, fact-checking, pre-bunking. Project: DOMINOES Digital cOMpetences INformatiOn EcoSystem ID: 2021-1-RO01-KA220-HED-000031158. 160. https://wordpress.projectdominoes.eu/wp-content/uploads/2023/07/DOMINOES-Handbook.final_.pdf#page=160

Burbidge, S. (2005). The governance deficit: Reflections on the future of public and private policing in Canada. *Canadian Journal of*

Criminology and Criminal Justice, 47(1), 63–86. https://doi.org/10.3138/cjccj.47.1.63

Burke, K. (2020). Democratic policing and officer well-being. *Frontiers in Psychology, 11*, 523876.

Bury, P. (2017). Barossa night: Cohesion in the British Army officer corps. *The British Journal of Sociology, 68*(2), 314–335. https://doi.org/10.1111/1468-4446.12236

Callaghan, T. C. (2017). *Mandating wellness programs for police officers*. Masters of Arts in Criminal Justice Thesis, University of the Fraser Valley.

Campeau, H., Levi, R., & Foglesong, T. (2021). Policing, recognition, and the bind of legal cynicism. *Social Problems, 68*(3), 658–674.

Canadian Association of Mental Health* (CAMH). (2018). *Police mental health*. A discussion paper, Oct, CAMH.

Cao, L. (2011). Visible minorities and confidence in the police. *Canadian Journal of Criminology and Criminal Justice, 53*(1), 1–26. https://doi.org/10.3138/cjccj.53.1.1

Carleton, R. N., Afifi, T. O., Turner, S., Taillieu, T., & Vaughan, A. (2020). Mental health training, attitudes toward support and screening positive for mental disorders. *Cognitive Behaviour Therapy, 49*(1), 55–73. https://doi.org/10.1080/16506073.2019.1575900

Carleton, R. N., Korol, S., Mason, J. E., Hozempa, K., & Anderson, G. (2018a). A longitudinal assessment of the road to mental readiness training among municipal police. *Cognitive Behaviour Therapy, 47*(6), 508–528. https://doi.org/10.1080/16506073.2018.1475504

Carlier, I. V., Lamberts, R. D., & Gersons, B. P. (1997). Risk factors for posttraumatic stress symptomatology in police officers: A prospective analysis. *The Journal of Nervous and Mental Disease, 185*(8), 498–506. https://doi.org/10.1097/00005053-1997080

Carrique, T. (2005). *Recruiting with vision: Cultivating a police service that reflects the community*. Masters thesis, Royal Roads University. ProQuest Dissertations Publishing.

Chan, D., Webb, D., Ryan, R. M., Tang, T., Yang, S. X., Ntoumanis, N., & Hagger, M. S. (2017). Preventing occupational injury among police officers: does motivation matter? *Occupational Medicine (Oxford, England), 67*(6), 435–441. https://doi.org/10.1093/occmed/kqx076

Chaney, C., & Robertson, R. V. (2013). Racism and police brutality in America. *Journal of African American Studies (New Brunswick, N.J.), 17*(4), 480–505. https://doi.org/10.1007/s12111-013-9246-5

Charles, L. L. (2007). Disarming people with words: Strategies of interactional communication that crisis (hostage) negotiators share with systemic clinicians. *Journal of Marital and Family Therapy, 33*(1), 51–68. https://doi.org/10.1111/j.1752-0606.2007.00006

Charles, S. (2009). *Professional integrity, modern racism, self-esteem, and universality-diversity orientation of police officers in a large urban police agency*. Education of Fordham University. ProQuest Dissertations Publishing.

Charman, S. (2017). *Police socialisation, identity and culture becoming blue*. Palgrave Macmillan.

Charman, S. (2020). Making sense of policing identities: The 'Deserving' and the 'Undeserving' in policing accounts of victimisation. *Policing & Society, 30*(1), 81–97. https://doi.org/10.1080/10439463.2019.1601721

Chidgey, K., Procter, N., Baker, A., & Grech, C. (2019). Police response to individuals displaying suicidal or self-harming behaviours: An integrative review. *Health & Social Care in the Community, 27*(3), e112–e124. https://doi.org/10.1111/hsc.12668

Clough, P., Earle, K., & Sewell, D. (2002). Mental toughness: The concept and its measurement. In I. Cockerill (Ed.), *Solutions in sport psychology* (pp. 32–43). Thomson.

Cohen, I. M., McCormick, A. V., & Rich, B. (2019). Creating a culture of police officer wellness. *Policing: A Journal of Policy and Practice, 13*(2), 213–229. https://doi.org/10.1093/police/paz001

Cohen, L., Dahlen, G., Escobar, A., Fejerskov, O., & Johnson, N. (2017). Why a radical overhaul of dentistry is needed. *Indian Journal of Dental Research, 28*, 471–474.

Conroy, R. J. (2017). *Beyond emotional intelligence: A correlational study of multifactor measures of performance and law enforcement leadership styles*. Dallas Baptist University. ProQuest Dissertations Publishing.

Cordner, G., & Cordner, A. (2011). Stuck on a plateau?: Obstacles to recruitment, selection, and retention of women police. *Police Quarterly, 14*(3), 207–226. https://doi.org/10.1177/1098611111413990

Corrigan, P. W. (2012). Research and the elimination of the stigma of mental illness. *British Journal of Psychiatry, 201*(1), 7–8. https://doi.org/10.1192/bjp.bp.111.103382

Corrigan, P. W., & Fong, M. W. (2014, February). Competing perspectives on erasing the stigma of illness: What says the dodo bird? *Social Science & Medicine, 103*, 110–117. https://doi.org/10.1016/j.socscimed.2013.05.027

Creamer, M., & Forbes, D. (2004). Treatment of posttraumatic stress disorder in military and veteran populations. *Psychotherapy (Chicago, Ill.), 41*(4), 388–398. https://doi.org/10.1037/0033-3204.41.4.388

Creswell, J. (2017). Mindfulness interventions. *Annual Review of Psychology, 68*, 491–516.

Crifasi, C., Pollack, K., & Webster, D. (2016). Effects of state-level policy changes on homicide and nonfatal shootings of law enforcement officers. *Injury Prevention, 22*(4), 274–278. https://doi.org/10.1136/injuryprev-2015-041825

Crust, L., & Clough, P. (2011). Developing mental toughness: From research to practice. *Journal of Sport Psychology in Action, 2*(1), 21–32. https://doi.org/10.1080/21520704.2011.563436

Cuttler, M. J., & Muchinsky, P. M. (2006). Prediction of law enforcement training performance and dysfunctional job performance with general mental ability, personality, and life history variables. *Criminal Justice and Behavior, 33*(1), 3–25.

Dalgaty, F., Guthrie, G., Walker, H., & Stirling, K. (2016). The value of mentorship in medical education. *The Clinical Teacher, 14*(2), 124–128. https://doi.org/10.1111/tct.12510

Dario, L., Fradella, H. F., Verhagen, M., & Parry, M. M. (2020). Assessing LGBT people's perceptions of police legitimacy. *Journal of Homosexuality, 67*(7), 885–915. https://doi.org/10.1080/00918369.2018.1560127

De Similien, R., & Okorafor, A. (2017). Suicide by cop: A psychiatric phenomenon. *American Journal of Psychiatry, 12*(1), 20–22. https://doi.org/10.1176/appi.ajp-rj.2017.120107

DeRosia, M. P. (2012). *Ethics training and practice within the Central Valley Police Department.* Walden University. ProQuest Dissertations Publishing.

Detrick, P., Chibnall, J. T., & Luebbert, M. C. (2004). The revised NEO personality inventory as a predictor of police academy performance. *Criminal Justice and Behavior, 31*, 676–694. https://doi.org/10.1177/0093854804268751

Di Nota, P., & Huhta, J. (2019). Complex motor learning and police training: Applied, cognitive, and clinical perspectives. *Frontiers in Psychology, 10*, 1797–1797. https://doi.org/10.3389/fpsyg.2019.01797

Dias, A. F., & Hilgers T. (2020). Community oriented policing theory and practice: global policy diffusion or local appropriation?. *Policing and Society*, 5, 1-9.

Dick, P. (2000). The social construction of the meaning of acute stressors: A qualitative study of the personal accounts of police officers using a stress counselling service. *Work & Stress, 14*(3), 226–244. https://doi.org/10.1080/02678370010026422

Dick, P. (2004). Between a rock and a hard place: The dilemmas of managing part-time working in the police service. *Personnel Review, 33*(3), 302–321. https://doi.org/10.1108/00483480410528841

Dick, P. (2005). Dirty work designations: How police officers account for their use of coercive force. *Human Relations, 58*(11), 1363–1390. https://doi.org/10.1177/0018726705060242

Dick, P. (2018). Police partnership working: Lessons from a co-located group pilot. *European Journal of Policing Studies*, 5. ISSN 2034-760X.

Mendoza J.,, "Olympic medals today: What is the medal count at 2024 Paris Games on Monday?", *USA Today*, August 5, 2024, https://www.usatoday.com/story/sports/olympics/2024/08/05/olympic-medals-today-medal-count-paris-games-aug-5/74668390007/

Dissmore, P. O. (2009). *Ethics for the military officer: Teaching ethics at the maneuver support center for engineer officers.* Assemblies of God Theological Seminary. ProQuest Dissertations Publishing.

Dobson, K. S., Szeto, A., & Knaak, S. (2019). The working mind: A meta-analysis of a workplace mental health and stigma reduction program. *Canadian Journal of Psychiatry, 64*(1_suppl), 39S–47S. https://doi.org/10.1177/0706743719842559

Dobson, K. S., Szeto, A., Knaak, S., Krupa, T., Kirsh, B., Luong, D., . . . Pietrus, M. (2018). Mental health initiatives in the workplace: Models, methods and results from the Mental Health Commission of

Canada. *World Psychiatry, 17*(3), 370–371. https://doi.org/10.1002/wps.20574
Duckworth, A. (2016). *Grit: The power of passion and perseverance* 234, Scribner, 2016.
Edwards, J. (2012). *Ethical decision-making: A treatise into the role of ethics in 21st century policing.* London Metropolitan University. ProQuest Dissertations Publishing.
Eisner, M., & Cohen, A. (2010). *Working together: Why great partnerships succeed.* Harper Collins.
Engel, R. (2003). Explaining suspects' resistance and disrespect toward police. *Journal of Criminal Justice, 31*(5), 475–492. https://doi.org/10.1016/S0047-2352(03)00052-7
English, B. (2008). "Climate for ethics" and occupational-organisational commitment conflict. *Journal of Management Development, 27*(9), 963–975. https://doi.org/10.1108/02621710810901309
Escamilla, A. A. (2015). *Are you in or out? A study of law enforcement officers' perceived quality of relationship with their leader and its effects on organizational commitment.* Our Lady of the Lake University. Texas: ProQuest Dissertations Publishing.
Estes, M. (2023). *Do better! Be better!*. eBooks2go.
Faggiani, D. (2006). Police talk: A scenario-based communications workbook for police recruits and officers. *Criminal Justice Review (Atlanta, Ga.), 31*(4), 381–382.
Fan, M. (2018). Body cameras, big data, and police accountability. *Law & Social Inquiry, 43*(4), 1236–1256. https://doi.org/10.1111/lsi.12354
Fekedulegn, D., Burchfiel, C. M., Ma, C. C., Andrew, M. E., Hartley, T. A., Charles, L. E., & Violanti, J. M. (2017). Fatigue and on-duty injury among police officers: The BCOPS study. *Journal of Safety Research, 60*, 43–51. https://doi.org/10.1016/j.jsr.2016.11.006
Ferguson, A. (2016). Policing predictive policing. *Washington University Law Review, 94*, 1109.
Fikretoglu, D., Liu, A., Nazarov, A., & Blackler, K. (2019). A group randomized control trial to test the efficacy of the Road to Mental Readiness (R2MR) program among Canadian military recruits. *BMC Psychiatry, 19*(1), 326–326. https://doi.org/10.1186/s12
Fikretoglu*, D., Liu, A., & Blackler, K. (2018b). *Feasibility findings from a pilot group randomized trial on the Road to Mental Readiness (R2MR)*

program. Scientific Report. DRDC- DDC-2018-R 018, Mar, Defence Research and Development Canada.

Fikretoglu*, D., Beatty, E., & Liu, A. (2014). *Comparing different versions of Road to Mental Readiness to determine optimal content testing instruction type, homework, and intelligence effects at two timepoints.* Scientific Report: DRDC-RDDC-2014-R164, Dec, Defense Research and Development Canada.

Fikretoglu*, D., D'Agata, M. T., Sullivan-Kwantes, W., & Richards, K. (2017). *Mental health and mental health service use attitudes among Canadian Armed Forces (CAF) recruits and officer cadets.* Scientific Report: DRDC-RDDC-2017-R027, Feb, Defence Research and Development Canada.

Fikretoglu*, D., Liu, A., & Blackler, K. (2016). *Testing different methods to optimize change in mental health service use attitudes: Findings and recommendations for the Road to Mental Readiness (R2MR) program at Basic Military Qualification.* Scientific Report DRDC-RDDC-2016-R025, Feb, Defence Research and Development Canada.

Fikretoglu*, D., Liu, A., & Blackler, K. (2018). *Testing the efficacy of Road to Mental Readiness (R2MR) mental health education and resilience training program during basic military qualification: A pilot group randomized control trial.* Scientific Report: DRDC-RDDC-2018-R158, Oct, Defence Research and Development Canada.

Fontaine, I. (2020, December 9). Neuroscience in support of resilience: Recommendations for self-care. *University of Ottawa Employee Webinar.* University of Ottawa Employee Webinar, Ottawa, Canada.

Ford, J. K. (2007). Building capability throughout a change effort: Leading the transformation of a police agency to community policing. *American Journal of Community Psychology, 39*(3–4), 321–334. https://doi.org/10.1007/s10464-007-9115-2

Forero, C. G., Gallardo-Pujol, D., Maydeu-Olivares, A., & Andrés-Pueyo, A. (2009). A longitudinal model for predicting performance of police officers using personality and behavioural data. *Criminal Justice and Behavior, 36*(6), 591–606. https://doi.org/10.1177/0093854809333406

Frank Klahm IV, C., Frank, J., & Liederbach, J. (2024). Understanding police use of force: Rethinking the link between conceptualization and measurement. *Policing: An International Journal of Police Strategies & Management, 37*(3), 558–578.

Gaither, R. B. (2017). *Ethical leadership and its impact on role modeling, strictness, openness, and job satisfaction of law enforcement officers.* Keiser University. ProQuest Dissertations Publishing.

Garbarino, S., Guglielmi, O., Puntoni, M., Bragazzi, N. L., & Magnavita, N. (2019). Sleep quality among police officers: Implications and insights from a systematic review and meta-analysis of the literature. *International Journal of Environmental Research*, 885. https://doi.org/10.3390/ijerph16050885

General Healthcare Resources, I. (2020, November 1). *PTA physical demand summary.* Retrieved from https://www.ghresources.com/wp-content/uploads/2014/06/Physical-Demands-Summary-PTA.doc

Giannasi, P. (2014). Policing and hate crime. In *The Routledge international handbook on hate crime* (pp. 331–342). Routledge. https://doi.org/10.4324/9780203578988

Gilberto, A. (2017). *An exploration of recovery from post-traumatic stress disorder in Canadian armed forces veterans: A qualitative inquiry using interpretive phenomenological analysis.* Doctoral dissertation, Brandon University, Faculty of Health Studies.

Gill, C., Weisburd, D., Telep, C., Vitter, Z., & Bennett, T. (2014). Community-oriented policing to reduce crime, disorder and fear and increase satisfaction and legitimacy among citizens: A systematic review. *Journal of Experimental Criminology, 10*(4), 399–428. https://doi.org/10.1007/s11292-014-9210-y

Gist, J. T., Ferdik, F., & Smith, H. P. (2023). A qualitative inquiry into the sources of resilience found among maximum security correctional officers. *Criminal Justice Policy Review, 34*(3), 291–315.

Giwa, S. (2018). Community policing in racialized communities: A potential role for police social work. *Journal of Human Behavior in the Social Environment, 28*(6), 710–730. https://doi.org/10.1080/10911359.2018.1456998

Goldsmith, M. (2016). The circle of engagement. *Leader to Leader, 81*, 31–35. https://doi.org/10.1002/ltl.20242

Goldsmith, M., & Reiter, M. (2015). *Triggers: Becoming the person you want to be.* Crown Business.

Gottfredson, D., Crosse, S., Tang, Z., Bauer, E., Harmon, M., Hagen, C., & Greene, A. (2020). Effects of school resource officers on school crime and responses to school crime. *Criminology & Public Policy, 19*(3), 905–940. https://doi.org/10.1111/1745-9133.12512

Graham, A. (2021). *Take back your weekends.* Elevate Press.

Granek*, J. A., Jarmasz, J., Boland, H., Guest, K., & Bailey, L. S. (2017). Mobile applications for personalized mental health resiliency training. *Inter-service/Industry Training, Simulation, and Education Conference (I/ITSEC), 16120,* DRDC-RDDC-2.

Graves, O. A. (2016). *Phenomenological study exploring mentoring received by Black Army officers to improve promotions.* University of Phoenix. ProQuest Dissertations Publishing.

Green, B. (2004). Post-traumatic stress disorder in UK police officers. *Current Medical Research and Opinion, 20*(1), 101–105. https://doi.org/10.1185/030079903125002748

Groff, E., Haberman, C., & Wood, J. D. (2020). The effects of body-worn cameras on police-citizen encounters and police activity: Evaluation of a pilot implementation in Philadelphia, PA. *Journal of Experimental Criminology, 16,* 463–480. https://doi.org/10.1007/s11292-019-09383-0

Grossmith*, L., Owens, C., Finn, W., Mann, D., Davies, T., & Baika, L. (2015). *Police, camera, evidence: London's cluster randomised controlled trial of Body Worn Video.* College of Policing and the Mayor's Office for Policing and Crime (MOPAC), London.

Guajardo, S. (2015). Women in policing: A longitudinal assessment of female officers in supervisory positions in the New York City police department. *Women & Criminal Justice, 26*(1), 20–36. https://doi.org/10.1080/08974454.2014.997418

Guajardo, S. A. (2015). Measuring diversity in police agencies. *Justice, 13*(1), 1–15. https://doi.org/10.1080/15377938.2014.893220

Guest*, K., Bailey, S., Khan, S., & Thompson, S. (2019). Performance and resilience coaching for military leadership. *S&T Organization-MP-HFM-302,* (15), 1–14.

Gutshall, C., Hampton, D. P., Sebetan, I. M., Stein, P. C., & Broxtermann, T. J. (2017). The effects of occupational stress on cognitive performance in police officers. *Police Practice & Research, 18*(5), 463–477. https://doi.org/10.1080/15614263.2017.1288120

Gutshall, C., Hampton, D., Sebetan, I. M., Stein, P., & Broxterma, T. J. (2017). The effects of occupational stress on cognitive performance in police officers. *Police Practice and Research, 18*, 463–477. https://doi.org/10.1080/15614263.2017.1288120

Haarr, R. N. (2005). Factors affecting the decision of police recruits to "Drop Out" of police work. *Police Quarterly, 8*(4), 431–453. https://doi.org/10.1177/1098611103261821

Halicioglu, M. B. (2010). *Examination of the relationship between self-directedness and outcomes of the online COP training program in the Turkish National Police context*. Michigan State University. ProQuest Dissertations Publishing.

Harvey*, M. S. (2019, February 23). *Mental health care in the CAF: Beyond R2MR*. Retrieved from WordPress: https://soleildotpress.wordpress.com/2019/02/23/continuum-model-of-mental-health-care-in-the-caf-the-road-2-mental-readiness-program/

Hassell, K. D., & Archbold, C. A. (2010). Widening the scope on complaints of police misconduct. *Policing: An International Journal of Police Strategies and Management, 33*(3), 473–489. https://doi.org/10.1108/13639511011066863

Hays, K. F. (2009). *Performance psychology in action: A casebook for working with athletes, performing artists, business leaders, and professionals in high-risk occupations* (Vols. ISBN: 978-1-4338-0443-4). American Psychological Association.

Helsby, J., Carton, S., Joseph, K., Mahmud, A., Park, Y., Navarrete, A., . . . Haynes, I. (2018). Early intervention systems: Predicting adverse interactions between police and the public. *Criminal Justice Policy Review, 29*(2), 180–209. https://doi.org/10.1177/0887403417695380

Hendrix, J. A., Taniguchi, T., Strom, K. J., Aagaard, B., & Johnson, N. (2019). Strategic policing philosophy and the acquisition of technology: Findings from a nationally representative survey of law enforcement. *Policing & Society, 29*(6), 727–743. https://doi.org/10.1080/10439463.2017.1322966

Henry-Noel, N., Bishop, M., Gwede, C., et al. (2019). Mentorship in medicine and other health professions. *Journal of Cancer Education, 34*, 629–637. https://doi.org/10.1007/s13187-018-1360-6

Hillier, R. (2010). *Leadership: 50 points of wisdom for today's leaders*. HarperCollins Canada.

Hillier, R. (n.d.). *Rick Hillier quotes*. (AZ Quotes). Retrieved from https://www.azquotes.com/author/64129-Rick_Hillier

Hinkle, J. C., Weisburd, D., Telep, C. W., & Petersen, K. (2020). Problem-oriented policing for reducing crime and disorder: An updated systematic review and meta-analysis. *Campbell Systematic Review, 16*(2). https://doi.org/10.1002/cl2.1089

Hohl, K., Bradford, B., & Stanko, E. A. (2010, May). Influencing trust and confidence in the London metropolitan police: Results from an experiment testing the effect of leaflet drops on public opinion. *The British Journal of Criminology, 50*(3), 491–513. https://doi.org/10.1093/bjc/azq005

Holmes, A. (2020). Marching with pride? Debates on uniformed police participating in Vancouver's LGBTQ pride parade. *Journal of Homosexuality, 7502386*(id5), 1–33. https://doi.org/10.1080/00918369.2019.1696107

Hurrell, J. J., Nelson, D. L., & Simmons, B. L. (1998). Measuring job stressors and strains: Where we have been, where we are, and where we need to go. *Journal of Occupational Health Psychology, 3*(4), 368–389. https://doi.org/10.1037//1076-8998.3.4.36

Jackson, J., Huq, A., Bradford, B., & Tyler, T. (2013). Monopolizing force? Police legitimacy and public attitudes toward the acceptability of violence. *Psychology, Public Policy, and Law, 19*(4), 479–497. https://doi.org/10.1037/a0033852

Jacoby, S. F., Kollar, L. L. M., Ridgeway, G., & Sumner, S. A. (2018). Health system and law enforcement synergies for injury surveillance, control and prevention: A scoping review. *Injury Prevention, 24*(4), 305–311. https://doi.org/10.1136/injuryprev-2017-042416

Jain, A., Deb, D., & Engelsma, J. (2021). Biometrics: Trust, but verify. *IEEE Transactions on Biometrics, Behavior, and Identity Science, 4*(3), 303–323.

Jain, H., Singh, P., & Agocs, C. (2000). Recruitment, selection and promotion of visible-minority and aboriginal police officers in selected Canadian police services. *Canadian Public Administration, 43*(1), 46–74. https://doi.org/10.1111/j.1754-7121.2000.tb015

Jain, S. P., & Agocs, C. (2000). Recruitment, selection and promotion of visible-minority and aboriginal police officers in selected

Canadian police services. *Canadian Public Administration, 43*(1), 46–74. https://doi.org/10.1111/j.1754-7121.2000.tb01560.x

Jefferis, E., Butcher, F., & Hanely, D. (2011). Measuring perceptions of police use of force. *Police Practice and Research, 12*(1), 81–96. https://doi.org/10.1080/15614263.2010.497656

Johnsen, B., Espevik, R., Saus, E., Sanden, S., Olsen, O., & Hystad S. W. (2017). Hardiness as a moderator and motivation for operational duties as mediator: The relation between operational self-efficacy, performance satisfaction, and perceived strain in a simulated police training scenario. *Journal of Police and Criminal Psychology, 32*, 331-9.

Kaufmann, M., Egbert, S., & Leese, M. (2019). Predictive policing and the politics of patterns. *The British Journal of Criminology, May, 59*(3), 674–692. https://doi.org/10.1093/bjc/azy060

Khorasheh, T., Naraine, R., Watson, T. W., Wright, A., Kallio, N., & Strike, C. (2019). A scoping review of harm reduction training for police officers [published correction appears in Drug Alcohol Rev. 2019 May;38(4):454–459]. *Drug and Alcohol Review, 38*(2), 131–150.

Kim, W. C., & Mauborgne, R. (2003). Tipping point leadership. *Harvard Business Review, 81*(4), 60–122.

King, S. (2011). "Ready to shoot and do shoot": Black working-class self-defense and community politics in Harlem, New York, during the 1920s. *Journal of Urban History, 37*(5), 757–774. https://doi.org/10.1177/0096144211413234

Kinley, J. (n.d.). *The 8 steps to resilience.* (Atlantic Institute for Resilience Inc.). Retrieved from www.Air-Institutes.com: https://pans.ns.ca/sites/default/files/8steps_to_resilience.pdf

Klahm, F., Frank, J., & Liederbach, J. (2024). Understanding police use of force: Rethinking the link between conceptualization and measurement. *Policing: An International Journal of Police Strategies & Management, 37*(3), 558–578.

Knaak, S., Luong, D., McLean, R., Szeto, A., & Dobson, K. S. (2019). Implementation, uptake, and culture change: Results of a key informant study of a workplace mental health training program in police organizations in Canada. *Canadian Journal of Psychiatry, 64*(1_suppl), 30S–38S. https://doi.org/10.1177/0706743719842565

Knights Jr, S. (2021). *Ethical decision-making framework in police officers' use of the force continuum*. Doctoral dissertation, Capella University, 1-179.

Knights, E., & Barath, I. (2017, November 16). These experienced officers are the gateway between the OPC Basic Constable Training (BCT) program and operational policing. *Blueline: Canada's Law Enforcement Magazine*.

Koper, C. S., Lum, C., & Hibdon, J. (2015). The uses and impacts of mobile computing technology in hot spots policing. *Evaluation Review, 39*(6), 587–624. https://doi.org/10.1177/0193841X16634482

Kowalski, C. (2018). *Strengthening the capabilities to lead police officers following exposure to trauma*. Royal Roads University. ProQuest Dissertations Publishing.

Krakauer, R. L., Stelnicki, A. M., & Carleton, R. N. (2020). Examining mental health knowledge, stigma, and service use intentions among public safety personnel. *Frontiers in Psychology, 11*, 949–949. https://doi.org/10.3389/fpsyg.2020.00949

Krewski, D., Westphal, M., Andersen, M. E., Paoli, G. M., Chiu, W. A., & Al-Zoughool, M. (2014). A framework for the next generation of risk science. *Environmental Health Perspectives, 122*, 796–805. http://dx.doi.org/10.1289/ehp.1307260

Kristina, M. (2009). Public satisfaction with police: The importance of procedural justice and police performance in police-citizen encounters. *Australian & New Zealand Journal of Criminology, 42*(2), 159–178. https://doi.org/10.1375/acri.42.2.159

Kwasniewski, J., McDonald, J., & Allen, J. (2006). Police training standard directed at improving performance excellence. In J. M. McDonald, *Gold medal policing: Mental readiness and performance excellence*, (pp. 209–215). Sloan Associate Press.

Larsen, L. B., Andersson, E. E., Tranberg, R., & Ramstrand, N. (2018). Multi-site musculoskeletal pain in Swedish police: Associations with discomfort from wearing mandatory equipment and prolonged sitting. *International Archives of Occupational and Environmental Health, 91*(4), 425–433. https://doi.org/10.1007/s00420-018-1292-9

Lasiewicki, P. A. (2007). *Achieving congruence between individual commitment to policing and organizational objectives in police departments.* University of Phoenix. ProQuest Dissertations Publishing.

Lechner, D. (2020, November 1). *Job demands analysis: Defining the physical demands of the work for post-offer and return-to-work functional testing.* Retrieved from https://aeasseincludes.assp.org/proceedings/2007/docs/750.pdf

Lee, J., Choi, H., Kim, J., Nam, J., Kang, H., Koh, S., & Oh, S. (2016). Self-resilience as a protective factor against development of post-traumatic stress disorder symptoms in police officers. *Annals of Occupational and Environmental Medicine, 28,* 1–7. https://link.springer.com/article/10.1186

Lepine, J., Podsakoff, N., & Lepine, M. (2005). A meta-analytic test of the challenge stressor-hindrance stressor framework: An explanation for inconsistent relationships among stressors and performance. *Academy of Management Journal, 48*(5), 764–775. https://doi.org/10.5465/AMJ.2005.18803921

Lewis, L. (2011). *Organizational change: Creating change through strategic communication* (Vol. 2). John Wiley & Sons, Incorporated.

Lewis, L. K., & Seibold, D. R. (1998). Reconceptualizing organizational change implementation as a communication problem: A review of literature and research agenda. *Annals of the International Communication Association, 21*(1), 93–152. https://doi.org/10.1080/23808985.1998.11678949

Lockey, S., Graham, L., Zheng, Y., Hesketh, I., Plater, M., & Gracey, S. (2021). The impact of workplace stressors on exhaustion and work engagement in policing. *The Police Journal: Theory, Practice and Principles, 32258,* 1–17. https://doi.org/10.1177/0032258X211016532

Losel, F., King, S., Bender, D., & Jugl, I. (2018). Protective factors against extremism and violent radicalization: A systematic review of research. *International Journal of Developmental Science, 12*(1–2), 89–102. https://doi.10.3233/DEV-170241

Lowmaster, S., & Morey, L. (2012). Predicting law enforcement officer job performance with the Personality Assessment Inventory. *Journal of Personality Assessment, 94*(3), 254–261. https://doi.org/10.1080/00223891.2011.648295

Lu, Y., Yang, K., & Thomas, M. B. (2021). Designing performance systems in anticipation of unintended consequences: Experiences and

lessons from the compstat-based performance regime in NYPD. *Administration & Society, 53*(6), 907–936. https://doi.org/10.1177/0095399720976532
Lumsden, K., & Goode, J. (2018). Policing research and the rise of the 'evidence-base': Police officer and staff understandings of research, its implementation and 'what works'. *Sociology, 52*(4), 813–829. https://doi.org/10.1177/0038038516664684
Lunney*, R. (2015, January 28). Performance ritual for street policing. *Blue Line Magazine*, p. 17.
Lyons, K., Radburn, C., Orr, R., & Pope, R. (2017). A profile of injuries sustained by law enforcement officers: A critical review. *International Journal of Environmental Research and Public Health, 14*(2), 142–162. https://doi.org/10.3390/ijerph14020142
MacClurg, M. (2020, June 3). Back to basics with Butch Harmon. *Golf Digest*. https://www.golfdigest.com/story/back-to-basics-with-butch-harmon
Maguen, S., Metzler, T. J., McCaslin, S. E., & Inslicht, S. S. (2009). Routine work environment stress and PTSD symptoms in police officers. *The Journal of Nervous and Mental Disease, 197*(10), 754–760. https://doi.org/10.1097/NMD.0b013e3181b975f8
Manning, P. (2003). *Policing contingencies*. University of Chicago Press.
Marins, E., David, G., & Del Vecchio, F. (2019). Characterization of the physical fitness of police officers: A systematic review. *Journal of Strength and Conditioning Research, 33*(10), 2860–2874. https://doi.org/10.1519/JSC.0000000000003177
Markos, K. M. (2017). *A conduit from public trust to legitimacy: Continuous ethics training in law enforcement*. University of La Verne. ProQuest Dissertations Publishing.
Martin, G. (2021). Protest, policing and law during COVID-19: On the legality of mass gatherings in a health crisis. *Alternative Law Journal, 46*(4), 275–281.
Martin, M., Marchand, A., Boyer, R., & Martin, N. (2009). Predictors of the development of posttraumatic stress disorder among police officers. *Journal of Trauma Dissociation, 10*(4), 451–468. https://doi.org/10.1080/15299730903143626
Martin, R. (2011). Police corruption: An analytical look into police ethics. *FBI Law Enforcement Bulletin, 80, p*. 11.

Mason, G., Maher, J., McCulloch, J., Pickering, S., Wickes, R., & McKay, C. (2017). *Policing hate crime: Understanding communities and prejudice*. Routledge.

Massinger, C., & Wood, N. (2016). Improving law enforcement cross cultural competencies through continued education. *Journal of Education and Learning, 5*(2), 258–264. http://dx.doi.org/10.5539/jel.v5n2p258

Mastison, F. (2015, February 16). On target: 20 police Marksman facts. *Tactical Life*. https://www.tactical-life.com/lifestyle/tactics/target-20-police-marksman-facts/

Mazerolle, L., Antrobus, E., Bennett, S., & Tyler, T. (2013). Shaping citizen perceptions of police legitimacy: A randomized field trial of procedural justice. *Criminology, 51*(1), 33–63. https://doi.org/10.1111/j.1745-9125.2012.00289.x

McAnally, K. M. (2017). Metacognitive monitoring and control in visual change detection: Implications for situation awareness and cognitive control. *PloS One, 12*(9), e0176032–e0176032. https://doi.org/10.1371/journal.pone.0176032

McCarthy, B., Hagan, J., & Herda, D. (2020). Neighborhood climates of legal cynicism and complaints about abuse of police power. *Criminology, 58*(3), 510–536. https://doi.org/10.1111/1745-9125.12246

McCreary, D. R., & Thompson, M. M. (2006). Development of two reliable and valid measures of stressors in policing: The operational and organizational police stress questionnaires. *International Journal of Stress Management, 13*(4), 494–518. https://doi.org/10.1037/1072-5245.13.4.494

McCreary, D., Fong, I., & Groll, D. L. (2017). Measuring policing stress meaningfully: Establishing norms and cut-off values for the Operational and Organizational Police Stress Questionnaires. *Police Practice and Research, 18*(6), 612–623. https://doi.org/10.1080/15614263.2017.1363965

McDonald, J. (1993). *Mental readiness training for air traffic control trainees: Course manual*. Transport Canada.

McDonald, J. (2021, May–August). Mental readiness: Focusing on the cutting edge. *Archives of Pediatric Neurosurgery, 3*(2), 95. https://doi.org/10.46900/apn.v3i2(May-August)

McDonald, J. (2022). Mental readiness for frontline workers in homelessness services in Ottawa, Canada. *International Journal on Homelessness, 2*(1), 80–104.

McDonald, J. M. (2006). *Gold medal policing: Mental readiness and performance excellence*, Sloan Associate Press.

McDonald, J., & Gyorkos, T. (2016). Operational Readiness for conducting global health research abroad. *Canadian Journal of Public Health, 107*(4–5), 387–389. https://doi.org/10.17269/cjph.107.5555

McDonald, J., & Hale, K. (2022). Mental readiness for frontline workers in homelessness services in Ottawa, Canada. *International Journal on Homelessness, 2*(1), 80–104.

McDonald, J., & Hoffman, R. (2008). *Gold medal policing overview to coach officers (ppt)*. Regularly presented at the Ontario Police College, 2008-2016.

McDonald, J., & Orlick, T. (1994). Excellence in surgery: Psychological considerations. *Performance Enhancement, 2*, 13–32. http://www.zoneofexcellence.ca/free/surgery.html

McDonald, J., & Paganelli, C. (2021). Exploration of mental readiness for enhancing dentistry in an inter-professional climate. *International Journal of Environmental Research and Public Health, 18*(13), 7038–7055. https://doi.org/10.3390/ijerph18137038

McDonald, J., Dahal, G. P., Tyshenko, M. G., Sloan, D. A. and Sharma, S. K., "Operational readiness: Links to Sherpas' peak performance in tourist mountain-guiding," In A. P. Adhikari, G. P. Dahal, I. Mahat, B. Regmi, K. Subedi, & S. Shrestha (Eds.), *Sustainable* livelihood systems *in Nepal: Principles,* practices *and* prospects. Kathmandu: International Union for Conservation of Nature, Nepal Country Office (IUCN Nepal), 2016, 281–308

McDonald, J., Hale, K., & Kirkwood, T. (2024). Excellence in Homelessness Service: Evidence-Based Frontline Practices, *International Journal on Homelessness, 4(3),* 1–19.

McDonald, J., Orlick, T., & Letts, M. (1995). Mental readiness in surgeons and its links to performance excellence in surgery. *Journal of Pediatric Orthopaedics, 15*(5), 691–697. https://doi.org/10.1097/01241398-199509000-00027

McLean, K., Alikhan, A., & Alpert, G. (2023). Re-examining the use of force continuum: Why resistance is not the only driver of use of force decisions. *Police Quarterly, 26*(1), 85–110.

Meehl, P. (1989). Law and the fireside inductions (with postscript): Some reflections of a clinical psychologist. *Behavioral Sciences & the Law, 7*(4), 521–550. https://doi.org/10.1002/bsl.2370070408

Ménard, J.-F. (2021). *Train (your brain) like an Olympian: Gold Medal Techniques to unleash your potential at work.* ECW Press.

Mental Health Commission of Canada* (MHCC). (2016, April 1). *Summary of Road To Mental Readiness (R2MR) evaluation results* (H. Canada, Producer). Retrieved from https://theworkingmind.ca/sites/default/files/r2mr_evaluation_results_summary_april_1_2016_en.pdf

Misis, M. L. (2012). *An examination of perceied stress levels and coping styles among rural law enforcement officers.* Doctoral dissertation, May, University of Southern Mississippi.

Miyamoto, I. (2021). Disinformation: Policy responses to building citizen resiliency. *Connections: The Quarterly Journal, 20*(2), 47–55. https://doi.org/10.11610/Connections.20.2.05

Moad, C. (2011). *Critical incidents: Responding to police officer trauma.* Criminal Justice Institute, Fayetteville Police Department, Fayetteville, Arkansas.

Mohler, G., Short, M., Brantingham, P., Schoenberg, F., & Tita, G. (2011). Self-exciting point process modeling of crime. *Journal of the American Statistical Association, 106*(493), 100–108.

Morabito, M. S. (2007). Horizons of context: Understanding the police decision to arrest people with mental illness. *Psychiatric Services (Washington, D.C.), 58*(12), 1582–1587. https://doi.org/10.1176/ps.2007.58.12.1582

Morrow, S. (2019). Social and news media's effects on law enforcement. *Global Journal of Forensic Science & Medicine, 1*(4), GJFSM.MS.ID.000516. https://doi.org/10.33552/AJGH.2019.01.000516

Moule Jr, R., Burruss, G., Gifford, F., Parry, M., & Fox, B. (2019). Legal socialization and subcultural norms: Examining linkages between perceptions of procedural justice, legal cynicism, and the code of the street. *Journal of Criminal, 61*, 26–39. https://doi.org/10.1016/j.jcrimjus.2019.03.001

Mount, G. R. (2007). Mental practice: Police performance in hostage negotiation. *Journal of Police Crisis Negotiations, 7*(2), 41–143. https://doi.org/10.1300/J173v07n02_11

Muennig, P., & Murphy, M. (2011). Does racism affect health? Evidence from the United States and the United Kingdom. *Journal of Health Politics, Policy and Law, 36*(1), 187–214. https://doi.org/10.1215/03616878-1191153

Nagengast. (2021). *Countering digital terrorism: A qualitative study on information sharing to deny digital radicalization and recruiting.* Doctoral Thesis, Colorado Technical University, Feb. ProQuest Dissertations Publishing.

National Law Enforcement Memorial Fund. (2014). National Law Enforcement Memorial Fund causes of law enforcement deaths. http://www.nleomf.org/facts/officer-fatalities-data/causes.html. The Washington Daybook. Federal Information & News Dispatch, LLC.

National Law Enforcement Officers Memorial Fund*, Causes of law enforcement deaths: Over the past decade (2014-2023), National Law Enforcement Officers Memorial Fund, 2024, https://nleomf.org/memorial/facts-figures/officer-fatality-data/causes-of-law-enforcement-deaths/

NAV Canada. (1998). *Situational awareness module: Participants manual.* NAV (Navigation) Canada.

Nelson, C., McDonald, J., Kyle, N., & Galipeau, J. (2006). Evaluation of police excellence. In J. McDonald (Ed.), *Gold medal policing*, pp. 201–209, Sloan Associate Press.

Norris, R. L. (2018). *Training for community policing: Constructing effective police education (Order No. 10846444).* Doctoral Dissertation. Saint Mary's College of California. ProQuest Dissertations & Theses Global (2124408064).

O'Neill, M., & McCarthy, D. (2014). (Re) negotiating police culture through partnership working: Trust, compromise and the 'new 'pragmatism. *Criminology & Criminal Justice, 14*(2), 143–159.

Occupational Health Clinics for Ontario Workers Inc. (2020, November 1). *Physical Demands Analysis (PDA).* Retrieved from https://www.ohcow.on.ca/edit/files/general_handouts/PhysicalDemandsAnalysis.pdf

Ontario Police College. (2009). *Police trainee field training manual*. Queen's Printer.

Orlick, T. (1986). *Psyching for sport: Mental training for athletes*. Human Kinetics.

Orlick, T. (1992). The psychology of personal excellence. *Contemporary Thought on Performance Enhancement, 1*, 110–122.

Orlick, T. (2003, October 25). *Wheel of excellence*. Retrieved from Zone of Excellence: http://www.zoneofexcellence.ca

Orlick, T., & Partington, J. (1988). Mental links to excellence. *The Sport Psychologist, 2*, 105–130.

Orr, M., & West, D. M. (2007). Citizen evaluations of local police: Personal experience or symbolic attitudes? *Administration & Society, 38*(6), 649–668. https://doi.org/10.1177/0095399706293989

Osterberg, E. C. (2020). *"We can't arrest our way out of this" police responses to gang violence in British Columbia's Lower Mainland*. Doctoral dissertation, University of British Columbia.

Owen, C. (2014). *Human-factors challenges in emergency management: Enhancing individual and team performance in fire and emergency services*. Ashgate Publishing, Ltd.

Page, J. W., Asken, M. J., Zwemer, C. F., & Guido, M. (2016). Brief mental skills training improves memory and performance in high stress police cadet training. *Journal of Police and Criminal Psychology, 31*(2), 122–126. https://doi.org/10.1007/s11896-015-9171-8

Pallas, E. (2016). *The relationship between emotional intelligence, transformational leadership style, and effectiveness among police supervisors*. Wilmington University (Delaware).

Palmiotto, M. (2017). *Police use of force: Important issues facing the police and the communities they serve*. CRC Press, Taylor & Francis Group.

Paterson, A. (2021). *Trauma and resilience in contemporary Australian policing: Is PTS inevitable for first responders?* Springer Nature.

Paton, D., & Violanti, J. M. (2006). Policing in the context of terrorism: Managing traumatic stress risk. *Traumatology (Tallahassee, Fla.), 12*(3), 236–247. https://doi.org/10.1177/1534765606294990

Patton, C., Asken, M., & Fremouw, W. J. (2017). The influence of police profanity on public perception of excessive force. *Journal of Police and Criminal Psychology, 32*, 340–357. https://doi.org/10.1007/s11896-017-9226-0

Peace, R. (2006). Probationer training for neighbourhood policing in England and Wales: Fit for purpose? *Policing: An International Journal of Police Strategies and Management, 29*(2), 335–346.

Peak, K., Bradshaw, R. V., & Glensor, R. W. (1992). Improving citizen perceptions of the police: "Back to the basics" with a community policing strategy. *Journal of Criminal Justice, 20*(1), 25–40. https://doi.org/10.1016/0047-2352(92)90032-5

Perea, S. D. (2019, March). Marijuana, law enforcement, mental health: A dangerous social experiment. https://www.policechiefmagazine.org/marijuana-law-enforcement-mental-health/?ref=6a709f431039dddb4f1512a2a1f010d8

Perry, J. L., Clough, P. J., Crust, L., Earle, K., & Nicholls, A. (2013). Factorial validity of the Mental Toughness Questionnaire-48. *Personality and Individual Differences, 54*(5), 587–592. https://doi.org/10.1016/j.paid.2012.11.020

Phelps, J. M., Strype, J., Le Bellu, S., Lahlou, S., & Aandal, J. (2018). Experiential learning and simulation-based training in Norwegian police education: Examining body-worn video as a tool to encourage reflection. *Policing: A Journal of Policy & Practice, 2*(1), 50–65. https://doi.org/10.1093/police/paw014

Phillips, N., & Cromwell, A. (2020). Building bridges in police-youth relations through experiential peacebuilding: How reduced threat and increased humanization impact racialized structural and direct violence in Baltimore. *Journal of Peace Education, 17*(3), 324–345. https://doi.org/10.1080/17400201.2020.1782181

Phinney, B. (2016). *Pathways to positive mental health: A comparison of previously deployed Canadian armed forces regular and reserve force members*. Masters of Arts in Psychology, Carleton University.

Picano, J. J., Roland, R. R., & Williams, T. J. (2022). Assessment and selection of high-risk operational personnel. *Military Psychology: Clinical and Operational Applications*, 326–343. https://books.google.ca/books?hl=en&lr=&id=3LtzEAAAQBAJ&oi=fnd&pg=PA326&ots=8wCTxIy4Tu&sig=nXzekuuaIHIrDGWTbP0V6fONc50&redir_esc=y#v=onepage&q&f=false

Pickering, S., McCulloch, J., & Wright-Neville, D. (2008). *Counter-terrorism policing*. Springer.

Pindek, S., & Spector, P. E. (2016). Organizational constraints: A meta-analysis of a major stressor. *Work & Stress, 30,* 7–25. https://doi.org/10.1080/02678373.2015.1137.

Piza, E. L., Caplan, J. M., Kennedy, L. W., & Gilchrist, A. (2015). The effects of merging proactive CCTV monitoring with directed police patrol: A randomized controlled trial. *Journal of Experimental Criminology, 11*(1), 43–69. https://doi.org/10.1007/s11292-014-9211-x

Plat, M., Frings-Dresen, M., & Sluiter, J. (2011). A systematic review of job-specific workers' health surveillance activities for fire-fighting, ambulance, police and military personnel. *International Archives of Occupational and Environmental Health, 84*(8), 839–857. https://doi.org/10.1007/s00420-011-0614-y

Podsakoff, N. P., LePine, J. A., & LePine, M. A. (2007). Differential challenge stressor-hindrance stressor relationships with job attitudes, turnover intentions, turnover, and withdrawal behavior: A meta-analysis. *Journal of Applied Psychology, 92*(2), 438–454. https://doi.org/10.1037/0021-9010.92.2.438

Poole, D. S. (2012). *A qualitative analysis of the effectiveness of professional ethics training standards in law enforcement.* Walden University. ProQuest Dissertations Publishing.

Preddy, J. (2018). *Building a cognitive readiness construct for violent police-public encounters.* Old Dominion University, Occupational/Tech Studies. Doctoral dissertation, Old Dominion University.

Prenzler, T., Porter, L., & Alpert, G. (2013). Reducing police use of force: Case studies and prospects. *Aggression and Violent Behavior, 18*(2), 343–356. https://doi.org/10.1016/j.avb.2012.12.004

Quinlan, T., & Derfoufi, Z. (2015). Counter-terrorism policing. In *Stop and search: The anatomy of a police power,* pp. 123–145. Palgrave Macmillan UK.

Raaijmakers, S. (2019). Artificial intelligence for law enforcement: Challenges and opportunities. *IEEE Security & Privacy, 17*(5), 7477.

Reid, K. (2019). *Medical narratives of military PTSD: Moving beyond the biomedical approach.* Masters of Arts in Psychology, Carleton University.

Renden, P. G., Savelsbergh, G. J. P., & Oudejans, R. D. (2015). Effects of reflex-based self-defence training on police performance in simulated high-pressure arrest situations. *Ergonomics, 60*(5), 669–679. https://doi.org/10.1080/00140139.2016.1205222

Reynolds, J., Mariani, M., & Goodman, D. (2001). *Police talk: A scenario-based communications workbook for police recruits and officers* (1st ed.). Pearson.

Risk Science International. (2022, January 25). *RSI*. Retrieved from https://risksciences.com/

Roach, J. (1982). Managing "key events" can be the fastest route to success. *Management Review, 71*(Apr), 56.

Roberts, R., Tarescavage, A., Ben-Porath, Y., & Roberts, M. (2019). Predicting post-probationary job performance of police officers using CPI and MMPI-2-RF test data obtained during pre-employment psychological screening. *Journal of Personality Assessment, 101*(5), 544–555. https://doi.org/10.1080/00223891.2018.1423990

Robinson, R. (2014). Purposive sampling. In A. Michalos (Ed.), *Encyclopedia of quality of life and well-being research*. Springer. https://doi.org/10.1007/978-94-007-0753-5_2337

Rogers, M., McNiel, D., & Binder, R. (2019). Effectiveness of police crisis intervention training programs. *The Journal of the American Academy of Psychiatry and the Law, 47*(4), 414–421. https://doi.org/10.29158/JAAPL.003863-19.

Rojek, J., Grieco, J., Meade, B., & Parsons, D. (2020). *National survey on officer safety training: Findings and implications*. National Police Foundation.

Roland*, R. R., & Bartone, P. T. (2015). Resilience research and training in the US and Canadian armed forces. *American Psychological Association Convention, Aug. 7*. Society for Military Psychology.

Rowe, M., & Ross, J. I. (2015, March). Comparing the recruitment of ethnic and racial minorities in police departments in England and Wales with the USA. *Policing: A Journal of Policy and Practice, 9*(1), 26–35. https://doi.org/10.1093/police/pau060

Sabat, S., & Mishra, S. (2010). Role of women in the management of police organisation: A paradigm shift. *International Journal of Learning and Change, 4*(4), 367–374.

Sandberg, S. (2015). Lean in-women, work and the will to lead. *NHRD Network Journal, 8*(2), 137–139. https://doi.org/10.1177/0974173920150225

Sanders, C., & Condon, C. (2017). Crime analysis and cognitive effects: the practice of policing through flows of data. *Global Crime, 18*(3), 237–255. https://doi.org/10.1080/17440572.2017.1323637

Sarkar, M. (2014, September). Psychological resilience in sport performers: A review of stressors and protective factors. *Journal of Sports Sciences, 32*(15), 1419–1434. https://doi.org/10.1080/02640414.2014.901551

Schomerus, G., Angermeyer, M., Baumeister, S., Stolzenburg, S., Link, B., & Phelan, J. (2015). An online intervention using information on the mental health-mental illness continuum to reduce stigma. *European Psychiatry, 32*, 21–27. https://doi.org/10.1016/j.eurpsy.2015.11.006

Sellbom, M., Corey, D. M., & Ben-Porath, Y. S. (2021). Examining the validity of the multidimensional personality questionnaire in the assessment of police candidates. *Assessment (Odessa, Fla.), 28*(1), 295–309. https://doi.org/10.1177/1073191119887443

Serier, J. G. (2011). *COP confidential: Police supervision and sub-culture.* Dissertations Publishing.

Sherman, L. (2013). The rise of evidence-based policing: Targeting, testing and tracking. In M. Tonry (Ed.), *Crime and justice* (Vols. 42, pp. 377–431). University of Chicago Press.

Sherman, L., & Murray, A. (2015). Evidence-based policing: From academics to professionals. *International Criminal Justice Review, 25*(1), 7–10. https://doi.org/10.1177/1057567715576174

Simons, D. J., & Schlosser, M. D. (2017). Inattentional blindness for a gun during a simulated police vehicle stop. *Cognitive Research: Principles and Implications, 2*(37), 1–8. https://doi.org/10.1186/s41235-017-0074-3

Sindall, K., Sturgis, P., & Jennings, W. (2012, July). Public confidence in the police: A time-series analysis. *The British Journal of Criminology, 52*(4), 744–764. https://doi.org/10.1093/bjc/azs010

Smart, S. M., Berry, M. A., & Rodriguez, D. N. (2014). Skilled observation and change blindness: A comparison of law enforcement and student samples. *Applied Cognitive Psychology, 28*(4), 590–596. https://doi.org/10.1002/acp.3021

Smith, H. A., Wolfe-Clark, A. L., & Bryan, C. J. (2016). An exploratory study of the mental toughness psychological skills profile psychometrics, and the mediating effect of social support sources on mental toughness and suicidal ideation among military police. *Journal of Police and Criminal Psychology, 31*(4), 295–303. https://doi.org/10.1007/s11896-016-9192-y

Söderström, T., Åström, J., Anderson, G., & Bowles, R. (2014). A framework for the design of computer-assisted simulation training for complex police situations. *Campus-Wide Information Systems, 31*(4), 242–253. https://doi.org/10.1108/CWIS-10-2013-0060

Sprafka, H., & Kranda, A. (2000). Best practices for institutionalizing mentoring into police departments. *International Association of Chiefs of Police.*

Stager P., Hameluck, D., & Jubis, R. (1989). Underlying factors in air traffic control incidents. In *Proceedings of the Human Factors Society Annual Meeting*, 33(2), 43-46. https://doi.org/10.1177/154193128903300209

Statistics Canada*. (2004). *Canadian community health survey: Mental health and well-being.* Public use microdata file, Statistics Canada, Health Statistics Division.

Steffens, N., Fonseca, M., Ryan, M., Rink, F., Stoker, J., & Pieterse, A. (2018). How feedback about leadership potential impacts ambition, organizational commitment, and performance. *The Leadership Quarterly, 29*(6), 637–647.

Stein, S., & Book, H. E. (2011). *The EQ edge: Emotional intelligence and your success* (3rd ed.). John Wiley & Sons Canada.

Stelnicki, A. M., Jamshidi, L., Fletcher, A. J., & Carleton, R. N. (2021). Evaluation of before operational stress: A program to support mental health and proactive psychological protection in public safety personnel. In L. E. van Zyl & S. Rothmann (Eds.), Positive organizational interventions: contemporary theories, approaches and applications. *Frontiers in psychology, 11, p. 511755.*

Stewart, M. L. (2011). *Subjects of prevention: Risk, threat, and anticipation in Canadian policing.* University of California, Davis. ProQuest Dissertations Publishing.

Szeto, A., Dobson, K. S., & Knaak, S. (2019). *The road to mental readiness for first responders: A meta-analysis of program outcomes* (Vol. 64). Canadian Journal of Psychiatry/Revue Canadienne de Psychiatrie.

Szeto, A., Dobson, K. S., Luong, D., Krupa, T., & Kirsh, B. (2019b). Workplace antistigma programs at the mental health Commission of Canada:

Part 1. processes and projects. *Canadian Journal of Psychiatry, 64*(1_suppl), 5S–12S. https://doi.org/10.1177/07067

Szeto, A., Dobson, K. S., Luong, D., Krupa, T., & Kirsh, B. (2019c). Workplace antistigma programs at the mental health commission of Canada: Part 2 lessons learned. *Canadian Journal of Psychiatry, 64*(1_suppl), 13S–17S. https://doi.org/10.1177/0706743719

Tam-Seto, L., Wood, V. M., Linden, B., & Stuart, H. (2018). A scoping review of mental health mobile apps for use by the military community. *mHealth, 4*, 57–57. https://doi.org/10.21037/mhealth.2018.12.01

Tarescavage, A. M., Brewster, J., Corey, D., & Ben-Porath, Y. S. (2015). Use of pre-hire Minnesota Multiphasic Personality Inventory-2-Restructured Form (MMPI-2-RF) police candidate scores to predict supervisor ratings of post-hire performance. *Assessment, 22*(4), 411–428. https://doi.org/10.1177/107319111454844

Tay, Y. (2020, November 26). Can't solve 21st century problems with 20th century ways of thinking: PwC Network's Blair Sheppard. *People Matters*.

Tengpongsthorn, W. (2017). Factors affecting the effectiveness of police performance in Metropolitan Police Bureau. *Kasetsart Journal of Social Sciences, 38*(1), 39–44. https://doi.org/10.1016/j.kjss.2016.07.001

Terrell, S. (2020). *Executive coaches who use Eq-i 2.0 in leadership development: A qualitative study*. Capella University. ProQuest Dissertations Publishing.

The Academy*. (2022). *Perishable skills program: South Bay regional public safety training*. (Plus ROI Online Marketing). Retrieved from https://theacademy.ca.gov/event/perishable-skills-program-7/

Tiesman, H., Heick, R., Konda, S., & Hendricks, S. (2015). Law enforcement officers' risk perceptions toward on-duty motor-vehicle events. *Policing, 38*(3), 563–577. https://doi.org/10.1108/PIJPSM-03-2015-0028

Tiesman, H., Hendricks, S., Bell, J., & Amandus, H. (2010). Eleven years of occupational mortality in law enforcement: The census of fatal occupational injuries, 1992–2002. *American Journal of Industrial Medicine, 53*(9), 940–949. https://doi.org/10.1002/ajim.20863

Tomes, C., Orr, R., & Pope, R. (2017). The impact of body armor on physical performance of law enforcement personnel: A systematic review. *Annals of Occupational and Environmental Medicine, 29*(1), 14–14. https://doi.org/10.1186/s40557-017-0169-9

Tongco MDC. 2007. Purposive sampling as a tool for informant selection. Ethnobotany Research & Applications, University of Hawaii at Manoa, 5:147-158. http://hdl.handle.net/10125/22.

Torres, C., & Kim, Y. (2019). The effects of caffeine on marksmanship accuracy and reaction time: A systematic review. *Ergonomics, 62*(8), 1023–1032. https://doi.org/10.1080/00140139.2019.1613572

Trounson*, J., & Pfeifer, J. (2017). *Corrections officer wellbeing: Training challenges and opportunities.* Department of Corrections.

Truxillo, D. M., Bennett, S. R., & Collins, M. L. (1998). College education and police job performance: A ten-year study. *Public Personnel Management, 27*(2), 269–280. https://doi.org/10.1177/009102609802700211

Tyshenko, M. G., McDonald, J., Kirkwood, T., & Ali-Ndi Ringnyu, C. (2025). Technical competencies in policing. In J. M. McDonald, *Gold Medal Policing: Operational Readiness and Performance Excellence*, 2nd ed. (pp. 526–536). Routledge.

Tyshenko, M. G., McDonald, J., Niyati Vyas, N., & Kirkwood, T. (2025). Physical competencies in policing. In J. M. McDonald, *Gold Medal Policing: Operational Readiness and Performance Excellence*, 2nd ed. (pp. 515–525). Routledge.

U.S. Bureau of Labor Statistics. (2020, November 1). *Occupational requirements survey: Visual overview for physical demands.*

Vallières, B., Hodgetts, H. M., Vachon, F., & Tremblay, S. (2016). Supporting dynamic change detection: Using the right tool for the task. *Cognitive Research: Principles and Implications, 1*(1), 1–20. https://doi.org/10.1186/s41235-016-0033-4

Van Ewijk, A. (2012). Diversity within police forces in Europe: A case for the comprehensive view. *Policing: A Journal of Policy and Practice, March, 6*(1), 76–92. https://doi.org/10.1093/police/par048

Vatin, D. (2020, November 4). *79 core competencies for your resume, resumegenius.* Retrieved from https://resumegenius.com/blog/resume-help/core-competencies-resume

Vermetten, E., Granek, J., Boland, H., Berge, E. T., Binsch, O., Carmi, L., . . . Jetly, R. (2020). Leveraging technology to improve military mental health: Novel uses of smartphone apps. *Journal of Military, Veteran and Family Health, 6*(S1), 36–43. https://doi.org/10.3138/jmvfh.2019-0034

Violanti, J. M., Charles, L. E., McCanlies, E., Hartley, T. A., Baughman, P., Andrew, M. E., . . . Ma, C. (2017). Police stressors and health: A state-of-the-art review. *Policing (Bradford, England), 40*(4), 642–656. https://doi.org/10.1108/PIJPSM-06-2016-0097

Violanti, J., Paton, D., Johnston, P., Burke, K., Clarke, J., & Keenan, D. (2008). Stress shield: A model of police resiliency. *Emergency Mental Health, 10*(2), 95–108. https://ovc.ojp.gov/sites/g/files/xyckuh226/files/media/document/res_stress_shield_resilience-508.pdf

Virtue, T., & Moir, S. (2022, February 12). *Tessa virtue and Scott Moir commentate RD at Beijing 2022.* (Olympic Broadcasting) Retrieved from https://twitter.com/wheelsofadream/status/1492526971225575425?lang=en

Vyas, N., McDonald, J., Kirkwood T. & Tyshenko, M. G. (2025). Predictors of police performance, In J. M. McDonald *Gold Medal Policing: Operational Readiness and Performance Excellence, 2nd ed.* (pp. 486–496). Routledge.

Vyas, N., McDonald, J., Kirkwood, T., Cheng, C., & Tyshenko, M. G. (2025). Police performance stressors, In J. M. McDonald *Gold Medal Policing: Operational Readiness and Performance Excellence, 2nd ed.* (pp. 497–504). Routledge.

Waggoner, L. B., Grant, D. A., Van Dongen, H., Belenky, G., & Vila, B. (2020). A combined field and laboratory design for assessing the impact of night shift work on police officer operational performance. *Sleep (New York, N.Y.), 43*(9). https://doi.org/10.1093/sleep/zsaa052

Ward, L. P., & Murphy, A. (2019). The impact of Marijuana legalization on law enforcement in states surrounding Colorado. *Police Quarterly, 22*(2), 217–242. https://doi.org/10.1177/1098611118819902

Waters, I., Hardy, N., Delgado, D., & Dahlmann, S. (2007). Ethnic minorities and the challenge of police recruitment. *Police Journal (Chichester), 80*(3), 191–216. https://doi.org/10.1350/pojo.2007.80.3.191

Wehr, K., Alpert, G., & Rojek, J. (2012). The fear of the ninja assassin: Understanding the role of agency culture in injurious and fatal on-duty vehicle collisions. *Journal of California Law Enforcement, 46*(2), 18–26.

White, D. (2006). A conceptual analysis of the hidden curriculum of police training in England and Wales. *Policing & Society, 16*(4), 386–404. https://doi.org/10.1080/10439460600968164

White, M. D., Gaub, J. E., Malm, A., & Padilla, K. E. (2021). Implicate or Exonerate? The impact of police body-worn cameras on the adjudication of drug and alcohol cases. *Policing: A Journal of Policy and Practice, 15*(2), 759–769. https://doi.org/10.1093/police/paz043

White, T. N., & Gaub, J. E. (2018). Examining body-worn camera integration and acceptance among police officers, citizens, and external stakeholders. *Criminology & Public Policy, 17*(3), 649–677. https://doi.org/10.1111/1745-9133.12376

Williams, C., McDonald, J., & Kyle, N. (2006). Challenges in female policing. In J. McDonald (Ed.), *Gold medal policing*, pp. 223–229. Sloan Associate Press.

Wills, J., & Schuldberg, D. (2016, April). Chronic trauma effects on personality traits in police officers. *Journal of Traumatic Stress, 29*(2), 185–189. https://doi.org/10.1002/jts.22089

Wilson, E., McDonald, J., & Allen, J. (2006). Sources of police stress. In J. McDonald (Ed.), *Gold medal policing: Mental readiness and performance excellence* (Vols. 216–222). Sloan Associate Press.

Wood, S. (2017). Police body cameras and professional responsibility: Public records and private evidence. *Preservation, Digital Technology & Culture, 46*(1), 41–51. https://doi.org/10.1515/pdtc-2016-0030

Wortley R. K. (2003, October). Measuring police attitudes toward discretion. *Criminal justice and behavior.* 30(5), 538–58.

Wyatt-Nichol, H., & Franks, G. (2009). Ethics training in law enforcement agencies. *Public Integrity, 12*(1), 39–50. https://doi.org/10.2753/PIN1099-9922120103

Yuksel, Y. (2013). *Understanding the role of culture and communication in implementing planned organizational change: The case of compstat in police organizations.* Dissertation. Rutgers University.

Zamorski, M. A., Rusu, C., Guest, K., & Fikretoglu, D. (2018). Exposure to mental health training and education in Canadian Armed Forces personnel. *Journal of Military, Veteran and Family Health, 4*(2), 91–100. https://doi.org/10.3138/jmvfh.2017-0046

Zimmerman, F. H. (2012). Cardiovascular disease and risk factors in law enforcement personnel: A comprehensive review. *Cardiology in Review, 20*(4), 159–166. https://doi.org/10.1097/CRD.0b013e318248d631

Acknowledgments

My biggest thank you must go to the frontline Patrol Constables, Sergeants, and Coach Officers whose anonymous and confidential interviews and guided questionnaires provided the substance for this investigation. Without their help, this research would have been impossible.

Preparation and testing of the interview process were aided by many officers who—while naturally skeptical and cautious—offered candid advice and extensive opportunities to participate in parade, ride alongs, and training days. My sincere appreciation to these officers of all ranks for the early support and personalized grounding I received during the pilot phases.

The University of Ottawa was a key starting point for this initiative, actively promoting collaborative community partnerships led by Director-Professor Melissa Brouwers in the School of Epidemiology and Public Health in the Faculty of Medicine. A special thanks to Emeritus Professor Daniel Krewski for his ongoing support and resources to explore risk assessments and risk management. A special thanks to former Deans Denise Alcock and Denis Prudhomme who provided initial collaboration. Early inspiration and leadership will be eternally attributed to Dr. Terry Orlick.

Ottawa Police Service (former) Deputy Chief Larry Hill first saw the opportunity in capturing corporate memory for the future of policing, under the direction of Chief Vince Bevan, with early support from (former) Superintendent Gilles Larochelle and (former) Inspector Mike Rice. I am grateful for the continued support from the Executive teams: current Chief Eric Stubbs, Deputy Chief Paul Burnett, and (former) Chiefs Charles Bordeleau and Vernon White. *Gold Medal Policing* core principles were actively embraced by Professional Development Centre leaders, including S/Sgts. Lynne Turnbull and Amy Bond, Sgts. Mike Besner and Grant Cotie, and Sgt. Peter Danyluk, who lead an ethics training initiative. A sincere thank you to Sgt. John Steinbachs and Cst. Kaleigh Knox in supplying frontline photos.

Ontario Police College instructors deserve heartfelt appreciation for integrating *Gold Medal Policing* into their teachings: Chief Instructor Irene Barath, and Instructors Ron Hoffman and Karen Mackenzie, under the leadership of Directors Paul Hebert, Bruce Herridge, and Rudy Gheysen.

Police alliances provided by the Canadian Police Research Centre, Canadian Association of Chiefs of Police, Canadian Police Association, Canadian Police Knowledge Network, Ottawa Police Association, and Justice Institute of British Columbia were immensely beneficial in promoting this research.

Corporation of the City of Ottawa offered early support of an inter-departmental partnership for a broader emergency measures mandate directed by General Managers Dick Stewart and Jocelyne St. Jean, under the direction of Deputy City Manager Steve Kanellakos. Contractual agreements were developed through the efforts of Ginette Champagne, Wendy Dewan, Francine Riopelle, and Aaron Burry.

Our research team was critically important, working exceedingly long hours in transcribing, coding, analyzing, and discussing data. The team included: Hwashin Hyun, Data Management and Analysis Coordinator; Theresa Gyorkos, Planning and Editorial Advisor; Michael G. Tyshenko, Senior Risk Analyst; Kathryn Waddington, Strategic Advisor; Elizabeth Siwicki, Photographer; Janice Neelands, External Logistics; and Sarah Visintini, Research Librarian. Other members who were dedicated to background reviewing, data inputting, and checking included: Mervat Abu-Alhassin, Chewe Ali-Ndi Ringnyu, Chuyai Cheng, Travis Kirkwood, Niyati Vyas, Wendy Wen, and Maria Williams. Anonymous external reviewers, who remain anonymous, provided exceptional feedback to refine the content, interpretations, and resources.

The publishing and editing teams made this research eminently more readable than it otherwise might have been— Routledge: Ellen Boyne, Editor for the Criminal Justice and Criminology List; Kate Taylor, Editorial Assistant; Thomas Sutton, Project Manager; Nigel Turner, Designer; Sarahjayne Smith, Production Editor; Daniel Andrew, Senior Project Manager (Deanta); Copy Editors: Sheila Oakley, Lakshmi Priya, and Nandhini Ravi. John Gagnon, President of Cielo Print Inc., and David Rile, Production Designer, provided quick access to images and files from *Gold Medal Policing, 1st Edition*. Early contributions will be forever remembered from Sloan Associate Press: David Sloan, Editorial-Production Director; Carol Gwinn, Copy Editor; and Anda Bruinsma, Senior Consultant.

Leadership advice was garnered from many executive leaders including: Vince Bevan, Terry Charbot, Karl Erfel, Debra Fraser, Pat Hayes, Larry Hill, Gilles Larocelle, Don Lyons, Marguerite Nadeau, Sue O'Sullivan, Andy Rhodes, Mike Rice, Ted Robinson, Raj Souccar, and Al Tario.

I have benefited from help and advice in multitudinous ways during my three-year(+) obsession: John Butler, Greg Danyklenko, Arlene Gregoire, Katherine Hale, John Lanktree, Mike Lebreton, Deirdre McDonald, Josette Noreau, Lynn Omholt-Jensen, Corinne Parker, Morina Reece, Greg Thompson, Barry Turner, Pauline Warren, and Ember. A thank you to my biweekly UK Writing Retreat group who encouraged a much needed focus: Julie Davies, Saire Jones, Karen Maher, Jennie Nowlan, and Katherine Waddington.

This investigation is not only the product of current research, colleagues, and partnerships. A personal note of thanks to my parents Hilde Reynolds and Carl McDonald for their constant encouragement throughout my life. Special gratitude to former Staff Sgt. Glenn Reynolds for teaching me the meaning of police integrity. I owe them a great deal.

Appendix A

Evidence-Based Rigor: Study Design

> **SPOILER ALERT**
>
> Collaborative and ethical research is key for reliable, evidence-based outcomes.

Abstract

What's New in 2nd edition: While the first edition was based on elite officers, the 2nd edition added new data from "excellent" coach officers recognized for their specialized training, evaluation and leadership skills. This edition fully constructs operational readiness, updates mental readiness and integrates physical and technical competencies. Resources are provided for further implementation and refinement in policing and other law enforcement professions. This chapter presents a comprehensive study design involving a collaborative partnership between the University of Ottawa, Ottawa Police Service, Ontario Police College, Routledge Publishing, and the principal investigator. The study conducted research on "operational readiness" and "high-performance" within policing, exploring over 10,000 journals from 2000 to 2022. Six dominant themes focusing on performance excellence and "physical, technical, and mental readiness" in policing were identified. A descriptive analysis of subjects, instruments, procedures, statistical testing, and investigative framework is provided. Key terms are defined for clarity and consistency, and influential factors are categorized.

Appendix A presents a comprehensive study design that includes an empirical Operational Readiness Framework, an extensive literature review, and ethical practices. It illustrates the rigor and evidence-based approach employed in this collaborative research effort.

This chapter discusses the study design structure in seven sections:

A. Collaborative partnerships
B. Study background
C. Study overview
D. Descriptive analysis
E. Operational definitions
F. Influential factors
G. Investigative framework

A. Collaborative partnerships

Business research in police partnerships has challenged conventional approaches[1]. It asks: "Why do some partnerships succeed and others not in producing both fruitful multi-agency collaboration and meaningful results for those targeted (in this case frontline officers)?" In policing, research suggests that partnerships that focused on a bottom-up approach to problem-solving value, reinforce, and enhance pragmatism[2]. We believe this six-tiered alliance is a success story worth acknowledging. These collaborations ensured evidence-based policing practices for the frontline.

Collaborative necessity

Collaborative contributions were fundamental to the impetus for publishing this second edition of *Gold Medal Policing*. Alliances were made in order to efficiently, ethically, and objectively collect and analyze new data on performance excellence in frontline policing with the same academic rigor and readability as the first edition. In turn, the evidence-based research attracted external opportunities for growth internationally.

Mutual benefits and equitable contributions

The University of Ottawa aims to efficiently conduct applied research and involve its students in teaching enrichments. Opportunities for collaborative research and publications with other institutions are conscientiously pursued. The university setting contributed objectivity, ethical approval, space, graduate student placements, professional resources, financial contributions, confidentiality, and anonymity to the subjects.

These collaborations ensured evidence-based policing practices for the frontline.

The Ottawa Police Service routinely and actively seeks better ways to target training and preparation, and to continue to bridge the management-frontline gap. By capturing and making available to others the effective practices and inner thoughts of some of their best officers, they have created a working tool for improving recruitment, selection, coach-officer training, and future research benchmarks. They provided open access and feedback occasion, and the opportunity to conduct coach officer and specialty training through their Professional Development Centre. Their coach officers were the source for collecting new data—chosen frontline leaders who set the bar for trainees.

The Ontario Police College was one of the first institutions to adopt *Gold Medal Policing, 1st Edition,* for their traditional, blended, and virtual training to a broader group of officers of all ranks including recruits, coaches, experienced officers upgrading, frontline supervisors, human resource personnel, and police instructors.

Routledge Publishing continue their drive to acquire more well-researched and practically useful policing books into their portfolio. A *Gold Medal Policing 2nd Edition* was assessed to be ideal. They accommodated the necessary academic rigor by: supporting multiple peer reviews; extending timelines to allow for further academic review; sharing logo rights with other collaborators; and offering their technical expertise, support, and flexibility in producing this book.

The author, with a proven background in research for high-risk professions and facilitating collaborative partnerships, has examined operational readiness in various fields, from surgery to high-altitude climbing. She developed an empirical approach to assess physical, technical, and mental readiness for peak performance. McDonald directed this research endeavor, resulting in the second edition of *Gold Medal Policing*.

Founding champions

In order to publish this book, a collaborative partnership was developed by high-level champions from each of the founding partnering groups. Recognition is awarded to:

> **University of Ottawa**: Dr. Daniel Krewski, Emeritus Professor under the direction of Dr. Melissa Brouwers, Director of the School of Epidemiology and Public Health in the Faculty of Medicine.
>
> **Ottawa Police Service**: Chief Eric Stubbs and Deputy Chief Paul Burnett, preceded by (Former) Deputy Chief Larry Hill under the direction of (Former) Chiefs Vince Bevan, Charles Bordeleau, and Vern Whyte.
>
> **Ontario Police College**: (Former) Chief Instructor Irene Barath, and (former) Instructors Ron Hoffman and Karen Mackenzie were instrumental in implementing Gold Medal Policing in their courses under the (former) direction of Bruce Herridge and Rudy Gheysen.
>
> **Routledge Publishing**: Ellen Boyne, Editor for the Criminal Justice and Criminology List; Kate Taylor, Editorial Assistant; Thomas Sutton, Project Manager; Sarahjayne Smith, Production Editor; and Daniel Andrew, Senior Project Manager (Deanta).
>
> **Principal Investigator and Author**: Judy McDonald, Associate Director with the McLaughlin Centre for Population Health Risk Assessment, and Adjunct Professor with the School of Epidemiology and Public

Health in the Faculty of Medicine at the University of Ottawa.

Other important project contributors

The active involvement of graduate students, research assistants, and subject experts contributed to acquiring an in-depth understanding of the current background research for this second edition. They were: Mervat Abu-Alhassin, Chewe Ali-Ndi Ringnyu, Chuyai Cheng, Travis Kirkwood, Michael G. Tyshenko, Niyati Vyas, and Maria Williams. See Appendices B–G for a condensed version[3,4,5,6,7,8] of their literature review papers.

Here are sample testimonials of their experiences.

Mervat Abu-Alhassin: *As an international pharmacist with a Master's in Epidemiology and Population Health Risk Assessment, I contributed to Police Mental Competencies and Road to Mental Readiness literature reviews. Our team developed an advanced coding system, assessing preparedness along a continuum. This experience broadened my perspective on population health and risk assessment, emphasizing the impact of frontline mental readiness on officer and public safety.*

Chuyao Cheng: *For students like me pursuing a career in public-health policy, learning the analytical techniques in this book is paramount. We must systematically deconstruct and analyze real-world situations, always remembering people are at the heart of what we do. I also sharpened my software skills by designing and revising graphs and tables. The author's meticulous attitude showed me the book's thorough research. It greatly benefited me, and I'm sure it will benefit you too.*

Niyati Vyas: *As a Clinical Research Associate with a Master's in Public Health and a graduate of Population Health Risk Assessment and Management, my venture into policing offered insights into officers' lives. Though not meeting them, I learned secondary searches, paper coding, and data review. This* *academic experience, guided by Judy, marks my first published contribution.*

Maria Williams: *I have a dentistry background and am pursuing a Master's in Public Health. In Gold Medal Policing, I acquired skills in Word Referencing, vital for my clinical research. Proficient in paraphrasing, I bring empathy from dentistry, grasping the mental demands of daily frontline challenges. This experience deepened my respect for policing's impact on officers' lives.*

B. Study background

This edition builds upon the foundation of *Gold Medal Policing*'s first edition to create comprehensive research on "operational readiness" and "high performance" within policing.

Gold-medal athletes: In the arena of measurable sports, rigorous mental-preparation techniques have been shown statistically to be the pivotal determinant of excellence at the elite level. Although numerous subsequent studies have been conducted[9,10,11,12,13,14], Orlick and Partington's unprecedented study[15] encompassed the entire 1984 Canadian Olympic team, presenting an exhaustive analysis of mental readiness. Their research uncovered common factors shared by top Olympians, before, during, and after peak performances. Statistical analysis of three readiness variables—physical, technical, and mental—underscored that mental readiness ($r = 0.40$, $p<.0001$) stood as the most significant predictor of final Olympic success. Noteworthy impediments to optimal Olympic performance included altering previously effective pre-performance routines, dealing with last-minute selections or changes, and being overcome by distractions. The repository of strategies distilled from adept athletes has profoundly impacted both Olympians and those with less experience, in clearly defining connections between mental readiness and consistent, remarkable performance.

Coach officer insights: Over the course of 14 years, from 2007 to 2020, I had the privilege of engaging with coach officers throughout Ontario, Canada. This involvement included instructing for Coach Officer Training across the province, collaborating and seeking input from a Coach Officer Advisory Group, and utilizing targeted group questionnaires to assess changes over the past two decades.

I also collaborated on a comprehensive training needs-analysis with the Ontario Police College and Ontario police services.

PHOTO APP A.1 AND A.2 A Coach Officer Advisory Group helped refine physical and technical performance indicators and gather feedback to ensure relevance. Credit: Judy McDonald

This analysis followed a multi-stage, multi-method strategy designed after the one used for the Advanced Patrol Training[16] to maximize the effectiveness and efficiency of the Coach Officer Program. As a result, changes were made to its design, delivery, and trainee evaluation processes in Ontario[17].

Literature review: Building upon the foundation of *Gold Medal Policing*'s first edition[18], comprehensive research on "operational readiness" and "high performance" within policing involved a review and narrowing down of relevant published articles spanning from 2000 to 2022. (Note: The complete list of the 343 reviewed articles is available in the "Bibliography.")

This thorough investigation spanned five databases, encompassing over 10,000 journals to explore topics centered on police "performance excellence" and "physical, technical, and mental readiness." To delve into the theme of "police mental readiness," a compilation of 106 synonyms across 14 categories was used as a source. A separate independent search was conducted for physical and technical readiness in policing. The multidisciplinary databases (and associated journals) from education, psychology, sociology, and international studies included ERIC, Psych Info, Sociofile, Sport Discuss, and PAIS.

Six dominant themes were revealed after this extensive examination of two decades' worth of articles on performance excellence and "physical, technical, and mental readiness" in policing. Relevant qualitative and quantitative data, including statistics, models, and charts, were extracted from the articles. The articles were carefully coded and organized to extract significant information, leading to comprehensive representation of emerging trends. A summarized overview of each theme is presented in Chapter 2, with condensed versions available in Appendices B–G.

1. Predictors of police performance[3]
2. Stressors impacting police performance
3. Critical analysis of "Road to Mental Readiness" (R2MR) Program[5]
4. Physical competencies in policing[6]
5. Technical competencies in policing
6. Mental competencies in policing

C. Study overview

This overview explains the utilization of coach officers to update mental-readiness results and define physical and technical competencies, ultimately enhancing this study on operational readiness in policing. The data were updated by combining the original data from "excellent frontline" officers with new data from "excellent coach" officers.

Academic aim and rationale
a) *The primary purpose* was to complete analyses on operational readiness in policing in three competencies—physical, technical, and mental readiness—by obtaining

physical and technical competencies from a Coach Officer Advisory Group.
b) *The secondary purpose* was to update the mental readiness from excellent coach officers.
c) *The final purpose* was to develop resources for practical implementations in policing and other law enforcement professions.
d) *Rationale*: To improve the operational readiness (performance) of frontline police officers by developing a model based on "excellent frontline" officers that will help frontline police officers achieve performance excellence by
- enhancing curriculum design and training
- increasing consistency (rather than relying solely on best practices)
- reducing mistakes
- decreasing inefficiencies

Overall changes to the second edition
By order of importance, this edition:

a. utilized the empirical Operational Readiness Framework to investigate performance excellence in policing with respect to three main competencies—physical, technical, and mental readiness (see Chapter 1: Insights from the Field)
b. conducted an extensive literature review of 343 current research on police in physical, technical, and mental readiness (see Chapter 2 and Appendices B–G)
c. provided current data and expertise on the importance of physical-, technical- and mental-readiness and performance stressors for frontline policing (see Chapters 3–7)
d. identified temporal changes in policing practices by comparing them in 2003 and 2019 (see Chapter 3 and 7)
e. updated the quotes shared by excellent officers and coach officers, including several officers' "Top 10" (throughout book and Appendices Q and S)
f. included improved evaluation tools developed from lessons learned in implementing many of the evidence-based

recommendations from the original *Gold Medal Policing* (see Chapters 9 and 10)
g. infused contemporary policing issues to expose varied applications for the Operational Readiness Framework, particularly with respect to preparing for challenging situations (see Chapter 3)
h. modified the book layout and terminology to improve the flow and consistent terminology for competencies, performance indicators, and practices (throughout)
i. expanded who can benefit by providing dedicated chapters and summaries for different readers from those in frontline, management, or academia (see Preface)
j. offered a broader scope based on context and application of an evidence-based framework and practices validated across multiple high-risk professions (see Chapter 1)

D. Descriptive analysis

Information is provided on subjects, instruments, sampling procedure, data collection, and statistical analysis, while also addressing limitations and potential investigator bias.

Subjects

To know what separates the *best* from the *rest*, you need to find the "gold-medal winners." Therefore, this was not a random sample but rather purposeful sampling[19,20] to investigate the preparedness of "excellent" frontline, uniformed officers. While the first edition was based on elite officers, this time "excellent" coach officers participated—policing influencers chosen to train, lead, evaluate, and determine the readiness of new recruits.

Coach officers were chosen from two sources.
- A Provincial Advisory Group was formed from 10 highly recognized coach officers. A Subject-Matter-Expert (SME) working group created benchmarks for physical and technical readiness by categorizing practices and performance indicators (see Chapter 4: Exceptional Officers Speak Out).

- Thirty-three coach officers, actively serving with the Ottawa Police Service, completed a guided questionnaire on the original findings for mental readiness. The original findings for mental readiness (from 48 "exceptional" frontline officers identified by both peers and supervisors) were compared with newly collected data (from 33 currently active coach officers). Irrespective of the population, excellence can be defined similarly with excellent practices that are comparable.

Instruments
The original study aimed to provide practical information for frontline police officers to enhance their mental readiness in facing operational challenges. This component focused on identifying effective mental training practices in policing, addressing two questions:
- How *do* frontline uniformed police officers perform their best in challenging operational situations?
- How *do* they prepare to be ready on demand, manage distracting situations, stay focused, and develop coping strategies?

In the second edition, the mental-readiness results from the first edition were formatted into a questionnaire that was guided by the principal investigator/author. Each of the 33 coach officers were required to answer open-ended questions, and rate (1–5) the significance of mental-readiness results, including challenging operational situations and performance blocks.

Sampling procedure
The sample consisted of "excellent coach" officers, following three stages:

a. *Set-up*: The Professional Development Centre manager for Ottawa Police Service arranged for the investigator to administer in-person, one-time-only questionnaires with two groups of currently active coach officers. The participants were guided through each of the questionnaire sections. The investigator responded to any questions. All questionnaires were submitted directly to the investigator, remaining confidential and anonymous.

b. *Sample:* Session #1 had 19 participants and 19 completed their questionnaires. Session #2 had 14 participants and 14 completed their questionnaires. Out of this original sample size of 33 coach officers, some of the items were not completed by all, which led to a maximum of five missing data. However, we did not attempt to impute the missing data. All 33 questionnaires were prepared for analysis by an independent research assistant and statistician. This resulted in a sample of 31 fully usable data for analyzing for performance blocks, and 28 for mental-readiness performance indicators and practices.

c. *Ethics*: As part of university study practice, this investigative phase was constructed in an ethical manner, adhering to strict standards. An information letter was provided to each participant, consent forms were signed and collected, and participants were free to not answer any questions found to be uncomfortable.

Data collection and statistical analysis

Two datasets from the first and second editions were merged and analyzed statistically as follows:

- The first edition was based on data from 48 "exceptional" frontline officers, identified anonymously and confidentially by both peers and supervisors. The second edition added new data from 33 "excellent" active coach officers. The newly collected data were compared with the original data for similarities and differences between the two datasets. Both datasets, comprising a total sample size of 81, were further analyzed using various statistical methods, including quantitative measures of overall operational readiness and qualitative measures such as percentage, consistency, correlation, influential factors, and classification, to update mental-readiness performance indicators and practices.

- Additionally, the data were proportionately weighted from the two groups and merged for further analysis.
- Finally, as a temporal study, z-scores were used to compare differences in overall operational readiness, mental-readiness practices, and performance blocks over the 17 years.

Limitations and attempts at controlling investigator bias

Many precautions were built into the study procedure to control for investigator bias, including the following:

a. *A sampling bias* of "excellent" officers was intentionally created as not representative of the broader population, to provide known practices for performance excellence.
b. *Demographics* linked to individual questionnaires identified in the first edition were not collected from coach officers. We knew it would be ideal to know age, gender, etc., but this was given up since being anonymous was more important to get reliable answers.
c. *Interviewer bias and effect* were attempted to be controlled, including the following:
    - Subjects were not known well by the investigator, nor was there any conflict of interest with this examined field.
    - All questions were systematically presented in a specific order and segmented for easier completion.
    - The investigator clarified or paraphrased as needed to ensure officers' comprehension.
    - No time limit was imposed, allowing officers to take the necessary time to complete the entire questionnaire.
d. *Analytical objectivity* was endeavored by having data inputted by independent reviewers and *not* by the investigator. A cross-checking procedure was used by the reviewers who independently coded the data from open-ended questions. An external statistician produced the calculations.
e. *Strict university study ethical standards* were adhered to including providing participants with information letters, obtaining signed consent forms, and allowing question

avoidance. All researchers in contact with the data passed a Security Police Clearance.

f. ***Participants self-reporting and recall bias*** were addressed by keeping the recall period within the past few months with questions that prompted detailed memories. Furthermore, as per Orlick and Partington's study (1988, p.108), it was concluded that manipulating the responses of high-level achievers would be extremely difficult, if not impossible, since these performers tend to be self-directed and act according to their own principles.

E. Operational definitions

The definitions below are used to operationally define basic terms used in the initial study on "mental readiness" and this second edition study of "operational readiness" in "frontline policing" and its links to "performance excellence." Key terms such as "challenging situations," "excellent" officers, and "disappointing" performances are defined to ensure clarity and consistency throughout the study.

Challenging situations: The officers interviewed were asked to list examples of high-performance challenging operational conditions in policing, like the challenge facing an athlete at an Olympic competition. A "challenging situation" referred to a call that was looked upon as complicated, stressful, or high risk. Furthermore, the officer would have to have been active in attending the call. These challenging calls are classified under seven circumstances and listed in rank order and described in detail (see Appendix H: Challenging Situations in Frontline Policing).

Coach officer: First Class Constable who is assigned to perform his duties as a training officer. Using adult learning principles, a coach officer's job is to assess and develop the essential skills and performance indicators for a frontline patrol officer. Coach Officer Training is designed to prepare coach officers to assist their trainees to apply the knowledge and skills acquired during basic training to the reality of policing.

Excellent officers *(Frontline definition)*: Over the course of 27 full-shift Ride Alongs plus 13 Training Days, frontline officers (Constables and Sergeants) were asked, "What is an 'excellent officer'?" It was *these* operational definitions that were ultimately used to anonymously and confidentially gather recommendations from frontline officers and Staff Sergeants for the sample group of high performers to be interviewed.

Frontline officers answered that "excellent street cops":

- are mentors, informal leaders, respected
- are high achievers; strive for success, are the best-of-the-best
- are outstanding at something (e.g., shooting, finding stolen cars, doing impaired charges)
- just work as good street cops
- are good diggers, hard workers, enthusiastic, motivated
- take their calls (do them quickly) and find lots of stuff on the side
- have high moral standards, ethics; are fair; are great guys/gals
- are good thinkers: very smart, good planners, good operators, resourceful, good coppers
- take care of paper work: very organized, very capable
- know their stuff, don't screw up, "catch the bad guy"
- have informants: know what's going on in the street
- have the ability not to be complacent
- self-dispatch, take calls in other people's zones
- enjoy coming to work, are safe officers to work with

Protect: "You have to want to find bad guys... It's about going after them and not being afraid to back down."

Good cop, protect—*You have to want to find bad guys, hunt them, stop crime and protect the person who's sleeping at night. It's about going after them and not being afraid to back down. On the policeman's war memorial in Washington, there's* *a saying: "While others fall to the wayside, someone has to stand tall and fight for the weaker."*

—Patrol

Respect: "Have respect for the members. Be a leader, keep your cool, don't blow it—and listen."

Good cop, respect—*Have respect for the members. Be a leader, keep your cool, and don't blow it—and listen. Be able to listen to other people, regardless of their sex or seniority. Have respect and show them how.*

—Traffic Escort

"Elite" officers: These are the best officers from across all specialty units with an "Elite" or exceptional reputation. This was based on the very top scoring by both peers and supervisors—a parallel to medal winners among Olympic athletes. There is a total of 13 identified as "Elite" out of the 48 "excellent officers" in the sample group.

Frontline officers: Six frontline uniformed police specialties were represented: Patrol, Neighborhood Resource Team (NRT, formerly Neighborhood Officer—NHO), School Resource Officer (SRO), Tactical, Canine, and Traffic Escort, based on meetings with Deputy Chiefs Paul Burnett and Larry Hill, Ottawa Police Service.

Frontline policing: Frontline policing refers to uniformed police specialty units performing high-stress work in challenging situations. Understanding the magnitude of responsibility for frontline police officers serves to emphasize the importance of being able to consistently perform at optimal levels in their high-risk workplace.

Frontline police dangers and stresses: Officers must perform in adverse conditions and face multiple demands such as high-level accountability, rotating shifts, and extensive overtime. Judgment, technical expertise, ethics, and stamina are vital. The following quotes illustrate the dangers and stresses inherent in policing:

Danger, ready—*You have to be ready because our line of work can be dangerous at any time. You always have to be physically and mentally ready. If you're not ready, "Go home, buddy."*

—>15 years on

Preparation, risk, courage—*Patrol guys have a more dangerous job than I do. When Tactical gets the call, Patrol's already arrived on the scene and… they didn't know what they were getting into and… they don't have the training and equipment we do. We train and rehearse scenarios before getting into them. They are FRONTLINE policing. I'll say it a 100-times, "Their job is a lot tougher and a lot more dangerous than my job."*

—Tactical

Feelings of being misunderstood and undervalued can be a common concern for frontline staff who are uniformed, in the field, and away from administration. Being "uniformed," for example, means being easily identified by the public and under day-to-day public scrutiny.

Mental readiness: Orlick[21] defined mental readiness as being "psyched," "totally ready," and "totally prepared." A high degree of mental readiness revolves around problem prevention and mental excellence. A detailed description of "mental readiness" is derived from Orlick's "Wheel of Excellence" which defines seven mental success elements demonstrated under high-performance challenging situations. Some modifications were made to the original terms to enhance their relevance to policing, as indicated in parentheses below. The seven elements are: Commitment, Self-Belief (Confidence), Positive Images (Positive Imagery), Mental Readiness (Mental Preparation), Full Focus, Distraction Control, and Constructive Evaluation (to include Coping)[15,21,22] (Appendix N: Orlick's Wheel of Excellence—Mental Success Elements).

Operational readiness: Operational readiness is comprised of physical-, technical-, and mental-readiness competencies.

It hinges on striking an appropriate balance between physical abilities, technical know-how, and mental skills. The importance of each competency is emphasized without overreach or underestimation. Generically, it can be defined as:

Physical readiness: Physical health and fitness; personal safety techniques; coordination of tasks; environmental stamina; and fatigue, food and hydration management.

Technical readiness: Knowledge and application of the field; verbal and written communication; knowledge of the service and community; and operational logistics and resources.

Mental readiness: Commitment; confidence; positive imagery; mental preparation; full focus; distraction control; and constructive evaluation and coping.

Performance blocks: The framework for defining performance blocks in this edition aligns with recent categorized measures from PSQ-Ops and PSQ-Org[23] with the following modifications and exceptions:

"Operational" stressors (formerly "Inherent") was simplified to include General Stressors and Rookie Errors.

Ethnic issues was moved to "Organizational" from "Operational" to align with McCreary et al. (2017). Conversely, "Operational" continues to include court appearances, team mistrust, and public disrespect, unlike McCreary et al. who incorporated them under "Organizational."

"External" stressors were kept as a distinct category, unlike McCreary et al. (2017) who incorporated them under "Organizational."

Climate conditions (renamed from environmental) and previous calls were moved to "Operational" from "External."

Performance excellence: Performance excellence is derived from understanding how "excellent street cops" operate at high levels in "challenging situations."

Respect: "Have respect for the members. Be a leader, keep your cool, don't blow it—and listen."

Good cop, respect—*Have respect for the members. Be a leader, keep your cool, and don't blow it—and listen. Be able to listen to other people, regardless of their sex or seniority. Have respect and show them how.*
—Traffic Escort

Successful performance: This is a "challenging situation" that the officer judged to be one of his or her best efforts. It refers to a call taken within the past few months where the officer had been active in attending the call.

Disappointing performance: This is a "challenging situation" that the officer judged to be disappointing or less than his or her best efforts. It refers to a call taken within the past few months where the officer had been active in attending the call.

F. Influential factors

Influential factors were identified in the initial study, ranging from background and training to rank and total years' experience. The excellent officers from the six frontline specialty units were analyzed based on three demographic factor areas for potential influence on performance—background, developmental ,and police distinction. Together, there are a total of 22 different individual factors (see Figure A.1).

Background factors

This area includes eight factors which officers are predisposed to upon entering a police service. Together with their respective descriptors, they are:

Education: 33% had university, 25% had college only, and 42% had high school only (i.e., University: Law and Criminology, Economics, Psychology, Physical Education, Education, Business, Recreation; College: Business, Police Foundations, Law and Security).

Gender: 77% (37) were male and 23% (11) were female officers.

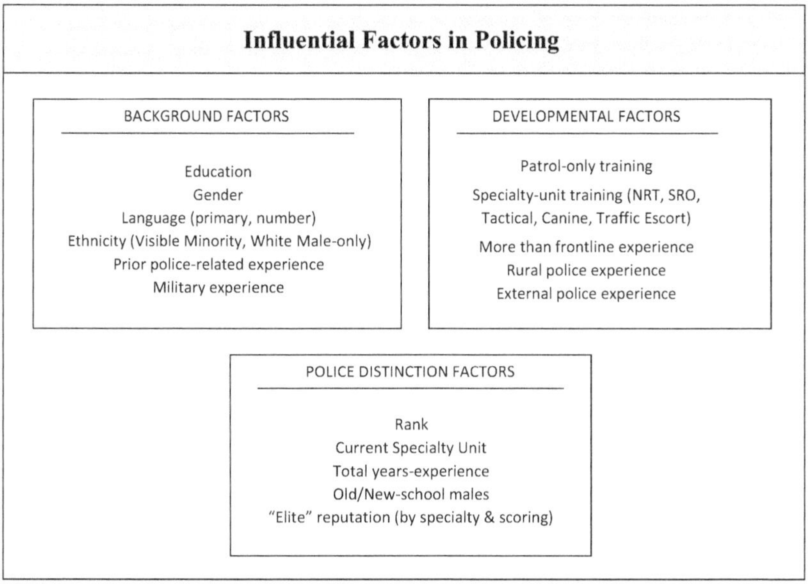

Influential Factors in Policing

BACKGROUND FACTORS

Education
Gender
Language (primary, number)
Ethnicity (Visible Minority, White Male-only)
Prior police-related experience
Military experience

DEVELOPMENTAL FACTORS

Patrol-only training
Specialty-unit training (NRT, SRO, Tactical, Canine, Traffic Escort)
More than frontline experience
Rural police experience
External police experience

POLICE DISTINCTION FACTORS

Rank
Current Specialty Unit
Total years-experience
Old/New-school males
"Elite" reputation (by specialty & scoring)

FIGURE A.1 Influential Factors in Policing

Primary language: 77% spoke English and 23% spoke a language other than English as their first language.

Number of languages: 52% spoke English only and 48% spoke two or more languages.

Ethnicity: 81% were Caucasian and 19% were Visible Minority/Aboriginal officers—this ratio occurred naturally.

Male ethnicity: 16% were Visible Minority/Aboriginal males and 84% "White Male Officers" (a total sample of 37 officers).

Prior police-related experience: 77% had no prior police experience and 23% had prior police-related experience upon entering the Service (i.e., auxiliary police, corrections officer, security, bar- tender, bouncer, prison guard, computer programming, hunting).

Military experience: 77% had no military training and 23% had military training (i.e., special operations forces, navy, army, infantry, SAR Tech, militia, Changing Guards, Air Cadets).

Developmental factors

This area includes nine factors which officers attained through former or current training and experience. Together with their respective descriptors, they are:

Patrol-only training: 21% had only Patrol experience.

Neighborhood Resource Team training: 21% had NRT experience.

School Resource Officer training: 15% had SRO experience.

Tactical training: 19% had Tactical experience.

Canine training: 10% had Canine experience.

Traffic Escort training: 17% had Traffic Escort experience.

More than frontline experience: 50% had more than frontline experience (i.e., Fraud, Major Crime, Youth, Community Centre, Outreach, Drugs, Police Association, Identification, Child Abuse, Property Room, Cellblock, Traffic Investigation, General Assignment, Training Centre, Range, Missing Persons).

Rural police experience: 50% had rural experience.

External police experience: 25% had external police experience from another police service (i.e., external police services that were urban, sub-urban, military, provincial and national Royal Canadian Mounted Police (RCMP).

Police Distinction factors

This area includes five factors which officers earn while serving in policing. These factors included: rank, current specialty unit, total years' experience, old/new school male, and elite (top scorers across specialties). Together with their respective descriptors, they are:

Rank: 79% were Constables/Senior Constables and 21% were Sergeants.

Current specialty unit: 37% were from Patrol (Central, East, West), 13% from NRT, 13% from SRO, 14% from Tactical, 10% from Canine, 13% from Traffic Escort—there was an intended dominance from Patrol,

Total years' experience: Total "years on" ranged from 3 to 30+, where 46% had over 15 years on, 27% had 10 to15 years on, 21% had 5 to 10 years on, and 6% had less than 5 years on.

"Old/New school" males: Of the male officers only, 70% were considered "Old School" or having been an officer for more than 15 years, while 30% were seen as "New School" with less than 10 years on.

"Elite" reputation (by specialty and scoring): 27% of the officers were jointly identified by their peers and supervisors as being "elite" or "exceptional" top scorers across all frontline units (i.e., similarly, while all athletes at the Olympics are excellent, only the top scorers receive a medal).

Differences in the point distribution of these readiness components are noted among certain groups. A lower percentage of weight would be expected where:

- the actual job description requires a lower standard
- a higher than average baseline is assumed
- skill levels and confidence are higher than most

For example, officers with tactical or military experience gave less weight to physical readiness (25% and 24%, respectively), possibly because they assume a higher physical baseline. Similarly, officers with prior police-related experience gave a lesser value to technical readiness (28%), possibly indicating more comfort in performing technical skills. Discussing such basic differences, regarding performance readiness between groups, lends itself to improved team building. (See Appendix K: Overall Importance of Operational Readiness by Factors for additional factors.)

G. Investigative framework

The Operational Readiness Framework assesses operational preparedness using both quantitative and qualitative measures. Balancing physical ability, technical knowledge, and mental mindset are key factors in overall performance excellence. An empirical approach has been developed to isolate and assess strategies. Based on numerous studies[24,25,26,27] and interactions with Olympians[15], profiles have been established for occupations that span surgery to policing to high-altitude climbing, arenas with life and death consequences. Mental-readiness skills have been determined to be a major contributor to peak performance and resiliency. Every occupation has detailed specificity regarding readiness and guidelines for preparedness.

Practical tools used for recruitment/selection, core competencies, training, mentoring, and evaluation have been utilized by various occupations which maximize multiple crossing-disciplinary techniques. Specialized training has been used extensively as a tool to best prepare top performers in their quest to achieve excellence.

This Operational Readiness Framework and investigative process are summarized as follows:

Categorize challenging operational situations. "Challenging" policing situations are collected from respected individuals when asked, *"What frontline situations are challenging (… and make you sit up a little straighter)?"*—akin to the challenges an athlete faces in an Olympic competition. The situations are classified against a template used in previous high-performance workplace research[24,26,28], into six situations—degree of difficulty, particular client behaviors, degree of complexity, first-of-its-kind/unfamiliarity, leading/mentoring responsibilities, and emotionally-charged pressures. They are also asked about performance blocks, categorized as inherent, organizational, external stressors, and rookie mistakes[18].

Identify readiness for performance excellence. Readiness is broadly and equitably defined by three essential competencies: physical, technical, and mental readiness. Standardized occupational functionality parameters are applied to define physical and technical readiness[29,30,31]. For mental readiness, the well-regarded Orlick's Wheel of Excellence[22] is employed to define mental readiness—which although crucial is historically overlooked and undefined.

> *Physical readiness*: Physical health and fitness; personal safety techniques; coordination of tasks; environmental stamina; and fatigue, food and hydration management.
>
> *Technical readiness*: Knowledge and application of the field; verbal and written communication; knowledge of the service and community; and operational logistics and resources.
>
> *Mental readiness*: Commitment; confidence; positive imagery; mental preparation; full focus; distraction control; and constructive evaluation and coping.

The significance of each competency is gauged using a weighted scale with a simple question:

"When you perform at your best in a challenging situation, how much do you believe your overall performance depends on your physical, technical, and mental readiness? Assign a weight across 100%."

This weighting approach results in a tailored profile aligning with the specific profession.

Assess success elements and practices with job-specificity. Typically, across most high-performance professions, physical and technical readiness practices are well defined, measured, and rigorously evaluated. Unfortunately, mental readiness tends to be underappreciated, lacking clear definition and emphasis. It is often assumed to be intuitive within the context of technical and physical competencies. An advisory group of coach officers refined the generic definitions into police-specific criteria. For mental readiness, "exceptional" frontline individuals are assessed against Orlick's seven mental-readiness success elements—Commitment, Self-Belief, Positive Imagery, Mental Preparation, Full Focus, Distraction Control, and Constructive Evaluation (refer to Appendix N: Orlick's Wheel of Excellence—Mental Readiness Success Elements). This process produces "performance indicators," exemplified by the strategies or "practices" of exceptional frontline leaders. They serve as benchmarks for the three competencies.

Customize to the profession. The readiness competencies—physical, technical, and mental—are harmonized with the profession's weighted profile determined in the earlier step. This customization generates a trio of performance indicators, both qualitative and quantitative, contributing to an all-encompassing operational readiness profile specific to the profession. This endeavor significantly contributes to achieving performance excellence. Best practices emerge through a process of isolating core practices (used by over 75% of excellent officers) and individual practices (used by less than 75% of excellent officers). Thus, a full complement of prescriptive, operational benchmarks of high-performance practices are established as an overall Operational Readiness Index.

FIGURE A.2 Operational Readiness Framework for High-Risk Professions

Quotes from "excellent" officers and coaches. Learning from others' mistakes and successes affords credible insight into what may or may not be a risky situation or decision. Open-ended inquiries prompted officers to freely discuss various practices and lived experiences shaping their preparedness. A substantial database of over 6,000 coded quotes from these informal leaders across six frontline specialty units, and coach officers province-wide, was generated through this study. This repository creatively preserves the experiential wisdom of seasoned officers. This resource allowed for easy access to diverse perspectives on performance matters like "hypervigilance," "court time," or "visualization." For instance, sample quotes for visualizing include:

> **Picture, checklist**—*I have a mental picture of my physical checklist. It's in-and-out visualizing. "Where are the other officers coming from? How are we going to set up?" If I'm missing something, there'll be an empty space—I can SEE it. Then it'll take me a few minutes to figure out what I'm missing. If time permits, I'll refer to the physical checklist—but usually it doesn't.*
>
> —>15 years on

Realistic, senses, reactions—*Make your training as realistically as possible. "How will I PERSONALLY react to that? How do I feel?" Live it! If you do encounter it later on, you'll be more prepared.*

—>15 years on

Gold Medal Policing stands as court-defensible, evidence-grounded research, uncovering the ways extraordinary frontline officers excel amid exacting situations. This framework allows the privilege of candidly exploring frontline policing through the perspectives of revered officers and coach officers and continues to enrich areas spanning recruitment, training, evaluation, and decision-making.

Notes

1 P. Dick, "Police partnership working: Lessons from a co-located group pilot," *European Journal of Policing Studies,* vol. 5, 2018.
2 M. O'Neill and McCarthy, D. J., "(Re) negotiating police culture through partnership working: Trust, compromise and the 'new' pragmatism," *Criminology & Criminal Justice,* vol. 14, no. 2, pp. 143–159, 2014.
3 N. Vyas, McDonald, J., Kirkwood, T. and Tyshenko, M. G., "Predictors of police performance," in *Gold medal policing*, 2nd ed. (pp. 497–504), Routledge, 2025.
4 N. Vyas, McDonald, J., Kirkwood, T. and Tyshenko, M. G., "Police performance stressors," in *Gold medal policing*, 2nd ed. (pp. 497–504), Routledge, 2025.
5 M. Abu-Alhassin, McDonald, J., Kirkwood, T. and Williams, M., "Critical analysis of Road to Mental Readiness (R2MR)," in *Gold medal policing*, 2nd ed. (pp. 505–514), Routledge, 2025.
6 M. G. Tyshenko, McDonald, J., Niyati Vyas, N. and Kirkwood, T., "Physical competencies in policing," in *Gold medal policing*, 2nd ed. (pp. 515–525), Routledge, 2025.
7 M. G. Tyshenko, McDonald, J., Kirkwood, T. and Ringnyu, C., "Technical competencies in policing," in *Gold medal policing*, 2nd ed. (pp. 526–536), Routledge, 2025.

8. M. Abu-Alhassin, McDonald, J., Kirkwood, T. and Williams, M., "Mental competencies in policing," in *Gold medal policing*, 2nd ed. (pp. 537–550), Routledge, 2025.
9. P. Clough, Earle, K. and Sewell, D., "Mental toughness: The concept and its measurement," in *Solutions in sport psychology*, Thomson, pp. 32–43, 2002.
10. J. L. Perry, Clough, P. J., Crust, L., Earle, K. and Nicholls, A., "Factorial validity of the Mental Toughness Questionnaire-48," *Personality and Individual Differences,* vol. 54, no. 5, pp. 587–592. https://doi.org/10.1016/j.paid.2012.11.020, 2013.
11. S. Stein and Book, H. E., *The EQ edge: Emotional intelligence and your success*, 3rd ed. John Wiley & Sons, 2011.
12. S. Terrell, "Executive coaches who use Eq-i 2.0 in leadership development: A qualitative study." ProQuest Dissertations Publishing, 2020.
13. J.-F. Ménard, *Train (your brain) like an Olympian: Gold Medal Techniques to unleash your potential at work.* ECW Press, p. 248, 2021.
14. M. Sarkar and Fletcher, D., "Psychological resilience in sport performers: A review of stressors and protective factors," *Journal of Sports Sciences,* vol. 32, no. 15, pp. 1419–1434. https://doi.org/10.1080/02640414.2014.901551, September 2014.
15. T. Orlick and Partington, J., "Mental links to excellence," *The Sport Psychologist,* vol. 2, pp. 105–130, 1988.
16. G. P. Brown and Hoffman, R., "The redesign of Advanced Patrol Training for police constables in Ontario: Making use of evaluation to maximize organizational effectiveness and efficiency," *Canadian Journal of Program Evaluation,* vol. 5, no. 1, pp. 83–100, 2000.
17. Ontario Police College, *Police trainee field training manual.* Queen's Printer, pp. 1–77, 2009.
18. J. McDonald, *Gold medal policing: Mental readiness and performance excellence.* New York: Sloan Associate Press, 2006.
19. M. D. C. Tongco, "Purposive sampling as a tool for informant selection." https://ethnobotanyjournal.org/index.php/era/article/view/126, 2007.
20. R. S. Robinson, "Purposive sampling," in *Encyclopedia of quality of life and well-being research.* Springer. https://doi.org/10.1007/978-94-007-0753-5_2337, 2014.

21 T. Orlick, "The psychology of personal excellence," *Contemporary Thought on Performance Enhancement,* vol. 1, pp. 110–122, 1992.
22 T. Orlick, "Wheel of excellence." http://www.zoneofexcellence.ca, October 25, 2003.
23 D. McCreary, Fong, I. and Groll, D. L., "Measuring policing stress meaningfully: Establishing norms and cut-off values for the Operational and Organizational Police Stress Questionnaires," *Police Practice and Research,* vol. 18, no. 6, pp. 612–623. https://doi.org/10.1080/15614263.2017.1363965, 2017.
24 J. McDonald, Dahal, G. P., Tyshenko, M. G., Sloan, D. A. and Sharma, S. K., "Operational readiness: Links to Sherpas' peak performance in tourist mountain-guiding," In A. P. Adhikari, G. P. Dahal, I. Mahat, B. Regmi, K. Subedi, & S. Shrestha (Eds.) *Sustainable livelihood systems in Nepal: Principles, practices and prospects.* Kathmandu: International Union for Conservation of Nature, Nepal Country Office (IUCN Nepal), pp. 281–308, 2015.
25 J. McDonald and Gyorkos, T., "Operational readiness for conducting global health research abroad," *Canadian Journal of Public Health,* vol. 107, no. 4–5, pp. 387–389. https://doi.org/10.17269/cjph.107.5555, 2016.
26 J. McDonald and Paganelli, C., "Exploration of mental readiness for enhancing dentistry in an inter-professional climate," *International Journal of Environmental Research and Public Health,* vol. 18, no. 13, pp. 7038–7055. https://doi.org/10.3390/ijerph18137038, 2021.
27 J. McDonald, Hale, K. & Kirkwood, T. (2024). Excellence in Homelessness Service: Evidence-Based Frontline Practices, *International Journal on Homelessness,* vol. 4, no. 3, pp. 1–19, 2024.
28 J. McDonald, Orlick, T. and Letts, M., "Mental readiness in surgeons and its links to performance excellence in surgery," *Journal of Pediatric Orthopaedics,* vol. 15, no. 5, pp. 691–697. https://doi.org/10.1097/01241398-199509000-00027, 1995.
29 D. Lechner, "Job Demands Analysis: Defining the physical demands of the work for post-offer and return-to-work functional testing." https://aeasseincludes.assp.org/proceedings/2007/docs/750.pdf, November 1, 2020.
30 Occupational Health Clinic for Ontario Workers Inc., Physical demand analysis (PDA), p. 1-10. https://www.ohcow.on.ca/edit/files/general_handouts/PhysicalDemandsAnalysis.pdf.

31 I. General Healthcare Resources, "PTA physical demand summary." https://www.ghresources.com/wp-content/uploads/2014/06/Physical-Demands-Summary-PTA.doc, November 1, 2020.

Appendix B

Predictors of Police Performance[1]

Niyati Vyas, *Masters Graduate*[2], Judy McDonald, *Research Supervisor*[2], Travis Kirkwood, *Masters Graduate*[2], and Michael G. Tyshenko, *Senior Risk Analyst*

1 Condensed version of original research paper.
2 School of Epidemiology and Public Health, Faculty of Medicine, University of Ottawa.

Abstract

This review explored the standards and measures that have been used to evaluate and predict excellence in frontline policing. Officers are accountable to and evaluated by their organization, the public and themselves. Four broad standards that ensure excellence at various phases of law enforcement include: selection criteria, organizational directives, training principles and leadership development. Sixteen excellence measures were identified within these four standards. This review contributed to the overall understanding of new and current trends in police operational readiness, and updating of Gold Medal Policing, 2nd edition

Introduction

Being accountable in law enforcement means meeting standards for quality, cost efficiency, productivity, performance, and citizen satisfaction[1]. Achieving public safety and ensuring ethical policing requires excellence. Official definitions for officer performance are needed to track their efficiency and for the transfer of knowledge. Some standards will be more or less appropriate, depending on the context, and the perspectives of officers, their organizations, and the public. But in the end, accountability rests with officers—yet there still remains a notable lack of performance research from a frontline perspective[2].

Purpose: To identify existing measures and standards used to evaluate frontline excellence in policing.

Search and analysis: International search of five databases revealed six themes, including "police excellence." A second refined search revealed 39 pertinent empirical articles for review with data, statistics, models, and charts pulled where relevant.

The prominent research for predicting police excellence was captured and weighed under four standards—selection criteria (39%) followed by organizational directives (29%) and trailed by training principles (16%) and leadership development (16%). A previous conceptual framework for reviewing "police evaluation"[2] was adapted for analyzing current findings and trends.

Findings

These four broad standards were further broken down into 16 measures briefly elaborated as follows.

Summary of Evaluation Standards and Measures to Predict Police Excellence

STANDARDS	Selection criteria	Organizational directives	Training principles	Leadership development
MEASURES	Psychological profiles	Community relations	Core competencies	Informal leaders
	Physical performance	Public confidence	Scenario-based training	Supervisor engagement
	Problem-solving	Appropriate use of force	Applied ethics	Females in authority
	Ethnic diversity	Wellness and performance	Critical thinking	Leadership styles

Selection criteria—to recruit people with desirable traits:

Psychological profiles are now preferred over background checks[2,3] in evaluating candidates due to increased power in predicting officer well-being or dysfunction;job performance collaboration and relationship building[4]. Successful officers show emotional stability and conscientiousness, and adopt coping styles fitted to the job[5,6]. Measures to check for anti-social traits[7] and incorporate self-reporting tools[8] (e.g., illegal drug use) have demonstrated performance improvement.

Physical performance interacts with personality traits, such as neuroticism and conscientiousness. These traits impact performance, such as firearm handling and driving performance[9]. Therefore, physical fitness has implications for basic policing functions (e.g., ability to handle average-sized adult men)[10].

Problem-solving (versus education): Newer evidence shows that higher education is not essential for policing excellence[11,12] and that it is much more important to ensure officers learn problem-solving skills that are useful in developing community-based solutions[12].

Ethnic diversity: Multicultural police-staff improve the force's communications, trust, and relatability to multicultural communities. This reduces negative perceptions of police during community encounters, de-escalates confrontations, and reduces use of excessive force[13,14,15].

Organizational directives—to focus officers' attention as priorities shift:

Community relations are central to certain policing styles, such as *community-oriented policing* (COP) and *problem-oriented policing* (POP). These emphasize the importance of: developing relationships between communities and law-enforcement[12]; proactively addressing long-term issues instead of reacting to short-term crises[16]; and prioritizing outcomes as success measures, such as community quality-of-life and the involvement of community in local problem-solving or decision-making[12].

Public confidence is affected by many factors[17], including: whether people have been previously victimized; an individual's political-social beliefs, visible minority status, and perception of crime rates; the current crime rates; public education levels; and the presence of visible minorities in police forces[18,19,20,21].

Appropriate use of force is very obviously a crucial measure of police performance. Use of force has implications for police brutality, "acceptable" deadly use of force, racial profiling, police militarization, cognitive decision-making, etc.[22,23]. Importantly, use of profanity can increase the chances and strength of reports of excessive force. This effect is exaggerated when either subjects or officers are female. Profanity negatively biases police-citizen interactions, and possibly triggers excessive force protests[22,23].

Wellness and performance: Anxiety has a negative influence on arrest and self-defense skills. In violent encounters, performance anxiety and insufficient training time combined to hurt performance. Wellness and performance can be improved by: using reality-based training scenarios[24]; promoting relaxation techniques[25]; addressing trauma through Crisis Intervention Teams; encouraging healthy coping skills[12]; and reducing shift work and consecutive night shifts[26]. In particular, relief from multiple night shifts can increase vigilance and reduce fatal vehicle accidents.

Training principles—to encourage critical thinking, flexibility and context-sensitive decision-making:

Core competencies have historically been too technical[27,28]. These must be replaced by competencies based on ethics, problem-solving, diversity, community focus, collaboration, and community understanding[27].

Scenario-based training is ideal for developing reflex-based self-defense training[24]. It improves skill in anticipating events, safety, ability to control suspects, trust during arrests, and community relations[22].

Applied ethics involves incorporating police ethics into officer training. This improves self-awareness, public interactions, community relations, and excessive force allegations. It can also impact officers' use of profanity, which can negatively impact citizens' evaluations of officers, but can also be practically useful to officers (e.g., gaining attention during arrests)[22].

Critical thinking is clearly important. Evidence shows that combining traditional education with critical-thinking training improves overall performance. Improvement was seen in: reading real-world situations and solving problems; communicating with locals in community settings; managing emotions and regulating behavior; using technology; and overall decision-making[12,29].

Leadership development—to promote ongoing career development:

Informal leaders are valuable, for example, when commanders or frontline officers participate in "citizen panels" at community meetings. Their know-how is effective in: answering questions on crime rates and responses; discussing successes and failures; explaining performance statistics[30]; and continuously evaluating and revising to fix unintended negative outcomes[31].

Supervisor engagement is important, because they are often balancing conflicting interests between themselves, their subordinates, senior management, and communities[32]. Therefore, two-way communication with these groups is crucial to generate new ideas and solutions quickly. One successful solution was to encourage supervisors to commute using the New York City subway (exposing senior staff first-hand to subway-specific challenges—such as youth gangs) which prompted innovative strategies for addressing high subway crime rates[30].

Female in authority: Generally, small female candidate pools for senior positions result in too few promotions[33,34]. Previous research shows that women's domestic roles impede career progression, rather than male-dominant cultures *per se*[35,36]. Women can also be deterred from senior roles due to inflexible hours, lack of career guidance, colleague prejudice, social pressure, and lack of confidence[37]. Ideal solutions have yet to be identified.

Leadership styles vary in law enforcement and are categorized to include[32]:

- morality-centric—equity, empathy, ethical justice, beneficence, and mutual respect
- transformational—equality, liberty, and justice with moral development of leaders
- transactional—personal ethics, beliefs, and moral values in the workplace
- pragmatic—contextualizes situations and considers particular impacts on individuals, organizations, and social environment
- stewardship—care-based with hierarchical structures of trust, support, encouragement, and mutual respect

Recommendations

Five recommendations were identified to advance the predictability of excellence in law enforcement.

1. *Update core competencies* for officers, based on newer measures known to predict performance. Selection criteria had the most prominent research highlighting the need to recognize harmful aggressive, impulsive, attention-seeking, and anti-social behavior. Seek officers who demonstrate calmness, maturity, responsibility, dutifulness, and controlled confidence[4,5,7,9,38,39].
2. *Enhance public trust and confidence,* and measure this using both traditional and newer community-policing metrics[12]. For example, combine number of citations, calls for police service, and average response times with creative problem-solving and activities that positively affect community safety. Account for the effect of public perceptions, local crime rates, and victimization in different neighborhoods for how they impact public confidence[17,18,21].
3. *Integrate problem-solving scenarios* during officer screening, training, finding community solutions, and shaping leaders in law enforcement[12,30]. Core values and good judgment can be screened and developed based on imaginary scenarios or real-world experience. A learner-centered[38] approach is ideal, and can be achieved by building on real-world frontline examples of issues that emerge (such as appropriate use of force, ethical decisions, and performing under pressure)[22,24].
4. *Expand wellness initiatives* to improve officers' physical and mental practices for controlling anxiety, sleep disorders, impaired alertness, and negative health outcomes[22,24]. Wellness is shown to improve skills such as driving performance, safety management, and injury prevention[26].
5. *Foster leadership informally and formally* throughout the organization. Recognize those who show courage, improve community relations, mentor, and promote gender and cross-cultural inclusion[30,32,33,34].

Notes

1. C. L. Alsabrook, Aryani, G. A. and Garrett, T. D., "The five principles of organizational excellence in police management," *Law and Order,* vol. 49, no. 6, pp. 109–114, 2001.
2. C. Nelson, McDonald, J., Kyle, N. and Galipeau, J., "Evaluation of police excellence," In J. McDonald (Ed.), *Gold medal policing*, pp. 201–209, Sloan Associate Press, 2006.
3. P. Meehl, "Law and the fireside inductions (with postscript): Some reflections of a clinical psychologist," *Behavioral Sciences & the Law,* vol. 7, no. 4, pp. 521–550. https://doi.org/10.1002/bsl.2370070408, 1989.
4. A. M. Tarescavage, Brewster, J., Corey, D. and Ben-Porath, Y. S., "Use of pre-hire Minnesota Multiphasic Personality Inventory-2-Restructured Form (MMPI-2-RF) police candidate scores to predict supervisor ratings of post-hire performance," *Assessment,* vol. 22, no. 4, pp. 411–428. https://doi.org/10.1177/1073191114548445, 2015.
5. P. Detrick, Chibnall, J. T. and Luebbert, M. C., "The revised NEO personality inventory as a predictor of police academy performance," *Criminal Justice and Behavior,* vol. 31, pp. 676–694. https://doi.org/10.1177/0093854804268751, 2004.
6. G. D. Bishop, Tong, E. M., Diong, S. M., Enkelmann, H. C., Why, Y. P., Khader, M. and Ang, J. C., "The relationship between coping and personality among police officers in Singapore," *Journal of Research in Personality,* vol. 35, no. 3, pp. 353–374. https://doi.org/10.1006/jrpe.2001.2319, 2001.
7. B. Arrigo and Claussen, N., "Police corruption and psychological testing: A strategy for preemployment screening," *International Journal of Offender Therapy and Comparative Criminology,* vol. 47, no. 3, pp. 272–290. https://doi.org/10.1177/0306624X03047003003, 2003.
8. R. Roberts, Tarescavage, A., Ben-Porath, Y. and Roberts, M., "Predicting post-probationary job performance of police officers using CPI and MMPI-2-RF test data obtained during pre-employment psychological screening," *Journal of Personality Assessment,* vol. 101, no. 5, pp. 544–555. https://doi.org/10.1080/00223891.2018.1423990, 2019.
9. C. G. Forero, Gallardo-Pujol, D., Maydeu-Olivares, A. and Andrés-Pueyo, A., "A longitudinal model for predicting performance of police officers using personality and behavioural data," *Criminal Justice and Behavior,*

vol. 36, no. 6, pp. 591–606. https://doi.org/10.1177/0093854809333406, 2009.
10. K. Peak, Bradshaw, R. V. and Glensor, R. W., "Improving citizen perceptions of the police: "Back to the basics" with a community policing strategy," *Journal of Criminal Justice,* vol. 20, no. 1, pp. 25–40. https://doi.org/10.1016/0047-2352(92)90032-5, 1992.
11. J. McDonald, *Gold medal policing: Mental readiness and performance excellence.* New York: Sloan Associate Press, 2006.
12. C. Massinger and Wood, N., "Improving law enforcement cross cultural competencies through continued education," *Journal of Education and Learning,* vol. 5, no. 2, pp. 258–264. http://dx.doi.org/10.5539/jel.v5n2p258, 2016.
13. M. Rowe and Ross, J. I., "Comparing the recruitment of ethnic and racial minorities in police departments in England and Wales with the USA," *Policing: A Journal of Policy and Practice,* vol. 9, no. 1, pp. 26–35. https://doi.org/10.1093/police/pau060, 2015.
14. I. Waters, Hardy, N., Delgado, D. and Dahlmann, S., "Ethnic minorities and the challenge of police recruitment," *Police Journal,* vol. 80, no. 3, pp. 191–216. https://doi.org/10.1350/pojo.2007.80.3.191, 2007.
15. S. P. Jain and Agocs, C., "Recruitment, selection and promotion of visible-minority and aboriginal police officers in selected Canadian police services," *Canadian Public Administration,* vol. 43, no. 1, pp. 46–74. https://doi.org/10.1111/j.1754-7121.2000.tb015, 2000.
16. J. C. Hinkle, Weisburd, D., Telep, C. W. and Petersen, K., "Problem-oriented policing for reducing crime and disorder: An updated systematic review and meta-analysis," *Campbell Systematic Review,* vol. 16, no. 2. https://doi.org/10.1002/cl2.1089, 2020.
17. K. Hohl, Bradford, B. and Stanko, E. A., "Influencing trust and confidence in the London metropolitan police: Results from an experiment testing the effect of leaflet drops on public opinion," *The British Journal of Criminology,* vol. 50, no. 3, pp. 491–513, https://doi.org/10.1093/bjc/azq005, May 2010.
18. K. Sindall, Sturgis, P. and Jennings, W., "Public confidence in the police: A time-series analysis," *The British Journal of Criminology,* vol. 52, no. 4, pp. 744–764, https://doi.org/10.1093/bjc/azs010, July 2012.
19. M. Kristina, "Public satisfaction with police: The importance of procedural justice and police performance in police-citizen encounters," *Australian & New Zealand Journal of Criminology,* vol. 42, no. 2, pp. 159–178. https://doi.org/10.1375/acri.42.2.159, 2009.

20 L. Cao, "Visible minorities and confidence in the police," *Canadian Journal of Criminology and Criminal Justice,* vol. 53, no. 1, pp. 1–26. https://doi.org/10.3138/cjccj.53.1.1, 2011.
21 M. Orr and West, D. M., "Citizen evaluations of local police: Personal experience or symbolic attitudes?," *Administration & Society,* vol. 38, no. 6, pp. 649–668. https://doi.org/10.1177/0095399706293989, 2007.
22 C. Patton, Asken, M. and Fremouw, W. J., "The influence of police profanity on public perception of excessive force," *Journal of Police and Criminal Psychology,* vol. 32, pp. 340–357. https://doi.org/10.1007/s11896-017-9226-0, 2017.
23 M. Palmiotto, *Police use of force: Important issues facing the police and the communities they serve.* CRC Press, Taylor & Francis Group 2016. https://doi.org/10.1201/9781315369921.
24 P. G. Renden, Savelsbergh G. J. P. and Oudejans, R. D., "Effects of reflex-based self-defence training on police performance in simulated high-pressure arrest situations," *Ergonomics,* vol. 60, no. 5, pp. 669–679. https://doi.org/10.1080/00140139.2016.1205222, 2015.
25 B. Arnetz, Nevedal, D.C., Lumley, M.A., Backman, L. and Lublin, A., "Trauma resilience training for police: Psycho physiological and performance effects," *Journal of Police and Criminal Psychology,* vol. 24, pp. 1–9. http://doi.org/10.1007/s11896-008-9030-y, 2009.
26 L. B. Waggoner, Grant, D. A., Van Dongen, H., Belenky, G. and Vila, B, "A combined field and laboratory design for assessing the impact of night shift work on police officer operational performance," *Sleep,* vol. 43, no. 9. https://doi.org/10.1093/sleep/zsaa052, 2020.
27 D. White, "A conceptual analysis of the hidden curriculum of police training in England and Wales," *Policing & Society,* vol. 16, no. 4, pp. 386–404. https://doi.org/10.1080/10439460600968164, 2006.
28 M. Sellbom, Corey, D. M. and Ben-Porath, Y. S., "Examining the validity of the Multidimensional Personality Questionnaire in the assessment of police candidates," *Assessment,* vol. 28, no. 1, pp. 295–309. https://doi.org/10.1177/1073191119887443, 2021.
29 D. M. Truxillo, Bennett, S. R. and Collins, M. L., "College education and police job performance: A ten-year study," *Public Personnel Management,* vol. 27, no. 2, pp. 269–280. https://doi.org/10.1177/009102609802700211, 1998.
30 W. C. Kim and Mauborgne, R., "Tipping point leadership," *Harvard Business Review,* vol. 81, no. 4, pp. 60–122, 2003.
31 Y. Lu, Yang, K. and Thomas, M. B., "Designing performance systems in anticipation of unintended consequences: Experiences and

lessons from the compstat-based performance regime in NYPD," *Administration & Society,* vol. 53, no. 6, pp. 907–936. https://doi.org/10.1177/0095399720976532, 2021.

32 J. G. Serier, "COP confidential: Police supervision and sub-culture." Dissertations Publishing, 2011.

33 G. Cordner and Cordner, A., "Stuck on a plateau?: Obstacles to recruitment, selection, and retention of women police," *Police Quarterly,* vol. 14, no. 3, pp. 207–226. https://doi.org/10.1177/1098611111413990, 2011.

34 S. Guajardo, "Women in policing: A longitudinal assessment of female officers in supervisory positions in the New York City police department," *Women & Criminal Justice,* vol. 26, no. 1, pp. 20–36. https://doi.org/10.1080/08974454.2014.997418, 2015.

35 P. Dick, "Between a rock and a hard place: The dilemmas of managing part-time working in the police service," *Personnel Review,* vol. 33, no. 3, pp. 302–321. https://doi.org/10.1108/00483480410528841, 2004.

36 C. Williams, McDonald, J. and Kyle, N., "Challenges in female policing," In J. McDonald (Ed.), *Gold medal policing*, pp. 223–229, Sloan Associate Press, 2006.

37 S. Sabat and Mishra, S., "Role of women in the management of police organisation: A paradigm shift," *International Journal of Learning and Change,* vol. 4, no. 4, pp. 367–374, 2010.

38 S. Charles, "Professional integrity, modern racism, self -esteem, and universality-diversity orientation of police officers in a large urban police agency." ProQuest Dissertations Publishing, Doctoral Dissertation, Fordham University. https://search.proquest.com/docview/304879604?accountid=14701, 2009.

39 S. Lowmaster and Morey, L., "Predicting law enforcement officer job performance with the Personality Assessment Inventory," *Journal of Personality Assessment,* vol. 94, no. 3, pp. 254–261. https://doi.org/10.1080/00223891.2011.648295, 2012.

Appendix C

Police Performance Stressors[1]

Niyati Vyas, *Masters Graduate*[2], Judy McDonald, *Research Supervisor*[2], Travis Kirkwood, *Masters Graduate*[1], and Michael G. Tyshenko, *Senior Risk Analyst*

1 Condensed version of original research paper.
2 School of Epidemiology and Public Health, Faculty of Medicine, University of Ottawa.

Abstract

This review identifies major sources of police officer stress. A modified framework categorized stressors as Operational, Organizational and External. An updated inventory of stressors highlighted: dominant findings within each category; heightened concerns from multiple general stressors; prevalence of previously under-researched family-life stress; and appearance of self-diagnostic police stress-questionnaires and military mental-health literacy programs. Certain officers were found to be impacted differentially, according to personal stressor awareness which impacts coping and job performance. Supports from coach officers, peers and the organization were stress protective and increased commitment. Recommendations include technological and inter-professional strategies. This assessment contributed to the overall understanding of current trends relating to police preparedness as part of publishing Gold Medal Policing, 2nd edition.

Introduction

Daily, experiences of frontline police officers cause stress to accumulate but the effects can be difficult to measure. Identifying stressors and blockers that impact high performance can advance the development of tools to manage stress. A total of 48 major performance blocks or stressors that interfered with optimal police performance were identified by "exceptional" officers in *Gold Medal Policing, 1st Edition* (GMP1)[1,2]. Have the perceptions and stress measures changed much over the last 20 years?

Attention to post-traumatic stress disorder (PTSD) and suicide in law enforcement has grown; consider that first responder groups have adapted the Road to Mental Readiness (R2MR) program, which was initially a military-based program[3,4,5]. It turns out that categories of police stressors are comparable to those encountered by athletes: there are *competitive/operational*, *organizational*, and *personal/external* distinctions[6]. R2MR suggests that identifying performance-impairing sources of excessive stress will tell how to look for key indicator symptoms and opportunities to offer targeted coping and resilience supports—such supports protect against stress effects, similar to positive mind-states of athletes. However, confidentiality in seeking help remains a barrier.

Chronic workplace stressors can reduce our physical, mental, and social well-being. This includes impacts on job satisfaction, motivation, and job performance[7,8]. Specific examples include time pressures, staff shortages, and ambiguities regarding workload; excessive training; roles and job control; lack of appropriate equipment; and work-family conflict. Detailed Operational and Organizational Police Stress Questionnaires (PSQ-Ops and PSQ-Org) exist with low-, moderate-, and high-stress cut-off scores[9,10].

Purpose: To identify major stress sources in frontline policing.

Search and data analysis Through extensive international search of five databases, six dominant themes were found, one being "police stress." Adding a second refined search produced 35 related empirical articles for this review. Qualitative and quantitative data, including models and charts, were pulled from the articles when relevant.

Findings

To organize current trends in "police stress," a framework was defined by primary and secondary stress sources, each organized into three broad categories:

> *Operational*: Inherent to the job—e.g., crises, arrests, shift work, court, public disrespect, potential risks.

Organizational: Stem from organizational structure, personnel, workload, supervisory action/inaction, and fewer resources.

External: Experienced beyond workplace bounds—e.g., fatigue, life conflicts, spousal fear, and work-life imbalance.

Detailed Summary of Police Performance Stressors					
CLASSIFICATIONS	PERFORMANCE STRESSORS			
^	Operational		Organizational	External
^	General	Rookie Errors*	^	^
Primary stressors >75% officers reported in GMP1 Frequently noted in current research	*Crisis* *Jaded/sceptical* *Lulls/routine* Shift work Personal fears* Public disrespect* Pain and injury**	Aggressiveness*		*Fatigue*
Secondary stressors <75% officers reported in GMP1 Less frequently noted in current research	*Court appearances* *Others' complacency* *Team/Peer mistrust* Work conflicts Car collisions* Climate conditions* External specialists* Getting lost* Lack of information* Previous calls*	Basic patrolling issues* Discipline problems* Lack community contacts* Lack of safety* More positivity* No action plan* No basic law* Other-officers' anxiety* Poor containment* Poor reports* Unrealistic expectations*	*Equipment limitations* *Ethnicity issues* *Female policing issues** *Leadership* *Mistrust administration* *Poor support* *Preferential treatment* *Training issues* *Workload Changes** Coaching issues* Lack of feedback* Politics* Promotional complacency* Public complaints* Other e.g., Laws*	*Day-to-day pressures* *Family conflicts*

Source: *Gold Medal Policing* (McDonald, 2006) (GMP1).

Found in both GMP1 and GMP2 reviews, *Found only in GMP1, **NOT found in GMP1

Impacts of stress. Research has shown that stress negatively affects police officers' behavior and physiology, impacting blood pressure, aggression, impulse control, anxiety, focus, motor skills, and working memory. It also adversely affects their perception and cognition, leading to impaired judgment, decision-making, and memory recall, as well as "burnout" and coping difficulties[11].

Stressors in policing can be either positive challenges, such as workload and job complexity, or hindrances, like role ambiguity and conflicts, affecting performance and motivation[12,13].

Measuring police stress. Various tools have been developed to measure police stress. Non-police-specific tools include models for family and work reintegration, as well as checklists assessing trauma history from various life events[14,15]). Police-specific measures include studies correlating officer exposure to stress with vigilance, aggression, and impulsiveness, as well as assessments considering traumatic experiences, coping strategies, social supports, and traumatic dissociation[11,16].

Additionally, police stress has been evaluated using tools like the California Psychological Inventory and various questionnaires related to stress, PTSD, and critical incidents. Findings from these studies suggest the need for targeted psychological support and coping strategies to help officers manage stress effectively[17].

Operational stressors are the stresses that come with the job, and can't always be avoided. They include crisis events, which can cause long-term mental suffering and feeling disconnected[7,16], can affect sleep, family life, personality, aggression, and other symptoms related to post-traumatic stress disorder[11,17,18,19,20]. Crises can include: death of a colleague; multiple simultaneous injuries or deaths (e.g., terrorist attack); shooting, near-shooting, or assault incidents; child trauma; and serious vehicle crashes[21]. Other operational stressors reported were *shift work and fatigue*[22,23,24,25]; *pain and injury*[26]; *personal fears* (of injury or death); *public disrespect* (sometimes hostile); and boring *routine and lulls*[1,15,27,28]. It was noticed that the impact of rookie errors was absent from any of the search literature yet was reported as 25% of all stressors by high-performing officers interviewed in GMP1. These officers agreed that rookie aggressiveness, such as overreacting and acting too quickly, was very problematic, needing immediate action.

Organizational stressors are when the workplace organization itself is a stressor. These can include: bad leadership and management; ineffective policies; lack of resources; bad partners; too much or unbalanced workload; ethnic minorities issues[29]; unclear roles and responsibilities; too much paperwork and bureaucracy; hoax calls; and dealing with public complaints[30,31]. Longitudinal studies have linked PTSD to feelings of lack of organizational support and a decrease in job commitment[15,24,32]. Internal support was highlighted as an important protective factor in mitigating stress and a function of overall job satisfaction[15,33].

External stressors happen outside of the job but cannot be fully separated from workplace stressors. Where sensitivity to police-family stress was previously lacking, it now appears more prevalent in current research. Stressors carry over from work to personal life, and back to work again. Fatigue is an example of a stressor that is often a normal part of the job. It can cause issues at work and at home, which can lead to conflicts and cause more stress, leading to more fatigue and less sleep—continuing in a vicious feedback loop[1,24]. Job loss and divorce are two large examples, among many others[15]. The effects of different stressors are greatest among patrol (versus non-patrol specialty-unit officers), rookie, visible-minority, Aboriginal, and female officers (all of whom face various specific stressors and discrimination)[24].

Recommendations

Five recommendations were identified to improve stress management in law enforcement.

1. *Develop confidential self-diagnostic technologies* to track track stressors that consistently influence their well-being and ability to perform their best[3,10.] Many stressors can combine and multiplysignificantly increasing their effect[17,24]. Many "combinatorial" interplays are not seen in the current

literature and are worth exploring in future research and tool designs.
2. ***Implement support initiatives*** for coach officers, mentors, fellow officers, and management-officer relationships, which are a necessity for actively building a more compassionate work environment in law enforcement[15].
3. ***Address sensitive issues*** often overlooked in most police research but shared in confidence in GMP1. Probing informal leaders at all levels can stimulate new directives for issues such as: promotional complacency[34]; differences in job satisfaction among patrol versus non-patrol officers; alienation of visible minority and Aboriginal officers[29]; and fundamental rookie errors.
4. ***Establish workplace health and fitness programs*** for all, which are commonly lacking. Strong physical health can positively impact heart-disease risk factors, mental well-being, energy levels, job satisfaction, and performance[35].
5. ***Promote work-life balance strategies*** to help mitigate life conflicts[15]. Creative solutions can come from anywhere, especially from inter-professional, non-police relationships[12,13].

Notes

1 J. McDonald, *Gold medal policing: Mental readiness and performance excellence*. New York: Sloan Associate Press, 2006.
2 E. Wilson, McDonald, J. and Allen, J., "Sources of police stress," In J. McDonald (Ed.), *Gold medal policing: Mental readiness and performance excellence*, pp. 216–222, New York: Sloan Associate Press, 2006.
3 Canadian Institute for Public Safety Research and Treatment, Road to mental readiness (R2MR) 2019 Review. https://www.cipsrt-icrtsp.ca/en/policy-brief/r2mr-2019-review, 2019.
4 R. N. Carleton, Korol, S., Mason, J. E., Hozempa, K. and Anderson, G., "A longitudinal assessment of the road to mental readiness training among municipal police," *Cognitive Behaviour Therapy*, vol. 47, no. 6, pp. 508–528. https://doi.org/10.1080/16506073.2018.1475504, 2018.
5 A. Szeto, Dobson, K. S. and Knaak, S., "The road to mental readiness for first responders: A meta-analysis of program outcomes," *Canadian*

Journal of Psychiatry/Revue Canadienne de Psychiatrie, vol. 64, pp. 18S–29S. https://doi.org/10.1177/0706743719, 2019.
6. M. Sarkar and Fletcher, D., "Psychological resilience in sport performers: A review of stressors and protective factors," *Journal of Sports Sciences*, vol. 32, no. 15, pp. 1419–1434. https://doi.org/10.1080/02640414.2014.901551, September 2014.
7. J. Andersen, Papazoglou, K., Arnetz, B. and Collins, P., "Mental preparedness as a pathway to police resilience and optimal functioning in the line of duty," *International Journal of Emergency Mental Health and Humience*, vol. 17, no. 3, pp. 624–627, 2015.
8. D. R. McCreary and Thompson, M. M., "Development of two reliable and valid measures of stressors in policing: The operational and organizational police stress questionnaires," *International Journal of Stress Management*, vol. 13, no. 4, pp. 494–518. https://doi.org/10.1037/1072-5245.13.4.494, 2006.
9. S. Pindek and Spector, P. E., "Organizational constraints: A meta-analysis of a major stressor," *Work & Stress*, vol. 30, pp. 7–25. https://doi.org/10.1080/02678373.2015.1137, 2016.
10. D. McCreary, Fong, I. and Groll, D. L., "Measuring policing stress meaningfully: Establishing norms and cut-off values for the Operational and Organizational Police Stress Questionnaires," *Police Practice and Research*, vol. 18, no. 6, pp. 612–623. https://doi.org/10.1080/15614263.2017.1363965, 2017.
11. C. Gutshall, Hampton, D., Sebetan, I. M., Stein, P. and Broxterma, T. J., "The effects of occupational stress on cognitive performance in police officers," *Police Practice and Research*, vol. 18, pp. 463–477. https://doi.org/10.1080/15614263.2017.1288120, 2017.
12. J. Lepine, Podsakoff, N. and Lepine, M., "A meta-analytic test of the challenge stressor-hindrance stressor framework: An explanation for inconsistent relationships among stressors and performance," *Academy of Management Journal*, vol. 48, no. 5, pp. 764–775. https://doi.org/10.5465/AMJ.2005.18803921, 2005.
13. Lockey, S., Graham, L., Zheng, Y., Hesketh, I., Plater, M. and Gracey, S., "The impact of workplace stressors on exhaustion and work engagement in policing," *The Police Journal: Theory, Practice and Principles*, vol. 32258, pp. 1–17. https://doi.org/10.1177/0032258X211016532, 2021.
14. A. R. Blais, Thompson, M. and McCreary, D. R., "The development and validation of the Army Post-Deployment Reintegration Scale," *Military Psychology*, vol. 21, no. 3, pp. 365–386. https://doi.org/10.1080/08995600902914727, 2009.

15 S. Maguen, Metzler, T. J., McCaslin, S. E. and Inslicht, S. S., "Routine work environment stress and PTSD symptoms in police officers," *The Journal of Nervous and Mental Disease,* vol. 197, no. 10, pp. 754–760. https://doi.org/10.1097/NMD.0b013e3181b975f8, 2009.
16 M. Martin, Marchand, A., Boyer, R. and Martin, N., "Predictors of the development of posttraumatic stress disorder among police officers," *Journal of Trauma Dissociation,* vol. 10, no. 4, pp. 451–468. https://doi.org/10.1080/15299730903143626, 2009.
17 J. Wills and Schuldberg, D., "Chronic trauma effects on personality traits in police officers," *Journal of Traumatic Stress,* vol. 29, no. 2, pp. 185–189. https://doi.org/10.1002/jts.22089, April 2016.
18 J. P. Andersen and Gustafsberg, H., "A training method to improve police use of force decision making: A randomized controlled trial," *SAGE Open,* vol. 6, no. 2, p. 215824401663870. https://doi.org/10.1177/2158244016638708, 2016.
19 G. Cordner and Cordner, A., "Stuck on a plateau?: Obstacles to recruitment, selection, and retention of women police," *Police Quarterly,* vol. 14, no. 3, pp. 207–226. https://doi.org/10.1177/1098611111413990, 2011.
20 B. Green, "Post-traumatic stress disorder in UK police officers," *Current Medical Research and Opinion,* vol. 20, no. 1, pp. 101–105. https://doi.org/10.1185/030079903125002748, 2004.
21 C. Moad, "Critical incidents: Responding to police officer trauma," Fayetteville, AR. https://www.cji.edu/wp-content/uploads/2019/04/chrismoad.pdf, 2011.
22 S. Garbarino, Guglielmi, O., Puntoni, M., Bragazzi, N. L. and Magnavita, N., "Sleep quality among police officers: Implications and insights from a systematic review and meta-analysis of the literature," *International Journal of Environmental Researc,* vol. 16, p. 885. https://doi.org/10.3390/ijerph16050885, 2019.
23 D. Fekedulegn, Burchfiel, C. M., Ma, C. C., Andrew, M. E., Hartley, T. A., Charles, L. E., Gu, J. K. and Violanti, J. M., "Fatigue and on-duty injury among police officers: The BCOPS study," *Journal of Safety Research,* vol. 60, pp. 43–51. https://doi.org/10.1016/j.jsr.2016.11.006, 2017.
24 J. M. Violanti, Charles, L. E., McCanlies, E., Hartley, T. A., Baughman, P., Andrew, M. E., Fekedulegn, D. and Ma, C., "Police stressors and health: A state-of-the-art review," *Policing,* vol. 40, no. 4, pp. 642–656. https://doi.org/10.1108/PIJPSM-06-2016-0097, 2017.
25 P. Dick, "The social construction of the meaning of acute stressors: A qualitative study of the personal accounts of police officers using a stress counselling service," *Work & Stress,* vol. 14, no. 3, pp. 226–244. https://doi.org/10.1080/02678370010026422, 2000.

26 D. Chan, Webb, D., RRyan, R. M., Tang, T., Yang, S. X., Ntoumanis, N. and Hagger, M. S., "Preventing occupational injury among police officers: Does motivation matter?," *Occupational Medicine,* vol. 67, no. 6, pp. 435–441. https://doi.org/10.1093/occmed/kqx076, 2017.
27 L. B. Larsen, Andersson, E. E., Tranberg, R. and Ramstrand, N., "Multisite musculoskeletal pain in Swedish police: Associations with discomfort from wearing mandatory equipment and prolonged sitting," *International Archives of Occupational and Environmental Health,* vol. 91, no. 4, pp. 425–433. https://doi.org/10.1007/s00420-018-1292-9, 2018.
28 I. V. Carlier, Lamberts, R. D. and Gersons, B. P., "Risk factors for post-traumatic stress symptomatology in police officers: A prospective analysis," *The Journal of Nervous and Mental Disease,* vol. 185, no. 8, pp. 498–506. https://doi.org/10.1097/00005053-1997080, 1997.
29 I. Waters, Hardy, N., Delgado, D. and Dahlmann, S., "Ethnic minorities and the challenge of police recruitment," *Police Journal,* vol. 80, no. 3, pp. 191–216. https://doi.org/10.1350/pojo.2007.80.3.191, 2007.
30 P. Brough, "Comparing the influence of traumatic and organizational stressors on the psychological health of police, fire, and ambulance officers," *International Journal of Stress Management,* vol. 11, no. 3, pp. 227–244. https://doi.org/10.1037/1072-5245.11.3.22, 2004.
31 J. J. J. Hurrell, Nelson, D. L. and Simmons, B. L., "Measuring job stressors and strains: where we have been, where we are, and where we need to go," *Journal of Occupational Health Psychology,* vol. 3, no. 4, pp. 368–389. https://doi.org/10.1037//1076-8998.3.4.36, 1998.
32 W. Tengpongsthorn, "Factors affecting the effectiveness of police performance in Metropolitan Police Bureau," *Kasetsart Journal of Social Sciences,* vol. 38, no. 1, pp. 39–44. https://doi.org/10.1016/j.kjss.2016.07.001., 2017.
33 R. N. Haarr, "Factors affecting the decision of police recruits to "drop out" of police work," *Police Quarterly,* vol. 8, no. 4, pp. 431–453. https://doi.org/10.1177/1098611103261821, 2005.
34 S. A. Guajardo, "Measuring diversity in police agencies," *Justice,* vol. 13, no. 1, pp. 1–15. https://doi.org/10.1080/15377938.2014.893220, 2015.
35 F. H. Zimmerman, "Cardiovascular disease and risk factors in law enforcement personnel: A comprehensive review," *Cardiology in Review,* vol. 20, no. 4, pp. 159–166. https://doi.org/10.1097/CRD.0b013e318248d631, 2012.

Appendix D

Critical Analysis of the "Road to Mental Readiness" (R2MR) Program[1]

Mervat Abu-Alhassin[2], *Masters Graduate*, Judy McDonald[2], *Research Supervisor*, Travis Kirkwood[2], *Masters Graduate*, and Maria Williams[2], *Masters Student*

1 Condensed version of original research paper
2 School of Epidemiology and Public Health, Faculty of Medicine, University of Ottawa.

Abstract

Risks of first responder suicide and post-traumatic stress disorder (PTSD) have garnered increased attention, partly for their links to employee wellness and productivity, and stressors inherent to occupations. Some evidence suggests 84-96% of Canadian military members would qualify for a disorder, yet claim not to use or need support services. This instigated the CAF launch of "Road to Mental Readiness" (R2MR), a program focused on mental health stigma; risk factor improvement; and literacy. This article is a R2MR critique, organized in five sections: program description; reported support and criticism; advancements; and R2MR fit with high performance. Publications reviewed include 37 peer-reviewed scientific articles, and 16 non-scientifically peer-reviewed or editorial analyses. Previous studies focused predominantly on military personnel, with a single empirical study on Canadian municipal police services[1]. This review contributed to the overall understanding of new and current trends in police operational readiness, and updating of Gold Medal Policing, 2nd edition.

Introduction

Worker wellness, mental health and job-specific stressors affect productivity, which is partly why they are gaining attention[2,3,4]. Previous military research shows the importance of seeking help in reducing operational stress injury (OSI) and post-traumatic stress disorder (PTSD)[5,6,7,8,9,10]. Canadian data showed that 84% and 96% of military members would be considered to have a disorder, but felt they did not "need" or use any services. The Canadian Armed Forces (CAF) began efforts in 2007 to reduce stigma and mental-illness risk factors, and improve mental-health literacy[11]. This eventually resulted in a military mental-health initiative called "Road to Mental Readiness," known as R2MR. It has been adapted for first responders and law enforcement personnel in Canada.

Purpose: To provide an academic summary of research conducted on the Canadian military mental-health program entitled "Road to Mental Readiness" (R2MR).

Framework: The critical review is organized in five sections:

- R2MR program description
- reported support for R2MR
- reported criticism of R2MR
- R2MR advancements
- R2MR fit with high performance

Search and data analysis: An extensive review of the research on R2MR produced 53 articles, 16 of which were editorial-style and not scientifically peer-reviewed articles, included only to describe the program and designated with "*" in the References. An analysis of the empirical evidence was critiqued in five main categories.

Findings

1) **R2MR program description**: R2MR is a four-hour, evidence-based, action-focused classroom program that is flexible and adaptive to real-world circumstances[12]. The three main components are: *stigma reduction*[13,14,15,16]; the *"Big 4"*

coping skills (goal setting, positive self-talk, visualization, and arousal control—with focus on tactical breathing)[17,18,19,20,21]; and the *Mental Health Continuum Model*[11,22,23,24,25], which considers a range of positive mental-health states, instead of just "healthy" and "sick."

2) **Evidence supporting R2MR**: The program has four main benefit areas: reducing the stigma of mental illness[17,18,19,20,26]; improving mental-health literacy[17,27]; reducing mental distress[8,28,29]; and providing early detection, intervention, reintegration, and system collaboration[26,30,31,32,33].

3) **Evidence criticizing R2MR**: The program has six main weaknesses, which are: minimal lasting effects[19,26,34,35,36,37,38]; program given at too low dose (not long enough, or often enough)[17,19]; highly trustworthy conditions are necessary—otherwise the program can cause stigma, mistrust, isolation, and conflicts of interest[7]; the original program was non-generalizable to other work contexts like prisons[39,40]; the diagnostic criteria only identify distress, which means underlying symptoms may be repeatedly missed[19,41]; and a lack of professional mental-health expertise by leaders and supervisors reduces their confidence to teach necessary skills[42].

4) **R2MR program advancements and adaptations**: Many updates to the program address previously identified weaknesses. Key examples include: *deployment-cycle training*, where military versions were adapted with specific pre-deployment, post-deployment, and leadership career stages[34,39]; *police stress management*, based on evidence supporting the use of R2MR for addressing OSI and PTSD among first responders[11,18,43]; and the *"Big 4" skills* taught to recruits and officers for maintaining mental health[44,45].

There is also an *R2MR for First Responders*[24,40,46] adaptation, which itself was adapted again to general workplaces (called *The Working Mind*[20,24,46,47]). There is a *"Mental Health Continuum" App*, which is a mobile application allowing military personnel to self-monitor health behaviors and needs[9,11,31,48]; and an *R2MR Performance Coaching Course*, which helps supervisors create daily psychological-skill practices to support the well-being of their team members[49].

FIGURE D.1 Extended Mental-Health Continuum

1 McDonald (2006)
2 Adapted from Road to Mental Readiness: Mental Health Continuum Model (Barath, 2017)

5) **R2MR fitting with research on high-performers**: For example, there is valuable research on athletes, where becoming a high performer requires *excellence*—not just a baseline or minimum level of skill. GMP1[1] built on this research[50,51,52] where the skills of police officers, who were considered "exceptional" by their colleagues and supervisors, were used to customize seven success elements for law enforcement excellence. Included in these elements are the R2MR skills of *setting clear objectives; 8 positive-imagery skills; psyching rituals* to get mentally "pumped up"; and *de-escalation* to keep situations calm and controlled.

Recommendations

1. *Enhance programming* for greater engagement with R2MR content[12]. The program addresses many workplace mental-health needs, but more training, rehearsal[13,14,15,17], and policy development are needed to better predict who will get PTSD (the same experiences don't affect everyone equally)[19].
2. *Conduct research regularly to validate training delivery* for maximum effect[19,26,34,35]. New improved measures for effectiveness, prediction, and keeping programming up to date are always needed. Research supporting applications of R2MR in other non-military contexts is also lacking[37].
3. *Address feelings of inadequacy* among supervisors and instructors by incorporating professional mental-health and

counseling support. They feel a need for support from experts who are trained in mental-health and behavioral therapy[42].
4. *Invest in e-tools* for personal assessments and best-practices to help address privacy concerns and mistrust. Observing mental-illness signs in others can be a very sensitive situation; e-tools can help[9,11,31,48].
5. *Develop performance readiness strategies* covering all risks, beyond just mental wellness. Different proficiency is needed for performance, depending on specific job and environment contexts[49].

Notes

*Editorial, non-peer reviewed

1 J. McDonald, *Gold medal policing: Mental readiness and performance excellence*. New York: Sloan Associate Press, 2006.
2 M. Creamer and Forbes, D., "Treatment of posttraumatic stress disorder in military and veteran populations," *Psychotherapy*, vol. 41, no. 4, pp. 388–398. https://doi.org/10.1037/0033-3204.41.4.388, 2004.
3 C. E. Agaibi and Wilson, J. P., "Trauma, PTSD and resilience: A review of the literature," *Trauma, Violence & Abuse*, vol. 6, no. 3, pp. 195–216. https://doi.org/10.1177/1524838005277438, 2005.
4 Statistics Canada*, "Canadian Community Health Survey: Mental health and well-being," https://www23.statcan.gc.ca/imdb/p2SV.pl?Function=getSurvey&Id=5285, 2003.
5 Canadian Association of Mental Health* (CAMH), "Police mental health," p. 1–14, https://www.camh.ca/-/media/files/pdfs---public-policy-submissions/police-mental-health-discussion-paper-oct2018-pdf.pdf, 2018.
6 J. A. Granek*, Jarmasz, J., Boland, H., Guest, K. and Bailey, L. S., "Mobile applications for personalized mental health resiliency training," in *Interservice/Industry Training, Simulation, and Education Conference (I/ITSEC)*. https://cradpdf.drdc-rddc.gc.ca/PDFS/unc269/p805213_A1b.pdf, 2017.
7 D. Fikretoglu, Liu, A., Nazarov, A. and Blackler, K., "A group randomized control trial to test the efficacy of the Road to Mental Readiness (R2MR) program among Canadian military recruits," *BMC Psychiatry*, vol. 19, no. 1, p. 326. https://doi.org/10.1186/s12, 2019.

8. K. Reid, "Medical narratives of military PTSD: Moving beyond the biomedical approach," Doctoral Dissertation, Carleton University. https://doi.org/10.22215/etd/2019-13638, 2019.
9. R. R. Roland* and Bartone, P. T., "Resilience research and training in the US and Canadian armed forces," in American Psychological Association convention, August 7, Toronto, 2015.
10. D. Fikretoglu, Liu, A. and Blackler, K., 2016. Testing different methods to optimize change in mental health service use attitudes. Defence Research and Development Canada Scientific Report DRDC-RDDC-2016-R025.https://cradpdf.drdc-rddc.gc.ca/PDFS/unc221/p803477_A1b.pdf.
11. Canadian Institute for Public Safety Research and Treatment*, Road to mental readiness (R2MR) 2019 Review. https://www.cipsrt-icrtsp.ca/en/policy-brief/r2mr-2019-review, 2019
12. Mental Health Commission of Canada* (MHCC), "Backgrounder: The road to mental readiness program." https://www.mentalhealthcommission.ca/wp-content/uploads/drupal/2017-09/MHCC_Backgrounder_R2MR_Crash_Course_eng.pdf, 2017.
13. P. W. Corrigan, "Research and the elimination of the stigma of mental illness," *British Journal of Psychiatry,* vol. 201, no. 1, pp. 7–8. https://doi.org/10.1192/bjp.bp.111.103382, 2012.
14. P. W. Corrigan and Fong, M. W., "Competing perspectives on erasing the stigma of illness: What says the dodo bird?,' *Social Science & Medicine,* vol. 103, pp. 110–117. https://doi.org/10.1016/j.socscimed.2013.05.027, February 2014.
15. B. Phinney, "Pathways to positive mental health: A comparison of previously deployed Canadian armed forces regular and reserve force members," Masters Dissertation, Carleton University, 2016.
16. D. Fikretoglu*, Liu, A. and Blackler, K., "Testing the efficacy of Road to Mental Readiness (R2MR) mental health education and resilience training program during basic military qualification: A pilot group randomized control trial," Scientific Report DRDC-RDDC-2016-R025, DRDC Toronto, Feb, 2016. 1–35. https://cradpdf.drdc-rddc.gc.ca/PDFS/unc221/p803477_A1b.pdf, 2018a.
17. R. L. Krakauer, Stelnicki, A. M. and Carleton, R. N., "Examining mental health knowledge, stigma, and service use intentions among public safety personnel," *Frontiers in Psychology,* vol. 11, p. 949. https://doi.org/10.3389/fpsyg.2020.00949, 2020.
18. S. Knaak, Luong, D., McLean, R., Szeto, A. and Dobson, K. S., "Implementation, uptake, and culture change: Results of a key

informant study of a workplace mental health training program in police organizations in Canada," *Canadian Journal of Psychiatry*, vol. 64, no. 1_suppl, pp. 30S–38S. https://doi.org/10.1177/0706743719842565, 2019.
19. R. N. Carleton, Korol, S., Mason, J. E., Hozempa, K. and Anderson, G., "A longitudinal assessment of the road to mental readiness training among municipal police," *Cognitive Behaviour Therapy*, vol. 47, no. 6, pp. 508–528. https://doi.org/10.1080/16506073.2018.1475504, 2018.
20. K. S. Dobson, Szeto, A., Knaak, S., Krupa, T., Kirsh, B., Luong, D., McLean, R. and Pietrus, M., "Mental health initiatives in the workplace: Models, methods and results from the Mental Health Commission of Canada," *World Psychiatry*, vol. 17, no. 3, pp. 370–371. https://doi.org/10.1002/wps.20574, 2018.
21. I. Barath*, "Police officer wellness training: The road to mental readiness," *FBI Law Enforcement Bulletin*, pp. 1–9. https://leb.fbi.gov/articles/perspective/perspective-police-officer-wellness-training, January 11, 2017.
22. G. Schomerus, Angermeyer, M., Baumeister, S., Stolzenburg, S., Link, B. and Phelan, J., "An online intervention using information on the mental health-mental illness continuum to reduce stigma," *European Psychiatry*, vol. 32, pp. 21–27. https://doi.org/10.1016/j.eurpsy.2015.11.006, 2015.
23. B. D. Adams, Davis, S. A., Brown, A. L., Filardo, E. A. and Thomson, M. H., "Post-traumatic stress disorder (PTSD) in emergency responders scoping study: Literature review," 2013 (DRDCRDDC-2014-C18). Ottawa, Ontario, Canada: Defence Research and Development Canada-Centre for Security Science. Retrieved from Defence Research and Development Canada: https://www.canada.ca/en/defence-research-development.html; 2013 Nov. https://cradpdf.drdc-rddc.gc.ca/PDFS/unc196/p538641_A1b.pdf.
24. A. Szeto, Dobson, K. S. and Knaak, S., "The Road to Mental Readiness for first responders: A meta-analysis of program outcomes," *Canadian Journal of Psychiatry/Revue Canadienne de Psychiatrie*, vol. 64, pp. 18S–29S. https://doi.org/10.1177/0706743719842562, 2019.
25. M. S. Harvey*, "Mental health care in the CAF: Beyond R2MR," https://soleildotpress.wordpress.com/2019/02/23/continuum-model-of-mental-health-care-in-the-caf-the-road-2-mental-readiness-program/, February 23, 2019.
26. R. N. Carleton, Afifi, T. O., Turner, S., Taillieu, T. and Vaughan, A., "Mental health training, attitudes toward support and screening positive for

mental disorders," *Cognitive Behaviour Therapy,* vol. 49, no. 1, pp. 55–73. https://doi.org/10.1080/16506073.2019.1575900, 2020.
27. M. A. Zamorski, Rusu, C., Guest, K. and Fikretoglu, D., "Exposure to mental health training and education in Canadian Armed Forces personnel," *Journal of Military, Veteran and Family Health,* vol. 4, no. 2, pp. 91–100. https://doi.org/10.3138/jmvfh.2017-0046, 2018.
28. J. Andersen, Papazoglou, K., Arnetz, B. and Collins, P., "Mental preparedness as a pathway to police resilience and optimal functioning in the line of duty," *International Journal of Emergency Mental Health and Humience,* vol. 17, no. 3, pp. 624–627, 2015.
29. T. C. Callaghan, *"Mandating wellness programs for police officers,"* Doctoral dissertation, University of the Fraser Valley, 2017.
30. I. M. Cohen, McCormick, A. V. and Rich, B., "Creating a culture of police officer wellness," *Policing: A Journal of Policy and Practice,* vol. 13, no. 2, pp. 213–229. https://doi.org/10.1093/police/paz001, 2019.
31. E. Vermetten, Granek, J., Boland, H., Berge, E. ten, Binsch, O., Carmi, L., Zohar, J., Wynn, G. and Jetly, R., "Leveraging technology to improve military mental health: Novel uses of smartphone apps," *Journal of Military, Veteran and Family Health,* vol. 6, no. S1, pp. 36–43. https://doi.org/10.3138/jmvfh.2019-0034, 2020.
32. A. Gilberto, "An exploration of recovery from post-traumatic stress disorder in Canadian armed forces veterans: A qualitative inquiry using interpretive phenomenological analysis," 2017, Doctoral Dissertation, University of the Fraser Valley, p. 1–39, 2017.
33. K. Blackler*, Fikretoglu D, Liu A. Feasibility findings from a pilot Group Randomized Control Trial on the Road to Mental Readiness (R2MR) program. Defence Research and Development Canada; 2018.
34. A. R. Blais, Thompson, M. and McCreary, D. R., "The development and validation of the Army Post-Deployment Reintegration Scale," *Military Psychology,* vol. 21, no. 3, pp. 365–386. https://doi.org/10.1080/08995600902914727, 2009.
35. J. Andersen, "The use of resilience programming to improve health and prevent PTSD and OSI among first responders," University of Toronto, Mississauga, 2007.
36. J. T. Gist, Ferdik, F. and Smith, H. P., "A qualitative inquiry into the sources of resilience found among maximum security correctional officers," *Criminal Justice Policy Review,* vol. 34, no. 3, pp. 291–315, 2023.
37. E. C. Osterberg, "'We can't arrest our way out of this' police responses to gang violence in British Columbia's Lower Mainland," Doctoral Dissertation, University of British Columbia, 2020.

38 A. M. Stelnicki, Jamshidi, L., Fletcher, A. J. and Carleton, R. N., "Evaluation of before operational stress: A program to support mental health and proactive psychological protection in public safety personnel," *Frontiers in Psychology*, vol. 12, no. 3218, 2021.
39 Trounson JS, Pfeifer JE. Corrections officer wellbeing: Training challenges and opportunities. Practice: The New Zealand Corrections Journal. Jul; *5(1)*, 22–28, 2017.
40 A. Szeto, Dobson, K. S., Luong, D., Krupa, T. and Kirsh, B., "Workplace antistigma programs at the Mental Health Commission of Canada: Part 2 lessons learned," *Canadian Journal of Psychiatry*, vol. 64, no. 1_suppl, pp. 13S–17S. https://doi.org/10.1177/0706743719, 2019c.
41 C. Kowalski, "Strengthening the capabilities to lead police officers following exposure to trauma." ProQuest Dissertations Publishing, Master's thesis, Royal Roads University (Canada), Nov, 1–106, 2018.
42 D. Fikretoglu*, Beatty, E. and Liu, A., "Comparing different versions of Road to Mental Readiness to determine optimal content Testing instruction type, homework, and intelligence effects at two timepoints," Scientific Report No. DRDC-RDDC-2014-R164, Defence Research and Development Canada, Dec, 2014.
43 S. Bailey*, Smith, S. and Williams, K., "Strive to thrive: Resiliency training for all levels of healthcare," in 6th Canadian Conference of Physician Health (CCPH), St. John's Newfoundland, October, 2019.
44 M. L. Misis, "An examination of perceied stress levels and coping styles among rural law enforcement officers," Doctoral dissertation, University of Southern Mississippi, May, 2012.
45 D. Fikretoglu*, D'Agata, M. T., Sullivan-Kwantes, W. and Richards, K., "Mental health and mental health service use attitudes among Canadian Armed Forces (CAF) recruits and officer cadets," Scientific Report: DRDC-RDDC-2017-R027, Defence Research and Development Canada, Feb, 2017.
46 A. Szeto, Dobson, K. S., Luong, D., Krupa, T. and Kirsh, B., "Workplace antistigma programs at the mental health Commission of Canada: Part 1. processes and projects," *Canadian Journal of Psychiatry*, vol. 64, no. 1_suppl, pp. 5S–12S. https://doi.org/10.1177/07067, 2019b.
47 K. S. Dobson, Szeto, A. and Knaak, S., "The working mind: A meta-analysis of a workplace mental health and stigma reduction program," *Canadian Journal of Psychiatry*, vol. 64, no. 1_suppl, pp. 39S–47S. https://doi.org/10.1177/0706743719842559, 2019.
48 L. Tam-Seto, Wood, V. M., Linden, B. and Stuart, H., "A scoping review of mental health mobile apps for use by the military community," *mHealth*, vol. 4, p. 57. https://doi.org/10.21037/mhealth.2018.12.01, 2018.

49 K. Guest*, Bailey, S., Khan, S. and Thompson, S., "Performance and resilience coaching for military leadership," Science and Technology Organization-MP-HFM, NATO-OTAN, 302(15), pp. 1–14, 2019.
50 Orlick, T., *Psyching for sport: Mental training for athletes.* Champaign, IL: Human Kinetics, 1986.
51 T. Orlick, "The psychology of personal excellence," *Contemporary Thought on Performance Enhancement,* vol. 1, pp. 110–122, 1992.
52 T. Orlick, "Wheel of excellence." http://www.zoneofexcellence.ca, October 25, 2003.

Appendix E

Physical Competencies in Policing[1]

Michael G. Tyshenko, *Senior Risk Analyst*, Judy McDonald, *Research Supervisor*[2], Niyati Vyas, *Masters Graduate*[2], and Travis Kirkwood, *Masters Graduate*[2]

1 Condensed version of original research paper.
2 School of Epidemiology and Public Health, Faculty of Medicine, University of Ottawa.

Abstract

This review explored the standards and measures that have been used to evaluate physical competencies in frontline policing. These are important, because policing is a high-risk profession with sometimes serious physical demands; being able to measure if officers are physically ready for frontline work helps design future training; and improve safety and effectiveness. Four broad standards that ensure physical readiness in law enforcement include: use of force, officer safety, physical demands, and vehicle operations. Eleven excellence measures were identified within these four standards. This review contributed to the overall understanding of new and current trends in police operational readiness, and updating of Gold Medal Policing, 2nd edition

Introduction

To find out whether officers are meeting job-related physical performance requirements, attention usually focuses on regular training for fitness, self-defense, and use of force[1]. This was also found to be true during a previous review of *Police Training Standards*, which was included in the first edition of *Gold Medal*

Policing[2]. Around the world, there are differences in the tasks police are expected to perform and the physical skills and practice that they need throughout their careers. And because policing is such a high-risk profession, it is important to have reliable ways of measuring their physical competencies and readiness for frontline work[3].

For example, some law enforcement programs require 14 hours of training per year with focus on firearms; arresting and controlling suspects; driver training and awareness; and strategic communication skills. But there is much more being researched in helping officers to be technically ready for the job[4].

The purpose of this review was to determine what standards and measures are used to evaluate physical competencies in policing.

Search and analysis. A rapid review of research on physical police competencies revealed 29 pertinent empirical articles with four main clusters of high-performance physical standards:

1. Use of force (39% of all articles)
2. Physical demands (24%)
3. Officer safety (21%)
4. Vehicle operations (15%)

Findings

In the research articles, the most common of these standards was *Use of Force,* found in **39%** of the articles. For *Officer Safety* it was **24%**; *Physical Demands* was **21%**; and Vehicle Operations was **15%**.

Within these four standards, 11 specific ways of measuring them were found. These are summarized in the table below.

	Summary of Police Physical Competencies			
STANDARDS	Use of Force	Officer Safety	Physical Demands	Vehicle Operations
MEASURES	Defensive tactics	Safety training	Fitness testing	Motor-vehicle events
	Force at mental-illness calls	Protective equipment	Environmental stamina	Officer compliance
	Equipment proficiency	Injury status		
	Cultural and gender challenges			

Use of force

The authority to use physical force is a serious responsibility for officers; it presents a constant ethical challenge and balancing act on the frontline. Sometimes, whether force is justified depends on who is watching, what their moral beliefs are, what the community believes, and what the social status is of the suspect (e.g., celebrity versus gang member)[5].

Defensive tactics are crucial for handling violent encounters with the public. Use of force instructors often state that officers are frequently not properly prepared for these encounters. Training needs to be longer and more regular and can be improved by: providing more resources (equipment, trainers); increasing motivation; focusing on useful tactics; improving real-life situational awareness, problem-solving, adaptability, decision confidence, and critical thinking[6].

The force that officers use should be proportional to the suspect's resistance levels. This can range from refusing to listen to orders to resisting and threatening with a deadly weapon. Officer force can be as minimal as simply "being there," and progressing through to giving verbal instructions, physical subduing and handcuffing, or using deadly force[7]. Unique individual biases, abilities, and personalities can affect understanding of what the "right" amount of force is. Training on examples of officers handling aggression helps identify the best strategies and sometimes avoids force completely by using communication skills[8].

Force at mental-illness calls. Of the 1,000 people fatally shot by police in the United States in 2018, 25% suffered mental illness. Readiness to deal with these individuals requires focused training. Additional benefits include increased officer satisfaction; making sure the suspects receive mental-health supports at psychiatric facilities; and improved perceptions of officers due to their reduced use of force[9].

Police also respond to self-harm and suicidal events, where using force requires careful balancing. A lot of factors can influence the outcome of these encounters. Overall, the suicidal individuals are more likely to: be males aged 35–40; be single or having relationship issues; have mental-illness histories; and have had recent contact with police prior to the crisis incident. They often are armed, show aggression, and threaten to injure either themselves, bystanders, or police. Officer education has shown to improve the outcomes[10].

Suicide-by-police is another risk, where individuals behave in a way, on purpose, that causes police to shoot at them. These are highly challenging situations, and make up approximately 10%–36% of police shootings[11]. They are more common in males suffering chronic depression, bipolar disorders, schizophrenia, substance use, personality disorders, and poor coping with recent stressors. They also tend to be unemployed, unmarried, poor, and previously suicidal. In the United States, victims are 98% male, 52% Caucasian, and average 32 years of age[12].

Suicide "triggers" include negative life events; domestic violence or relationship break-ups; terminal illness; financial troubles; and lawsuits. These factors are involved in 70% of suicide cases[12].

Equipment proficiency. Marksmanship excellence is critical. It is constantly promoted, maintained, and improved in law enforcement. It is complicated by city layouts, short-distance shots (usually under 75 yards), and strict rules for engagement. When required, hostile suspects should be neutralized with minimal shots to avoid collateral damage via wounded suspects[13]. During long workdays, it is important to be trained and ready to maintain accuracy and quickness. Caffeine is commonly used to combat tiredness, and research shows that it supports reaction-time but not accuracy[14].

Taser training is somewhat controversial. Not all agencies agree on the policies for how they should be used. The supporting evidence is minimal for helping to make these decisions. It has been difficult to measure how much Tasers improve safety by replacing lethal force. The media join and enhance the controversy. Police departments focus instead on where Tasers fit in to the overall continuum of use of force, and how policies on their use can achieve increased safety and effectiveness. This may involve getting the thoughts of the communities being served[15].

Officer safety

Safety training for officers typically focuses on officer survival; threats; lethal and non-lethal situations; contact with people suffering from mental illness; active-shooter response; and driving. Most training places attention on preventing assaults and attacks on officers. This is surprising when you consider that way more officer deaths and serious injuries occur due to vehicle collisions. However, it is argued that the fact fewer officers get shot may be proof that the training works. Either way, it is encouraged that risk assessments be used to make sure officer training more accurately matches with the evidence of risks officers face[16].

Protective equipment use, such as body armor, is controversial. Some studies have shown that the chance of officers dying from being shot decreased 57% if wearing body armor. Ambush or unprovoked attacks produce a three-fold increase in likelihood of fatality. Becoming disarmed results in a two-fold increase. Different situational factors influence how lethal assaults are; but in all cases mandatory-wear policies for body armor are recommended for reducing officer mortality[17]. However, body armor is bulky and heavy, and shown to diminish physical performance. It makes work feel more demanding, increases how long tasks take to complete, and reduces balance and stability. It may also affect marksmanship. The decision to wear body armor should be made carefully, depending on the fitness of the officer, how it interacts with all the other equipment they carry (gun, handcuffs, radio, etc.), and the overall ergonomic fit[18].

Injury status impacts performance. The unpredictable, high-risk work of policing leads to physical injuries, especially to the upper body—soft tissue sprains and strains. Assaults and trying to handle non-compliant offenders are the most common causes[19].

Physical demands

Fitness testing is a way to estimate if officers are physically able to perform important police-work tasks. Generally, police are just slightly above average in: muscular strength and endurance; body composition (fat versus muscle); power; flexibility; speed; agility; and cardiorespiratory fitness. Ongoing fitness training is always recommended; it benefits overall health and also the success of police-specific tasks[20].

Increased equipment loads reduce agility and power, which are necessary for rare but extremely important high-intensity frontline duties. Burdens on movement can increase risk of injury or death in the line of duty[21]. Culture and gender also pose challenges to fitness expectations. In Canada, visible minority and Indigenous communities have previously expressed that policing is not an acceptable profession for women, because of its high physical requirements[22].

Environmental stamina. Occupations like emergency medical services, policing, and military operations have safety and health encounters required for the job. These exposures include: sense-related, bacteria and viruses, weather conditions, cardiovascular exertion, in addition to basic fitness demands. Quality of sleep and stress resilience related to incident recall in debriefs was also noted[23]. Some examples of how these are addressed include: vaccine protocols, and training for respiratory endurance, muscle resistance and physical readiness. Some health and safety trainings have also incorporated psychological tasks[24].

Vehicle operations

Motor-vehicle training is critical related to events that are the leading cause of on-duty death for law enforcement officers, which include roadside incidents[16,25]. Officers spend many hours conducting vehicle patrols, where unique risks include: rough weather conditions, high speeds, in-car distractions, and work along major highways[26].

Officer compliance. Despite the known risks and frequency of motor-vehicle-related events (MVEs), officers tend to be complacent and not take the risks as seriously as they should[27]. As noted previously, officer training should align better with the actual risks they are likely to encounter[16]. When departments focus on MVE reduction, officers become more aware of the true risks—this makes them more willing to accept protective equipment and behaviors (e.g., speed caps and restrictive driving policies)[28].

Recommendations

1. *Increase training time and frequency* to enhance equipment proficiencies[29]. Improving officer marksmanship and tactics requires repetition to form muscle memory—this is critical in facing violent encounters. Quality of practice is improved by pairing physical training with critical thinking, mental adaptability, situational awareness, and decision-making confidence.
2. *Prioritize competence in handling mental-illness calls*, an urgent ethical and social priority. Suicide calls, suicide-by-cop shootings, and suspects with psychiatric illnesses are not new for officers. But expectations have evolved toward using less force and showing greater empathy while making sure individuals get the mental support they need. Safely directing use of force to communications, or reducing the severity of force (e.g., with Tasers instead of guns) requires careful policies based on evidence.
3. *Implement tailor-made scenario training* covering: officer survival; lethal and non-lethal threats to officers; contact with the mentally ill; active-shooter response; and complex driving maneuvers. Safety awareness also extends to: caring for casualties and injuries out in the frontline; officer-rescue tactics; anticipation of ambush attacks; and crowd-control strategies.

4. ***Analyze risk versus protection***, considering factors from public threats of violence, to hours behind the wheel. Officer acceptance and use of protective behaviors and equipment are highly dependent on risk perception. While personal protective equipment continues to get better, the policies for use remain controversial due to impacts on exertion, reaction time, performance, and the strain on physical posture.
5. ***Attend to reputed physical demands*** in policing defined by the endurance, complex motor-skills, and situation tactics needed to perform forceful maneuvers (such are subduing a suspect to the ground, and handcuffing). These may be impacted by environmental conditions (heat/cold, rain, smells, germs), cultural and gender biases, and the risk of injury.
6. ***Emphasize protective driving measures.*** In 2005, a 20-year review of police training standards revealed that research focuses *a lot* on officer use of force. This is still true. However, vehicle fatalities and roadside incidents remain the most common threats, proving that police driving is complex, and officers need to be encouraged to commit to measures for reducing driving incidents.

Notes

1 J. Kwasniewski, McDonald, J. and Allen, J., "Police training standard directed at improving performance excellence" In J. McDonald (Ed.), *Gold medal policing*, (pp. 209–215), New York: Sloan Associate Press, 2006.
2 J. M. McDonald, *Gold medal policing: Mental readiness and performance excellence*. Ottawa: Sloan Associate Press, 2006.
3 The Academy, "Perishable skills: South Bay regional public safety training," Plus ROI Online Marketing. https://theacademy.ca.gov/perishable_skills/#:~:text=In%20January%202002%20POST%20implemented,Tactical%20Firearms%204%20hour%20minimum, 2022.
4 P. Di Nota and Huhta, J., "Complex motor learning and police training: Applied, cognitive, and clinical perspectives," *Frontiers in Psychology*, vol. 10, p. 1797. https://doi.org/10.3389/fpsyg.2019.01797, 2019.

5 P. Dick, "Dirty work designations: How police officers account for their use of coercive force," *Human Relations,* vol. 58, no. 11, pp. 1363–1390. https://doi.org/10.1177/0018726705060242, 2005.

6 J. Preddy, "Building a cognitive readiness Construct for violent police-public encounters." ProQuest Dissertations Publishing, Doctoral Dissertation, Old Dominion University, DOI: 10.25777/t8jr-8n49.n https://digitalcommons.odu.edu/stemps_etds/40, 2018.

7 E. Jefferis, Butcher, F. and Hanely, D., "Measuring perceptions of police use of force," *Police Practice and Research,* vol. 12, no. 1, pp. 81–96. https://doi.org/10.1080/15614263.2010.497656, 2011.

8 T. Prenzler, Porter, L. and Alpert, G., "Reducing police use of force: Case studies and prospects," *Aggression and Violent Behavior,* vol. 18, no. 2, pp. 343–356. https://doi.org/10.1016/j.avb.2012.12.004, 2013.

9 M. Rogers, McNiel, D. and Binder, R., "Effectiveness of police crisis intervention training programs," *The Journal of the American Academy of Psychiatry and the Law,* vol. 47, no. 4, pp. 414–421. https://doi.org/10.29158/JAAPL.003863-19, 2019.

10 K. Chidgey, Procter, N., Baker, A. and Grech, C., "Police response to individuals displaying suicidal or self-harming behaviours: An integrative review," *Health & Social Care in the Community,* vol. 27, no. 3, pp. e112–e124. https://doi.org/10.1111/hsc.12668, 2019.

11 S. Bresler, Scalora, M., Elbogen, E. and Moore, Y., "Attempted suicide by cop: A case study of traumatic brain injury and the insanity defense," *Journal of Forensic Sciences,* vol. 48, no. 1, pp. 1–5. https://doi.org/10.1520/JFS2001045, 2003.

12 R. De Similien and Okorafor, A., "Suicide by cop: A psychiatric phenomenon," *American Journal of Psychiatry,* vol. 12, no. 1, pp. 20–22. https://doi.org/10.1176/appi.ajp-rj.2017.120107, 2017.

13 F. Mastison, "On target: 20 police marksman facts," Tactical Life. https://www.tactical-life.com/lifestyle/tactics/target-20-police-marksman-facts/, February 16, 2015.

14 C. Torres and Kim, Y., "The effects of caffeine on marksmanship accuracy and reaction time: A systematic review," *Ergonomics,* vol. 62, no. 8, pp. 1023–1032. https://doi.org/10.1080/00140139.2019.1613572, 2019.

15 K. Adams and Jennison, V., "What we do not know about police use of Tasers™," *Policing: An International Journal,* vol. 30, no. 3, pp. 447–465. https://doi.org/10.1108/13639510710778831, 2007.

16 J. Rojek, Grieco, J., Meade, B. and Parsons, D., "National survey on officer safetyTraining: Findings and implications," National Police Foundation, Washington, DC, 2020.
17 C. Crifasi, Pollack, K. and Webster, D., "Effects of state-level policy changes on homicide and nonfatal shootings of law enforcement officers," *Injury Prevention,* vol. 22, no. 4, pp. 274–278. https://doi.org/10.1136/injuryprev-2015-041825, 2016.
18 C. Tomes, Orr, R. and Pope, R., "The impact of body armor on physical performance of law enforcement personnel: A systematic review," *Annals of Occupational and Environmental Medicine,* vol. 29, no. 1, p. 14. https://doi.org/10.1186/s40557-017-0169-9, 2017.
19 K. Lyons, Radburn, C., Orr, R. and Pope, R., "A profile of injuries sustained by law enforcement officers: A critical review," *International Journal of Environmental Research and Public Health,* vol. 14, no. 2, pp. 142–162. https://doi.org/10.3390/ijerph14020142, 2017.
20 E. Marins, David, G. and Del Vecchio, F., "Characterization of the physical fitness of police officers: A systematic review," *Journal of Strength and Conditioning Research,* vol. 33, no. 10, pp. 2860–2874. https://doi.org/10.1519/JSC.0000000000003177, 2019.
21 J. Helsby, Carton, S., Joseph, K., Mahmud, A., Park, Y., Navarrete, A., Ackermann, K., Walsh, J. and Haynes, I., "Early intervention systems: Predicting adverse interactions between police and the public," *Criminal Justice Policy Review,* vol. 29, no. 2, pp. 180–209. https://doi.org/10.1177/0887403417695380, 2018.
22 H. Jain, Singh, P. and Agocs, C., "Recruitment, selection and promotion of visible-minority and aboriginal police officers in selected Canadian police services," *Canadian Public Administration,* vol. 43, no. 1, pp. 46–74. https://doi.org/10.1111/j.1754-7121.2000.tb015, 2000.
23 C. L. Gutshall, Hampton, D. P., Jr., Sebetan, I. M., Stein, P. C. and Broxtermann, T. J., "The effects of occupational stress on cognitive performance in police officers," *Police Practice & Research: An International Journal*, vol. 18, no. 5, pp. 463–477, 2017.
24 M. Plat, Frings-Dresen, M. and Sluiter, J., "A systematic review of job-specific workers' health surveillance activities for fire-fighting, ambulance, police and military personnel," *International Archives of Occupational and Environmental Health,* vol. 84, no. 8, pp. 839–857. https://doi.org/10.1007/s00420-011-0614-y, 2011.
25 National Law Enforcement Officers Memorial Fund, Causes of law enforcement deaths: Over the past decade (2014-2023), National Law Enforcement Officers Memorial Fund, https://nleomf.org/memorial

/facts-figures/officer-fatality-data/causes-of-law-enforcement-deaths/, 2024

26 H. Tiesman, Hendricks, S., Bell, J. and Amandus, H., "Eleven years of occupational mortality in law enforcement: The census of fatal occupational injuries, 1992-2002," *American Journal of Industrial Medicine,* vol. 53, no. 9, pp. 940–949. https://doi.org/10.1002/ajim.20863, 2010.

27 K. Wehr, Alpert, G. and Rojek, J., "The fear of the ninja assassin: Understanding the role of agency culture in injurious and fatal on-duty vehicle collisions," *Journal of California Law Enforcement,* vol. 46, no. 2, pp. 18–26, 2012.

28 H. Tiesman, Heick, R., Konda, S. and Hendricks, S., "Law enforcement officers' risk perceptions toward on-duty motor-vehicle events," *Policing,* vol. 38, no. 3, pp. 563–577. https://doi.org/10.1108/PIJPSM-03-2015-0028, 2015.

29 Mental Health Commission of Canada* (MHCC), "Summary of Road To Mental Readiness (R2MR) evaluation results." https://theworkingmind.ca/sites/default/files/r2mr_evaluation_results_summary_april_1_2016_en.pdf, April 1, 2016.

Appendix F

Technical Competencies in Policing[1]

Michael G. Tyshenko, *Senior Risk Analyst,*
Judy McDonald, *Research Supervisor*[2], Niyati Vyas,
Masters Graduate[2], Travis Kirkwood, *Masters Graduate*[2],
and Chewe Ali-Ndi Ringnyu, *Masters Student*[2]

1 Condensed version of original research paper.
2 School of Epidemiology and Public Health, Faculty of Medicine, University of Ottawa.

Abstract

This review explored the standards and measures that have been used to evaluate technical competencies in frontline policing. Officers need technical competency to adeptly execute tactical, analytical, knowledge sharing, and legal tasks associated with their day-to-day duties. Four broad standards that ensure technical readiness in law enforcement include: Knowledge of police organizations, knowledge and application of the law, community understanding, and verbal and written communication. thirteen measures were identified within these four standards. This review contributed to the overall understanding of new and current trends in police operational readiness, and updating of Gold Medal Policing, 2nd edition

Introduction

Day-to-day, police officers use technical skills in their work crucial for meeting various job demands. Agencies must train these skills in officers, and measure them. This review summarizes methods for measuring how prepared officers are for technical excellence in their job. A key finding is that communications skills make dangerous situations safer (e.g., giving clear instructions, collaborating with firefighters or nurses). Specific skills include: active listening; problem solving; persuasion and conflict management.

Purpose: To determine what standards and measures are related to technical police competency.

Search and analysis: A rapid literature review was completed to determine what standards and measures for technical competencies for policing excellence were being reflected across five databases. The search revealed 51 pertinent empirical articles for review with data, statistics, models, and charts pulled where relevant. Four sub-themes or *standards* for technical excellence were identified:
- knowledge of police organizations (40% of all articles)
- community understanding (27%)
- knowledge and application of the law (25%)
- verbal and written communication (8%)

Findings

These four broad standards were further broken down into 13 measures briefly elaborated as follows.

	Summary of Police Technical Competencies			
STANDARDS	*Knowledge of police organization*	*Understand community*	*Knowledge and application of law*	*Verbal and written communication*
MEASURES	Policing philosophy	Special-interest groups	Local, provincial, federal laws	Articulation
	Policies, procedures, protocols	Street-drug use	Situational tactics	Note-taking and reporting
	Organizational culture	The media	Technology resources	
	Counter-terrorism impacts	Community partners		

Knowledge of police organization

Policing philosophy must reflect new "big data" analytics—computing power and massive amounts of information can identify useful patterns in crime and how police resources should be deployed. It shifts policing philosophy away from rigid hierarchies toward complex networks[1]. Modern policing also emphasizes:

Community-Oriented Policing, involving communities in crime prevention, improving satisfaction; sense of order; and trust in police[2,3,4].

Problem-Oriented Policing plans solutions to long-term problems, instead of reacting to short-term events.

Public-private Policing is another growing trend, but there are problems; private police are accountable to people who hire them, while public police serve the public and elected politicians[5] (e.g., NYPD Shield program[6,7]).

Policies, procedures, and protocol can improve by adapting to societal changes and new technologies, and evolving cultures and communication practices in police agencies[8,9]. Despite being favored, implementation often fails[10]. This supports crime-mapping; planning and clear goals; accountability to communities; flexibility; focus on outcomes; and basing decisions on evidence. This requires two-way channels of communication, instead of rigid one-way orders[11]. It also requires more diversity of officers, to better represent the communities they serve[12]. Diversity (gender, migrant background) improves trust and positive views of police[13,14].

Organizational culture (e.g., training) needs to focus on students, encouraging critical thinking and experience-based learning. Compared to previous focus on teacher lectures, student-centered training strategies improve decision-making[15].

Counter-terrorism impacts can be significant. Agencies explore ways to combat terrorists' ability to rapidly recruit people globally using social media and propaganda[16]. The threat and fear of terrorism contribute to depression and post-traumatic stress disorder (PTSD)[17]. This can be improved by making sure stress is treated as an ongoing process, and that officers and agencies must continually learn, adapt, and cope[18,19,20].

Understand community

Geographic awareness is a skill officers develop gradually by working in specific locations. They gain an ability to identify "hotspots" and predict where crime problems will occur[21]. This knowledge needs to be measured and used in computer algorithms[22]. This would help anticipate crime locations and inform strategies and placement of police resources to respond quickly when crimes occur[21].

Special-interest groups include those with *mental-health needs*, who are more likely to be arrested, often just to manage their behaviors while suffering disturbances in public[23,24]. Better strategies are needed to ensure they receive care[24]. *Anti-racism* efforts cite research on police racism, brutality, and misconduct[25,26,27,28]. Strategies are needed to respond to public criticisms[29]. *LBGTQ2S+ hate crimes* by officers and the public are an ongoing issue. To improve everyone's safety, better strategies are needed to ensure LBGTQ2S+ victimization is taken more seriously in police responses[30,31].

Street-drug use: Recently officers have been forced to learn and adapt in responding to rising overdose and deaths from opioids. PowerPoint presentations on harm reduction are commonly included into training, but improved training methods and measurement of effectiveness are needed[32].

The media amplify misinformation, fueling hatred and violence against police. Resisting arrest, and physical assault and murder of officers is more common. Calls to de-police communities have grown, along with beliefs that police are racist. Media with low reporting standards increase the chances people become violent. Improved media relations are needed[33].

Community partners can be valuable. For example, there are benefits to injury control and prevention when police and healthcare providers share information regarding road-traffic injuries[34].

Knowledge and application of the law

Local, provincial, and federal laws shift over time. The effects of changes must be measured, to inform ongoing police training and strategies for responding to the secondary effects (e.g., legalization of cannabis and risks of juvenile use; increased potency; psychotic episodes)[35,36].

Technology resources can improve traditional police work and also support new strategies, but do come with a high degree of complexity[37]. Computer software can forecast when and where crimes will take place, and virtual simulations can be designed to train officers' in-the-moment decision-making[22,38]. Key technologies that have been widely used include body cameras[39,40,41,42]; crime mapping technologies; closed-circuit television (CCTV) monitoring[43,44]; social media[45,46]; data-mining software; car cameras; and license-plate readers[47].

Verbal and written communication

Articulation, the ability to communicate clearly and confidently, improves police outcomes. Indeed, law enforcement often disarms people with words (e.g., hostage negotiations). There are methods for training communication to de-escalate explosive situations and resolve conflicts[48,49]. Articulation skills also improve note-taking; assertiveness; and sensitivity for safely handling calls involving domestic violence, sexual harassment, and disabilities[49,50].

Note-taking and reporting are basic job functions. Concise, convincing reporting is essential for police work and criminal justice. Much time is spent finalizing reports; writing skills can increase speed and quality[49].

Recommendations

1. *Deploy mobile technology effectively.* Technological advancements can aid in frontline risk management but implementation comes with a high degree of difficulty. Poor deployment can not only fail to achieve intended goals, but may *create* additional harm for all concerned. When combined with proactive old-fashioned policing in high-risk areas, street-level crime is reduced[51].
2. *Strengthen articulation training for rookies*: On-scene debriefs and simulation training reinforce effective "police talk" for rookies. Well-articulated, deliberate interactions help de-escalate toward peaceful resolutions. Student-centered police training engages critical situational analysis and choosing best responses. More self-directed field-training materials are needed[48,49,50].
3. *Facilitate collaborative information-sharing.* Police must meet public interest via interactive platforms for two-way communication[2,11]. This improves community relations and public image branding. Frontline officers are encouraged to collaborate and share information with other service providers for greater efficiency and preventive efforts. Website portals host mapping technologies, best-practices, training opportunities, and inter-organizational information sharing.
4. *Invest in specialized counter-terrorism training.* Threats of terrorism contribute to risk of depression and PTSD. Investments have been made to increase mental-health literacy and access to services within police services[16,17,18].
5. *Embrace community-policing strategies.* Local community involvement in crime prevention is outgrowing traditional law enforcement[2]. Media publicity can both intensify police controversy and, conversely, bridge good communications. Community-policing strategies improve citizen satisfaction, perceptions of disorder, and police legitimacy[3].

Notes

1. M. Kaufmann, Egbert, S. and Leese, M., "Predictive policing and the politics of patterns," *The British Journal of Criminology,* Vol. 59, no. 3, pp. 674–692, https://doi.org/10.1093/bjc/azy060, 2019.
2. C. Massinger and Wood, N., "Improving law enforcement cross cultural competencies through continued education," *Journal of Education and Learning,* vol. 5, no. 2, pp. 258–264, 2016.
3. C. Gill, Weisburd, D., Telep, C., Vitter, Z. and Bennett, T., "Community-oriented policing to reduce crime, disorder and fear and increase satisfaction and legitimacy among citizens: A systematic review," *Journal of Experimental Criminology,* vol. 10, no. 4, pp. 399–428. https://doi.org/10.1007/s11292-014-9210-y, 2014.
4. A. F. Dias and Hilgers T. Community oriented policing theory and practice: global policy diffusion or local appropriation?. Policing and Society. Jun 5: 1–9, 2020.
5. S. Burbidge, "The governance deficit: Reflections on the future of public and private policing in Canada," *Canadian Journal of Criminology and Criminal Justice,* vol. 47, no. 1, pp. 63–86. https://doi.org/10.3138/cjccj.47.1.63, 2005.
6. C. Andreeva, The evolution of information-sharing in EU counter-terrorism post-2015: a paradigm shift?. InCollective Securitization and Crisification of EU Policy Change (pp. 134-159). Routledge, 2022.
7. V. Amadeo and Iannone, S., "Successful public-private partnerships: The NYPD shield model," *Journal of Business Continuity & Emergency Planning,* vol. 10, no. 2, pp. 106–117, 2007.
8. Y. Yuksel, "Understanding the role of culture and communication in implementing planned organizational change: the case of compstat in police organizations," PhD Dissertation, Rutgers University, New Brunswick, NJ, 2013.
9. L. Lewis, *Organizational change: Creating change through strategic communication,* vol. 2. Hoboken, NJ: John Wiley & Sons, 2011.
10. L. K. Lewis and Seibold, D. R., "Reconceptualizing organizational change implementation as a communication problem: A review of literature and research agenda," *Annals of the International Communication Association,* vol. 21, no. 1, pp. 93–152. https://doi.org/10.1080/23808985.1998.11678949, 1998.

11 W. J. Bratton and Malinowski, S. W., "Police performance management in practice: Taking COMPSTAT to the next level," *Policing: A Journal of Policy and Practice,* vol. 2, no. 3, pp. 259–265. https://doi.org/10.1093/police/pan036, 2008.

12 T. Carrique, "Recruiting with vision: Cultivating a police service that reflects the community." ProQuest Dissertations Publishing, Masters thesis, Royal Roads University, 2005.

13 A. Van Ewijk, "Diversity within police forces in Europe: A case for the comprehensive view," *Policing: A Journal of Policy and Practice,* vol. 6, no. 1, pp. 76–92. https://doi.org/10.1093/police/par048, 2012.

14 S. P. Jain and Agocs, C., "Recruitment, selection and promotion of visible-minority and aboriginal police officers in selected Canadian police services," *Canadian Public Administration,* vol. 43, no. 1, pp. 46–74, 2000.

15 R. L. Norris, "Training for community policing: Constructing effective police education (Order No. 10846444)." ProQuest Dissertations & Theses Global (2124408064), Doctoral Dissertation, Saint Mary's College of California, https://www.proquest.com/docview/2124408064?pq-origsite=gscholar&fromopenview=true&sourcetype=Dissertations%20&%20Theses, 2018.

16 Nagengast, "Countering digital terrorism: A qualitative study on information sharing to deny digital radicalization and recruiting." ProQuest Dissertations Publishing Doctoral Dissertation, Colorado Technical University, Feb 2021.

17 D. Paton and Violanti, J. M., "Policing in the context of terrorism: Managing traumatic stress risk," *Traumatology,* vol. 12, no. 3, pp. 236–247. https://doi.org/10.1177/1534765606294990, 2006.

18 F. Losel, King, S., Bender, D. and Jugl, I., "Protective factors against extremism and violent radicalization: A systematic review of research," *International Journal of Developmental Science,* vol. 12, no. 1–2, pp. 89–102. https://doi.10.3233/DEV-170241, 2018.

19 R. N. Carleton, Korol, S., Mason, J. E., Hozempa, K. and Anderson, G., "A longitudinal assessment of the road to mental readiness training among municipal police," *Cognitive Behaviour Therapy,* vol. 47, no. 6, pp. 508–528. https://doi.org/10.1080/16506073.2018.1475504, 2018a.

20 D. Fikretoglu*, D'Agata, M. T., Sullivan-Kwantes, W. and Richards, K., "Mental health and mental health service use attitudes among Canadian Armed Forces (CAF) recruits and officer cadets," Scientific Report: DRDC-RDDC-2017-R027, Defence Research and Development Canada, Feb 2017.

21. G. Bichler and Gaines, L., "An examination of police officers' insights into problem identification and problem solving," *Crime and Delinquency*, vol. 51, no. 1, pp. 53–74. https://doi.org/10.1177/0011128704265936, 2005.
22. M. Bennett, Lyria and Chan, J., "Algorithmic prediction in policing: Assumptions, evaluation, and accountability," *Policing and Society*, vol. 28, no. 7, pp. 806–822, https://doi.org/10.1080/10439463.2016.1253695, 2018.
23. M. S. Morabito, "Horizons of context: Understanding the police decision to arrest people with mental illness," *Psychiatric Services,* vol. 58, no. 12, pp. 1582–1587. https://doi.org/10.1176/ps.2007.58.12.1582, 2007.
24. R. D. Borschmann, Gillard, S., Turner, K., Chambers, M. and O'Brien, A., "Section 136 of the Mental Health Act: A new literature review," *Medicine, Science and the Law,* vol. 50, no. 1, pp. 34–39. https://doi.org/10.1258/msl.2009.009004, 2010.
25. C. Chaney and Robertson, R. V., "Racism and police brutality in America," *Journal of African American Studies*, vol. 17, no. 4, pp. 480–505. https://doi.org/10.1007/s12111-013-9246-5, 2013.
26. K. D. Hassell and Archbold, C. A., "Widening the scope on complaints of police misconduct," *Policing: An International Journal of Police Strategies and Management,* vol. 33, no. 3, pp. 473–489. https://doi.org/10.1108/13639511011066863, 2010.
27. S. King, "'Ready to shoot and do shoot': Black working-class self-defense and community politics in Harlem, New York, during the 1920s," *Journal of Urban History*, vol. 37, no. 5, pp. 757–774. https://doi.org/10.1177/0096144211413234, 2011.
28. P. Muennig and Murphy, M., "Does racism affect health? Evidence from the United States and the United Kingdom," *Journal of Health Politics, Policy and Law*, vol. 36, no. 1, pp. 187–214. https://doi.org/10.1215/03616878-1191153, 2011.
29. J. McDonald, *Gold medal policing: Mental readiness and performance excellence.* New York: Sloan Associate Press, 2006.
30. L. Dario, Fradella, H. F., Verhagen, M. and Parry, M. M., "Assessing LGBT people's perceptions of police legitimacy," *Journal of Homosexuality,* vol. 67, no. 7, pp. 885–915. https://doi.org/10.1080/00918369.2018.1560127, 2020.
31. A. Holmes, "Marching with pride? Debates on uniformed police participating in Vancouver's LGBTQ pride parade," *Journal of Homosexuality*, vol. 7502386, no. id5, pp. 1–33. https://doi.org/10.1080/00918369.2019.1696107, 2020.

32 T. Khorasheh, Naraine, R., Watson, T. W., Wright, A., Kallio, N. and Strike, C., "A scoping review of harm reduction training for police officers," *Drug and Alcohol Review,* vol. 38, no. 2, pp. 131–150, 2019.

33 S. Morrow, "Social and news media's effects on law enforcement," *Global Journal of Forensic Science & Medicine,* vol. 1, no. 4, p. GJFSM.MS.ID.000516. https://doi.org/10.33552/AJGH.2019.01.000516, 2019.

34 S. F. Jacoby, Kollar, L. L. M., Ridgeway, G. and Sumner, S. A., "Health system and law enforcement synergies for injury surveillance, control and prevention: A scoping review," *Injury Prevention,* vol. 24, no. 4, pp. 305–311. https://doi.org/10.1136/injuryprev-2017-042416, 2018.

35 S. D. Perea, "Marijuana, law enforcement, mental health: A dangerous social experiment." https://www.policechiefmagazine.org/marijuana-law-enforcement-mental-health/?ref=6a709f431039dddb4f1512a2a1f010d8, March 2019.

36 L. P. A. Ward and Murphy, A., "The impact of Marijuana legalization on law enforcement in states surrounding Colorado," *Police Quarterly,* vol. 22, no. 2, pp. 217–242. https://doi.org/10.1177/1098611118819902, 2019.

37 T. N. White and Gaub, J. E., "Examining body-worn camera integration and acceptance among police officers, citizens, and external stakeholders," *Criminology & Public Policy,* vol. 17, no. 3, pp. 649–677. https://doi.org/10.1111/1745-9133.12376, 2018.

38 T. Söderström, Åström, J., Anderson, G. and Bowles, R., "A framework for the design of computer-assisted simulation training for complex police situations," *Campus-Wide Information Systems,* vol. 31, no. 4, pp. 242–253. https://doi.org/10.1108/CWIS-10-2013-0060, 2014.

39 B. Ariel, Farrar, W. A. and Sutherland, A., "The effect of police body-worn cameras on use of force and citizens' complaints against the police: A randomized controlled trial," *Journal of Quantitative Criminology,* vol. 31, no. 3, pp. 509–535. https://doi.org/10.1007/s10940-014-9236-3, 2014.

40 M. D. White, Gaub, J. E., Malm, A. and Padilla, K. E., "Implicate or exonerate? The impact of police body-worn cameras on the adjudication of drug and alcohol cases," *Policing: A Journal of Policy and Practice,* vol. 15, pp. 759–769, 2019.

41 J. M. Phelps, Strype, J., Le Bellu, S., Lahlou, S. and Aandal, J., "Experiential learning and simulation-based training in Norwegian police education: Examining body-worn video as a tool to encourage reflection," *Policing: A Journal of Policy & Practice,* vol. 2, no. 1, pp. 50–65. https://doi.org/10.1093/police/paw014, 2018.

42 L. Grossmith, Owens, C., Finn, W., Mann, D., Davies, T. and Baika, L., "Police, camera, evidence: London's cluster randomised controlled

trial of Body Worn Video," College of Policing and the Mayor's Office for Policing and Crime (MOPAC), London, 2015.
43 E. L. Piza, Caplan, J. M., Kennedy, L. W. and Gilchrist, A., "The effects of merging proactive CCTV monitoring with directed police patrol: A randomized controlled trial," *Journal of Experimental Criminology,* vol. 11, no. 1, pp. 43–69. https://doi.org/10.1007/s11292-014-9211-x, 2015.
44 E. Groff, Haberman, C. and Wood, J. D., "The effects of body-worn cameras on police-citizen encounters and police activity: evaluation of a pilot implementation in Philadelphia, PA," *Journal of Experimental Criminology,* vol. 16, pp. 463–480. https://doi.org/10.1007/s11292-019-09383-0, 2020.
45 M. Beshears, Beshears, M. L. and Bond, M., "Improving police social media use practices," *International Journal of Social Science Studies,* vol. 7, no. 5. http://ijsss.redflame.com, 2019.
46 C. Sanders and Condon, C., "Crime analysis and cognitive effects: The practice of policing through flows of data," *Global Crime,* vol. 18, no. 3, pp. 237–255. https://doi.org/10.1080/17440572.2017.1323637, 2017.
47 J. A. Hendrix, Taniguchi, T., Strom, K. J., Aagaard, B. and Johnson, N., "Strategic policing philosophy and the acquisition of technology: Findings from a nationally representative survey of law enforcement," *Policing & Society,* vol. 29, no. 6, pp. 727–743. https://doi.org/10.1080/10439463.2017.1322966, 2019.
48 L. L. Charles, "Disarming people with words: strategies of interactional communication that crisis (hostage) negotiators share with systemic clinicians," *Journal of Marital and Family Therapy,* vol. 33, no. 1, pp. 51–68. https://doi.org/10.1111/j.1752-0606.2007.00006, 2007.
49 J. Reynolds, Mariani, M. and Goodman, D., *Police talk: A scenario-based communications workbook for police recruits and officers,* 1st ed. London: Pearson, p. 128, 2001.
50 D. Faggiani, "Police talk: A scenario-based communications workbook for police recruits and officers," *Criminal Justice Review,* vol. 31, no. 4, pp. 381–382, 2006.
51 C. S. Koper, Lum, C. and Hibdon, J., "The uses and impacts of mobile computing technology in hot spots policing," *Evaluation Review*, vol. 39, no. 6, pp. 587–624. https://doi.org/10.1177/0193841X16634482, 2015.

Appendix G

Mental Competencies in Policing[1]

Mervat Abu-Alhassin, *Masters Graduate*[2],
Judy McDonald, *Research Supervisor*[2], Travis
Kirkwood, *Masters Graduate*[2], Maria Williams, Masters
Student[2] and Chuyao Cheng, *Masters Graduate*[2]

1 Condensed version of original research paper.
2 School of Epidemiology and Public Health, Faculty of Medicine, University of Ottawa.

Abstract

This review explored the standards and measures that have been used to evaluate mental readiness competencies in frontline policing. Orlick's 'Wheel of Excellence' (2003), with an established application in policing and other high-performance professions, was used to identify current mental-readiness standards in research for law enforcement[1, 2]. The model has seven mental success-elements or standards which include: Commitment, Self-Belief, Positive Images, Mental Preparation, Full Focus, Distraction Control and Constructive Evaluation. Within these standards, 23 measures were identified. This review contributed to the overall understanding of new and current trends in police operational readiness, and updating of Gold Medal Policing, 2nd edition.

Introduction

Mental readiness is critical for police performance and success. World-class athletes, like police, also perform under high pressure. Orlick's "Wheel of Excellence"[3,4] describes the main elements of athletic success[5], which can effectively be applied to review success and excellence in policing research. The elements are

Summary of Police Mental Competencies

STANDARDS	Commitment	Evaluation and Coping	Self-Belief	Distraction Control	Full Focus	Positive Imagery	Mental Preparation
MEASURES	Ethics	Formal evaluation	Quality training and practice	Emotional control	Situational awareness	Motor-imagery training	Rituals
	Ethics training	Public feedback	Support systems	Car-collision avoidance	Anticipation	Stress reduction	Goal setting
	Leadership connection	Debriefs	Recognition and thanks	Refocusing			
	Job engagement	Coping	Maturity and culturally-grounded				
	Competitiveness	Leadership directives					

Commitment, Self-Belief, Positive Imagery, Mental Preparation, Full Focus, Distraction Control, and Constructive Evaluation.

Purpose: To determine what standards and measures relate to mental readiness competency in policing.

Search and data analysis: An international search of five databases revealed six themes, including "police mental competencies." A second refined search revealed 64 pertinent empirical articles for review with data, statistics, models, and charts pulled where relevant.

The seven (mental) success elements from the Wheel of Excellence[3,4] were used as standards for coding the literature—Commitment·Self-Belief·Positive Imagery·Mental Preparation·Full Focus·Distraction Control·and Constructive Evaluation. Coping was added as part of the Evaluation standard to capture post-performance stress management. These elements are supported by four other existing models for organizing mental readiness: Mental Toughness Questionnaire-48 (MTQ48)[6,7,8]; Emotional Intelligence Model (EQ)[9,10]; Train (your brain) like an Olympian[11]; and "Psychological Resilience in Sport Performers"[12].

Findings

These seven broad standards were further broken down into 23 measures briefly elaborated as follows.

In the research articles, the most common element was *Commitment* (30% of all articles). Also common were *Constructive Evaluation* and *Coping* (22%), and *Self-Belief* (17%). The other articles covered *Distraction Control* (12%), *Full Focus* (10%), *Positive Imagery* (5%), and *Mental Preparation* (4%).

Commitment

Ethics has to do with moral goodness[13]. In policing, this requires openness, honesty, following the values of *service*, and maintaining public trust[14]. Police have a lot of freedom during their shifts, which implies confidence in their ethical decision-making.

Biases are complicated and can prevent ethical behavior. They are impacted by officer maturity, camaraderie, rank, personality, race, and gender[15,16,17,18,19,20].

Ethics training can improve decision-making[21]. But training must be continuous because lessons slowly fade[16]; even when officers learn and understand training, it doesn't guarantee that they will implement the lessons and perform ethically[22]. Training strategies include frameworks that help assess potential ethical risks and steps for coming up with the best possible response options. Real-life examples are also useful for officers to see what effective reactions in ethically challenging situations look like, and which behaviors are clearly legal versus questionable[23]. Strong leadership can be effective for modeling ethical behaviors and attitudes[23,24]. Ultimately, effective ethics training has to lead to officers following laws and regulations which have been established (e.g., firearms, driving, community relations, and use of force)[22,24,25].

Leadership connection. In addition to ethics, effective leadership improves officers' enthusiasm, performance, development, social supports, and overall commitment to their jobs[13,26,27,28,29]. Effective leaders demonstrate openness, respect for organizational principles, and enhance organizational culture and commitment to its vision[30].

Job engagement is linked to connection[26], satisfaction, retaining qualified officers[27], ethical leadership[30], and openness to using new innovative online training methods[31].

Competitiveness and personality hardiness also predict job satisfaction and motivation[32].

Evaluation and Coping

Coping is important to protect against stress injuries from repetitive traumas from police work. Trainings that improve self-confidence and frontline mental skills, along with job satisfaction, social supports, and debriefs with colleagues[33], can improve wellness and decrease risks of post-traumatic stress disorder (PTSD) or suicide[34,35]. Acts of terrorism are unique stressors, and officers benefit from "lessons learned" debriefs in adapting to terrorist acts[35,36]. *Debriefs* are particularly effective, and especially after violent events. *Impromptu debriefings* shortly after events reduce stress, improve strategic reflection and community relations[37]. *Video-cued-recall debriefs* can provide point-of-view learning using head and body camera footage for evaluation[38,39,40].

Public feedback is necessary for effectively policing communities, which officers are ultimately accountable to[16,41]. Listening to residents' concerns is critical[19]. Lost community trust can bring rioting, robberies, and violence[16].

Formal assessments are valuable for monitoring officer performance, and also for understanding individual personality and life-histories, which can help guide hiring and predicting future performance[16,42].

Leadership directives are valuable, because police cultures are difficult to change, but the right leaders can support mental and physical wellness, debriefings with colleagues, mindfulness, and various peer-support programs[33].

Self-Belief

Quality training and practice can create expectations for success, which reduce officer doubt and help them maintain positive commitment through failures and other challenges[26].

Self-directness is another predictor of performance, especially for Community-Oriented-Policing (COP) Basic Training outcomes[31].

Support systems, especially *mentoring*, provide many benefits to individuals' careers and the police agency. Mentors gain satisfaction from contributing value to the organization, while protégés benefit directly from shared wisdom and resource supports[43]. There are sometimes questions about how appropriate certain mentors' qualities are, such as whether they address racial diversity challenges[44,45].

Camaraderie and rituals build unity and teamwork[46]. Training together strategically helps officers learn each other's strengths and weaknesses[21]. Risks include isolation of visible-minorities and reinforcing unethical cultures. Faith can be a source of guidance in navigating life's complexities, to enhance ethics training[21].

Recognition and thanks. Officers who feel less valued often report lower well-being and higher fatigue and stress. When they coach new recruits, they may impose their negative beliefs[47].

Maturity and culturally grounded. As mentioned, older officers have higher self-esteem and have more positive and confident interactions with diverse groups and cultures[17].

Mental Preparation

Rituals, such as tactical breathing, squad meetings, and positive self-talk, can be helpful. They can provide clear thought and relaxation, and improve bonding and handling stressful events[46,48].

Goal setting can improve performance and also help manage stress. Goals should be specific, measurable, attainable, relevant, and time-bound (SMART)[49].

Distraction Control

Emotional control decreases stress and depressive symptoms, and improves communications, performance, memory, and positive mind-set[50,51]. It also increases healthy coping such as seeking peer support and self-care, instead of aggression or avoiding the problem[52]. Skills include controlled breathing and training to focus attention on important cues while ignoring all kinds of internal and external distractions[49].

Car collision avoidance is critical to reducing officer injury and death[53]. When departments make officers aware of vehicle-related risks, they are more likely to accept protective rules and equipment use[54,55].

Refocusing during tasks improves performance, and is improved by self-talk, visualizing next steps, tactical breathing, and involving others[33,56].

Full Focus

Situational awareness can be improved with training on observational skills, which improve safety by noticing nervous behaviors in suspects and noticing weapons, and improve performance by saving mental resources for the most important details. Awareness can be improved by programs and technologies aimed at addressing *attention blindness*[57,58,59]; *sources of police stress*;[50,56] and *change-detection*[60].

Anticipation can help with more targeted and proactive policing efforts, increasing cooperation with community and preventing work stress[52,61]. *Emotional intelligence* also helps, and predicts officer performance and survival[62].

Positive Imagery

Motor-imagery training. This is valuable for many skills, including firearm control which can be practiced "mentally" even while injured. Guided-imagery training can support relaxation and improve performance, attention, confidence, and emotional control[51,63]. *Stress reduction* is closely related, and can be improved by, for example, repeatedly listening to critical incident scenarios and visualizing the ideal response[49,50].

Recommendations

1. ***Identify and refine less-dominant success elements.*** Orlick's success elements exist already in police research[3,4], sometimes in different forms and names. Commitment, Evaluation, and Self-Belief were the most dominant. Combine Positive Imagery with Mental Preparation and Full Focus with Distraction Control for more effective training and evaluation.
2. ***Emphasize ethics*** to address complex moral dilemmas, misconduct, and professional discipline. Personal and organizational biases (e.g., victimization, racism, and priorities) impact

ethical decision-making. Self-esteem, maturity, and comfort with cultural diversity are significant. Commitment to laws and regulations is critical[17,21,29,30,64].
3. *Inspire officer commitment* through successful police leaders who: role model openness and accountability; foster meaningful leader-member exchanges; generate job engagement and performance; and capitalize on what guides best performances. Trainers who feel undervalued can impose negative beliefs and confidence levels on a recruit's career[18].
4. *Focus on emotional control* for managing distractions and good leadership; improving memory; preventing mental-health issues; and sustaining interpersonal skills for career development. Public disrespect, complaints, and court testimony are stressful situations that would benefit from refocusing practices. Visualization, controlled breathing, and positive self-talk have gained popularity as rituals for stress reduction. Simulated training positively impacts learning, performance, and stress-reduction[32].
5. *Cultivate resiliency* through individual and organizational responsibility. It supports: coping with acts of terrorism; preventing operational stress injuries; and improving performance[35,36]. Historically, police culture has resisted formal interventions following workplace trauma. Preferred alternative practices are: preventive mental skills on scene; habitual drills/training; informal peer-debriefing after an incident; and lessons learned from body-cam footage[33]. Factors associated with wellness and decreased risk conditions for PTSD include: self-confidence; self-directed learning; social support; job satisfaction; and gratitude[34,35]. Mandatory versus voluntary annual physical- and mental-wellness check-ups for police personnel are debated[33].

Notes

* Not scientifically peer-reviewed publications
1 J. McDonald, *Gold medal policing: Mental readiness and performance excellence*. New York: Sloan Associate Press, 2006.

2 S. Amyot, McDonald, J. and Allen, J., "Current measures of police mental training," In J. McDonald (Ed.), *Gold medal policing: Mental readiness and performance excellence*, (pp. 230–238), New York: Sloan Associate Press, 2006.
3 T. Orlick, The psychology of personal excellence. Contemporary thought on performance enhancement. 1(1), 109–122, 1992.
4 T. Orlick, "Wheel of excellence." http://www.zoneofexcellence.ca, October 25, 2003.
5 T. Orlick, *Psyching for sport: Mental training for athletes.* Champaign, IL: Human Kinetics, 1986.
6 AQR International, "Mental Toughness Questionnaire: A user guide," Rossett. https://aqrinternational.co.uk/wp-content/uploads/2018/02/MTQ-User-Manual-2017-4.00.pdf, 2017.
7 P. Clough, Earle, K. and Sewell, D., "Mental toughness: The concept and its measurement," In I. Cockerill (Ed.), *Solutions in sport psychology.* London: Thomson, pp. 32–43, 2002.
8 J. L. Perry, Clough, P. J., Crust, L., Earle, K. and Nicholls, A., "Factorial validity of the Mental Toughness Questionnaire-48," *Personality and Individual Differences,* vol. 54, no. 5, pp. 587–592. https://doi.org/10.1016/j.paid.2012.11.020, 2013.
9 S. Stein and Book, H. E., *The EQ edge: Emotional intelligence and your success*, 3rd ed. Toronto: John Wiley & Sons, 2011.
10 S. Terrell, "Executive coaches who use Eq-i 2.0 in leadership development: A qualitative study." ProQuest Dissertations Publishing, Doctoral Dissertation, Capella University, 1–137, 2020.
11 J.-F. Ménard, *Train (your brain) like an Olympian: Gold Medal Techniques to unleash your potential at work.* Toronto: ECW Press, 2021, p. 248.
12 K. Guest, Bailey, S., Khan, S. and Thompson, S., "Performance and resilience coaching for military leadership," S & T Organization-MP-HFM, 2019, p. 302.
13 B. English, "'Climate for ethics' and occupational-organisational commitment conflict," *Journal of Management Development,* vol. 27, no. 9, pp. 963–975. https://doi.org/10.1108/02621710810901309, 2008.
14 British College of Policing, "Integrity and transparency." https://www.college.police.uk/What-we-do/Ethics/integrity-and-transparency/Pages/Integrity-and-Transparency.aspx, February 12, 2022.
15 J. Edwards, "Ethical decision-making: A treatise into the role of ethics in 21st century policing." ProQuest Dissertations Publishing, Doctoral

dissertation, London Metropolitan University, https://repository.londonmet.ac.uk/id/eprint/7492, 2012.
16 M. P. DeRosia, "Ethics training and practice within the Central Valley Police Department." ProQuest Dissertations Publishing, Doctoral dissertation, Walden University, 1–147, 2012.
17 S. Charles, "Professional integrity, modern racism, self-esteem, and universality-diversity orientation of police officers in a large urban police agency." ProQuest Dissertations Publishing, Doctoral Dissertation, Fordham University, 2009.
18 S. Charman, "Making sense of policing identities: The 'deserving' and the 'undeserving' in policing accounts of victimisation," *Policing & Society*, vol. 30, no. 1, pp. 81–97. https://doi.org/10.1080/10439463.2019.1601721, 2020.
19 A. Armenta, "Between public service and social control: Policing dilemmas in the era of immigration enforcement," *Social Problems*, vol. 63, no. 1, pp. 111–126. https://doi.org/10.1093/socpro/spv024, 2016.
20 R. Martin, "Police corruption: An analytical look into police ethics," *FBI Law Enforcement Bulletin*, vol. 80, no. 11. https://leb.fbi.gov/articles/featured-articles/police-corruption-an-analytical-look-into-police-ethics, 2011.
21 P. O. Dissmore, "Ethics for the military officer: Teaching ethics at the maneuver support center for engineer officers." ProQuest Dissertations Publishing, Doctoral Dissertation, Assemblies of God Theological Seminary, 1–251, 2009.
22 D. S. Poole, "A qualitative analysis of the effectiveness of professional ethics training standards in law enforcement." ProQuest Dissertations Publishing, Doctoral dissertation, Walden University, 1–194, 2012.
23 H. Wyatt-Nichol and Franks, G., "Ethics training in law enforcement agencies," *Public Integrity*, vol. 12, no. 1, pp. 39–50. https://doi.org/10.2753/PIN1099-9922120103, 2009.
24 K. M. Markos, "A conduit from public trust to legitimacy: Continuous ethics training in law enforcement." ProQuest Dissertations Publishing, Doctoral dissertation, University of La Verne, 1–152, 2017.
25 The Academy*, "Perishable skills training." https://theacademy.ca.gov/perishable_skills#:~:text=In%20January%202002%20POST%20implemented,Tactical%20Firearms%204%20hour%20minimum, January 20, 2020.
26 M. Bettschart, Herrmann, M., Wolf, B. M. and Brandstätter, V., "The seed of goal-related doubts: A longitudinal investigation of the roles of failure and expectation of success among police trainee applicants,"

Frontiers in Psychology, vol. 10, p. 2151. https://doi.org/10.3389/fpsyg.2019.02151.

27. A. A. Escamilla, "Are you in or out? A study of law enforcement officers' perceived quality of relationship with their leader and its effects on organizational commitment." ProQuest Dissertations Publishing, TX, Doctoral Dissertation, Our Lady of the Lake University, 1–124, 2015.

28. J. K. Ford, "Building capability throughout a change effort: Leading the transformation of a police agency to community policing," *American Journal of Community Psychology,* vol. 39, no. 3–4, pp. 321–334. https://doi.org/10.1007/s10464-007-9115-2, 2007.

29. P. A. Lasiewicki, "Achieving congruence between individual commitment to policing and organizational objectives in police departments." ProQuest Dissertations Publishing, Doctoral Dissertation, University of Phoenix, 1–435, 2007.

30. R. B. Gaither, "Ethical Leadership and Its Impact on Role Modeling, Strictness, Openness, and Job Satisfaction of Law Enforcement Officers." ProQuest Dissertations Publishing, Doctoral dissertation, Keiser University, 1–113, 2017.

31. M. B. Halicioglu, "Examination of the relationship between self-directedness and outcomes of the online COP training program in the Turkish National Police context." ProQuest Dissertations Publishing, 2010, *Journal of police and Criminal Psychology*, 32:331-9, Dec 2017.

32. B. H. Johnsen, Espevik, R., Saus, E. R., Sanden, S. and Olsen, O. K., "Hardiness as a moderator and motivation for operational duties as mediator: The relation between operational self-efficacy, performance satisfaction, and perceive," Doctoral Dissertation, Michigan State University, 1–262, 2017.

33. I. Cohen, McCormick, A. V. and Rich, B., "Creating a culture of police officer wellness," *Policing: A Journal of Policy and Practice,* vol. 13, no. 2, pp. 213–229. https://doi.org/10.1093/police/paz001, 2019.

34. H. A. Smith, Wolfe-Clark, A. L. and Bryan, C. J., "An exploratory study of the mental toughness psychological skills profile psychometrics, and the mediating effect of social support sources on mental toughness and suicidal ideation among military police," *Journal of Police and Criminal Psychology,* vol. 31, no. 4, pp. 295–303. https://doi.org/10.1007/s11896-016-9192-y, 2016.

35. M. Andrew, Violanti, J. M., Gu, J. K., Fekedulegn, D. and Li, S., "Police work stressors and cardiac vagal control," *American Journal of Human Biology,* vol. 29, no. 5. https://doi.org/10.1002/ajhb.22996, 2017.

36 D. Paton and Violanti, J. M., "Policing in the context of terrorism: Managing traumatic stress risk," *Traumatology,* vol. 12, no. 3, pp. 236–247. https://doi.org/10.1177/1534765606294990, 2006.

37 C. Gutshall, Hampton, D., Sebetan, I. M., Stein, P. and Broxterma, T. J., "The effects of occupational stress on cognitive performance in police officers," *Police Practice and Research,* vol. 18, pp. 463–477, https://doi.org/10.1080/15614263.2017.1288120, 2017.

38 L. Grossmith*, Owens, C., Finn, W., Mann, D., Davies, T. and Baika, L., "Police, camera, evidence: London's cluster randomised controlled trial of Body Worn Video," London. https://www.london.gov.uk/sites/default/files/bwv_report_nov_2015.pdf, 2015.

39 M. D. White, Gaub, J. E., Malm, A. and Padilla, K. E., "Implicate or exonerate? The impact of police body-worn cameras on the adjudication of drug and alcohol cases," *Policing: A Journal of Policy and Practice,* vol. 15, no. 2, pp. 759–769. https://doi.org/10.1093/police/paz043, 2021.

40 V. Blackhall, Walker, K. G., Whiteley, I. and Wilson, P., "Use of head camera-cued recall and debrief to externalise expertise: A systematic review of literature from multiple fields of practice," *BMJ Simulation & Technology Enhanced Learning,* vol. 5, no. 3, pp. 121–129. https://doi.org/10.1136/bmjstel-2018-000341, 2019.

41 D. J. Bordua and Tifft, L. L., "Citizen interviews, organizational feedback, and police-community relations decisions," *Law & Society Review,* vol. 6, no. 2, pp. 155–182. https://doi.org/10.2307/3052850, 1971.

42 M. J. Cuttler and Muchinsky, P. M., "Prediction of law enforcement training performance and dysfunctional job performance with general mental ability, personality, and life history variables," *Criminal Justice and behavior,* vol. 33, no. 1, pp. 3–25, 2006.

43 H. Sprafka* and Kranda, A. H., "Institutionalizing mentoring in police departments," *Police Chief,* vol. 75, no. 1, p. 46, 2008.

44 L. W. Bewley, "Seasons of leadership development: An analysis of a multi-dimensional model of mentoring among career groups of United States Army officers." ProQuest Dissertations Publishing, Doctoral dissertation, University of Alabama at Birmingham, 1–115, 2005.

45 O. A. Graves, "Phenomenological study exploring mentoring received by Black Army officers to improve promotions." ProQuest Dissertations Publishing, Doctoral dissertation, University of Phoenix, 1–259, 2016.

46 R. Lunney*, "Performance ritual for street policing," *Blue Line Magazine,* Vols. 205–227, no. 3, p. 17, 2015.

47 S. Charman, *Police socialisation, identity and culture becoming Blue.* New York: Palgrave Macmillan, 2017.
48 P. Bury, "Barossa night: Cohesion in the British Army officer corps," *The British Journal of Sociology,* vol. 68, no. 2, pp. 314–335. https://doi.org/10.1111/1468-4446.12236, 2017.
49 R. L. Krakauer, Stelnicki, A. M. and Carleton, R. N., "Examining mental health knowledge, stigma, and service use intentions among public safety personnel," *Frontiers in Psychology,* vol. 11, p. 949. https://doi.org/10.3389/fpsyg.2020.00949, 2020.
50 J. P. Andersen and Gustafsberg, H., "A training method to improve police use of force decision making: A randomized controlled trial," *SAGE Open,* vol. 6, no. 2, p. 2158244016638708. https://doi.org/10.1177/2158244016638708, 2016.
51 J. W. Page, Asken, M. J., Zwemer, C. F. and Guido, M., "Brief mental skills training improves memory and performance in high stress police cadet training," *Journal of Police and Criminal Psychology,* vol. 31, no. 2, pp. 122–126. https://doi.org/10.1007/s11896-015-9171-8, 2016.
52 M. Berking, Meier, C. and Wupperman, P., "Enhancing emotion-regulation skills in police officers: Results of a pilot-controlled study," *Behavior Therapy,* vol. 41, no. 3, pp. 329–339. https://doi.org/10.1016/j.beth.2009.08.001, 2010.
53 National Law Enforcement Officers Memorial Fund, Causes of law enforcement deaths: Over the past decade (2014-2023), National Law Enforcement Officers Memorial Fund, https://nleomf.org/memorial/facts-figures/officer-fatality-data/causes-of-law-enforcement-deaths/, 2024
54 K. Wehr, Alpert, G. and Rojek, J., "The fear of the ninja assassin: Understanding the role of agency culture in injurious and fatal on-duty vehicle collisions," *Journal of California Law Enforcement,* vol. 46, no. 2, pp. 18–26, 2012.
55 H. Tiesman, Hendricks, S., Bell, J. and Amandus, H., "Eleven years of occupational mortality in law enforcement: The census of fatal occupational injuries, 1992-2002," *American Journal of Industrial Medicine,* vol. 53, no. 9, pp. 940–949. https://doi.org/10.1002/ajim.20863, 2010.
56 E. Wilson, McDonald, J. and Allen, J., "Sources of police stress," In J. McDonald (Ed.), *Gold medal policing: Mental readiness and performance excellence.* New York: Sloan Associate Press, pp. 216–222, 2006.
57 D. J. Simons and Schlosser, M. D., "Inattentional blindness for a gun during a simulated police vehicle stop," *Cognitive Research: Principles*

and Implications, vol. 2, no. 37, pp. 1–8. https://doi.org/10.1186/s41235-017-0074-3, 2017.

58 K. I. McAnally, Morris, A. P. and Best, C., "Metacognitive monitoring and control in visual change detection: Implications for situation awareness and cognitive control," *PLoS One,* vol. 12, no. 9, p. e0176032. https://doi.org/10.1371/journal.pone.0176032, 2017.

59 B. Vallières, Hodgetts, H. M., Vachon, F. and Tremblay, S., "Supporting dynamic change detection: Using the right tool for the task," *Cognitive Research: Principles and Implications,* vol. 1, no. 1, pp. 1–20. https://doi.org/10.1186/s41235-016-0033-4, 2016.

60 S. M. Smart, Berry, M. A. and Rodriguez, D. N., "Skilled observation and change blindness: A comparison of law enforcement and student samples," *Applied Cognitive Psychology,* vol. 28, no. 4, pp. 590–596. https://doi.org/10.1002/acp.3021, 2014.

61 M. L. Stewart, "Subjects of prevention: Risk, threat, and anticipation in Canadian policing." ProQuest Dissertations Publishing, Doctoral dissertation, University of California, 1–287, 2011.

62 R. J. Conroy, Beyond emotional intelligence: A correlational study of multifactor measures of performance and law enforcement leadership styles. ProQuest Dissertations Publishing, Doctoral Dissertation, Dallas Baptist University, 1–287, 2017.

63 G. R. Mount, "Mental practice: Police performance in hostage negotiation," *Journal of Police Crisis Negotiations,* vol. 7, no. 2, pp. 41–143. https://doi.org/10.1300/J173v07n02_11, 2007.

64 K. Breevaart, Bakker, A. B. and Demerouti, E., "Leader-member exchange, work engagement, and job performance," *Journal of Managerial Psychology,* vol. 30, no. 7, pp. 754–770. https://doi.org/10.1108/JMP-03-2013-0088, 2015.

Appendix H

Challenging situations in frontline policing

Knowing your strengths and limitations can bolster your self-confidence. Review the list of challenges below from "excellent" officers identified by their peers and supervisors (add to each category as needed). For each challenging situation, decide and mark as follows:

- ~~strike out~~ if it is not applicable
- circle if you would find it difficult to handle
- <u>underline</u> if you generally feel comfortable handling it

Building a personalized profile of demanding situations will aid in discovering new strategies and refining of existing ones. Some challenges may persist as limitations, necessitating specialized or dedicated attention. Other situations you are adept at managing can open avenues for mentoring others and uncovering potential areas of expertise for career development.

Challenging Situations in Frontline Policing

Heightened risk: "confirmed" weapon call • suicide attempted with weapon • "legitimate" hostage taking • domestics • stolen cars pursuits • B & E in progress • barricaded person call • dynamic entry • lock down (for bomb threat) • bar or drug blitz • high-risk tracks • explosive detection scenario • high speed escort • high-risk vehicle takedowns • bank robberies • live fire in the mix • 6.5-hour day in an intersection • delay in/access to back-up • nothing is "routine" • not recognizing the potential risks • when it's the "real deal" • feeling nervous with "tunnel-vision warp"

Complicated: complex entry (double entry, distraction devices) • demonstration (prostitute) "sweep" • call volume for service • school drug search • long canine tracks • intersections on Level 5 Escort • sexual assaults at school • involvement of external agencies, parents, officers • mass traffic accident chaos • multi-injuries • handling a lot all at once • bound by protocol/guidelines • racing to call while radio is blaring, computer is going, calls coming in, still getting updates • hate crimes • suspected terrorism • being quick and observant • circumstances bound by protocol, guidelines, and changes • school fight-at-large with re-offenders • getting a good witness statement • limited resources

Challenging Situations in Frontline Policing

Emotionally charged: accident or incident with an officer ("a whole different dynamic—especially if you know them") • policy versus "what's right" • special relationship pressures with subjects (e.g., relative, friend) • emotional relationship • graphically violent situations • injury or violence against a child • personal physical or mental fatigue • low team morale • parental involvement • feeling like a politician • handler-canine issues • complacency at repetitive calls • not looking foolish with peers • promotional process with A-types • personal fear • "I wish this wasn't my call" feeling • feeling misunderstood or undervalued • team pressure, like being the last guy on the truck

Coaching/Leadership: official Coach Officer role • liabilities with young officers • simulations • range training • team projects • recruit not performing but father is the Supt/Chief • first day with a new recruit • coaching someone more skilled requires more preparation • feeling the added responsibility as leader • when you miss a step • keeping it current to avoid boredom from repetition • dealing with a "tv cop" outlook • pressures when mentoring • assessing a poor trainee • trainee not willing to accept feedback • balancing coaching with other duties • managing time and priorities to address key skills • building rapport while assessing • managing expectations

Unfamiliar: common rookie pressure situations • "every day is different" • threat that this could be the "big one" • traumatic situations—afterwards "nobody gave a shit" • working with dogs • unfamiliar building or neighborhoods • first time drawing gun or shooting • anywhere I haven't been tested yet • a search without warrant for weapons • the unknown • lacking necessary skills • inexperienced area and not recognizing the potential risks

High-risk individual: MHA/EDP (Mental Health Act/Emotionally Disturbed Person) • drunk call • large groups fights between persons who know each other • evidence of criminal record • known HIV positive • groups with a violent reputation (known to carry gun, fight police, be full patch HA)

Unprecedented: first-of-its-kind procedure • using new equipment • implementing new procedures or policies • striving for exceptional results • world-class sniper training • being someone driven to "find the stolen car" • training for extreme circumstances • constantly set new traps to challenge dogs • having a request for your personal expertise • needing perfect timing • trying something not typical

Appendix I

Temporal changes in performance blocks 2003–2019

Temporal Changes in Police Performance Blocks from 2003 to 2019 by Block Type

Block Type	Performance Block	31 "Excellent" Coach Officers (1) 2019 (%)	48 "Excellent" Frontline Officers (2) 2003 (%)	Difference (1–2)	Block Weighted Average (%)	Block Impact (Immediate Need, Serious, Individual)	Specialized Strategies
Operational General Blocks	Crises	74	100	−26	90	Immediate Need	79*
	Personal fear	52	100	−48	81	Immediate Need	
	Shift work fatigue	84	78	6	80	Immediate Need	69*
	Jaded & skeptical	68	79	−11	75	Serious	
	Public disrespect	39	90	−51	70	Serious (−)	73
	Downtime and routine tasks	45	79	−34	66	Serious (−)	71
	Climate conditions	73	48	25	58	Serious (+)	
	Car collisions	29	75	−46	57	Serious (−)	73
	Peer mistrust	39	65	−26	55	Serious	
	Lack of information	77	31	46	49	Individual	
	Court appearances	42	50	−8	47	Individual (−)	72
	Work conflicts	70	17	53	38	Individual	
	Others' complacency	65	15	50	35	Individual	
	Previous call	43	8	35	22	Individual	
	External specialist attitudes	29	6	23	15	Individual	
	Getting lost	13	13	0	13	Individual	

554 ■ Appendix I

Operational Rookie Error	Aggressiveness	68	88	−20	80	Immediate Need
	General patrol issues	88	42	46	60	Serious (+)
	Lack of safety	87	40	47	58	Serious (+)
	Poor reports	77	38	39	53	Serious (+)
	Unrealistic expectations	81	31	50	51	Serious (+)
	Poor containment	53	38	15	44	Individual
	Rookie anxiety	65	27	38	42	Individual
	No action plan	84	10	74	39	Individual
	Discipline problems	74	13	61	37	Individual
	Negativity	60	4	56	26	Individual
	No basic law	52	4	48	23	Individual
	Lack community contacts	35	8	27	19	Individual
Organizational Blocks	Workload volume	90	65	25	75	Serious	64*
	Lack of leadership	87	48	39	63	Serious (+)
	Bureaucracy	73	54	19	61	Serious
	Fewer resources	73	52	21	60	Serious
	Public complaints	60	48	12	53	Serious (−)	68
	Female-policing coping issues	6	82	−76	52	Serious (−)	68
	Training issues	63	42	21	50	Serious (+)	45*
	Changes	57	40	17	47	Individual
	Poor support	57	38	19	45	Individual
	Lack management feedback	70	29	41	45	Individual
	Equipment limitations	74	23	51	43	Individual
	Politics	60	31	29	42	Individual
	Not being promoted	32	35	−3	34	Individual	59
	Coach issues	77	5	72	33	Individual
	Ethnicity issues	19	22	−3	21	Individual
External Blocks	Family conflicts	57	42	15	48	Individual
	Day-to-day pressures	63	10	53	31	Individual

*These blocks are significantly greater than their associated specialized strategies.

(+) Blocks that shifted up in impact level; e.g., from Individual to Serious

(−) Blocks that shifted down in impact level; e.g., from Immediate to Serious

Appendix J

Calculations for the differences in the importance of readiness in policing over 17 years

\multicolumn{5}{c}{Calculations for the differences in the importance of readiness in policing over 17 years}				
DESCRIPTION	MEASURES	COMPETENCIES			
		Physical Readiness	Technical Readiness	Mental Readiness	Total
28 "Excellent" frontline officers (1) 2019	Mean % Standard Error Standard Deviation	24 1.89 10.02	26 1.47 7.77	50 11.93 40	100
48 "Excellent" frontline officers (2) 2003	Mean % Standard Error Standard Deviation	28 1.58 10.98	32 1.52 10.55	40 1.12 7.77	100
Difference (1–2)		−4	−6	+10	
Weighted Average [(1) *28/76)] + [(2) *48/76)]	Mean % Standard Error Standard Deviation	26 1.70 10.63	30 1.50 9.53	44 1.54 9.30	100

Appendix K

Overall importance of operational readiness by factor

\multicolumn{6}{c}{Overall Importance of Operational Readiness by Factor}
FACTORS	GROUPS	PHYSICAL %	TECHNICAL %	MENTAL %	TOTAL %
Overall group average	All	28	32	40	100
Prior police-related experience	No police-related experience Police-related experience	27 29	33 28 *p=.082**	40 43	100 100
Tactical experience	No Tactical experience Tactical experience	29 22 *p=.014**	31 35	40 43	100 100
Military experience	Non-military Military	29 24 *p=.054**	32 31	39 45	100 100
Male ethnicity	White male Visible Minorities-Aboriginal	26 34 *p=.042**	32 32	42 34	100 100
Overall ethnicity	White Visible Minorities-Aboriginal	27 33	32 32	41 35	100 100
Rural experience	Non-rural experience Rural experience	*p=.052** 25 30 *p=.022***	31 33	44 37	100 100

Note on p-value: The smaller the value, the stronger the evidence for differences between groups by the given factor.

*potential for difference p<0.1

**significant difference p<0.05

Appendix L
Successful performance readiness by factor

Successful Performance Readiness by Factor

FACTORS	GROUPS	PHYSICAL /10—%	TECHNICAL /10—%	MENTAL /10—%
Overall group average (%)	All	88	88	88
Primary language	English only Two or more languages	86 94 *p=.038***	87 92	88 90
Elite by group/scoring	Non-elite Elite	88 88	91 81 *p=.044**	90 83 *p=.067**
Military experience	Non-military Military	86 94 *p=.058**	87 93	87 93 *p=.083**
Gender (F/M)	Female Male	92 87 *p=.097**	91 87	88 88
Ethnicity	White Visible Minorities-Aboriginal	88 88	87 92 *p=.064**	90 82
Tactical experience	No Tactical experience Tactical experience	88 87	90 81 *p=.096**	88 88

Police-related experience	No police-related experience	89	90	90
	Police-related experience	84	84	81
				p=.015**
SRO experience	No SRO experience	88	89	90
	SRO experience	86	82	81
				p=.077*
Number of languages	English Language Other than English	86	87	91
		90	90	85
				p=.086*

Note on p-value: The smaller the value, the stronger the evidence for differences between groups by the given factor.

*Potential difference p<0.1.

**Significant difference p<0.05.

Appendix M

Disappointing performance readiness by factor

Disappointing Performance Readiness by Factor				
FACTORS	GROUPS	PHYSICAL /10—%	TECHNICAL /10—%	MENTAL /10—%
Overall group average	All	88	78	64
Rank	Constable/ Senior Constable Sergeant	87 90	78 76	61 77 $p=051$
Elite by group/ scoring	Non-elite Elite	91 79 $p=.025**$	80 71	67 56 $p=.074*$
Gender (F/M)	Female Male	94 86 $p=.082*$	69 80	62 65
Police-related experience	No police-related exp Police-related exp	89 83 $p=.088*$	79 71	64 64
Rural experience	Non-rural experience Rural experience	89 87	82 74 $p=.084*$	67 62

Note on p-value: The smaller the value, the stronger the evidence for differences between groups by the given factor.

* Potential for difference p<0.1

** Significant difference p<0.05

Appendix N

Orlick's Wheel of Excellence: Mental readiness success elements

Orlick's "Wheel of Excellence" (Orlick 1992, 2003) introduces a conceptual model which outlines seven mental success elements of excellence that allow human beings to excel. The success elements include: Commitment, Self-Belief, Positive Images, Mental Readiness, Full Focus, Distraction Control, and Constructive Evaluation.

This study verifies the presence of the seven mental success elements in "excellent" frontline officers and coach officers during challenging policing situations (as defined in Chapter 1). Some modifications were made to the original terms to enhance their relevance to policing, as indicated in parentheses below. They are described as follows:

Commitment and Self-Belief (or Confidence) are stipulated by Orlick (1992, 2003) as the underlying core of excellence and can become the central focus in one's life without becoming the only focus. Commitment implies that an individual has a strong personal reason to excel, or a powerful driving desire to be the best that he or she can possibly be. This ensures that the individual puts in the quality or quantity of work required to excel, and dedicates the necessary time to fully develop the critical mental readying skills required for the successful pursuit of excellence (pp. 8, 9).

The series of mental readying skills that produce a superior performance at critical events are defined as follows (Orlick & Partington, 1988).

Positive Images (or Positive Imagery) allows one to pre-experience or re-experience desired performance skills or results in one's mind. It is used in preparing to get what is wanted out of training, perfecting skills within the training sessions, making technical corrections, imagining oneself being successful in competition, and seeing oneself achieving the ultimate goal. It is a skill that needs to be very well developed and used daily to achieve quality (i.e., seeing and feeling) and control in the visualization.

Mental Readiness (or Mental Preparation) is developing systematic procedures for drawing upon one's strengths in important competitions. It includes the use of mental imagery, warming up well physically, rituals, positive thoughts, and reminders to focus on what has previously worked well. This pre-event plan must be well developed, refined, well-practiced, and followed consistently to ensure a constructive focus going into the event.

Full Focus is developing the ability to stay centered in the present, focused on the task at hand. One connects totally to what one is doing and only on what is within one's immediate control for the duration of the task, to the exclusion of irrelevant thoughts or input. A poor focus is one in which the individual dwells on factors over which he or she has no direct control. For example, concentrating on the desired outcome, other competitors, or other distractions can actually decrease performance. Success depends on refining this skill to form a focus plan for use during the event.

Distraction Control is defined by Orlick as the ability to deal with "things that are expected or unexpected that can pull you off track." This requires strategies for getting back on track quickly when faced with distractions, negative input, or random bad luck. It may mean avoiding the scoreboard, deciding not to watch everyone else, or using a headphones. Under high-level stress, the likelihood of a negative impact on performance is greater; consequently, more refocusing skills are needed.

Constructive Evaluation (and Coping) is a procedure developed for extracting the important lessons from every critical event. Proper debriefing, based on these lessons, allows one to continually adapt or refine one's mental approach, thus attaining an ever-higher level of personal excellence.

Notes

T. Orlick and Partington, J. Mental links to excellence. The sport psychologist. Jun 1; 2(2), 105–130, 1988.

T. Orlick. The psychology of personal excellence. Contemporary thought on performance enhancement. 1(1), 109–122, 1992.

T. Orlick. Wheel of excellence, http://www.zoneofexcellence.ca/free/wheel.html, 2003.

T. Orlick. *In pursuit of excellence.* Human Kinetics; Nov 13, 2015.

Appendix O

Temporal changes in mental readiness practices 2003–2019

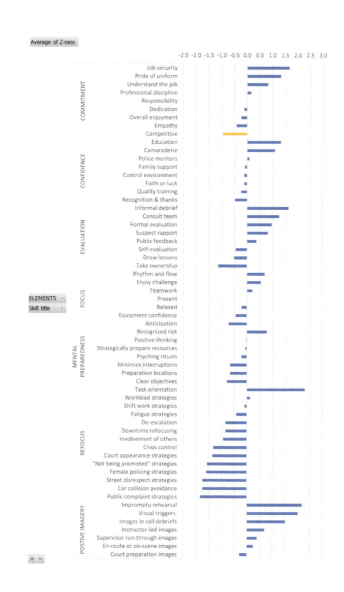

Appendix P

Police field training assessment and progress report

Field Training Assessment Progress Report # _____ Weeks _____

Trainee: _____ Coach Officer: _____ Date: _____

PLEASE NOTE: *"COMPETENT" PERFORMANCE MEANS THAT IN YOUR OPINION BACKED UP BY EXAMPLES FROM THE DAILY LOG, THE TRAINEE DEMONSTRATES A SATISFACTORY COMPETENCY IN THE PERFORMANCE INDICATOR.*

	Performance Indicators in Field Training	Practices that demonstrate Performance Indicators	Examples from Daily Log (Trainee is to assist in providing examples)
TECHNICAL (30%)	**Proficiency in Law** ☐ Comprehension ☐ Progressive competency ☐ Competent	Has knowledge and application of local, provincial, federal laws; understands court procedures and process; knows arrest authorities; knows and applies use of force principles; conducts effective apprehensions.	
	Verbal Communication ☐ Comprehension ☐ Progressive competence ☐ Competent	Prevents conflicts; de-escalates (Tac com); exhibits good articulation; uses appropriate tone; demonstrates active listening; builds community rapport; shows effective interviewing.	
	Written Communication ☐ Comprehension ☐ Progressive competence ☐ Competent	Follows systematic note taking (according to policy); submits timely reports; completes suitable report writing (i.e., general occurrences, arrest reports, use of force reports).	
	Knowledge of Police Service and Community ☐ Comprehension ☐ Progressive competence ☐ Competent	Understands the police service (organizational structure, reporting relationships, vision and mission); knows and complies with policies and procedures; communicates well internally; understands community composition (geographic locations, landmarks, diversity); accesses community resources.	
PHYSICAL	**Officer Safety** ☐ Comprehension ☐ Progressive competence ☐ Competent	Performs proper handcuffing; completes thorough body searches (including sensitive areas); has good health, fitness and wellness (amidst shiftwork, fatigue and injury); endures containment in environmental conditions; has a strong safety-sense	

Adapted from the Ontario Police College Field Training Manual (2009)
Based on McDonald, Gold Medal Policing (2025)

Performance Indicators in Field Training	Practices that demonstrate Performance Indicators	Examples from Daily Log (Trainee is to assist in providing examples)
Use of Force ☐ Comprehension ☐ Progressive competence ☐ Competent	Uses firearms properly and can perform gunpoint arrest; has equipment readiness; shows evidence of defensive tactics; has physical control with appropriate use of force response option; understands 'reasonableness.'	
Police Vehicle Operations ☐ Comprehension ☐ Progressive competence ☐ Competent	Operates vehicle safely (collision avoidance, uses lights and sirens in emergency response, pursuits); can multitask while driving (e.g. talk on radio, gather information, plates); reverses cruiser using back window not only mirrors; is effective patrolling the environment; positions vehicle appropriately during traffic stops.	
Commitment ☐ Comprehension ☐ Progressive competence ☐ Competent	Empathetic (cares about helping); professional discipline (time management, initiative, ethics); proper protocol (values authority, follows orders, punctual, appropriate physical appearance); appears satisfied to be in policing; shows responsible leadership; understands "the job" and what's expected; demonstrates loyalty (dedication, pride of uniform); shows motivation to succeed	
Confidence ☐ Comprehension ☐ Progressive competence ☐ Competent	Carries out quality training and practice; controls environment by showing independence and leadership (takes charge); has police mentors; seeks support (family, camaraderie); knows strengths and limitations; is grounded and appears credible, professional with the public.	
Mental Preparation ☐ Comprehension ☐ Progressive competence ☐ Competent	Visualizes/role plays to rehearse "what-and-then" scenarios; strategically plans resources (safety, equipment, communications, procedures, electronics); thinks positively; sets clear objectives, plans); recognizes risks; establishes rituals with designated locations;	
Full Focus/Refocus ☐ Comprehension ☐ Progressive competence ☐ Competent	Is present and mindful (alert, observant, relaxed rhythm, anticipates); looks confident wearing equipment; shows trust in teamwork and involving others; de-escalates and controls pace of situation in a "crisis;" stays task-oriented and not complacent; manages common distractions (e.g., public disrespect, public complaints, workload, court); uses common-sense, practical resolutions; can refocuses after downtime and during routine tasks	
Evaluate and Cope ☐ Comprehension ☐ Progressive competence ☐ Competent	Self-evaluates; seeks feedback from others (e.g., team, coach, public, supervisor); doesn't get defensive; accountable for own actions; draws lessons; copes well with challenging situations	

PHYSICAL (26%) — MENTAL (44%)

Adapted from the Ontario Police College Field Training Manual (2009)
Based on McDonald, Gold Medal Policing (2025)

Trainee Comments/Remedial Action:

_____
_____
_____
_____
_____
_____
_____

Print Name: _____ Signature: _____

Coach Officer Comments/Remedial Action:

_____
_____
_____
_____
_____
_____
_____

Print Name: _____ Signature: _____

Adapted from the Ontario Police College Field Training Manual (2009)
Based on McDonald, Gold Medal Policing (2025)

Appendix Q

Officer X's top 10
Gold Medal Policing quotes and lessons

"OFFICER X'S" TOP 10 GOLD MEDAL POLICING QUOTES

Gold Medal Policing (GMP) **was** aimed at capturing exceptional policing practices from a <u>frontline</u> perspective. Quotes demonstrate the value of frank dialogue to serve both young and seasoned officers. Anonymously, an officer compiled the list of *GMP* quotes below that meant the most <u>to him</u>. Please review *GMP* and choose <u>five</u> other quotes that resonated for <u>you</u>, then list them on the following page. Also review the associated research findings and draw lessons-learned helpful for training purposes.

TEN   *I try to deal with everything with a little wit and humor. I'm just my typical obnoxious self—which is apparently quite funny to some people. One kid said, "Ah, Miss? Are police officers allowed to just walk up and call you a c---sucker?" I said, "I don't know. Are you a c---sucker?" The whole class just LOST it. At that point they're thinking, "Oh, she's kind of funny."* — School Resource

     <u>Lesson:</u> This was my absolute favorite! It's funny but also has a deep and immediate ring of authenticity. Valid and useful tip—also comes from a female officer.

NINE   *I still carry the lessons my coach officer taught me. Like report writing—a lot of people don't do them properly. The key is detail, but not too much. Always give a background. Don't just go in there and tell a story because there's always something that happened before. In a domestic report, for example, do they have children together? Is there a history of assaults? I received a commendation for my report writing and it has everything to do with my coach officer.* —Neighborhood Resource

     <u>Lesson:</u> Reinforces the lasting impact of coach officers.

EIGHT   *I took a little from both of my coach officers. One was extremely strong administratively. He had a certain way of doing his notes. He knew what reports had to be done and who to contact. The other was very, very personable—he could talk to absolutely anybody.* —Patrol

     <u>Lesson:</u> More reminder of positive impact of a coach officer.

SEVEN   *If you have to do it for the first time, it's a crisis. Just try to resist the urge to light your hair on fire and run around. Try to be cool.* ——Elite Officer

     <u>Lesson:</u> Resonator for all officers. We have all been in that position.

SIX   *Fear works for you; it keeps you on your toes. Fear brings me to life and awakens my every sense—my being. It makes me more alert and more aware. I use fear to my advantage. I don't let it overtake me, but I use it to my advantage.* —Patrol > 10 yrs on

     <u>Lesson:</u> Coping with the terrain—resonates.

GOLD MEDAL POLICING QUOTES cont'd

FIVE *People who are good at their job learn from their mistakes. I can't stand working with officers who never learn from their mistakes—they're always right. You're going to make mistakes. I've made hundreds of mistakes—and some pretty serious ones—but I learned from them. I accepted the ribbing and the lumps, and I moved on. That's what makes the difference in good students, parents… and people. You have to be humble and know that you are going to make mistakes—some of them serious.* —5 to10 years on

   Lesson: A great message about experiential life-long learning.

FOUR *If they hired me for my life experience and the pre-requisite is to keep my mouth shut and work 25 years, then they should have hired me when I was 21. I've got life experience and I've got an opinion. I'm not 21 years old. If I was 21, I would keep my mouth shut. But they hired me because I've been places. I've got a sense of what works and what doesn't work. If you can't take someone with six-years-on respectfully giving a suggestion, that's not my problem. It's about you.* —Neighborhood Resource, Female

   Lesson: Our new officers are not the same as when I joined. They have experience, they think, they evaluate and they have useful and valid opinions.

THREE *I critique my own behavior: "What did I do there that I could do better?" I pay attention to other people—I don't critique them openly but I may critique them to myself. I do my best to keep my mind open and learn something new everyday.* —5 to 10 years on

   Lesson: The power of officer self-examination and commitment to the job—Wow!

TWO *An old, old, old officer taught me to never run to a fight. I walk and I watch because if there's a knife or anything going on, I'm going to see it. If you're running, everybody runs with you and it gets their anxiety up. Calm equals calm and panicky equals panicky.* —School Resource

   Lesson: Officers learning from an experienced officer (like a coach officer). Good message about human behavior on the frontline.

ONE *If I screw up, I want you to say, "You f---ed up." I love listening to other people's opinions, no matter who it is.* —> 15 years on

   Lesson: Same ring of authenticity as the first one—but not as funny. It is poignant because the officer is a veteran.

MY TOP 5 GOLD MEDAL POLICING QUOTES

Gold Medal Policing was aimed at capturing exceptional policing practices from a frontline perspective, and demonstrating the value of frank dialogue to serve both young and seasoned officers. Choose five quotes that resonated for you. Review the associated research findings and draw lessons-learned that could be helpful for training purposes. You need only flag it in your book then reference the **page #** and the *"Start… end of the quote."* (PLEASE CHECK BACK OF SHEET FOR SECTION OF BOOK FOR YOU TO REVIEW)

FIVE   p.____: _____

    Lesson: _____

FOUR   p.____: _____

    Lesson: _____

THREE   p.____: _____

    Lesson: _____

TWO   p.____: _____

    Lesson: _____

ONE   p.____: _____

    Lesson: _____

SECTIONS OF BOOK FOR YOU TO REVIEW

Begin reading these pages, looking for quotes that are meaningful to you.

You are welcome to include other pages in addition to these.

Last name	Pages	Content

MENTAL READINESS

- ☐ ____-____ p. _____ Commitment & Self-Belief
- ☐ ____-____ p. _____ Positive Images & Mental Preparation
- ☐ ____-____ p. _____ Mental Preparation
- ☐ ____-____ p. _____ Full Focus & Distraction Control
- ☐ ____-____ p. _____ Distraction Control
- ☐ ____-____ p. _____ Constructive Evaluation & Performance Blocks
- ☐ ____-____ p. _____ Performance Blocks

PHYSICAL READINES

- ☐ ____-____ p. _____ Officer Safety
- ☐ ____-____ p. _____ Use of Force
- ☐ ____-____ p. _____ Vehicle Operations

TECHNICAL READINESS

- ☐ ____-____ p. _____ Proficiency in Law
- ☐ ____-____ p. _____ Verbal Communication
- ☐ ____-____ p. _____ Written Communication
- ☐ ____-____ p. _____ Knowledge of Police Service and Community

How would you breakdown the importance of readiness when you perform with excellence?

Physical readiness: _____%

Technical readiness: _____%

Mental readiness: _____%

TOTAL 100%

Do you have a quote(s) you would like to contribute? Identifier: _____ (e.g., years on, M/F, specialty)

McDonald, Gold Medal Policing, 2025

Appendix R

Police simulation training focus assessment

Simulation Training Focus Assessment

☐ Scenario #1: _____   ☐ Scenario #2: _____   ☐ Scenario #3: _____

Self-evaluation *(At the conclusion of simulation training or as take-home)*
Complete and assess level achieved for each performance indicator as: *Satisfactory/Unsatisfactory/Unable to rate*

Full Focus Assessment (Performance Indicators)	Examples of practices *Did I...*	Specific details to describe performance (include both correct and incorrect actions) *I...*	Improvement/Refocus strategies *(Next time I will) Remember....*
Anticipation ☐ Satisfactory ☐ Unsatisfactory ☐ Unable to rate	1. Prepare in advance? 2. Consider "What if" options? 3. Take preventive actions to avoid incidents? 4. Become proactive/take initiative?		
Equipment confidence ☐ Satisfactory ☐ Unsatisfactory ☐ Unable to rate	1. Clean/check my gun recently? 2. Find using e-com/e-aids easy? 3. Clearly articulate force options? 4. "Appear comfortable and competent with my duty belt (required equipment)?	(*Sample for) #4. Struggled and was awkward drawing gun.	(*Sample for) #4. "Smooth is fast." Practice a good draw every time I remove my gun from the holster.
Presence ☐ Satisfactory ☐ Unsatisfactory ☐ Unable to rate	1. Report good observations? 2. Display alertness? 3. "Show good judgement? 4. Reads people well?	(*Sample for) #3. Gained a stable position on the ground before getting up.	(*Sample for) #3. Focus on good hand and feet skills—take time to create a solid stance.
Teamwork ☐ Satisfactory ☐ Unsatisfactory ☐ Unable to rate	1. Exhibit trust in my peers? 2. Communicate with and involve other officer(s)? 3. Demonstrate officer safety? 4. Listen and show empathy/good people skills?		
Comfort ☐ Satisfactory ☐ Unsatisfactory ☐ Unable to rate	1. Enjoy the challenge? 2. Appear relaxed? 3. Feel in-sync with the rhythm and flow of the situation? 4. Prioritize activity sequences?		
Complacency control ☐ Satisfactory ☐ Unsatisfactory ☐ Unable to rate	1. Shift tasks/update resources to avoid boredom in down time? 2. Take control when there was an unnecessary lull? 3. Have a positive attitude through a frustrating time? 4. Take a "time out" when needed?		

J. McDonald, University of Ottawa, Canada; adapted from *Gold Medal Policing*, 2025, 2006.

Appendix S

Officer X's Top 10 Commitment and Confidence quotes in Gold Medal Policing

Gold Medal Policing was aimed at capturing exceptional policing practices from a *frontline* perspective through frank dialogue. An officer compiled this list of quotes saying that they represented the self-awareness that inspires *their* feeling of commitment and self-confidence in policing. Are there quotes that inspire you? What is your level of commitment and confidence today? What inspires you?

TEN *My thought process is that if you're prepared for the worst, then everything is so much easier to handle.*
—Neighbourhood Resource

NINE *One thing I despise is when we don't respect each other on the job. I don't care if you don't like each other—we're not all going to be best buddies and go drinking after work. When you're working, you do your share, and you respect your partner—him or her.*
—Patrol Sergeant

EIGHT *The problem with policing is: policy and "what's right" can be two separate things. For example, we take the oath and we're not allowed to talk about anything on the job but I had a case where a biker affiliate was recruiting 17-year-old girls into prostitution. I did everything I could to try to convince one of these girls not to go back. I spent two hours trying to get through to her. I wasn't allowed to tell her what I did, but could I sleep at night if I didn't tell her what she is getting herself involved in? She went back to the bikers and told them everything—they might sue us. I could be hung out to dry on the police perspective but I will continue to do the right thing, as opposed to what policy states. At least I can sleep knowing this girl had the chance.*
—School Resource

SEVEN *People who are good at their job learn from their mistakes. I can't stand working with officers who never learn from their mistakes—they're always right. You're going to make* mistakes. I've made hundreds of mistakes—and some pretty serious ones—but I learned from them. I accepted the ribbing and the lumps and I moved on. That's what makes the difference in good students, parents…people. You have to be humble and know that you are going to make mistakes, some of them serious.

—Female <10 years on

SIX It makes it that much easier if your partner understands that shift work comes with the career. It may be an issue when kids arrive, but you work around that. It is stressful on the body and we see stuff that 90% of the public doesn't see. That creeps up on you once in a while but you deal with it by talking about it.

—Patrol <10 years on

FIVE My biggest thing is keeping perspective. Yes, you saw a bad thing but it's part of life. Babies die, people get killed in car accidents or by other people. Keep perspective of what your role is.

—Sergeant >15 years on

FOUR You can't plan for what you can't control. I plan my days around an agenda I can work with. I won't try to fit two litres into a one litre jar. It can't be done but I try to please as many people as I can. Sometimes you don't have a choice. It's not in your agenda but you have to go deal with your emergency.

—Officer >15 years on

THREE Officers are so scared to get in shit. This police department focuses more on community rights than preparing officers for stressful situations. They should be training us about the signs of a fleeing felon, or how to find a scent after losing a track. They should talk about that in training. Nobody's prepared for that.

—Canine

TWO The survival technique for me is—don't put up with it.

—Female <10 years on

ONE Knowledge of the law is so incredibly important. If I had to, I could probably arrest you for something right now. It is so much fun out there when you know. Someone says, "You can't do this!" Guess what, I can.

—Patrol >10 years on

Gold Medal Policing, McDonald, 2025

Appendix T

Coach Officers' 25 teaching tips

Coach Officers' 25 teaching tips

These coaching tips were gathered over 10 years while instructing in the Facilitating and Assessing Police Learning Course at the Ontario Police College.

1. Opening with unspoken, written words (e.g., on a title page) can set tone and clarity to what follows (e.g., "Vision inspired, mission-focused, value driven").
2. Sharing what YOU know makes a difference; e.g., *"This is GOLD!" "THIS [action] tells you everything." "DON'T EVER do [this]… you'll be in harm's way."*
3. Working in a dangerous environment requires passion and knowledge. It may ground and surprise others when you share: *"I love dealing with this stuff." "It's rewarding." "Let's have some fun!"*
4. Instructor-led-scenarios can induce realistic stressful conditions to improve the quality of training in a classroom situation.
5. Finding time under stress to be prepared is a learned skill—be it a meticulous weapon checks or producing a detailed lesson plan.
6. Mentally rehearsing movements reinforces the importance of understanding maneuvers before conducting the physical drill.
7. When instructing common skills (where an audience will assume their proficiency), a humble approach can make a leader's expertise more evident—teaching, measuring and evaluating a skill is different than performing it.
8. Group expertise is maximized through impromptu Q&As and spontaneous story opportunities. Posing a challenge (man against machine) is an intuitive trigger to win.
9. A demonstration can become more personalized by pre-empting it with a scoring system to encourage self-evaluation and competitiveness (i.e., show test standards based on age, gender, etc. so individuals can self-determine their personal score).
10. If you are the "creator" of a truly unique idea, there may be merit in sharing the start-up and inspiration for the product.
11. State the obvious when instructing on skills that have become automatic (e.g., making a "protein latte" …*with no milk*).
12. A real-time, free-flow demonstration can add a "Wow factor" and speak louder than words in selling a new concept (prior to analyzing each component).
13. In contrast, progressively teaching skills (without the intimidation of seeing the complete task) can keep confidence high for advancing a novice.
14. During highly complex instruction, a silent audience is difficult to read whether they are concentrating or confused.

McDonald, Gold Medal Policing (2025)

15. Humor is a matter of style. Wit, pictures, unexpected honesty, and procedures using a wild example (e.g., a "Bigfoot Call")—all can make a point and deflect stress in a difficult situation.
16. Recognize that outside feedback may be more accurate than an instructor's own internal perception. We are not always the best judge of our performance.
17. Being outside your "comfort zone" requires you to sharpen your skills to perform under pressure—and builds confidence and efficiency for the next "unexpected" teaching situation.
18. A presentation may lend itself to more than just the intended agenda and audience—be open to lessons learned by others. (e.g., web-search methods, ppt techniques, photography).
19. Upgrade a quiz by inserting: little known historical facts, international content, new controversial evidence.
20. Gain "buy-in" with mandatory or new essential procedures. Personalize the need. Design simple solutions (e.g., 5-step cue cards). Show that it works.
21. Show confidence in an audience by building in realistic challenges and surprises into a scenario.
22. With technical hiccups, recognize your options: persist on the same path OR let it go and improvise—assess the merits of both.
23. After a web search, pick the best tool, then do the real homework. Adapt tried-and-true lesson plans with terms familiar to your audience (e.g., "muscle memory," use of a cell phone).
24. In an open venue, voice projection and body positioning require planning and practice.
25. You do not have to be the best at a skill to be a great teacher.

What are your tips to a new Coach Officer?

26. _____

27. _____

28. _____

29. _____

30. _____

McDonald, Gold Medal Policing (2025)

Index

Note: Page locators in **Bold** indicates tables

Page locators in *italics* indicates figures

academic 9, 174, 390; *see* study design
action plan *see* no action plan
active listening 27, 171, 185, 189–190, 361, **362**, 414
administration, mistrust **23**, 498; *see also* bureaucracy
aggressiveness **23**, 51, 68, *70*, **71**, 91, 94, 143, 287, **366**, 374, **498**; differences in *95*; temporal changes 555; unexpected aggressiveness 143; weighted average **89**
analysis 13, 24–25, 32, 158, 415, 454, 465–468, 487, 497, 506, 516, 527, 539
anticipation **30**, 275, **277**, 277–279, **357**, 543
anxiety *see* rookie anxiety
applied ethics **20**, 487, 489
apprehensions, effective 171, 183–185, 361, **362**; *see also* arrest
appropriate use of force **20**, 487, 488; *see also* physical control with appropriate use of force
arrest 25, 51, 69, 71, 76, 79, 108, 143, 177, 183–185, 193, 196, 246, 248, 258, 265; authorities 171–172, 179–181, 361, **362**; bad guys 215; beyond-arrest thinking 393; criminal 228; gunpoint 126, 144, 146–147, 363; individuals with mental illnesses 213; officer safety during 127; post-arrest 183; powers 204; requirement of *180*; resisting 202, 214; wrongful 50, 174; *see also* handcuffing
analysis 13, 24–25, 32, 158, 415, 454, 465–468, 487, 497, 506, 516, 527, 539
articulation **20**, 28, 171, 201, 203, 398, **527**, 530; and appropriate tone 171, 185, 188–189, 361, **362**, 414; *see also* voice
artificial intelligence (AI) 404; algorithms 394; controversy 369; facial recognition 369; integration with mental training 369, 389, 393, 415; transparent integration 415
athletes *see* Olympic athletes

background factors: education *see* education; ethnicity *see* ethnicity; gender *see* gender; language *see* language; military experience 48, 111, *111*, 112, *112*, 242, 314–316, **315**, 374, 384, 475, *476*, 557, 559; prior police-related experience 47, *111*, 112, 132, 134, 136, 250, 314, **315**, 320, 384, 475, **475**, 557, 558
back-up 40, 109, 183, **264**
belief *see* confidence; self-belief
beyond-arrest thinking 393
body cam 27, *173*, 312, 369, 393, 403; video-cued-recall debriefs 541
body language 276, 395
body search 126, 127, 130–132, **362**, 363, 414
boredom 44–45, 68, 142, 300; *see also* complacency; downtime (lulls) and routine tasks
Box, George 6
bureaucracy 73, *74*, 240, 365, **366**, 391; difference in *95*; weighted average **89**; *see also* paperwork
"buy-in" procedures 334, 392, 401

California Psychological Inventory (CPI-434) 50
camaraderie support 127, 133–134, 234, 243–245, *245*, 250–251, 320, 323, 356, **357**, 413; *see also* teamwork
Canine 108, *111*, **315**, 475, *476*; articulation and appropriate tone 188–189; body search 131, 132; car collisions 61; collision-avoidance strategies 156; containment in environmental conditions 141, 142; court appearance strategies 177; crisis 56; effective apprehensions 184; equipment maintenance

148–149; fatigue strategies 137; firearms and gunpoint arrest 148; lights and sirens 158; multitasking 160, 161; opportunities to visualize 259; patrolling the environment 163; personal fears and skepticism 64; physical control with appropriate use of force 152; physical discipline 133, 134; shift work strategies 135; team dynamics 66; use-of-force principles 182, 183; vehicle reversing 162

car collision avoidance **30**, 91, **157**, 286, **292**, 294, 320, **357**, 368, 415, 542; collision-avoidance strategies 154, 156–157, **157**, *285*, 287, **292**, **357**, **366**, 368, 415

car collisions 23, **30**, *53*, 54, 61–62, 91, **157**, **292**, 294, 320, 356, **358**, **366**, 498, 554; difference in *95*; temporal changes **554**; weighted average **89**; *see also* cruiser and vehicle operations

career/succession planning 340–341, 370, 380, 385, 387, 392, 398, 404, 406, 415

challenging situations: categorizing 38–49, 96–98; coaching/leadership *see* coaching; leadership; complex/complicated situations 6, 37, *40*, 41–42, 136, 145, 155, 172, 174, 179, 233, 277, 292, 336, 551; defined 469; emotionally charged situations 39, *40*, 43–44, 337, 551–552; heightened-risk situations 39–41, *40*, 148, 278, 336, 551; high-risk individuals *40*, 47–48, 551; unfamiliar situations *40*, 46–47, 66, 213, 314, 337, 551–552; unprecedented circumstances *40*, 48–49, 337, 551–552

changes 23, 42, *74*, 83, 105, 173–174, 190, 342, **366**, 413, 498; differences in *95*; heart rate 55, 339; organizational 94; policy 84; politics 84; to schedule 57; shift 56, 138; social 204; technological 388; temporal changes in 553–555; in training 213; weighted average **89**; *see also* trends

cheat sheets 197, 198, 210, 258; *see also* checklist 11, 264, 277, 386; court 260; mental 253, 256, **256**, 257, 259; personal 261; physical 179, 257, 260; self-directed 395

climate conditions **23**, 52, *53*, 54, 88, **366**, 498; differences in *95*; environmental stamina **26**, 103, 517, 520; temporal changes **554**; weighted average **89**

Coach Officer Advisory Group 2, 5, 115, 361

Coach officers 5, 12–13, 31, 36–37, 104, 115, 118, 127, 144, 146–147, 172, 196, 202–203, 206, 225, 229, 249, 271, 323, 345–346, 352, 399, 411; competencies for 10; concerns 82; consultations 120; defined 469; excellent 118, 401, 554–555; issues 391, 401; official role 44; performance indicators 126, 171; *see also specific performance indicators*; program 384, 400, 404, 406; questionnaires 120; responsibility 237; role of 9; selection 370, 401; teaching tips 380, 579–580; trainees and 11; training 9

coaching 13, 22, *40*, 82, 337, 341, 406, 413, 552; benchmarks 382, 384; challenges 39, *40*, 45; co-coaching 400; decisions 229; dynamics 36; immediate 341; issues **23**, 75, 82, **366**, **498**; others 45; reimagining 36; responsibilities 39; sports 11; *see also* leader/leading/leadership; mentor

collaborative, partnerships 457–460; *see also* partnershipscollision-avoidance strategies *see* car collision avoidance strategies

collision/crash *see* car collisions

commitment 2, 29, **30**, 104, 118, 141, 150, 227–243, 306, **317**, 318, **319**, 323, 354, **357–358**, 359, **360**, 371–372, 375, 383, 392, 404, 413, 414, 539–540, 563, 566–568; competitiveness 242, 318, 323, 339, 370, 383, 415, 538, 540; consistent 376; courage and physical 227–244; defined 228; empathy **26**, 179, *195*, 204, 229–231, 250, 281, 355, **357**, 372, 376, 380, 383, 392, 396; ethics *see* ethics; ethics

training **30**, 229, 234, 343, 538, 540; exceptional 228; extraordinary 401; firm *290*; inconsistent 321; inspiring 342, 348; job engagement 538; job satisfaction 21–22, 83, 229, 230, 235–236, **267**, 314, **319**, 355, **357**, 380, 388, 415; leadership connection **30**, 538, 540; long-term 380; loyalty 229, 240–242, 281; motivated to succeed 229, 242–244; *see also* competitiveness; job security; to ongoing preparedness 208; organizational 35, 235–236; professional 241, 262; professional discipline 228, 229, 231–235, **232**, 262, 313, 355, **357**, 380, 383, 406; quotes in Gold Medal Policing 576–577; responsible leadership 229, 236–238, 321, 355, **357**, 380, 406; team **289**; understanding "the job" 229, 238–240, **238**, 318, 323, 355, **357**, 415; unwavering 203
communication 179, 230, 299, 318, 334, 335, 368, 396; centre 36; constant 339, 343; e-communications 280; empathetic 183, 191; external 148, 192–194, **317**, 318, **319**, 373, 415; insufficient 73; internal 203, 210–213, **211**, 263; interpersonal 127; open 369; overcoming 194; public 68; radio 155, 159, 280; skills 10, 12, 371; tactical 25, 182; training 204; verbal *see* verbal communication; written *see* written communication
community composition 203, 213–216, **362**; *see also* knowledge of community
community engagement 21, 181, 191, 214, 216, 266, 394
community partners **28**, 337, 527, 529
community policies 20, 28, 73, 191, 203, 207–210, 324, 354, **362**, 393, 403; *see also* knowledge of police service, community
community policing 20, 28, 73, 191, 323, 354, 393, 403, 531
community rapport and humor 162, 171, 185, 191–194, 361, **362**, 414; community leaders 341; community relations **20**, 172, 204, 214, 487, 488; *see also* lack community contacts

Community Resource Officer (CRO) 46, *111*, 142, 156, 176, 311, **315**, 319, 476; court appearance strategies **176**; unfamiliar situations 46
Community-Oriented-Policing (COP) 204, 488, 528
competitiveness 243, 318, 323, 339, 370, 371, 383, 415, 538, 540
complacency 38, 43, 60, **80**, 143, 154, 164, 247, 278, 283, **299**, 300, 397; false-alarm 61; *vs.* hyper-vigilance 60; implied 92; promotional 22, **23**, 80, 388, 498; risk of 213; *see also* boredom; others' complacency
complaints 4, 48, 68, 77, 153, 214, 242; misconduct 59; public *see* public complaints
complex/complicated situations 6, 37, *40*, 41–42, 136, 145, 155, 172, 174, 179, 233, 280, 292, 336, 551
concentration *see* full focus
conclusions 352–378
confidence 10, 49, 76, 80, 104, 109–110, 118, 127, 132, 163, 175, 179–181, 226, *228*, 233–234, 244–252, 259, 264, 274, **298**, 303, **303**, 305, 320, 347, 354, **357–358**, 360, 365, 369, 389, 401–402, 413, 567; building 131, 186, 323, 340, 368; control environment 244, *245*, 247–249, **289**, **357**; decision-making 145; education *see* education; enhancing 20; equipment 275, 279–281, *279*, **289**, **319**, 354, **357**, 373, 395, 415; faith or luck 244, *245*, **358**; grounded *245*, 252–253, 395; issues 370; laws, authority 175; physical 86; police mentors 244, 245, *245*, 249, 356, **357**, 368, 404; public **20**; quality training **30**, 244–246, *245*, 356, **357**, 413; quotes in Gold Medal Policing 576–577; seek support *see* camaraderie support; family, support; self-confidence 251, 260, 312, 356; steps to amass 244–245; training 82, 182; *see also* recognition and thanks; self-belief
conflicts and de-escalation prevention 171, 185–188, 361, **362**, 414
constructive evaluation 29, **30**, 104, 119, 225–226, *228*, 262, 306–313, **317**, 319, **319**, 323, 354–355, **357–358**, **360**, 361, 371–372, 398, 404, 413,

563, 567; consult team 312; coping *see* coping; debriefs *see* debriefs; draw lessons 312–313; feedback from others 307, 309–312; formal evaluation 30, 208, 214, *307*, 309, **319**, 323, **358**, 373, 385, 415, 538, 541; leadership directives **30**, 380, 541; public feedback **30**, 252, *307*, 309, 311–313, **317**, 318, 356, **358**, 372, 389, 413, 538, 541; self-evaluation 307–309, *307*, 356, 385
contacts **23**, *70*, **71**, **89**, *95*, **366**, 498, 555; *see also* lack community contacts
containment: operations 126, 127, 141–143, 363, 414; poor *see* poor containment
control environment 244, *245*, 247–249, **289**, **357**
coping 104, 313–315, 338, 356, **358**, 369, 540, 563; difficulties 50; external support 241; family 241; female-policing 75, 77–80, **78**, **80**, 88–89, **89**, 94, *95*, *285*, 286, **292**, **305**, 305–307, 370; in high-stress situations 386; mechanisms 62, 134, 235, 237; ownership and draw lessons 313–315; with shift work 57; strategies 5, 77, 94, 138, 155, 262, 320, 397, 415; time management 133
core competencies **20**, 478, 487, 489
counter-terrorism 28, **28**, 204, 393, 402, 527, 528
court 83; accountability 62; fatigue 63; justice *see* court appearances; justice; preparation 196; *see also* court appearance strategies; procedures 172, 175–179, 361, **362**; testimonies 196; time 199; wasted resources 63
court appearances **23**, *53*, 54, 62–63, 82, 88, 96, 172, 175, 199, 323, 365, **366**, 408; anticipating 258; differences in *95*; paid 177; temporal changes 555; weighted average **89**; *see also* court preparation/strategies
court appearances strategies, preparation for *184*; strategies 92, 175, **176**, 195, *285*, 286, **292**, 297, 356, **357**
court procedures 172, 175–179, 361, **362**

crises/crisis **23**, 49, 51–52, *53*, 54–56, 88, 127, 133, 323, 325, 344, 347–348, 363, **366**, 497; defined 337; differences in *95*; extraordinary 181; temporal changes 554; weighted average **89**
crisis refocusing 88, 284, *285*, 287, 290, 291–**292**, **294**, 294–296, 355, **357**, 397; management 333, 335, 338–339; opportunity in 348; reaction **294**
Critical Incident History Questionnaire (CIHQ) 50
critical thinking 8, **20**, 26, 145, 487, 489
cruiser 69–70, 79, 126, 130, 157, 160, 162–164, 184, 197, 246; coordination 161; public reactions to 61; winter-driving 62; *see also* vehicle operations
culture 94, 172, 190, 214, 375, 404; adjustment 370; challenges **26**, 127, 516; clashes 75, 85; diversity 229, 249; factors 59, 145; issues 303; maturity and culturally-grounded 12, **30**, 68, 229, 234, 538, 542; multicultural 488; organizational **28**, 52, 73, 204, 236, 527, 528; positive cultural shifts 4, 26; *see also* ethnicity
curriculum 8, 380, 392–393, 398, 404

day-to-day pressures **23**, 85, 87, **89**, 94, 365, **366**, **498**, 555
debriefs 28, **30**, 208, 258, 268, 276, 309, 312, 324, 396, 538, 540; impromptu 541; incident 128, 310; informal *307*, 309–311, 323, 356, **358**, 398, 413; informal social 259; parade 311; peer 31, 312; policy-debrief 209; video-cued-recall 541; visualized 258, 320; workout 132
decision-making 6, 9, 26, 50, 63, 109, 143, 175, 181, 213, 252, 265, 276, 295, 340, 342, 405; biased 369, 389; civilian-led 83; coaching 227; collaborative 191; confidence 145; critical 344; equipment 83; ethical 21, 229; hasty 295; informed 4, 172, 173, 318, 332–333; life-altering 146; on-the-spot 179; professional 173; quick 60, 154, 159; rapid 144, 146, 155; real-time 173; training programs 394; uninformed 337

dedication 148, 227, 228, 240–242, 355, **357**, 383, 390; demanding 2; networking 194; unwavering 146
de-escalation 28, 145, 170, 284–285, *285*, 287, **287**, **357**, 361, **362**, 368; *see also* conflicts and de-escalation prevention
defending 13, 69, 133–134, **291**, 297, 298
defensive tactics **26**, 126, 144, 149–150, **362**, 363, 517
definitions 469–473
desired feedback 311
developmental factors: Canine *111*, **315**, 476, 485; *see also* Canine; Community Resource Officers 46, *111*, 142, 156, 176, **315**, 316, 321, 476; external police *111*, 243, **315**, 316, 475, 487; more than frontline *111*, 272, **315**, 321, 374, 475, *475*; patrol-only experience 41, *111*, 136, 156, 302, 305, **315**, 318, **319**, 325, 367, 372, 415; rural police 40, *111*, 114–115, 189, 242, **315**, 315, 321, 326, 374, 384, *475*, 557, 562; School Resource Officer *see* School Resource Officer; Tactical *see* Tactical; Traffic Escort *see* Traffic Escort
diet *see* eating/diet
disappointing performance 49, 102, 103, 111–114, 120, 122, 353, 469, 474, 561, 562
discipline problems **23**, *70*, **71**, 94, **366**, 498; differences in *95*; temporal changes 555; weighted average **89**
discipline, professional 228, 229, 231–235, **232**, 262, 277, 355, **357**, 380, 383, 406
dispatch/dispatcher 65, 72, 143, 152, 158–161, 190, 211–213, 248, 264, 269, 277
disrespect *see* public disrespect
distinction factors: current specialty unit *110*, **315**, 314, 475, 477; elite reputation *110*, **315**, 314, 475, 477; old/new-school males *110*, **315**, 314, 475, 477; rank *110*, **315**, 314, 371, 475, 477, 561; total years experience *110*, **315**, 314, 475, 477
distraction control 29, 104, 118, 225–226, 284–305, *285*, 323, 354–355, 359, **360**, 367, 372, 384, 390,
413, 538, 562; emotional control **30**, 144, 259, 284, 287, **287**, 396–397, 542; strategies 37; training 392–393; *see also* Generic Control Practices; Specialized Control Practices; stress management/reduction
distractions/hindrances 22, 31, 50, 51, 60, 75, 204, 284, 296, 372; unexpected disruptions 227; *see also* performance blocks; stressors
distraction control 284–305
downtime (lulls) and routine tasks *53*, 54, 60, 88–89, 376; temporal changes in 564; weighted average **89**
downtime (lulls) and routine tasks refocusing 89, *285*, 288, **292**, 299–300, **299**, 357, 368, 397
drinking/drunk 59, 72, 136–137, 237, **291**, 301, 338
driving 43, 48, 61–62, 152, 154–155, 198, 203, **273**, 274, 281, 283–284, 402; aggressive 68; control 270; cruiser winter 62; defensive 162, 269; driver training 25, 127; drunk 49, 215; friendly 281; impaired 143, 215; maneuvers 26; measures 27; multitasking while 154; restrictive policies 154; rookies 69; safe 125, 155, *155*, 189, 285; tactics while 152
drugs 47, 143, 278–279, 395; abusing 58; addiction 278; drug-related calls 181; raid 81, 130; seizing 235; street-drug use **28**, 214, 527, 529; trading 248; warrants 41

eating/diet 56, 57, 138, 272, 388
education *111*, 131, 244, *245*, 251–252, 292, 305, **315**, 316, **319**, 320–321, 343, **358**, 374, 378, 384, 415, 474, 488; backgrounds 244; college 176, 255, 282; formal 374; higher 373; levels 114, 374; officer-centered 204; resources 186; school 42, 282; university 271
elite officer 230, 238, 242, 259, 262, 310, **317**, 372, 401, 415; defined 471; factor 318; non-Elite officers 316, 318, 372; profile 371–374; project 371; unfamiliar situations 46
elite sport 2, 9–11, 29, 105, 271, 324, 394
emergency 68, 85, 106, 126, 158, 160, 199, 212, 263, 282, 296; *see also* lights and sirens

emotional control/intelligence 30, 144, 259, 284, 287, **287**, 396–397, 542
emotionally charged situations 40, *40*, 43–44, 336, 479
empathy/empathetic 26, 179, *195*, 204, 229–231, *250*, 281, 355, **357**, 372, 376, 380, 383, 392
endurance 4, 128, 141, 318, 340; physical 4, 337; respiratory 128; *see also* fitness; physical discipline
engagement 25, 205, 310, 339, 342–343; community 21, 172, 185, 216, 217, 272, 394; job **30**, 540; supervisor **20**, 498
enjoyment 75, **135**, 174, 229, 266, 267, 275, 282–284, **291**, 301, 302, 325, **357**, 373; *see* job satisfaction/engagement
en-route or on-scene images *254*, 255, **357**
environmental stamina *see* climate conditions
equipment: checking 148; confidence 275, 279–281, *279*, **289**, *319*, 355, **357**, 373, 401, 415; decision-making 85; limitations *see* equipment limitations; proficiency **26**, 125, 518; protective **26**, 185, 519, 521, 522
equipment limitations **23**, 66, *74*, 83, **366**, 497; differences in *95*; temporal changes 554; weighted average **89**
ethics 20, **30**, 33, 120, *151*, 205, **264**, 280, 538, 539; applied **20**, 487, 489; behavior 11, 145, 234; challenge 229; clarity 333; considerations 150, 173, 205; decision-making 21, 229; issues 343; leadership 236; training **30**, 234, 240, 244, 538, 540; work 231–232, **232**, 239
ethnicity **23**, *74*, 75, 83–84, 94, *111*, 320–321, **367**, 371, 374, 475, 498, 556; differences in *95*; ethnic diversity **20**, 488; internal 405; male **315**, 475, 477, 557; overall 557; weighted average **89**; *see also* culture
evaluation and coping *see* constructive evaluation
evidence 14–15, 107, 147, 198, **298**, 379, 401, 412; -based approach 3, 7, 31, 456–482; based mental-readiness 361; based performance indicators 116; based tactics 412; body-cam 393, 403; criticizing R2MR 24;

digital 393; documented 202; protecting 141; supporting R2MR 24; traffic 203
excellent/exceptional officer 4, 8, 11, 231, 400, 411–412, 554–555
executive/senior management 333–334, 340, 349
executive summary 411–418
Extended Mental-Health Continuum *24*
external blocks/performance stressors 500; day-to-day pressures **23**, 85, 87, **89**, 94, 365, **366**, **498**, 554; family conflicts 21, 51, 85, **89**, *95*, 96, 98, **238**, **366**, 383, 406, 497, 555; fatigue *see* fatigue
external police *111*, 243, **315**, 316, 475, 479
external specialists **23**, *53*, 54, 66, 92, 192, **264**, **366**, 372, 498; differences in *95*; temporal changes 555; weighted average **89**

facial recognition 369; *see also* artificial intelligence
faith or luck 244, *245*, **358**
family: conflicts 21, 51, 85, **89**, *95*, 96, **238**, 361, **366**, 406, 499, 530; coping 241–242; shift work and 250; support **135**, 241, *245*, 249–251, 356, **357**, 413
fatigue **23**, 36–37, 43, 50, 96, 121, 127, 132, 146, 159, 165, 227, **238**, 285, 292, 318, 372, 402, 500; court 63; factor 137; mental 85, 337; motorcycle 57; physical 137, 337; resiliency 50; rituals 137; shift-work 52, *53*, 54, 56–58, **89**, 91, *95*, 97, 285, **292**, 363, **366**, 554
fatigue strategies **136**, 137, *285*, 286, **292**, **317**, 318, **319**, 355, **357**, 371–372, 415
fears *see* personal fears
feedback 9, 10, 36, 44, 49, 309, 389, 392, 394, 396; accepting 190; desired 311; formal evaluations 309; informal debriefs 309–312; lack of feedback **23**, 73, *74*, 83, **89**, *95*, 202, **366**, 555; not-typical 215; police instructor 19; positive 215; public **30**, 251, *306*, 310–312, **317**, 318, 356, **358**, 372, 390, 413; suspect rapport 310–312; team advice 309
female policing coping strategies **78**, 94, *285*, 286, **292**, **305**, 305–306, *319*

female policing issues **23**, 48, *74*, 75, 77–80, 88–89, 94, **238**, 239, 285, 293, **366**, 372, 378, 415, 498, 555; differences in *95*; females with concerns relating to 78; males with concerns regarding 78; weighted average 89; *see also* gender
females in authority **20**, 487, 490
Field Training Assessment tool 116, 361, 380, 566–568
firearms 25, 146, 148, 189, 246, **362**, 363; coaches 147; dilemma 147; fear 146; information gathering 147; marksmanship 146, 254, 275, 323, 396; measured response for 158; oversights 148; related situations 146; safety habits 147; skill-sharing 146; tactical 127; threat assessment 147
fitness **20**, 22, 126, 127, 132–143, **317**, 354, 362, 414, 488, 501; testing **26**, 517, 520; *see also* gym; physical discipline; well-being
focus *see* full focus and concentration
force at mental-illness calls 26, **26**, 127, 145, 518
formal recognition 390–391
framework, investigative *see* investigative framework
frontline officer 5, 10, 13, 36, 37, 52, 117, 280, 336, 345, 374–375, 385, 389–390, 401; crisis, defined 54, 337; defined 471; excellent 8, 231, 400, 411–412, 554–555; exceptional 4, 31, 120; navigating challenges 8–9; safety 143; seasoned 37
frontline-recognition plan 380, 389–392; formal recognition 390–391; frontline "buy-in" procedures 392; frontline organizational problem-solving 391–392
full focus 274–283, 563, 567; anticipation **30**, 277, **357**, 543–544; emotional intelligence 29, 275, 282–284, 332, 336, 543; enjoyment 75, **135**, 174, 235, 266, 275, 282–284, **301**, 302, 304, 323, 355, **357**, 373; equipment confidence 275, 279–281, *279*, **289**, *319*, 355, **357**, 373, 395, 415; present and mindful 276–277, 355, **357**; relaxation 155, 241–242, 254, 259, 270–271, 274, 275,

282–284, **287**, **293**, **299**, 300, **357**; rhythm and flow 274, 275, 282–284, **357**; situational awareness 30, 143, 145, 150, 158, 159, 164, *164*, 190, 196, 276, 395–396, **538**, 543; teamwork and trust 275, 281–282, **357**

gear 27, 67, 143, 159, 212, *279*; protective 131; shifting 58, 86; tactical 128; winter-gear planning 67; *see also* equipment
gender 77, **78**, **96**, *110*, 234, **315**, 314–316, 384, 400, 415, 475; challenges **26**, 127, 128, 517; conflict 238; differences 50, 374; disparities 59; factors 27, 319; female-policing *see* female policing; -related performance 77
Generic Control Practices: de-escalation 28, 145, 183, 284–285, *285*, **287**, 287–289, 355–356, **357**, 361, **362**, 368; involvement of others 284, *285*, 286, 287, **289**, 289–291, 356, **357**, 368; task orientation *285*, 286, 287, 291, **291**, 358
getting lost *see* lost, getting
goal setting 10, **30**, 538, 542
Gold Medal Policing 4, 8, 19, 31, 117, 333, 381, 389, 406, 411–412, 417, 457–459, 461–462, 482, 497, 515–516; commitment and confidence quotes in 576–577; quotes and lessons 570–573
gunpoint arrest 126, 144, 146–148, 363
gym 133–134, 259, 261, **273**, 273, 274; *see also* fitness

handcuffing 126, 127, 129–130, 191, **362**, 363, 414, 517
Harmon, B. 263
hate crime 4, 39, 205, 207, 214, 389, 393, 403–404
heightened-risk situations 39–41, *40*, 148, 278, 336–337, 551
high-risk individuals *40*, 47–48, 552
Hillier, R. 348
humor 59, 63, 69, **267**, 267, 282, **287**, 289, **299**; internal 52; sick sense of 240; *see also* community rapport and humor
hyper-vigilance 60; *see also* vigilance

588 ■ Index

imagery/images *see positive imagery or* visualization
impromptu rehearsal *254*, 254, 259, **317**, 318, **358**, 415
influential factors 11, *110*, 119, 314–321, 474–482, *475*; background factors *see* background factors; developmental factors *see* developmental factors; distinction factors *see* distinction factors
informal debriefs *307*, 309, 311, 323, 356, **358**, 398, 413
informal leadership 4, **20**, 22, 36, 205–207, 345, 403, 487, 489
injury: management strategies 132, 140; pain and **23**, 498; risk of 127–128, 150; status **26**, 517, 520
instructor-led images *254*, 255, 258–259, **358**
internal communication 203, 210–213, **211**, 263
interruptions *see* distractions; minimize interruptions
interviewing, effective 171, 185, 194–195, 361, **362**, 414
investigative framework 478–481
involvement of others 284, *285*, 286, 287, **289**, 289–291, 356, **357**, 368; *see also* teamwork

jaded, feeling **23**, *53*, 91, 94, 239–240, 365, **366**, 367, 383, 498; difference in *95*; temporal changes 554; weighted average **89**
job satisfaction/engagement 21–22, 83, 229, 235–236, **267**, 312, **319**, 355, **357**, 380, 388, 415; job engagement **30**, 538, 540; *see also* enjoyment
job security 229, 231, 242–243, **287**, 321–322, **358**, 375
jokes *see* humor
justice 62, **176**, 198; finding closure to 242; procedural 59; uphold 205

knowledge, application of the law and 171, 173–175, 361, **362**; local, provincial and federal laws **28**, 171, 527, 530; situational tactics **28**, 213, 527; technology resources **28**, 527, 530; *see also* proficiency in law
knowledge of community 117, 171, 213–215, 361, 414, 566; community composition and resources 213–216, **362**

knowledge of police organization/service 203–215, 527; counter-terrorism impacts 28, **28**, 204, 393, 402, 527, 528; internal communication 203, 210–213, **211**, 263; organizational culture **28**, 52, 73, 204, 236, 527, 528; police organizations 204–207, **362**; policies and procedures 20, **28**, 28, 73, 191, 203, 207–210, 324, 354, **362**, 393, 403, 527–528; policing philosophy **28**, 527

lack community contacts **23**, *70*, **71**, **366**, 498; differences in *95*; temporal changes 555; weighted average **89**
lack of feedback **23**, *73*, *74*, 87, **89**, *95*, 209, **366**, 554
lack of information **23**, *53*, 69, 95, **366**, 374, 509; differences in *95*; temporal changes 554; weighted average **89**
lack of leadership **23**, *74*, 76, 88, **89**, *95*, 365, **366**, 391, 498, 555
lack of safety **23**, *70*, **71**, 88, **366**, 498; differences in *95*; temporal changes 555; weighted average **89**
language 115, 164, 188, 190, 202, 314, 371, 373, 384, 400; body 276, 395; multiple 46, *110*, **315**, 320, 474, 475, 559–560; primary *110*, 138, 143, **315**, 320, 475, 559
law *see* knowledge, application of the law; proficiency in law
leader/leading/leadership 6, 13, **23**, 32, *39*, *40*, 44, 81, 84, 229, 251, 265, 312, 332–351, 385, 412, 552; abilities 340, 401; business 9; coach-officer 115 *see also* Coach officers; community 341; connection **30**, 538, 540; development 19, **20**, 21, 181, 345, 415, 487, 489–490; directives **30**, 379–408, 541; effective 205, 339, 345; endurance 340; engagement 342–343; ethical 235, 333; fostering 346, 491; frontline 7, 21, 343, 344; frontline patrol 337; good 284, 334, 344, 396; ineffective 336; informal 4, 22, 36, 205–206, 490; informal patrol 345, 405; instructor-led images *254*, 255, 258–259, **358**; issues 337; lack of **23**, *73*, *74*, 88, **89**, *95*, 365, **366**, 391, 498, 555; natural 345, 346; pressures

339; proactive career planning 415; problems 83; responsible 229, 236–238, 321, 355, **357**, 380; roles 190; selfless 344, 345; senior 333; skills 11; spontaneous 345–346; strategies 369; styles **20**, 488, 490; support 369, 415; team building and partnerships 340–342; training 183; true 333, 335; *see also* coaching

lessons, draw *see* constructive evaluation

lights and sirens 62, 126, 147, 154, 157–158, 160, 270, 278

literature review 19, 172, 411, 462; Critical Analysis of the "Road to Mental Readiness" (R2MR) Program 505–509; Mental Competencies in Policing 537–544; Physical Competencies in Policing 515–522; Police Performance Stressors 496–501; Predictors of Police Performance 486–491; Technical Competencies in Policing 526–531

Lombardi, Vince 4

lost, getting **23**, *53*, 54, 66, 92, 94, 213, **366**, 498; differences in *95*; temporal changes 555; weighted average **89**

loyalty 229, 240–242, 281

luck *see* faith or luck

lulls *see* downtime (lulls) and routine tasks

marksmanship *see* firearms

maturity and culturally-grounded 12, **30**, 68, 229, 234, 538, 542

media **28**, 205, 207, 527, 529; attention 336; issues 336–337; negative reports 29; news 214; scrutiny 333; social 27, 172, 191, 214; social interactions 29

mental competencies 537–550; *see also* mental readiness

mental health 24, 31, 48; advocacy groups 213; awareness 37; challenges 205; Extended Mental-Health Continuum 24; issues 4, 284, 396; needs 528; physical and 132; post-traumatic stress syndrome 21, 24, 28, 31, 36, 50, 75, 85, 205, 497–500, 505–509, 528, 540, 544; programs 323; risks 205

mental preparation 29, 104, 115, 118, 152, 225, 226, 261–273, 318, 323, 354–355, 359, **360**, 371–372, 404, 413, 563, 567; clear objectives and plan 261, 268–269, 355, **357**; goal setting 10, **30**, 538, 542; minimize interruptions 262, 269–270, **287**, 323; positive thinking 253, 255, 262, 266–268, **267**, 304, 355, **357**; psyching 262, **267**, 271, **319**, **357**, 373, 415; *see also* preparation location; rituals; recognize risk 262, 270–271, 313, 321, 355, **357**; rituals *see* rituals; strategic resource plan 262–265, **264**, 355, **357**

mental readiness 1, 4–6, 8, 14, 19, 29–31, **30**, 49, 119, 224–331, **317**, **319**, 353, 359, 361, 394, 405, 411–413, 537–544, 563; artificial intelligence integration and 369, 415; assessment 413; competencies 400; defined 104, 472, 473; differences in overall importance *104*, 556; in disappointing performances 113, *113*, 561; by factors 110, *111*, 559–560; influencing 400; as influential factor 11; mental competencies 537–550; never getting old 110; occupational differences **106**, 106; overall importance 103, *104*, **104**, 557; performance indicators 117, 118–119, 353–354, **357**, **360**, 413; police-specific 4–5; reminders 109; skills 4, 13, 115, 375; in successful performances 111–114, *112*, 559–560; in successful *vs.* disappointing performances *114*, 115; by tactical experience 112, *111*; *see also* influential factors

mentor 244, *245*, 249, 356, **357**, 368, 404; *see also* coaching

methodology *see* study design

military 25, 162, 240, 265, 343, 475; based R2MR program 21; Canadian 87, 335; experience 48, 110, 111, *112*, 242, **315**, 314, 374, 384, 475–476, 557; personnel 146; research 4–5, 24, 318, 321; security 9

mindful 143, 276, 355, **357**, 387; *see also* full focus

minimize interruptions 261, 269–270, **287**, 323

mission xxx, 171, 203, 268, 272, *290*, 342, 346, 396, 412

mistrust: administration **23**, 498; team/peer **23**, 52, *53*, 65, **89**, *95*, 365, 366, 367, 498, 554
more than frontline experience *110*, 272, **315**, 321, 374, *475*, 476
motivation 21, 52, 133, 145, 227, 233, 272, 282, 342, 348, 355, 375, 383, 402; homicide 393, 403; internal 203; lack of 80, 369; skills 339–340; to succeed 229, 242–244; team 334; *see also* commitment
motor-imagery training **30**, 538, 543
multiple language 46, *110*, **315**, 320, 475, 559–560
multitasking 12, 75, 154, 159–161, 256, 282, **362**, 363
music rituals 272

negativity **23**, *70*, **71**, 72, 94, **366**, 370, 499; differences in *95*; temporal changes 555; weighted average **89**
Neighborhood Resource Team (NRT) 107, 109, *110*, **315**, 475, 476; active listening 191; arrest authorities 179, 180; body search 130; collision-avoidance strategies 156; commitment 227; community composition and resources 214, 215; complex situations 42; control environment 247, 248; court appearance strategies 177; day-to-day pressure 87; effective apprehensions 184, 185; empathy 230; external communication 192–194; hate crime 207; injury management strategies 140; job satisfaction 236; knowledge and application of laws 173, 174; leadership 346; lights and sirens 157, 160; long-term rest strategies 140; motivated to succeed 242; multitasking 159, 161; officer safety 127; operational rookie errors 72–73; personal fears and skepticism 65; physical discipline 133; power 205–206; prevention of conflicts and de-escalation 187, 188; professional discipline 233; public complaints 76; quality training 246; reasonableness 153; reassurance 206; resource shortcomings 67; responsible leadership 236; review and interpret internal resources 210; still remembers 207; suitable reports 202–203; timely reports 200–201; understand "the job" 240; unprecedented circumstances 48–49; use-of-force principles 183; visual triggers 256, 258
networking/liaison 194, 212, 215–216, 250; liaison 263, *265*, 371
no action plan **23**, *70*, **71**, 92, 94, **366**, 370, 498; differences in *95*; temporal changes 555; weighted average **89**
no basic law **23**, *70*, **71**, **366**, 498; differences in *95*; temporal changes 555; weighted average **89**
not being promoted 75, 74, 80–82, 88, 94, 285, **358**, 365, **366**, 371, 391; differences in *95*; promotional complacency 22, **23**, 80, 388, 498; temporal changes 554; weighted average **89**
not being promoted refocusing *285*, 286, **293**, 294, **303**, 303–305
note-taking and reporting 143, 186, 527, 530; safety 69, 197; suitable/timely reports 171, 196, 201–203, 361, **362**; systematic 171, 196–198, 361, **362**
nutrition *see* eating/diet

objectives and plan 262, 268–269, 355, **357**
offense-defense mastery 370
officer safety 26, **26**, 117, 127–143, 146, 165, 194, 236, 264, 310, 318–319, 372, 415, 519–520, 566; during arrest 127; body search 126, 127, 130–131, **362**, 363, 414; common-sense approach 143–144, 363, 414; communication and 186; containment operations 126, 127, 141–143, 363, 414; fitness *see* fitness; physical discipline; handcuffing 126, 127, 129–130, 191, **362**, 363, 414, 517; honesty 237; injury status **26**, 517, 520; protective equipment **26**, 185, 517, 519, 521; safety training **26**, 128, 517, 519, 520; toute la gang 237; US national officer-safety survey 154
Okazawa, Yoshinori 266
Olympic athletes 2, 5, 29, 38, **106**, 106, 117, 148, 227, 276, 317, 354, 394, 412
Ontario Police College (OPC) 413, 458, 459

Index ■ 591

operational general blocks/stressors 52, 499; car collisions *see* car collisions; climate conditions 23, 52, *53*, 54, **89**, *95*, **366**, 498, 554; court appearances *see* court appearances; crises *see* crises/crisis; downtime and routine tasks *see* downtime (lulls) and routine tasks; external specialists 23, *53*, 54, 66, **89**, 92, *95*, 192, **264**, **366**, 371–372, 498, 555; getting lost 23, *53*, 54, 66, **90**, 92, 94, *95*, 213, **366**, 498, 555; lack of information 23, *53*, 66, **90**, 92, *95*, 365, **366**, 498, 554; others' complacency 23, 52, *53*, 65, **90**, 92, *95*, 365, **366**, 498, 555; pain and injury 23, 498; personal fears 23, 43, 52, *53*, 54–55, 63–65, **89**, 89, 94, *95*, 270, 365, **366**, 370, 498, 554; previous calls 23, *53*, 54, **89**, *95*, **366**, 498, 555; public disrespect *see* public disrespect; shift-work fatigue *see* shift work, fatigue; team/peer mistrust 23, 52, *53*, 65, **89**, *95*, 365, 367, **366**, 498, 554; work conflicts 23, *53*, 66, **90**, 92, 94, *95*, **366**, 498, 555

operational performance blocks/stressors: operational general blocks *see* operational general blocks/stressors; operational rookie errors *see* rookie errors

operational readiness 2, 9, 14, 19, 389, 412; defined 472–473; evidence-based approaches to address 31; expansion to 6; Operational Readiness Framework 6–8, *8*, 411, 412, 457; performance indicators 115; *see also* mental readiness; physical readiness; technical readiness

Operational Readiness Framework (ORF) 6–8, *8*, 411, 412, 457

Operational Readiness Index (ORI) *8*, 353, 361, 413

organizational blocks/stressors 52, 500; bureaucracy 73, 74, **89**, *95*, 240, 365, **366**, 391; changes *see* changes; coaching issues 23, 75, 82, **366**, 498; equipment limitations 23, 66, 74, 83, **89**, *95*, **366**, 498, 554; ethnicity issues *see* ethnicity; female policing issues *see* female policing;

lack of feedback 23, 73, 74, 83, **89**, *95*, **366**, 554; lack of leadership 23, 73, 74, 88, **89**, *95*, 365, **366**, 391, 498, 555; mistrust administration 23, 498; politics 23, 75, 74, 82, 84, **89**, *95*, 205, 206, 336, **366**, 498, 554; poor support 23, 74, **89**, *95*, **366**, 498, 554; preferential treatment 23, 77, 498; promotional complacency 22, 23, 80, 388, 498; public complaints *see* public complaints; training issues 23, 74, 88, **89**, 91, *95*, **366**, 367, 498, **554**; workload *see* workload

organizational culture 28, 52, 73, 204, 236, 527, 528; *see also* knowledge of police organization

organizational directives 20, **20**, 488–489; appropriate use of force **20**, 488, 489; community relations **20**, 172, 204, 214, 488; public confidence **20**, 487, 488; wellness and performance **20**, 21, 487, 489, 491

Orlick, T. 29, 105, 117–118, 225–226, *226*, 354, 403, 413, 562–563; *see also* Wheel of Excellence

others' complacency 23, 52, *53*, 65, 92, 365, **366**, 498; differences in *95*; temporal changes 555; weighted average **89**; *see also* complacency

Ottawa Police Service (OPS) 39, 333, 391, 413, 458, 459

ownership 312–314, **357**

packing rituals *279*, 280

pain 23, 498; *see also* injury; personal fears

paperwork 83, 177, 202, 249, 302; *see also* bureaucracy

partnership 19, 199, 214, 272, 281, 334, 341–342; building 339; collaborative 457–460; incompatible 73; public-private 204; strategic 411; team building and 340

Patrol 107–109, *110*, **315**, 475, 476; active listening 191; arrest authorities 181; articulation and appropriate tone 189; attitude and actions 343; body search 131; car collisions 61; coach issues 82; coaching/leading 45; collision-avoidance strategies

157; commitment 227–228; community composition and resources 216; complex situations 42; containment in environmental conditions 142; court appearance strategies 178; court appearances 63–64; crisis 54; defensive tactics 150; downtime and routine tasks 61; effective apprehensions 185; emotionally charged situations 44; empathy 231; engagement 343; equipment maintenance 149–150; external communication 193, 194; family priorities 85–86; fatigue strategies 137–138; feeling grounded 252; female-policing coping issues 78–79; firearms and gunpoint arrest 146, 147; flexible 265; informal leadership 206–207; injury management strategies 140; internal communication 211–213; knowledge and application of laws 173–174; leadership 346; leadership 84; lights and sirens 159; long-term rest strategies 138–139; loyalty 241–242; motivated to succeed 243–244; multitasking 160–161; not being promoted 80, 81; operational rookie errors 69; paperwork *vs.* quality 83; patrolling the environment 162–163; personal fears and skepticism 63–64; physical discipline 134; police mentors 249; policy changes 84; politics 84; prevention of conflicts and de-escalation 186–187; professional discipline 235; proper handcuffing 130; public disrespect 59–60; quality training 246, 247; reasonableness 153; responsible leadership 237–238; review and interpret internal resources 209–210; seek support 251; shift work strategies 135; shift-work fatigue 58; suitable reports 202; systematic note-taking 197–198; team dynamics 65, 66; timely reports 199, 200; understand "the job" 239, 240; unfamiliar situations 47; unsupported 84; use-of-force principles 181–182; visual triggers 256, 257; workload 76; written communication 196

patrol issues, general **23**, 70, **71**, **366**, 367, 498; differences in *95*; temporal changes 555; weighted average **89**

Patrol Sergeant: attitude and actions 348; car collisions 62; community composition and resources 215; downtime and routine tasks 61; engagement 343; fatigue strategies 136–137; feeling grounded 252; leadership 345; mental preparation 261; not being promoted 80–81; police mentors 249; public complaints 76; review and interpret internal resources 208, 209; safety sense 143; scene management 263, 264; sergeants' perspectives 344–345; supervisors' dilemma 347; timely support 206; understand "the job" 239

patrolling environment 127, 154, 162–163, 249, **362**, 363

patrol-only experience 41, 136, 156, 301, 305, **315**, 316, **319**, 319, 320, 367, 372, 415

pay 63, 82, 153, 176, 182, 243, **287**, 401

performance blocks/stressors 49–98, 363–368, 414–415, 496–504; changes in performance blocks over time 87–98; external performance blocks 85–87; operational performance blocks 52–72; organizational Blocks 73–85; *see also specific stressors*

performance indicators (PIs) 8, 10, 103, 118, 226, **357–358**, 361, 566–568; coach-officer 126, 171; evidence-based 116; mental readiness 117; physical readiness 117, **362**, 363; technical readiness 117, 361–**362**, 362; *see also specific entries*

perishable skills 25, 127, 165

personal fears **23**, 43, 52, **53**, 54–55, 63–65, 88, 94, 270, 363, **366**, 370, 498; difference in *95*; temporal changes 554; weighted average **89**

physical competencies 515–525 *see also* physical readiness

physical control with appropriate use of force 126, 144, 150–152, **362**, 363

physical demands 26, 52, 127, 132, 266; environmental stamina 26, 103, 517, 520; fitness testing 26, 517, 520
physical discipline 132–134, 313, **319**, 372, 373, 387, 415; fatigue strategies 132, 136–138, **136**; injury management strategies 132, 140; long-term rest strategies 132, 138–139; shift work strategies 132, 134–136, **135**
physical performance 8, **20**, 487; see also physical readiness
physical readiness 1–2, 4–5, 7–8, 14, 19, 25–27, **26**, 49, 125–169, **317**, 353, 361, 373, 411, 413, 415, 515–521; artificial intelligence integration and 369; cold 108; defined 103, 473; differences in overall importance 105, *105*, 556; in disappointing performances 113, *113*, 561; by factors 110–111, *110*, 559–560; occupational differences **106**, 106; overall importance 103, **104**, *104*, 557; performance indicators 115–118, 361, **362**, 363, 414 see also officer safety; use of force; vehicle operations; stress shield 108; in successful performances 111–112, *112*, 559–560; in successful vs. disappointing performances 114, *114*; by tactical experience 111, *111*
plan see objectives and plan; resource plan
police mentors 244, *245*, 249, 356, **357**, 367–368, 404
police service/force see knowledge of police service
Police Stress Questionnaire-Operational (PSQ-op) 22, 50
Police Stress Questionnaire-Organizational (PSQ-org) 22, 50
policies, procedures, protocols **28**, 528; policy-debrief 209
policing philosophy **28**, 527–528
politics 23, *74*, 75, 82, 84, 205, 206, 336, **366**, 498; differences in *95*; temporal changes 554; weighted average **89**
poor containment **23**, 51, 69, *70*, **71**, **366**, 498; differences in *95*; temporal changes 555; weighted average **89**

poor reports **23**, *70*, **71**, 88, 367, **366**, 498; differences in *95*; temporal changes 554; weighted average **89**
poor support **23**, *74*, **89**, *95*, **366**, 498, 554
positive feedback 215
positive imagery 104, 118, 120, 225, 226, 253–260, *254*, 306, 321, 323, 354–355, **360**, 371, 404, 413, 543, 562–563; call debrief images *254*, 255, **358**; court preparation images 196, 255, 356, **357**; en-route or on-scene images *254*, 255, **357**; impromptu rehearsal *254*, 255, 259, **317**, 318, **358**, 415; instructor-led images *254*, 255, 259, **358**; motor-imagery training 30, 538, 543; physical competencies 515–525; stress reduction **30**, 259, 538, 543; visual triggers 148, 253, *254*, 255, 256, 258, **358**; vivid images 255, **256**, 356
positive thinking 253, 255, 262, 266–268, **267**, 304, 355, **357**
post-traumatic stress syndrome (PTSD) 21, 24, 28, 31, 36, 75, 85, 205, 496–501, 505–509, 528, 540, 544; PTSD Checklist Civilian (PCL-C) 50
predictors of police performance 486–496
preferential treatment **23**, 77, 498
pregnancy **78**; see also female policing
preparation location 263, 271, **273**, 273–274, **357**
preparation rituals 320, 402; see also rituals
present see mindful
pre-shift rituals 272, **273**
previous calls **23**, *53*, 54, **366**, 498; differences in *95*; temporal changes 555; weighted average **89**
pride of uniform 227–228, 231, 240–242, 323, **357**
primary language *110*, 138, 143, **315**, 320, 475, 559–560
prior police-related experience 47, *110*, 112, 132, 134, 136, 250, 309, 314, **315**, 320, 384, 475, 557–559
Problem-Oriented Policing 204, 488, 528

problem-solving 27, 404, 488; creative tactics 20–21; frontline organizational 391; integrate scenarios 21; skills 144, 146, 394
professional discipline *see* discipline, professional
proficiency in law 117, 172–184, 566; arrest authorities 172, 179–181, 361, **362**; court appearance *see* court appearance; court procedures 172, 175–179, 361, **362**; effective apprehensions 171, 183–185, **362**, 373; knowledge and application of the law *see* knowledge, application of the law and; use-of-force principles 171, 172, 181–183, 361, **362**
profiles *see specific profiles*
promotional complacency 22, **23**, 80, 388, 498; *see also* not being promoted refocusing
protective equipment **26**, 185, 517, 519, 521
psyching 263, **267**, 271, **319**, **357**, 373, 415; *see also* preparation location; rituals
psychology/psychological 9, 252; attributes 225; profiles **20**, 487; well-being 128; *see also* Orlick
PTSD *see* post-traumatic stress syndrome
public complaints **23**, **74**, 75, 76, 88, 91, 150, 153, 190, 285, 294, **366**, 369, 381, 498, 555; weighted average **89**
public complaints refocusing 91, *285*, 286, **293**, **298**, 298–299, **358**; addressing 196; differences in *95*; managing 29, 320, 323; preventing 186, **286**; strategies **77**
public confidence **20**, 86, 487, 488
public disrespect **23**, 51–52, *53*, 54, 58–60, 88–91, 94, 214, **293**, **296**, 356, 365, **366**, 368–370, 396, 497; differences in *95*; disrespect 192, 193, 247, 285, 291, 296; rudeness 58; temporal changes 554; weighted average **89**
public disrespect refocusing, preventing 277; proactive with 277; refocusing *285*, 286, **293**, **296**, 296–298, **357**; strategies 91
public feedback **30**, 251, *307*, 310–312, **317**, 318, 356, **358**, 372, 389, 413
publication 306; opportunities 404–405; physical 127; technical 172
Public-private Policing 204, 528
pucker factor *see* crises/crisis

Qinwen, Zheng 2
qualitative analysis 7, 119–120, 318, 353, 371, 413, 463, 467, 478, 480
quality training **30**, 244, 245–247, *245*, 356, **357**, 413; and practice **30**, 244–247, *245*, 356, **357**, 413, 538, 541; *see also* training principles
quantitative analysis 7, 103, 120, 353, 371, 413, 463, 467, 478, 480
questionnaire 5, 8, 22, 29, 50, 120, 462, 465–466; *see also* effective interviewing
quotes 108, 236–237, 333, 493, 571–574; Anonymous Testimonial Database 388; candid 8, 394; direct 107; interviews 118, 119, 225; notable 119; sample 38

R2MR *see* Road to Mental Readiness (R2MR)
radio communication 155, 160, 280; *see also* verbal communication; voice
rapport 69–70; building 45, 194, 196–197, 372; community rapport and humor 162, 171, 185, 191–194, 361, **362**, 414; suspect 309–311, **317**, 318, 356, **358**, 415
reasonableness 126, 144, 153–154, **362**, 363
recognition and thanks **30**, 38, 82, 115, 150, 229, 245, *245*, 251–252, 356, **357**, 390, 401; facial 369; formal 390–391; frontline "buy-in" procedures 392; frontline organizational problem-solving 391; frontline-recognition plan 380, 389; internal 389; lack of 97; overdose 214; public 390; risk 321
recommendations 379–410; 508, 543–544; to address police stressors 22, 25; to advance mental competencies 29; to advance performance excellence 20; to advance predictability of excellence 419; to advance technical competencies 27, 29; to enhance frontline policing 416–417; to improve

stress management 500–501; from R2MR literature analysis 25–27; to strengthen frontline policing 380, 406–408
recruitment/selection 204, 374, 380, 404, 411; opportunities for 381; procedures 94, 370; targeting 373, 381; *see also* selection criteria
refocus *see* distraction control
rehearsal *see* impromptu rehearsal
relaxation 155, 241–242, 254, 259, 270–271, 274, 275, 282–283, **287**, **294**, **299**, 300, **357**
reporting *see* poor reports; written communication
research review 31, 51; *see also* literature review
resilience/resilient 4, 31, 37, 339, 381, 386, 394; emotional 155; fatigue 50; personal 214; readiness *vs.* 312; stress 128; trauma 128, 313
resource plan, strategic 262–265, **265**, **264**, 355, **357**
resources, fewer 66–68
responsible leadership 229, 236–238, 321, 355, **357**, 380, 406
retention 199, 204, **238**, 380, 381
retire 301
reviewer 19, 381, 389
Rhodes, Andy 36, 230
rhythm and flow 274, 275, 282–283, **357**
ride along xxxvii–xlviii, 382
risk 3, 25, 46, 115, 128, 143–144, 147, 156, 162, 183, 229, 236, 261, 312, 396; accident 162; of alerting suspects 157; assessment 6, 128, 160, 276; avoiding 335, 342; of complacency 213; defining 6; depression 28; ethical 234; familiarity with 38; heightened-risk situations 39–41, *40*, 148, 276, 336–337, 551; high-risk areas 28; high-risk calls 181; high-risk individual *40*, 47–48; high-risk operational personnel 4, 318, 337; high-risk professions 5, 7, *8*, 9, 36, 38, 60; high-risk subjects 39; high-risk vehicle stops 84; inherent 52, 146; of injuries 128–129, 150; job 375; lives at 3; mental-health 205; minimizing 127, 132; needless 68; non-risk takers 66; political 336–337; post-traumatic stress

disorder 28, 31, 312; protection *vs.* 27; recognizing 261, 270–271, 313, 321, 355, **357**; road 162; science research 5, 6; taking 334; threat 237; unexpected 55–56; unique 154–155
rituals **30**, 144, 211, 226, 253, 261, **267**, 311, **357**, 396, 538, 541; crisis refocusing 296; equipment checking 148; fatigue 137; music 271–273; packing 280–281, *279*; performance 271; personally planned 282; physical 148; preparation 320, 402; pre-shift 272, **273**; psyching 271; shift 261; sleep pattern with 138
Road to Mental Readiness (R2MR) 21, 24–25, 37, 205, 323, 505–514
role model 9, 249, 380, 382, 384, 399
rookie anxiety 23, *70*, **71**, 366, 498; differences in *95*; temporal changes 555; weighted average **89**
rookie errors: aggressiveness 23, 51, 68, *70*, **71**, *89*, 91, 94, *95*, 143, 287, 365, 366, 498, **555**; discipline problems 23, *70*, **71**, *89*, 94, *95*, 366, 499, 555; general patrol issues 23, *70*, **71**, *89*, *95*, 366, 367, 499, 555; lack community contacts 23, *70*, **71**, *89*, *95*, 366, 499, 555; lack of safety 23, *70*, **71**, 88, **89**, *95*, 366, 499, 555; negativity 23, *70*, **71**, 73, **90**, *94*, 95, 366, 368, 499, 555; no action plan 23, *70*, **71**, *89*, 94, **366**, 370, 499, 555; no basic law 23, *70*, **71**, *89*, *95*, 366, 499, 555; poor containment 23, 53, *70*, **71**, 72, **89**, *95*, **366**, 499, 555; poor reports 23, *70*, **71**, 88, **89**, *95*, 366, 367, 499, 554; rookie anxiety 23, *70*, **71**, *89*, *95*, 366, 499, 555; unrealistic expectations 23, *70*, **71**, 72–73, 88, **89**, 91, *95*, 366, 367, 382, 499, 555
routine tasks *see* downtime (lulls) and routine tasks
Routledge, Taylor & Francis Group 413, 458, 459
rudeness *see* public disrespect
rural experience 40, *110*, 113–115, 208, 242, **315**, 316, 321, 374, 384, *475*, **557**, 561

safety: habits 147; lack of 23, *70*, **71**, 88, **89**, *95*, 366, 499, 555; note-taking

and reporting 69, 197; training **26**, 128, **517**, 519, 520; vehicle 154–159, 361, *362*; *see also* officer safety
safety training **26**, 128, **517**, 519, 520
Sandberg, Sheryl 4
satisfaction *see* enjoyment; job satisfaction/engagement
scenario-based training **20**, 487, 489
School Resource: control environment 247–248; empathy 230; internal communication 213; professional discipline 232, 234; responsible leadership 236; review and interpret internal resources 208; seek support 249–251; suitable reports 202
School Resource Officer (SRO) *110*, 112, **315**, 475, 476; collision-avoidance strategies 156; complex situations 42; court appearance strategies 177; effective apprehensions 184; effective interviewing 195; emotionally charged situations 43–44; external communication 192, 193; female-policing coping issues 77–80; knowledge and application of laws 173–175; not being promoted 80; operational rookie errors 73; patrolling the environment 162; personal fears and skepticism 65; physical control with appropriate use of force 153–154; proper handcuffing 129; public disrespect 59; reasonableness 153; shift-work fatigue 56, 57; shift work strategies 134; staff shortage 83; use-of-force principles 181
selection criteria 20, **21**, 487; ethnic diversity **21**, 488; physical performance *8*, **21**, 488; problem-solving 488; *see also* problem-solving; psychological profiles **21**, 487; *see also* recruitment/selection
self-belief 29, **30**, 225, 318, **319**, 354, 356, 404, 541–542, 562; *see also* confidence; maturity and culturally-grounded 12, **30**, 68, 229, 234, 538, 542; quality training and practice **30**, 244–247, *245*, 356, **357**, 413, 538, 541; recognition and thanks *see* recognition and thanks; support systems **30**, 249, 538, 541

self-confidence 251, 260, 312, 356
self-directed checklist 395–396
self-evaluation 307–308, *307*, 356–357, 385; assessment 8, 380, 385, 386, 396
selfless leadership 344, 345
Sergeant 109; coaching/leading 45; leadership 346; opportunities to visualize 258; post-shift 86; review and interpret internal resources 210; team dynamics 66; workload 75
service: service *see* knowledge of police organization; organizational culture
shared traits 12, 120–121, 132, 226, 229, 236, 266, 272, 273, 282, 374, 381
shift work **23**, 51–53, 78, 80, 85, 126, 127, 203–205, **238**, 293, 313, 323; coping with 57; demands 383; difference in *95*; environment 388; family and 250; fatigue 52, *53*, 56–58, 88, 94, 284, **293**, 363, **366**; shift rituals 261; weighted average **89**
shift work strategies, shift rituals 261; strategies 132, 134–136, **135**, *285*, 286, **293**, **357**, 367, 386–387
simulation 10, 28; critical-incident 393; virtual 173
Simulation-Training Focus Assessment 380, 386, 395, 396, 530
sirens *see* lights and sirens
situational awareness **30**, 143, 145, 149–150, 158, 159, *164*, 164, 190, 196, 276, 395–396, 538, 543; geographic awareness 213, 529
skepticism *see* jaded, feeling
sleep 43–44, 58, 61, 133, 136, 288; adequate 128; deprivation and exhaustion 134; disciplined **135**, 136, **136**, 138; disorders 21, 36; disturbances 52; fatigue *see* fatigue; interrupted 57; lack of 156; patterns **136**; quality 52; scheduled 138
special-interest groups **28**, 213–214, 527, 529–530
specialists *see* external specialists
Specialized Control Practices: car collisions avoidance 154, 156–157, **157**, *285*, 286, **293**, **357**, **366**, 368–369, 415; court appearance strategies 92, 175, **176**, *285*, 286, **293**, **357**; crises refocusing 88, 284, *285*, 286,

290, **291–293**, 294–296, 355–356, **357**, 397; downtime and routine task refocusing 91, *285*, 286, **293**, **299**, 299–301, 356, 367, 397; fatigue strategies 132, 136–138, **136**, *285*, 286, **293**, **317**, **319**, 318, 356, **357**, 372–374, 415; female-policing coping strategies *285*, 285, **293**, 298, **303**, 305–306; "not being promoted" refocusing **303**, 303–304, **358**, 365, **366**; public complaint refocusing 91, *285*, 286, **293**, **298**, 298–299, **358**; public disrespect refocusing *285*, 286, **293**, **296**, 296–298, **357**; shift-work strategies 132, 134–136, **135**, *285*, 286, **293**, **358**, 367, 387; workload strategies **76**, 91, *285*, 286, **293**, **301**, 302, **319**, 323, **358**, 415, 499
spoiler alert 1, 18, 35, 102, 125, 170, 224, 332, 352, 379, 456
spontaneous leadership 345
sport psychologist, Okazawa 266; *see also* Orlick
sport *see* elite sport
standardized assessment 38–39, 225
stigma 24, 37, 506; *see also* mental health
strategies: challenges and performance blocks 96–98; from current research for enhancing performance 32–33; for leadership 348–350; for measuring readiness and success 120–122; for mental readiness 324–326; for navigating science of peak performance 13–15; for physical readiness 165–167; for technical readiness 216–218
street-drug use **28**, 214, 527, 529
stress management/reduction **30**, 259, 538, 543; *see also* distraction control
stressors 496–504; *see also* distractions; performance blocks; *specific stressors*
study design, evidence-based rigor 456–485; background factors 474–476; collaborative contributions 457; collaborative partnerships 457; data collection and statistical analysis 467–468; descriptive analysis 465–469; developmental factors 476; founding champions 459; important project contributors 460–461; influential factors 474–478; instruments 466; investigative framework 478–482; investigator bias 468–469; mutual benefits and equitable contributions 458–459; operational definitions 468–469; police distinction factors 477–478; sampling procedure 466–467; structure 456–482; study background 461–463; study overview 463–465; subjects 465–466
success elements (SE) *see* commitment; confidence; constructive evaluation; distraction control; full focus; mental preparation; positive imagery; Wheel of Excellence; *specific elements*
successful performance 111–114, 558
succession planning *see* career/succession planning
suitable reports 171, 196, 201–203, 361, **362**
supervisor engagement **20**, 487, 490
supervisor run-through images *254*, 255, 259–260, **358**
support systems **30**, 249, 538, 541; *see also* poor support
suspect rapport 309–312, **317**, 318, 356, **358**, 415
systematic note-taking 171, 196–198, 362, **362**

tac com *see* conflicts and de-escalation prevention
Tactical 107, *110*, 115, 127, **315**, 475, 476; arrest authorities 179; coaching/leading 45; collision-avoidance strategies 156–157; complex situations 42; containment in environmental conditions 141–143; control environment 247–248; court appearance strategies 176, 178; downtime and routine tasks 60; effective interviewing 194–195; emotionally charged situations 43, 44; feeling grounded 251–253; firearms and gunpoint arrest 147; flexible 265; heightened-risk situations 40–41; injury management strategies 140;

internal communication 210–213; leadership 345–346; lights and sirens 158; long-term rest strategies 138–139; loyalty 240; officer safety 127; operational rookie errors 68, 70; opportunities to visualize 258–261; physical control with appropriate use of force 154; physical discipline 132–134; police mentors 249; professional discipline 231, 232; proper handcuffing 130; quality training 245–247; resource shortcomings 66–68; responsible leadership 236; review and interpret internal resources 208–210; safety sense 143–144; sergeants' perspectives 345; training 84–85; understand "the job" 239; unfamiliar situations 47; use-of-force principles 181; vehicle reversing 162; visual triggers 256–258

Tactical Sergeant: articulation and appropriate tone 189; handcuffing 129–130; sergeants' perspectives 345; supervisors' dilemma 346–347; workload 75–76

task orientation *285*, 286, 287, 291, **291**, **358**

taxpayer 58

team/peer mistrust **23**, 52, *53*, 65, 365, 368, 498; differences in *95*; temporal changes 554; weighted average **89**

teamwork: advice 291; building and partnerships 340–342; commitment **289**; on individual accountability 368; motivation 334; and trust 275, 281–282, **357**; unexpected cooperation 298; well-being 344; workload 75; *see also* camaraderie support; team/peer mistrust

technical competencies 526–536; *see also* technical readiness

technical readiness 1–2, 7–8, 14, 19, 27–29, **28**, 49, 170–223, **317**, 353, 373, 389, 411, 413, 526–531; artificial intelligence integration and 369; back-ups 108; defined 103, 473; differences in overall importance 104, *105*, 557; in disappointing performances 113–114, *114*, 561; by factors 111, *111*, 561; knowledge of law 108; occupational differences 106, **106**; overall importance 103, *104*, **104**, 557; performance indicators 116, 117, 358, 361, **362**, 414; *see also* knowledge of police service, community and; proficiency in law; verbal communication; written communication; in successful performances 112–113, *113*, 559–562; in successful *vs.* disappointing performances 114–115, *114*; by tactical experience 110, *111*

technology 148, 173, 354, 393, 413; mobile 27; resources **28**, 527, 529; to spot fake news 191

temporal changes *see* changes

terrorism 28, 39, 172, 204, 266, 312, 333, 336–337; counter-terrorism 28, **28**, 204, 393, 402, 528, 531

thanks *see* recognition and thanks

timely reports 171, 196, 199–201, 307, 361, **362**

tools *see* training tools

Traffic Escort *110*, **315**, 475, 476; active listening 189–191; arrest authorities 179–181; articulation and appropriate tone 188; body search 131; court appearances 62–63; crisis 55–56; equipment maintenance 148; external communication 193; fatigue strategies 136; feeling grounded 251–253; firearms and gunpoint arrest 147; heightened-risk situations 40; lights and sirens 158; long-term rest strategies 138; loyalty 240–242; monotony 86; motivated to succeed 242; motorcycle tiredness 57; not being promoted 80; opportunities to visualize 258–261; personal fears and skepticism 64; physical confidence 86; politics 206; prevention of conflicts and de-escalation 186; seek support 249–251; shift work 205; shift-work fatigue 57; shift work strategies 134; spouse conflict 86; suitable reports 202–203; systematic

note-taking 196–198; traffic stops 164; visual triggers 256, 258
Traffic Escort Sergeant 345
traffic stops, strategic 153, 163–164, 362, **363**
training issues 23, *74*, 88, 91, 366, **366**, 498; difference in *95*; temporal changes 554; weighted average **89**
training principles 20, **20**, 487, 489–490; applied ethics **20**, 487, 489; core competencies **20**, 478, 487, 489; critical thinking 8, **20**, 26, 145, 487, 489; scenario-based training **20**, 487, 489; *see also* quality training
training tools: challenging situations 551–552; Coach Officers' 25 teaching tips 578–580; Officer X's Top 10 Commitment and Confidence quotes 576–577; Officer X's top 10 Gold Medal Policing quotes and lessons 569–570; Police field training assessment and progress report 565–568; Police simulation training focus assessment 574–575
trends 94, 105–106, *105*, 314–316, 321–323, *322*, 463, 499, 526–528, 537, 553–556; *see also* changes
triggers *see* visual triggers
trust *see* teamwork

understand community 27; community partners **28**, 336, 527, 529; media *see* media; special-interest groups **28**, 213, 528, 529; street-drug use **28**, 213, 528, 529
understanding "the job" 229, 238–239, **238**, 318, 323, 356, **357**, 415
unfamiliar situations *40*, 46–47, 66, 213, 314, 337, 552
uniform 58, 66, **71**, 81, 109, 157, 186, 193, 214–215, 280, *283*; pride of 227–228, 231, 240–241, 322, **357**
University of Ottawa 413, 458, 459
unprecedented circumstances *40*, 48–49, 336, 337, 552
unrealistic expectations **23**, *70*, **71**, 72–73, 88, 91, **366**, 367, 382, 498; differences in *95*; temporal changes 555; weighted average **89**
use of force **20**, 21, **26**, 64, 105, 117, 126, 144–153, 190, 196, 354, **362**, 567; continuum 145; cultural and gender challenges **26**, 126, 517; defensive tactics **26**, 126, 144, 150–151, **362**, 363, 517–518; equipment proficiency **26**, 126, 517, 518; equipment readiness 149–150; evaluating 145; evidence-based 25; excessive 50; firearms *see* firearms; force at mental-illness calls 25, **26**, 126, 145, 518; gunpoint arrest 126, 145–147, **362**; instructors 144–149; measures 343, 347; physical control with appropriate 126, 144, 150–152, **362**, 363; principles 171, 173, 181–183, **362**, 363; proficiency 414; reasonableness 126, 144, 152–153, **362**, 363; research 126; training 25, 152, 395–396; unwarranted 152

vehicle operations 25, **26**, 117, 125, 126, 154–164, **362**, 414, 520, 567; collision-avoidance strategies *see* car collisions; lights and sirens 62–63, 126, 147, 153, 158–160, 270, 278; motor-vehicle events **26**, 517, 520; multitasking 12, 75, 154, 160–162, 256, 282, 362, **363**; officer compliance **26**, 517, 520; patrolling environment 126, 154, 162–163, 249, **362**, 363; strategic traffic stops 154, 162–163, **362**, 363; vehicle reversing 154, 161–162, **362**, 363; vehicle safety 154–159, **362**, 363
vehicle reversing 154, 161–162, **362**, 363
vehicle safety 154–164, **362**, 363
verbal communication 27, **28**, 104, 117, 171, 185–195, **317**, 354, 473, 530, 566; active listening 27, 171, 185, 186, 190–191, 361, **362**, 414; articulation and appropriate tone 171, 185, 188–190, 361, **362**, 414; community rapport and humor 162, 171, 185, 192–194, 361, **362**, 414; conflicts and de-escalation prevention 171, 185–188, 361, **362**, 414; effective interviewing 171, 185, 186, 194–195, 361, **362**, 414; radio communication 155, 159–160, 280; *see also* voice
victim 11, 47, 145, 202, 214, 229, **238**, 248, 264–265, 268, 290, 311, 347
vigilance 60, 141, 162, 164, 196, 237

Virtue, Tessa 227
visual triggers 148, 253, *254*, 254, 255, 257–258, **358**
visualize/visualization *see* positive imagery
vivid images/imagery 255, 256, **256**, 356
voice: calm 186, 187, 206; radio voice 160, 188–189; tone of 56, 69, 159–160, 186–189, 191, 206, 212; *see also* articulation

Watch Items 353, 368, 388, 405, 414–415; artificial intelligence integration with mental training 369–370; generalized strategies, downside to 368–369; individual accountability, teamwork on 369; initiatives for women, public protocol, and offense-defense mastery 370; promotional realities 369–370; recruit selection and training 370; workload dynamics, shift in 369
weather *see* climate conditions
well-being 3, 22, 36–39, 49, 126–127, 132–143, 227, 312, 415; cardiovascular 128; emotional 140; physical 128; psychological 128; sensory 128; team 345; *see also* fitness
wellness *see* fitness; well-being
Wheel of Excellence 224–226, *226*, 562–563; *see also* Orlick
witness 42, 153, 176, 191, 201, 263, **264**
work conflicts **23**, *53*, 66, 92, 94, **366**, 498; differences in *95*; temporal changes 555; weighted average **89**
workload **23**, 50–51, 60, 75–76, 160, 313, 337, 365, 367, 390–391; addressing 415; ambiguous 21; demands 81; dynamics 369; patrol-only 372–373; unfair 73; workload volume *74*, **89**, *95*, 285, **293**, 293, **366**, 555
workload strategies **76**, 91, *285*, 286, **293**, 301, **302**, **319**, 323, **357**, 415, 498; sharing 400; team 76
written communication 27, **28**, 104, 117, 171–172, 196–203, 361, **362**, 473, 530, 566; suitable reports 171, 196, 201–203, 361, **362**; systematic note-taking 171, 196–198, 361, **362**; timely reports 171, 196, 199–201, 307, 361, **362**
wrongful arrest 50, 174